# Learn Microsoft Transaction Server Development Using Visual C++ 6.0

Nathan Wallace

Wordware Publishing, Inc.

**Library of Congress Cataloging-in-Publication Data**

Wallace, Nathan
Learn Microsoft Transaction Server development using Visual C++ 6.0 / by Nathan Wallace.
p. cm.
Includes index.
ISBN 1-55622-629-2 (pbk.)
1. Application software—Development. 2. Microsoft Transaction server.
3. Microsoft Visual C++. I. Title.
QA76.76.D47W356 1999
005.2'76—dc21

99-26758
CIP



2320 Los Rios Boulevard
Plano, Texas 75074



Printed in the United States of America

ISBN 1-55622-629-2
10 9 8 7 6 5 4 3 2 1
9905



All inquiries for volume purchases of this book should be addressed to Wordware Publishing, Inc., at the above address. Telephone inquiries may be made by calling:

(972) 423-0090

# Dedication

To Phil. From Antioch to High Alphaeus, you're still the man I want at my back when the wild winds blow.

# Acknowledgments

Like so many complex undertakings, this book would not have existed without support from many people besides the guy who tickled the keyboard. I'd like to take a moment to thank Beth Kohler, who tried to make vague sense of my frantic scribblings. Any leftover typos or illogic is entirely mine.

A big thank you to Russell Stultz, owner of Wordware Publishing, for his care and thoughtfulness in a business all too often filled with the reverse.

Thanks to Andrew Troelsen for performing a technical review of the manuscript.

And a final thanks to my wife, Laura, for her kindness, support, and patience during the creative process.

Above all, I need to thank the Totoro, because without him, I wouldn't be here at all!

# Contents

## *A note to our readers:*

Wordware Publishing, Inc. is offering a complete series of ActiveX/COM-oriented books for Visual C++ programmers. Much of the information within these books overlaps to ensure that each book stands alone. However, each focuses on a specific ActiveX/COM-related technology. Therefore, each book provides an essential set of resources for programmers who must either write stand-alone COM programs or include one or more COM modules as part of other

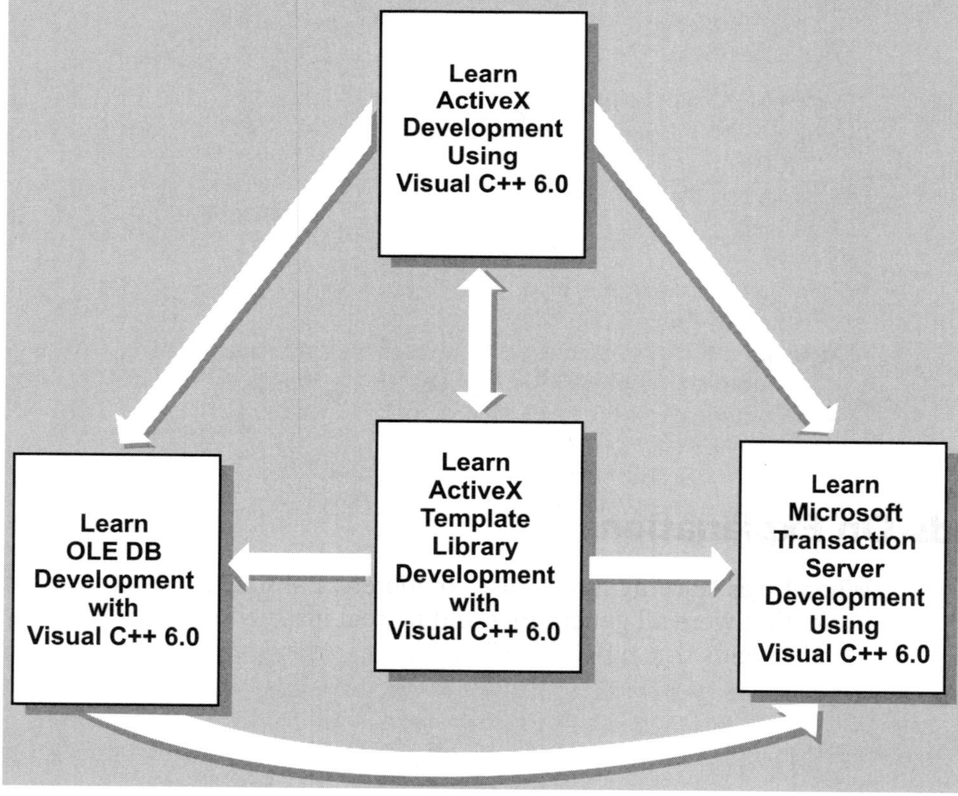

# Introduction

Welcome to *Learn Microsoft Transaction Server Development Using Visual C++ 6.0.*

This book is the result of many hours of labor at the computer, and over the various online and printed documentation for Microsoft Transaction Server. I became intrigued with MTS when version 2 was released, since for the first time it was freely available rather than an expensive add-on. When support for MTS was added to Visual C++ 6.0, I proposed doing a book on it, and the industry agreed one was needed. I hope you enjoy the book, and find it as exciting as I do!

## Who Can Use This Book?

Anyone can use this book, provided they are at least familiar with the syntax of Visual C++ as a language and know something about SQL programming (the book does not cover this aspect of MTS at all due to space limitations). You can be a rank beginner with COM, ATL, and/or MFC and still make full use of this book; the chapters are carefully presented in an order of increasing complexity to allow you to come up to speed as you learn about ATL, MFC, MTS, and COM together. If you are knowledgeable in one or more areas but not in others, then you can skip around as you develop increasingly powerful projects in a hands-on fashion.

## Hands-On Explanations

When I was learning how to use computers, I absolutely hated computer books that were all generalities and no real instructions. This book completely avoids that pitfall by using detailed, step-by-step guides to creating all the projects and support systems needed by MFC. You can identify where the hands-on stuff starts with the icon at the left.

If you're looking for precise details of how to create an MTS component, develop an MTS application, or write an MTS Active Server Page, flip through the chapter until you see this symbol, fire up your computer, and dive in!

The other thing I've disliked about computer books (even some that I've written) is that they contain lots and lots of code, and then an explanatory paragraph or two which has little connection with the code. You find a line

you don't understand in the listing, and search for hours trying to see where it is explained or why it seems unusual. This book remedies this problem with the line-by-line approach. You can identify where this information starts with the icon at the left.

These sections first contain a numbered code listing, and then a breakdown of every major line or group of lines that isn't automatically generated. The explanations tell you what the code does and why it's important (although they don't do a blow-by-blow coverage because that's the province of the source code comments).

# What's In This Book?

## Chapter 1—A COM Primer

Before you can start using C++ to write MTS servers, you need a good working understanding of what the Component Object Model is, how it works, and why it matters. This chapter will give you all that information, and in the process bring you up to speed on both the history and underlying technologies behind COM, Automation, and ActiveX. (If you already know all you want about COM, Automation, and ActiveX, feel free to move on to Chapter 2 or 3.)

## Chapter 2—An ATL Primer

ATL stands for "ActiveX Template Library," a name that encompasses a lot of territory. First, it invokes ActiveX, which in this context means all of COM except the forthcoming COM+. The template portion of ATL's name indicates that this system uses the C++ template mechanism heavily, along with a lot of very sophisticated macros. The library part of ATL indicates that, unlike some other template-based systems, ATL provides extensive source code rather than binary OBJ files. This source code is modified to produce the final code, resulting in executables that are both quite small for what they do and very fast, with minimum dependencies on external DLL files. There is a lot to ATL, and it often confuses beginners to either COM or itself. There is enough material in the ATL system for two or three full-sized books; this particular book is going to focus on the basics. This chapter will cover how ATL fits into Visual C++ and what its various wizard dialogs do. A brief look is taken at the templates and macros ATL uses, but because these are more advanced topics, they won't be covered in great detail. (Individual chapters will cover the specific macros and template classes they use.) When you've finished reading this chapter, you'll be ready to start creating powerful ATL-based COM servers and ActiveX controls for use with MTS applications!

## Chapter 3—An MFC Primer

MFC stands for the Microsoft Foundation Classes. MFC is a set of C++ objects that encapsulate access to a number of Windows programming aspects, including the GDI (Graphical Device Interface), file operations, window creation and message handling, and various specialized aspects of the OS. One of these specialized aspects is ActiveX; support for it is added via existing support for COM (the Component Object Model, discussed in Chapter 1). MFC's main claim to fame is its provision of C++ objects rather than raw API calls for Windows programming, and this holds true for ActiveX as well. There is a lot to MFC, and it often confuses beginners to either COM or itself. There is enough material in the MFC system for two or three full-sized books; this particular book is going to focus on the basics. This chapter will cover how MFC fits into Visual C++, and what its various wizard dialogs do. A brief look is taken at the classes MFC uses, but because these are more advanced topics, they won't be covered in great detail. (Individual chapters will cover the specific classes they use.) When you've finished reading this chapter, you'll be ready to start creating MFC-based COM servers for MTS!

## Chapter 4—An MTS Primer

Microsoft Transaction Server programming consists of using a set of powerful COM interfaces (which is why we went into all the details on COM earlier in the book). These interfaces (along with a couple of API calls) are what developers use to make their database components work with MTS seamlessly. This chapter will give you complete information on these API calls and interfaces, and in the process explain what MTS is and how it works. There is one important point to remember, however: MTS has absolutely no database functionality of its own! Instead, it relies on the powerful Microsoft technology known as ADO (ActiveX Data Objects) for actual programmatic connection to MTS-aware databases like SQL Server and Oracle.

## Chapter 5—An ADO Primer

Microsoft has two high-level database technologies: OLE DB (which isn't an acronym) and MTS (which is, and stands for Microsoft Transaction Server). Both of these powerful database systems rely on a single technology to connect with end users: ActiveX Data Objects (ADO). ADO is a set of COM objects (i.e., interfaces) designed to connect with database systems via the OLE DB technology, but users don't need to know anything about OLE DB to use ADO. Instead, they simply create appropriate ADO objects and make method calls on them to connect with databases and obtain and set information. For OLE DB developers, ADO is the vehicle their users need to connect with the OLE DB providers and consumers they create. For MTS programmers, ADO is the system which they use to interact with databases under the umbrella of MTS. (ADO itself has several advanced capabilities, including

RDS (Remote Data Service) and MD (Multi-Dimensional) database interactions, which we won't go into here.)

Either way, database programmers using Microsoft technology need a detailed reference about ADO. This chapter provides that reference, with a complete write-up on all the collections, objects, methods, and events of the ADO system. Dive in, and your database development will never be the same!

## Chapter 6—Creating ATL MTS Components

At this point, you understand how to use COM, ATL, MFC, MTS, and ADO. All these acronyms add up to the most powerful database technology the PC world has ever seen. Now it is time to do some actual programming and put all this information into practice. This chapter will provide you with a set of COM components written in ATL that utilize Microsoft Transaction Server to work with a SQL Server database for a fictitious online video store. In the process, you'll create two ATL MTS components, an ATL ActiveX control with MTS functionality, and an ATL ASP component with MTS features. (For those who prefer to work in MFC, Chapter 7 reproduces these projects in that development framework.) Chapter 8 then provides you with three projects that develop applications using these elements: one in ATL, one in MFC, and one in HTML and Active Server Pages. Chapter 9 then takes you through the steps to install the MTS components and configure them with MTS Explorer, and illustrates running the three applications.

## Chapter 7—Creating MFC MTS Components

At this point, you understand how to use COM, ATL, MFC, MTS, and ADO. All these acronyms add up to the most powerful database technology the PC world has ever seen. Now it is time to do some actual programming and put all this information into practice. This chapter will provide you with a set of COM components written in MFC that utilize Microsoft Transaction Server to work with a SQL Server database for a fictitious online video store. In the process, you'll create two MFC MTS components, an MFC ActiveX control with MTS functionality, and an MFC ASP component with MTS features. (For those who prefer to work in ATL, Chapter 6 reproduces these projects in that development framework.) Chapter 8 then provides you with three projects that develop applications using these elements: one in ATL, one in MFC, and one in HTML and Active Server Pages. Chapter 9 then takes you through the steps to install the MTS components and configure them with MTS Explorer, and illustrates running the three applications.

## Chapter 8—Creating MTS Applications in ATL and MFC

At this point, if you've been working your way through the book one chapter at a time, you have created either four ATL or four MFC MTS components (or both) to access a SQL Server 6 or 7 database group representing the customers and videos of a fictitious broadband Internet online video store. What remains to do is to create applications that use these components. This chapter will present three different versions of such an application: one each in MFC and ATL that represents the storefront's access to the customers and video databases, as well as an ability to process a phone order for a video. Also, for those who have access to Internet Information Server (IIS) and Active Server Pages (ASP), an additional application written in HTML and ASP using the ActiveX control to simulate online Internet ordering is presented as well. Chapter 9 will guide you through setting up the MTS-aware components in MTS Explorer and show you how to run the applications and test their MTS functionality. Chapter 10 will then show you how to support and deploy the components over the Internet.

### Chapter 9—Installing and Using MTS Components and Applications with MTS Explorer and SQL Server 7

Unlike many types of computer applications (even COM ones), an MTS application does not live on its own. Instead, MTS applications must have their components installed in the MTS run-time environment, so that MTS knows how to configure and support them. The utility that permits this configuration is called the MTS Explorer; a version of it exists on all operating systems that support MTS. With MTS Explorer, a developer or IT manager can install MTS-aware COM components; set their properties in regard to transactions, memory usage, and security; and even create self-installing executable files that automatically set up MTS components on a remote machine without further user or administrator intervention. This chapter takes you through the steps needed to install components in MTS Explorer, configure them into packages, and set the properties of the packages to support the expected behavior of the components. Finally, this chapter will guide you through running the three MTS applications created in Chapter 8. When you're done, you'll be ready to move out into the world of MTS and make your own components and applications.

### Chapter 10—Putting MTS on the Internet

At this point, you're fully up to speed on all that Visual C++ 5.0 and/or 6.0 have to offer in terms of MTS. You can create and use MTS components and applications with the best of them, you understand the issues involved in creating MTS Automation Servers and ActiveX controls and clients in both ATL and MFC, and you're an ace with both the MTS Explorer and the underlying concepts behind MTS. So what's left? The Internet, that's what! More and more database developers are tasked by their clients to put DBMS (and thus MTS) functionality onto Web pages, either on a local intranet or the big, bad Internet/World Wide Web itself. Doing this requires an understanding of arcane issues totally unrelated to MTS or COM, and so this chapter will fill that essential gap. This chapter will add mastery of the LPK_Tool application for creating HTML License Keys, understanding of the ActiveX Control Pad and ActiveX SDK's Code Signing tools, and familiarity with the two major tools of Internet and World Wide Web functionality, FTP and Internet Explorer, to your MTS/COM skills inventory.

## Source Code Duplication

One of the thornier issues for a computer programming book author is: source code or no source code, and if so, how much source code? I've read and written books that try many different approaches to this dilemma. This book goes to one extreme: I include full source code for every project, even if it duplicates a previous project substantially. I do this so that a reader who is only interested in one type of project does not have to go hunting for the code he or she wants. For those reading the book through, this is a bit redundant, but hopefully not too much so. I feel the utility for the average "deadline reader" (like me!) is worth it.

## Project Source Code and the CD

The CD distributed with this book contains complete project source code for all the material in the book, along with several third-party applications and utilities. Since each hands-on section assumes you start from scratch, you don't need any of these files to do the projects, but they're there if you want them.

Use the DOS XCOPY /S command to copy the files to your hard drive and set the files' read-only attributes to False. For more information, see the page opposite the inside back cover.

It's also a good idea to look at the README.TXT file on the CD for any last-minute typos, bug fixes, or updates to the book. Despite our best efforts, there are always a few loose ends!

## Get Updates on the World Wide Web!

The author maintains a web presence, and this book is one of the ones kept current there. The URL is: **http://www.ciupkc.com/books/lmtsdcpp/default.htm**. Along with the README.TXT file on the CD, this is the place to go for updates on bug and typo fixes, new and more sophisticated versions of the book's projects, and a host of information on ActiveX, Visual C++, and WWW programming. Please drop by!

## MTS Forever!

This book is not intended to be the most definitive resource on MTS out there; what it does do, and do well, is bring you up to speed on the techniques needed to create a robust, fully functional set of MTS components and applications in the C++ development framework of your choice, and then demonstrates the truly amazing power of MTS in a real-world setting. So go ahead, join the MTS revolution! We're way past the sky; it's Alpha Centauri or bust!

Chapter One

# A COM Primer

Before you can start using C++ to write MTS servers, you need a good working understanding of what the Component Object Model is, how it works, and why it matters. This chapter will give you all that information, and in the process bring you up to speed on both the history and underlying technologies behind COM, Automation, and ActiveX. (If you already know all you want about COM, Automation, and ActiveX, feel free to move on to Chapter 2 or 3, depending on whether you want to program in ATL or MFC.)

## What is COM?

COM is an acronym for the Component Object Model. It was developed at Microsoft to allow applications to share data and program code while running on an end user's computer. Initially a limited system for allowing programs like Word and Excel to display each other's files, it now has become a centerpiece technology of the Windows operating system. Internet Explorer 5.0, Internet Information Server, Microsoft Transaction Server, Active Server Pages, and Universal Data Access are only some of the current releases from Microsoft that depend wholly or partially on COM.

The Component Object Model is a specification for writing applications that can be used by other applications. The specification provides details on how compilers must output their executable files for the applications to communicate, and on how the operating system must support this communication. One of the benefits of this approach is that it permits COM to be language- and even platform-independent, so that a COM application written in Visual Basic can easily work with one written in Java or C++.

Since COM stands for Component Object Model, you would expect objects to be involved with it somehow. COM provides for six key features of object-oriented programming (OOP):

- **Identity** This means that each COM component must be identified as different from all other COM components. This is done by their GUID attributes.

- **State** This means that COM components must keep track of changes made to their status in some way. COM components have at least the information on their usage count, and many keep internal data as well.
- **Behavior** This means that COM components must implement methods to provide standard and custom functionality of some sort. They do this via their interfaces.
- **Encapsulation** This means that the internal data and functionality used by a COM component is hidden from its users, available as a "black box." Since COM only supports functions and then only their names and parameters, it nicely supports encapsulation. All the internal functions and data of COM components are completely inaccessible to users.
- **Inheritance** This means that one COM component can be derived from another, using the ancestor component's functions while adding its own. COM supports inheritance but in a special way.
- **Polymorphism** This means that any two COM components that implement the same interaction can be used interchangeably. COM fully supports this capability.

The *component* part of COM's name is the major driving force behind the technology. Although initially conceived as a way for Microsoft applications to display and edit each other's data, COM has since become the leading mechanism for creating reusable applications. This is in some part due to the advent of the Internet, which provided a new and unexpected market for component software. Also, Bill Gates, the CEO of Microsoft, has long been a proponent of "component software," which he viewed as applications created by end users out of many smaller "applets," or components. COM was written to some degree to further this strategy.

## How Did COM Happen?

COM did not come about as part of a single development process. Instead, it began in Windows 3.0, with the object linking and embedding (OLE) system. OLE 1, as it is now known, allowed one application, such as Word and Excel, to display another application's data without the user having to explicitly open up the second application. Although it was exciting in its time, OLE 1 had two serious limitations: The embedded data could not be edited in the containing document, and there was no standardized system for storing the embedded information.

These limitations of OLE 1 caused Microsoft to produce OLE 2, which was considered a name (pronounced "oh lay two") rather than an acronym. OLE 2 came out with Windows 3.1. OLE 2 was the first true COM technology, since the COM specification was not available when OLE 1.0 was released; OLE 1.0 used a different system. OLE 2 produced a new and unique form of data called a *compound document*, which included information from any number of OLE-supporting applications in one file, and supported editing, updating, and printing all within any one of the contributing applications.

Although OLE 2 was a quantum jump ahead of OLE 1, it still had its own limitations, the most noticeable of which was the requirement to open a new window whenever editing of an embedded data element was required. This led to the development of the next release of OLE, called OLE Automation. This technology allowed editing inside the application where the data was embedded (called in-place editing), but also added two other major improvements over OLE 2 to the implementation of COM: It provided access to COM services from non-C++ application development environments like Visual Basic, and it provided for the creation of COM-based components that existed outside the world of compound documents. Automation was supported in Windows 3.11.

This last enhancement was to have the most lasting impact on COM, because to this point Mr. Gates' dream of component software was still not realized with the OLE implementation of COM. Instead, it had become a reality through a most unexpected mechanism: the VBX control. VBX controls were add-ins for the Visual Basic development environment, created in C++ initially and later in VB itself. They allowed VB programmers to create useful software elements like custom list boxes or printer utilities, and distribute the binary file only for reuse by other programmers, either for free or after payment for a license. But VBX controls were not implemented in COM, and while they were soon available for C++, problems remained in this crossover system. Also, Borland released its breakthrough Delphi product, which also featured proprietary reusable binary components called VCL controls.

The COM team was tasked with making a reusable control that worked on COM principles rather than proprietary ones. They succeeded, and the OCX control joined the COM family. It was quickly supported in C++, Visual Basic, and Delphi and seemed to be the end of the line for COM, since it had finally achieved its goal of reusable component software at the binary level.

Then along came Java and the Internet. Just as no one expects the Spanish Inquisition (as they used to say on Monty Python), no one expected Java or the Internet, in particular the World Wide Web, to explode onto the computer stage with the force of a hydrogen bomb. Microsoft had long assumed that its dominance of the PC desktop was beyond challenge, but Java and the web browser, coupled with the Internet, represented a whole new way of approaching personal computing, one controlled by Sun and Netscape rather than Microsoft. Microsoft scrambled to meet the Java/WWW challenge, and Bill Gates developed the Internet Initiative. This led to the retooling of COM into ActiveX, with compound documents becoming ActiveX documents, OCX controls becoming ActiveX controls, and so forth. ActiveX COM elements were enhanced for Internet use, with added security features, smaller code sizes, and data elements designed for asynchronous downloading. Soon Java was corralled into the COM camp, with support for ActiveX added in

Microsoft's Visual J++ environment for Java programming. An enhanced version of Automation was added to Microsoft's web browser, Internet Explorer, and called ActiveX scripting. Despite legal and government squabbles, ActiveX soon became a dominant technology for the Internet and World Wide Web, and continues to gain in strength both there and on the emerging corporate and public intranet/extranet systems.

OLE 1, OLE 2, OLE Automation, OCX controls, ActiveX, and COM+ are all implementations of COM that are part of the Windows operating system. They allow developers to actually create and use COM components in various ways without having to write all the COM support code themselves. COM functionality is provided via various API functions that developers include in their programs along with appropriate references, just like the core Windows API.

Although Windows was COM's original home, it has begun to branch out recently. Microsoft has released an implementation of COM for the Solaris variant of the UNIX operating system, and currently has a version under development for the Apple Macintosh.

COM has now become a central element of Microsoft's product line. Once relegated to the application data-sharing niche, then to the VBX-replacement slot, and finally to the Java-competitor position, COM has been made the core technology for a host of new releases:

- **Internet Explorer 5.0** This cutting-edge web browser includes full support for ActiveX controls and in fact uses one for its display interface.
- **Windows 98** Along with its integration of IE 4 into the operating system, Windows 98 also supports the Active Desktop, a COM-based system for placing web-enabled applications on the Windows desktop.
- **Internet Information Server** Microsoft's entry in the web server wars, IIS includes many powerful COM-based systems, including Active Server Pages, ISAPI Extensions, and ISAPI Filters.
- **Microsoft Transaction Server** A database-oriented system, MTS uses COM to allow the combination of transactions from many different database systems and vendors, as well as non-database actions, into single activities that succeed or fail and can be "rolled back" (returned to a valid previous state in the database) without losing information if they fail.
- **OLE DB** Harking back to the OLE 2 roots of COM, OLE DB allows non-database applications to interact with database-oriented technologies (like MTS) using the same techniques as ODBC databases.

## Why Do We Need COM?

As you look at all the technologies that are part of COM now, you may wonder why there has been all the bother. After all, programmers have been exchanging code for years, long before Microsoft was around; why the big fuss? The answer lies in four separate aspects of PC software creation: how computer code is turned into working programs, how developers actually write programs, how memory is used in Windows, and how Windows DLL files work.

The core of a computer program is a set of text files called its source code. Since you're reading this book, you are very likely a programmer yourself and have written many such files. You know how much of an investment each project takes in terms of your time, your expertise, and your company's resources. Source code is literally money in the bank, a sizable investment. The concept of giving this away to other companies, perhaps even competing companies, is hardly a good idea.

But prior to COM, giving away source code was precisely how programmers had to exchange their code! A prime example is the C and C++ libraries used for many years prior to COM. These are binary files (LIB) rather than source code (C or CPP), but in most cases they were accompanied by their C and CPP source code simply because without it the libraries were not very useful. Quite often, they had to be rewritten for the needs of each project or the style of individual developers.

The reason for this lies in the incompatibility of binary computer code at the compiler level. Each compiler produces a set of machine language instructions (binary numbers) that are designed to be fed by the operating system into the CPU of the computer in structured ways to produce program behavior. While there are standards for programming languages like C++, there are currently no standards for the binary output of compilers. Thus, without the source code to draw upon, one development environment has no way to effectively interpret and use the binary output of another programming system, even one that uses the same language.

Even more difficulty lies in the area of reusing binary files at the application level. Once source code has been turned into a binary executable file, it has no natural capability to import and use binary files produced by another application as part of its own running machine language code. There is no "road map" as to what the various number codes mean inside a machine language file. A number may represent a data item, a processor directive, or an internal value used in some calculation; the outside program has no way to know this.

An example of this problem is the need for filters for word processing documents. Each modern word processor application stores its information in a binary format, including not only the text characters typed in by the writer, but also formatting data, fonts, graphics, annotations, and so on. Each program has a different format for storing this information; the result is that a WordPerfect WP file cannot be used automatically by Microsoft Word, and vice versa.

This problem was solved by the adoption of open formats. Each word processing application company published its internal data format freely; this allowed competing and complementary products to create filters that used the data format specification as a road map to read in, display, and manipulate the other application's binary data. Once the road map was available, writing the filtering code was easy; this allowed binary compatibility between the different applications' data files.

This led to the conclusion that what programmers needed was a version of their own open formats and roadmap-based filters. Once there is a standard way to create binary computer files, and a well-known road map to interpret them, writing filtering programs to use any sort of binary information is fairly easy, whether the data is a word processing document or code for use inside another application.

Interestingly enough, the developers of the Windows 3.0 operating system at Microsoft ran into this problem from a different angle; they needed to share low-level system functions like graphics and file management between parts of the OS being developed by different teams. Their solution, also developed for efficiency reasons, was the DLL, or dynamic-link library. Initially only available to the operating system, DLLs would become the mechanism used to implement COM itself.

A *dynamic-link library* is an executable file, like an EXE, that is never allowed to run on its own. Instead, it is loaded into memory by the Windows operating system when requested by an actual application. The requesting application then uses code from the DLL just as if the DLL's code had been included in its own binary file; this is the long-desired binary compatibility for applications!

As long as reusable software components are not easily available, a company must spend money time and again to "reinvent the wheel," redoing simple user interface or sorting programming just because a previous project was not available as source code, or the code did not fit the programming style of the current development team.

The NIH syndrome (Not Invented Here) has been a major stumbling block to the adoption of software components; it manifests itself as the attitude of developers that any code they did not personally write is inferior at best. Analysts have suggested that this tendency by programmers to distrust the work of others continues to be a major obstacle to the adoption of any standard for reusable code. Reusable code at the binary level gets around this syndrome by isolating programmers from the internal behavior of components, making the components into cost-effective "black boxes."

Once again, the DLL file concept I mentioned above provides this sort of functionality. DLLs provide a list of "exported functions," which developers can call with a simple API mechanism, but give no hint as to their internal implementation. DLL files serve as perfect "black boxes" for reusable code. The only difficulty, initially, was that they were creatable only at Microsoft and usable only inside Windows itself. That eventually changed, and at about the same time as when COM itself was initially released.

Without some form of component reuse at the operating system level, each application must contain all of its executable code, even the code that does simple calculation or graphics tasks, such as drawing a line. This can result in "code bloat," huge executable files occupying limited hard drive and RAM space. The DLL system mentioned previously also solved this problem.

The Windows operating system actually inserts a DLL's code into the same memory space as the application that calls it. A DLL makes a group of functions available (called exported functions) to Windows; whenever the binary code of the application using the DLL wants to use one of these exported functions, it first uses the LoadLibrary API call to cause the DLL code to be placed in memory, obtains the function address via another API call, and then invokes the function, just as if it had written the code itself.

In Windows 3.x, DLL code actually resided in physical RAM only once; if more than one application was using the same DLL at the same time, the operating system did some fancy pointer arithmetic to keep them both happy. Windows 95 no longer uses this system except for some operating system DLLs, mainly for performance reasons and because RAM is so much more plentiful and cheaper than a few years ago. But what makes DLLs useful for ending space bloat is the fact that once the application is through with them it can unload them and free up the RAM while continuing to execute.

Although DLL files solved the space bloat problem, the reinventing-the-wheel problem, and the binary incompatibility problem, they had difficulties of their own. Their locations were "hard coded," or else they had to reside in the WINDOWS\SYSTEM directory. They also had no way to let an application know which version of the DLL was currently on a computer, which could result in inconsistent behavior when an older version of an application tried to use the new version's functions.

An even worse problem with DLL files lay in how they were reused by multiple applications from different vendors. Both vendors might buy a DLL from a third party and distribute it, but the second vendor's application would use a newer version of the DLL in question. When it was installed, the other application that used the previous DLL version would break, because it either expected functions to exist that were no longer supported or because the supported functions worked in different ways.

This "broken application" problem was what led, more than any of the other concerns, to the creation of COM. COM took the DLL mechanism and upgraded its behavior to a consistent standard that still met the other three needs of reusable component software (binary compatibility, effective reusability, and efficient executable size) and also supported versioning and enforcement of backwards compatibility that prevented new COM components from breaking applications that used older ones.

# How COM Works

COM, in its basic incarnation, consists of six elements working in a somewhat intricate but relatively straightforward way to produce reusable component software. These elements are the server application, the ClassFactory implementation, the interface specification, the reference count mechanism, the Windows COM system, and the client application.

## The COM Server

The server application is where you, the COM component developer, put your work. It is an executable file, in either DLL or EXE format, that contains all the code to create and maintain the COM elements you provide to COM clients. When a COM client asks the COM system for one of the interfaces your server supports, the COM system will load your server into memory and run it. A server must provide some very specific functions and behaviors to allow the COM system to use it successfully; Chapter 3 explains what these functions and behaviors are and how to satisfy their requirements.

## The COM ClassFactory

A ClassFactory is an implementation of one of the requirements for a COM server: the need to return an interface pointer when the COM system requests it. The ClassFactory can be a C++ class, but it does not have to be; the only requirement is that a ClassFactory's behavior be implemented at the specific entry points COM expects. The client for a COM server never sees any aspect of the ClassFactory; only the COM system uses it. ClassFactories also have some specific requirements in their behavior.

## The COM Interface

The COM interface is the only part of the functionality of a COM server that is visible to a COM client application. For this reason, considerable confusion has arisen as to just what interfaces really are. Simply put, an *interface* is a specification of what functions a given server provides for a COM component with a specific name. This name is not a text string like most programs use, but rather a special number called (in general) a GUID. A COM server is expected to provide implementation code for all the interfaces it exposes to clients; how it does the implementation is not specified. When asked for an interface pointer, a server provides a pointer to the client via the server's

ClassFactory. The client will dereference this pointer and make function calls on its implementation. What actually happens is that these function calls are processed into the VTable, which is simply a list of function pointers. These function pointers, when called, execute the implementation code in the server's application.

This is where the confusion often arises. While from the client's standpoint an interface is an object, in fact its pointer is a link to a set of function pointers and nothing more. The server does not actually provide a pointer to its internal implementation object (if any) when asked for an interface pointer, but rather the pointer to a set of functions. The interface specifies which functions and in what order, but other than that has no information about how those functions are implemented. So in fact an interface has no physical existence; instead, what exists are the implementations of whatever functions it has agreed to provide and a special pointer that gives clients access to these functions. All COM interfaces derive from IUnknown, the standard interface which the system rests upon. COM interfaces based on IUnknown are called "custom" interfaces, because their functions are non-standard, implemented differently in each new interface.

## The COM Reference Count

COM servers are loaded into memory by the COM system. For this reason, clients cannot manage the memory used by the servers. To help the COM system decide when a server is no longer needed in memory, the reference counting mechanism is another required implementation for all COM servers. The reference counting system adds two methods to every COM interface: AddRef and Release.

The AddRef method is used to increment an internal counter that keeps track of how many times an interface has been requested by the client. The call to AddRef must be made by the implementation of the ClassFactory in a server; what type of internal counting the method uses is up to the individual developer. When a client is finished with an interface pointer, it is required to call the Release method on that pointer; this method is expected to decrement the same internal counter used by AddRef. This way, the COM server always knows how many clients are using it at any given time.

At appropriate times, the COM system checks with each server to see whether it thinks it should no longer be in memory. The server is required to be able to accurately know how many interfaces are still in use by clients; if this value is 0, it must inform the COM system it is no longer needed and can be unloaded, but otherwise it must tell the COM system that it needs to stay in memory.

### The COM System in Windows

Since clients for COM servers are never allowed to know about either the server's DLL or EXE file, or the ClassFactory implementation, clearly some other application must be able to deal with these essential aspects of using COM. Windows provides a set of API calls, similar to those used for Windows operating system API functions, that initializes the COM internal system for a client and allows it to initially request an interface pointer for a given GUID "name." When the client application is done with using COM services, another API call shuts down COM for that application.

### The COM Client

The COM client application is where all the other five pieces of the COM puzzle fit together. COM clients initialize the COM system, make the API call to obtain a specific interface pointer for a specific server, and then use the functions supported by that interface as they wish. When they are done with a given interface, they call its Release method to tell the server they are done with it. When they are finished with using COM services, they shut down their access to the COM system.

What makes COM work, and work so well, is that neither the server nor the client need to know anything about each other! As long as both follow the rules for COM behavior, they can mesh together as if one single developer wrote both applications.

## COM is Static, Automation is Dynamic

Remember that COM was developed to allow Microsoft programs to communicate with each other, and only for that reason. It therefore was not oriented towards client/server interactions, but more towards peer interactions between applications. A concept had been growing for some time, however, that the big, feature-laden application was a dinosaur that was about to be done in by a new breed of program called component software.

*Component software* was conceived as a combination of many smaller elements, sometimes referred to as *applets*, which would be connected by end users in a simple scripting language like Perl. The scripted portion of the component software would create the applet objects as needed, and tell them what to do in response to user interactions. This type of embedding came to be called Automating. Microsoft began to seriously consider supporting component software, and developed a system using a variant of its Visual Basic language. This system was based on COM, which then was implemented as OLE 2. It was called OLE Automation, but is now usually just called Automation. It has become, to many users, the dominant version of COM in use today.

Basic COM is entirely fixed at compile time in its function invocations. The only way to call a function on a server's interface pointer in the client is to give the client a header file or two that gives precise type information about that server's interfaces. If the server has since changed, and supports more interfaces than are present in the header files the client is using, the client will never know about those interfaces and so can never ask for them or use their functions. This type of interface function calling is called *static invocation*.

Automation, on the other hand, is not fixed at compile time in what functions it can call on a given interface pointer. Instead, it can ask the Automation server for a list of its available interfaces and functions, check them against the source code of its script, and connect the script's function calls with the actual interface functions entirely at run time. This type of interface function calling is known as *dynamic invocation*. The information as to which functions a given Automation server supports and their parameters and data types are stored for each Automation server in a file called a *Type Library*. A Type Library can be thought of as a compiled version of a C .h header file, optimized for use by the Automation system. Compilers that create Automation servers also create their Type Libraries; clients that support Automation servers have the capacity to locate and obtain Type Library information, usually as part of their development framework.

IDispatch is a COM interface, derived from IUnknown just like custom interfaces, which supports Automation via four functions: GetTypeInfoCount, GetTypeInfo, GetIDsOfNames, and Invoke. Each of these functions must be invoked using original static invocation in the client's executable file.

What makes Automation work is that the GetIDsOfNames and Invoke functions can and do call any Automation-enabled function of their Idispatch-derived custom interface, by obtaining a number called a DISPID from GetIDsOfNames against a textual version of the function's name and passing that number along with any appropriate parameters to Invoke. To allow the client to figure out which of the custom functions is being called, a complementary component called a script parser must be provided. This component takes the text file, called a script, and turns it into symbols that the client can understand and translate via GetIDsOfNames and Invoke into real Automation interface function calls in its executable code. The client itself is responsible for obtaining data from the script, storing it internally, and reporting it when asked, but these are not COM issues. Since the functions of an Automation server's IDispatch Interface are dynamic rather than static, the IDispatch Interface became known as a Dispinterface rather than an interface to highlight this distinction. A later development merged interface and Dispinterface capabilities into one object; these are called *dual interfaces*.

To make Automation servers more programmer-friendly, the COM team added two new terms to the COM vocabulary: properties (data stored inside the instance of a given IDispatch-derived Automation server) and methods

(COM functions given a new name). Although properties seemed to work like C++ class member variables to the developers of Visual Basic, Java, or VBScript, in fact they were a trick supplied by Automation based on getting and setting functions. (This made them harder to use for C++ programmers, and this is one reason Automation is not as popular among the C++ community.)

## Automation Opens COM to the World

The scripting language used for OLE Automation was called VBA, or Visual Basic for Applications. Major applications like Word and Excel were given Automation capabilities, and still have them. But the market for component software never materialized, perhaps because of the massive increase in memory and hard drive capacities coupled with drastically reduced costs as the PC market exploded. OLE Automation probably would have been only a niche version of COM had not two additional factors intervened: Visual Basic and the Internet. The latter aspect led to the merging of Automation with the Windows Desktop, and to the next evolutionary step of COM: COM+.

Visual Basic was Microsoft's entry into the RAD market (rapid application development) where application user interfaces and even program functionality can be quickly laid out and coded, in exchange for somewhat poor runtime performance. Once the prototype was created in VB, it would be recoded in C++ for speed and executable size.

But Visual Basic became a larger success than Microsoft probably anticipated, to the point that its sales revenue became a factor in the company's strategy. One major thing had been left out of Visual Basic at that point: access to OLE and COM. The VB development team was assigned the task of supplying this access for the next version of Visual Basic.

Because at that time Visual Basic was not compiled into executable machine code, but instead tokenized and then interpreted by the VB runtime module, using the C++ static invocation system for VB was not possible. On the other hand, by treating the tokens in the parsed VB source code like a VBA script, OLE Automation could very easily provide COM functionality to Visual Basic programs. This provided a substantial new market for OLE Automation, and it became known simply as Automation since many of its uses had little to do with the compound documents that were the focus of OLE.

Another player entered the PC world at about this time: the Internet. Taken from its comfortable academic niche and thrust into the mainstream of the world's lifestyle via the user-friendly World Wide Web and Mosaic and Netscape browser applications, the Internet upset everyone's calculations as to the future of PC computing development. Adding to the furor was Sun's powerful and revolutionary Java language, which was platform-independent and could send its code over the Internet safely to run on client machines worldwide from a single source.

Microsoft retaliated with two powerful new products: Visual J++, its version of a Java compiler that provided increasing support for Windows at the cost of losing platform-independence, and Internet Explorer, a web browser to compete with Netscape Navigator.

Visual J++ features the ability for its Java programs to both import and use Automation-enabled COM servers, and to even create COM servers that support Automation. Like Visual Basic, it too must rely on the Automation dynamic invocation system to connect its Java code with the COM system.

But the most important fallout of the Internet for COM was the decision to emulate the JavaScript capability of Netscape Navigator in Microsoft's web browser, Internet Explorer. IE 3 offered relatively complete support for JavaScript, but also had its own scripting language, VBScript, based of course on Visual Basic for Applications. VBScript was part of HTML, and ran on the client machine that had downloaded a web page with included SCRIPT tags. The scripts in VBScript were designed along classic Automation lines, controlling the IE browser and creating and using applets, in this case Java applets and special COM Automation servers called ActiveX controls.

But it is vital to remember that no matter how sophisticated and user-friendly Automation technology becomes, it is still based on four static-invocation functions of the COM IDispatch Interface.

## From Automation to OCX to ActiveX

When Automation was released, many developers saw it as the culmination of COM. It provided access to COM for Visual Basic, allowed creating COM servers not tied to compound documents, and added considerable support for compound documents as well. Many felt things couldn't get better than Automation. But trouble was brewing on the horizon, as the increasing popularity of the Visual Basic development environment led to a new type of software component, the VBX control. VBX controls had two important features that Automation servers did not: a user interface and the ability to communicate with their clients (called containers). The unprecedented success of VBX controls led Microsoft to task the COM team with creating an Automation equivalent. The result was the OCX control specification, which supported all the functionality of VBX controls with COM technology with the added bonus of being 32-bit. Then, before OCX controls really got their feet on the ground, the arrival of the Internet and Java caused them to be recast as ActiveX controls, with both added and removed functionality.

Automation was a powerful COM technology, with many useful features. But it had limitations as well. Perhaps the most serious feature that Automation lacked was the ability for a non-compound document server to display a user interface. While compound document servers could create visual images, manipulate them, and even interact with their containing application via in-place editing, Automation servers could do none of these things. Also, even with in-place editing, there was no effective mechanism for a server to contact its client or container with information asynchronously (like the Windows messaging system).

These limitations tended to keep COM and Automation from becoming mainstream development tools. Programmers moved instead towards Visual C++ and its MFC system for application development, and to Visual Basic for rapid prototyping and hobbyist computer programming. In these environments, emphasis soon shifted towards components that had a sophisticated graphical user interface along with underlying program functionality. In Visual C++, these components were provided by Microsoft and became known as common controls. In Visual Basic, however, these elements were called VBX controls, and they paved the way for a whole new form of component software.

A VBX control is a type of DLL application written with special support to allow it to hook into the Visual Basic system. VBX controls supported two important features: a graphical user interface and the ability to communicate with their containing application (which became known as a container). This allowed VBX controls to behave like C++ common controls, but with one big difference: They could be created by outside developers, using an SDK released by Microsoft.

It seems likely that Microsoft had no concept when it released the SDK for VBX control creation, initially for C++ and then for VB itself, just what genie it was releasing from its bottle. Within a year, the VBX control market exploded into a multimillion dollar industry, and took sales of the Visual Basic product along with it. Soon, bulletin boards around the world were filled with sophisticated freeware and shareware applications written in VB using the thousands of powerful third-party VBX controls now available.

The C++ development community agitated for the ability to use VBX controls, and they got it, although not as cleanly as some would have liked. There were several inherent limitations of VBX controls that made them unsuitable for use in other environments:

- VBX controls are inherently 16-bit. This meant that a massive porting job would be needed to move them to the 32-bit environment of Windows 95 and Windows NT, which Microsoft viewed as the future of Windows.
- VBX controls don't use the Windows messaging system. This meant that to use them outside of VB, an interpreter had to be added to convert their VB-specific communication system to the standard Windows arrangement.
- VBX controls had only eight available functions. This meant that to define a custom method for a VBX control, you had to define the clumsy Action property, which was hard to use in VB, let alone any other language.

- The VBX control event mechanism, because of its tie to the VB system, was inflexible; adding new events was difficult, if not impossible.

All these problems led Microsoft to decide that a general system for controls was needed, and COM and Automation were the obvious technologies to implement it. The result was the OCX control, released in 1994 as a specification and SDK.

OCX controls were specialized Automation DLL servers (you cannot create an EXE OCX control) with the extension OCX rather than DLL on their filenames. OCX controls could only be used by applications that were written as OCX control containers.

Like Automation servers, OCX controls exposed properties and methods, which could be called by the container as desired. Unlike Automation servers, however, OCX controls had a graphical user interface displayed in the control container, and they had the ability to asynchronously send messages to the container in response either to user actions or to internal state changes.

Soon OCX controls were everywhere, from Visual C++ to Delphi to Java, and were viewed by the developer community as another COM triumph. But there were storm clouds on the horizon, named the Internet and Java. Their winds of change would blow OCX controls away, and replace them with something both similar and very different: the ActiveX control.

When AOL dumped millions of its users on the academic network called the Internet in late 1994, no one really understood what it would mean for PC software development. But when combined with the brand-new graphical information display technology called HTML and the World Wide Web, the Internet became the wildfire technology of the last half of the 1990s. The Netscape web browser became synonymous with the WWW, and it was not a Microsoft product. Microsoft's competing browser, Internet Explorer, lagged behind in capability and was virtually ignored by the developer community.

Then in 1995, Sun Microsystems released the Java programming language. It provided for the first time a secure way to send programs over the Internet and WWW, producing Java applets which were very similar to OCX controls but which worked either by themselves or as part of an HTML web page. In combination with the JavaScript programming language, they behaved very much like Automation servers in web pages or stand-alone applications. Java, unlike COM, was platform-independent; it ran on Windows, UNIX workstations, and the Macintosh. Java was touted as the language of the future, and together with Netscape, it became a serious candidate to challenge the dominance of Microsoft Windows on the PC desktop.

Microsoft was take by surprise by the WWW and Java, but it soon came back fighting. Its response to Netscape was Internet Explorer version 3, which featured both a JavaScript clone called JScript and its own programming language called VBScript. To counter the Java initiative, Microsoft produced a version of COM called ActiveX. ActiveX encompassed most existing COM and Automation technologies; OCX controls became known as ActiveX controls, for example. Compound documents were called ActiveX documents, and COM servers and Automation servers were renamed ActiveX servers or ActiveX code components.

Although initially resisted, soon the innate power of ActiveX moved it to the forefront of both Web development and component software programming. As ActiveX matured, the name was shifted to a smaller set of technologies, principally those involving the Internet and WWW. The COM name reappeared, now oriented towards a host of new technologies like Transaction Server, OLE DB, and the Windows DNA system. Internet Explorer moved to version 4 and into the operating system itself in Windows 98. ActiveX controls, however, have remained unchanged since their release in 1996.

## ActiveX Controls are Automation Servers with a User Interface

By now you may be a bit tired of hearing that ActiveX controls have a user interface. After all, what's so special about that? What makes the ability to create a user interface so special is that ActiveX controls are not compound documents. A compound document, the previous user interface system supported for COM servers, is a very limited display. It is literally a "window into another application," and as such does not need to know about things like resizing, background colors, font settings, or display optimization. Controls, on the other hand, are designed to blend in with a consistent user interface around them. They need to understand how to resize when needed, and often need to support display optimization to enhance application performance.

The ActiveX control at its basic level maintains its own display window, complete with a device context. While this window is a child window of the container, it nonetheless has its own message queue, and refreshes itself when needed. This has some good and bad points. The good points are that ActiveX controls are responsible for drawing themselves, taking this job away from the container, and that they can receive messages using the normal Windows messaging system if needed. The bad points are that ActiveX controls must be rectangular, and cannot be transparent or easily overlaid with non-windowed elements of their container's display. To get around these limitations, an ActiveX control can be made windowless.

Windowless ActiveX controls are a relatively recent innovation; some ActiveX control containers may not support them. Those that do provide the windowless control with its display window, and also take care of sending and receiving Windows messages for it. What the container gets in return for this effort is a control that can be non-rectangular, and even transparent if desired. Also, the control will often redisplay faster due to less overhead internally.

ActiveX controls must always draw themselves, and thus are fully responsible for what the user sees on their window. This requires their container to provide them with all the messages that might require refreshing their display. This can range from a simple paint message to resize requests or more advanced data acquisition calls (needed to store the image of the control in the container as a metafile).

Why this matters is that some drawing commands don't work on a device context for a metafile. The ActiveX control must be able to distinguish between normal drawing requests and those that are needed to create a metafile and alter its drawing code appropriately.

The other major effect of having a user interface for ActiveX controls is that they must be able to change size when their container changes its size. The ActiveX system supports three types of sizing for ActiveX controls:

- **Autosizing** This type of sizing makes the control entirely responsible for its own display extents. The container will tell the control its own extents and let the control figure out how big it wants to be.
- **Content Sizing** This type of sizing makes the container responsible for setting the size of the control initially, but allows the control to decide on its final size.
- **Integral Sizing** This type of sizing makes the container responsible for the size of the control. The control must resize itself to the desired values.

Aside from these sizing aspects, ActiveX controls must also decide which mapping mode they will use in their drawing operations. The default is MM_TEXT, but this can be changed if the control wishes.

## Stock Properties and Property Pages Standardize ActiveX Control Behavior

Automation servers are quite free-form; aside from the needed methods of IDispatch, they are free to support whatever properties and methods they like. Since their clients presumably have access to their Type Library, they will know what custom elements are supported and deal with them appropriately. But ActiveX controls are designed to be used in a general environment, sometimes with little prior knowledge about their behavior. To help compensate for this, the ActiveX system provides stock and ambient properties and methods to help ActiveX controls blend in with their containers and function consistently for end users.

Custom properties and methods of ActiveX controls are just that: custom; to save on naming overhead, if a property or method isn't qualified as stock or ambient, it is custom by default. They are implemented by the control and are different for each given control, based on its unique functionality. List-oriented controls will expose a property that is an iterator over their internal list of items. Graphical controls will provide an image property to set their displayed graphic. The custom methods of a control are likewise unique; the list control will provide methods to add and delete items from its list, while the graphical control will expose methods to resize its image and change its orientation.

From the container standpoint, the custom methods and properties of an ActiveX control are available, just like Automation-based properties and methods. End users will access the custom properties and methods with scripts or program code, which will be sent to the control via the usual Automation system (either Dispinterface or dual interface, depending on how the control is implemented). From a display standpoint, custom methods and properties have no effect (although they may change what is displayed, they are not central to how the display of the control is rendered).

The Windows system (where most ActiveX controls live and work) has consistency as one of its major features. Once a user has learned how to manipulate scroll bars, buttons, list boxes, radio buttons, check boxes, and so on in one application, he can reasonably expect the same user interface behaviors from other Windows applications. As long as the Windows applications are all using common controls or API-based user interface elements, this will be the case. But ActiveX controls (and their precursors, VBX controls) have their own custom user interfaces in many cases. The behavior of these elements can differ widely despite a similar appearance, resulting in considerable user confusion.

To help work around this, ActiveX controls are provided by the ActiveX system with a list of so-called stock properties and methods. These stock features are designed to allow both containers and users to have a consistent and understandable set of appearances and behaviors from ActiveX controls. Stock properties are covered in Chapters 6 and 7.

ActiveX controls live on in the display of their container. This means that they have two choices in their own appearance: They can be a complete iconoclast, and set their colors, fonts, and other styles solely to please themselves, or they can set their display values to match those of the container except when it would interfere with their own functionality. In order for an ActiveX control to set its own internal display values to match those of its container, however, it must have some way of obtaining the container's values. This system is called *ambient properties*.

Ambient properties are actually properties of the ActiveX control container, and they are exposed to the control itself via a special COM interface the control must implement. An ActiveX control container will obtain this interface from the control when the control is first loaded, and call its functions with the initial values of the ambient properties it supports. Also, whenever one of these ambient properties changes, the ActiveX control will be informed of the new value by another call to the interface's notification function. A basic ActiveX control with properties of all sorts is the focus of Chapters 6 and 9.

Another thorny aspect of the various properties of ActiveX controls is making them available to end users for setting at run time. To help with this task, ActiveX provides the Property Page system. This system is similar to the property sheet dialogs introduced in Windows 95; these are tabbed dialogs that group similar properties together and provide consistent, Windows UI-based methods for manipulating them. Property Pages are covered in Chapters 6 and 9.

## Connection Points Allow Events to be Sent from ActiveX Controls to Containers

The need for two-way communication between programs has been around since Windows programming began. In Windows, the system to provide this functionality is the callback function. For COM, however, the interface is the clear choice to implement communication between servers and clients; these interfaces are known as outgoing and incoming interfaces. The problems lie in keeping track of obtaining and notifying many incoming and outgoing interfaces between clients and servers. To handle this difficulty, ActiveX provides the Connection Point system.

The Windows system by its very design needs some way for applications to communicate with Windows itself. Probably the most well-known example is the so-called Window procedure, required for every window created by an application. This function is called by Windows to deal with dispatched messages. Another common callback function is the one used to enumerate window objects (like those on the desktop).

This system works because Windows is the operating system, and thus exempt from the problems of interprocess communication. Also, the functions involved are strictly standardized so that Windows can support them. To provide a generalized interprocess method of inter-application communication, a COM interface is the vehicle of choice.

Since ActiveX controls are COM servers via Automation and OCX, it makes sense for them to use interfaces for their communication with their containers and vice versa. The communication system that ActiveX implements is provided by sink interfaces (incoming) and source interfaces (outgoing).

*Sink interfaces* are called that because they sink, or consume, notifications from a client to a server. In technical terms, all server interfaces (COM and Automation) are sink interfaces since they are called by the client or container. They are incoming because they leave the client and come in to the server.

*Source interfaces* are called that because they source, or provide, notifications from a server to a client. They are outgoing because they go out to the client from the server, reversing the normal interaction. These interfaces are what is unique to the ActiveX system, since COM and Automation servers and clients do not have them. It is the source interface that tells a client/container that something of importance has happened in the server; this notification is called an event. Events are covered in Chapters 6 and 7. In order for a server to use an outgoing interface, the client must implement it and provide a registration of this implementation so the COM system can find it. This makes a client into a server, and vice versa, to support source interfaces. For this reason, the implementation of a source interface in the client then becomes a sink interface (because it is consuming event notifications from the server).

The problem that arises with the sink and source interface system lies in the concepts of one-to-many, many-to-one, and many-to-many connection topologies:

- **One to Many** This topology results from a single implementation of an outgoing interface being used by two or more servers in a single client. The client must be able to determine which server has sent a notification to the single outgoing interface.
- **Many to One** This topology results from a single server supporting two or more outgoing interfaces which are implemented on a single client. The client must keep track of all of the incoming notifications for all the implemented source interfaces.
- **Many to Many** This topology is a combination of the above two; it occurs when two or more servers are providing notification to the same client on the same outgoing interface, but to two different instances of that interface in the client. The server and the client both must keep track of which instance has been sent and which notification has been received.

To prevent a confusing multiplicity of sink and source implementations, ActiveX provides the IConnectionPoint and IConnectionPointContainer interfaces; these are collectively known as Connection Points. These two statically invoked COM interfaces allow clients and servers to inform each other of what sink and source interfaces they support, and hook up the implemented ones to allow effective two-way communication. Connection Points are covered in Chapters 6 and 7.

## Persistence Allows ActiveX Controls to Save Their State Over Time

Compound documents save their information in special DocObject files, which are also called structured storages and are supported by OLE interfaces and functions. Automation did not need this complexity, since Automation servers rarely needed to save their state; those that did, used files or other custom implementations. ActiveX controls, however, need the same generalized information persistence as compound documents, since they are designed to be edited in one environment and displayed in another. This capability is called *persistence*. The ActiveX system implemented three interfaces to encapsulate persistence: IPersistStorage, IPersistStream, and IPersistPropertyBag. Each of these interfaces has a unique place in the ActiveX data storage arrangement; they are all covered in Chapters 6 and 9. All persistence is the responsibility of the container; the control only is required to support the interfaces that provide the data.

An ActiveX *storage* is very similar to a folder on a hard drive (also called a directory). It holds no data in and of itself, but serves to contain other data (folders and files) in a single logical and isolated unit. The IPersistStorageXXX interfaces provide storage support for ActiveX controls, allowing them to create and manipulate persistence storages as needed, adding other storages and streams to them.

An ActiveX *stream* is equivalent to a file on a hard drive. It contains data in a format appropriate to whatever application created it, but cannot contain other files or folders. The IPersistStreamXXX interfaces provide stream support for ActiveX controls, allowing them to create, read, and write persistence data streams as needed.

Both of the previous persistence implementations are binary, and meant for use in applications that can deal with binary data (like Microsoft Word). Other applications, like Visual Basic or Internet Explorer, need their persistence data stored as text with named associations. To implement this type of persistence, ActiveX provides the IPersistPropertyBagXXX interfaces. These interfaces permit ActiveX controls to read and write their data as HTML <PARAM> tags or named fields in FRM or other text files as needed.

## Where We Go From Here

This chapter has been a whirlwind tour of some of the most powerful and complex technology in the modern computing environment. This book, due to space limitations, cannot cover all the wonders of COM; instead, it focuses on teaching you how to create Microsoft Transaction Server components in Microsoft Visual C++ 6.0 and ATL 3.0 and ATL 2.1, and using the Microsoft Foundation Classes libraries. If you need a more detailed coverage of COM itself, both theoretically and structurally, check out the author's web site at **http://www.ciupkc.com/books/**. There are references to several good books on COM and COM-related subjects there.

Meanwhile, the next chapter takes us into the wonderful world of ATL and of the Visual C++ IDE which hosts it. We'll learn how to create projects in Visual C++ 6.0, and how to use the various ATL wizards and dialogs to automate a great deal of the COM programming we need to do. So fire up Visual C++ 6.0, turn the page, and step into the new millenium of COM development a little early! (If you don't use ATL but MFC instead, move on to Chapter 3, which does the same job for Microsoft Foundation Classes.)

Chapter Two

# An ATL Primer

ATL stands for "ActiveX Template Library," a name that encompasses a lot of territory. First, it invokes ActiveX, which in this context means all of COM except the forthcoming COM+. The *template* portion of ATL's name indicates that this system uses the C++ template mechanism heavily, along with a lot of very sophisticated macros. The *library* part of ATL indicates that, unlike some other template-based systems, ATL provides extensive source code rather than binary OBJ files. This source code is modified to produce the final code, resulting in executables that are both quite small for what they do and very fast, with minimum dependencies on external DLL files.

There is a lot to ATL, and it often confuses beginners to either COM or itself. There is enough material in the ATL system for two or three full-sized books; this particular book is going to focus on the basics. This chapter will cover how ATL fits into Visual C++ and what its various wizard dialogs do. A brief look is taken at the templates and macros ATL uses, but because these are more advanced topics, they won't be covered in great detail. (Individual chapters will cover the specific macros and template classes they use.) When you've finished reading this chapter, you'll be ready to start creating powerful ATL-based MTS servers and ActiveX controls!

As of Visual C++ 6.0, ATL enters version 3.0. Most of the features of 3.0 are the same as those of 2.1, and so the following sections are written from the perspective of an ATL 2.1 user. A section at the end of the chapter covers the new features of ATL version 3.0.

## ATL in Visual C++

ATL does not work by itself; it is designed for, and only works with, Microsoft Visual C++ 4.2, 5.0, or 6.0. It enhances the Integrated Development Environment of Visual C++ with wizard dialogs and automatic code generators. It also provides extensive online help and a detailed tutorial and sample project.

## Getting ATL for Older Visual C++ Versions

If you have purchased either Microsoft C++ 5.0 or 6.0, then you automatically have ATL; it is part of the application. If you have version 4.0, then you may not have the ATL system, since it was developed after that application's release. Also, even if you have ATL 1.0 for Visual C++ 4.2, you should obtain version 2.1 to use this book.

Fortunately, Microsoft has released version 2.1 of ATL as a free download for owners of Visual C++ 4.2b or higher. To get the self-installing executable for ATL 2.1, activate a web browser and go to the URL **http://www.microsoft.com/visualc/prodinfo/archives/download/default.htm**. Figure 2-1 shows this web site, which provides considerable information about ATL as well as the download link.

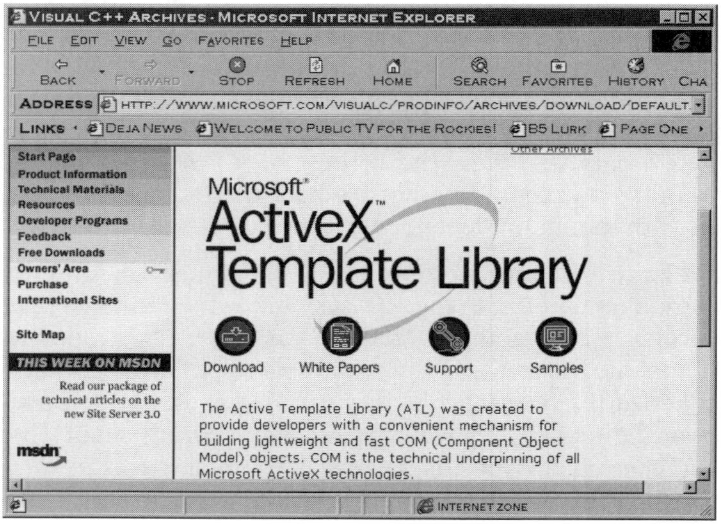


*Figure 2-1 Downloading ATL from the Microsoft web site*

Once you download the file, run it either by double-clicking on it in Explorer, or using the Run dialog from the Start menu. It will extract itself and allow you to choose various simple installation options. Once it is finished, reboot your computer and you will find ATL installed and ready for use in Visual C++.

## ATL's Online Documentation

As mentioned above, ATL is a complex system. It has many useful features that can make COM programming easier and faster, but at a price in time and effort to familiarize yourself with it. Since you've purchased (or are considering purchasing) this book, you are obviously interested in ATL. One very good way to learn about it is to work through all the online documentation installed with it (either by default in Visual C++ 5.0 or 6.0, or when you install version 2.1 after downloading it).

To access the online documents for ATL, use the Help menu option and select Search. In the edit control, enter ATL and press the Search button. A number of results will appear; scroll down until you see the " " option. Clicking on it will bring up a group of topics as shown in Figure 2-2; the best place to start

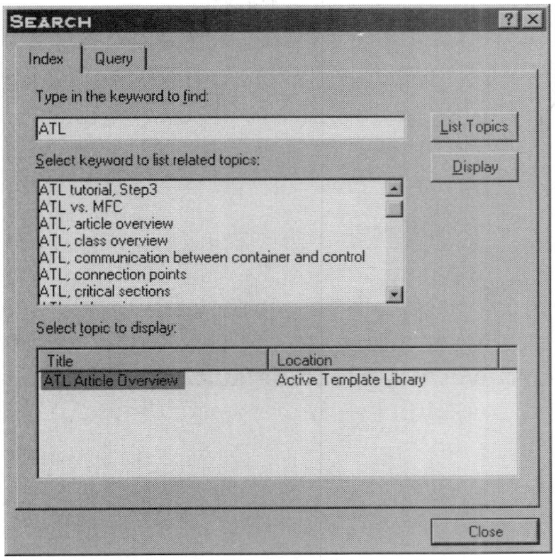


***Figure 2-2***
*The ATL online documentation in Visual C++*

is "ATL Article Overview"; select it and press the Display button. From there all the ATL documents are hyperlinked into one detailed unit, which you can browse and print at your leisure.

# Creating ATL Projects with the ATL AppWizard

An ATL project starts with the ATL AppWizard. It is found in the ubiquitous New dialog of Visual C++, and provides a simple wizard dialog that hides a lot of power behind its plain face. With this wizard and its attendant confirmation dialog, you unleash all the power of ATL.

## *The New Dialog*

To start an ATL project, select File|New from the Visual C++ menu. The New dialog appears; select the Projects tab to produce the display shown in Figure 2-3. By clicking on the ATL COM AppWizard entry as illustrated in the figure, you enable entry of the project name (which should be different from the planned name(s) of any interfaces to avoid conflicts) and selection of its directory on the hard drive of the development computer. When you have entered this information, pressing OK will start the actual ATL AppWizard.

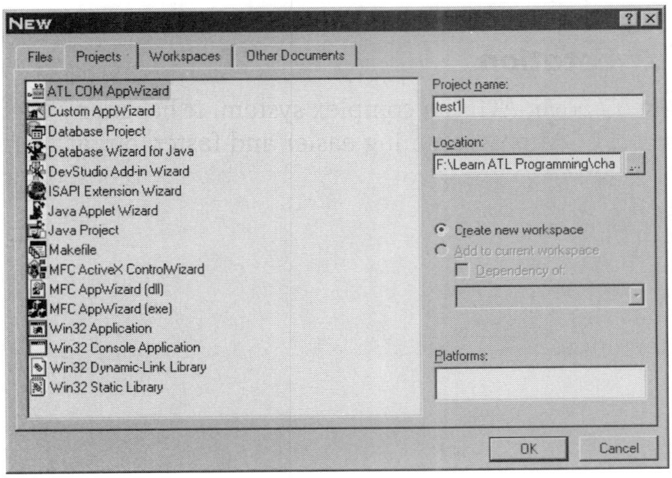


***Figure 2-3***
*The Visual C++ New dialog creating a new ATL AppWizard project*

## The ATL AppWizard

Once you press OK in the New dialog, the ATL AppWizard dialog appears, very similar in appearance to Figure 2-4. It contains only one page, with a small number of choices. As illustrated in the figure, you can select a DLL, an EXE, or an NT Service basic project type. You also have two check boxes to enable support for Microsoft Foundation Classes (MFC) and to enable the inclusion of proxy/stub functions directly in the server DLL (if a DLL project is selected) rather than requiring them in a separate DLL as is the standard approach. Once you have made the desired choices, press the Finish button to bring up the confirmation dialog.

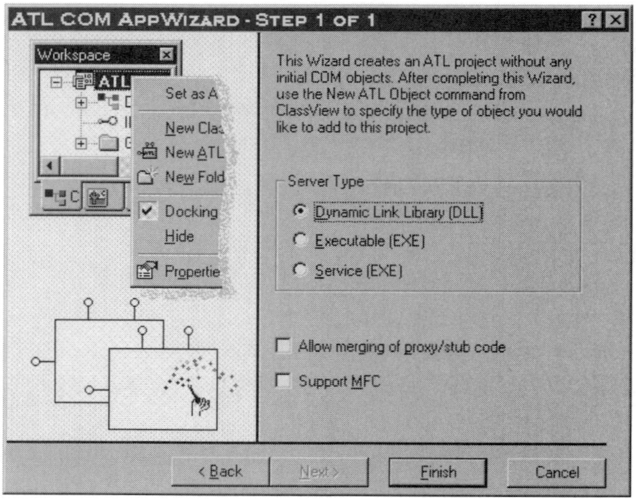


*Figure 2-4* The ATL AppWizard dialog

## The Confirmation Dialog

Pressing Finish in the ATL AppWizard brings up a confirmation dialog, as shown in Figure 2-5. This dialog lists the project name, the name of the COM server which will be generated and its file type (EXE or DLL), which file contains the DLL initialization code if there is one, what the IDL filename is, and what filename contains proxy/stub makefile code. Pressing OK actually generates the new ATL project with the selected options and displayed filenames.

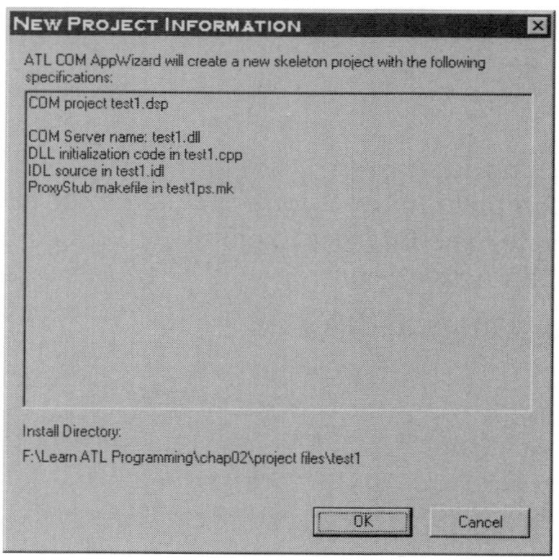


*Figure 2-5* The ATL AppWizard confirmation dialog

# Adding COM Interfaces with the ATL Object Wizard

Once you have created your ATL project via the ATL AppWizard, all you really have is a shell that does nothing. The AppWizard does not add any COM functionality! Instead, you must do that yourself. Fortunately, ATL provides (as of version 2.0) the ATL Object Wizard dialog system to help with this task. You access it via the Insert|New ATL Object menu option, which brings up the Object Wizard dialog box. There are four types of interfaces you can create using the version 2.0 ATL Object Wizard, each of which is discussed below. Once you've decided which type of interface object to use, select it in the dialog box and press Next to move to the tabbed dialog of the ATL Object Wizard.

## The Object Wizard Objects

The top-level choice in the left-hand list box brings up a group of six objects, as illustrated in Figure 2-6. These six objects are all basic COM interfaces, ranging from the Simple Object, which is a pure IUnknown Interface, to the Microsoft Transaction Server Component, which is a powerful COM interface capable of working in the MTS database management system. This book covers the MTS object in great detail; the others are topics outside our scope.

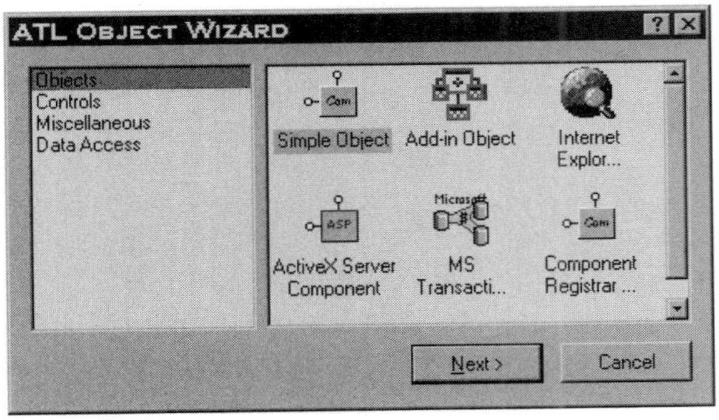


***Figure 2-6*** *Basic and specialized COM interface objects in the ATL Object Wizard*

## The Object Wizard Controls

The Controls entry brings up the three ActiveX control objects. The Full control object is just that, a complete ActiveX control suitable for use with Visual C++, Visual Basic, or Delphi. The Internet Explorer ActiveX control object is a "lightweight" version of an ActiveX control, which reduces its size for Internet download but does not seriously degrade its functionality. The Property Page object implements the ActiveX control Property Page system. This book covers all three of these controls in detail for our MTS ActiveX controls.

***Figure 2-7*** *ActiveX control and Property Page objects in the ATL Object Wizard*

## The Object Wizard Miscellaneous Elements

If you select the Miscellaneous entry in the left-hand list box, you'll see a display very much like that of Figure 2-8. It contains one entry in version 2.0, a Dialog object. This object allows ATL projects to display standard Windows dialog boxes, which can be edited in Visual C++'s dialog editor just like MFC dialogs. We won't use this in this book, but you might want to in one of your own projects.

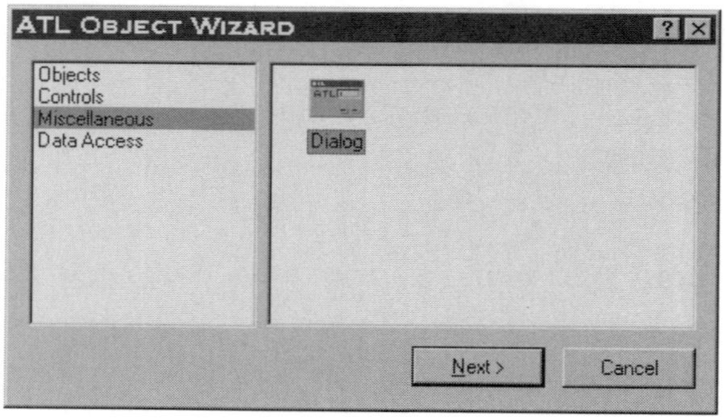


*Figure 2-8*
*The ATL Dialog object in the ATL Object Wizard*

## The Object Wizard Data Access Elements

The Data Access entry in the left-hand list box brings up the display shown in Figure 2-9. It also has only one entry in version 2.0: the OLE DB Provider object. This is an advanced interface that allows any type of data to be accessed using ActiveX Data Objects in a manner identical to a relational database. This book does not cover this object.

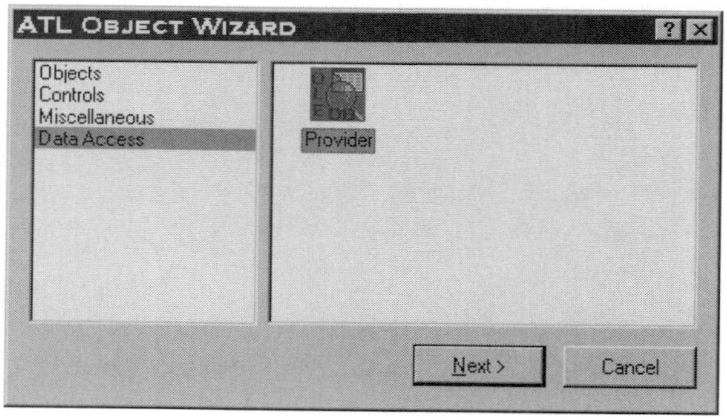


*Figure 2-9*
*The OLE DB Provider object in the ATL Object Wizard*

## The Object Wizard Names Tab

Once you've selected the type of interface object to create for your ATL project and pressed the Next button, you'll see a display similar to that of Figure 2-10. This is the Names tab of the ATL Object Wizard tabbed dialog box. All you need to do is enter a unique name in the Short Name edit control. The wizard then automatically fills in all the other edit controls for you. While you can alter these values, it is best not to, to avoid name

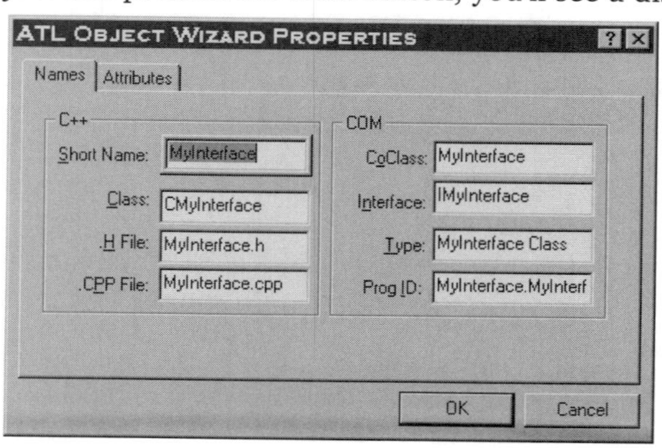


*Figure 2-10*
*Setting the names for an ATL interface object with the ATL Object Wizard*

conflicts later. Once you've done this, select the Attributes tab to set basic properties for your COM interface.

## The Object Wizard Attributes Tab

Selecting the Attributes tab of the ATL Object Wizard tabbed dialog box shows you a display very much like that of Figure 2-11. There are four basic attributes you can select for a COM interface from this tab of the dialog: the Threading Model (a complex topic involving using two or more copies of the same COM interface at the same time in the same process), whether the interface is a custom (basic COM) one or a dual one (usable by Automation clients), whether or not the interface can be aggregated (used "blind" by another COM interface, a topic not covered in this book), and which of three specialized features the interface will support: ISupportErrorInfo (Rich Error Information for Automation), Connection Points (interfaces for ActiveX events), and the Free Threaded Marshaler (a very advanced topic for speeding up threading for COM servers that is not covered in this book).

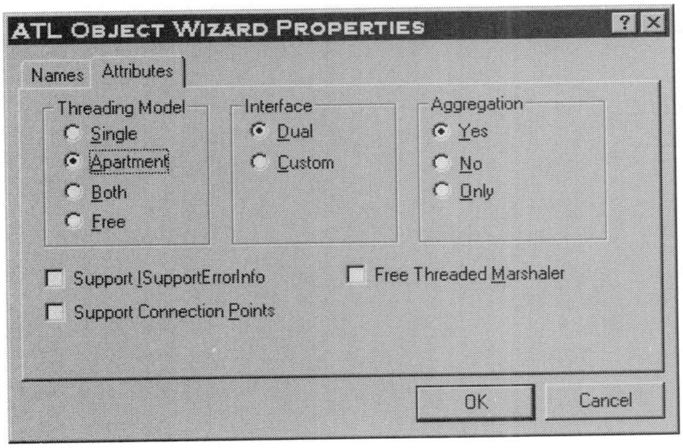


***Figure 2-11*** *Setting basic attributes for an ATL interface object with the ATL Object Wizard*

## Specialized Object Wizard Tabs

The above two tabs are always present for ATL interface objects. Other objects, like ActiveX controls, will have additional tabs. These will be covered in the appropriate chapters where they are used. When you have set the desired names and options for the ATL interface object, press OK to add it to the current ATL project.

# Creating Functions and Properties with the ATL Interface Wizards

Even after you've added an interface to your ATL project, you have a lot of work cut out for you. The interface you added contains only basic methods and properties, which in many cases do little or nothing. You must add your own custom methods and properties to the interface. This is intricate work, and again ATL comes to our rescue in version 2.0 with two wizard dialogs. These dialogs are rather hidden, only available from the shortcut (right-click) menu for a COM interface in the ClassView pane of the Project Viewer window of Visual C++.

## The ClassView Shortcut Menu

Figure 2-12 shows the shortcut (right-click) menu for a COM interface in the ClassView pane of the Project Viewer window of Visual C++. It has a number of useful options, but the ones we are interested in are Add Property and Add Method. Selecting Add Method brings up the Add Method Wizard for the ATL COM interface; selecting Add Property brings up the Add Property Wizard for the ATL Automation Dispinterface (covered in Chapter 4).

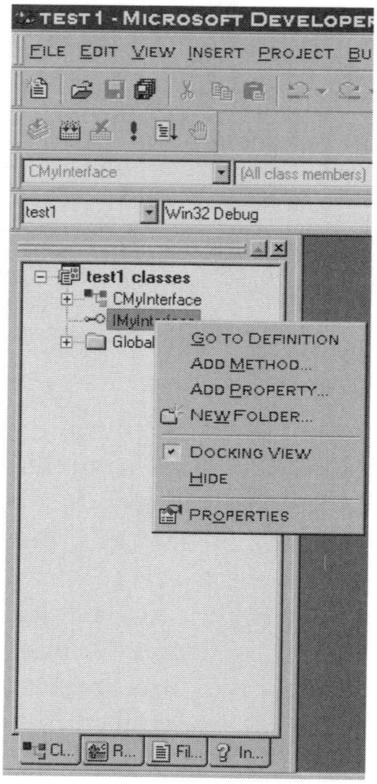


*Figure 2-12* *The shortcut menu for an ATL interface in the ClassView pane of Visual C++*

## The Add Method to Interface Dialog

Selecting Add Method from the ATL COM interface shortcut menu brings up the wizard dialog shown in Figure 2-13. As illustrated by the figure, the return type of the method is fixed as HRESULT; this is explained in Chapter 4. You enter a unique name for the method and set any desired parameters it will receive using IDL syntax. The read-only edit control at the bottom of the dialog will, as you press various buttons and make various entries, update itself with the IDL source code your actions have generated. To add the method to the selected interface, simply press OK. To add specialized IDL attributes for the method function, press the Attributes button (covered in a section below) before you press OK.

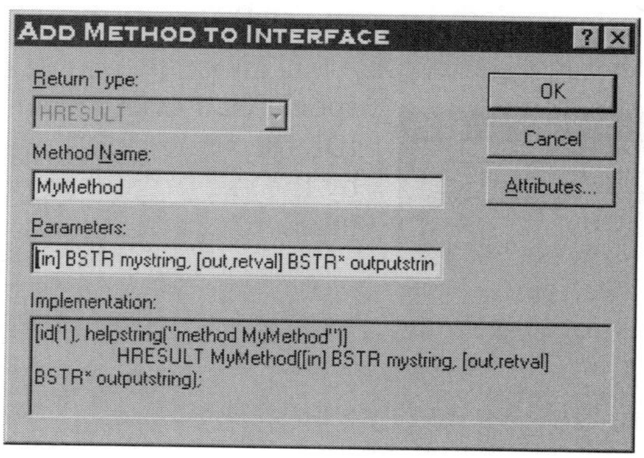


*Figure 2-13* *The Add Method Wizard dialog in ATL*

## The Add Property to Interface Dialog

Selecting Add Property from the ATL COM interface shortcut menu brings up the wizard dialog shown in Figure 2-14. As illustrated by the figure, the return type of the method is fixed as HRESULT; this is explained in Chapter 4. You enter a unique name for the property and set any desired parameters it will receive using IDL syntax. More importantly, you can select the Property Type value from the combo box; this list contains all the Automation data types ATL supports. While the function itself won't return this data type in C++, other languages like VBScript or Delphi Pascal will treat the property as if it does return that data type. The Get and Put Function check boxes allow you to determine whether the property is read/write, read-only, or write-only. The read-only edit control at the bottom of the dialog will, as you press various buttons and make various entries, update itself with the IDL source code your actions have generated. To add the method to the selected interface, simply press OK. To add specialized IDL attributes for the method function, press the Attributes button (covered below) before you press OK.

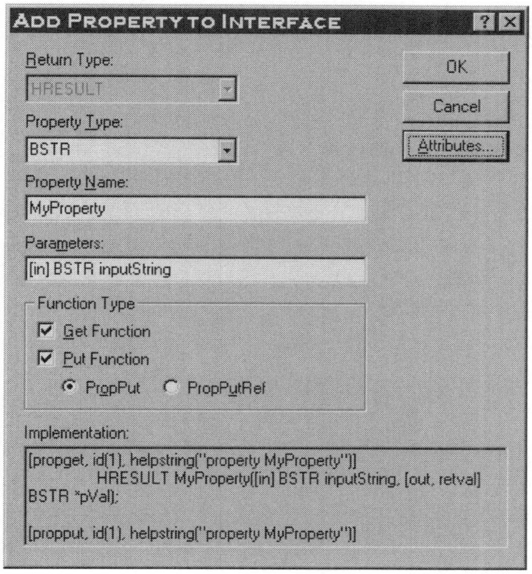


***Figure 2-14*** *The Add Property Wizard dialog in ATL*

## The Edit Attributes Dialog

In either wizard dialog, you can press the Attributes button to bring up a dialog very similar to that shown in Figure 2-15. This dialog is used to add specialized information to the IDL file source code generated by the wizard for the property or method. The left-hand combo box allows you to select from the available attributes; once you have selected one, you can enter a desired initial value in a right-hand edit control or combo box. The read-only edit control will show you what your choices have done to the IDL source

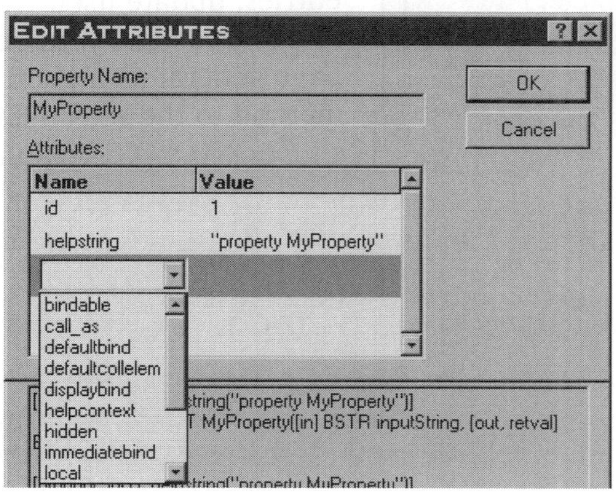


***Figure 2-15*** *The Add Property Wizard's Edit Attributes dialog in ATL*

code for the property or method. Press OK to add your changes to the generated IDL source code or Cancel to abort them. You can also edit to some degree the generated attributes already shown.

# Some Advanced Topics for ATL Projects

ATL is oriented towards COM development, and since more and more of Microsoft's technologies use COM, ATL has acquired more and more capabilities. Among these are proxy generation of specialized classes for Smart Pointers and Connection Points; advanced server projects like MTS, ASP, Visual C++ Add-Ins, and Component Registrars; and OLE DB Providers.

## *The Proxy Generator*

Although ATL code is generated with many automatic elements, in some cases the basic ATL system cannot create needed code. To help with this, the ATL Proxy Generator component was developed. The Proxy Generator outputs code that transforms one type of interface into another so that it can be more easily used in ATL. As of this writing, the Proxy Generator can handle two types of proxies: Smart Pointers (special wrapper classes that avoid most of the grunt work of using COM interfaces in C++) and Connection Points (specialized interfaces used for events in ActiveX controls). It is located on the Insert menu, under Components and Controls. You will use this component several times during the course of this book; since it is very specialized, it is covered when it is used rather than here.

## *Advanced Servers*

The Microsoft Transaction Server interface object is the focus of this book's non-ActiveX code; it contains about the same functionality as a basic COM Automation server, but also includes full support for MTS headers and acquiring the Object Context interface pointer (explained in Chapter 4 and beyond).

# ATL Code (Templates and Macros, Oh My!)

ATL's code is not straightforward. As we'll see in examining the various files output by the ATL wizards, there are many unusual software constructs in them. The two most common, and most powerful, are templates and macros.

## *Templates Create Custom Classes from Standard C++ Code*

Templates are what ATL is all about. Simply put, a template is a special software syntax used in C++ to allow generation of code from a basic pattern or template. This template has generic symbols for its variables, which therefore end up being untyped. When a template is given real variables with real types, the template "fills in" these actual data types and variables and performs the indicated actions on them. What makes ATL work is that this system also works for class variables. You can write a template that generates a custom class from a template, replacing key variables and functions in the template class with the imported class's functionality, while maintaining all the standard code of the template class unchanged. You'll see a number of concrete examples in later chapters as to how this works in COM server projects.

### Macros Expand into Customized Code

Macros came before templates; they do much the same thing but in a simpler way. A macro is expanded during the preprocessor step of compilation, and adds its code to that of the basic source file, replacing parameters of the macro with real variables from the macro's invocation. Unlike templates, however, macros are typed and so cannot be generic. You'll see a number of key macros in the coming chapters; where each is used, a detailed explanation and source listing is provided to help you understand how the ATL code works.

## What's New with ATL Version 3.0?

With the release of Visual C++ 6.0, a new version of ATL has been released as well: 3.0. It has a number of important changes, some of which are only used at the advanced level, a number of which affect intermediate developers, and a few of which will impact all users. The most fundamental changes are the addition of two new shortcut menu entries: adding an event handler for Windows messages and adding a Connection Point interface (rather than having to use the Proxy Generator). Also, a number of new ATL objects are provided in the Object Wizard, and there is a change to the basic ATL AppWizard itself. For intermediate users, there are some changes to the functionality of a number of ATL classes, as well as the addition of some new classes. At the advanced level, there are new macros, changes to how templates work, and support for ATL in MFC projects.

### Version 3.0 Changes to the ATL AppWizard

Figure 2-16 shows the ATL AppWizard dialog for version 3.0. You'll notice it looks very much like the one for version 2.1, except for the new check box at the bottom labeled Support MTS. This check box enables automatic support in the server for the Microsoft Transaction Server system when it is checked. This is somewhat subtle: It does not make the server an MTS-aware component; you have to do that yourself by adding an MTS Object from the ObjectWizard; it does, however, put in the proper header files for compilation of MTS objects, interfaces, and API calls rather than requiring you to find and include them by hand. It also causes the MTSEX.DLL dynamic-link library to be delay-loaded when the server is loaded, for efficiency.

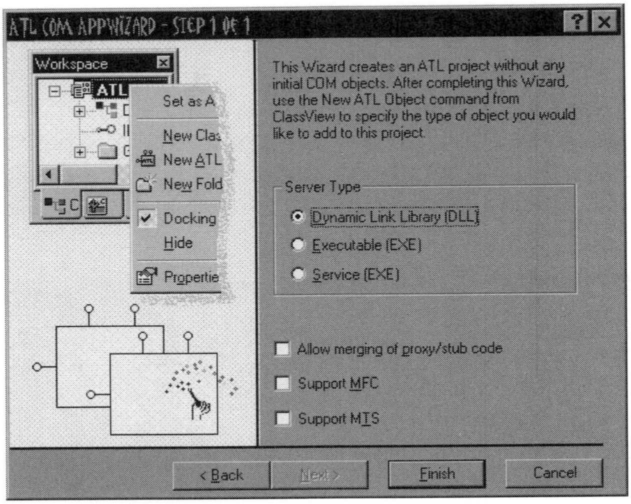


*Figure 2-16 The ATL AppWizard dialog for version 3.0*

## Version 3.0 Changes to the ATL Object Wizard

The changes to the ATL Object Wizard are more substantial, because a number of new and different ATL objects have been made available. Each page of the wizard is covered below, along with a brief synopsis of its new objects.

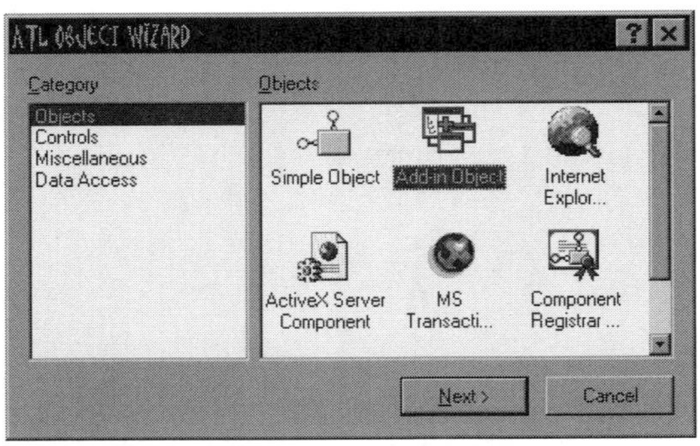


*Figure 2-17 The ATL Object Wizard dialog for version 3.0 showing the first six objects*

Figure 2-17 shows the ATL Object Wizard dialog's Objects page, with the top six objects visible. They are the same as the ones for ATL 2.1, but have somewhat more elegant icons.

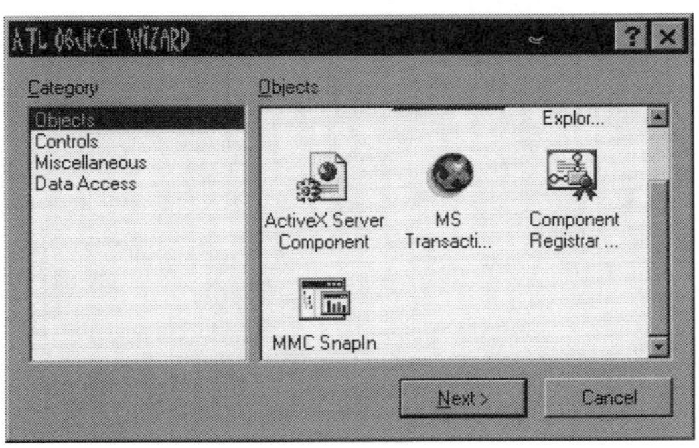


*Figure 2-18 The ATL Object Wizard dialog for version 3.0 showing the MMC SnapIn object*

Figure 2-18 shows the seventh object in the Objects page, the MMC SnapIn object. This ATL object is new for Version 3.0, and is used to create a component that can connect with the Windows NT Microsoft Management Console application. The object provides support for all the common interfaces needed to interact with the MMC UI; the developer provides the code to actually manage some aspect of NT behavior. This book does not cover MMC SnapIn components.

Figure 2-19 shows the ATL Object Wizard dialog's Controls page, with the top six objects visible. There are significant changes from the 2.1 version, as follows:

- The Internet Explorer Control is now the Lite Control. It otherwise has the same capabilities.
- The Full Control and Property Page objects have new icons but otherwise work the same.

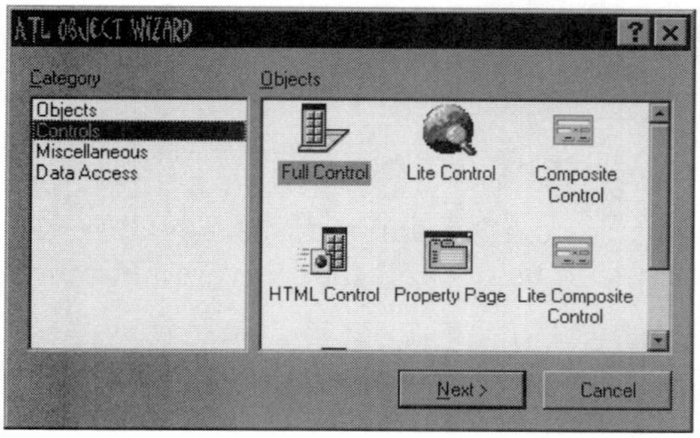


***Figure 2-19*** *The ATL Object Wizard dialog for version 3.0 showing the first six control objects*

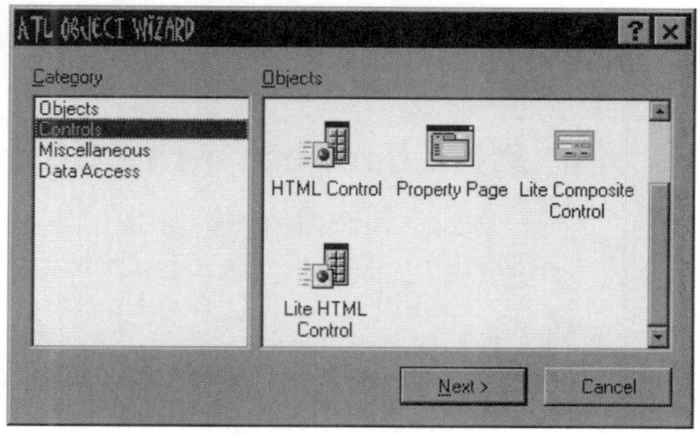


***Figure 2-20*** *The ATL Object Wizard dialog for version 3.0 showing the Lite HTML Control object*

Four new controls have been added (the fourth is shown in Figure 2-20). They are:

- **Composite Control** This object is a dialog-based template that allows visual creation of control user interfaces from existing Windows common controls. It is a full control otherwise.
- **Lite Composite Control** This object is identical in behavior to the Composite control, but only supports the interfaces of a Lite (Internet Explorer) control for faster downloading and performance.
- **HTML Control** This object is a dialog-based template hosting the WebBrowser control and connecting its DHTML text with COM interfaces in C++ to allow using DHTML as a user interface. This book does not cover DHTML components.
- **Lite HTML Control** This object is identical in behavior to the HTML control, but only supports the interfaces of a Lite (Internet Explorer) control for faster downloading and performance. This book does not cover DHTML components.

The Miscellaneous page has no changes; it still only contains the Dialog object for giving an ATL server a user interface.

Figure 2-21 shows the Object Wizard dialog's Data Access page, with both the Consumer and Provider objects shown. The Provider object was supported in

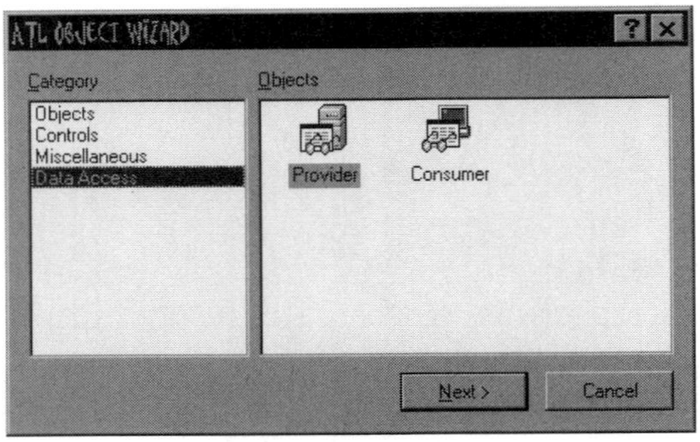


*Figure 2-21*
*The ATL Object Wizard dialog for version 3.0 showing the Consumer and Provider OLE DB objects*

version 2.1; version 3.0 adds a Consumer object as well. This book does not cover OLE DB components.

## Version 3.0 Changes to the ClassView Context Menus

There are three exciting new context ("shortcut") menu options available for many ATL classes; each is given a discussion below and then covered in more detail when it is used in later chapters.

### The Add Windows Message Handler Option

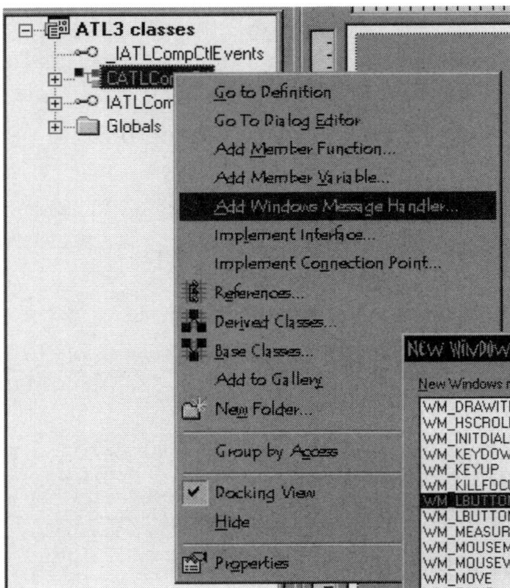


*Figure 2-22*
*The ATL ClassView context menu showing the Add Windows Message Handler option*

Figure 2-22 shows the ATL ClassView Context menu displaying the Add Windows Message Handler option. Selecting it brings up the dialog box shown in Figure 2-23.

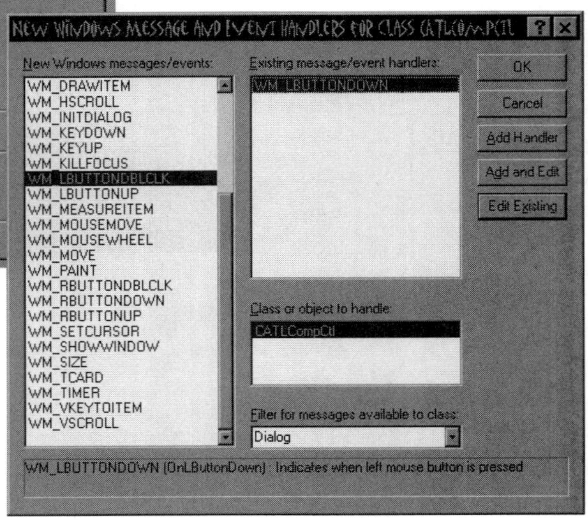


*Figure 2-23*
*The ATL New Windows Message Handler Wizard dialog*

**Warning:** This option is only available for classes which "wrap" a window, such as Dialog objects and Composite, Lite Composite, HTML, and Lite HTML controls. Other objects will not have this option since they do not normally receive Windows messages.

The New Windows Message Handler Wizard allows you to select from all appropriate Windows messages the ATL class can receive, displayed in the left-hand list box. You move a message to the right-hand list box by pressing either the Add Handler button or the Add and Edit button. (The latter choice will bring up code where the event handler is added so you can enter custom statements to respond to the message.) You can edit an existing handler by pressing the Edit Existing button. To accept the new event handler, press OK. To exit without saving the changes made in the wizard, press Cancel (unless you've pressed Add and Edit; this constitutes pressing OK first and cannot be undone).

### *The Implement Connection Point Option*

Figure 2-24 shows the ATL ClassView context menu displaying the Implement Connection Point option. Selecting it brings up the dialog box shown in Figure 2-25.

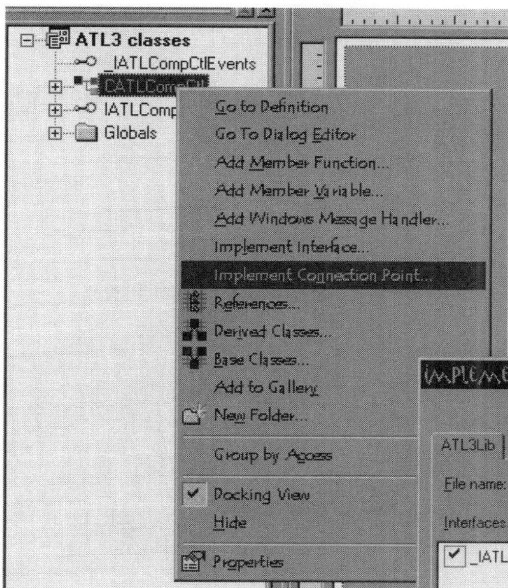


***Figure 2-24** The ATL ClassView context menu showing the Implement Connection Point option*

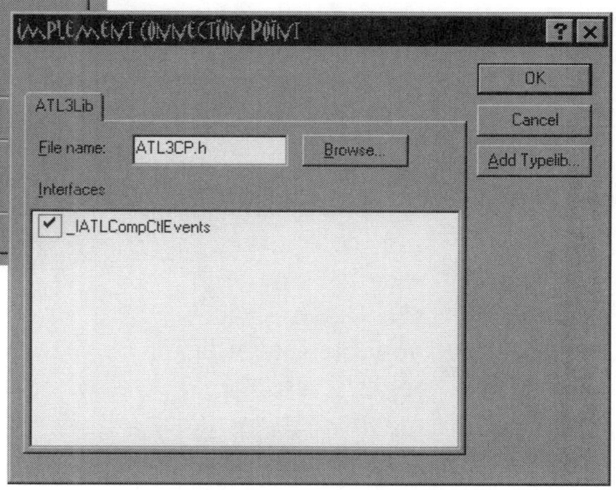


***Figure 2-25** The ATL Connection Point Wizard dialog*

**Warning:** This option is only available after you have compiled your ATL project at least once or, at the minimum, compiled its IDL file to produce a Type Library. Otherwise, an error dialog will appear when you try to select this option.

The Implement Connection Point Wizard replaces the Proxy Generator, which previously had to be used to compile a header file implementing an inline function dealing with adding support for a Connection Point to an ATL object.

### The Implement Interface Option

Figure 2-26 shows the ATL ClassView context menu displaying the Implement Interface option. Selecting it brings up the Implement Interface Wizard dialog box; press the Add TypeLib button to bring up the dialog shown in Figure 2-27.

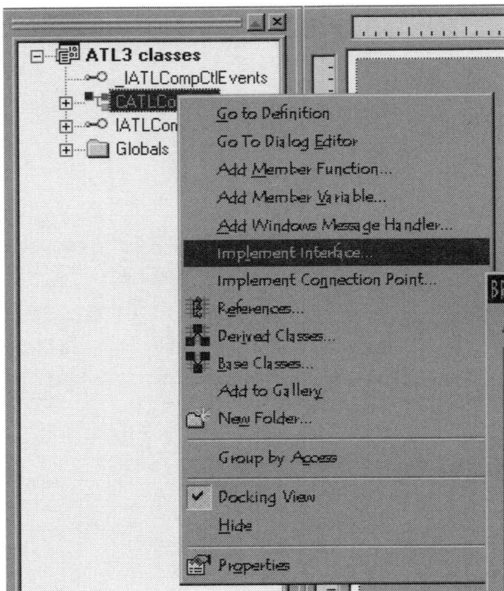


*Figure 2-26*
*The ATL ClassView context menu showing the Implement Interface option*

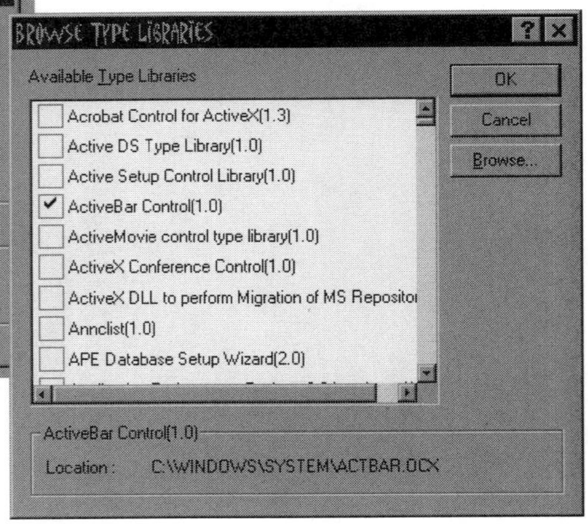


*Figure 2-27*
*The ATL Add TypeLib Wizard dialog*

Shown in the dialog are all the Type Libraries registered on the current development computer. Selecting one will make its interfaces available for implementation in the current class; you can select as many as you need. Pressing OK brings up the dialog box shown in Figure 2-28.

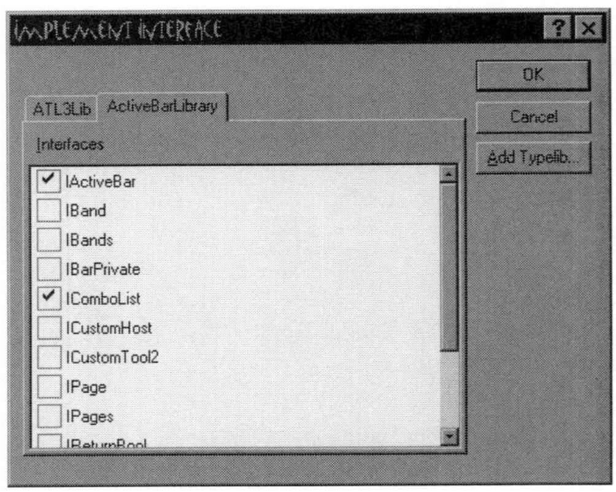


*Figure 2-28*
*The ATL Implement Interfaces Wizard dialog*

The figure shows a sample list of the interfaces supported by a chosen Type Library's server. Selecting them will cause "stub" code to be placed for them in the current object, allowing a developer to automatically aggregate or contain the interface as desired.

## Where We Go From Here

Now that you're familiar with the basic mechanics of ATL in Visual C++, you are ready to add your understanding of COM to this knowledge and start creating MTS ActiveX controls and servers. Chapter 4 begins the process with basic MTS programming information. (Chapter 3 goes over MFC; you can skip it if you don't use that environment.) Put on your Component Object Model hardhat and fire up the ATL rivet gun: MTS awaits!

Chapter Three

# An MFC Primer

MFC stands for the Microsoft Foundation Classes. MFC is a set of C++ objects that encapsulate access to a number of Windows programming aspects, including the GDI (Graphical Device Interface), file operations, window creation and message handling, and various specialized aspects of the OS. One of these specialized aspects is ActiveX; support for it is added via existing support for COM (the Component Object Model, discussed in Chapter 1). MFC's main claim to fame is its provision of C++ objects rather than raw API calls for Windows programming, and this holds true for ActiveX as well.

There is a lot to MFC, and it often confuses beginners to either COM or itself. There is enough material in the MFC system for two or three full-sized books; this particular book is going to focus on the basics. This chapter will cover how MFC fits into Visual C++ and what its various wizard dialogs do. A brief look is taken at the classes MFC uses, but because these are more advanced topics, they won't be covered in great detail. (Individual chapters will cover the specific classes they use.) When you've finished reading this chapter, you'll be ready to start creating basic MFC-based MTS servers and ActiveX controls!

## MFC in Visual C++

MFC does not work by itself; it is designed for, and only works with, Microsoft Visual C++. It enhances the Integrated Development Environment of Visual C++ with wizard dialogs and automatic code generators. It also provides extensive online help and many detailed sample projects.

### *MFC's Online Documentation*

As mentioned above, MFC is a complex system. It has many useful features that can make ActiveX programming easier and faster, but at a price in time and effort to familiarize yourself with it. Since you've purchased (or are considering purchasing) this book, you are obviously interested in MFC and

ActiveX. One very good way to learn about it is to work through all the online documentation installed with it.

To access the online documents for MFC, use the Help menu option and select Search. In the edit control, enter MFC and press the Search button. A number of results will appear; scroll down until you see the feature you are interested in. Clicking on it will bring up a group of topics; the best place to start is "MFC Article Overview"; select it and press the Display button. From there all the MFC documents are hyperlinked into one detailed unit, which you can browse and print at your leisure.

# Creating MFC Projects with the MFC AppWizard

An MFC project starts with the MFC AppWizard. It is found in the ubiquitous New dialog of Visual C++, and provides a simple wizard dialog that hides a lot of power behind its plain face. With this wizard and its attendant confirmation dialog, you unleash all the power of MFC for ActiveX programming.

## The New Dialog

To start an MFC project, select File|New from the Visual C++ menu. The New dialog appears; select the Projects tab to produce the display shown in Figure 3-1. By clicking on the MFC ActiveX ControlWizard entry as illustrated in the figure, you enable entry of the project name (which should be different from the planned name(s) of any other controls to avoid conflicts) and selection of its directory on the hard drive of the development computer. When you have entered this information, pressing OK will start the actual MFC ActiveX ControlWizard.

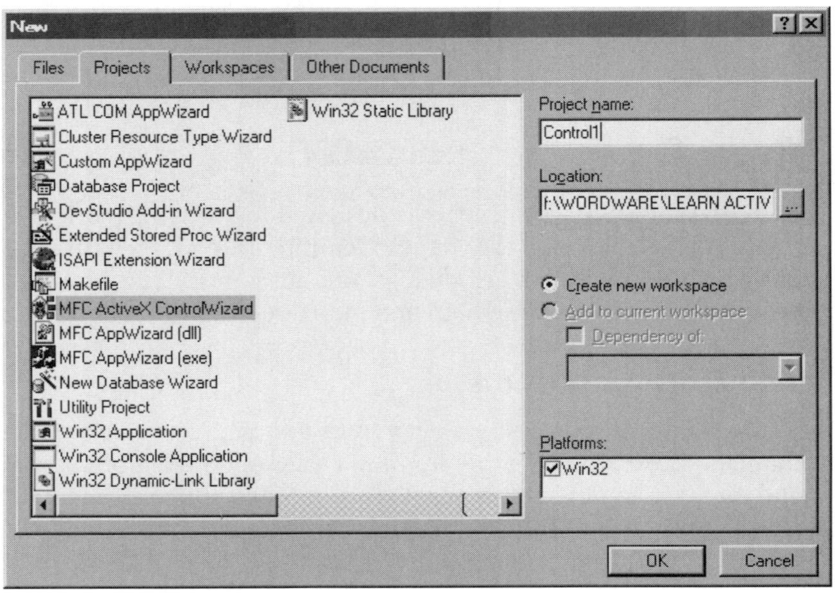


*Figure 3-1 The Visual C++ New dialog creating a new MFC ActiveX ControlWizard project*

## The MFC ActiveX ControlWizard

Once you press OK in the New dialog, the MFC ActiveX ControlWizard dialog appears, very similar in appearance to Figure 3-2. It contains two pages, with a number of choices. As illustrated by the figure, you can enter how many controls you want to create in the project (default is 1), whether or not to use a runtime license (a means of protecting openly distributed controls from being reused after they are downloaded for display), whether or not to generate source file comments (default is yes, a good idea), and whether or not to create a basic WinHelp helpfile project (default is no). Once you have made the desired choices, press the Next button to bring up the second page of the wizard.

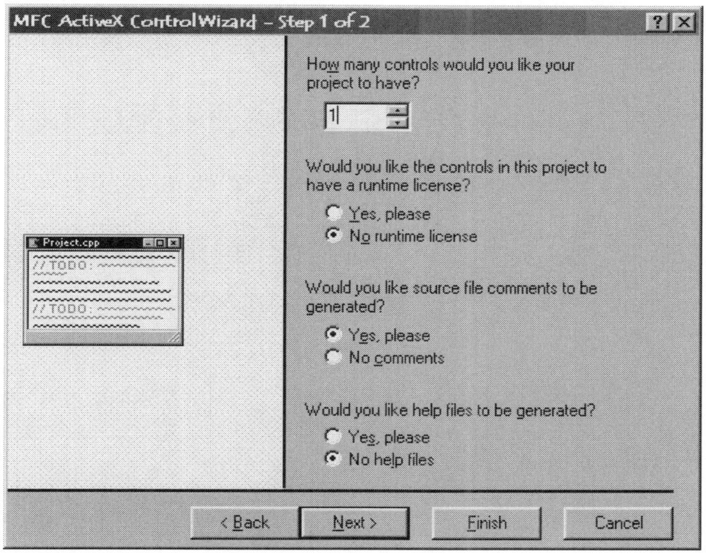


***Figure 3-2*** *The MFC ActiveX ControlWizard dialog first page*

Pressing Next brings up the second page of the wizard, as shown in Figure 3-3. As illustrated in the figure, you select the active control for its settings from a drop-down list. For each control you can edit its filenames (shown in Figure 3-4) or set a number of specialized options. You can also select a base Windows common control to use as the basis for the currently selected ActiveX control and set a

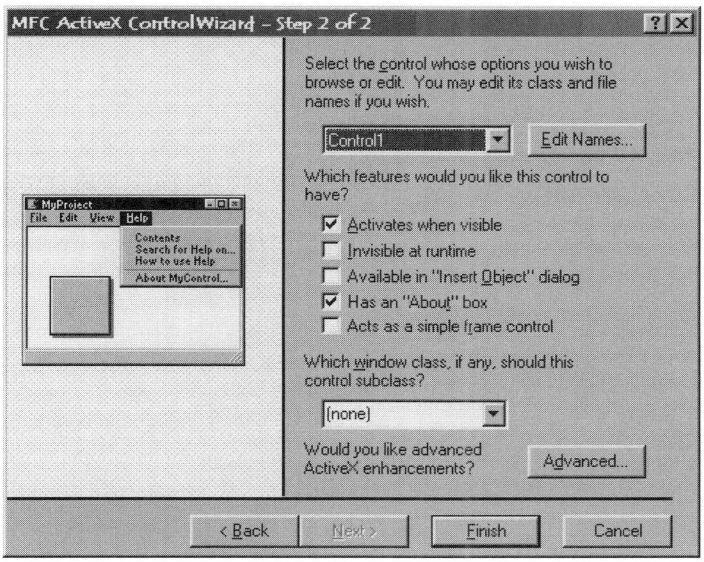


***Figure 3-3*** *The MFC ActiveX ControlWizard dialog second page*

number of advanced options. Once you have made the desired choices, press the Finish button to bring up the confirmation dialog.

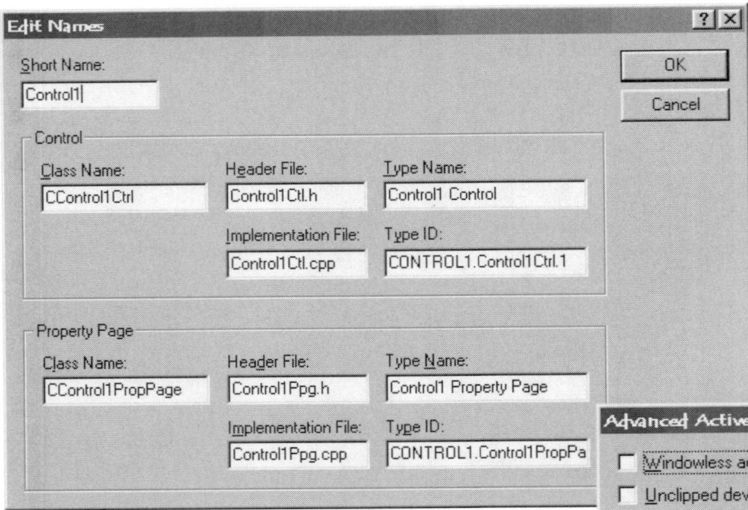


*Figure 3-4* *The MFC ActiveX Control-Wizard names entry dialog*

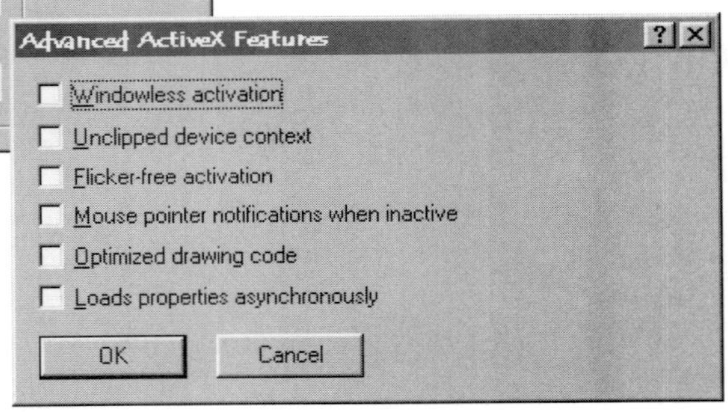


*Figure 3-5* *The MFC ActiveX ControlWizard advanced options dialog*

## The Confirmation Dialog

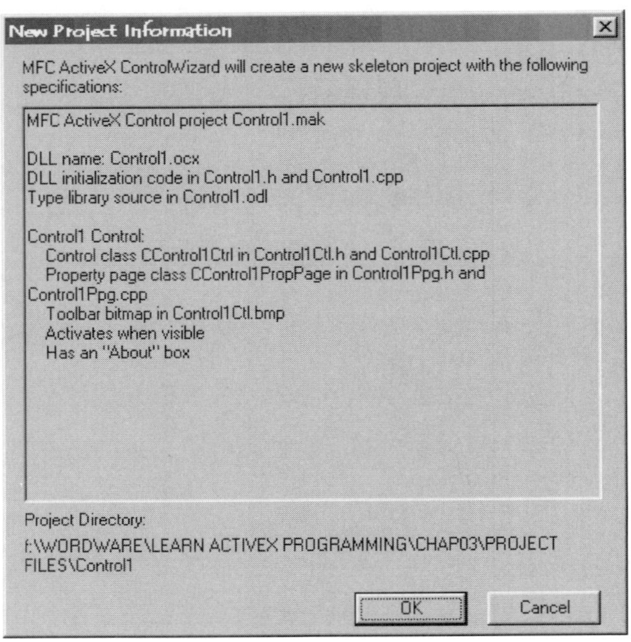


*Figure 3-6* *The MFC ActiveX ControlWizard confirmation dialog*

Pressing OK in the ControlWizard brings up a confirmation dialog, as shown in Figure 3-6. This dialog lists the project name, the name of the ActiveX control that will be generated, and its default Property Page, as well as the filenames for these objects. Pressing OK actually generates the new MFC project with the selected options and displayed filenames.

# Working MFC Magic with the ClassWizard

Once you have created your MFC project via the MFC ActiveX ControlWizard, all you really have is a shell that does nothing. The ControlWizard does not add any ActiveX functionality! Instead, you must do that yourself. Fortunately, MFC provides the enormously powerful ClassWizard dialog system to help with this task. You access it via the View|ClassWizard menu option as shown in Figure 3-7, which brings up the ClassWizard dialog box. There are five tabs for the ClassWizard, each of which is discussed below.

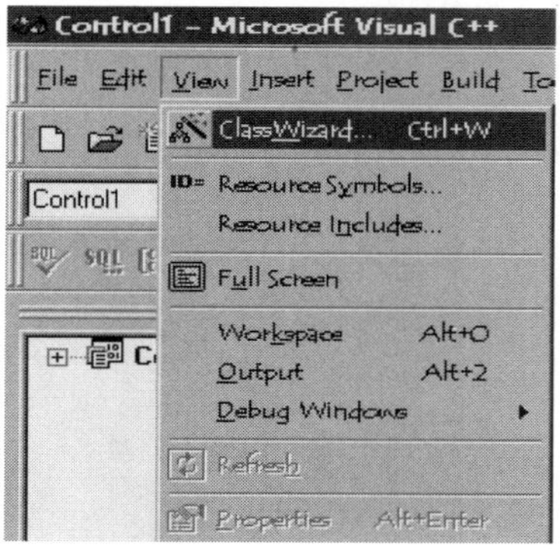


*Figure 3-7*
*The MFC ClassWizard menu option*

## The ClassWizard Message Maps Tab

The leftmost tab covers MFC Message Maps, as illustrated in Figure 3-8. These are specialized macros and functions that connect Windows messages with the currently selected ActiveX control's MFC class.

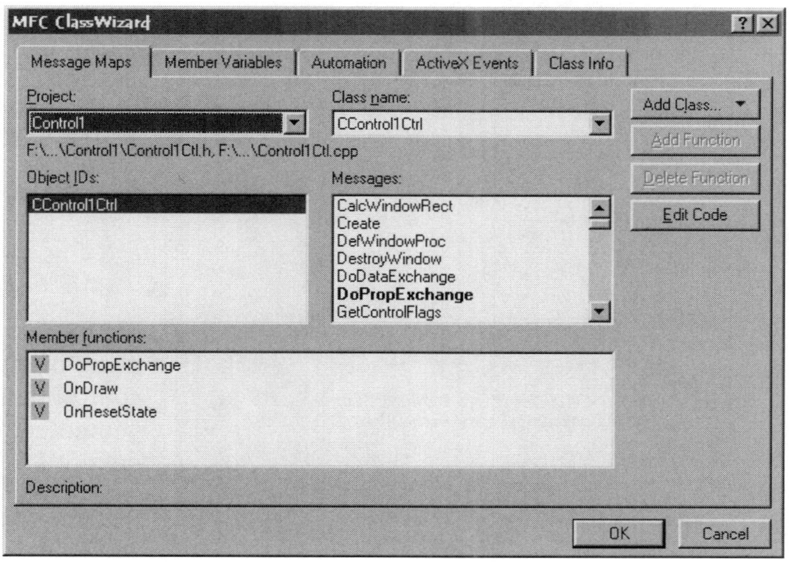


*Figure 3-8*
*The MFC ClassWizard Message Maps tab*

## The ClassWizard Member Variables Tab

The second tab of the ClassWizard is the Member Variables tab, as shown in Figure 3-9. Member variables are used in several ways in ActiveX MFC programming: to store information for control use, to connect with exposed

ActiveX control properties, and to move information in and out of Windows controls on ActiveX control Property Pages.

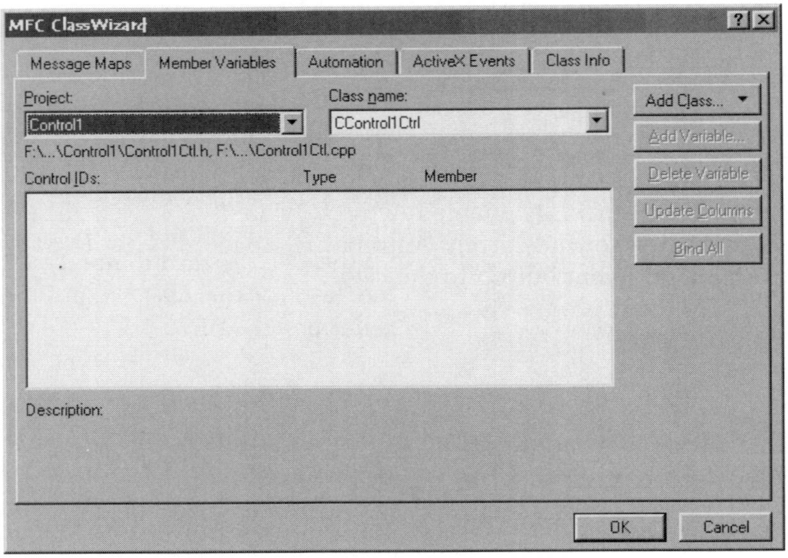


*Figure 3-9*
*The MFC ClassWizard Member Variables tab*

## The ClassWizard Automation Tab

When you select the Automation Tab of the MFC ClassWizard, you'll see a display very much like that of Figure 3-10. It contains two drop-down lists, one of all the projects in the current workspace on the left and one of all the classes in the current project on the right. If the currently selected class in the right-hand combo box is Automation-enabled (by default all ActiveX control

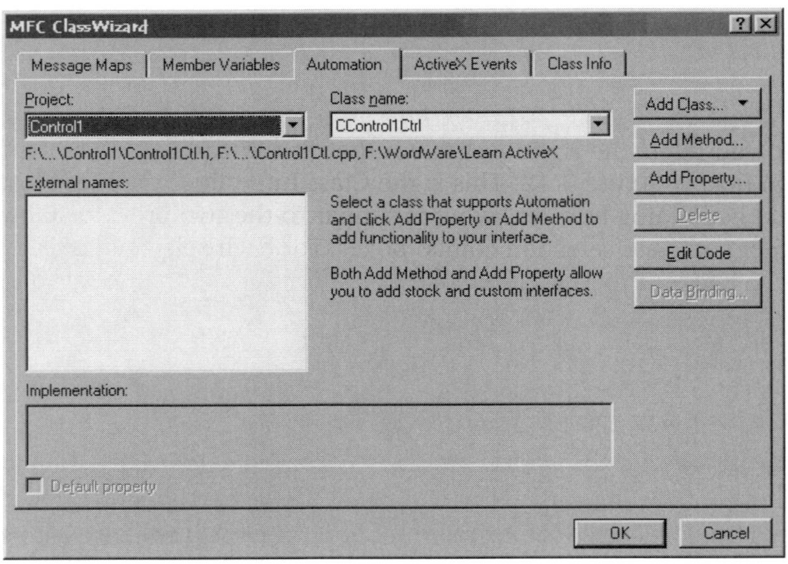


*Figure 3-10*
*The MFC ClassWizard Automation tab*

classes are), then the various buttons to the right are enabled as well. They are used to add custom and stock methods and properties to the ActiveX control.

## The ClassWizard ActiveX Events Tab

The ActiveX Events tab of the MFC ClassWizard brings up the display shown in Figure 3-11. It has the same basic layout as the Automation tab covered above, with its project and class selection combo boxes. Its left-hand list box gives all the currently enabled ActiveX events (which are different from Windows events) for the current Automation-enabled class. To add a new event, use the Add Event button to the right.

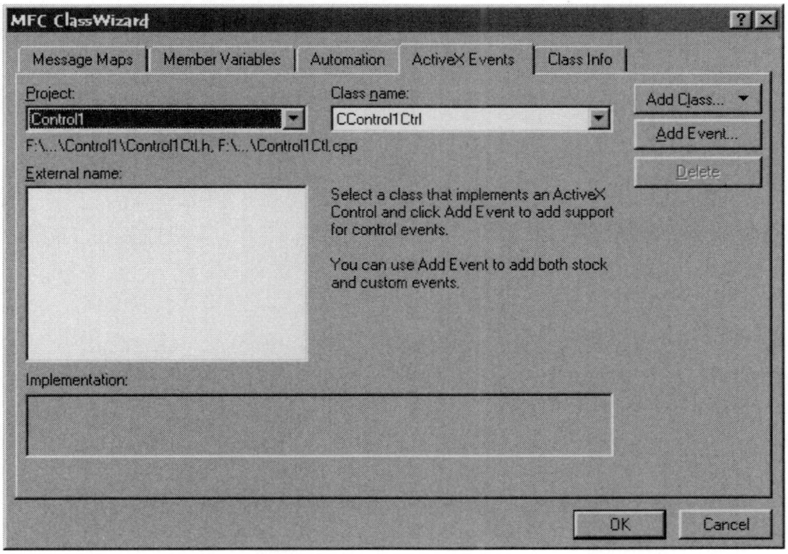


***Figure 3-11*** *The MFC ClassWizard ActiveX Events tab*

## The ClassWizard Class Info Tab

If you select the rightmost tab of the ClassWizard, you'll see a display similar to that of Figure 3-12. This is the Class Info tab of the MFC ClassWizard tabbed dialog box. Its layout is similar to the two previous tabs, with its project and class selection combo boxes. For each selected class, the tab displays the header file, source file, base class, and resource file information. It also allows selection of a Windows message filter class, and of "foreign" classes and variables for use in the class currently selected.

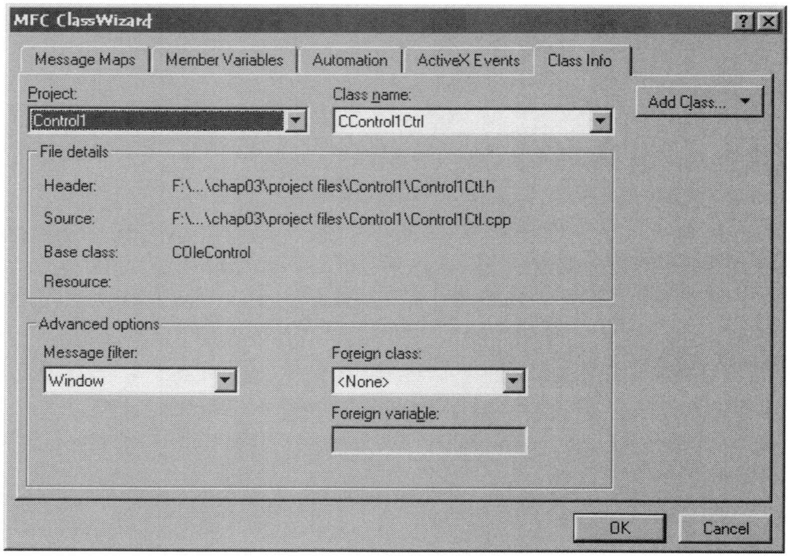


***Figure 3-12*** *The MFC ClassWizard Class Info tab*

# Augmenting ActiveX Control Features with ClassWizard Dialogs

There are a number of important dialogs accessed through ClassWizard's various tabs; each one is shown below with a quick tour of its major features.

## *The ClassWizard New Class Dialog*

Figure 3-13 shows the New Class dialog for the MFC ClassWizard. It is accessed from the Automation tab of the wizard via the Add Class button's New Class menu option. While in normal ActiveX programming with MFC you won't use this dialog, it is a vital way to add Automation/ActiveX features to a basic MFC project. To use the New Class dialog, simply enter a new class name in the upper edit control, then select a base class from the middle combo box (CCmdTarget is a good one). Finally, decide whether to use basic

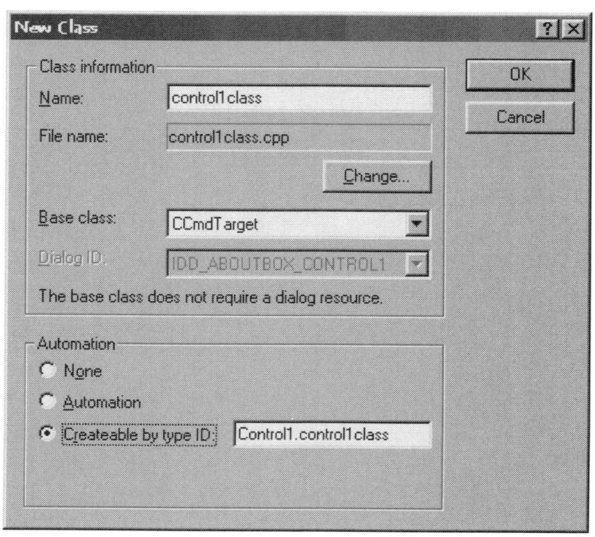


***Figure 3-13*** *The MFC ClassWizard New Class dialog in Visual C++ 6.0*

Automation or TypeID support (shown in the figure). TypeID support is best for most Automation projects.

## The ClassWizard Add Method Dialog

Selecting the Add Method button from the ClassWizard Automation tab brings up the Add Method dialog shown in Figure 3-14. As illustrated in the figure, there are stock methods available from the upper combo box, or you can enter a new name for a custom method. An internal name will be created, which you can edit if desired. The return type is void for stock methods, but you can set it to other values if desired (the MFC system will actually move these in and out as parameters). Finally, you can add any desired parameters to the method via the two combo boxes at the bottom of the dialog.

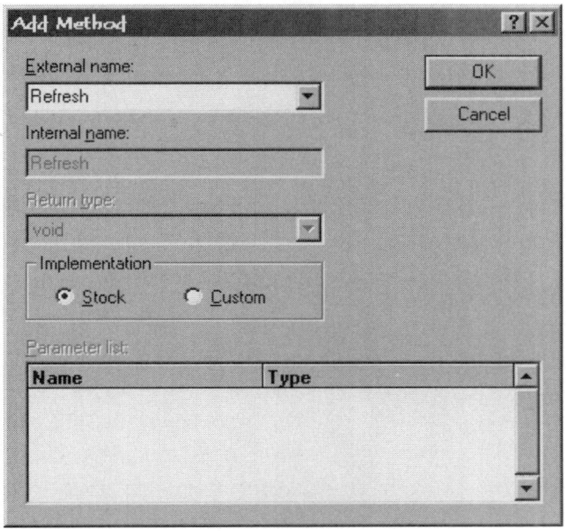


*Figure 3-14 The MFC ClassWizard Add Method dialog in Visual C++ 6.0*

## The ClassWizard Add Property Dialog

Selecting the Add Property button from the ClassWizard Automation tab brings up the Add Property dialog shown in Figure 3-15. As illustrated in the figure, this is a much more involved dialog box. First, you must enter an external name for the property; this is what clients of your control or other Automation class will work with. Then you must select a data type for the property from the available list in the combo box. The MFC system will add automatic support for Get and Put functions if you select that radio button in the Implementation section; if you select Member Variable, these function edit controls are disabled. The MFC dialog also allows you to

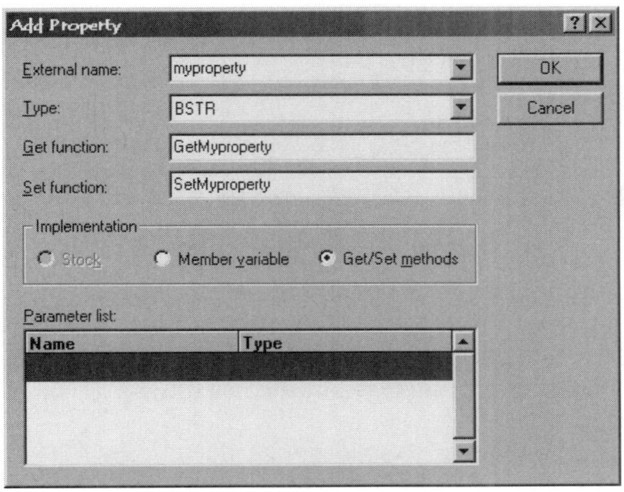


*Figure 3-15 The MFC ClassWizard Add Property dialog in Visual C++ 6.0*

select from a number of stock properties; in this case, the Implementation radio button is automatically Stock and you cannot change it. Finally, you can add parameters of any supported data type to the property; this is because ActiveX/Automation properties are actually functions.

### The ClassWizard Add Event Dialog

Selecting the Add Event button from the ClassWizard ActiveX Events tab brings up the Add Event dialog shown in Figure 3-16. As illustrated in the figure, you can either select a stock event (two are supported) or enter a new external name for a custom one. An internal name based on the external name is automatically generated; you can edit it if you like. If you select a custom implementation, you can also add parameters of any supported data type to the event; this is because ActiveX events are really just method functions exchanged between clients and controls.

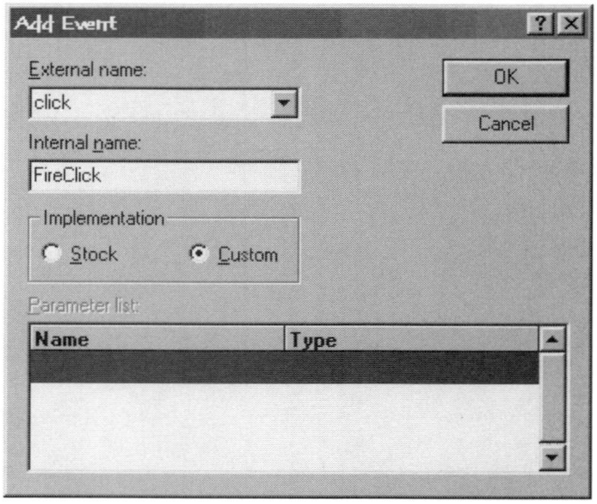


***Figure 3-16*** *The MFC ClassWizard Add Event dialog in Visual C++ 6.0*

## Some Advanced Topics for MFC ActiveX Control Projects

There are three other topics that MFC ActiveX developers need to understand beyond those covered already in this chapter: connecting Windows events to ActiveX controls, editing Property Page dialogs, and connecting Property Page dialog controls to ActiveX control properties. Each is explained below.

### Using Windows Events with ClassWizard

Figure 3-17 shows the MFC ClassWizard Message Maps tab. It lists all the Windows messages a given MFC class (in the upper left-hand list box) can receive in the upper right-hand list box. Selecting one of these messages will enable the Add Function button on the right-hand side as shown in the figure. Clicking on it will bring up a dialog allowing editing of the default name given to the event handler; once this dialog has been accepted, the new event and its handler function are shown in the lower list box display. You can then write custom code in the actual handler itself (the Edit Code button is a handy way to find the exact function in the class file).

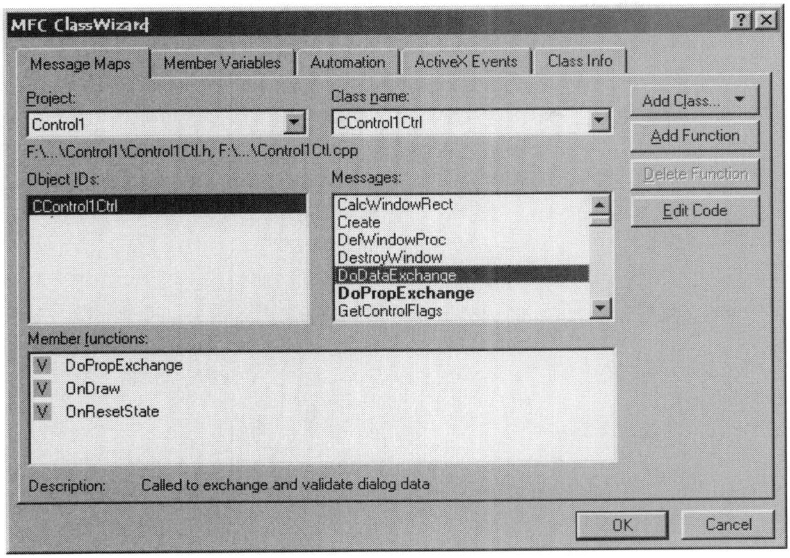


***Figure 3-17** The MFC ClassWizard Message Maps tab in Visual C++ 6.0*

## Editing Property Pages

MFC automatically creates a Property Page dialog resource for all ActiveX control projects. It is editable in the Dialog Editor for Visual C++, as shown in Figure 3-18 below. You use the standard dialog box editing techniques to put on Windows common controls, position them, and change their captions and other properties using the Edit Properties dialog box also shown in the figure. (Note its little "push pin" button; if you click on it, this button "flips up" and the dialog stays on top even when you edit the main dialog resource. Otherwise, the Edit Properties dialog box is hidden once you return to editing the main display.)

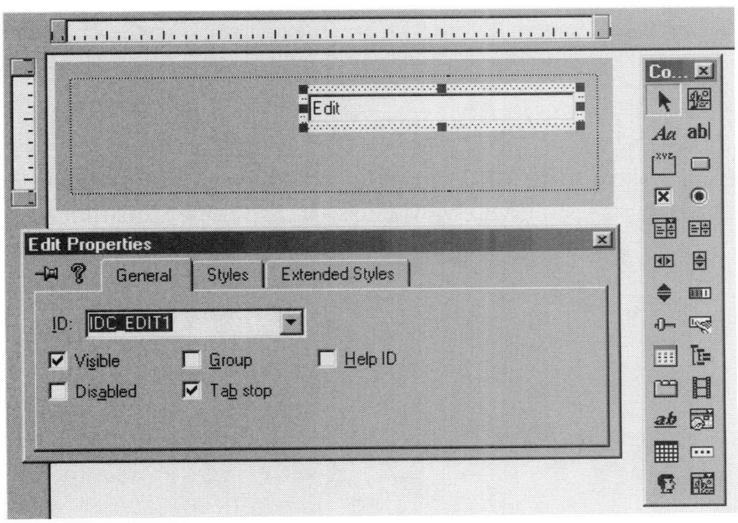


***Figure 3-18** The Dialog Editor in Visual C++ 6.0*

## Connecting Property Page Controls to ActiveX Control Properties with ClassWizard

Once you have a Property Page dialog all ready to go, MFC will happily display it for you, but it lets you decide which controls connect to what ActiveX control properties. Unlike the ATL system, MFC provides help in this connection process via the ClassWizard. Its Member Variables tab shown in Figure 3-19 illustrates how this works. As illustrated in the figure, once you have a control on your Property Page dialog that can be connected to an ActiveX control property, its identifier is listed in the lower list box of the dialog page. To connect it with an ActiveX control property, simply select the desired control identifier and click on the Add Variable button to the right.

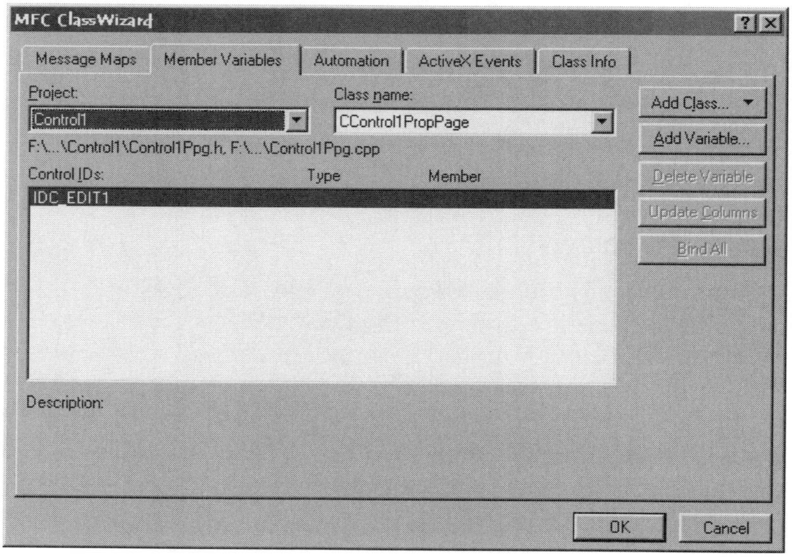


*Figure 3-19*
*The MFC ClassWizard Member Variables tab in Visual C++ 6.0*

Once you do this, the Add Member Variable dialog appears as shown in Figure 3-20. The upper edit control allows you to enter the desired name; note that it already contains the appropriate prefix for the Hungarian notation used by MFC. Once you enter the desired name, select either a Value category or a Reference one; the former passes the data from the control as a value, while the latter puts it in directly as a pointer. Next, select the variable type, which can be any of those Automation supports

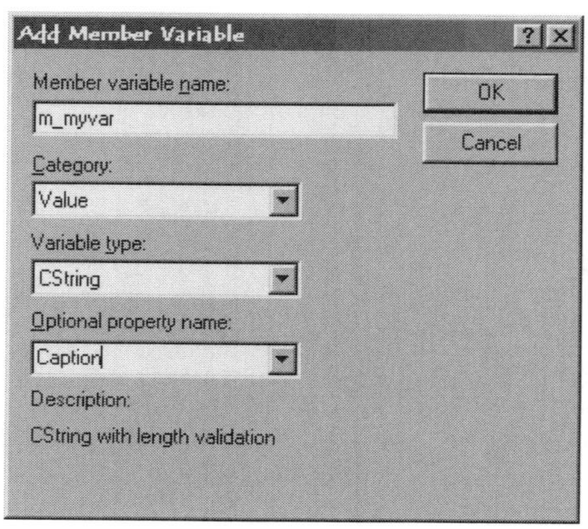


*Figure 3-20*
*The MFC ClassWizard Add Member Variable dialog in Visual C++ 6.0*

plus some MFC specialties like CString. Then select the optional property name from those available, including both custom and stock properties.

## MFC Code (Classes and Macros, Oh My!)

MFC's code is not straightforward. As we'll see in examining the various files output by the MFC wizards, there are many unusual software constructs in them. The two most common, and most powerful, are classes and macros.

### *MFC Classes Encapsulate Much Windows Functionality in C++ Wrappers*

MFC is a collection of C++ classes that encapsulate much of the functionality of Windows programming in the C++ metaphor (the actual Windows API is C-based, and so are just functions rather than classes). This was done initially to speed developers' understanding of the powerful but very complex and often unintuitive Windows programming process. The MFC system is a compromise; it does use C++ classes and syntax, but doesn't do much more. Other vendors such as Inprise (aka Borland) have other wrapper classes that are much more sophisticated, but developers pay a price in that they pretty much do things the way the framework wants them to, rather than their own way. MFC's compromise allows much developer flexibility while providing considerable C++ capability.

### *Macros Expand into Customized Code*

A *macro* is a defined identifier that represents a block of source code. A macro is expanded during the preprocessor step of compilation and adds its code to that of the basic source file, replacing parameters of the macro with real variables from the macro's invocation. Unlike C++ templates, however, macros are typed and so cannot be generic. You'll see a number of key macros in the coming chapters; it is often useful to select them in the IDE and examine their online help entry.

## Where We Go From Here

Now that you're familiar with the basic mechanics of MFC in Visual C++, you are ready to add your understanding of COM to this knowledge and start creating MTS ActiveX controls and servers. Chapter 4 begins with a detailed overview of MTS programming and administration. Put on your Component Object Model hardhat and fire up the MFC assembly line: MTS awaits!

Chapter Four

# An MTS Primer

Microsoft Transaction Server programming consists of using a set of powerful COM interfaces (which is why we went into all the details on COM earlier in the book). These interfaces (along with a couple of API calls) are what developers use to make their database components work with MTS seamlessly. This chapter will give you complete information on these API calls and interfaces, and in the process explain what MTS is and how it works.

There is one important point to remember, however: MTS has absolutely no database functionality of its own! Instead, it relies on the powerful Microsoft technology known as ADO (ActiveX Data Objects) for actual programmatic connection to MTS-aware databases like SQL Server and Oracle. Chapter 5 covers ADO in complete detail.

## Overview of Microsoft Transaction Server

Before we get down and dirty with the interfaces that make up MTS, it's important to understand what MTS is, what it does, and why this is important.

### *MTS is Generic "Middleware"*

To understand what MTS is, you first have to have a good picture of the way most modern PC databases work in the real world. There are two models that are prevalent: two-tier and three-tier. Both models are based on client/server architecture, where one or more computers provide a user interface (the client(s)), and (usually) one computer provides the database(s) used by the client(s) (the server). Figure 4-1 shows the basic two-tier architecture at work.

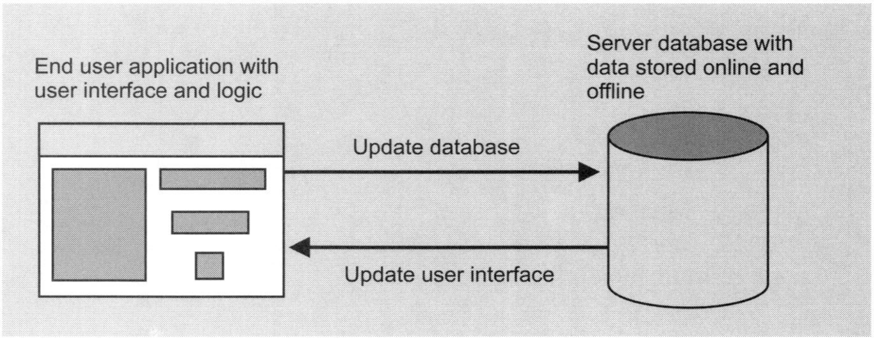


*Figure 4-1*
*Two-tier client/server architecture*

As you see in the figure, two-tier systems connect directly to their database(s). This has several advantages: It is faster, because each copy of the user interface has all the instructions to go right to the data store and obtain or change information; it is easier to create, because the flow of work is very contained and can be modeled in a straightforward way; and it can be easier to control for security purposes, since access to the user interface is all that must be restricted. However, this model has several major drawbacks: If the logic of the application needs to be changed, every copy of the application containing the user interface must be changed, even if only a few users need the change; if the underlying database changes, every copy of the application must be changed; and finally, if additional databases must be added, the interaction problems with existing code can quickly explode into exponentially unmanageable dimensions.

For this reason, as technology became available to support component software (like CORBA and COM), database systems began to adopt the three-tier model, shown in Figure 4-2.

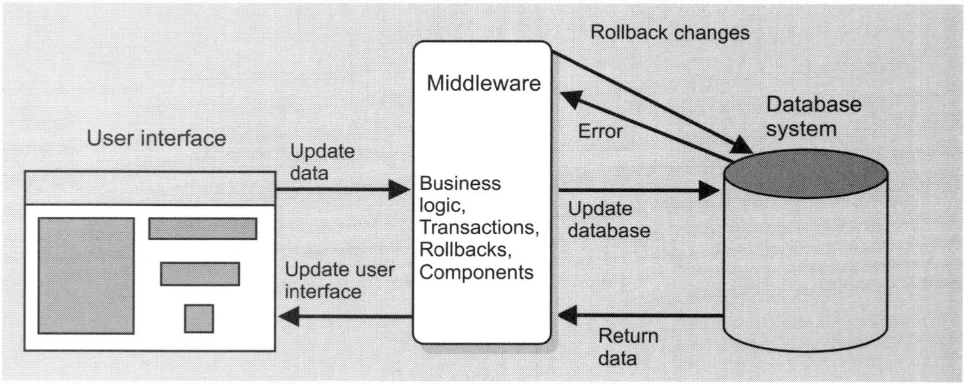


*Figure 4-2*
*Three-tier client/server architecture*

This figure shows the alternative solution provided by component software: the creation of a “middle” layer between the user-interface applications and the actual database systems. This third level of software came to be known as *middleware*. Its job is to encapsulate much of the logical and security programming contained in the applications of a two-tier system. At first, this may not seem such a major improvement, but it allows many options not possible before. For example, if an additional feature is needed, only a few of the elements of the middleware need to be changed and distributed; users who don't need the change will not need to have their user interface updated. Similarly, if the underlying database is changed, only appropriate middleware components need to be changed, rather than the user interface applications. Finally, if another database is needed, it can be accessed via the middleware by simply adding new components rather than having to rewrite one monolithic application.

## MTS Provides Support for Heterogenous Transactions

A *transaction* is a database system interaction which encapsulates two or more changes to the underlying information. Transactions are implementations of the four most important properties for database systems in a client/server environment, known by their acronym ACID. Figure 4-3 illustrates the four ACID properties.

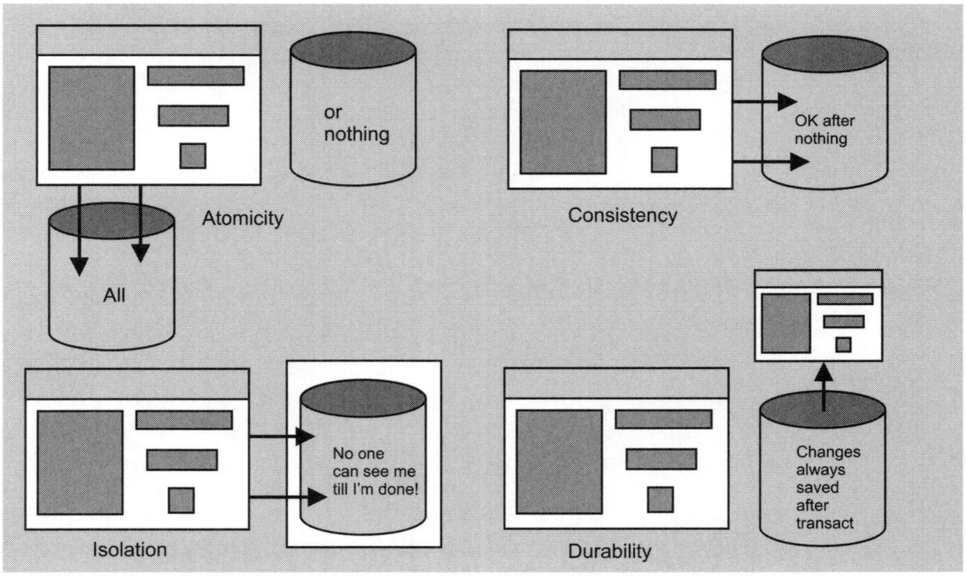


***Figure 4-3*** *ACID properties of database systems*

Table 4-1 lists the ACID properties and explains their importance.

| | |
|---|---|
| **Atomicity** | A transaction will either *commit* or *abort*. If a transaction commits, all of its effects remain; if it aborts, all of its effects are undone. As an example, in the case of a funds transfer by an ATM system, a movement of funds to one account will fail if there isn't sufficient money in the source account, and neither account will be changed. Otherwise, the funds transfer will succeed and both accounts will be updated. If intermediate changes need to be undone in the case of a failed transaction, this is called *rolling back* the changes. |

| | |
|---|---|
| **Consistency** | A transaction is a correct transformation of the system *state*; it preserves the state information so that all subsequent transactions follow the expected behaviors. An example of a consistent transaction would be the proper deletion of money from a source account during a funds transfer and the proper addition of money to the destination account. The state of the bank's total money is unchanged; none has been added or lost. If either the deletion or addition were not done, then the state of the bank's money would have changed inappropriately (too much or too little) and further transactions would not behave properly. |
| **Isolation** | Concurrent transactions are isolated from the updates of other incomplete transactions; these updates do not constitute a consistent state. This property is often called *serializability*. In the funds transfer example, no checks would be drawn on the accounts being used in the transfer until after the transfer was complete; otherwise, in the event the transfer failed after the destination account was updated but before this change was rolled back, a check might clear inappropriately by being drawn against nonexistent funds. |
| **Durability** | Once a transaction commits, its effects will persist even if there are system failures. *Persistence* is the term used to describe permanent storage (usually a hard drive, although for some systems a tape drive or CD-R system is used) which maintains the state of the entire database from transaction to transaction. For the funds transfer example, if the power at the bank fails right after the transfer was completed, in a durable transaction, the correct account totals are still present in the database when power is restored. A non-durable system might lose the transfer information, resulting in a loss of consistency as well (see above). |

***Table 4-1*** *ACID properties explained*

After you read down the above table, you understand why transactions are such a big deal. For any real-world database application, they are essential to deal with invalid entries, system crashes, power failures, and so on. Database applications rely on transactions to make sure that their users receive valid and timely information regardless of outside conditions or user mistakes.

Given the importance of transactions, it is understandable that the primary programming language of modern databases, SQL (Structured Query Language, pronounced "sequel"), offers support for transactions. Figure 4-4 shows a diagram of a set of SQL transactions for our example ATM application.

Aside from the syntax issue, notice one vital point: A transaction cannot encompass interactions with more than one database in SQL. The funds transfer interactions both used the same database (checking) on a local bank server and thus could be part of the same transaction. The savings transfer to checking, however, could not (even though they are both at the same bank) because the savings database and checking database are different. This prevented SQL from rolling back the savings transfer even though there wasn't enough money in the account.

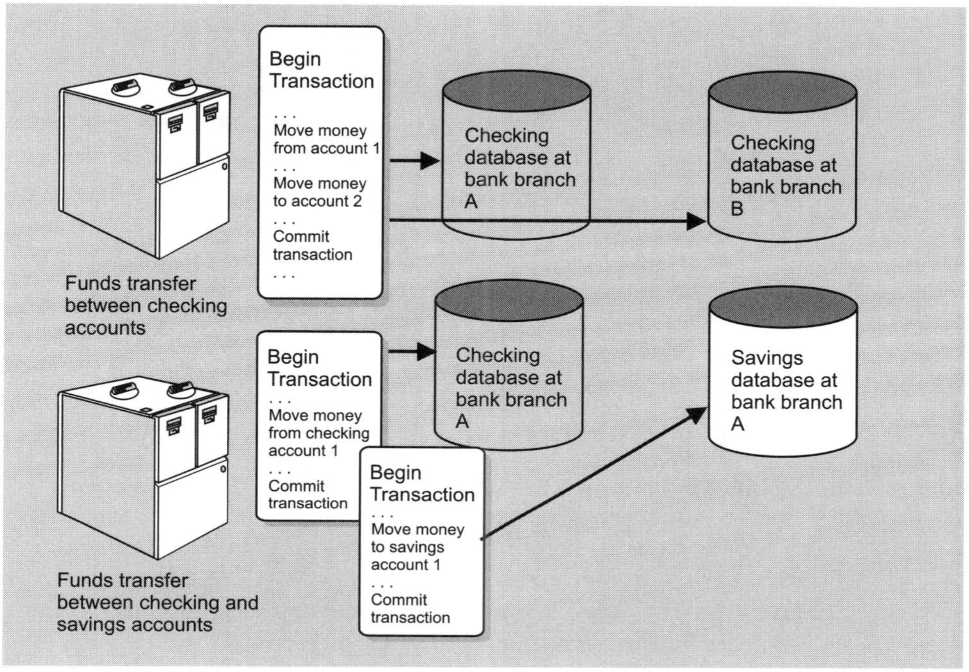


***Figure 4-4***
*A SQL transaction*

Middleware to the rescue! Figure 4-5 shows the checking/savings transaction using a custom middleware program.

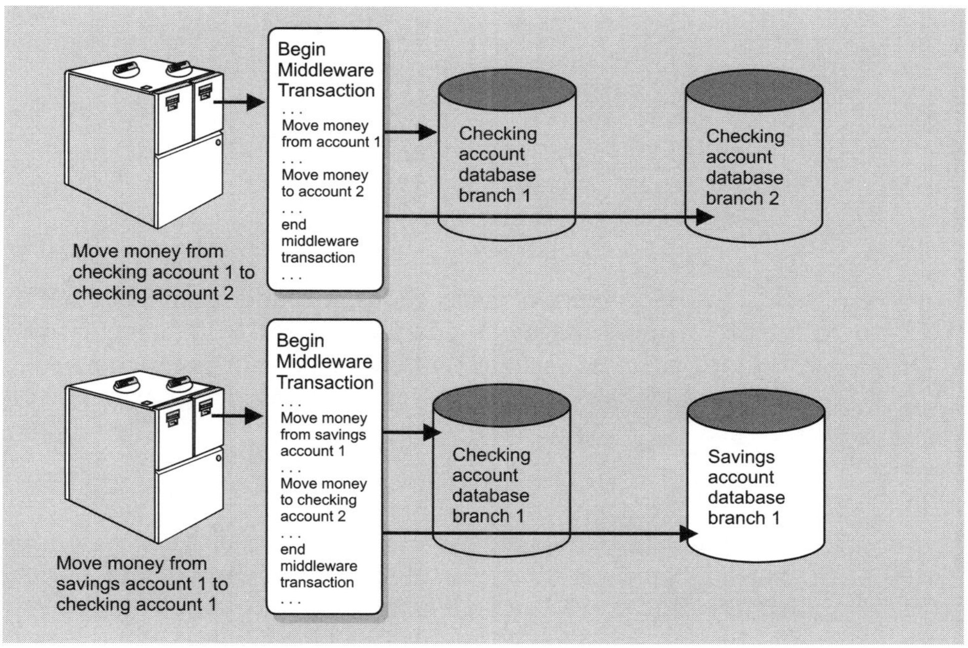


***Figure 4-5***
*A middleware/ MTS transaction*

Now, with the addition of the custom middleware program, the two SQL transactions are merged. Thus, when one fails, so does the other, resulting in a consistent state in both the savings and checking databases. These multiple-database transactions are sometimes heterogenous transactions, and support for them is a large part of what middleware supplies.

MTS does exactly the same job as the middleware, as shown in the figure. It also allows merging the two SQL transactions, using its own programming API rather than SQL syntax itself. Via its internal communication objects, MTS can determine whether a given component of a transaction has succeeded or failed, and either let the process continue or automatically roll it back.

## MTS Allows Everyone to Play in the Three-Tier Game

The bad news from the above example is that the middleware program in question cost $5 million to write and administer for a year. Obviously, the mom and pop video store isn't going to be able to afford middleware (even MTS-based), so their hope to offer online ordering from their web site goes up in smoke, right? Wrong! MTS lets everyone play in the three-tier client/server olympics, as shown in Figure 4-6.

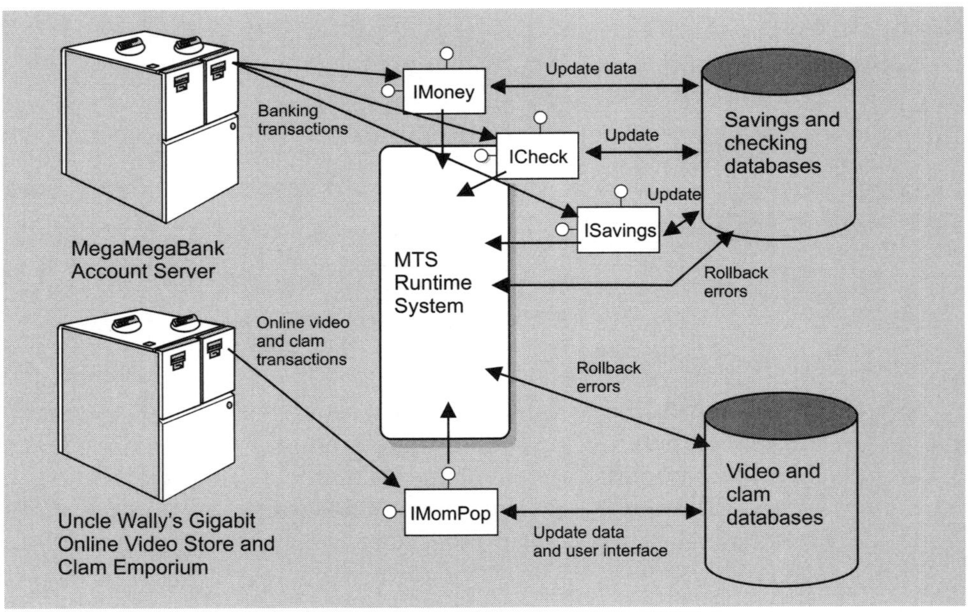


***Figure 4-6*** *MTS versus custom middleware*

This figure shows how the same MTS run time is used by both the bank (which replaced its expensive middleware program with MTS and saved a bundle) and Uncle Wally's Video Emporium to support web-based video rentals over a (hypothetical) Internet 2-gigabit broadband network. Because MTS is generic rather than custom middleware, programmers for any application can easily use it at virtually no cost (it's part of the operating system or available as a free download). And because MTS uses simple API calls under the COM umbrella, virtually any professional PC programmer can write an MTS component (particularly after they've read this book).

# The Architecture of MTS

MTS consists of five parts, each of which is required for the whole to work: the MTS run time, one or more MTS-aware RDBMS systems, one or more MTS-aware COM components, an MTS-aware client application, and one or more MTS packages, created using the MTS Explorer (covered in detail in Chapter 9). Figure 4-7 shows how this architecture works; each segment is covered in its own section below.

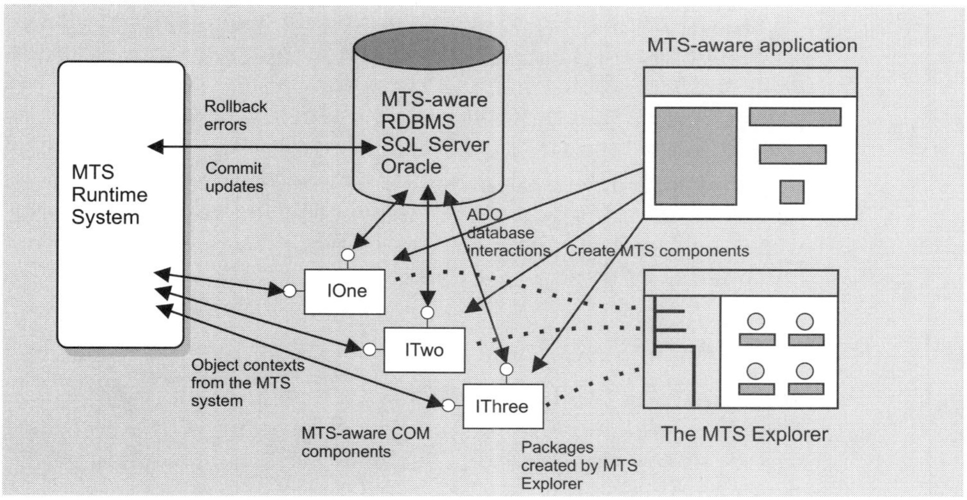


***Figure 4-7***
*The MTS architecture*

## *The MTS Run-time Module*

The MTS run-time module is what must be installed on both the client and server computer for an MTS three-tier application to work. It provides the DLL files and other system elements that let all the rest of the application do its job. MTS comes with well-done help files that guide users through installation and setup of the system, so we won't spend lots of space on that here.

## *MTS-Aware RDBMS*

MTS does not, as noted above, contain any RDBMS (Relational Database Management System) feature of its own. Instead, it must rely on commercial systems for this part of the application. At present, there are three options for the RDBMS element: Microsoft SQL Server version 6 or higher, Oracle version 7 or higher, or a custom system created with the MTS Software Development

Kit (SDK). This book will exclusively use the SQL Server RDBMS, but its examples can be used with Oracle or a custom system with minimal changes.

## MTS-Aware COM Components

This is what half this book is about: writing COM servers that are MTS-aware. They must simultaneously be COM components (as explained in the first three chapters), understand both the behavior and API of MTS, and be ADO (ActiveX Data Object) elements, since MTS is only accessible at present via ADO operations. Chapter 5 gives complete details on ADO; Chapter 6 covers MTS-aware COM server creation in ATL; and Chapter 7 covers MTS-aware COM server creation in MFC.

One vital point to notice in the previous figure is that when an MTS COM component interface pointer is first created in memory, it is considered *activated*, and when it has exited its last method call inside the MTS system, it is considered *deactivated*. Deactivated MTS components are normally removed from memory (their IUnknown::Release method is invoked by MTS, causing COM to delete them). Right now, these distinctions are only used if the IObjectControl interface is implemented for IObjectContext acquisition (see the next section). In a soon-to-be-released version of MTS, however, an interface pointer that is deactivated may not be destroyed from memory; instead it may be "pooled," allowing MTS to avoid a lot of overhead and making it much more efficient and scalable.

## MTS-Aware Clients

An MTS-aware COM component is of no value on its own; it needs a home. The MTS-aware application provides this, along with a user interface to allow customers or employees to take advantage of all the shiny MTS features in the COM components. While the MTS-aware client does not itself have to include anything other than the MTS-aware COM components to be a fully functional part of an MTS application, it can choose to include some specialized MTS features, or even function as an MTS component itself. Chapter 8 covers MTS-aware application development in ATL and MFC.

## MTS Packages

Even with all the above functionality, an MTS application will not work without the last piece of the puzzle: an MTS package. *Packages* are groups of COM components (one or more) that participate in the same transaction and have been registered with MTS so that when an attempt is made to create them via the COM system, they are actually created by the MTS system instead. MTS packages are created from the MTS Explorer and are fully covered in Chapter 9.

# Object Contexts are the Key to MTS Programming

The lovely model for MTS applications has to eventually devolve to something a programmer can access. This access point is the Object Context, represented by a COM interface: IObjectContext. Object Contexts are made available via two API calls, and have a number of vital methods that handle most of the features of MTS (principally completing or aborting transactions). In addition, there are several other interfaces that work in conjunction with IObjectContext in various support roles. Each is covered in detail below, but no actual program code is provided; that is found in the following programming chapters.

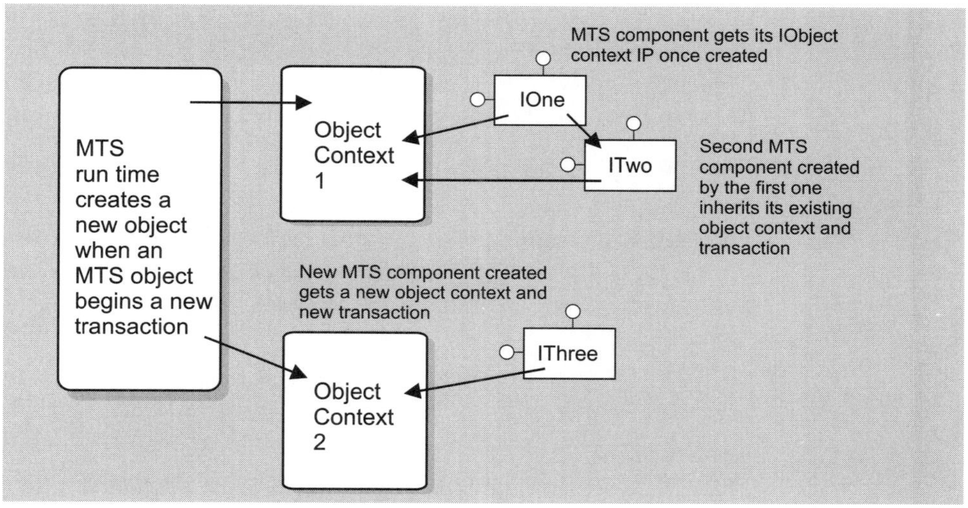


***Figure 4-8*** *Object contexts in MTS*

## The Object Context API Calls

There are only two ways to obtain an Object Context in an MTS component or application: via the IObjectControl interface (which is actually implemented by the MTS system and called by the MTS-aware element) or via the GetObjectContext API call. In the rare case where an MTS object pointer needs to be moved around (with its attendant Object Context), the SafeRef API function is needed. Each is covered completely below.

### GetObjectContext API Call

This API function obtains a reference to the IObjectContext interface on the ObjectContext associated with the current MTS object. The header file for the GetObjectContext function is MTX.H. An object should never attempt to pass its IObjectContext reference to another object; it will no longer be a valid reference. When an object obtains a reference to its ObjectContext, it must release the ObjectContext object when it's finished with it, via a call to its standard COM function IUnknown::Release (see Chapter 1).

The syntax for this function is:

```
HRESULT GetObjectContext (
    IObjectContext** ppInstanceContext
);
```

The parameters for this function are:

[out] *ppInstanceContext*
: This parameter is a reference to the IObjectContext Interface on the object's context. If the object's component hasn't been imported into an MTS package or if GetObjectContext is called from a constructor or an IUnknown method, this will be set to a NULL pointer. An object's MTS Object Context is not accessible from an object's constructor or from any IUnknown method implementation (QueryInterface, AddRef, or Release).

Possible return values from the function are:

S_OK
: This HRESULT indicates a reference to the IObjectContext Interface on the current object's context is returned in the *ppInstanceContext* parameter.

E_INVALIDARG
: This HRESULT indicates the argument passed in the *ppInstanceContext* parameter is invalid.

E_UNEXPECTED
: This HRESULT indicates an unexpected error occurred. This is usually associated with running out of memory.

CONTEXT_E_NOCONTEXT
: This HRESULT indicates the current object doesn't have a context associated with it, because either the component wasn't imported into a package or the object wasn't created with one of the MTS CreateInstance methods (see IObjectContext later in this chapter). This error will also be returned if the GetObjectContext method was called from the constructor or from an IUnknown method (this is the reason for the IObjectControl Interface explained later in this chapter).

## SafeRef API Call

This function is used by an object to obtain a reference to itself (as an interface pointer) that's safe to pass outside its context (i.e., that will maintain the IObjectContext pointer as valid when obtained properly). The header file for the SafeRef function is MTX.H. When an MTS component interface wants to pass a self-reference (i.e., an interface pointer) to a client or another interface (for example, for use as a callback), it should always call SafeRef first and then pass the interface pointer returned by this call. This interface pointer will be able to obtain a valid IObjectContext pointer and make calls on it that work correctly. An object should never pass a **this** pointer or an interface pointer to itself obtained through an internal call to QueryInterface, to a client, or to any other interface. Once such a reference is passed outside the object's MTS context, it's no longer a valid reference inside the MTS system. Calling SafeRef on a reference that is already safe returns the safe reference unchanged, except that the reference count on the interface is incremented. When a client calls QueryInterface on a reference that's safe, MTS automatically ensures that the reference returned to the client is also a safe reference. An MTS component that obtains a safe reference interface pointer must release the interface pointer via the COM IUnknown::Release function when done. Safe interface pointers have values that are different from their unsafe counterparts.

The syntax for this function is:

```
void* SafeRef (
REFIID riid
    UNKNOWN* pUnk
);
```

The parameters for this function are:

[in] *riid*
: This parameter is a reference to the interface ID of the interface that the current object wants to pass to another object or client.

[in] *pUnk*
: This parameter is a reference to an interface for the current object (such as a **this** pointer).

The possible return values for this function are:

Non-NULL
: This return value is a pointer to the interface specified in the *riid* parameter that's safe to pass outside the current interface's *object context*.

NULL
: This return value indicates the COM interface is requesting a safe reference on an interface other than itself, or the interface requested in the *riid* parameter is not implemented by the current COM server.

## The Object Context Interfaces

Most MTS programming centers around a single COM interface: IObjectContext. Aside from the API calls above, this interface encapsulates three-quarters of the functionality of MTS at present. Along with its various methods, IObjectContext is supported by several additional COM interfaces that provide context-safe interface pointers for Microsoft Internet Information Server (IIS) system elements, a GUID for the current transaction, and a way to obtain the IObjectContext interface pointer prior to method calls into MTS components. Each is covered completely below.

## IGetContextProperties Interface

The IGetContextProperties interface provides access to interface pointers for the five IIS intrinsic elements while still inside an MTS object context. This is important both because obtaining access to the IIS intrinsic objects is somewhat difficult, and because doing so inside an MTS object context requires sending the returned interface pointers through MTS (which could not be done via standard techniques). The header file for the IGetContextProperties interface is MTX.H. The IGetContextProperties interface exposes the following methods:

| Method | Description |
|---|---|
| Count | This method returns the number of properties associated with the context object. |
| EnumNames | This method returns a reference to an enumerator that you can use to iterate through all the context object properties. |
| GetProperty | This method returns a context object property. |

## Count Method

This method of IGetContextProperties returns the number of IIS intrinsic elements that are currently available.

The syntax for the method is:

```
HRESULT IGetContextProperties::Count (
long * plCount);
Parameters
```

The parameter for the method is:

[out] *plCount*
  This parameter returns the number of IIS intrinsic elements currently existing in the object context.

Possible return values for the method are:

S_OK
  This return value indicates that a valid count is returned in the *plCount* parameter.

E_INVALIDARG
  This return value indicates that the valid count could not be returned, usually because of running out of memory.

## EnumNames Method

This method of IGetContextProperties returns a reference to an enumerator that developers can use to iterate through all the IIS intrinsic elements currently available inside the MTS object context. You use the EnumNames method to obtain an interface pointer to an enumerator object (based on the COM IEnumXXX interfaces). The returned IEnumNames COM interface exposes several methods developers can use to iterate through a list of BSTRs that are the names of the IIS intrinsic elements. Sending each name to the GetProperty method will obtain an interface pointer to the intrinsic IIS element it represents. Remember that IEnumNames is a descendant of the standard COM enumerator interface, and has all of its standard methods as well; also remember that when the IEnumNames interface has done its job, the developer must explicitly call IUnknown::Release on it for COM reference counting purposes.

The syntax for the method is:

```
HRESULT IGetContextProperties::EnumNames (
    IEnumNames ** ppenum);
```

The parameter for the method is:

[out] *ppenum*
: This parameter is a reference to the IEnumNames interface on a new enumerator object that a developer can use to iterate through all the IIS intrinsic objects, using standard IEnumXXX methods (for BSTRs).

Possible return values for the method are:

S_OK
: This return value indicates that a reference to the requested enumerator is returned in the *ppenum* parameter.

E_INVALIDARG
: This return value indicates that the requested enumerator could not be returned, usually because of running out of memory.

## GetProperty Method

This method of IGetContextProperties returns an interface pointer to an IIS intrinsic element, based on the name in the first parameter. Developers can use GetProperty to retrieve the following IIS intrinsic objects:

- Request
- Response
- Server
- Application
- Session

To retrieve an IIS object, call QueryInterface using the VT_DISPATCH member of the returned VARIANT for an interface pointer to the IIS object.

**Note:** This interface is not available in MTS 1.0.

The syntax for the method is:

```
HRESULT IGetContextProperties::GetProperty (
BSTR            name
VARIANT *     pProperty);
```

The parameters for the method are:

[in] *name*
    This parameter is the name of the IIS intrinsic element to be retrieved.

[out] *pProperty*
    This parameter is a pointer to the returned IIS intrinsic element.

Possible return values for the method are:

S_OK
    This return value indicates the IIS intrinsic element was returned successfully.

S_FALSE
    This return value indicates the IIS intrinsic element given in *name* was not found (but is valid).

E_INVALIDARG
    This return value indicates the *name* parameter was invalid (not an IIS intrinsic element or a bad pointer).

### IObjectContextActivity Interface

The IObjectContextActivity interface is used to retrieve a unique identifier associated with the current MTS activity. (MTS activities are groups of MTS components that participate in the current transaction and are guaranteed thread-safe, but are not necessarily implemented on a specific threading model or specific thread.) This activity identifier is a GUID, and is only valid for the lifetime of the current MTS activity. The header file for the IObjectContextActivity is MTX.H. Developers must also link MTXGUID.LIB to their project to use IObjectContextActivity. An application obtains a reference to an object's IObjectContextActivity interface by calling QueryInterface on the object's IObjectContext interface pointer. The usual need for an activity identifier is by an MTS component that implements per-activity critical section locking (rather than per-thread locking).

The IObjectContextActivity interface provides the following method.

| Method | Description |
|---|---|
| GetActivityId | This method retrieves the GUID associated with the current activity. |

## GetActivityId Method

This method retrieves the GUID associated with the current MTS activity. This GUID value can be used to determine which such MTS activity a given instance of an MTS COM component is currently participating in, to allow entry to critical sections or other thread-dependent code.

The syntax for the method is:

```
HRESULT IObjectContextActivity::GetActivityId(
GUID * pActivityId);
```

The parameter for the method is:

[out] *pActivityId*
: This parameter is a reference to the GUID associated with the current MTS activity.

Possible return values for the method are:

S_OK
: This return value indicates that the GUID of the current MTS activity is returned in the parameter *pActivityId*.

E_INVALIDARG
: This return value indicates that the argument passed in the *pActivityId* parameter is a NULL pointer.

E_UNEXPECTED
: This return value indicates that an unexpected error occurred (usually involving memory).

## IObjectContext Interface

The IObjectContext interface provides access to the object context for an MTS component. The header file for the IObjectContext interface is MTX.H. Applications obtain a reference to the IObjectContext interface by calling the GetObjectContext function. Since it is a COM interface, an application must call IUnknown::Release on IObjectContext when done using it. IObjectContext is the primary interaction point between MTS components and the MTS system; it includes functions to inform MTS that the component's work is completed successfully and therefore can be committed, to inhibit a transaction from being committed, either temporarily or permanently, to create other MTS components in memory and include their work within the scope of the current object's transaction, to find out if the account of a calling application or component is in a particular security role, to determine if security is enabled for the current transaction at all, and to find out if the component is executing within a transaction.

The IObjectContext interface exposes the following methods:

| Method | Description |
|---|---|
| CreateInstance | This method creates another MTS object. |
| DisableCommit | This method declares that the component hasn't finished its work and that its transactional updates are in an inconsistent state. The component retains its state across method calls (i.e., MTS will not destroy and re-create the component, as it might otherwise), and any attempts to commit the transaction before the component calls EnableCommit or SetComplete will result in the current transaction being aborted by MTS internally. |
| EnableCommit | This method declares that the component's work isn't necessarily finished, but its transactional updates are in a consistent state. This method allows the transaction to be committed, but the object retains its state across method calls (i.e., MTS won't destroy and re-create the component as it might otherwise) until the component calls SetComplete or SetAbort, or until the current transaction is completed. |
| IsCallerInRole | This method indicates whether the object's direct caller is in a specified security role (either directly or as part of a group). |
| IsInTransaction | This method informs the caller whether the object is executing within a transaction. |
| IsSecurityEnabled | This method tells callers whether security is enabled. MTS security is enabled unless the object is running in the client's process, or unless the OS involved is Windows 95/98. |
| SetAbort | This method informs MTS that the component has completed its work and can be deactivated (removed from memory) on returning from the currently executing method, but that its transactional updates are in an inconsistent state or that an unrecoverable error occurred. This means that the transaction in which the component was executing must be aborted; none of its results will be committed to the underlying database(s). If any component executing within a transaction returns to its client after calling SetAbort, the entire transaction is guaranteed to abort. |
| SetComplete | This method tells MTS that the component has completed its work and can be deactivated (removed from memory) on returning from the currently executing method. For components that are executing within the scope of a transaction, it also indicates that the object's transactional updates can be committed to the underlying database(s). When a component that is the root (initial component) of a transaction calls SetComplete, MTS attempts to commit the transaction on return from the current method. |

**Note:** Calls by a component to any of the IObjectContext methods DisableCommit, EnableCommit, SetComplete, or SetAbort from within a method call cause one or both of two flags (Done and Consistent) to be set in the underlying implementation of IObjectContext. Table 4.2 shows how these flags are affected by the various method calls. These flags aren't evaluated by the MTS runtime environment until the component's currently executing method returns to its calling application. The net effect therefore is that a component can call these methods any number of times from within one of its own methods, but the last call before the component returns to its calling application is the one that will take effect. The Done flag, which allows a component to be deactivated and its transaction to commit or abort, is only evaluated after the component returns from the call that first entered its object context (this is called the root component).

| Method | Done | Consistent |
|---|---|---|
| **SetAbort** | TRUE | FALSE |
| **EnableCommit** | FALSE | TRUE |
| **SetComplete** | TRUE | TRUE |
| **DisableCommit** | FALSE | FALSE |

***Table 4-2*** *Method call effects on internal flags of MTS IObjectContext*

## CreateInstance Method

This function creates an MTS object as a COM interface pointer. However, the interface will have an object context only if its server is registered with MTS (via the MTS Explorer, see Chapter 9). When an application creates an interface pointer by using CreateInstance, the new interface's object context is derived from the current object's object context. The new interface pointer always executes within the same MTS activity (see above) as the component that created it. If the current component has a transaction, the transaction attribute of the new interface's component determines whether or not the new interface will execute within the scope of that transaction. If the component's transaction attribute is set to either Requires a Transaction or Supports Transactions, the new interface inherits its creator's transaction. If the component's transaction attribute is set to Requires a New Transaction, MTS initiates a new transaction for the new interface. If the component's transaction attribute is set to Does Not Support Transactions, the new interface doesn't execute under any transaction, regardless of whether one already exists or not. If the Microsoft Distributed Transaction Coordinator (DTC) is not running and the interface is transactional, the interface is successfully created. However, method calls to that interface will fail with CONTEXT_E_TMNOTAVAILABLE. Any interface that reports this error should be destroyed using IUnknown::Release immediately and the current MTS session aborted.

**Note:** MTS always uses standard marshaling. Even if a component exposes the IMarshal interface, its IMarshal methods will never be called by the MTS run-time environment, so custom marshaling is not available using MTS. Also, an application or component cannot create MTS interfaces as part of a COM aggregation (see Chapter 1). MTS interfaces can, however, be contained normally (again, see Chapter 1)

The syntax for the method is:

```
HRESULT IObjectContext::CreateInstance (
    REFCLSID rclsid,
    REFIID riid,
    LPVOID FAR* ppvObj
);
```

The parameters for the method are:

[in] *rclsid*
: This parameter is a reference to the CLSID for the server of the interface to instantiate.

[in] *riid*
: This parameter is a reference to the interface ID of the MTS-aware COM interface to be created.

[out] *ppvObj*
: This parameter holds the requested interface pointer if it is returned successfully.

Possible return values for the method are:

S_OK
: This return value indicates that the interface pointer was created and returned in the *ppvObj* parameter.

REGDB_E_CLASSNOTREG
: This return value indicates that the server specified by *rclsid* is not registered as a COM server in the Windows Registry.

E_OUTOFMEMORY
: This return value indicates insufficient memory to load the request COM server.

E_INVALIDARG
: This return value indicates that the argument passed in the *ppvObj* parameter is invalid.

E_UNEXPECTED
: This return value indicates that an unexpected error occurred. This is usually caused when an MTS component interface passes its IObjectContext interface pointer to another interface, and the other interface calls CreateInstance using this pointer. An IObjectContext pointer is

not valid outside the MTS object context of the interface that originally obtained it (to get around this, see SafeRef).

## DisableCommit Method

This function tells MTS that the object's transactional updates are inconsistent and can't be committed in their present state. An MTS component interface that invokes DisableCommit is *stateful*; this means that it will be persisted in memory until it calls SetAbort or EnableCommit, even between method calls. (Otherwise, MTS has the option to transparently destroy and re-create the interface between method calls.) The purpose of the DisableCommit method is to prevent a transaction from committing prematurely between method calls to a stateful MTS component interface, due to MTS's option to destroy its instance in memory (and thus its internal state). When an interface method invokes DisableCommit, it indicates that its work is inconsistent and that the interface can't complete its work until it receives further method invocations from other elements of the application. Calling DisableCommit also indicates that the MTS component interface needs to maintain its state to perform that work. Once an MTS component interface has called DisableCommit, if another component attempts to commit the transaction before that component has called EnableCommit or SetComplete, the transaction will be aborted automatically by MTS (this means that components working together which use DisableCommit must be sensitive to the current state of the transaction).

The syntax for the method is:

```
HRESULT IObjectContext::DisableCommit ( );
```

Possible return values for the method are:

S_OK
: This return value indicates that the call to DisableCommit succeeded. The interface's transactional updates can't be committed until the current interface calls either EnableCommit or SetComplete.

E_UNEXPECTED
: This return value indicates that an unexpected error occurred. This usually happens if one interface passes its IObjectContext pointer to another interface and the other interface calls DisableCommit using this pointer. An IObjectContext pointer is not valid outside the object context of the interface that originally obtained it; to get around this, see the SafeRef API function.

CONTEXT_E_NOCONTEXT
: This return value indicates that the current interface doesn't have an MTS object context associated with it. Normally this is due to the interface pointer not being obtained with one of the MTS CreateInstance methods.

## EnableCommit Method

This function is the inverse of DisableCommit; it declares that the current interface's work is not necessarily finished, but that its transactional updates are consistent and could be committed in their present form. When an MTS component interface calls EnableCommit, this allows the transaction in which it is participating to be committed by MTS (avoiding an automatic abort if an attempt is made to commit the current transaction; see above), but the interface maintains its internal state across calls from its clients until the interface calls SetComplete or SetAbort or until the current transaction completes. EnableCommit is the default state when an interface is activated (created in memory by MTS). This is why an interface should always call SetComplete or SetAbort before returning from a method, unless a developer wants the interface to maintain its internal state for the next call from a client.

The syntax for the method is:

```
HRESULT IObjectContext::EnableCommit ( );
```

Possible return values for the method are:

S_OK
: This return value indicates that the call to EnableCommit succeeded and the interface's transactional updates can now be committed.

E_UNEXPECTED
: This return value indicates that an unexpected error occurred. This usually happens when one interface passes its IObjectContext pointer to another interface and the other interface calls EnableCommit using this pointer. An IObjectContext pointer is not valid outside the object context of the interface that originally obtained it; to get around this limitation, see the SafeRef API call.

## IsCallerInRole Method

This function tells a caller whether an interface's *direct caller* (see below) is in a specified security role (either individually or as part of a group). A *security role* is a symbolic name that represents a user or group of users who have specific access permissions to all components in a given MTS package. Developers define roles when they create a component (via internal strings; see Chapters 6 and 7), and roles are mapped to individual users or groups at deployment time (via the MTS Explorer; see Chapter 9). IsCallerInRole only applies to the direct caller of the currently executing method. (The *direct caller* is the process calling into the current server process. It can be either a base client process or a server process.) IsCallerInRole doesn't apply to the process that initiated the call sequence from which the current method was called, or to any other callers in that sequence.

**Warning:** Because IsCallerInRole returns True when the interface that invokes it is executing in a client's process (in which case MTS security is not enabled), any MTS component that wants to use IsCallerInRole should first call IsSecurityEnabled before calling IsCallerInRole. If security isn't enabled, IsCallerInRole does not return useful information and other arrangements must be made to verify proper user information.

The syntax for the method is:

```
HRESULT IObjectContext::IsCallerInRole (
BSTR bstrRole,
    BOOL* pfIsInRole
);
```

The parameters for the method are:

[in] *bstrRole*
: This parameter is the name of the role in which a component wants to determine whether the caller is acting.

[out] *pfIsInRole*
: This parameter contains True if the caller is in the specified role in *bstrRole*, False if not. It will also be set to True if security is not enabled.

Possible return values for the method are:

S_OK
: This return value indicates that the role specified in the *bstrRole* parameter is a recognized role, and the Boolean result returned in the *pfIsInRole* parameter indicates whether or not the caller is in that role.

CONTEXT_E_ROLENOTFOUND
: This return value indicates that the role specified in the *bstrRole* parameter does not exist on the server being used.

E_INVALIDARG
: This return value indicates that one or more of the arguments passed in is invalid.

E_UNEXPECTED
: This return value indicates that an unexpected error occurred. This normally is caused if one interface passes its IObjectContext pointer to another interface and the other interface calls IsCallerInRole using this pointer. An IObjectContext pointer is not valid outside the object context of the interface that originally obtained it; see SafeRef for a solution to this problem.

## IsInTransaction Method

This function informs callers whether the current MTS component interface is executing in an MTS transaction. Components can use this method to make sure that an interface that requires a transaction never runs without one. A common problem is a component that requires a transaction being improperly configured in the MTS Explorer; the component can use this method to determine that an interface from that component doesn't have a transaction when it is supposed to. Then the component can return an error to alert the user to the problem, who will in turn alert the proper administrator to correct it.

The syntax for the method is:

```
BOOL IObjectContext::IsInTransaction ( );
```

Possible return values for the method are:

TRUE
: This return value indicates that the current interface is executing within an MTS transaction.

FALSE
: This return value indicates that the current interface is not executing within an MTS transaction.

## IsSecurityEnabled Method

This function informs callers as to whether or not MTS security is enabled for the current MTS component interface. MTS security is enabled unless the interface is running in the client's process or MTS is running in Windows 95/98. MTS security is enabled only if an MTS component interface is running in a server process. This could be either because the interface's component was configured to run in a client's process (via the MTS Explorer; see Chapter 9) or because the component and the client are in the same MTS package. If the interface is running in the client's process, there is no security checking and IsSecurityEnabled will always return FALSE.

The syntax for the method is:

```
BOOL IObjectContext::IsSecurityEnabled ( );
```

Possible return values for the method are:

TRUE
: This return value indicates that MTS security is enabled for this MTS component interface.

FALSE
: This return value indicates that MTS security is not enabled for this MTS component interface.

## SetAbort Method

This function tells MTS that the transaction in which the MTS component interface is executing must be aborted and that the interface should be deactivated (removed from memory) on returning from the currently executing method call. For this reason, an MTS component interface is deactivated automatically on return from the method in which it called SetAbort. If the MTS component interface is an *automatic transaction root* (see below), MTS aborts the transaction at this point and rolls back any changes made to the underlying database(s). If the MTS component interface is transactional, but not the root of an automatic transaction, the transaction in which it is participating is guaranteed to abort, but will not actually be aborted until the root MTS component interface is deactivated. (An object is an *automatic transaction root* if the MTS run-time environment has to initiate a new transaction for it. This is the case when the MTS component that provides the interface pointer is configured (via the MTS Explorer) to Require a Transaction and the object's creator doesn't have one, or when the component is configured likewise to Require a New Transaction.)

**Note:** An MTS component can call SetAbort in error handlers to ensure that a transaction aborts when an error occurs. An MTS component can also call SetAbort at the beginning of a method to protect itself from committing prematurely in the event of an unexpected return and then call SetComplete just before the method returns, if all goes well. This is a form of "worst case" error handling that can prevent database corruption while debugging MTS components.

The syntax for the method is:

```
HRESULT IObjectContext::SetAbort ( );
```

Possible return values for the method are:

S_OK
: This return value indicates that the call to SetAbort succeeded and the current MTS transaction will be aborted.

E_UNEXPECTED
: This return value indicates that an unexpected error occurred. This normally is caused when one interface passes its IObjectContext pointer to another interface and the other interface calls SetAbort using this pointer. An IObjectContext pointer is not valid outside the object context of the interface that originally obtained it. To get around this problem, see the SafeRef API call.

## SetComplete Method

This function tells MTS that the current MTS component interface has completed its work and should be deactivated (removed from memory) when the currently executing method returns to the client. For MTS component interfaces that are executing within the scope of a transaction, it also indicates that the interface's transactional updates can be committed to the underlying database(s). For this reason, the interface is deactivated automatically on return from the method in which it called SetComplete. If the MTS component interface is an *automatic transaction root* (see below), MTS attempts to commit the transaction and update the underlying database(s). However, if any MTS component interface that was participating in the current transaction has called SetAbort, or has called DisableCommit and has not subsequently called EnableCommit or SetComplete, the transaction will be aborted instead. (An MTS component interface is an *automatic transaction root* if the MTS run-time environment has to initiate a new transaction for it. This is caused when the component that provides the interface pointer is configured (via the MTS Explorer) to Require a Transaction and the interface's creator doesn't have one, or when the component is configured likewise to Require a New Transaction.)

**Note:** If an MTS component interface doesn't need to maintain its internal state after it returns from a method call (i.e., be kept in memory), it should call SetComplete from each method call just before it returns so that the interface can be automatically deactivated (removed from memory) as soon as it returns and its resources can be reclaimed.

The syntax for the method is:

```
HRESULT IObjectContext::SetComplete ( );
```

Possible return values for the method are:

S_OK
: This return value indicates that the call to SetComplete succeeded.

E_UNEXPECTED
: This return value indicates that an unexpected error occurred. This usually happens when an interface passes its IObjectContext pointer to another interface and the other interface calls SetComplete using this pointer. An IObjectContext pointer is not valid outside the object context of the interface that originally obtained it. To get around this difficulty, see the SafeRef API function.

## *IObjectControl Interface*

As noted in the above sections, one of the major problems with object contexts in MTS is that, for a given MTS component interface, its current IObjectContext interface pointer is not available during the initialization of its own interface pointer (i.e., in its constructor); this is due to the way MTS interacts with the COM API to actually create MTS components in memory. This can lead to implementation difficulties if a given MTS component interface needs object context information prior to the invocation of its own methods. To work around this problem, a developer simply needs to implement the IObjectControl interface. The header file for the IObjectControl interface is MTX.H. Implementing this interface is optional; if an MTS component does implement the IObjectControl interface, the MTS run-time environment automatically calls the IObjectControl methods on the component at the appropriate times as explained below. When an MTS component supports the IObjectControl interface, MTS calls the IObjectControl::Activate method once for each time an interface of the component is activated (created in memory). The reason this is important is that, inside this call, the IObjectContext interface is now available to the component's interface and will remain valid until the Deactivate method is called by the MTS run time. The Activate method is called before any of the object's other methods are called by clients or other MTS components. Similarly, the MTS run time calls the component's IObjectControl::Deactivate method each time an interface pointer supported by the component is deactivated (removed from memory). This can be the result of the MTS component interface returning from a method in which it calls SetComplete or SetAbort, or due to the root of the object's transaction causing the transaction to complete. After calling the Deactivate method, the MTS run-time environment calls the IObjectControl::CanBePooled method. If this method returns TRUE from an MTS component, the deactivated object is placed in an object pool for reuse rather than being freed from memory. If the CanBePooled method returns FALSE, the object is released in the usual way and removed from memory. On systems that don't support object pooling, the value returned by this method is ignored by MTS

**Warning:** Only the MTS run-time environment can invoke the IObjectControl methods. If a client or other MTS component interface attempts to obtain an interface pointer for the IObjectControl interface, QueryInterface or CreateInstance will return E_NOINTERFACE.

The IObjectControl interface exposes the following methods:

| Method | Description |
|---|---|
| Activate | This method allows an MTS component to perform its own unique initialization whenever it is activated (created in memory). This method is called by the MTS run-time environment before any other methods are called on a given interface pointer supported by the component. |
| CanBePooled | This method permits an MTS component to notify the MTS run-time environment of whether it can be pooled for reuse (i.e., have its interface pointer kept around rather than being destroyed). A component's implementation of this method should return TRUE if it wants instances of this component to be pooled or FALSE if not. Components that need to be destroyed and re-created to reset internal states should always return TRUE. |
| Deactivate | This method is used by an MTS component to perform its own unique cleanup before it is destroyed. This method is called by the MTS run-time environment whenever an object is deactivated (potentially about to be removed from memory). |

## Activate Method

If an MTS component chooses to support the IObjectControl interface, it must implement this method. IObjectControl::Activate is called by the MTS run-time environment before any other methods are called on a given interface pointer. Whenever a client (either an application or another MTS component) calls an MTS component that isn't already activated (i.e., instantiated in memory), the MTS run-time environment automatically activates the object. The principal reason for implementing the Activate method is to obtain a reference to an interface's MTS object context IObjectContext interface pointer and store it in a member variable. Then the object context interface is available to any method that requires it, without needing to acquire a new one and then release it every time it is used. If an interface intends to enable object recycling (returning TRUE from the CanBePooled method), the Activate method must be able to handle both newly created and recycled interface pointers. When the Activate method returns, there should be no distinguishable difference between a new object and a recycled one. This means in practice two things: First, any internal state information of the component must be reset by each call to Activate, but any memory allocations must be able to determine if their elements are already instantiated; and secondly, any stored IObjectContext interface pointer must be released and reacquired since such interface pointers are no longer usable by recycled interfaces.

The syntax for the method is:

```
HRESULT IObjectControl::Activate ( );
```

Possible return values for the method are:

S_OK

This result means that the Activate method succeeded. Components should return this value to indicate internal state initialization succeeded.

Failure HRESULT

If any other result is returned by the Activate method, it should indicate why an interface was unable to initialize itself; the MTS system will indicate failure and normally the calling element (client or other MTS component) will abort execution.

## CanBePooled Method

If an MTS component chooses to support the IObjectControl interface, it must implement this method. This method allows an MTS interface pointer to notify the MTS run-time environment of whether it can be pooled for reuse. The implementation should return TRUE if a developer wants the interface pointer to be pooled for reuse or FALSE if not. When an interface pointer returns TRUE from CanBePooled, it indicates to the MTS run-time environment that it can be added to an object pool after deactivation rather than being destroyed (i.e., removed from memory). Whenever an instance of the interface is required (i.e., another interface pointer), one is drawn from the pool rather than created by the ClassFactory via a call to COM's CoCreateInstance API function (see Chapter 1). The way MTS interface pointer recycling works is that an interface pointer removes all its state information in its Deactivate method and is returned to the MTS interface pointer pool. Later, when an instance of the same component is needed via an interface pointer, the stored interface pointer can be reused. Its Activate method must be able to tell whether the interface pointer is a newly minted one or a retread from the MTS pool, however.

**Note:** MTS interface pointer pooling requires that an object must be accessible on different threads each time it is activated by MTS. Such recycling isn't possible under the apartment threading model because although an object can be instantiated on any thread in the single-threaded apartment model (STA), it can only be used by the same thread on which it was first created in memory. If a developer wants instances of a component (i.e., interface pointers) to be recyclable in MTS via object pooling, he should register the component with the ThreadingModel Registry value set to Both. This indicates to MTS that the component's interface pointers can be called from different threads. In MTS, objects without this setting will run under the STA model and won't be recycled even if they return TRUE from the CanBePooled method. However, if the developer configures a component to support both threading models, the component can take advantage of recycling.

**Warning:** MTS 2.0 does not support object pooling, but it is slated for a near-term revision, possibly the one released with Windows 2000. Therefore, all MTS components that want to take advantage of this feature should include support for it now.

The syntax for the method is:

```
BOOL IObjectControl::CanBePooled ( );
```

Possible return values for the method are:

TRUE
: This return value notifies the MTS run-time environment that it can pool this interface pointer on deactivation for later reuse.

FALSE
: This return value notifies the MTS run-time environment that it should not pool this interface pointer on deactivation, but should release its last reference to the interface pointer so that the implementation object will be destroyed.

### *Deactivate Method*

If an MTS component chooses to support the IObjectControl interface, it must implement this method. This method allows an MTS interface pointer to perform any state maintenance required before it is recycled (see above) or destroyed (removed from memory). This method is called by the MTS run-time environment whenever an interface pointer is deactivated, that is, when it returns from a method in which it called SetComplete or SetAbort, when the transaction in which it executed is committed or aborted, or when the last client to hold a reference on it releases its reference. If the component supports recycling (returns TRUE from the CanBePooled method), an interface pointer should use the Deactivate method to reset the object's state to the state in which the Activate method expects to find it. If you have one, you must also use the Deactivate method to release the interface pointer's IObjectContext interface pointer. An interface pointer can't do this in the Release method or the class's destructor, because the IObjectContext interface isn't accessible from the destructor or any of the IUnknown methods due to the way MTS overlays the COM system.

The syntax for the method is:

```
void IObjectControl::Deactivate ( );
```

This method has no parameters or return values.

## Shared Properties Provide Thread-Safe State for MTS Components

Shared properties in MTS address the one major hole left by the MTS transaction paradigm: state interactions between MTS components engaged in a current MTS activity. A simple way to illustrate the problem is this: Suppose an application needs to update a counter of items which is maintained in a stateful MTS component and which may be inconsistent inside a given instance of the component until processing is complete. The problem arises when an instance of the same component is accessed by another MTS element; it may use the inconsistent state information and thus corrupt the entire application's state. Shared properties avoid this problem by having MTS maintain the state information rather than MTS components. MTS sees to it that no other component on any thread can access the shared properties until their current user has been deactivated.

Shared properties work in MTS via a three-level hierarchy which is illustrated in Figure 4-9.

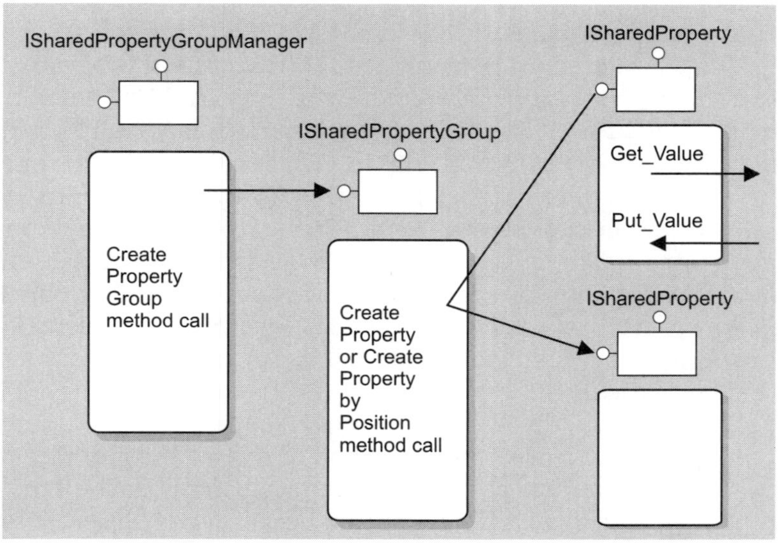


***Figure 4-9*** *Shared properties in MTS*

As seen in the figure, the top level of the MTS shared property system is the ISharedPropertyGroupManager COM interface. This interface is where all MTS components must go to obtain shared property data. However, to avoid the problem of name collisions from multiple MTS components participating in the same transaction, ISharedPropertyGroupManager only provides access to the ISharedPropertyGroup COM interface rather than to shared properties directly. Since each ISharedPropertyGroup must be identified by a unique name, this provides a workable namespace system for actual shared properties with the same name. Finally, from a given ISharedPropertyGroup interface, an MTS component can obtain a given ISharedProperty COM interface pointer via either a unique textual name or via a number value. Each such interface supports one specific shared data item, obtained from its Value property, either directly or via get_ and put_ methods.

## The Shared Property Interfaces

Unlike object contexts, which are supported both by API calls and COM interfaces, MTS shared properties are only accessible via a hierarchy of COM interfaces as shown in Figure 4-9. Each is detailed below; example code for using them is found in Chapters 6 and 7.

**Warning:** An MTS component interface should never attempt to pass a shared property group interface pointer (any of the three plus the enumerator) to another interface pointer. If the interface pointer is passed outside of the interface that acquired it, it's no longer a valid reference and will return errors only.

### ISharedProperty Interface

The ISharedProperty interface is used by MTS components to set or retrieve the value of a shared property in the MTS system. A shared property can contain any data type that can be represented by a VARIANT (see Chapter 1). The header file for the ISharedProperty interface is MTXSPM.H. MTS components must also link MTXGUID.LIB to their project to use this interface. To access the ISharedProperty interface, an MTS component must instantiate it via either the ISharedPropertyGroup::CreateProperty method or the ISharedPropertyGroup::CreatePropertyByPosition method. For this reason, an ISharedProperty interface can be created or accessed only from an ISharedPropertyGroup interface pointer. Since ISharedProperty is a COM interface, an MTS component must call its IUnknown::Release method when finished using it.

**Warning:** The online documentation for this interface is defective; the MTS 2.0 update in Service Pack 1 has the correct versions.

The ISharedProperty interface exposes the following methods.

| Method | Description |
|---|---|
| **get_Value** | This method retrieves the value of a shared property; it is an accessor for the Value property of the interface. |
| **put_Value** | The method sets the value of a shared property; it is an accessor for the Value property of the interface. |

### get_Value Method

This method retrieves the value of a shared property; it is an accessor for the Value property of the interface.

The syntax for the method is:

```
HRESULT ISharedProperty::get_Value (
    VARIANT* pVal
);
```

The parameter for the method is:

[out] *pVal*
: This parameter is a reference to a VARIANT in which the value of the shared property will be returned.

Possible return values for the method are:

S_OK
: This return value indicates that a reference to a VARIANT containing the value of the shared property was returned in the *pVal* parameter.

E_INVALIDARG
: This return value indicates that the argument passed in the *pVal* parameter is invalid.

### put_Value Method

This method assigns the value of a shared property; it is an accessor for the Value property of the interface.

The syntax for the method is:

```
HRESULT ISharedProperty::put_Value (
    VARIANT value
);
```

The parameter for the method is:

[in] *value*
: This parameter contains a VARIANT containing the value to assign to the SharedProperty interface's internal storage.

Possible return values for the method are:

S_OK
: This return value indicates that the shared property's value has been set to *value*.

E_INVALIDARG
: This parameter indicates that the argument passed in the *value* parameter has the VT_BYREF bit set.

DISP_E_ARRAYISLOCKED
: This return value indicates that the argument passed in the *value* parameter contains an array that is locked.

DISP_E_BADVARTYPE
: This return value indicates that the argument passed in the *value* parameter isn't a valid VARIANT type.

### Value Property

This is the way non-C++ clients access the ISharedProperty's stored data; only C++ applications need to use the get_ and put_ accessor functions.

## The ISharedPropertyGroup Interface

As noted previously, the ISharedPropertyGroup interface is used to create and access the shared properties in a shared property group.The header file for the ISharedPropertyGroup interface is MTXSPM.H. An MTS component must also link MTXGUID.LIB to its project to use this interface. Clients can only access the ISharedPropertyGroup interface via the ISharedPropertyGroup-Manager::CreatePropertyGroup method, which means that in practice, the MTS component must obtain an ISharedPropertyGroupManager interface pointer first. Since ISharedPropertyGroup is a COM interface, an MTS component must call its IUnknown::Release method when finished using it.

| Method | Description |
|---|---|
| CreateProperty | This method creates a new shared property identified by a string expression that's unique within its property group. Shared properties created this way cannot be accessed using get_PropertyByPosition. |
| CreatePropertyByPosition | This method creates a new shared property identified by a numeric index within its property group. Shared properties created this way cannot be accessed using get_Property. |
| get_Property | This method returns a reference to a shared property as an ISharedProperty interface pointer, given the string name by which the property is identified. The property must previously have been created with CreateProperty. |
| get_PropertyByPosition | This method returns a reference to a shared property as an ISharedProperty interface pointer, given its numeric index in the shared property group. The property must previously have been created by CreatePropertyByPosition. |

### CreateProperty Method

This method creates and returns a reference to a new ISharedProperty interface pointer with a specified name. If a shared property by that name already exists, CreateProperty returns an interface pointer to the existing property.

When an application creates a shared property, its value is set to the default, which is a VARIANT of type VT_I4, with a value of 0.

**Warning:** If an application creates a shared property with the CreateProperty method, it (and other applications) can access that property only by using the get_Property method. An application can't assign a numeric index to the same property and then access it by using the get_PropertyByPosition method. For this reason, the same shared property group can contain some shared property objects that are identified by name and others that are identified by position.

The syntax for the method is:

```
HRESULT ISharedPropertyGroup::CreateProperty (
    BSTR name,
    VARIANT_BOOL* pfExists;
    ISharedProperty** ppProp,
);
```

The parameters for the method are:

[in] *name*
: This parameter contains the name of the property to create. An application can later use this name to obtain a reference to this property by using the get_Property method (see below).

[out] *pfExists*
: This parameter contains a reference to a Boolean value that's set to VARIANT_TRUE on return from this method if the shared property specified in the *name* parameter existed prior to this call, and VARIANT_FALSE if the property was created by this call.

[out] *ppProp*
: This parameter contains an interface pointer to an ISharedProperty element with the name specified in the *name* parameter, or NULL if an error is encountered.

Possible return values for the method are:

S_OK
: This return value indicates a reference to a shared property with the name specified in the *name* parameter was returned in the parameter *ppProp*.

E_INVALIDARG
: This return value indicates that one or more of the arguments passed in was invalid.

### CreatePropertyByPosition Method

This method creates a new shared property identified by a numeric index that's unique within the property group (as opposed to CreateProperty, which uses a unique string value) and returns an ISharedProperty interface pointer to it. If a shared property with the specified index already exists, CreatePropertyByPosition returns an interface pointer to the existing one. When you create a shared property, its value is set to the default, which is a VARIANT of type VT_I4, with a value of 0.

**Warning:** If an application creates a shared property with the CreatePropertyByPosition method, it (and other applications) can access that property only by using the get_PropertyByPosition method. An application can't assign a string value to the same property and then access it by using the get_Property method. For this reason, the same shared property group can contain some shared property objects that are identified by name and others that are identified by position.

The syntax for the method is:

```
HRESULT ISharedPropertyGroup::CreatePropertyByPosition (
    INT index,
    VARIANT_BOOL* pfExists;
    ISharedProperty** ppProp,
);
```

The parameters for the method are:

[in] *index*
This parameter is the numeric index within the shared property group by which the new property will be referenced. An application can use this index later to retrieve the shared property with the get_PropertyByPosition method.

[out] *pfExists*
This parameter is a reference to a Boolean value. If *pfExists* is set to VARIANT_TRUE on return from this method, the shared property specified by *index* existed prior to this call. If it is set to VARIANT_FALSE, the property was created by this call.

[out] *ppProp*
This parameter contains an ISharedProperty interface pointer identified by the numeric index passed in the *index* parameter, or NULL if an error is encountered.

Possible return values for the method are:

S_OK
This return value indicates that a reference to the shared property

occupying the position specified in the *index* parameter is returned in the *ppProp* parameter.

E_INVALIDARG
: This return value indicates that one or more of the arguments passed in is invalid.

## get_Property Method

This method returns an ISharedProperty interface pointer to an existing shared property identified by a string name. An application can use only the get_Property method to access properties that were created with the CreateProperty method. To access properties that were created with the CreatePropertyByPosition method, it must use the get_PropertyByPosition method.

The syntax for the method is:

```
HRESULT ISharedPropertyGroup::get_Property (
    BSTR name,
    ISharedProperty** ppProperty,
);
```

The parameters for the method are:

[in] *name*
: This parameter contains the unique name of the shared property to retrieve.

[out] *ppProperty*
: This parameter contains an ISharedProperty interface pointer to the shared property specified in the *name* parameter, or NULL if the property doesn't exist.

Possible return values for the method are:

S_OK
: This return value indicates that the shared property specified by *name* was found and an ISharedProperty interface pointer to it was returned in the *ppProperty* parameter.

E_INVALIDARG
: This return value indicates that either the argument passed in the *ppProperty* parameter was a null pointer, or there is no property in the shared property group with the name specified in the *name* parameter.

## get_PropertyByPosition Method

This function returns an ISharedProperty interface pointer to an existing shared property identified by its numeric index within the property group. An application can use only the get_PropertyByPosition method to access properties that were created with the CreatePropertyByPosition method. To access properties that were created with the CreateProperty method, an application must use the get_Property method.

The syntax for the method is:

```
HRESULT ISharedPropertyGroup::get_PropertyByPosition (
    INT index,
    ISharedProperty** ppProperty,
);
```

The parameters for the method are:

[in] *index*
: This parameter contains the numeric index within the shared property group of the property to retrieve.

[out] *ppProperty*
: The parameter contains an ISharedProperty interface pointer to the shared property specified by the *index* parameter, or NULL if the property doesn't exist.

Possible return values for the method are:

S_OK
: This return value indicates that the shared property specified by *index* was found and an ISharedProperty interface pointer to it was returned in the *ppProperty* parameter.

E_INVALIDARG
: This return value indicates that either the argument passed in the *ppProperty* parameter was a null pointer, or there is no property in the shared property group with the index number specified in the *index* parameter.

### Property Property

This property is used by non-C++ languages to access a name-based shared property; it is used the same as get_Property except that the get_ portion is left off.

### PropertyByPosition Property

This property is used by non-C++ languages to access a number-based shared property; it is used the same as get_PropertyByPosition except that the get_ portion is left off.

### The ISharedPropertyGroupManager Interface

The ISharedPropertyGroupManager interface is used to create shared property groups and to obtain access to existing shared property groups. The header file for the ISharedPropertyGroupManager interface is MTXSPM.H. An application must also link MTXGUID.LIB to its project to use this interface.

An application can access the ISharedPropertyGroupManager interface via the IObjectContext::CreateInstance method or by COM's CoCreateInstance; it makes no difference which is used since shared properties don't have an object context (and thus don't participate in transactions). However, the ISharedPropertyGroupManager should only be instantiated inside an MTS component that does have object context to avoid process and access problems (see below). ISharedPropertyGroupManager is an MTS resource dispenser that MTS components can use to share state among multiple objects within a server process. MTS components can't use global variables in a distributed environment because of concurrency and name collision issues. The ISharedPropertyGroupManager component eliminates name collisions by providing shared property groups, which establish unique name spaces for the shared properties they contain. The ISharedPropertyGroupManager component also implements locks and semaphores to protect shared properties from simultaneous access, which could result in lost updates and could leave the properties in an unpredictable state. Shared properties can be shared only by objects running in the same process, which means that they all have to be registered with MTS as being part of the same MTS package, and they must individually all have the same process activation attribute (either client or server, as explained in Chapter 6). For this reason, an MTS application should always instantiate the ISharedPropertyGroupManager, ISharedPropertyGroup, and ISharedProperty interface pointers from MTS components rather than from a base client, otherwise the activation attributes may differ. In fact, when an application sets the isolation mode (see Table 4-3 below) to LockMethod, the ISharedPropertyGroupManager requires access to the calling object's IObjectContext. Under these circumstances, an application can't create a shared property group from within a constructor or from a non-MTS interface pointer because IObjectContext isn't available during object construction and a non-MTS interface doesn't have an IObjectContext.

The ISharedPropertyGroupManager interface exposes the following methods and properties:

| Method | Description |
|---|---|
| CreatePropertyGroup | This method creates a new ISharedPropertyGroup with a string name as an identifier. If a group with the specified name already exists, CreatePropertyGroup returns a reference to the existing group. Unlike shared properties, shared property groups cannot be created with a number identifier. |
| get_Group | This method returns an ISharedPropertyGroup interface pointer to an existing shared property group, given a string name by which it can be identified. Unlike shared properties, shared property groups cannot be created with a number identifier. |

| Method | Description |
|---|---|
| get__NewEnum | This method returns an interface pointer to an enumerator that iterates through a list of all the shared property groups in a given process. (Note that _NewEnum, with a leading underscore, is the name of the property.) |

### CreatePropertyGroup Method

This method creates and returns an ISharedPropertyGroup interface pointer to a new shared property group. If a property group with the specified name already exists, CreatePropertyGroup returns an interface pointer to the existing group. The CreatePropertyGroup method sets the value in *pfExists* to VARIANT_TRUE if the property group it returns in the *ppGroup* parameter existed prior to the current call. The CreatePropertyGroup method sets the value in *pfExists* to VARIANT_FALSE if the returned property group was created by the current call.

**Note:** The *isolation mode* and *release mode* (see Tables 4-3 and 4-4) internal values are assigned when the property group is originally created and aren't changed if a subsequent call passes different values in these parameters (because it doesn't realize the shared property group already exists). The caller should always determine if *pfExists* is set to VARIANT_TRUE; in this case, the caller should check the values returned in *plIsoMode* and *plRelMode* to determine the isolation and release modes in effect for the property group in case they are different from the ones it planned.

The syntax for the method is:

```
HRESULT ISharedPropertyGroup::CreatePropertyGroup (
    BSTR name,
    LONG* plIsoMode,
    LONG* plRelMode,
    VARIANT_BOOL* pfExists,
    ISharedPropertyGroup** ppGroup,
);
```

The parameters for the method are:

[in] *name*
: This parameter contains the name of the shared property group to create or access if already created.

[in, out] *plIsoMode*
: This parameter contains a reference to a LONG that specifies the isolation mode for the properties in the new shared property group (see Table 4-3). If the value of the *pfExists* parameter is set to VARIANT_TRUE on return from this method, the *plIsoMode* value passed in is ignored and the

value returned in this parameter is the isolation mode that was assigned when the property group was created.

[in, out] *plRelMode*

This parameter contains a reference to a LONG that specifies the release mode for the properties in the new shared property group (see Table 4-4). If the value of the *pfExists* parameter is set to VARIANT_TRUE on return from this method, the *plRelMode* value passed in is ignored and the value returned in this parameter is the release mode that was assigned when the property group was created.

[out] *pfExists*

This parameter contains a reference to a BOOL that's set to VARIANT_TRUE on return from this method if the shared property group specified in the *name* parameter existed prior to this call, and VARIANT_FALSE if the property group was created by this call.

[out] *ppGroup*

This parameter contains an ISharedPropertyGroup interface pointer for a shared property group identified by the BSTR passed in the *name* parameter, or NULL if an error is encountered.

| Constant | Value | Description |
|---|---|---|
| **LockSetGet** | 0 | This value locks a property during a get_Value or put_Value call, assuring that every get or set operation on a shared property is atomic. This setting doesn't prevent other clients from concurrently accessing other properties in the same group. (This is also the default setting if not explicitly specified.) |
| **LockMethod** | 1 | This setting locks all of the properties in the shared property group for exclusive use by the caller as long as the caller's current method is executing. Use this mode when there are interdependencies among properties, or in cases where a client may have to update a property immediately after reading it before it can be accessed again. This value also requires access to the IObjectContext interface for a given caller, so it cannot be used from a base client or other MTS situation without an object context. |

***Table 4-3*** *Isolation mode constants*

| Constant | Value | Description |
|---|---|---|
| **Standard** | 0 | This release mode setting indicates that when all clients have released their references on the property group, the property group is automatically destroyed. (This is the default COM mode as well; interfaces that hold ISharedPropertyXXX interface pointers on a property group must still call Release on them for COM purposes.) |

| Constant | Value | Description |
|---|---|---|
| **Process** | 1 | This release mode indicates that the property group isn't destroyed until the process in which it was created has terminated. (Interfaces that hold ISharedPropertyXXX interface pointers on a property group must still call Release on them for COM purposes; MTS will hold a hidden reference to keep them in memory.) |

***Table 4-4*** *Release mode constants*

Possible return values for the method are:

S_OK
: This return value indicates that an ISharedPropertyGroup interface pointer to the shared property group specified in the *name* parameter is returned in the *ppGroup* parameter.

CONTEXT_E_NOCONTEXT
: This return value indicates that the caller isn't executing under the MTS run-time environment. A caller must be executing under MTS to use ISharedPropertyGroupManager.

E_INVALIDARG
: This return value indicates that at least one of the parameters is invalid, or the same interface pointer instance is attempting to create the same property group more than once.

## get_Group Method

This method returns an ISharedPropertyGroup interface pointer to an existing shared property group; it is an accessor for the Group property.

The syntax for the method is:

```
HRESULT ISharedPropertyGroupManager::get_Group (
    BSTR name,
    ISharedPropertyGroup** ppGroup,
);
```

The parameters for the method are:

[in]*name*
: This parameter is the name of the shared property group to retrieve.

[out] *ppGroup*
: This parameter is an ISharedPropertyGroup interface pointer to the shared property group specified in the *name* parameter, or NULL if the property group doesn't exist.

Possible return values for the method are:

S_OK
: This return value indicates that the shared property group exists, and an

ISharedPropertyGroup interface pointer to it is returned in the *ppGroup* parameter.

E_INVALIDARG
This return value indicates that the shared property group with the name specified in the *name* parameter doesn't exist (for this reason, it is often better to use CreatePropertyGroup instead, since it will return either the existing ISharedPropertyGroup interface pointer or a new one, rather than an error).

## get__NewEnum Method

This function returns an IEnumXXX interface pointer to an enumerator that an application can use to iterate through all the shared property groups in a process. Once this IEnumXXX interface pointer is retrieved from get__NewEnum, the application should immediately call QueryInterface on the returned IUnknown for the IEnumVARIANT interface. This interface pointer exposes several methods an application can use to iterate through a list of BSTRs representing shared property group names. Once the application has the name, it can use the get_Group method to obtain an ISharedPropertyGroup interface pointer to the shared property group it represents. Since the IEnumXXX interface pointer is a COM object, the application must call IUnknown::Release as soon as it is finished using it, as well as on the IEnumVARIANT interface pointer too.

**Warning:** When an application uses an IEnumVARIANT from get__NewEnum to enumerate the shared property groups, all groups in existence at that point will be included. However, if an application keeps this interface pointer in use, then calls CreatePropertyGroup to add a new group, the existing enumerator won't include the new group even if the application calls its Reset or Clone methods. To include the new group, the application must call IUnknown::Release on the existing enumerator, and then create a new enumerator by again calling get__NewEnum.

**Note:** get__NewEnum has two underscore characters between get and NewEnum.

The syntax for the method is:

```
HRESULT ISharedPropertyGroupManager::get__NewEnum (
    IUnknown** ppEnumerator
);
```

The parameter for the method is:

[out] *ppEnumerator*
This parameter contains an interface pointer to the IUnknown interface on a new IEnumXXX enumerator interface that an application can use to iterate through the list of all the shared property groups in the process.

Possible return values for the method are:

S_OK
This parameter indicates that an IUnknown interface pointer to the requested enumerator was returned in the *ppEnumerator* parameter. Normally, no other result will be returned since the enumerator will always be created even if there isn't anything to enumerate.

### Group Property

This property is a read-only property accessed via the get_Group accessor function described above for non-C++ languages; it otherwise works the same way.

### _NewEnum Property

This property is a read-only property accessed via the get__NewEnum accessor function described above for non-C++ languages; it otherwise works the same way.

# Miscellaneous MTS Interfaces

Aside from object context and shared properties, there are two remaining aspects to MTS 2.0 which are accessible by MTS components and clients: MTS security and MTS base clients. Each has its interface explained in detail below.

## ISecurityProperty Interface

The ISecurityProperty interface is used to determine the security ID of the current object's caller or creator. The header file for the ISecurityProperty interface is MTX.H. An application must also link MTXGUID.LIB to its project to use this interface. You obtain a reference to an object's ISecurityProperty interface by calling QueryInterface on the object's IObjectContext interface (see above). The principal value of ISecurityProperty is that, unlike the simple IsCallerInRole method of IObjectContext, ISecurityProperty lets you examine NT Security ID values directly.

The ISecurityProperty interface provides the following methods:

| Method | Description |
|---|---|
| GetDirectCallerSID | This method retrieves the security ID of the external process that called the currently executing method. |

| Method | Description |
|---|---|
| GetDirectCreatorSID | This method retrieves the security ID of the external process that directly created the current object. |
| GetOriginalCallerSID | This method retrieves the security ID of the base process that initiated the call sequence from which the current method was called. |
| GetOriginalCreatorSID | This method retrieves the security ID of the base process that initiated the activity in which the current object is executing. |
| ReleaseSID | This method releases the security ID returned by one of the other ISecurityProperty methods. |

## GetDirectCallerSID Method

This method retrieves the Windows NT security ID of the external process that called the currently executing method. An application should use the GetDirectCallerSID method to determine the security ID of the process that called the object's currently executing method. Figure 4-10 illustrates the functionality of the GetDirectCallerSID method.

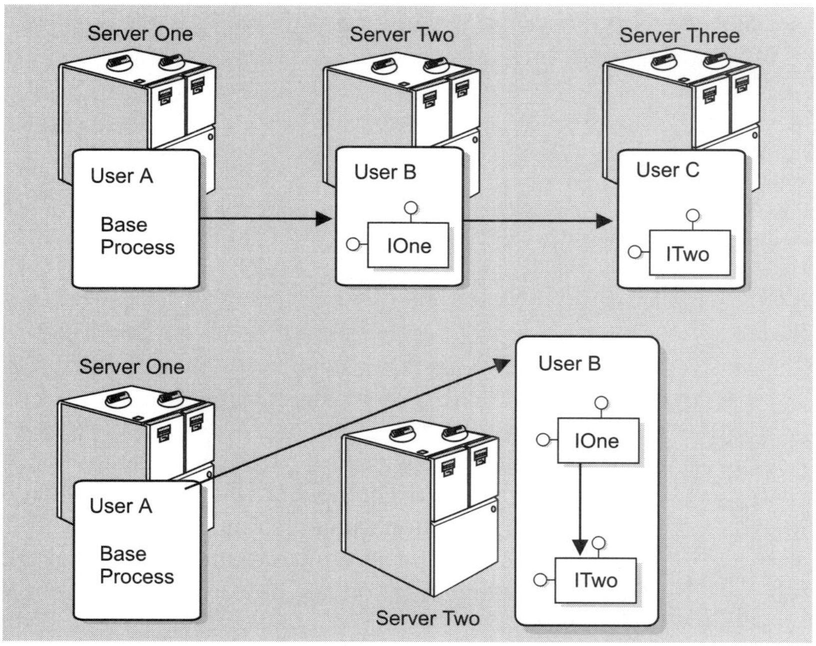


***Figure 4-10*** *A direct caller in MTS in two scenarios*

As shown in the upper part of the figure, an MTS base process running on server one, as user A, calls into MTS component interface IOne on server two, running as user B. Then interface IOne calls into interface ITwo, running on server three. If interface ITwo calls GetDirectCallerSID, the security ID of user B is returned. It is important to remember that security can only be enforced across process boundaries. This means that the security ID returned by GetDirectCallerSID is the security ID associated with the process that called into the process in which the current interface is running, not necessarily the immediate caller into the interface itself. If an interface calls into another interface within the same process, when the second interface calls GetDirectCallerSID, it will get the the security ID of the most immediate caller outside its own process boundary, not the the security ID of the interface that directly called into it. The lower part of the figure illustrates this; an MTS base process, running on server one as user A, calls into interface IOne on server two, running as user B. Then interface IOne calls into interface ITwo, running in the same process as interface IOne, also on server two. When interface ITwo calls GetDirectCallerSID, the security ID of user A is returned, not the the security ID of user B.

**Warning:** An application must call ReleaseSID on a security ID when it is finished using it. Security IDs are not a COM interface; they do not support IUnknown::Release.

The syntax for the method is:

```
HRESULT ISecurityProperty::GetDirectCallerSID (
PSID* ppSid
);
```

The parameter for the method is:

[out] *ppSid*
: This parameter is a reference to the security ID of the process from which the current method was invoked.

Possible return values for the method are:

S_OK
: This return value indicates that the security ID of the process that called the current method is returned in the parameter *ppSid*.

E_INVALIDARG
: This return value indicates that the argument passed in the *ppSid* parameter is a null pointer.

E_UNEXPECTED
: This return value indicates that an unexpected error occurred, often involving memory.

## GetDirectCreatorSID Method

This method retrieves the security ID of the current object's immediate (out-of-process) creator. An application should use the GetDirectCreatorSID method to determine the security ID of the process that created the current interface instance. Figure 4-11 illustrates the functionality of the GetDirectCreatorSID method.

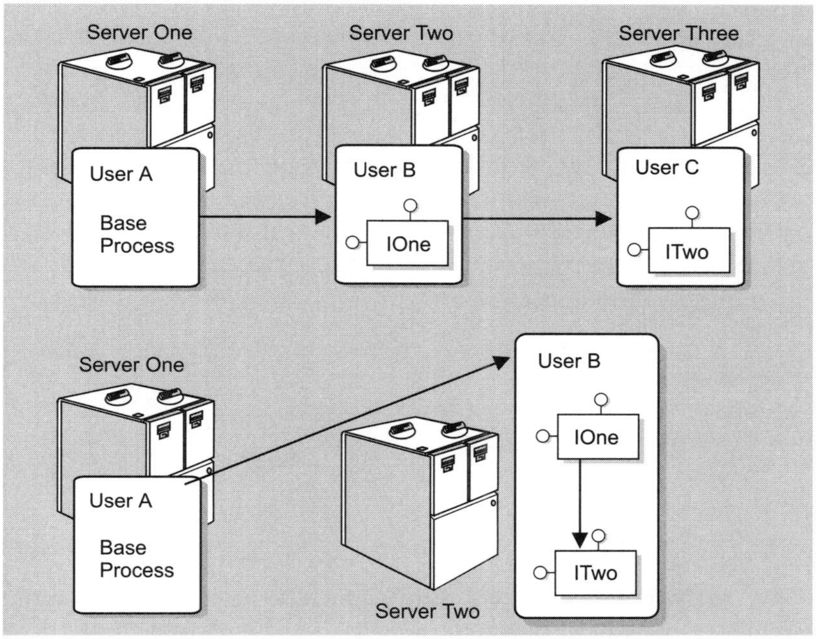


***Figure 4-11***
*A direct creator in MTS in two scenarios*

As shown in the upper part of the figure, an MTS base process running on server one, as user A, creates interface IOne on server two, running as user B. Then interface IOne creates interface ITwo, running on server three. If interface ITwo calls GetDirectCreatorSID, the security ID of user B is returned. It is important to remember that security can only be enforced across process boundaries. This means that if an interface creates another interface within the same process, when the second interface calls GetDirectCreatorSID, it will get the the security ID of the most immediate creator outside its own process boundary, not the security ID of the interface that actually created it. This is illustrated by the lower part of the figure; an MTS base client running on server one, as user A, creates interface IOne on server two, running as user B. Then interface IOne creates interface ITwo, running in the same process as interface IOne, also on server two. When interface ITwo calls GetDirect-CreatorSID, the security ID of user A is returned, not the security ID of user B.

**Warning:** An application must call ReleaseSID on a security ID when it is finished using it. Security IDs are not a COM interface; they do not support IUnknown::Release.

The syntax for the method is:

```
HRESULT ISecurityProperty::GetDirectCreatorSID (
PSID* ppSid
);
```

The parameter for the method is:

[out] *ppSid*
: This parameter contains a reference to the security ID of the process that directly created the current interface.

Possible return values for the method are:

S_OK
: This return value indicates that the security ID of the process that directly created the current interface is returned in the parameter *ppSid.*

E_INVALIDARG
: This return value indicates that the argument passed in the *ppSid* parameter is a null pointer.

E_FAIL
: This return value indicates that an unexpected error occurred, usually involving memory.

## GetOriginalCallerSID Method

This method retrieves the security ID of the base process that initiated the sequence of calls from which the call into the current interface originated. Applications should use the GetOriginalCallerSID method to determine the security ID of the original process that initiated the call sequence from which the current method was called (but see the Warning below for possible ways this call could fail). Figure 4-12 illustrates the functionality of the GetOriginalCallerSID method.

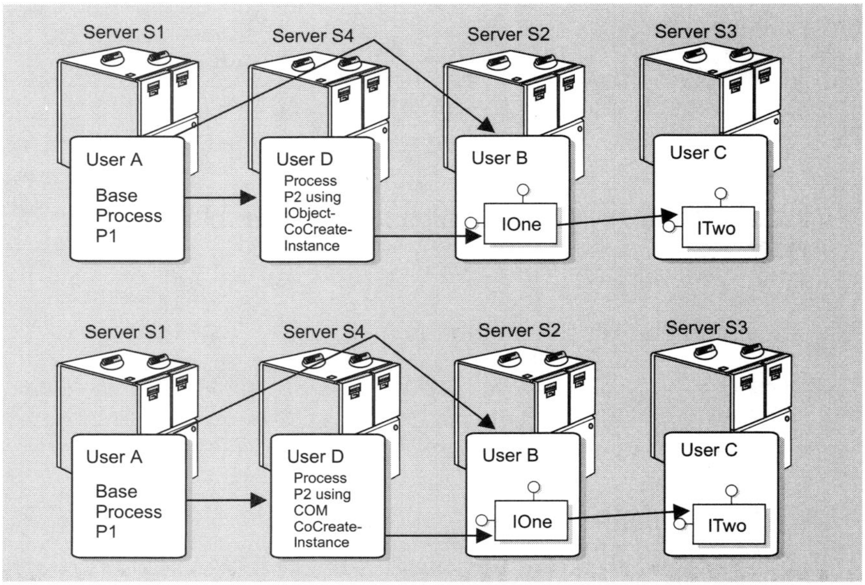


**Figure 4-12** *A original caller in MTS in two scenarios*

As illustrated in the upper part of the figure, an MTS base process P1, running on server S1 as user A, creates interface IOne on server S2, running as user B. Then base process P1 passes its reference on interface IOne to base process P2, running on server S3 as user C. Base process P2 uses that reference to call into interface IOne again. Interface IOne calls into interface ITwo, running on server S4. If interface ITwo then calls GetOriginalCallerSID, the security ID of user D is returned. Usually, an object's original caller is the same process as its original creator. The only situation in which the original caller and the original creator would be different is one in which the original creator passes a reference to another process, and the other process initiates the call sequence (as in the figure, just to make the point and be difficult).

**Warning:** The path to the original caller is broken if any interface along the chain was created by some means other than IObjectContext::CreateInstance or ITransactionContext::CreateInstance.

As shown in the lower part of the figure (which reproduces the same calls as in the upper part with one critical difference), if MTS base process P1 instead uses the base COM CoCreateInstance to create interface IOne, when interface ITwo calls GetOriginalCallerSID, the security ID it gets back will be the security ID of user B, not user D. This is because the call sequence is traced back through the object context system, and MTS can only create a context for an interface that's created with either IObjectContext::CreateInstance or ITransactionContext::CreateInstance.

**Warning:** An application must call ReleaseSID on a security ID when it is finished using it. Security IDs are not a COM interface; they do not support IUnknown::Release.

The syntax for the method is:

```
HRESULT ISecurityProperty::GetOriginalCallerSID (
PSID* ppSid
);
```

The parameter for the method is:

[out] *ppSid*

This parameter contains a reference to the security ID of the base process that initiated the call sequence from which the current method was called.

Possible return values for the method are:

S_OK

This return value indicates that the security ID of the base process that originated the call into the current object is returned in the parameter *ppSid*.

E_INVALIDARG

This return value indicates that the argument passed in the *ppSid* parameter is a null pointer.

E_FAIL

This return value indicates an unexpected error occurred, usually involving memory.

### *GetOriginalCreatorSID Method*

This method retrieves the security ID of the original base process that initiated the activity in which the current interface is executing. An application should use the GetOriginalCreatorSID method to determine the security ID of the process that initiated the MTS activity in which the current interface is executing (but see the Warning below for a situation where the function will not return the desired information). Figure 4-13 illustrates the functionality of the GetOriginalCreatorSID method.

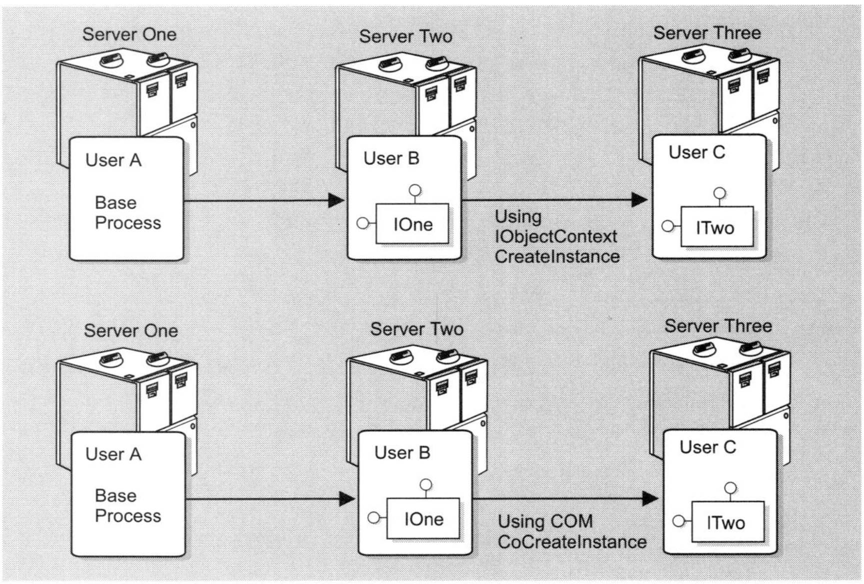


***Figure 4-13***
*An original creator in MTS in two scenarios*

As illustrated in the upper part of the figure, an MTS base process running on server one, as user A, creates interface IOne on server two, running as user B. Then interface IOne creates interface ITwo, running on server three. If interface ITwo calls GetOriginalCreatorSID, the security ID of user A is returned.

**Warning:** The path to the original creator is broken if an interface is created by some means other than IObjectContext::CreateInstance or ITransactionContext::CreateInstance.

As shown in the lower part of the figure (which reproduces the same calls as the upper part with one critical difference), if the base process on server one uses the COM function CoCreateInstance to create interface IOne, when interface ITwo calls GetOriginalCreatorSID, the security ID it gets back will be the security ID of user B, not user A. This is because the creation sequence is traced back through the object context system, and MTS can only create a context for an interface that's created with either IObjectContext::Create-Instance or ITransactionContext::CreateInstance.

**Warning:** An application must call ReleaseSID on a security ID when it is finished using it. Security IDs are not a COM interface; they do not support IUnknown::Release.

The syntax for the method is:

```
HRESULT ISecurityProperty::GetOriginalCreatorSID (
PSID* ppSid
);
```

The parameter for the method is:

[out] *ppSid*
: This parameter contains a reference to the security ID of the base process that initiated the activity in which the current interface is executing.

Possible return values for the method are:

S_OK
: This return value indicates that the security ID of the original creator is returned in the parameter *ppSid*.

E_INVALIDARG
: This return value indicates that the argument passed in the *ppSid* parameter is a null pointer.

E_FAIL
: This return value indicates that an unexpected error occurred, usually involving memory.

### *ReleaseSID Method*

This function releases a security ID that was obtained from the GetDirectCallerSID, GetDirectCreatorSID, GetOriginalCallerSID, or GetOriginalCreatorSID method. An application must always invoke the ReleaseSID method to release any security ID pointers returned by the GetDirectCallerSID, GetDirectCreatorSID, GetOriginalCallerSID, and GetOriginalCreatorSID methods of the ISecurityProperty interface.

The syntax for the method is:

```
HRESULT ISecurityProperty::ReleaseSID (
PSID pSid
);
```

The parameter for the method is:

[in] *pSid*
This parameter contains a reference to a security ID that was obtained by invoking one of the ISecurityProperty methods.

Possible return values for the method are:

S_OK
This return value indicates that the security ID, passed in the *pSid* parameter, was released.

E_INVALIDARG
This return value indicates that the argument passed in the *pSid* parameter is not a reference to a security ID.

## ITransactionContextEx Interface

Most MTS components are created as such by their developers and then composed into an MTS package by the administrator on their server and client machines via the MTS Explorer (see Chapter 9). This has the nice side effect of removing the need for an MTS client to have any knowledge of MTS; all this behavior is handled by the MTS COM components and the MTS Explorer. In some cases, however, it is necessary for the MTS client application to create an MTS transaction that is not supported for the participating COM components and the MTS Explorer. To do this, the ITransactionContextEx interface is used by a *base client* (see the Note below) to compose the work of one or more MTS objects into an atomic transaction and to commit or abort the transaction. The header file for the ITransactionContextEx interface is TXCTX.H. The client must also link MTXGUID.LIB to its project to use this interface. Figure 4-14 illustrates the functionality of the ITransactionContextEx interface.

As shown in the figure, an application can create an MTS transaction without ever going near the MTS Explorer by instantiating an ITransactionContextEx interface pointer using the standard COM CoCreateInstance call, and then end the transaction by calling Commit or Abort on the interface pointer. The base client itself never executes within the MTS transaction, however. The TransactionContextEx component is a standard MTS component already built into the MTS system. The component's transaction attribute is set to Requires a New Transaction, which means that an ITransactionContextEx object is always the root of a transaction. When a base client instantiates an MTS-registered COM interface by using the ITransactionContextEx::CreateInstance method, the new interface and its descendants will participate in the

ITransactionContextEx interface's transaction unless the new interface's transaction attribute is set to Requires a New Transaction or Does Not Support Transactions. The net gain by using ITransactionContextEx is that MTS components that were not created in a package with MTS Explorer can still participate in the same transaction.

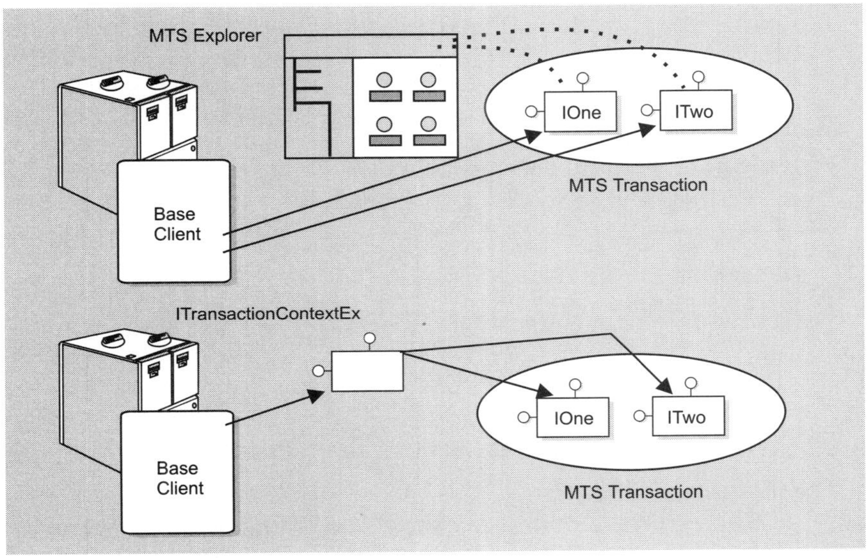


***Figure 4-14** ITransactionContextEx at work*

**Note:** A *base client* is a COM client that runs outside the Microsoft Transaction Server run-time environment, but that instantiates Microsoft Transaction Server objects.

The ITransactionContextEx interface exposes the following methods:

| Method | Description |
|---|---|
| Abort | This method aborts the work of all MTS interfaces participating in the current transaction. The transaction is completed on return from this method but all its changes are rolled back. |
| Commit | This method attempts to commit the work of all MTS interfaces participating in the current transaction. If any of the MTS interfaces participating in the transaction have called SetAbort or DisableCommit, or if a system error has occurred, the transaction will be aborted. Otherwise, the transaction will be committed. In either case, the transaction is completed on return from this method. |
| CreateInstance | This method instantiates another MTS interface. If the component that provides the interface is configured to support or require a transaction, then the new object runs under the transaction of the TransactionContextEx object. If the component is set to require a new transaction, a new transaction is begun automatically. |

### Abort Method

This method aborts the current ITransactionContextEx transaction. When a base client calls Abort, all interfaces that participated in the transaction are automatically deactivated. Any database updates made by those objects are rolled back. The transaction is completed on return from this method. If another call is made on the TransactionContextEx interface pointer after the TransactionContextEx interface has returned from a call in which it called the Abort method, a new transaction is started.

**Warning:** The online documentation for this interface is defective; the MTS 2.0 update in Service Pack 1 has the correct versions.

The syntax for the method is:

```
HRESULT ITransactionContextEx::Abort ( );
```

Possible return values for the method are:

S_OK
: This return value indicates that the transaction was aborted.

E_FAIL
: This return value indicates that the TransactionContextEx object isn't running under an MTS process. This usually happens if the TransactionContextEx component's Registry entry has been corrupted.

E_UNEXPECTED
: This return value indicates that an unexpected error occurred, usually involving one of the database connections.

### Commit Method

This method attempts to commit the current ITransactionContextEx transaction. Calling Commit doesn't guarantee that a transaction will be committed. If any MTS interface that was part of the transaction has returned from a method after calling SetAbort, the transaction will be aborted. If any interface that was part of the transaction has called DisableCommit and hasn't yet called EnableCommit or SetComplete, the transaction will also be aborted. Any error that causes Microsoft DTC to abort a transaction will also abort an MTS transaction. When a base client calls Commit, regardless of whether the transaction commits or aborts, the transaction is completed on return from this method and all interfaces that participated in the transaction are automatically deactivated. If another call comes in after the TransactionContextEx interface has returned from a call in which it called the Commit method, a new transaction is started.

**Warning:** The online documentation for this interface is defective; the MTS 2.0 update in Service Pack 1 has the correct versions.

The syntax for the method is:

```
HRESULT ITransactionContextEx::Commit ( );
```

Possible return values for the method are:

S_OK
: This return value indicates that the transaction was committed.

E_FAIL
: This return value indicates that the TransactionContextEx object isn't running under an MTS process. This usually happens if the Transaction-ContextEx component's Registry entry has been corrupted.

E_UNEXPECTED
: This return value indicates an unexpected error occurred, usually involving a database connection.

CONTEXT_E_ABORTED
: This return value indicates that despite the desire for committing it, the transaction was aborted for one of the reasons noted above.

### *CreateInstance Method*

This method instantiates an MTS interface that will execute within the scope of the transaction that was initiated with the creation of the Transaction-ContextEx interface. When a base client uses the ITransactionContextEx::CreateInstance method to instantiate an MTS interface, the new interface executes within the transaction context's activity. If the transaction attribute of the new object's component is set to either Supports Transactions or Requires a Transaction, the new interface also inherits the transaction initiated with the creation of the TransactionContextEx object. However, if the component that provides the new interface has its transaction attribute set to Does Not Support Transactions, the object neither inherits the transaction nor passes it on to interfaces it subsequently creates. If the component that provides the new interface has its transaction attribute set to Requires a New Transaction, the MTS run-time environment initiates a new transaction for the new interface, and that transaction is the one that's inherited by interfaces it subsequently creates.

**Warning:** If the Microsoft Distributed Transaction Coordinator is not running and the interface is transactional, the interface pointer is successfully created. However, method calls to that interface pointer will fail with CONTEXT_E_TMNOTAVAILABLE. In this case the interface pointer should have its IUnknown::Release method called at once and the current transaction aborted and execution halted.

**Note:** MTS always uses standard marshaling. Even if a component exposes the IMarshal interface, its IMarshal methods will never be called by the MTS run-time environment. Also, applications can't create MTS interfaces as part of an aggregation (see Chapter 1).

The syntax for the method is:

```
HRESULT ITransactionContextEx::CreateInstance (
    REFCLSID rclsid,
    REFIID riid,
    LPVOID FAR* ppvObj
);
```

The parameters for the method are:

[in] *rclsid*

This parameter is a reference to the CLSID of the COM server for the interface to instantiate.

[in] *riid*

This parameter is a reference to the interface ID of the interface to instantiate.

[out] *ppvObj*

This parameter contains an interface pointer from the COM server specified by the *rclsid* argument, supporting the interface specified by the *riid* argument.

Possible return values for the method are:

S_OK

This return value indicates that an interface pointer to the element is returned in the *ppvObj* parameter.

REGDB_E_CLASSNOTREG

This return value indicates that the component specified by *rclsid* is not registered as a COM component.

E_OUTOFMEMORY

This return value indicates that there is insufficient memory available to instantiate the interface.

E_INVALIDARG
: This return value indicates that the argument passed in the *ppvObj* parameter is invalid.

E_UNEXPECTED
: This return value indicates that an unexpected error occurred, which will be server dependent since there is an explicit out of memory error HRESULT supported.

## Where We Go From Here

At this point, you may be surprised at how much you know about MTS. This is because MTS, despite its power, is really a rather simple system. But as noted in the introduction, MTS is useless by itself; it needs a complementary database access technology to work. This technology at present is ActiveX Data Objects, or ADO. The next chapter brings you fully up to speed on this critical bit of MTS information.

Chapter Five

# An ADO Primer

Microsoft has two high-level database technologies: OLE DB (which isn't an acronym) and MTS (which is, and stands for Microsoft Transaction Server). Both of these powerful database systems rely on a single technology to connect with end users: ActiveX Data Objects (ADO). ADO is a set of COM objects (i.e., interfaces) designed to connect with database systems via the OLE DB technology, but users don't need to know anything about OLE DB to use ADO. Instead, they simply create appropriate ADO objects and make method calls on them to connect with databases and obtain and set information. For OLE DB developers, ADO is the vehicle their users need to connect with the OLE DB providers and consumers they create. For MTS programmers, ADO is the system they use to interact with databases under the umbrella of MTS. (ADO itself has several advanced capabilities, including RDS (Remote Data Service) and MD (Multi-Dimensional) database interactions, which we won't go into here.)

Either way, database programmers using Microsoft technology need a detailed reference about ADO. This chapter provides that reference, with a complete writeup on all the collections, objects, methods, and events of the ADO system. Dive in, and your database development will never be the same!

## ADO Collections

Collections are groups of things that share at least one similar feature, like a coin collection. In ADO, *collections* are objects (i.e., interfaces) used to store and provide access to groups of other ADO objects (i.e., interface pointers) that contain specific information or capabilities important to their owning ADO element (like the Errors collection for the Connection object). Each such collection allows clients to access single elements from groups of IPs using either a compile-time name, a run-time string, or a run-time integer. This allows the ADO system to provide general information to its clients while staying inside the COM metaphor. The collections supported in ADO 2.0 are Errors, Fields, Parameters, and Properties. Each has its own section below. In addition, each collection object supports a single property, as explained below. Each specific collection will implement its own specialized methods as well, with some overlap to the methods of other collections. Except for the Errors collection, each collection is fixed in number of elements and content when its owning ADO object is created by the system.

### Count Property (All Collections)

This property is common to all ADO collections. It gives a Long value which is the number of objects (i.e., interface pointers) in the current collection. A value of 0 indicates no IPs in the collection. Although Count is 1-based, the Item method used to retrieve collection objects is 0-based, so loops using Count should subtract 1 from it (i.e., (for x=0;x++;x<MyCollection.Count)).

## The Errors Collection

Any operation involving ADO objects can generate one or more errors. As each error occurs, one or more Error objects are placed in the Errors collection of the current Connection object. When another ADO operation generates an error, the Errors collection is cleared, and the new set of Error objects is placed in the Errors collection. Each Error object represents a specific OLE DB error, not an ADO run-time error (ADO errors are exposed to the run-time exception-handling mechanism). ADO operations that don't generate an error have no effect on the Errors collection. Developers can use the Clear method to manually clear an Errors collection.The set of Error objects in the Errors collection describes all errors that occurred in response to a single SQL statement. Enumerating the specific errors in the Errors collection enables an application's error-handling routines to more precisely determine the cause and origin of an error, and take appropriate steps to recover. Some properties and methods return warnings that appear as Error objects in the Errors collection but do not halt an application's execution. Before an application calls the Resync, UpdateBatch, or CancelBatch methods on a Recordset object or the Open method on a Connection object, or sets the Filter property on a Recordset object, it should call the Clear method on the Errors collection so that it can check the Count property of the Errors collection to test for returned warnings.

The Errors collection supports two methods: Clear and Item.

### Clear Method (Errors Collection)

This method removes all of the objects in the Errors collection. An application should use the Clear method on the Errors collection to remove all existing Error objects from the collection. When an error occurs, ADO automatically clears the Errors collection and fills it with Error objects based on the new error.

The method has the following syntax:

```
pErrorscollection->Clear();
```

The method has no parameters.

### Item Method (Errors Collection)

This method returns a specific member of a collection by name or ordinal number. An application should use the Item method to return a specific object in a collection. If the method cannot find an object in the collection corresponding to the *Index* argument, an ADO error occurs.

The method has the following syntax:

```
pError = pErrorscollection->Item(Index);
```

The method returns an interface pointer to an ADO Error object.

The method has the following parameter:

*Index*
: This parameter is a Variant that evaluates either to the name or to the ordinal number of an object in a collection.

**Warning** Some collections don't support named objects; for these collections, an application must use ordinal number references.

## The Fields Collection

A Recordset object has a Fields collection made up of Field objects. Each Field object corresponds to a column in the Recordset. An application should populate the Fields collection before opening the Recordset by calling the Refresh method on the Fields collection.

The Fields collection supports four methods: Append, Delete, Item, and Refresh.

### Append Method (Fields Collection)

This method appends a new Field object to the collection, which may be created before it is appended. An application must set the CursorLocation property to adUseClient before calling the fields.Append method. Calling the Fields.Append method for an open Recordset, or a Recordset where the ActiveConnection property has been set, will cause an ADO error.

The method has the following syntax:

```
pfields->Append(Name, Type, DefinedSize, Attrib);
```

The method has the following parameters:

*Name*
: This parameter is a String holding the name of the new Field object, which must not be the same name as any other object in pfields.

*Type*
: This parameter is a DataTypeEnum, whose default value is adEmpty; it holds the data type of the new field.

*DefinedSize*
: This optional parameter is a Long which is the defined size in characters or bytes of the new field. The default value for this parameter is derived from Type. (The default Type is adEmpty, and therefore the default DefinedSize is unspecified.)

*Attrib*
: This optional parameter is a FieldAttributeEnum that specifies attributes for the new Field. The default value for this parameter is adFldDefault. If this value is not specified, the Field will contain attributes derived from Type.

### Delete Method (Fields Collection)

This method deletes an object from the Fields collection. Calling the Fields.Delete method on an open Recordset causes an ADO error.

The method has the following syntax:

```
pfields->Delete(Field);
```

The method has the following parameter:

*Field*
: This parameter is a Variant designating the Field object to delete, which must be the name of the Field object; it cannot be an ordinal position or the Field object itself.

### Item Method (Fields Collection)

This method returns a specific member of a collection by name or ordinal number. An application should use the Item method to return a specific object in a collection. If the method cannot find an object in the collection corresponding to the *Index* argument, an ADO error occurs.

The method has the following syntax:

```
pField = pFieldscollection->Item(Index);
```

The method returns an interface pointer to an ADO Field object.

The method has the following parameter:

*Index*

This parameter is a Variant that evaluates either to the name or to the ordinal number of an object in a collection.

**Warning** Some collections don't support named objects; for these collections, an application must use ordinal number references.

### Refresh Method (Fields Collection)

This method updates the Field objects in a Fields collection to reflect objects available from and specific to the OLE DB provider.

The method has the following syntax:

```
pFieldscollection->Refresh();
```

The method has no parameters.

**Note** In ADO 2.0, using the Refresh method on the Fields collection has no visible effect. To retrieve changes from the underlying database structure, an application must use either the Requery method or, if the Recordset object does not support bookmarks, the MoveFirst method.

## The Parameters Collection

A Command object has a Parameters collection made up of Parameter objects (interface pointers). Using the Refresh method on a Command object's Parameters collection retrieves parameter information for the stored procedure or parameterized query specified in the Command object. Some providers do not support stored procedure calls or parameterized queries; calling the Refresh method on the Parameters collection when using such a provider will return an error. If an application has not defined its own Parameter objects and it accesses the Parameters collection before calling the Refresh method, ADO will automatically call the method and populate the collection for it. For this reason, an application can minimize calls to the provider to improve performance if it knows the properties of the parameters associated with the stored procedure or parameterized query it wishes to call. An application can use the CreateParameter method to create Parameter objects with the appropriate property settings and use the Append method to add them to the Parameters collection. This lets the application set and return parameter values without having to call the provider for the parameter information. If an application is writing to a provider that does not supply parameter information, it must manually populate the Parameters collection using the CreateParameter method to be able to use parameters at all. An application should use the Delete method to remove Parameter objects from the Parameters collection if necessary.

The Parameters collection supports four methods: Append, Delete, Item, and Refresh.

### Append Method (Parameters Collection)

Use the Append method to add a new Parameter object to the Parameters collection of a Command object. The application must set the Type property of the Parameter object before appending it to the Parameters collection. If an application selects a variable-length data type, it must also set the Size property to a value greater than zero.

The method has the following syntax:

```
pParameters->Append(object);
```

The method has the following parameter:

*object*
: This parameter is the Parameter interface pointer to be appended.

### Delete Method (Parameters Collection)

This method deletes an object from the Parameters collection. The application must use the Parameter object's Name property or its collection index when calling the Delete method; an object variable is not a valid argument.

The method has the following syntax:

```
pParameters->Delete(Index);
```

The method has the following parameter:

*Index*
: This parameter is a String representing the name of the Parameter object the application wants to delete, or the object's ordinal position (index) in the collection.

### Item Method (Parameters Collection)

This method returns a specific member of a collection by name or ordinal number. An application should use the Item method to return a specific object in a collection. If the method cannot find an object in the collection corresponding to the *Index* argument, an ADO error occurs.

The method has the following syntax:

```
pParameter = pParameterscollection->Item(Index);
```

The method returns an interface pointer to an ADO Parameter object.

The method has the following parameter:

*Index*

This parameter is a Variant that evaluates either to the name or to the ordinal number of an object in a collection.

**Warning** Some collections don't support named objects; for these collections, an application must use ordinal number references.

### Refresh Method (Parameters Collection)

Using the Refresh method on a Command object's Parameters collection retrieves provider-side parameter information for the stored procedure or parameterized query specified in the Command object. The collection will be empty for providers that do not support stored procedure calls or parameterized queries.

An application should set the ActiveConnection property of the Command object to a valid Connection object, the CommandText property to a valid command, and the CommandType property to adCmdStoredProc before calling the Refresh method. If an application accesses the Parameters collection before calling the Refresh method, ADO will automatically call the method and populate the collection for it.

The method has the following syntax:

```
pParameterscollection->Refresh();
```

The method has no parameters.

**Note** If an application uses the Refresh method to obtain parameter information from the provider and it returns one or more variable-length data type Parameter objects, ADO may allocate memory for the parameters based on their maximum potential size, which will cause an error when executed. An application should explicitly set the Size property for these parameters before calling the Execute method to prevent errors.

## The Properties Collection

Some ADO objects (interface pointers) have a Properties collection made up of Property objects. Each Property object corresponds to a characteristic of the ADO object specific to the provider currently in use.

The Properties collection supports two methods: Item and Refresh.

### Item Method (Properties Collection)

This method returns a specific member of a collection by name or ordinal number. An application should use the Item method to return a specific object in a collection. If the method cannot find an object in the collection corresponding to the *Index* argument, an ADO error occurs.

The method has the following syntax:

```
pProperty = pPropertiescollection->Item(Index);
```

The method returns an interface pointer to an ADO Property object.

The method has the following parameter:

*Index*
This parameter is a Variant that evaluates either to the name or to the ordinal number of an object in a collection.

**Warning** Some collections don't support named objects; for these collections, an application must use ordinal number references.

### Refresh Method (Properties Collection)

Using the Refresh method on a Properties collection of some objects populates the collection with the dynamic properties the provider exposes in the form of Property Interface pointers (objects). These properties provide information about functionality specific to the provider beyond the built-in properties ADO supports; consult the specific OLE DB provider documentation for specific property information.

The method has the following syntax:

```
pPropertiescollection->Refresh();
```

The method has no parameters.

## The ADO Connection Object

An ADO Connection object represents a unique session with a data source (an OLE DB provider). In the case of a client/server database system, it may be an actual network connection to the server. To execute a query without using a Command object, an application can pass a query string to the Execute method of a Connection object. (A Command object is still required when an application wants to persist the command text and re-execute it, or use query parameters.) Applications can create Connection objects independently of any other previously defined object.

One of the more interesting uses of Connection objects is that they permit an application to execute commands or stored procedures as if they were native methods on the Connection object. To execute such a command, an application must give the command a name using the Command object Name property, then set the Command object's ActiveConnection property to the connection. Next, the application must include a program statement where the command name is used as if it were a method on the Connection object, followed by any parameters, followed by a Recordset object if any rows are returned. The application can also set the Recordset properties to customize the resulting Recordset. To execute a stored procedure, an application simply must contain a program statement where the stored procedure name is used as if it were a method on the Connection object, followed by any parameters. (ADO will make a "best guess" of parameter types.)

Using the collections, methods, and properties of a Connection object, an application can do any or all of the following:

- Configure the connection before opening it with the ConnectionString, ConnectionTimeout, and Mode properties.
- Set the CursorLocation property to invoke the Client Cursor Provider, which supports batch updates.
- Set the default database for the connection with the DefaultDatabase property.
- Set the level of isolation for the transactions opened on the connection with the IsolationLevel property.
- Specify an OLE DB provider with the Provider property.
- Establish, and later break, the physical connection to the data source with the Open and Close methods.
- Execute a command on the connection with the Execute method and configure the execution with the CommandTimeout property.
- Manage transactions on the open connection, including nested transactions if the provider supports them, with the BeginTrans, CommitTrans, and RollbackTrans methods and the Attributes property.
- Examine errors returned from the data source with the Errors collection.
- Read the version from the ADO implementation in use with the Version property.
- Obtain schema information about its database with the OpenSchema method.

**Warning** Depending on the functionality supported by the OLE DB provider in use, some collections, methods, or properties of a Connection object may not be available.

Each of the properties and methods of the Connection object is discussed below.

## Attributes Property (Connection Object)

This property is read/write, and sets or returns a Long value which is the sum of any one or more of the XactAttributeEnum values in Table 5-1 below (default is zero).

| Constant | Description |
|---|---|
| adXactCommitRetaining | This value indicates that calling CommitTrans automatically starts a new transaction. Not all providers support this feature. |
| adXactAbortRetaining | This value indicates that calling RollbackTrans automatically starts a new transaction. Not all providers support this feature. |

***Table 5-1*** *XactAttributeEnum values*

## CommandTimeout Property (Connection Object)

This property indicates how long the ADO run-time system should wait while executing a command before terminating the attempt and generating an error (presumably due to a network connection failure). The property is read/write (even after a connection is opened), with a default value of 30 seconds. If the interval set in the CommandTimeout property elapses before the command completes execution, an error occurs and ADO cancels the command. If an application sets the property to zero, ADO will wait indefinitely until the execution is complete.

**Note** The CommandTimeout setting on a Connection object has no effect on the CommandTimeout setting on a Command object on the same Connection; that is, the Command object's CommandTimeout property does not inherit the value of the Connection object's CommandTimeout value.

**Warning** If an application uses CommandTimeout functionality without support from the underlying OLE DB provider, results are unpredictable.

## ConnectionString Property (Connection Object)

This property contains the information used to establish a connection to a data source (i.e., an OLE DB provider). The property is a String, and is read/write until a connection is opened and read-only thereafter. Applications use the ConnectionString property to specify a data source by passing a detailed series of *argument* = *value* statements separated by semicolons, as explained below. After an application has set the ConnectionString property and opened the Connection object, the provider may alter the contents of the property by mapping the ADO-defined argument names to their provider equivalents. The ConnectionString property automatically inherits the value used for the *ConnectionString* argument of the Open method, so an application can override the current ConnectionString property during the Open method call. ADO supports four arguments for the ConnectionString property which are listed in Table 5-2; any other arguments pass directly to the provider without any processing by ADO.

| Argument | Description |
|---|---|
| Provider= | This argument specifies the name of an OLE DB provider to use for the connection. |
| File Name= | This argument specifies the name of a provider-specific file containing preset connection information. |
| Remote Provider= | This argument specifies the name of a provider to use when opening a client-side connection. This argument is used by the Remote Data Service only. |
| Remote Server= | This argument specifies the path name of the server to use when opening a client-side connection. This argument is used by the Remote Data Service only. |

***Table 5-2*** *ConnectionString arguments processed by ADO*

**Warning** Because the *File Name*= argument causes ADO to load the associated provider, an application cannot pass both the *Provider*= and *File Name*= arguments to a ConnectionString.

## ConnectionTimeout Property (Connection Object)

This property indicates how long the ADO run time should wait while establishing a connection before terminating the attempt and generating an error (usually due to a failed network transmission). The property is a Long value with a default of 15 seconds; the property is read/write until a connection is opened and read-only afterwards. If an application sets the property to zero, ADO will wait indefinitely until the connection is opened.

**Warning** If an application uses ConnectionTimeout functionality without support from the underlying OLE DB provider, results are unpredictable.

## CursorLocation Property (Connection Object)

This property determines the location of the cursor engine to be used by ADO, based on various cursor libraries accessible to the OLE DB provider in use. The property is a Long value which is read/write regardless of whether a connection is open or not, but the setting affects connections established only after the property has been set; changing this property has no effect on existing connections. The cursor obtained via an Execute call will automatically inherit the setting of this property. Table 5-3 gives the possible values of this property:

| Constant | Description |
|---|---|
| adUseNone | This value indicates that no cursor services are used; it is obsolete and should be used only for the sake of backward compatibility with legacy code. |
| adUseClient | This value indicates that the connection uses client-side cursors supplied by a local cursor library. Since local cursor engines often will allow features that driver-supplied cursors may not, using this setting may enable extra features. (adUseClientBatch is an alternative value for this constant.) |
| adUseServer | This value is the default; it indicates that the connection uses OLE DB provider- or driver-supplied cursors. Some features of the Microsoft Client Cursor Provider (such as disassociated recordsets) cannot be simulated with server-side cursors, but other provider-specific features may be supported instead. |

***Table 5-3*** *CursorLocation property values*

### *DefaultDatabase Property (Connection Object)*

This property indicates the default database for a Connection object. This property is a String that evaluates to the name of a database available from the current OLE DB provider. If there is a default database, SQL strings sent as commands may use an unqualified syntax to access objects in that database. To access objects in a database other than the one specified in the DefaultDatabase property, SQL strings must qualify object names with the desired database name. Upon connection, the provider will write default database information to the DefaultDatabase property if it uses the property.

**Warning** Some OLE DB providers allow only one database per connection, in which case an application cannot change the DefaultDatabase property. Also, some OLE DB providers may not support this feature, and will return an error or an empty string.

### *IsolationLevel Property (Connection Object)*

This property indicates the level of isolation for a Connection object. The property contains one or more of the IsolationLevelEnum values shown in Table 5-4 below. The setting does not take effect until the next time an application calls the BeginTrans method.

**Warning** If the level of isolation an application requests is unavailable, the OLE DB provider may return the next greater level of isolation.

| Constant | Description |
|---|---|
| adXactUnspecified | This value indicates that the provider is using a different isolation level than specified, but that the level cannot be determined. |
| adXactChaos | This value is the default; it indicates that an application cannot overwrite pending changes from more highly isolated transactions. |
| adXactBrowse | This value indicates that from one transaction an application can view uncommitted changes in other transactions. |
| adXactReadUncommitted | This value is the same as adXactBrowse. |
| adXactCursorStability | This value indicates that from one transaction an application can view changes in other transactions only after they've been committed. |
| adXactReadCommitted | This value is the same as adXactCursorStability. |
| adXactRepeatableRead | This value indicates that from one transaction an application cannot see changes made in other transactions, but that requerying can bring new recordsets. |
| adXactIsolated | This value indicates that transactions are conducted in isolation of other transactions. |
| adXactSerializable | This value is the same as adXactIsolated. |

***Table 5-4*** *IsolationLevelEnum values*

## *Mode Property (Connection Object)*

This property indicates the available permissions for modifying data in a connection. The property is one of the ConnectModeEnum values listed in Table 5-5 below; it is read/write when the connection is not open and read-only when a connection is open.

| Constant | Description |
|---|---|
| adModeUnknown | This value is the default, and indicates that the permissions have not yet been set or cannot be determined. |
| adModeRead | This value indicates read-only permissions. |
| adModeWrite | This value indicates write-only permissions. |
| adModeReadWrite | This value indicates read/write permissions. |
| adModeShareDenyRead | This value indicates that ADO prevents others from opening the connection with read permissions. |
| adModeShareDenyWrite | This value indicates that ADO prevents others from opening the connection with write permissions. |

| Constant | Description |
|---|---|
| adModeShareExclusive | This value indicates that ADO prevents others from opening the connection. |
| adModeShareDenyNone | This value indicates that ADO prevents others from opening the connection with any permissions. |

***Table 5-5*** *ConnectModeEnum and ConnectOptionEnum values*

## Provider Property (Connection Object)

This property indicates the name of the OLE DB provider for a Connection object. The property is a String value which is read/write when a connection is closed and read-only when it is open. If no provider is specified, the property will default to MSDASQL (Microsoft OLE DB Provider for ODBC). The setting does not take effect until an application either opens the Connection object or accesses the Properties collection of the Connection object.

**Warning** This property can also be set by the contents of the ConnectionString property or the *ConnectionString* argument of the Open method; however, specifying a provider in more than one place while calling the Open method can have unpredictable results. If an invalid setting is placed in the property, an ADO error occurs.

## State Property (Connection Object)

This is a read-only Long property which indicates whether the Connection object is currently open (interacting with an OLE DB provider) or closed (not interacting with an OLE DB provider). The possible values are listed in Table 5-6.

| Constant | Description |
|---|---|
| adStateClosed | This value is the default; it indicates that the Connection object is closed. |
| adStateOpen | This value indicates that the Connection object is open. |

***Table 5-6*** *Connection object State property values*

## Version Property (Connection Object)

This property indicates the ADO version number as a String value. An application should use it to determine which ADO implementation is currently available on a given client or server computer, and degrade gracefully if a lesser version than expected is found.

**Note** The version information of a given OLE DB provider will usually be available as a dynamic Property object in the Properties collection.

## *BeginTrans Method (Connection Object)*

An application should use the BeginTrans, CommitTrans, and RollbackTrans methods with a Connection object when it wants to save or cancel a series of changes made to the source data as a single unit. Once an application calls the BeginTrans method, the OLE DB provider will no longer instantaneously commit any changes the application makes until it calls CommitTrans or RollbackTrans to end the transaction. For OLE DB providers that support nested transactions, calling the BeginTrans method within an open transaction starts a new, nested transaction. The return value indicates the level of nesting: A return value of 1 indicates the application has opened a top-level transaction (that is, the transaction is not nested within another transaction), 2 indicates that the application has opened a second-level transaction (a transaction nested within a top-level transaction), and so forth. Calling CommitTrans or RollbackTrans affects only the most recently opened transaction; the application must close or roll back the current transaction before it can resolve any higher-level transactions. (Note that rolling back a nested transaction does not automatically force a rollback of a higher-level one.) Calling the CommitTrans method saves changes made within an open transaction on the connection and ends the transaction. Calling the RollbackTrans method reverses any changes made within an open transaction and ends the transaction. Calling either method when there is no open transaction generates an ADO error.

**Note** Depending on the Connection object's Attributes property, calling either the CommitTrans or RollbackTrans methods may automatically start a new transaction. If the Attributes property is set to adXactCommitRetaining, the OLE DB provider automatically starts a new transaction after a CommitTrans call. If the Attributes property is set to adXactAbortRetaining, the OLE DB provider automatically starts a new transaction after a RollbackTrans call.

**Warning** Not all OLE DB providers support transactions. To determine if a given OLE DB provider does support transactions, check that the provider-defined Transaction DDL property appears in the Connection object's Properties collection. If an application calls any of the transaction-oriented Connection object methods for an OLE DB provider that does not support transactions, an ADO error will result.

The method has the following two syntaxes:

```
level = pConnection->BeginTrans();
pConnection->BeginTrans();
```

The method can be called as a function that returns a Long value indicating the nesting level of the transaction.

The method has no parameters.

### CommitTrans Method (Connection Object)

An application should use the BeginTrans, CommitTrans, and RollbackTrans methods with a Connection object when it wants to save or cancel a series of changes made to the source data as a single unit. Once an application calls the BeginTrans method, the OLE DB provider will no longer instantaneously commit any changes the application makes until it calls CommitTrans or RollbackTrans to end the transaction. For OLE DB providers that support nested transactions, calling the BeginTrans method within an open transaction starts a new, nested transaction. The return value indicates the level of nesting: A return value of 1 indicates the application has opened a top-level transaction (that is, the transaction is not nested within another transaction), 2 indicates that the application has opened a second-level transaction (a transaction nested within a top-level transaction), and so forth. Calling CommitTrans or RollbackTrans affects only the most recently opened transaction; the application must close or roll back the current transaction before it can resolve any higher-level transactions. (Note that rolling back a nested transaction does not automatically force a rollback of a higher-level one.) Calling the CommitTrans method saves changes made within an open transaction on the connection and ends the transaction. Calling the RollbackTrans method reverses any changes made within an open transaction and ends the transaction. Calling either method when there is no open transaction generates an ADO error.

**Note** Depending on the Connection object's Attributes property, calling either the CommitTrans or RollbackTrans methods may automatically start a new transaction. If the Attributes property is set to adXactCommitRetaining, the OLE DB provider automatically starts a new transaction after a CommitTrans call. If the Attributes property is set to adXactAbortRetaining, the OLE DB provider automatically starts a new transaction after a RollbackTrans call.

**Warning** Not all OLE DB providers support transactions. To determine if a given OLE DB provider does support transactions, check that the provider-defined Transaction DDL property appears in the Connection object's Properties collection. If an application calls any of the transaction-oriented Connection object methods for an OLE DB provider that does not support transactions, an ADO error will result.

The method has the following syntax:

```
pConnection->CommitTrans();
```

The method has no parameters.

### Cancel Method (Connection Object)

Applications should use the Cancel method to terminate execution of an asynchronous Execute or Open method call (that is, the method was invoked with the adConnectAsync, adExecuteAsync, or adFetchAsync option). Cancel will return an ADO error if adRunAsync was not used in the terminated method.

The method has the following syntax:

```
pConnection->Cancel();
```

The method has no parameters.

### Close Method (Connection Object)

Applications should use the Close method on a Connection object to free any associated system resources needed while it is active. Closing a Connection object does not remove it from memory; the application can change its property settings and open it again later. Using the Close method to close a Connection object also closes any active Recordset objects associated with the connection. A Command object associated with the Connection object the application is closing will persist, but it will no longer be associated with a Connection object; that is, its ActiveConnection property will be set to Nothing. Also, the Command object's Parameters collection will be cleared of any provider-defined parameters. An application can later call the Open method to re-establish the connection to the same or another data source. While the Connection object is closed, calling any methods that require an open connection to the data source will generate an ADO error. Closing a Connection object while there are open Recordset objects on the connection rolls back any pending changes in all of the Recordset objects. Explicitly closing a Connection object (calling the Close method) while a transaction is in progress generates an ADO error. If a Connection object falls out of scope while a transaction is in progress, ADO automatically rolls back the transaction.

The method has the following syntax:

```
pConnection->Close();
```

The method has no parameters.

## Execute Method (Connection Object)

An application should use the Execute method on a Connection object to execute whatever query the application passes to the method in the CommandText argument on the specified connection. If the CommandText argument specifies a row-returning query, any results the execution generates are stored in a new Recordset object. If the command is not a row-returning query, the provider returns a closed Recordset object. The returned Recordset object is always a read-only, forward-only cursor. If an application needs a Recordset object with more functionality, it should first create a Recordset object with the desired property settings, then use the Recordset object's Open method to execute the query and return the desired cursor type. The contents of the CommandText argument are specific to the provider and can be standard SQL syntax or any special command format that the provider supports. An ExecuteComplete event will be issued when this operation concludes.

The method has the following syntax for a non–row-returning command string:

```
pConnection->Execute(CommandText, RecordsAffected, Options);
```

The method has the following syntax for a row-returning command string:

```
pRecordset = pConnection->Execute(CommandText, RecordsAffected, Options);
```

The method returns a Recordset interface pointer reference for the second syntax.

The method has the following parameters for both syntax options:

*CommandText*
This parameter contains a String with the SQL statement, table name, stored procedure, or provider-specific text to execute.

*RecordsAffected*
This optional parameter contains a Long variable via which the provider returns the number of records that the operation affected.

*Options*
This optional parameter contains a Long value that indicates how the provider should evaluate the CommandText argument. It can be one of the values in Table 5-7:

| Constant | Description |
| --- | --- |
| adCmdText | This value indicates that the OLE DB provider should evaluate *CommandText* as a textual definition of a command. |
| adCmdTable | This value indicates that ADO should generate a SQL query to return all rows from the table named in *CommandText*. |
| adCmdTableDirect | This value indicates that the OLE DB provider should return all rows from the table named in *CommandText*. |

| Constant | Description |
|---|---|
| adCmdTable | This value indicates that the OLE DB provider should evaluate *CommandText* as a table name. |
| adCmdStoredProc | This value indicates that the OLE DB provider should evaluate *CommandText* as a stored procedure. |
| adCmdUnknown | This value indicates that the type of command in the *CommandText* argument is not known. |
| adExecuteAsync | This value indicates that the command should execute asynchronously. |
| adFetchAsync | This value indicates that the remaining rows after the initial quantity specified in the CacheSize property should be fetched asynchronously. |

***Table 5-7*** *Execute method Options parameter values*

## Open Method (Connection Object)

Applications should use the Open method on a Connection object to establish the physical connection to a data source (usually an OLE DB provider). After this method successfully completes, the connection is live and the application can issue commands against it and process the results. The application can use the optional *ConnectionString* argument to specify a string containing a series of *argument* = *value* statements separated by semicolons. The ConnectionString property automatically inherits the value used for the *ConnectionString* argument. Therefore, the application can either set the ConnectionString property of the Connection object before opening it, or use the *ConnectionString* argument to set or override the current connection parameters during the Open method call. If an application chooses to pass user and password information both in the *ConnectionString* argument and in the optional *UserID* and *Password* arguments, the *UserID* and *Password* arguments will override the values specified in *ConnectionString*. When an application has concluded its operations over an open Connection, it should use the Close method to free any associated system resources, as noted above.

The method has the following syntax:

```
pConnection->Open(ConnectionString, UserID, Password, OpenOptions);
```

The method has the following parameters:

*ConnectionString*

Optional. A String containing connection information. See the ConnectionString property for details on valid settings.

*UserID*

This optional parameter contains a String with a user name to use when establishing the connection.

*Password*

This optional parameter contains a String with a password to use when establishing the connection.

*OpenOptions*

This optional parameter contains a ConnectOptionEnum value. If set to adConnectAsync, the connection will be opened asynchronously. A ConnectComplete event will be issued when the connection is available in this case.

## OpenSchema Method (Connection Object)

Applications should use this method to obtain database schema information from the OLE DB provider. The OpenSchema method returns information about the data source, such as information about the tables on the server and the columns in the tables. The *Criteria* argument is an array of values that can be used to limit the results of a schema query. Each schema query has a different set of parameters that it supports. The actual schemas are defined by the OLE DB specification under the IDBSchemaRowset interface. The constant adSchemaProviderSpecific is used for the QueryType argument if the OLE DB provider defines its own nonstandard schema queries. When this constant is used, the *SchemaID* argument is required to pass the GUID of the schema query to execute. If QueryType is set to adSchemaProviderSpecific but SchemaID is not provided, an ADO error will result. OLE DB providers are not required to support all of the OLE DB standard schema queries. Specifically, only adSchemaTables, adSchemaColumns, and adSchemaProviderTypes are required by the OLE DB specification.

The method has the following syntax:

```
pRecordset = pConnection->OpenSchema(QueryType, Criteria, SchemaID);
```

The method returns a Recordset object that contains schema information, which will be opened as a read-only, static cursor.

The method has the following parameters:

*QueryType*

This parameter contains the type of schema query to run; it can be any of the constants listed in Table 5-8.

*Criteria*

This parameter is optional; if included it is an array of query constraints for each QueryType option shown in Table 5-8.

*SchemaID*

This parameter contains the GUID for a provider-schema schema query not defined by the OLE DB specification. This parameter is required if QueryType is set to adSchemaProviderSpecific; otherwise, it is not used.

| | |
|---|---|
| adSchemaAsserts | CONSTRAINT_CATALOG<br>CONSTRAINT_SCHEMA<br>CONSTRAINT_NAME |
| adSchemaCatalogs | CATALOG_NAME |
| adSchemaCharacterSets | CHARACTER_SET_CATALOG<br>CHARACTER_SET_SCHEMA<br>CHARACTER_SET_NAME |
| adSchemaCheckConstraints | CONSTRAINT_CATALOG<br>CONSTRAINT_SCHEMA<br>CONSTRAINT_NAME |
| adSchemaCollations | COLLATION_CATALOG<br>COLLATION_SCHEMA<br>COLLATION_NAME |
| adSchemaColumnDomainUsage | DOMAIN_CATALOG<br>DOMAIN_SCHEMA<br>DOMAIN_NAME<br>COLUMN_NAME |
| adSchemaColumnPrivileges | TABLE_CATALOG<br>TABLE_SCHEMA<br>TABLE_NAME<br>COLUMN_NAME<br>GRANTOR<br>GRANTEE |
| adSchemaColumns | TABLE_CATALOG<br>TABLE_SCHEMA<br>TABLE_NAME<br>COLUMN_NAME |
| adSchemaConstraintColumnUsage | TABLE_CATALOG<br>TABLE_SCHEMA<br>TABLE_NAME<br>COLUMN_NAME |
| adSchemaConstraintTableUsage | TABLE_CATALOG<br>TABLE_SCHEMA<br>TABLE_NAME |
| adSchemaForeignKeys | PK_TABLE_CATALOG<br>PK_TABLE_SCHEMA<br>PK_TABLE_NAME<br>FK_TABLE_CATALOG<br>FK_TABLE_SCHEMA<br>FK_TABLE_NAME |

| | |
|---|---|
| adSchemaIndexes | TABLE_CATALOG<br>TABLE_SCHEMA<br>INDEX_NAME<br>TYPE<br>TABLE_NAME |
| adSchemaKeyColumnUsage | CONSTRAINT_CATALOG<br>CONSTRAINT_SCHEMA<br>CONSTRAINT_NAME<br>TABLE_CATALOG<br>TABLE_SCHEMA<br>TABLE_NAME<br>COLUMN_NAME |
| adSchemaPrimaryKeys | PK_TABLE_CATALOG<br>PK_TABLE_SCHEMA<br>PK_TABLE_NAME |
| adSchemaProcedureColumns | PROCEDURE_CATALOG<br>PROCEDURE_SCHEMA<br>PROCEDURE_NAME<br>COLUMN_NAME |
| adSchemaProcedureParameters | PROCEDURE_CATALOG<br>PROCEDURE_SCHEMA<br>PROCEDURE_NAME<br>PARAMETER_NAME |
| adSchemaProcedures | PROCEDURE_CATALOG<br>PROCEDURE_SCHEMA<br>PROCEDURE_NAME<br>PARAMETER_TYPE |
| adSchemaProviderSpecific | <see above> |
| adSchemaProviderTypes | DATA_TYPE<br>BEST_MATCH |
| adSchemaReferentialConstraints | CONSTRAINT_CATALOG<br>CONSTRAINT_SCHEMA<br>CONSTRAINT_NAME |
| adSchemaSchemata | CATALOG_NAME<br>SCHEMA_NAME<br>SCHEMA_OWNER |
| adSchemaSQLLanguages | <none> |
| adSchemaStatistics | TABLE_CATALOG<br>TABLE_SCHEMA<br>TABLE_NAME |

| | |
|---|---|
| adSchemaTableConstraints | CONSTRAINT_CATALOG<br>CONSTRAINT_SCHEMA<br>CONSTRAINT_NAME<br>TABLE_CATALOG<br>TABLE_SCHEMA<br>TABLE_NAME<br>CONSTRAINT_TYPE |
| adSchemaTablePrivileges | TABLE_CATALOG<br>TABLE_SCHEMA<br>TABLE_NAME<br>GRANTOR<br>GRANTEE |
| adSchemaTables | TABLE_CATALOG<br>TABLE_SCHEMA<br>TABLE_NAME<br>TABLE_TYPE |
| adSchemaTranslations | TRANSLATION_CATALOG<br>TRANSLATION_SCHEMA<br>TRANSLATION_NAME |
| adSchemaUsagePrivileges | OBJECT_CATALOG<br>OBJECT_SCHEMA<br>OBJECT_NAME<br>OBJECT_TYPE<br>GRANTOR<br>GRANTEE |
| adSchemaViewColumnUsage | VIEW_CATALOG<br>VIEW_SCHEMA<br>VIEW_NAME |
| adSchemaViewTableUsage | VIEW_CATALOG<br>VIEW_SCHEMA<br>VIEW_NAME |
| adSchemaViews | TABLE_CATALOG<br>TABLE_SCHEMA<br>TABLE_NAME |

***Table 5-8*** *OpenSchema QueryType and Criteria parameter values*

## RollbackTrans Method (Connection Object)

An application should use the BeginTrans, CommitTrans, and RollbackTrans methods with a Connection object when it wants to save or cancel a series of changes made to the source data as a single unit. Once an application calls the BeginTrans method, the OLE DB provider will no longer instantaneously commit any changes the application makes until it calls CommitTrans or RollbackTrans to end the transaction. For OLE DB providers that support nested transactions, calling the BeginTrans method within an open transaction starts a new, nested transaction. The return value indicates the level of nesting: A return value of 1 indicates the application has opened a top-level transaction (that is, the transaction is not nested within another transaction), 2 indicates that the application has opened a second-level transaction (a transaction nested within a top-level transaction), and so forth. Calling CommitTrans or RollbackTrans affects only the most recently opened transaction; the application must close or roll back the current transaction before it can resolve any higher-level transactions. (Note that rolling back a nested transaction does not automatically force a rollback of a higher-level one.) Calling the CommitTrans method saves changes made within an open transaction on the connection and ends the transaction. Calling the RollbackTrans method reverses any changes made within an open transaction and ends the transaction. Calling either method when there is no open transaction generates an ADO error.

**Note** Depending on the Connection object's Attributes property, calling either the CommitTrans or RollbackTrans methods may automatically start a new transaction. If the Attributes property is set to adXactCommitRetaining, the OLE DB provider automatically starts a new transaction after a CommitTrans call. If the Attributes property is set to adXactAbortRetaining, the OLE DB provider automatically starts a new transaction after a RollbackTrans call.

**Warning** Not all OLE DB providers support transactions. To determine if a given OLE DB provider does support transactions, check that the provider-defined Transaction DDL property appears in the Connection object's Properties collection. If an application calls any of the transaction-oriented Connection object methods for an OLE DB provider that does not support transactions, an ADO error will result.

The method has the following syntax:

```
pConnection->RollbackTrans();
```

The method has no parameters.

## The ADO Command Object

Applications have three uses for a Command object: to query a database and return records in a Recordset object, to execute a bulk operation, and to manipulate the structure of a database. A Command object is required when an application wants to persist command text and re-execute it, or use query parameters. To create a Command object independently of a previously defined Connection object, an application should first set its

ActiveConnection property to a valid connection string. ADO will still create a Connection object, but it doesn't assign that object to an object variable. To associate multiple Command objects with the same connection, an application should explicitly create and open a Connection object; this assigns the Connection object to an object variable. If an application does not set the Command objects' ActiveConnection property to the Connection object variable, ADO creates a new Connection object for each Command object, even if an application uses the same connection string. To execute a Command, simply call it by its Name property on the associated Connection object. The Command must have its ActiveConnection property set to the Connection object. If the Command has parameters, pass values for them as arguments to the method. With the collections, methods, and properties of a Command object, an application can do the following:

- Define the executable text of the command (for example, a SQL statement) with the CommandText property.
- Define parameterized queries or stored procedure arguments with Parameter objects and the Parameters collection.
- Execute a command and return a Recordset object if appropriate with the Execute method.
- Specify the type of command with the CommandType property prior to execution to optimize performance.
- Control whether or not the provider saves a prepared (or compiled) version of the command prior to execution with the Prepared property.
- Set the number of seconds a provider will wait for a command to execute with the CommandTimeout property.
- Associate an open connection with a Command object by setting its ActiveConnection property.
- Set the Name property to identify the Command object as a method on the associated Connection object.
- Pass a Command object to the Source property of a Recordset in order to obtain data.

## CommandText Property (Command Object)

This property contains the text of a command that an application wants to issue against an OLE DB provider. The property is a String value containing an OLE DB provider command, such as a SQL statement, a table name, or a stored procedure call; its default value is the empty string. Usually, the value of CommandText will be a SQL statement, but it can also be any other type of command statement recognized by the OLE DB provider, such as a stored procedure call. A SQL statement must be of the particular dialect or version supported by the OLE DB provider's query processor. If the Prepared property of the Command object is set to True and the Command object is bound to an open connection when an application sets the CommandText property, ADO prepares the query (that is, a compiled form of the query is stored by the OLE DB provider) when an application calls the Execute or Open methods. Depending on the CommandType property setting, ADO may alter the CommandText property. An application can read the CommandText property at any time to check the actual text that ADO will use during execution.

### CommandTimeout Property (Command Object)

This property indicates how long the ADO run time should wait while executing a command before terminating the attempt and generating an error (usually due to a failed network transmission). The property is a Long value with a default of 30 seconds; the property is read/write regardless of whether a connection is open or closed. If an application sets the property to zero, ADO will wait indefinitely until the command is completed.

**Warning** If an application uses CommandTimeout functionality without support from the underlying OLE DB provider, results are unpredictable.

### CommandType Property (Command Object)

Applications should use the CommandType property to optimize evaluation of the CommandText property. If the CommandType property value equals adCmdUnknown (the default value), an application may experience diminished performance because ADO must make calls to the provider to determine if the CommandText property is a SQL statement, a stored procedure, or a table name. If an application knows what type of command it is using, setting the CommandType property instructs ADO to go directly to the relevant code. If the CommandType property does not match the type of command in the CommandText property, an ADO error occurs when you call the Execute method. CommandType can be one or more of the CommandTypeEnum values in Table 5-9.

**Note** The adExecuteNoRecords constant improves performance by minimizing internal processing. This constant never stands alone; it is always combined with adCmdText or adCmdStoredProc. An ADO error results if adExecuteNoRecords is used with the Recordset.Open method or a Command object used by that method.

| Constant | Description |
|---|---|
| adCmdText | This value indicates that ADO should evaluate CommandText as a textual definition of a command or stored procedure call. |
| adCmdTable | This value indicates that ADO should evaluate CommandText as a table name whose columns are all returned by an internally generated SQL query. |

| Constant | Description |
|---|---|
| adCmdTableDirect | This value indicates that ADO should evaluate CommandText as a table name whose columns are all returned. |
| adCmdStoredProc | This value indicates that ADO should evaluate CommandText as a stored procedure name. |
| adCmdUnknown | This value is the default; it indicates that the type of command in the CommandText property is not known and that ADO cannot perform any internal processing prior to sending the command to the OLE DB provider. |
| adCommandFile | This value indicates that ADO should evaluate CommandText as the filename of a persisted Recordset. |
| adExecuteNoRecords | This value indicates that CommandText is a command or stored procedure that does not return rows; if any rows are retrieved, they are discarded and not returned. This constant is always combined with adCmdText or adCmdStoredProc. |

***Table 5-9** CommandTypeEnum values*

## *Prepared Property (Command Object)*

This property indicates whether or not an OLE DB provider should save a compiled version of a command before execution.The property is a read/write Boolean value. Setting it to True may slow a command's first execution, but once the OLE DB provider compiles a command, the provider will use the compiled version of the command for any subsequent executions, which will result in improved performance.

**Warning** If the OLE DB provider does not support command preparation, it may return an error as soon as this property is set to True. If it does not return an error, the OLE DB provider simply ignores the request to prepare the command and sets the Prepared property to False.

## *State Property (Command Object)*

This is a read-only Long property which indicates whether the Command object is currently open (interacting with an OLE DB provider) or closed (not interacting with an OLE DB provider). The possible values are listed in Table 5-10.

| Constant | Description |
|---|---|
| adStateClosed | This value is the default; it indicates that the Command object is closed. |
| adStateOpen | This value indicates that the Command object is open. |

***Table 5-10** Command object State property values*

## Cancel Method (Command Object)

An application should use the Cancel method to terminate execution of an asynchronous Execute or Open method call (that is, the method was invoked with the adConnectAsync, adExecuteAsync, or adFetchAsync option). Cancel will return a run-time error if adRunAsync was not used in the method it is trying to terminate.

The method has the following syntax:

```
pCommand->Cancel();
```

The method has no parameters.

## CreateParameter Method (Command Object)

An application should use the CreateParameter method to create a new Parameter object with the specified name, type, direction, size, and value. Any values an application passes in the arguments are written to the corresponding Parameter properties. This method does not automatically append the Parameter object to the Parameters collection of a Command object; the application must explicitly do so using the Append method described earlier in this chapter. This lets the application set additional properties whose values ADO will validate when it appends the Parameter object to the collection. If no parameters are included, a default Parameter object is created.

The method has the following syntax:

```
pParameter = command->CreateParameter(Name, Type, Direction, Size, Value);
```

The method returns a Parameter object (interface pointer).

The method has the following parameters:

*Name*
: This optional parameter is a String representing the name of the Parameter object.

*Type*
: This optional parameter is a Long value specifying the data type of the Parameter object, with values as noted for the Type property.

*Direction*
: This optional parameter is a Long value specifying the type of Parameter object, with values as noted for the Direction property.

*Size*
: This optional parameter is a Long value specifying the maximum length for the parameter value in characters or bytes.

*Value*
: This optional parameter is a Variant specifying the Value property for the Parameter object.

## *Execute Method (Command Object)*

An application should use the Execute method on a Command object to execute the query specified in the CommandText property against the current OLE DB provider. If the CommandText property specifies a row-returning query, any results the execution generates are stored in a new Recordset object. If the command is not a row-returning query, the OLE DB provider returns a closed Recordset object. Some application languages allow an application to ignore this return value if no Recordset is desired. If the query has parameters, the current values for the Command object's parameters are used unless the application chooses to override these with parameter values passed with the Execute call. An application can override a subset of the parameters by omitting new values for some of the parameters when calling the Execute method. The order in which the application should specify the parameters is the same order in which the method passes them. An ExecuteComplete event will be issued when this operation concludes.

**Warning** Output parameters will not return correct values when passed in the *Parameters* parameter.

The method has the following syntax for a row-returning Command object:

```
pRecordset = pCommand.Execute(RecordsAffected, Parameters, Options);
```

The method has the following syntax for a non—row-returning Command object:

```
pCommand.Execute(RecordsAffected, Parameters, Options);
```

The method returns a Recordset object reference.

The method has the following parameters:

*RecordsAffected*
: This optional parameter is a Long variable from which the provider returns the number of records that the operation affected.

*Parameters*
: This optional parameter is a Variant array of parameter values passed with a SQL statement. (It is important to remember that output parameters will not return correct values when passed in this argument.)

*Options*
: This optional parameter is a Long value that indicates how the provider should evaluate the CommandText property of the Command object. It can contain one or more of the constants in Table 5-11.

| Constant | Description |
|---|---|
| adCmdText | Indicates that the provider should evaluate *CommandText* as a textual definition of a command, such as a SQL statement. |
| adCmdTable | Indicates that ADO should generate a SQL query to return all rows from the table named in *CommandText*. |
| adCmdTableDirect | Indicates that the provider should return all rows from the table named in *CommandText*. |
| adCmdStoredProc | Indicates that the provider should evaluate *CommandText* as a stored procedure. |
| adCmdUnknown | Indicates that the type of command in *CommandText* is not known. |
| adExecuteAsync | Indicates that the command should execute asynchronously. |
| adFetchAsync | Indicates that the remaining rows after the initial quantity specified in the CacheSize property should be fetched asynchronously. |

***Table 5-11*** *Command object Execute method Options values*

## The ADO Recordset Object

An application should use Recordset objects to manipulate data from an OLE DB provider. All Recordset objects are constructed using records (rows) and fields (columns). The most important property for a Recordset is CursorType; it must be set prior to opening the Recordset either directly in the application's program statements, or via passing a CursorType argument with the Open method. Some OLE DB providers don't support all cursor types; an application should check the documentation for the specific OLE DB provider. If an application doesn't specify a cursor type, ADO opens a forward-only cursor by default. There are four different Recordset cursor types defined in ADO:

- **Dynamic cursor** This cursor allows an application to view additions, changes, and deletions by other users, and allows all types of movement through the Recordset that don't rely on bookmarks. It also allows bookmarks if the OLE DB provider supports them.
- **Keyset cursor** This cursor behaves like a dynamic cursor except that it prevents an application from seeing records that other users add and prevents access to records that other users delete. Data changes by other users will still be visible. It always supports bookmarks and therefore allows all types of movement through the Recordset.
- **Static cursor** This cursor provides a static copy of a set of records for an application to use to find data or generate reports. It always allows bookmarks and therefore allows all types of movement through the Recordset. Additions, changes, or deletions by other users will not be visible. This is the only type of cursor allowed when an application opens a client-side (ADOR) Recordset object.

- **Forward-only cursor** This cursor behaves identically to a dynamic cursor except that it allows an application to scroll only forward through records. This improves performance in situations where an application needs to make only a single pass through a Recordset.

When used with some providers (such as the Microsoft ODBC Provider for OLE DB in conjunction with Microsoft SQL Server), an application can create Recordset objects independently of a previously defined Connection object by passing a connection string with the Open method. ADO still creates a Connection object, but it doesn't assign that object to an object variable. However, if an application is opening multiple Recordset objects over the same connection, it should explicitly create and open a Connection object; this assigns the Connection object to an object variable. If an application does not use this object variable when opening its Recordset objects, ADO creates a new Connection object for each new Recordset, even if the application passes the same connection string. An application can create as many Recordset objects as needed, subject to memory limitations.

When an application opens a Recordset, the current record is positioned to the first record (if any) and the BOF and EOF properties are set to False. If there are no records, the BOF and EOF property settings are True. An application can use the MoveFirst, MoveLast, MoveNext, and MovePrevious methods, as well as the Move method, and the AbsolutePosition, AbsolutePage, and Filter properties to reposition the current record, assuming the provider supports the relevant functionality. Forward-only Recordset objects support only the MoveNext method. When an application uses the MoveXXX methods to visit each record (or enumerate the Recordset), it can use the BOF and EOF properties to see if it has moved beyond the beginning or end of the Recordset.

Recordset objects can support two types of updating: *immediate* and *batched*. In *immediate* updating, all changes to data are written immediately to the underlying data source once an application calls the Update method. An application can also pass arrays of values as parameters with the AddNew and Update methods and simultaneously update several fields in a record. If an OLE DB provider supports *batch* updating, an application can have the provider cache changes to more than one record and then transmit them in a single call to the database with the UpdateBatch method. This applies to changes made with the AddNew, Update, and Delete methods. After an application calls the UpdateBatch method, it can use the Status property to check for any data conflicts in order to resolve them.

## AbsolutePage Property (Recordset Object)

An application should use the AbsolutePage property to identify the page number on which the current record is located. First, the application should use the PageSize property to logically divide the Recordset object into a series of pages, each of which has the number of records equal to PageSize (except for the last page, which may have fewer records). The OLE DB provider must support the appropriate functionality for this property to be available. Like the AbsolutePosition property, AbsolutePage is 1-based and equals 1 when the current record is the first record in the Recordset. Aside from a read-only Long numeric page value, AbsolutePage can also have one of the (negative) constant values in Table 5-12:

| Constant | Description |
|---|---|
| adPosUnknown | This value indicates that the Recordset is empty, the current position is unknown, or the provider does not support the AbsolutePage property. |
| adPosBOF | This value indicates that the current record pointer is at BOF (that is, the BOF property is True). |
| adPosEOF | This value indicates that the current record pointer is at EOF (that is, the EOF property is True). |

***Table 5-12*** *Recordset object AbsolutePage property values*

### AbsolutePosition Property (Recordset Object)

An application should use the AbsolutePosition property to move to a record based on its ordinal position in the Recordset object or to determine the ordinal position of the current record. The OLE DB provider must support the appropriate functionality for this property to be available. Like the AbsolutePage property, AbsolutePosition is 1-based and equals 1 when the current record is the first record in the Recordset. An application can obtain the total number of records in the Recordset object from the RecordCount property. When an application sets the AbsolutePosition property, even if it is to a record in the current cache, ADO reloads the cache with a new group of records starting with the record it specified. The CacheSize property determines the size of this group. Aside from a read/write Long numeric record value, AbsolutePosition can also have one of the (negative) constant values in Table 5-13:

| Constant | Description |
|---|---|
| adPosUnknown | This value indicates that the Recordset is empty, the current position is unknown, or the provider does not support the AbsolutePosition property. |
| adPosBOF | This value indicates that the current record pointer is at BOF (that is, the BOF property is True). |
| adPosEOF | This value indicates that the current record pointer is at EOF (that is, the EOF property is True). |

***Table 5-13*** *Recordset object AbsolutePosition property values*

**Warning** An application should not use the AbsolutePosition property as a surrogate record number. The position of a given record changes when an application deletes a preceding record. There is also no assurance that a given record will have the same AbsolutePosition if the Recordset object is requeried or reopened. Bookmarks are still the recommended way of retaining and returning to a given position and are the only way of positioning across all types of Recordset objects.

## *ActiveConnection Property (Recordset Object)*

This property indicates to which Connection object the specified Command or Recordset object currently belongs.The read/write value is a String containing the definition for a connection or a Connection object; the default value is a Null reference.

## *BOF/EOF Property (Recordset Object)*

An application should use the BOF and EOF properties to determine whether a Recordset object contains records or whether it has gone beyond the limits of a Recordset object when it moves from record to record. BOF indicates that the current record position is before the first record in a Recordset object; the BOF property returns True (–1) if the current record position is before the first record and False (0) if the current record position is on or after the first record. The EOF property returns True if the current record position is after the last record and False if the current record position is on or before the last record. If either the BOF or EOF property is True, there is no current record. If an application opens a Recordset object containing no records, the BOF and EOF properties are set to True, and the Recordset object's RecordCount property setting is zero. When an application opens a Recordset object that contains at least one record, the first record is the current record and the BOF and EOF properties are False. If an application deletes the last remaining record in the Recordset object, the BOF and EOF properties may remain False until an application attempts to reposition the current record. Table 5-14 shows which MoveXXX methods are allowed with different combinations of the BOF and EOF properties.

| | MoveFirst, MoveLast | MovePrevious, Move < 0 | Move 0 | MoveNext, Move > 0 |
|---|---|---|---|---|
| **BOF=True, EOF=False** | Allowed | Error | Error | Allowed |
| **BOF=False, EOF=True** | Allowed | Allowed | Error | Error |
| **Both True** | Error | Error | Error | Error |
| **Both False** | Allowed | Allowed | Allowed | Allowed |

***Table 5-14*** *MoveXXX method calls permitted by EOF/BOF state combinations*

Allowing a MoveXXX method doesn't guarantee that the method will successfully locate a record; it only means that calling the specified MoveXXX method won't generate an ADO error.

Table 5-15 shows what happens to the BOF and EOF property settings when an application calls various MoveXXX methods that are unable to successfully locate a record (due to going past the first or last record in the data source).

| | BOF | EOF |
|---|---|---|
| **MoveFirst, MoveLast** | Set to True | Set to True |
| **Move 0** | No change | No change |
| **MovePrevious, Move < 0** | Set to True | No change |
| **MoveNext, Move > 0** | No change | Set to True |

***Table 5-15*** *EOF/BOF changes due to failed MoveXXX method calls*

## Bookmark Property (Recordset Object)

An application should use the Bookmark property to save the position of the current record and return to that record at any time. Bookmarks are available only in Recordset objects that support bookmark functionality via the current OLE DB provider. When an application opens a Recordset object, each of its records has a unique bookmark. To save the bookmark for the current record, an application should assign the value of the Bookmark property to a variable. Then to quickly return to that record at any time after moving to a different record, the application should set the Recordset object's Bookmark property to the value of that variable. If an application uses the Clone method to create a copy of a Recordset object, the Bookmark property settings for the original and the duplicate Recordset objects are identical and an application can use them interchangeably. However, an application cannot use bookmarks from different Recordset objects interchangeably, even if they were created from the same source or command. The property is read/write and uses a Variant expression that evaluates to a valid bookmark on the current OLE DB provider.

**Warning** The application may not be able to view the value of a bookmark since it may be represented in a non-displayable way by the OLE DB provider in use. Also, applications should not expect bookmarks to be directly comparable—two bookmarks that refer to the same record may have different values because of the OLE DB provider's implementation.

## CacheSize Property (Recordset Object)

Applications should use the CacheSize property to control how many records the OLE DB provider keeps in its buffer and how many to retrieve at one time into local memory. The property is a Long value that must be greater than 0;

the default is 1. After first opening the Recordset object, the OLE DB provider retrieves the first CacheSize records into local memory. As an application moves through the Recordset object, the OLE DB provider returns the data from the local memory buffer. As soon as the application moves past the last record in the cache, the provider retrieves the next CacheSize records from the data source into the cache. The value of this property can be adjusted during the life of the Recordset object, but changing this value only affects the number of records in the cache after subsequent retrievals from the data source. Changing the property value alone will not change the current contents of the cache. If there are fewer records to retrieve than CacheSize specifies, the provider returns the remaining records; no error occurs. Records retrieved from the cache do not reflect concurrent changes that other users may make to the source data; to force an update of all the cached data, use the Resync method.

**Warning** A CacheSize setting of 0 is not allowed and returns an ADO error.

## *CursorLocation Property (Recordset Object)*

This property determines the location of the cursor engine to be used by ADO, based on various cursor libraries accessible to the OLE DB provider in use. The property is a Long value which is read/write regardless of whether a Connection is open or not, but the setting affects connections established only after the property has been set; changing this property has no effect on existing connections. The cursor obtained via an Execute call will automatically inherit the setting of this property. Table 5-16 gives the possible values of this property:

| Constant | Description |
|---|---|
| adUseNone | This value indicates that no cursor services are used; it is obsolete and should be used only for the sake of backward compatibility with legacy code. |
| adUseClient | This value indicates that the connection uses client-side cursors supplied by a local cursor library. Since local cursor engines often will allow features that driver-supplied cursors may not, using this setting may enable extra features. (adUseClientBatch is an alternative value for this constant.) |
| adUseServer | This value is the default; it indicates that the connection uses OLE DB provider- or driver-supplied cursors. Some features of the Microsoft Client Cursor Provider (such as disassociated recordsets) cannot be simulated with server-side cursors, but other provider-specific features may be supported instead. |

***Table 5-16*** *Recordset object CursorLocation property values*

## CursorType Property (Recordset Object)

Applications should use the CursorType property to specify the type of cursor that should be used when opening the Recordset object. Only a setting of adUseStatic is supported if the CursorLocation property is set to adUseClient. If an unsupported value is set, then no error will result; the closest supported CursorType will be used instead. If an OLE DB provider does not support the requested cursor type, the provider may return another cursor type. The CursorType property will change to match the actual cursor type in use when the Recordset object is open. To verify specific functionality of the returned cursor, use the Supports method. Although Supports(adUpdateBatch) may be true for dynamic and forward-only cursors, for batch updates an application should use either a keyset or static cursor. Also, the application should set the LockType property to adLockBatchOptimistic, and the CursorLocation property to adUseClient to enable the Microsoft Client Cursor Engine, which is required for batch updates.

After an application closes the Recordset, the CursorType property reverts to its original setting. The CursorType property is read/write when the Recordset is closed and read-only when it is open. The property is composed of only one of the CursorTypeEnum values in Table 5-17.

| Constant | Description |
|---|---|
| adOpenForwardOnly | This value is the default and is a forward-only cursor. This is identical to a static cursor except that an application can only scroll forward through records. |
| adOpenKeyset | This value is for a keyset cursor. It works like a dynamic cursor, except that an application can't see records that other users add, although records that other users delete are inaccessible from the Recordset. |
| adOpenDynamic | This value is for a dynamic cursor. Under it, all additions, changes, and deletions by other users are visible, and all types of movement through the Recordset are allowed, except for bookmarks if the OLE DB provider doesn't support them. |
| adOpenStatic | This value is for a static cursor. This is a static copy of a set of records that an application can use to find data or generate reports. |

***Table 5-17*** *Recordset object CursorTypeEnum values*

## EditMode Property (Recordset Object)

An application should use the EditMode property to determine the editing status of the current record. The application can test for pending changes if an editing process has been interrupted and determine whether it needs to use the Update or CancelUpdate method. ADO maintains an editing buffer associated with the current record. This property indicates whether changes have been made to this buffer, or whether a new record has been created. The property contains one of the EditModeEnum values in Table 5-18.

| Constant | Description |
|---|---|
| adEditNone | This value indicates that no editing operation is in progress. |
| adEditInProgress | This value indicates that data in the current record has been modified but not yet saved. |
| adEditAdd | This value indicates that the AddNew method has been invoked, and the current record in the copy buffer is a new record that hasn't been saved in the database. |
| adEditDelete | This value indicates that the current record has been deleted. |

***Table 5-18*** *Recordset object EditModeEnum values*

## *Filter Property (Recordset Object)*

Use the Filter property to selectively screen out records in a Recordset object. The filtered Recordset becomes the current cursor. This affects other properties such as AbsolutePosition, AbsolutePage, RecordCount, and PageCount that return values based on the current cursor, because setting the Filter property to a specific value will move the current record to the first record that satisfies the new value. The criteria string is made up of clauses in the form *FieldName Operator Value* (for example, "Genus = 'Pinniped'"). An application can create compound clauses by concatenating individual clauses with AND (for example, "Species = Genus AND Habitat = 'Arctic'") or OR (for example, "Genus = 'Pinniped' OR Genus = 'Cetacean'"). *FieldName* must be a valid field name from the Recordset. If the field name contains spaces, the application must enclose the name in square brackets. *Operator* must be one of the following: <, >, <=, >=, <>, =, or LIKE. *Value* is the value with which the OLE DB provider will compare the field values (for example, 'Pinniped', #7/27/52#, 158.158 or $158.00). An application should use single quotes with strings and pound signs (#) with dates. For numbers, an application can use decimal points, dollar signs, and scientific notation. If *Operator* is LIKE, *Value* can use wild cards. Only the asterisk (*) and percent sign (%) wild cards are allowed, and they must be the last character in the string. *Value* cannot be Null. There is no precedence between AND and OR. Clauses can be grouped within parentheses. However, an application cannot group clauses joined by an OR and then join the group to another clause with an AND.

The filter constants make it easier to resolve individual record conflicts during batch update mode by allowing an application to view only those records that were affected during the last UpdateBatch method call. Setting the Filter property itself may fail because of a conflict with the underlying data (for example, a record has already been deleted by another user); in such a case, the provider returns warnings to the Errors collection but does not halt program execution. An ADO error occurs only if there are conflicts on all the requested records. An application can use the Status property to locate records with conflicts. Setting the Filter property to an empty string ("") has the same effect as using the adFilterNone constant. Whenever the Filter property is set, the current record position moves to the first record in the filtered subset of records in the Recordset. Similarly, when the Filter property is cleared, the current record position moves to the first record in the Recordset. The property holds a Variant value, which can contain only one of the following types of data:

- Criteria string—a string made up of one or more individual clauses concatenated with AND or OR operators.
- Array of bookmarks—an array of unique bookmark values that point to records in the Recordset object.
- One of the FilterGroupEnum values in Table 5-19:

| Constant | Description |
|---|---|
| adFilterAffectedRecords | This value allows an application to view only records affected by the last Delete, Resync, UpdateBatch, or CancelBatch call. |
| adFilterConflictingRecords | This value allows an application to view the records that failed the last batch update attempt. |
| adFilterFetchedRecords | This value allows an application to view records in the current cache, that is, the results of the last call to retrieve records from the database. |
| adFilterNone | This value removes the current filter and restores all records to view. |
| adFilterPendingRecords | This value allows an application to view only records that have changed but have not yet been sent to the server. It is applicable only for batch update mode. |

***Table 5-19*** *Recordset object FilterGroupEnum values*

## LockType Property (Recordset Object)

An application should set the LockType property before opening a Recordset to specify what type of locking the OLE DB provider should use when opening it. An application should read the property to return the type of locking in use on an open Recordset object it did not create, or if it is unsure whether the current OLE DB provider supports a given LockType setting. The LockType property is read/write when the Recordset is closed and read-only when it is open. Not all OLE DB providers support all lock types. If an OLE DB provider cannot support the requested LockType setting, it will substitute another type of locking rather than raising an ADO error. To determine the actual locking functionality available in a Recordset object, an application should use the Supports method with adUpdate and adUpdateBatch. The property contains only one of the LockTypeEnum values in Table 5-20.

| Constant | Description |
|---|---|
| adLockReadOnly | This value is the default. It indicates read-only access; the application cannot alter the data. |
| adLockPessimistic | This value indicates pessimistic locking, record by record. In this case, the OLE DB provider does what is necessary to ensure successful editing of the records, usually by locking records at the data source immediately upon editing. |
| adLockOptimistic | This value indicates optimistic locking, record by record. In this case, the OLE DB provider uses optimistic locking, locking records only when an application calls the Update method. |
| adLockBatchOptimistic | This value indicates optimistic batch updates. It is required for batch update mode as opposed to immediate update mode. |

***Table 5-20*** *Recordset object LockTypeEnum values*

**Warning** The adLockPessimistic setting is not supported if the CursorLocation property is set to adUseClient.

## *MarshalOptions Property (Recordset Object)*

This property indicates which records are to be marshaled back to the server. When using a client-side (ADOR) Recordset, records that have been modified on the client are written back to the middle tier or web server through a technique called *marshaling*, the process of packaging and sending interface method parameters across thread or process boundaries. Setting the MarshalOptions property can improve performance when modified remote data is marshaled for updating back to the middle tier or web server. The property contains a Long value that can only be one of the constants in Table 5-21.

| Constant | Description |
|---|---|
| adMarshalAll | This value is the default; it indicates that all rows are returned to the server. |
| adMarshalModifiedOnly | This value indicates that only modified rows are returned to the server. |

***Table 5-21*** *Recordset object MarshalOptions values*

## *MaxRecords Property (Recordset Object)*

An application should use the MaxRecords property to limit the number of records the OLE DB provider returns from the data source. A value of 0 means the OLE DB provider returns all requested records. The property is read/write when the Recordset is closed and read-only when it is open, and is a Long value with a default of 0 (no limit).

### PageCount Property (Recordset Object)

An application should use the PageCount property to determine how many pages of data are in the Recordset object. *Pages* are groups of records whose size equals the PageSize property setting. Even if the last page is incomplete, because there are fewer records than the PageSize value, it counts as an additional page in the PageCount value. If the Recordset object does not support this property, the value will be –1 to indicate that the PageCount is indeterminable. The property is read-only and is a Long value.

### PageSize Property (Recordset Object)

An application should use the PageSize property to determine how many records make up a logical page of data. Establishing a page size allows an application to use the AbsolutePage property to move to the first record of a particular page. This is useful in web server scenarios when an application want to allow the user to page through data, viewing a certain number of records at a time. This property can be set at any time, and its value will be used for calculating the location of the first record of a particular page. The property is a Long value with a default of 10.

### RecordCount Property (Recordset Object)

An application should use the RecordCount property to find out how many records are in a Recordset object. The property returns –1 when ADO cannot determine the number of records. If the Recordset object supports approximate positioning or bookmarks, this value will be the exact number of records in the Recordset regardless of whether it has been fully populated. If the Recordset object does not support approximate positioning, this property may be a significant drain on resources because all records will have to be retrieved and counted to return an accurate RecordCount value. The property is a read-only Long value.

**Warning** Reading the RecordCount property on a closed Recordset causes an error.

### Sort Property (Recordset Object)

An application should use this property to set one or more field names on which the Recordset is sorted and specify whether each field is sorted in ascending or descending order. The data is not physically rearranged, but is simply accessed in the sorted order. A temporary index will be created for each field specified in the Sort property if the CursorLocation property is set to adUseClient and an index does not already exist. Setting the Sort property to an empty string will reset the rows to their original order and delete temporary indexes; existing indexes will not be deleted. The property is always read/write, and contains a String of comma-separated field names to sort on, where each name is a field in the Recordset, each of which is optionally followed by a blank and the keyword ASCENDING or DESCENDING, which specifies the field sort order. If no keyword is specified, the default is descending order.

## Source Property (Recordset Object)

An application should use the Source property to specify a data source for a Recordset object using a Command object variable, a SQL statement, a stored procedure, or a table name. If an application sets the Source property to a Command object, the ActiveConnection property of the Recordset object will inherit the value of the ActiveConnection property for the specified Command object. Reading the Source property does not return a Command object; instead, it returns the CommandText property of the Command object to which the application set the Source property. If the Source property is a SQL statement, a stored procedure, or a table name, an application can optimize performance by passing the appropriate *Options* argument with the Open method call. The Source property is read/write for closed Recordset objects and read-only for open Recordset objects.The property is set to a String value or Command object reference, but can only return a String value.

## State Property (Recordset Object)

This property describes for a Recordset object executing an asynchronous method whether the current state of the object is connecting, executing, or fetching; otherwise, it simply reports whether the Recordset is open (comnmunicating with the OLE DB provider) or closed (not communicating with the OLE DB provider). The property can have a combination of values; if a statement is executing, this property will have a combined value of adStateOpen and adStateExecuting. This property is read-only and returns a Long value that can be one or more of the constants in Table 5-22.

| Constant | Description |
|---|---|
| adStateClosed | This value indicates that the Recordset is closed. |
| adStateOpen | This value indicates that the Recordset is open. |
| adStateConnecting | This value indicates that the Recordset object is connecting. |
| adStateExecuting | This value indicates that the Recordset object is executing a command. |
| adStateFetching | This value indicates that the rows of the Recordset object are being fetched. |

***Table 5-22** Recordset object State property values*

## Status Property (Recordset Object)

Applications should use the Status property to see what changes are pending for records modified during batch updating. Applications can also use the Status property to view the status of records that fail during bulk operations, such as when they call the Resync, UpdateBatch, or CancelBatch methods on a Recordset object, or set the Filter property on a Recordset object to an array of bookmarks. The property is read-only and contains a combination of one or more of the RecordStatusEnum values in Table 5-23.

| Constant | Description |
|---|---|
| adRecOK | This value indicates that the record was successfully updated. |
| adRecNew | This value indicates that the record is new. |
| adRecModified | This value indicates that the record was modified. |
| adRecDeleted | This value indicates that the record was deleted. |
| adRecUnmodified | This value indicates that the record was not modified. |
| adRecInvalid | This value indicates that the record was not saved because its bookmark is invalid. |
| adRecMultipleChanges | This value indicates that the record was not saved because it would have affected multiple records. |
| adRecPendingChanges | This value indicates that the record was not saved because it refers to a pending insert. |
| adRecCanceled | This value indicates that the record was not saved because the operation was canceled. |
| adRecCantRelease | This value indicates that the new record was not saved because of existing record locks. |
| adRecConcurrencyViolation | This value indicates that the record was not saved because optimistic concurrency was in use. |
| adRecIntegrityViolation | This value indicates that the record was not saved because the user violated integrity constraints. |
| adRecMaxChangesExceeded | This value indicates that the record was not saved because there were too many pending changes. |
| adRecObjectOpen | This value indicates that the record was not saved because of a conflict with an open storage object. |
| adRecOutOfMemory | This value indicates that the record was not saved because the computer has run out of memory. |
| adRecPermissionDenied | This value indicates that the record was not saved because the user has insufficient permissions. |
| adRecSchemaViolation | This value indicates that the record was not saved because it violates the structure of the underlying database. |
| adRecDBDeleted | This value indicates that the record has already been deleted from the data source. |

***Table 5-23*** *Recordset object RecordStatusEnum values*

## AddNew Method (Recordset Object)

An application should use the AddNew method to create and initialize a new record. First, however, it should use the Supports method with adAddNew to verify whether it can add records to the current Recordset object. After it makes the call to AddNew method, the new record becomes the current record and remains current after the call to the Update method. If the Recordset object does not support bookmarks, an application may not be able to access the new record once it moves to another record. Depending on the cursor type, an application may need to call the Requery method to make the new record accessible. If an application calls AddNew while editing the current record or while adding a new record, ADO calls the Update method to save any changes and then creates the new record. The behavior of the AddNew method depends on the updating mode of the Recordset object and whether or not an application chooses to pass the *FieldList* and *Values* arguments. In immediate update mode (the provider writes changes to the underlying data source once the application calls the Update method), calling the AddNew method without arguments sets the EditMode property to adEditAdd. The OLE DB provider caches any field value changes locally. Calling the Update method posts the new record to the database and resets the EditMode property to adEditNone. If an application chooses to pass the *FieldList* and *Values* arguments, ADO immediately posts the new record to the database (no Update call is necessary); the EditMode property value does not change (adEditNone). In batch update mode (the OLE DB provider caches multiple changes and writes them to the underlying data source only when you call the UpdateBatch method), calling the AddNew method without arguments sets the EditMode property to adEditAdd. The OLE DB provider caches any field value changes locally. Calling the Update method adds the new record to the current Recordset and resets the EditMode property to adEditNone, but the OLE DB provider does not post the changes to the underlying database until the application calls the UpdateBatch method. If an application chooses to pass the *FieldList* and *Values* arguments, ADO sends the new record to the provider for storage in a cache; the application then needs to call the UpdateBatch method to post the new record to the underlying database.

The method has the following syntax:

```
pRecordset.AddNew(FieldList, Values);
```

The method has the following parameters:

*FieldList*
: This optional parameter is a single name or an array of names or ordinal positions of the fields in the new record.

*Values*
: This optional parameter is a single value or an array of values for the

fields in the new record. If *FieldList* is an array, *Values* must also be an array with the same number of members; otherwise, an ADO error occurs. The order of field names must match the order of field values in each array.

## *Cancel Method (Recordset Object)*

An application should use the Cancel method to terminate execution of an asynchronous Execute or Open method call (that is, the method was invoked with the adConnectAsync, adExecuteAsync, or adFetchAsync option). Cancel will return an ADO error if adRunAsync was not used in the method it is trying to terminate.

The method has the following syntax:

```
pRecordset->Cancel();
```

The method has no parameters.

## *CancelBatch Method (Recordset Object)*

An application should use the CancelBatch method to cancel any pending updates in a recordset in batch update mode. If the Recordset is in immediate update mode, calling CancelBatch without adAffectCurrent generates an ADO error. If the application is editing the current record or is adding a new record when it calls CancelBatch, ADO first calls the CancelUpdate method to cancel any cached changes; after that, all pending changes in the recordset are canceled. It is possible that the current record will be indeterminable after a CancelBatch call, especially if the application was in the process of adding a new record. For this reason, it is prudent to set the current record position to a known location in the Recordset after the CancelBatch call.

The method has the following syntax:

```
pRecordset->CancelBatch(AffectRecords);
```

The method has the following parameter:

*AffectRecords*
This optional parameter is an AffectEnum value that determines how many records the CancelBatch method will affect. The value is one of the constants in Table 5-24:

| Constant | Description |
|---|---|
| adAffectCurrent | This value indicates that ADO should cancel pending updates only for the current record. |
| adAffectGroup | This value indicates that ADO should cancel pending updates for records that satisfy the current Filter property setting. You must set the Filter property to one of the valid predefined constants in order to use this option. |

| Constant | Description |
|---|---|
| adAffectAll | This default value indicates that ADO should cancel pending updates for all the records in the Recordset object, including any hidden by the current Filter property setting. |

***Table 5-24*** *Recordset object CancelBatch method AffectEnum values*

## CancelUpdate Method (Recordset Object)

An application should use the CancelUpdate method to cancel any changes made to the current record or to discard a newly added record. An application cannot undo changes to the current record or to a new record after it calls the Update method unless the changes are either part of a transaction that the application can roll back with the RollbackTrans method or part of a batch update that it can cancel with the CancelBatch method. If the application is adding a new record when it calls the CancelUpdate method, the record that was current prior to the AddNew call becomes the current record again. If an application has not changed the current record or added a new record, calling the CancelUpdate method generates an ADO error.

The method has the following syntax:

```
pRecordset->CancelUpdate();
```

The method has no parameters.

## Clone Method (Recordset Object)

An application should use the Clone method to create multiple, duplicate Recordset objects, particularly if it wants to be able to maintain more than one current record in a given set of records. Using the Clone method is more efficient than creating and opening a new Recordset object with the same definition as the original. The current record of a newly created clone is set to the first record. Changes the application may make to one Recordset object are visible in all of its clones regardless of cursor type. However, once an application executes Requery on the original Recordset, the clones will no longer be synchronized to the original. Closing the original Recordset does not close its copies; closing a copy does not close the original or any of the other copies. An application can only clone a Recordset object that supports bookmarks. Bookmark values are interchangeable; that is, a bookmark reference from one Recordset object refers to the same record in any of its clones.

The method has the following syntax:

```
pDuplicateRecordset = pOriginalRecordset->Clone(LockType);
```

The method returns a Recordset interface pointer reference.

The method has the following parameter:

*LockType*

This optional parameter is a LockTypeEnum value (given in Table 5-25) that specifies either the lock type of the original Recordset or a read-only Recordset.

| Constant | Description |
|---|---|
| adLockReadOnly | This default value indicates that the clone is created as read-only. |
| adLockUnspecified | This default value indicates that the clone is created with the same lock type as the original. |

***Table 5-25*** *Recordset object LockTypeEnum values*

## Delete Method (Recordset Object)

An application should use the Delete method to mark the current record or a group of records in a Recordset object for deletion. If the Recordset object doesn't allow record deletion, an ADO error occurs. If the application is in immediate update mode, deletions occur in the database immediately. Otherwise, the records are marked for deletion from the cache and the actual deletion happens when the application calls the UpdateBatch method. (Applications can use the Filter property to view the deleted records.) Retrieving field values from the deleted record generates an ADO error. After deleting the current record, the deleted record remains current until an application chooses to move to a different record. Once the application chooses to move away from the deleted record, that deleted record is no longer accessible. If an application should nest deletions in a transaction, however, it can recover deleted records with the RollbackTrans method. If an application is in batch update mode, it can cancel a pending deletion or group of pending deletions with the CancelBatch method. If the attempt to delete records fails because of a conflict with the underlying data (for example, a record has already been deleted by another user), the provider returns warnings to the Errors collection but does not halt program execution with an ADO error. However, an ADO error does occur if there are conflicts on all the requested records.

The method has the following syntax:

```
pRecordset->Delete(AffectRecords);
```

The method has the following parameter:

*AffectRecords*

This parameter is an AffectEnum value that determines how many records the Delete method will affect. The AffectEnum constants are given in Table 5-26.

| Constant | Description |
|---|---|
| adAffectCurrent | This default value indicates that ADO should delete only the current record. |
| adAffectGroup | This value indicates that ADO should delete the records that satisfy the current Filter property setting. An application must set the Filter property to one of the valid predefined constants in order to use this option. |

***Table 5-26** Recordset object AffectEnum values*

## Move Method (Recordset Object)

An application should use this method to move the position of the current record in a Recordset object. The Move method is supported on all Recordset objects. If the *NumRecords* argument is greater than zero, the current record position moves forward (toward the end of the recordset). If *NumRecords* is less than zero, the current record position moves backward (toward the beginning of the recordset). If the Move call would move the current record position to a point before the first record, ADO sets the current record to the position before the first record in the recordset (BOF is True). An attempt to move backward when the BOF property is already True generates an ADO error. If the Move call would move the current record position to a point after the last record, ADO sets the current record to the position after the last record in the recordset (EOF is True). An attempt to move forward when the EOF property is already True generates an ADO error. Calling the Move method from an empty Recordset object generates an error. If an application chooses to pass the *Start* argument, the move is relative to the record with this bookmark, assuming the Recordset object supports bookmarks. If this parameter is not specified, the move is relative to the current record. If an application is using the CacheSize property to locally cache records from the provider, passing a *NumRecords* argument that moves the current record position outside the current group of cached records forces ADO to retrieve a new group of records starting from the destination record. The CacheSize property determines the size of the newly retrieved group, and the destination record is the first record retrieved. If the Recordset object is forward-only, an application can still pass a *NumRecords* argument less than zero as long as the destination is within the current set of cached records. If the Move call would move the current record position to a record before the first cached record, an ADO error will occur. This technique allows an application to use a record cache that supports full scrolling over a provider that supports only forward scrolling. Because cached records are loaded into memory, however, an application should avoid caching more records than is necessary. Even if a forward-only Recordset object supports backward moves using this technique from the vantage point of the end user, calling the MovePrevious method on any forward-only Recordset interface pointer in program statements still generates an ADO error.

The method has the following syntax:

```
pRecordset->Move(NumRecords, Start);
```

The method has the following parameters:

*NumRecords*
: This parameter is a signed Long expression specifying the number of records the current record position moves.

*Start*
: This optional parameter is a String or Variant that evaluates to a bookmark. An application can also use one of the BookmarkEnum values in Table 5-27:

| Constant | Description |
|---|---|
| adBookmarkCurrent | This default value indicates that ADO should start at the current record. |
| adBookmarkFirst | This value indicates that ADO should start at the first record. |
| adBookmarkLast | This value indicates that ADO should start at the last record. |

***Table 5-27*** *Recordset object BookmarkEnum values*

## MoveFirst Method (Recordset Object)

An application should use the MoveFirst method to move the current record position to the first record in the Recordset. The Recordset object must support bookmarks or backward cursor movement; otherwise, the method call will generate an ADO error. If the Recordset is forward-only and an application wants to support both forward and backward scrolling, it can use the CacheSize property to create a record cache that will support backward cursor movement through the Move method. Because cached records are loaded into memory, an application should avoid caching more records than is necessary. An application can call the MoveFirst method in a forward-only Recordset object; doing so may cause the OLE DB provider to re-execute the command that generated the Recordset object.

The method has the following syntax:

```
pRecordset.MoveFirst();
```

The method has no parameters.

## MoveLast Method (Recordset Object)

An application should use the MoveLast method to move the current record position to the last record in the Recordset. The Recordset object must support bookmarks or backward cursor movement; otherwise, the method call will generate an ADO error. If the Recordset is forward-only and an application wants to support both forward and backward scrolling, it can use the CacheSize property to create a record cache that will support backward cursor movement through the Move method. Because cached records are loaded into memory, an application should avoid caching more records than is necessary.

The method has the following syntax:

```
pRecordset.MoveLast();
```

The method has no parameters.

## MoveNext Method (Recordset Object)

An application should use the MoveNext method to move the current record position one record forward (toward the bottom of the Recordset). If the last record is the current record and an application calls the MoveNext method, ADO sets the current record to the position after the last record in the Recordset (EOF is True). An attempt to move forward when the EOF property is already True generates an ADO error. If the Recordset is forward-only and an application wants to support both forward and backward scrolling, it can use the CacheSize property to create a record cache that will support backward cursor movement through the Move method. Because cached records are loaded into memory, an application should avoid caching more records than is necessary.

The method has the following syntax:

```
pRecordset.MoveNext();
```

The method has no parameters.

## MovePrevious Method (Recordset Object)

An application should use the MovePrevious method to move the current record position one record backward (toward the top of the recordset). The Recordset object must support bookmarks or backward cursor movement; otherwise, the method call will generate an ADO error. If the first record is the current record and an application calls the MovePrevious method, ADO sets the current record to the position before the first record in the recordset (BOF is True). An attempt to move backward when the BOF property is already True generates an ADO error. If the Recordset object does not support either bookmarks or backward cursor movement, the MovePrevious method will generate an ADO error. If the Recordset is forward-only and an application wants to support both forward and backward scrolling, it can use the CacheSize property to create a record cache that will support backward cursor movement through the Move method. Because cached records are loaded into memory, an application should avoid caching more records than is necessary.

The method has the following syntax:

```
pRecordset.MovePrevious();
```

The method has no parameters.

## NextRecordset Method (Recordset Object)

An application should use the NextRecordset method to return the results of the next command in a compound command statement or of a stored procedure that returns multiple results. If you open a Recordset object based on a compound command statement using the Execute method on a Command or the Open method on a Recordset, ADO executes only the first command and returns the results to the Recordset. To access the results of subsequent commands in the statement, call the NextRecordset method. As long as there are additional results, the NextRecordset method will continue to return Recordset objects. If a row-returning command returns no records, the returned Recordset object will be empty; test for this case by verifying that the BOF and EOF properties are both True. If a non–row-returning command executes successfully, the returned Recordset object will be closed, which an application can verify by testing the State property on the Recordset. When there are no more results, the Recordset will be set to Null. If an edit is in progress while in immediate update mode, calling the NextRecordset method generates an ADO error; an application should call the Update or CancelUpdate method first. If an application needs to pass parameters for more than one command in the compound statement by filling the Parameters collection or by passing an array with the original Open or Execute call, the parameters must be in the same order in the collection or array as their respective commands in the command series. An application must finish reading all the results before reading output parameter values. When an application calls the NextRecordset method, ADO executes only the next command in the statement. If an application explicitly closes the Recordset object before stepping through the entire command statement, ADO never executes the remaining commands.

The method has the following syntax:

```
pRecordset2 = pRecordset1->NextRecordset(RecordsAffected);
```

The method returns a Recordset object. In the syntax model, pRecordset1 and pRecordset2 can be the same Recordset object, or the application can use separate objects.

The method has the following parameter:

*RecordsAffected*
: This optional parameter is a Long variable to which the OLE DB provider returns the number of records that the current operation affected.

## Open Method (Recordset Object)

An application shoud use the Open method on a Recordset object to open a cursor that represents records from a base table, the results of a query, or a previously saved Recordset. The application should use the optional Source argument to specify a data source using one of the following: a Command object variable, a SQL statement, a stored procedure, a table name, or a complete file path name. The *ActiveConnection* argument corresponds to the ActiveConnection property and specifies in which connection to open the Recordset object. If an application chooses to pass a connection definition for this argument, ADO opens a new connection using the specified parameters. An application can change the value of this property after opening the Recordset to send updates to another provider. Or, an application can set this property to Null to disconnect the Recordset from any provider (after calling Release, see Chapter 1). For the other arguments that correspond directly to properties of a Recordset object (*Source*, *CursorType*, and *LockType*), the relationship of the arguments to the properties is as follows:

- The property is read/write before the Recordset object is opened.
- The property settings are used unless an application passes the corresponding arguments when executing the Open method. If an application chooses to pass an argument, it overrides the corresponding property setting, and the property setting is updated with the argument value.
- After an application opens the Recordset object, these properties become read-only.

For Recordset objects whose Source property is set to a valid Command object, the ActiveConnection property is read-only, even if the Recordset object isn't open. If an application passes a Command object in the *Source* argument and also passes an *ActiveConnection* argument, an ADO error occurs. The ActiveConnection property of the Command object must already be set to a valid Connection object or connection string. If an application passes something other than a Command object in the *Source* argument, an ADO error occurs. An application can use the *Options* argument to optimize evaluation of the *Source* argument. If the *Options* argument is not defined, an application may experience diminished performance because ADO must make calls to the OLE DB provider to determine if the argument is a SQL statement, a stored procedure, or a table name. If an application knows what Source type it is using, setting the *Options* argument instructs ADO to jump directly to the relevant code. If the *Options* argument does not match the Source type, an ADO error occurs. The default for the *Options* argument is adCommandFile if no connection is associated with the recordset. This will typically be the case for persisted Recordset objects. If the data source returns no records, the provider sets both the BOF and EOF properties to True, and the current record position is undefined. An application can still add new data to this empty Recordset object if the cursor type allows it. When an application has concluded its operations over an open Recordset object, it should use the Close method to free any associated system resources. Closing an object does not remove it from memory; an application can change its property settings and use the Open method to open it again later. To completely eliminate an object from memory, set the object variable to Null after calling Release (see Chapter 1). An application can call Open with no operands, and before the ActiveConnection property is set, to create an instance of a Recordset created by appending fields to the Recordset Fields collection.

The method has the following syntax:

```
pRecordset->Open(Source, ActiveConnection, CursorType, LockType, Options);
```

The method has the following parameters:

*Source*
: This optional parameter is a Variant that evaluates to a valid Command object variable name, a SQL statement, a table name, a stored procedure call, or the filename of a persisted Recordset.

*ActiveConnection*
: This optional parameter is either a Variant that evaluates to a valid Connection object variable name or a String containing ConnectionString parameters.

*CursorType*
: This optional parameter is a CursorTypeEnum value (listed in Table 5-28) that determines the type of cursor the provider should use when opening the Recordset.

| Constant | Description |
|---|---|
| adOpenForwardOnly | This default value opens a forward-only–type cursor. |
| adOpenKeyset | This value opens a keyset-type cursor. |
| adOpenDynamic | This value opens a dynamic-type cursor. |
| adOpenStatic | This value opens a static-type cursor. |

***Table 5-28*** *Recordset object CursorTypeEnum values*

*LockType*
: This optional parameter is a LockTypeEnum value (given in Table 5-29) that determines what type of locking (concurrency) the provider should use when opening the Recordset.

| Constant | Description |
|---|---|
| adLockReadOnly | This value is the default and indicates read-only access; the application cannot alter the data. |
| adLockPessimistic | This value indicates pessimistic locking, record by record. In this case, the OLE DB provider does what is necessary to ensure successful editing of the records, usually by locking records at the data source immediately upon editing. |
| adLockOptimistic | This value indicates optimistic locking, record by record. In this case, the OLE DB provider uses optimistic locking, locking records only when an application calls the Update method. |

| Constant | Description |
|---|---|
| adLockBatchOptimistic | This value indicates optimistic batch updates. It is required for batch update mode as opposed to immediate update mode. |

***Table 5-29*** *Recordset object LockTypeEnum values*

*Options*

This optional parameter is a Long value that indicates how the OLE DB provider should evaluate the *Source* argument if it represents something other than a Command object, or that the Recordset should be restored from a file where it was previously saved. This parameter is one of the constants in Table 5-30:

| Constant | Description |
|---|---|
| adCmdText | This value indicates that the OLE DB provider should evaluate *CommandText* as a textual definition of a command. |
| adCmdTable | This value indicates that ADO should generate a SQL query to return all rows from the table named in *CommandText*. |
| adCmdTableDirect | This value indicates that the OLE DB provider should return all rows from the table named in *CommandText*. |
| adCmdTable | This value indicates that the OLE DB provider should evaluate *CommandText* as a table name. |
| adCmdStoredProc | This value indicates that the OLE DB provider should evaluate *CommandText* as a stored procedure. |
| adCmdUnknown | This value indicates that the type of command in the *CommandText* argument is not known. |
| adExecuteAsync | This value indicates that the command should execute asynchronously. |
| adFetchAsync | This value indicates that the remaining rows after the initial quantity specified in the CacheSize property should be fetched asynchronously. |

***Table 5-30*** *Recordset object CommandTypeEnum values*

## Requery Method (Recordset Object)

An application should use the Requery method to refresh the entire contents of a Recordset object from the data source by reissuing the original command and retrieving the data a second time. Calling this method is equivalent to calling the Close and Open methods in succession. If you are editing the current record or adding a new record, an error occurs. While the Recordset object is open, the properties that define the nature of the cursor (CursorType, LockType, MaxRecords, etc.) are read-only. Thus, the Requery method can only refresh the current cursor. To change any of the cursor properties and view the results, an application must use the Close method so that the properties become read/write again. An application can then change the property settings and call the Open method to reopen the cursor.

The method has the following syntax:

```
pRecordset->Requery(Options);
```

The method has the following parameter:

*Options*
This optional parameter is a bitmask indicating options affecting this operation. If this parameter is set to adExecuteAsync, this operation will execute asynchronously and a RecordsetChangeComplete event will be issued when it concludes.

## Resync Method (Recordset Object)

An application should use the Resync method to resynchronize records in the current Recordset with the underlying database. This is useful if an application is using either a static or forward-only cursor but also wants to see any changes in the underlying database. Unlike the Requery method, the Resync method does not re-execute the Recordset object's underlying command; new records in the underlying database will not be visible. If the attempt to resynchronize fails because of a conflict with the underlying data, the provider returns warnings to the Errors collection and an ADO error occurs. In this case, an application should use the Filter property (adFilterConflictingRecords) and the Status property to locate records with conflicts.

The method has the following syntax:

```
pRecordset->Resync(AffectRecords, ResyncValues);
```

The method has the following parameter:

*AffectRecords*
This optional parameter is an AffectEnum value (listed in Table 5-31) that determines how many records the Resync method will affect.

| Constant | Description |
|---|---|
| adAffectCurrent | This value indicates that ADO should refresh only the current record. |
| adAffectGroup | This value indicates that ADO should refresh the records that satisfy the current Filter property setting. An application must set the Filter property to one of the valid predefined constants in order to use this option. |
| adAffectAll | This default value indicates that ADO should refresh all the records in the Recordset object, including any hidden by the current Filter property setting. |

**Table 5-31** *Recordset object AffectEnum values*

*ResyncValues*
This optional parameter is a ResyncEnum value (given in Table 5-32) that specifies whether underlying values are overwritten.

| Constant | Description |
|---|---|
| adResyncAllValues | This default value indicates that data is overwritten, and pending updates are canceled. |
| adResyncUnderlyingValues | This value indicates that data is not overwritten, and pending updates are not canceled. |

***Table 5-32*** *Recordset object ResyncEnum values*

## *Save Method (Recordset Object)*

An application should use this method to save (persist) the Recordset in a file. The Save method can only be invoked on an open Recordset. Use the Open method to later restore the Recordset from *FileName*. If the Filter property is in effect for the Recordset, then only the rows accessible under the filter are saved. If the Recordset is hierarchical, then the current child recordset and its children are saved, but not the parent recordset. The first time an application saves the Recordset, it must specify the *FileName* parameter. If you subsequently invoke Save, omit *FileName* or else a run-time error will occur. If it subsequently invokes Save with a new *FileName*, the Recordset is saved to the new file. However, the new file and the original file will both be open, since Save does not close Recordset or *FileName*, so an application can continue to work with the Recordset and save its most recent changes. *FileName* remains open until the Recordset is closed, during which time other applications can read but not write to *FileName*. If the Save method is called while an asynchronous Recordset fetch, execute, or update operation is in progress, then Save waits until the asynchronous operation is complete. When the Save method is done, the current row position will be the first row of the Recordset.

The method has the following syntax:

```
pRecordset->Save(FileName, PersistFormat);
```

The method has the following parameters:

*FileName*
: This optional parameter is a complete path name of the file where the Recordset is to be saved.

*PersistFormat*
: This optional parameter is the format in which the Recordset is to be saved. In ADO 2.0 the only valid value is adPersistADTG.

**Warning** For reasons of security, the Save method cannot be used from a script executed by Microsoft Internet Explorer.

## Supports Method (Recordset Object)

An application should use this method to determine whether a specified Recordset object supports a particular type of functionality.

The method has the following syntax:

```
bMyboolean = pRecordset->Supports(CursorOptions);
```

The method returns a Boolean value that indicates whether all of the features identified by the CursorOptions argument are supported by the provider.

The method has the following parameter:

*CursorOptions*
: This parameter is a Long expression that consists of one or more of the CursorOptionEnum values given in Table 5-33.

| Constant | Description |
|---|---|
| adAddNew | This value indicates that the application can use the AddNew method to add new records. |
| adApproxPosition | This value indicates that the application can read and set the AbsolutePosition and AbsolutePage properties. |
| adBookmark | This value indicates that the application can use the Bookmark property to gain access to specific records. |
| adDelete | This value indicates that the application can use the Delete method to delete records. |
| adHoldRecords | This value indicates that the application can retrieve more records or change the next retrieve position without committing all pending changes. |
| adMovePrevious | This value indicates that the application can use the MoveFirst and MovePrevious methods, and Move or GetRows methods to move the current record position backward without requiring bookmarks. |
| adResync | This value indicates that the application can update the cursor with the data visible in the underlying database, using the Resync method. |
| adUpdate | This value indicates that the application can use the Update method to modify existing data. |
| adUpdateBatch | This value indicates that the application can use batch updating (UpdateBatch and CancelBatch methods) to transmit changes to the provider in groups. |

***Table 5-33*** *Recordset object CursorOptionEnum values*

## Update Method (Recordset Object)

An application can use this method to set field values, by doing one of the following:

- Assign values to a Field object's Value property and calling the Update method.
- Passing a field name and a value as arguments with the Update call.
- Passing an array of field names and an array of values with the Update call.

When an application chooses to use arrays of fields and values, there must be an equal number of elements in both arrays. Also, the order of field names must match the order of field values. If the number and order of fields and values do not match, an ADO error occurs. If the Recordset object supports batch updating, then an application can cache multiple changes to one or more records locally until it chooses to call the UpdateBatch method. If an application is editing the current record or adding a new record when it calls the UpdateBatch method, ADO will automatically call the Update method to save any pending changes to the current record before transmitting the batched changes to the provider. If an application chooses to move from the record it is adding or editing before calling the Update method, ADO will automatically call Update to save the changes. An application must call the CancelUpdate method if it wants to cancel any changes made to the current record or to discard a newly added record. The current record remains current after the application calls the Update method.

The method has the following syntax:

```
pRecordset->Update(Fields, Values);
```

The method has the following parameters:

*Fields*
: This optional parameter is a Variant representing a single name or a Variant array representing names or ordinal positions of the field or fields an application may wish to modify.

*Values*
: This optional parameter is a Variant representing a single value or a Variant array representing values for the field or fields in the new record.

## UpdateBatch Method (Recordset Object)

An application should use the UpdateBatch method when modifying a Recordset object in batch update mode to transmit all changes made in a Recordset object to the underlying database. If the Recordset object supports batch updating, then an application can cache multiple changes to one or more records locally until it calls the UpdateBatch method. If an application is editing the current record or adding a new record when it calls the UpdateBatch method, ADO will automatically call the Update method to save any pending changes to the current record before transmitting the batched changes to the OLE DB provider. An application should use batch updating only with either a keyset or static cursor. If the attempt to transmit changes fails because of a conflict with the underlying data, the OLE DB provider returns warnings to the Errors collection but does not halt program execution with an ADO error unless there are conflicts on all the requested records. In this case, an application should use the Filter property (adFilterAffectedRecords) and the Status property to locate records with conflicts. To cancel all pending batch updates, an application should use the CancelBatch method.

The method has the following syntax:

```
pRecordset->UpdateBatch(AffectRecords);
```

The method has the following parameter:

*AffectRecords*
: This optional parameter is an AffectEnum value (given in Table 5-34) that determines how many records the UpdateBatch method will affect.

| Constant | Description |
|---|---|
| adAffectCurrent | This value indicates that ADO should refresh only the current record. |
| adAffectGroup | This value indicates that ADO should refresh the records that satisfy the current Filter property setting. An application must set the Filter property to one of the valid predefined constants in order to use this option. |
| adAffectAll | This default value indicates that ADO should refresh all the records in the Recordset object, including any hidden by the current Filter property setting. |

***Table 5-34*** *Recordset object AffectEnum values*

## The ADO Field Object

A Recordset object has a Fields collection made up of Field objects. Each Field object corresponds to a column in the Recordset. Applications should use the Value property of Field objects to set or return data for the current record. With the collections, methods, and properties of a Field object, an application can:

- Return the name of a field with the Name property.
- View or change the data in the field with the Value property.
- Return the basic characteristics of a field with the Type, Precision, and NumericScale properties.
- Return the declared size of a field with the DefinedSize property.
- Return the actual size of the data in a given field with the ActualSize property.
- Determine what types of functionality are supported for a given field with the Attributes property and Properties collection.

- Manipulate the values of fields containing long binary or long character data with the AppendChunk and GetChunk methods.
- If the provider supports batch updates, resolve discrepancies in field values during batch updating with the OriginalValue and UnderlyingValue properties.

All of the metadata properties (Name, Type, DefinedSize, Precision, and NumericScale) are available before opening the Field object's Recordset; this is useful for dynamically constructing forms.

## *ActualSize Property (Field Object)*

An application should use the ActualSize property to return the actual length of a Field object's value. For all fields, the ActualSize property is read-only. If ADO cannot determine the length of the Field object's value, the ActualSize property returns adUnknown.

## *Attributes Property (Field Object)*

For a Field object, the Attributes property is read-only; its value can be the sum of any one or more of the FieldAttributeEnum values in Table 5-35.

| Constant | Description |
|---|---|
| adFldMayDefer | This value indicates that the field is deferred—that is, the field values are not retrieved from the data source with the whole record, but only when an application explicitly accesses them. |
| adFldUpdatable | This value indicates that an application can write to the field. |
| adFldUnknownUpdatable | This value indicates that the OLE DB provider cannot determine if you can write to the field. |
| adFldFixed | This value indicates that the field contains fixed-length data. |
| adFldIsNullable | This value indicates that the field accepts Null values. |
| adFldMayBeNull | This value indicates that an application can read Null values from the field. |
| adFldLong | This value indicates that the field is a Long binary field. Also indicates that an application can use the AppendChunk and GetChunk methods. |
| adFldRowID | This value indicates that the field contains a persistent row identifier that cannot be written to and has no meaningful value except to identify the row (such as a record number, unique identifier, and so forth). |
| adFldRowVersion | This value indicates that the field contains some kind of time or date stamp used to track updates. |
| adFldCacheDeferred | This value indicates that the OLE DB provider caches field values and that subsequent reads are done from the cache. |

***Table 5-35*** *Field object FieldAttributeEnum values*

## DefinedSize Property (Field Object)

Applications should use the DefinedSize property to determine the data capacity of a Field object. The DefinedSize and ActualSize properties are different.

## Name Property (Field Object)

An application should use the Name property to assign a name to or retrieve the name of a Command, Field, Parameter, or Property object. For Parameter objects not yet appended to the Parameters collection, the Name property is read/write. For appended Parameter objects and all other objects, the Name property is read-only. Names do not have to be unique within a collection. An application can retrieve the Name property of an object by an ordinal reference, after which it can refer to the object directly by name.

## NumericScale Property (Field Object)

An application should use the NumericScale property to determine how many digits to the right of the decimal point will be used to represent values for a numeric Parameter or Field object. The NumericScale property is read-only.

## OriginalValue Property (Field Object)

An application should use the OriginalValue property to return the original field value for a field from the current record. In immediate update mode (the OLE DB provider writes changes to the underlying data source once an application calls the Update method), the OriginalValue property returns the field value that existed prior to any changes (that is, since the last Update method call). This is the same value that the CancelUpdate method uses to replace the Value property. In batch update mode (the OLE DB provider caches multiple changes and writes them to the underlying data source only when an application calls the UpdateBatch method), the OriginalValue property returns the field value that existed prior to any changes (that is, since the last UpdateBatch method call). This is the same value that the CancelBatch method uses to replace the Value property. When an application uses this property with the UnderlyingValue property, it can resolve conflicts that arise from batch updates.

## Precision Property (Field Object)

An application should use the Precision property to determine the maximum number of digits used to represent values for a numeric Parameter or Field object. The property is a Byte value, indicating the maximum total number of digits used to represent values. The value is read-only.

## Type Property (Field Object)

This read-only property indicates the operational type or data type of a Field object. It contains one of the DataTypeEnum values in Table 5-36. The corresponding OLE DB type indicator is shown in parentheses.

| Constant | Description |
|---|---|
| adArray | This value indicates that the type is joined in a logical OR together with another type to indicate that the data is a safe-array of that type (DBTYPE_ARRAY). |
| adBigInt | This value indicates that the type is an 8-byte signed integer (DBTYPE_I8). |
| adBinary | This value indicates that the type is a binary value (DBTYPE_BYTES). |
| adBoolean | This value indicates that the type is a Boolean value (DBTYPE_BOOL). |
| adByRef | This value indicates that the type is joined in a logical OR together with another type to indicate that the data is a pointer to data of the other type (DBTYPE_BYREF). |
| adBSTR | This value indicates that the type is a null-terminated character string (Unicode) (DBTYPE_BSTR). |
| adChar | This value indicates that the type is a String value (DBTYPE_STR). |
| adCurrency | This value indicates that the type is a currency value (DBTYPE_CY). Currency is a fixed-point number with four digits to the right of the decimal point. It is stored in an 8-byte signed integer scaled by 10,000. |
| adDate | This value indicates that the type is a Date value (DBTYPE_DATE). A date is stored as a Double, the whole part of which is the number of days since December 30, 1899, and the fractional part of which is the fraction of a day. |
| adDBDate | This value indicates that the type is a date value (*yyyymmdd*) (DBTYPE_DBDATE). |
| adDBTime | This value indicates that the type is a time value (*hhmmss*) (DBTYPE_DBTIME). |
| adDBTimeStamp | This value indicates that the type is a date-time stamp (*yyyymmddhhmmss* plus a fraction in billionths) (DBTYPE_DBTIMESTAMP). |
| adDecimal | This value indicates that the type is an exact numeric value with a fixed precision and scale (DBTYPE_DECIMAL). |
| adDouble | This value indicates that the type is a double-precision floating-point value (DBTYPE_R8). |
| adEmpty | This value indicates that no type value was specified (DBTYPE_EMPTY). |
| adError | This value indicates that the type is a 32-bit error code (DBTYPE_ERROR). |

| Constant | Description |
|---|---|
| adGUID | This value indicates that the type is a globally unique identifier (GUID) (DBTYPE_GUID). |
| adIDispatch | This value indicates that the type is a pointer to an IDispatch interface on an OLE object (DBTYPE_IDISPATCH). |
| adInteger | This value indicates that the type is a 4-byte signed integer (DBTYPE_I4). |
| adIUnknown | This value indicates that the type is a pointer to an IUnknown interface on an OLE object (DBTYPE_IUNKNOWN). |
| adNumeric | This value indicates that the type is an exact numeric value with a fixed precision and scale (DBTYPE_NUMERIC). |
| adSingle | This value indicates that the type is a single-precision floating-point value (DBTYPE_R4). |
| adSmallInt | This value indicates that the type is a 2-byte signed integer (DBTYPE_I2). |
| adTinyInt | This value indicates that the type is a 1-byte signed integer (DBTYPE_I1). |
| adUnsignedBigInt | This value indicates that the type is an 8-byte unsigned integer (DBTYPE_UI8). |
| adUnsignedInt | This value indicates that the type is a 4-byte unsigned integer (DBTYPE_UI4). |
| adUnsignedSmallInt | This value indicates that the type is a 2-byte unsigned integer (DBTYPE_UI2). |
| adUnsignedTinyInt | This value indicates that the type is a 1-byte unsigned integer (DBTYPE_UI1). |
| adUserDefined | This value indicates that the type is a user-defined variable (DBTYPE_UDT). |
| adVariant | This value indicates that the type is an Automation Variant (DBTYPE_VARIANT). |
| adVector | This value indicates that the type is joined in a logical OR together with another type to indicate that the data is a DBVECTOR structure, as defined by OLE DB, that contains a count of elements and a pointer to data of the other type (DBTYPE_VECTOR). |
| adWChar | This value indicates that the type is a null-terminated Unicode character string (DBTYPE_WSTR). |

***Table 5-36*** *Field object DataTypeEnum values*

## *UnderlyingValue Property (Field Object)*

An application should use the UnderlyingValue property to return the current field value from the database. The field value in the UnderlyingValue property is the value that is visible to an application's transaction and may be the result of a recent update by another transaction. This may differ from the

OriginalValue property, which reflects the value that was originally returned to the Recordset. This is similar to using the Resync method, but the UnderlyingValue property returns only the value for a specific field from the current record. This is the same value that the Resync method uses to replace the Value property.

### Value Property (Field Object)

An application should use the Value property to set or return data from Field objects. ADO allows setting and returning Long amounts of binary data with the Value property. Otherwise, the rules for manipulating Value depend on the data type (see Table 5-36).

### AppendChunk Method (Field Object)

An application should use the AppendChunk method on a Field object to fill it with Long binary or character data. In situations where system memory is limited, an application can use the AppendChunk method to manipulate Long values in portions rather than in their entirety. If the adFldLong bit in the Attributes property of a Field object is set to True, an application can use the AppendChunk method for that field. The first AppendChunk call on a Field object writes data to the field, overwriting any existing data. Subsequent AppendChunk calls add to existing data. If an application is appending data to one field and then chooses to set or read the value of another field in the current record, ADO assumes that the application is done appending data to the first field. If an application calls the AppendChunk method on the first field again, ADO interprets the call as a new AppendChunk operation and overwrites the existing data. Accessing fields in other Recordset objects that are not clones of the first Recordset object will not disrupt AppendChunk operations. If there is no current record when an application calls AppendChunk on a Field object, an ADO error occurs.

The method has the following syntax:

```
pField->AppendChunk(Data);
```

The method has the following parameter:

*Data*
: This parameter is a Variant containing the data the application wants to append to the Field object.

### GetChunk Method (Field Object)

An application should use the the GetChunk method on a Field object to retrieve part or all of its Long binary or character data. In situations where system memory is limited, an application can use the GetChunk method to manipulate Long values in portions rather than in their entirety. The data that a GetChunk call returns is assigned to pMyVariant. If *Size* is greater than the remaining data, the GetChunk method returns only the remaining data without padding pMyVariant with empty spaces. If the field is empty, the GetChunk method returns Null. Each subsequent GetChunk call retrieves data starting from where the previous GetChunk call left off. However, if an application is retrieving data from one field and then it chooses to set or read the value of another field in the current record, ADO assumes the application is done retrieving data from the first field. If an application calls the GetChunk method on the first field again, ADO interprets the call as a new GetChunk operation and starts reading from the beginning of the data. Accessing fields in other Recordset objects that are not clones of the first Recordset object will not disrupt GetChunk operations. If the adFldLong bit in the Attributes property of a Field object is set to True, an application can use the GetChunk method for that field. If there is no current record when an application uses the GetChunk method on a Field object, an ADO error occurs.

The method has the following syntax:

```
pMyVariant = pField->GetChunk(Size);
```

The method returns a Variant.

The method has the following parameter:

*Size*

This parameter is a Long expression equal to the number of bytes or characters an application wants to retrieve.

## The ADO Error Object

Any operation involving ADO objects can generate one or more OLE DB provider errors. As each error occurs, one or more Error objects are placed in the Errors collection of the Connection object. When another ADO operation generates an error, the Errors collection is cleared, and the new set of Error objects is placed in the Errors collection. Each Error object represents a specific provider error, not an ADO error. An application can read an Error object's properties to obtain specific details about each error, including the following:

- The Description property, which contains the text of the error.
- The Number property, which contains the Long integer value of the error constant.
- The Source property, which identifies the object that raised the error. This is particularly useful when an application has several Error objects in the Errors collection following a request to a data source.
- The SQLState and NativeError properties, which provide information from SQL data sources.

When an OLE DB provider error occurs, it is placed in the Errors collection of the Connection object. ADO supports the return of multiple errors by a single

ADO operation to allow for error information specific to the provider. The Errors collection on the Connection object is cleared and populated only when the OLE DB provider generates a new error, or when the Clear method is called. Some properties and methods return warnings that appear as Error objects in the Errors collection but do not halt a program's execution with an ADO error. Before an application calls the Resync, UpdateBatch, or CancelBatch methods on a Recordset object or the Open method on a Connection object, or sets the Filter property on a Recordset object, it should first call the Clear method on the Errors collection so that it can read the Count property of the Errors collection to test for returned warnings.

**Note** All properties of the Error object are read-only.

## Description Property (Error Object)

An application should use the Description property to obtain a short description of the error. It should display this property to alert the user to an error that it cannot or does not want to handle. The string will come from either ADO or an OLE DB provider. OLE DB providers are responsible for passing specific error text to ADO. ADO adds an Error object to the Errors collection for each OLE DB provider error or warning it receives. Applications should enumerate the Errors collection to trace the errors that the OLE DB provider passes. The property holds a String value.

## NativeError Property (Error Object)

Applications should use the NativeError property to retrieve the database-specific error information for a particular Error object. When using the Microsoft ODBC provider for OLE DB with a Microsoft® SQL Server™ database, native error codes that originate from SQL Server pass through ODBC and the ODBC provider to the ADO NativeError property. The property holds a Long value.

## Number Property (Error Object)

Applications should use the Number property to determine which error occurred. The value of the property is a unique number that corresponds to the error condition (defined by the OLE DB provider). The property holds a Long value.

## Source Property (Error Object)

Applications should use the Source property on an Error object to determine the name of the object or application that originally generated an error. This could be the object's class name or programmatic ID. For errors in ADODB, the property value will be ADODB.*ObjectName*, where *ObjectName* is the name of the object that triggered the error. The property holds a String value.

### SQLState Property (Error Object)

Applications should use the SQLState property to read the five-character error code that the provider returns when an error occurs during the processing of a SQL statement. When using the Microsoft OLE DB Provider for ODBC with a Microsoft SQL Server database, SQL state error codes originate from ODBC based either on errors specific to ODBC or on errors that originate from Microsoft SQL Server and are then mapped to ODBC errors. These error codes are documented in the ANSI SQL standard, but may be implemented differently by different data sources. The property holds a String value.

## The ADO Property Object

ADO objects have two types of properties: built-in and dynamic. *Built-in* properties are those properties implemented in ADO and immediately available to any new object. They do not appear as Property objects in an object's Properties collection, so although an application can change their values, it cannot modify their characteristics. *Dynamic* properties are defined by the underlying OLE DB provider, and appear in the Properties collection for the appropriate ADO object. For example, a property specific to the provider may indicate if a Recordset object supports transactions or updating. These additional properties will appear as Property objects in that Recordset object's Properties collection. Dynamic properties can be referenced only through the collection. An application must consult the documentation for each OLE DB provider as to the names, data types, and semantics of its dynamic properties. A dynamic Property object in ADO has four built-in properties of its own:

- The Attributes property is a Long value that indicates characteristics of the property specific to the OLE DB provider.
- The Name property is a String that identifies the property.
- The Type property is an integer that specifies the property data type.
- The Value property is a Variant that contains the property setting.

### Attributes Property (Property Object)

For a Property object, the Attributes property is read-only. Its value can be the sum of any one or more of the PropertyAttributesEnum values in Table 5-37:

| Constant | Description |
|---|---|
| adPropNotSupported | This value indicates that the property is not supported by the provider. |
| adPropRequired | This value indicates that the user must specify a value for this property before the data source is initialized. |
| adPropOptional | This value indicates that the user does not need to specify a value for this property before the data source is initialized. |

| Constant | Description |
|---|---|
| adPropRead | This value indicates that the user can read the property. |
| adPropWrite | This value indicates that the user can set the property. |

***Table 5-37*** *Property object PropertyAttributesEnum values*

## Name Property (Property Object)

Applications should use the Name property to retrieve the name of a Property object. The Name property is read-only. Names do not have to be unique within a collection. An application can retrieve the Name property of a Property object by an ordinal reference, after which it can refer to the object directly by name. For example, if MyConnection.Properties(15).Name yields TransactionState, an application can subsequently refer to this property as MyConnection.Properties("TransactionState").

## Type Property (Property Object)

This read-only property indicates the operational type or data type of a Property object. It contains one of the DataTypeEnum values in Table 5-38. The corresponding OLE DB type indicator is shown in parentheses.

| Constant | Description |
|---|---|
| adArray | This value indicates that the type is joined in a logical OR together with another type to indicate that the data is a safe-array of that type (DBTYPE_ARRAY). |
| adBigInt | This value indicates that the type is an 8-byte signed integer (DBTYPE_I8). |
| adBinary | This value indicates that the type is a binary value (DBTYPE_BYTES). |
| adBoolean | This value indicates that the type is a Boolean value (DBTYPE_BOOL). |
| adByRef | This value indicates that the type is joined in a logical OR together with another type to indicate that the data is a pointer to data of the other type (DBTYPE_BYREF). |
| adBSTR | This value indicates that the type is a null-terminated character string (Unicode) (DBTYPE_BSTR). |
| adChar | This value indicates that the type is a String value (DBTYPE_STR). |
| adCurrency | This value indicates that the type is a currency value (DBTYPE_CY). Currency is a fixed-point number with four digits to the right of the decimal point. It is stored in an 8-byte signed integer scaled by 10,000. |
| adDate | This value indicates that the type is a Date value (DBTYPE_DATE). A date is stored as a Double, the whole part of which is the number of days since December 30, 1899, and the fractional part of which is the fraction of a day. |

| Constant | Description |
|---|---|
| adDBDate | This value indicates that the type is a date value (*yyyymmdd*) (DBTYPE_DBDATE). |
| adDBTime | This value indicates that the type is a time value (*hhmmss*) (DBTYPE_DBTIME). |
| adDBTimeStamp | This value indicates that the type is a date-time stamp (*yyyymmddhhmmss* plus a fraction in billionths) (DBTYPE_DBTIMESTAMP). |
| adDecimal | This value indicates that the type is an exact numeric value with a fixed precision and scale (DBTYPE_DECIMAL). |
| adDouble | This value indicates that the type is a double-precision floating-point value (DBTYPE_R8). |
| adEmpty | This value indicates that no type value was specified (DBTYPE_EMPTY). |
| adError | This value indicates that the type is a 32-bit error code (DBTYPE_ERROR). |
| adGUID | This value indicates that the type is a globally unique identifier (GUID) (DBTYPE_GUID). |
| adIDispatch | This value indicates that the type is a pointer to an IDispatch interface on an OLE object (DBTYPE_IDISPATCH). |
| adInteger | This value indicates that the type is a 4-byte signed integer (DBTYPE_I4). |
| adIUnknown | This value indicates that the type is a pointer to an IUnknown interface on an OLE object (DBTYPE_IUNKNOWN). |
| adNumeric | This value indicates that the type is an exact numeric value with a fixed precision and scale (DBTYPE_NUMERIC). |
| adSingle | This value indicates that the type is a single-precision floating-point value (DBTYPE_R4). |
| adSmallInt | This value indicates that the type is a 2-byte signed integer (DBTYPE_I2). |
| adTinyInt | This value indicates that the type is a 1-byte signed integer (DBTYPE_I1). |
| adUnsignedBigInt | This value indicates that the type is an 8-byte unsigned integer (DBTYPE_UI8). |
| adUnsignedInt | This value indicates that the type is a 4-byte unsigned integer (DBTYPE_UI4). |
| adUnsignedSmallInt | This value indicates that the type is a 2-byte unsigned integer (DBTYPE_UI2). |
| adUnsignedTinyInt | This value indicates that the type is a 1-byte unsigned integer (DBTYPE_UI1). |
| adUserDefined | This value indicates that the type is a user-defined variable (DBTYPE_UDT). |
| adVariant | This value indicates that the type is an Automation Variant (DBTYPE_VARIANT). |

| Constant | Description |
|---|---|
| adVector | This value indicates that the type is joined in a logical OR together with another type to indicate that the data is a DBVECTOR structure, as defined by OLE DB, that contains a count of elements and a pointer to data of the other type (DBTYPE_VECTOR). |
| adWChar | This value indicates that the type is a null-terminated Unicode character string (DBTYPE_WSTR). |

***Table 5-38*** *Property object DataTypeEnum values*

### *Value Property (Property Object)*

Applications should use the Value property to set or return property settings with Property objects; the property is a Variant and can contain any appropriate data as indicated in Table 5-38. ADO allows setting and returning Long binary data with the Value property.

## *The ADO Parameter Object*

Many providers support parameterized commands. These are commands in which the desired action is defined once, but variables (or parameters) are used to alter some details of the command. For example, a SQL SELECT statement could use a parameter to define the matching criteria of a WHERE clause, and another to define the column name for a SORT BY clause. Parameter objects represent parameters associated with parameterized queries, or the in/out arguments and the return values of stored procedures. If an application knows the names and properties of the parameters associated with the stored procedure or parameterized query it wishes to call, it can use the CreateParameter method to create Parameter objects with the appropriate property settings and use the Append method to add them to the Parameters collection. This lets an application set and return parameter values without having to call the Refresh method on the Parameters collection to retrieve the parameter information from the OLE DB provider, a lengthy and resource-intensive operation. With the collections, methods, and properties of a Parameter object, an application can:

- Set or return the name of a parameter with the Name property.
- Set or return the value of a parameter with the Value property.
- Set or return parameter characteristics with the Attributes, Precision, NumericScale, Size, and Type properties.

## Attributes Property (Parameter Object)

The Attributes property describes several behavioral capabilities of the Parameter object; its value can be the sum of any one or more of the ParameterAttributesEnum values in Table 5-39. The property is read-only.

| Constant | Description |
|---|---|
| adParamSigned | This default value indicates that the parameter accepts signed values. |
| adParamNullable | This value indicates that the parameter accepts Null values. |
| adParamLong | This value indicates that the parameter accepts Long binary data. |

***Table 5-39*** *Parameter object ParameterAttributesEnum values*

## Name Property (Parameter Object)

Applications should use the Name property to assign a name to or retrieve the name of a Parameter object. For Parameter objects not yet appended to the Parameters collection, the Name property is read/write. For appended Parameter objects, the Name property is read-only. Names do not have to be unique within a collection. An application can retrieve the Name property of an object by an ordinal reference, after which it can refer to the object directly by name. For example, if MyConnection.Parameters(13).Name yields BinaryParameter, an application can subsequently refer to this parameter as MyConnection.Parameters("BinaryParameter").

## NumericScale Property (Parameter Object)

An application should use the NumericScale property to determine how many digits to the right of the decimal point will be used to represent values for a numeric Parameter object.

For Parameter objects, the NumericScale property is read/write.

## Precision Property (Parameter Object)

An application should use the Precision property to determine the maximum number of digits used to represent values for a numeric Parameter object. The property is read-only and a Long value.

## Size Property (Parameter Object)

Applications should use the Size property to determine the maximum size for values written to or read from the Value property of a Parameter object. The Size property is read/write. If an application chooses to specify a variable-length data type for a Parameter object (for example, any String type, such as adVarChar), it must set the object's Size property before appending it to the Parameters collection; otherwise an ADO error occurs. If an application has already appended the Parameter object to the Parameters collection of a

Command object and it chooses to change its type to a variable-length data type, it must set the Parameter object's Size property before executing the Command object; otherwise an ADO error occurs. If an application uses the Refresh method to obtain parameter information from the OLE DB provider and it returns one or more variable-length data type Parameter objects, ADO may allocate memory for the parameters based on their maximum potential size, which could cause an error during execution. To prevent an error, an application should explicitly set the Size property for all parameters before executing the command.

## Type Property (Parameter Object)

This read-write property indicates the operational type or data type of a Parameter object. It contains one of the DataTypeEnum values in Table 5-40. The corresponding OLE DB type indicator is shown in parentheses.

| Constant | Description |
|---|---|
| adArray | This value indicates that the type is joined in a logical OR together with another type to indicate that the data is a safe-array of that type (DBTYPE_ARRAY). |
| adBigInt | This value indicates that the type is an 8-byte signed integer (DBTYPE_I8). |
| adBinary | This value indicates that the type is a binary value (DBTYPE_BYTES). |
| adBoolean | This value indicates that the type is a Boolean value (DBTYPE_BOOL). |
| adByRef | This value indicates that the type is joined in a logical OR together with another type to indicate that the data is a pointer to data of the other type (DBTYPE_BYREF). |
| adBSTR | This value indicates that the type is a null-terminated character string (Unicode) (DBTYPE_BSTR). |
| adChar | This value indicates that the type is a String value (DBTYPE_STR). |
| adCurrency | This value indicates that the type is a currency value (DBTYPE_CY). Currency is a fixed-point number with four digits to the right of the decimal point. It is stored in an 8-byte signed integer scaled by 10,000. |
| adDate | This value indicates that the type is a Date value (DBTYPE_DATE). A date is stored as a Double, the whole part of which is the number of days since December 30, 1899, and the fractional part of which is the fraction of a day. |
| adDBDate | This value indicates that the type is a date value (*yyyymmdd*) (DBTYPE_DBDATE). |
| adDBTime | This value indicates that the type is a time value (*hhmmss*) (DBTYPE_DBTIME). |
| adDBTimeStamp | This value indicates that the type is a date-time stamp (*yyyymmddhhmmss* plus a fraction in billionths) (DBTYPE_DBTIMESTAMP). |

| Constant | Description |
|---|---|
| adDecimal | This value indicates that the type is an exact numeric value with a fixed precision and scale (DBTYPE_DECIMAL). |
| adDouble | This value indicates that the type is a double-precision floating-point value (DBTYPE_R8). |
| adEmpty | This value indicates that no type value was specified (DBTYPE_EMPTY). |
| adError | This value indicates that the type is a 32-bit error code (DBTYPE_ERROR). |
| adGUID | This value indicates that the type is a globally unique identifier (GUID) (DBTYPE_GUID). |
| adIDispatch | This value indicates that the type is a pointer to an IDispatch interface on an OLE object (DBTYPE_IDISPATCH). |
| adInteger | This value indicates that the type is a 4-byte signed integer (DBTYPE_I4). |
| adIUnknown | This value indicates that the type is a pointer to an IUnknown interface on an OLE object (DBTYPE_IUNKNOWN). |
| adLongVarBinary | This value indicates that the type is a Long binary value. |
| adLongVarChar | This value indicates that the type is a Long String value. |
| adLongVarWChar | This value indicates that the type is a Long null-terminated string value. |
| adNumeric | This value indicates that the type is an exact numeric value with a fixed precision and scale (DBTYPE_NUMERIC). |
| adSingle | This value indicates that the type is a single-precision floating-point value (DBTYPE_R4). |
| adSmallInt | This value indicates that the type is a 2-byte signed integer (DBTYPE_I2). |
| adTinyInt | This value indicates that the type is a 1-byte signed integer (DBTYPE_I1). |
| adUnsignedBigInt | This value indicates that the type is an 8-byte unsigned integer (DBTYPE_UI8). |
| adUnsignedInt | This value indicates that the type is a 4-byte unsigned integer (DBTYPE_UI4). |
| adUnsignedSmallInt | This value indicates that the type is a 2-byte unsigned integer (DBTYPE_UI2). |
| adUnsignedTinyInt | This value indicates that the type is a 1-byte unsigned integer (DBTYPE_UI1). |
| adUserDefined | This value indicates that the type is a user-defined variable (DBTYPE_UDT). |
| adVarBinary | This value indicates that the type is a binary value. |
| adVarChar | This value indicates that the type is a String value. |
| adVariant | This value indicates that the type is an Automation Variant (DBTYPE_VARIANT). |

| Constant | Description |
|---|---|
| adVector | This value indicates that the type is joined in a logical OR together with another type to indicate that the data is a DBVECTOR structure, as defined by OLE DB, that contains a count of elements and a pointer to data of the other type (DBTYPE_VECTOR). |
| adVarWChar | This value indicates that the type is a null-terminated Unicode character string. |
| adWChar | This value indicates that the type is a null-terminated Unicode character string (DBTYPE_WSTR). |

***Table 5-40*** *Parameter object DataTypeEnum values*

### *Value Property (Parameter Object)*

Applications should use the Value property to set or return parameter values with Parameter objects. The property holds a Variant which can assume any of the allowed data types in Table 5-40. ADO allows setting and returning Long binary data with the Value property.

## ADO Events

*Events* are notifications between applications, or between the operating system and applications, that some state of the application or system has changed. An example are windows messages in response to a mouse action; these result in mouse events. ADO has its own unique set of events, each of which has a section below that explains when it happens, what information it provides, and what ADO-using applications should do about the event.

### *BeginTransComplete Event*

This event handler is called after the associated operation on the Connection object finishes executing; BeginTransComplete is called after the BeginTrans operation. In Visual C++ multiple Connection objects can share the same event handling method. The method implementation should use the returned Connection object to determine which object (interface pointer) caused the event. If the Attributes property is set to adXactCommitRetaining or adXactAbortRetaining, a new transaction is started after committing or rolling back a transaction. A BeginTransComplete event handler routine should ignore all but the first transaction start event.

The event handler function has the following syntax:

```
BeginTransComplete(TransactionLevel, pError, adStatus, pConnection);
```

The event handler function has the following parameters:

*TransactionLevel*

This parameter is a Long which contains the new transaction level of the BeginTrans operation that caused this event.

*pError*

This parameter is an Error object which describes the error that occurred if the value of EventStatusEnum is adStatusErrorsOccurred; otherwise it is not set.

*adStatus*

This parameter is an EventStatusEnum status value, which when any of these methods is called is set to adStatusOK if the operation that caused the event was successful, or adStatusErrorsOccurred if the operation failed. The event handler can prevent subsequent notifications by setting this parameter to adStatusUnwantedEvent before the method returns.

*pConnection*

This parameter is the Connection object for which this event occurred.

## CommitTransComplete Event

This event handler is called after the associated operation on the Connection object finishes executing; CommitTransComplete is called after the CommitTrans operation. In Visual C++ multiple Connection objects can share the same event handling method. The method implementation should use the returned Connection object to determine which object (interface pointer) caused the event. If the Attributes property is set to adXactCommitRetaining or adXactAbortRetaining, a new transaction is started after committing or rolling back a transaction.

The event handler function has the following syntax:

```
CommitTransComplete(pError, adStatus, pConnection);
```

The event handler function has the following parameters:

*pError*

This parameter is an Error object which describes the error that occurred if the value of EventStatusEnum is adStatusErrorsOccurred; otherwise it is not set.

*adStatus*

This parameter is an EventStatusEnum status value which is set to adStatusOK if the operation that caused the event was successful, or adStatusErrorsOccurred if the operation failed. In RollbackTransComplete, an application can prevent subsequent notifications by setting this parameter to adStatusUnwantedEvent before the method returns.

*pConnection*

This parameter is the Connection object for which this event occurred.

## ConnectComplete Event

This event handler is called after a connection starts. The Disconnect event is called after a connection ends.

The event handler function has the following syntax:

```
ConnectComplete(pError, adStatus, pConnection);
```

The event handler function has the following parameters:

*pError*
: This parameter is an Error object which describes the error that occurred if the value of *adStatus* is adStatusErrorsOccurred; otherwise it is not set.

*adStatus*
: This parameter is an EventStatusEnum status value which is set to adStatusOK if the operation that caused the event was successful, or adStatusErrorsOccurred if the operation failed. When ConnectComplete is called, this parameter is set to adStatusCancel if a WillConnect method has requested cancellation of the pending connection. Before ConnectComplete returns, an application can set this parameter to adStatusUnwantedEvent to prevent subsequent notifications.

*pConnection*
: This parameter is the Connection object for which this event applies.

## Disconnect Event

This event handler is called after a connection ends. The ConnectComplete event handler is called after a connection starts.

The event handler function has the following syntax:

```
Disconnect(pError, adStatus, pConnection);
```

The event handler function has the following parameters:

*pError*
: This parameter is an Error object which describes the error that occurred if the value of *adStatus* is adStatusErrorsOccurred; otherwise it is not set.

*adStatus*
: This parameter is an EventStatusEnum status value which is set to adStatusOK if the operation that caused the event was successful, or adStatusErrorsOccurred if the operation failed. Before Disconnect returns, an application can set this parameter to adStatusUnwantedEvent to prevent subsequent notifications.

*pConnection*
: This parameter is the Connection object for which this event applies.

## EndOfRecordset Event

This event handler is called when there is an attempt to move to a row past the end of the Recordset. An EndOfRecordset event may also occur if the Recordset.MoveNext operation fails for other reasons. This event handler is called when the application attempts to move past the end of the records in the *pRecordset* parameter, perhaps as a result of calling MoveNext. However, while in this event handler the application could retrieve more records from a database and append them to the end of *pRecordset*. In that case, the event handler implementation would set *fMoreData* to VARIANT_TRUE, and return from EndOfRecordset. Then the application could safely call MoveNext again to access the newly retrieved records.

The event handler function has the following syntax:

```
EndOfRecordset(fMoreData, adStatus, pRecordset);
```

The event handler function has the following parameters:

*fMoreData*
: This parameter is a VARIANT_BOOL flag which makes it possible to append new records to *pRecordset* while processing this event. Before EndOfRecordset returns, the implementation should add the new data, then set this parameter to True to indicate that there is a new end to the Recordset.

*adStatus*
: This parameter is an EventStatusEnum status value which is set to adStatusOK if the operation that caused the event was successful. It is set to adStatusCantDeny if this method cannot request cancellation of the operation that caused this event. Before EndOfRecordset returns, an application can set this parameter to adStatusUnwantedEvent to prevent subsequent notifications.

*pRecordset*
: This parameter is the Recordset object for which this event occurred.

## ExecuteComplete Event

This event handler is called after a command has finished executing. An ExecuteComplete event can occur due to Connection.Execute, Command.Execute, Recordset.Open, or Recordset.NextRecordset.

The event handler function has the following syntax:

```
ExecuteComplete(RecordsAffected, pError, adStatus, pCommand, pRecordset,
pConnection);
```

The event handler function has the following parameters:

*RecordsAffected*
This parameter is a Long containing the number of records affected by the command.

*pError*
This parameter is an Error object which describes the error that occurred if the value of adStatus is adStatusErrorsOccurred; otherwise it is not set.

*adStatus*
This parameter is an EventStatusEnum status value which is set to adStatusOK if the operation that caused the event was successful, or adStatusErrorsOccurred if the operation failed. Before this method returns, an application can set this parameter to adStatusUnwantedEvent to prevent subsequent notifications.

*pCommand*
This parameter is the Command object that was executed. If the execution was not via a Command object, then this parameter is empty.

*pRecordset*
This parameter is a Recordset object containing the result of the execution, which may be empty.

*pConnection*
This parameter is a Connection object on which the command was executed.

## FetchComplete Event

This event handler is called after all the records in a lengthy asynchronous operation have been retrieved (fetched) into the Recordset. It is normally used to dismiss a visual progress indicator for the operation.

The event handler function has the following syntax:

```
FetchComplete(pError, adStatus, pRecordset);
```

The event handler function has the following parameters:

*pError*
This parameter is an Error object which describes the error that occurred if the value of *adStatus* is adStatusErrorsOccurred; otherwise it is not set.

*adStatus*
This parameter is an EventStatusEnum status value which is set to adStatusOK if the operation that caused the event was successful, or adStatusErrorsOccurred if the operation failed. Before this method returns, an application can set this parameter to adStatusUnwantedEvent to prevent subsequent notifications.

*pRecordset*

This parameter is a Recordset object containing the result of the fetch operation, which may be empty.

## FetchProgress Event

This event handler is called periodically during a lengthy asynchronous operation to report how many rows have currently been retrieved (fetched) into the current Recordset. Its normal use is to update a progress bar or other visual display to maintain a user comfort level during the lengthy operation to prevent their aborting it.

The event handler function has the following syntax:

```
FetchProgress(Progress, MaxProgress, pRecordset);
```

The event handler function has the following parameters:

*Progress*

This parameter is a Long containing the number of records that have currently been retrieved.

*MaxProgress*

This parameter is a Long containing the maximum number of records expected to be retrieved.

*pRecordset*

This parameter is a Recordset object for which the records are being retrieved.

## FieldChangeComplete Event

This event handler is called after the value of one or more Field objects has changed. A FieldChangeComplete event can occur due to the following Recordset operations: calls to Value and Update with field and value array parameters.

The event handler function has the following syntax:

```
FieldChangeComplete(cFields, Fields, pError, adStatus, pRecordset);
```

The event handler function has the following parameters:

*cFields*

This parameter is a Long which is the number of Field objects in *Fields*.

*Fields*

This parameter is an array of Variants which contains Field objects with pending changes.

*pError*

This parameter is an Error object which describes the error that occurred if the value of *adStatus* is adStatusErrorsOccurred; otherwise it is not set.

*adStatus*

This parameter is an EventStatusEnum status value which is set to adStatusOK if the operation that caused the event was successful, or adStatusErrorsOccurred if the operation failed. Before FieldChangeComplete returns, an application can set this parameter to adStatusUnwantedEvent to prevent subsequent notifications.

*pRecordset*

This parameter is a Recordset object for which this event occurred.

## InfoMessage Event

This event handler is called whenever a ConnectionEvent operation completes successfully and additional information is returned by an OLE DB provider.

The event handler function has the following syntax:

```
InfoMessage(pError, adStatus, pConnection);
```

The event handler function has the following parameters:

*pError*

This parameter is an Error object which describes the ADO error that occurred if the value of *adStatus* is adStatusErrorsOccurred; otherwise it is not set. Multiple OLE DB provider warnings can be returned, which can be found by enumerating the Errors collection.

*adStatus*

This parameter is an EventStatusEnum status value which is set to adStatusOK if the operation that caused the event was successful, or adStatusErrorsOccurred if the operation failed. Before this method returns, an application can set this parameter to adStatusUnwantedEvent to prevent subsequent notifications.

*pConnection*

This parameter is a Connection object on which the command was executed.

## MoveComplete Event

The MoveComplete method is called after the current position in the Recordset changes. A MoveComplete event can occur due to the following Recordset method calls (depending on whether they cause the position to change): Open, Move, MoveFirst, MoveLast, MoveNext, MovePrevious, Bookmark, AddNew, Delete, Requery, and Resync.

The event handler function has the following syntax:

```
MoveComplete(adReason, pError, adStatus, pRecordset);
```

The event handler function has the following parameters:

*adReason*
: This parameter is an EventReasonEnum value which specifies the reason for this event. Its value can be adRsnMoveFirst, adRsnMoveLast, adRsnMoveNext, adRsnMovePrevious, adRsnMove, or adRsnRequery. Each such enumeration value corresponds to the name of the method which caused the event to fire (i.e., a value of adRsnMoveLast means that a call was made to MoveLast, resulting in a position change that fired the event).

*pError*
: This parameter is an Error object which describes the error that occurred if the value of *adStatus* is adStatusErrorsOccurred; otherwise it is not set.

*adStatus*
: This parameter is an EventStatusEnum status value which is set to adStatusOK if the operation that caused the event was successful, or adStatusErrorsOccurred if the operation failed. Before MoveComplete returns, an application can set this parameter to adStatusUnwantedEvent to prevent subsequent notifications.

*pRecordset*
: This parameter is a Recordset object for which this event occurred.

## OnError Event

This method is called whenever an error occurs during an ADO object operation (this is different from the errors that are put in the Errors collection; those come from the OLE DB provider itself).

The event handler function has the following syntax:

```
onError(SCode, Description, Source, CancelDisplay);
```

The event handler function has the following parameters:

*SCode*
: This parameter is an integer which contains the status code (HRESULT) of the error.

*Description*
: This parameter is a String which contains a description of the error.

*Source*
: This parameter is a String which contains the SQL query or command that caused the error.

*CancelDisplay*
: This parameter is a Boolean which if set to True prevents the error from being displayed in a dialog box (useful for remote server applications where there is no one to see and dismiss the dialog box).

## OnReadyStateChange Event

This event handler is called whenever the value of the ReadyState property changes. The ReadyState property reflects the progress of an RDS.DataControl object as it asynchronously fetches data into its Recordset object. Use the onReadyStateChange event handler to monitor changes in the ReadyState property whenever they occur, rather than periodically checking the property's value.

The event handler function has the following syntax:

**onReadyStateChange();**

The event handler function has no parameter.

## RecordChangeComplete Event

This event handler is called after one or more records change. A RecordChangeComplete event can occur due to the following Recordset operations: Update, Delete, CancelUpdate, AddNew, UpdateBatch, and CancelBatch (depending on whether they actually change one or more records).

The event handler function has the following syntax:

**RecordChangeComplete(***adReason*, *cRecords*, *pError*, *adStatus*, *pRecordset***);**

The event handler function has the following parameters:

*adReason*
: This parameter is an EventReasonEnum value which specifies the reason for this event. Its value can be adRsnAddNew, adRsnDelete, adRsnUpdate, adRsnUndoUpdate, adRsnUndoAddNew, adRsnUndoDelete, or adRsnFirstChange, with the value of the enumeration giving the name of the method that fired the event (i.e., adRsnDelete means that a Delete method call caused the event to fire).

*cRecords*
: This parameter is a Long which is the number of records changing (affected).

*pError*
: This parameter is an Error object which describes the error that occurred if the value of *adStatus* is adStatusErrorsOccurred; otherwise it is not set.

*adStatus*
: This parameter is an EventStatusEnum status value which is set to adStatusOK if the operation that caused the event was successful, or adStatusErrorsOccurred if the operation failed. Before RecordChangeComplete returns, an application can set this parameter to adStatusUnwantedEvent to prevent subsequent notifications.

*pRecordset*
This parameter is a Recordset object containing the result of the change.

## RecordsetChangeComplete Event

This event handler is called after the Recordset has changed. A RecordsetChangeComplete event can occur due to the following Recordset operations: Requery, Resync, Close, Open, and Filter (depending on whether they change the Recordset).

The event handler function has the following syntax:

```
RecordsetChangeComplete(adReason, pError, adStatus, pRecordset);
```

The event handler function has the following parameters:

*adReason*
This parameter is an EventReasonEnum value that specifies the reason for this event. Its value can be adRsnReQuery, adRsnReSynch, adRsnClose, or adRsnOpen, with the name of the enumeration giving the name of the method which fired the event (i.e., adRsnClose means that the Close method call fired the current event).

*pError*
This parameter is an Error object which describes the error that occurred if the value of *adStatus* is adStatusErrorsOccurred; otherwise it is not set.

*adStatus*
This parameter is an EventStatusEnum status value which is set to adStatusOK if the operation that caused the event was successful, adStatusErrorsOccurred if the operation failed, or adStatusCancel if the operation associated with the previously accepted WillChangeRecordset event has been canceled. Before RecordsetChangeComplete returns, an application can set this parameter to adStatusUnwantedEvent to prevent subsequent notifications.

*pRecordset*
This parameter is a Recordset object for which this event occurred.

## RollbackTransComplete Event

This event handler will be called after the associated operation on the Connection object finishes executing. RollbackTransComplete is called after the RollbackTrans operation. In Visual C++ multiple Connections can share the same event handling method. The event handler uses the returned Connection object to determine which object caused the event. If the Attributes property is set to adXactCommitRetaining or adXactAbortRetaining, a new transaction is started after committing or rolling back a transaction.

The event handler function has the following syntax:

```
RollbackTransComplete(pError, adStatus, pConnection);
```

The event handler function has the following parameters:

*pError*
: This parameter is an Error object which describes the error that occurred if the value of *EventStatusEnum* is adStatusErrorsOccurred; otherwise it is not set.

*adStatus*
: This parameter is an EventStatusEnum status value which is set to adStatusOK if the operation that caused the event was successful, or adStatusErrorsOccurred if the operation failed. In RollbackTransComplete, an application can prevent subsequent notifications by setting this parameter to adStatusUnwantedEvent before the method returns.

*pConnection*
: This parameter is the Connection object for which this event occurred.

## WillChangeField Event

This event handler is called before a pending operation changes the value of one or more Field objects in the Recordset. A WillChangeField event can occur due to the following Recordset operations: calls to Value and Update with field and value array parameters.

The event handler function has the following syntax:

```
WillChangeField(cFields, Fields, adStatus, pRecordset);
```

The event handler function has the following parameters:

*cFields*
: This parameter is a Long which is the number of Field objects in *Fields*.

*Fields*
: This parameter is an array of Variants which contains Field objects with pending changes.

*adStatus*
: This parameter is an EventStatusEnum status value which is set to adStatusOK if the operation that caused the event was successful. It is set to adStatusCantDeny if this method cannot request cancellation of the pending operation. Before WillChangeField returns, an application can set this parameter to adStatusCancel to request cancellation of the pending operation.

*pRecordset*
: This parameter is a Recordset object for which this event occurred.

## WillChangeRecord Event

This event handler is called before one or more records (rows) in the Recordset change. A WillChangeRecord event can occur due to the following Recordset operations: Update, Delete, CancelUpdate, AddNew, UpdateBatch, and CancelBatch (depending on whether they actually change one or more records). During the WillChangeRecord event, the Recordset Filter property is set to adFilterAffectedRecords. It is illegal to change this property while processing the event.

The event handler function has the following syntax:

```
WillChangeRecord(adReason, cRecords, adStatus, pRecordset);
```

The event handler function has the following parameters:

*adReason*
: This parameter is an EventReasonEnum value which specifies the reason for this event. Its value can be adRsnAddNew, adRsnDelete, adRsnUpdate, adRsnUndoUpdate, adRsnUndoAddNew, adRsnUndoDelete, or adRsnFirstChange, with the value of the enumeration giving the name of the method that fired the event (i.e., adRsnDelete means that a Delete method call caused the event to fire).

*cRecords*
: This parameter is a Long which is the number of records changing (affected).

*adStatus*
: This parameter is an EventStatusEnum status value which is set to adStatusOK if the operation that caused the event was successful. It is set to adStatusCantDeny if this method cannot request cancellation of the pending operation. Before WillChangeRecord returns, an application can set this parameter to adStatusCancel to request cancellation of the operation that caused this event.

*pRecordset*
: This parameter is a Recordset object for which this event occurred.

## WillChangeRecordset Event

This event handler is called before a pending operation changes the Recordset. A WillChangeRecordset event can occur due to the following Recordset operations: Requery, Resync, Close, Open, and Filter (depending on whether they change the Recordset).

The event handler function has the following syntax:

```
WillChangeRecordset(adReason, adStatus, pRecordset);
```

The event handler function has the following parameters:

*adReason*

This parameter is an EventReasonEnum value that specifies the reason for this event. Its value can be adRsnReQuery, adRsnReSynch, adRsnClose, or adRsnOpen, with the name of the enumeration giving the name of the method which fired the event (i.e., adRsnClose means that the Close method call fired the current event).

*adStatus*

This parameter is an EventStatusEnum status value which is set to adStatusOK if the operation that caused the event was successful. It is set to adStatusCantDeny if this method cannot request cancellation of the pending operation. Before WillChangeRecordset returns, an application can set this parameter to adStatusCancel to request cancellation of the pending operation. Before WillChangeRecordset returns, an application can set this parameter to adStatusUnwantedEvent to prevent subsequent notifications.

*pRecordset*

This parameter is a Recordset for which this event occurred.

## WillConnect Event

This event handler is called before a connection starts. The parameters to be used in the pending connection are supplied as input parameters and can be changed before the method returns. This event handler may return a request that the pending connection be canceled. When this method is called, the ConnectionString, UserID, Password, and Options parameters are set to the values established by the operation that caused this event. When this method is canceled, ConnectComplete will be called with its *adStatus* parameter set to adStatusErrorsOccurred.

The event handler function has the following syntax:

```
WillConnect(ConnectionString, UserID, Password, Options, adStatus,
pConnection);
```

The event handler function has the following parameters:

*ConnectionString*

This parameter is a String containing connection information for the pending connection.

*UserID*

This parameter is a String containing a user name for the pending connection.

*Password*

This parameter is a String containing a password for the pending connection.

*Options*
This parameter is a Long value that indicates how the provider should evaluate *ConnectionString*, using the CommandTypeEnum values.

*adStatus*
This parameter is an EventStatusEnum status value. When this event handler is called, this parameter is set to adStatusOK if the operation that caused the event was successful. This parameter is set to adStatusCantDeny if this method cannot request cancellation of the pending operation. Before this method returns, an application can set this parameter to adStatusUnwantedEvent to prevent subsequent notifications. Alternatively, an application can set this parameter to adStatusCancel to request the connection operation that caused cancellation of this notification.

*pConnection*
This parameter is the Connection object for which this event notification applies.

## WillExecute Event

This event handler is called just before a pending command executes on the current Connection object. The event gives the application an opportunity to examine and modify the pending execution parameters. This method may return a request that the pending command be canceled. A WillExecute event may occur due to Connection.Execute, Command.Execute, or Recordset.Open. The corresponding *pConnection*, *pCommand*, or *pRecordset* parameter will be set to the object causing the event and the remaining two will be set to Null.

The event handler function has the following syntax:

```
WillExecute(Source, CursorType, LockType, Options, adStatus, pCommand,
pRecordset, pConnection);
```

The event handler function has the following parameters:

*Source*
This parameter is a String which contains a SQL command or a stored procedure name.

*CursorType*
This parameter is a CursorTypeEnum which contains the type of cursor for the recordset that will be opened. This parameter cannot be changed if it is set to adOpenUnspecified when this method is called.

*LockType*
This parameter is a LockTypeEnum which contains the lock type for the recordset that will be opened. This parameter cannot be changed if it is set to adLockUnspecified when this method is called.

*Options*

This parameter is a Long value which contains settings that can be used to execute the command or open the recordset.

*adStatus*

This parameter is an EventStatusEnum status value which may be adStatusCantDeny or adStatusOK when this method is called. If it is adStatusCantDeny, this method may not request cancellation of the pending operation. Before this method returns, it can set this parameter to adStatusUnwantedEvent to prevent subsequent notifications, or adStatusCancel to request cancellation of the operation that caused this event.

*pCommand*

This parameter is the Command object for which this event notification applies.

*pRecordset*

This parameter is the Recordset object for which this event notification applies.

*pConnection*

This parameter is the Connection object for which this event notification applies.

## WillMove Event

The WillMove method is called before a pending operation changes the current position in the Recordset. A WillMove event can occur due to the following Recordset method calls (depending on whether they cause the position to change): Open, Move, MoveFirst, MoveLast, MoveNext, MovePrevious, Bookmark, AddNew, Delete, Requery, and Resync.

The event handler function has the following syntax:

```
WillMove(adReason, adStatus, pRecordset);
```

The event handler function has the following parameters:

*adReason*

This parameter is an EventReasonEnum value which specifies the reason for this event. Its value can be adRsnMoveFirst, adRsnMoveLast, adRsnMoveNext, adRsnMovePrevious, adRsnMove, or adRsnRequery. Each such enumeration value corresponds to the name of the method which caused the event to fire (i.e., a value of adRsnMoveLast means that a call was made to MoveLast, resulting in a position change that fired the event).

*adStatus*

This parameter is an EventStatusEnum status value which is set to adStatusOK if the operation that caused the event was successful. It is set to adStatusCantDeny if this method cannot request cancellation of the pending operation. Before WillMove returns, an application can set this parameter to adStatusCancel to request cancellation of the pending operation.

*pRecordset*

This parameter is a Recordset object for which this event occurred.

## Where We Go From Here

At this point, you're up to speed on COM, ATL, MFC, MTS, and ADO. With this alphabet soup under your belt, it is time to fire up Visual C++ and start doing some real programming! The next three chapters take you through MTS development in ATL and MFC, for both components and clients. After that come two more chapters that show you how to install and administer MTS components and clients, and how to deploy them on the Internet and WWW.

Chapter Six

# Creating ATL MTS Components

At this point, you understand how to use COM, ATL, MFC, MTS, and ADO. All these acronyms add up to the most powerful database technology the PC world has ever seen. Now it is time to do some actual programming and put all this information into practice. This chapter will provide you with a set of COM components written in ATL that utilize Microsoft Transaction Server to work with a SQL Server database for a fictitious online video store. In the process, you'll create two ATL MTS components, an ATL ActiveX control with MTS functionality, and an ATL ASP component with MTS features. (For those who prefer to work in MFC, Chapter 7 reproduces these projects in that development framework.) Chapter 8 then provides you with three projects that develop applications using these elements: one in ATL, one in MFC, and one in HTML and Active Server Pages. Chapter 9 then takes you through the steps to install the MTS components and configure them with MTS Explorer, and illustrates running the three applications.

## Uncle Wally's Gigabit Online Video Store and Clam Emporium

For purposes of this book, we'll create a fictional world in which many users of the Internet have access to broadband connections at the megabit or gigabit level, and a service industry has sprung up similar to the "mom and pop" video rental stores of the early 1980s, one which provides access to videos (actually DVDs) online rather than by renting physical tapes. The service exists in two portions: a storefront-based operation where customers come in and set up their accounts and perhaps order videos for later viewing, and an online operation where existing customers connect to the business's web site and order their videos directly online, using their account and password. The business uses MTS to ensure that customers' accounts don't conflict, that videos that are ordered are actually available, and that a given account has the available credit to purchase the video desired.

This arrangement uses four MTS-aware components: two MTS COM servers, one for handling customer accounts and one for handling videos in stock; an ASP COM server to deal with the actual mechanics of ordering online; and an ActiveX control to serve as the front end for the MTS and ASP COM elements, either in a storefront application or via an online HTML page. The storefront applications are compiled and do the same jobs as the ASP component (in fact, they call it just like an ASP page would!).

# Creating an MTS COM Component with ATL

Our first step will be to use ATL to create an MTS COM server that handles customer accounts for Wally's. The following sections take you through the user interface portions of creating the project in my well-received step-by-step system, then show you the code you need to write and an analysis using the line-by-line approach.

## Step-By-Step

Start Visual C++ 5.0 or 6.0. From the File menu, select New. The New dialog box opens; click on ATL COM AppWizard. Select an appropriate directory, then enter a project name of **ATLMTSWallysAccount**. Figure 6-1 shows how the New dialog should appear when you are done. Press OK to open the ATL COM AppWizard.

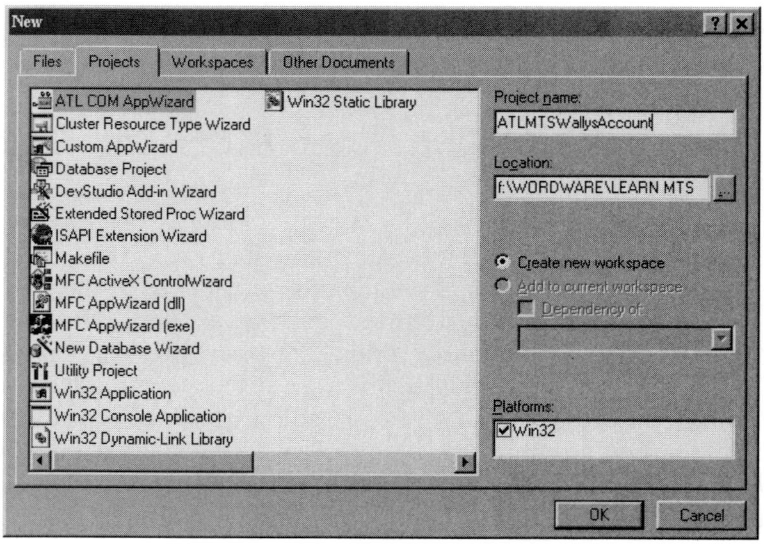


*Figure 6-1*
*The New dialog box creating the ATLMTSWallysAccount ATL project*

In the ATL AppWizard, select the DLL project, and make sure that the Support MFC, Merge Proxy/Stub Code, and Support MTS check boxes are checked; Figure 6-2 illustrates how the dialog should appear when you are done. Press Finish.

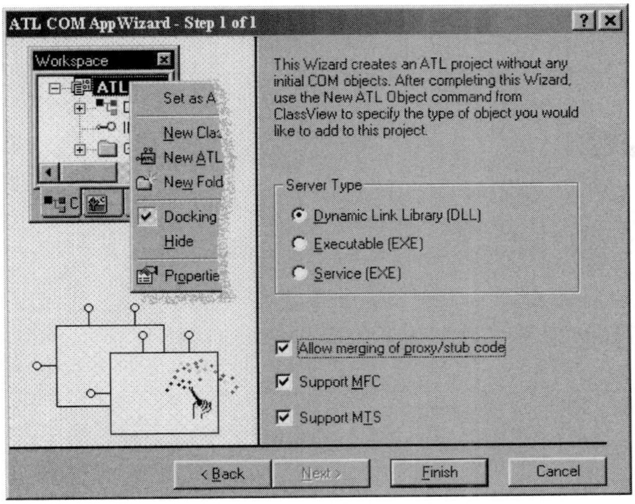


***Figure 6-2***
*Setting the MTS COM server project properties*

A confirmation dialog box appears as shown in Figure 6-3; press OK to create the ATL project.

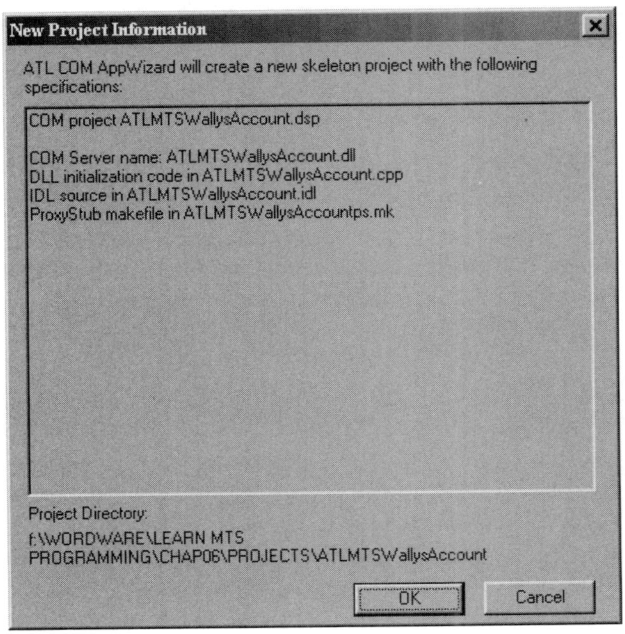


***Figure 6-3***
*The confirmation dialog*

From the Insert menu, select New ATL Object. The ATL Object Wizard dialog appears, as shown in Figure 6-4. Select the Objects entry in the left-hand list box, and the MS Transaction Server Component entry in the right-hand list box. Press Next to move to the settings pages of the wizard.

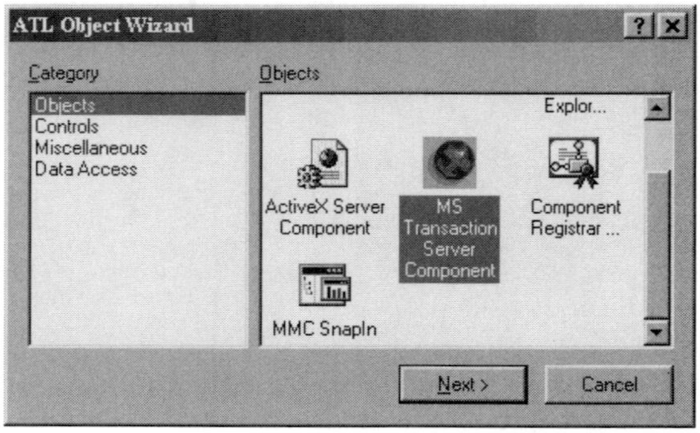


***Figure 6-4** Selecting an MS Transaction Server Component object in the ATL Object Wizard*

Select the Names tab of the next wizard dialog if it is not selected by default. As shown in Figure 6-5, enter AccountsHandler as the name of the control implementation class; the other boxes will fill in automatically. Accept the default values and select the MTS tab.

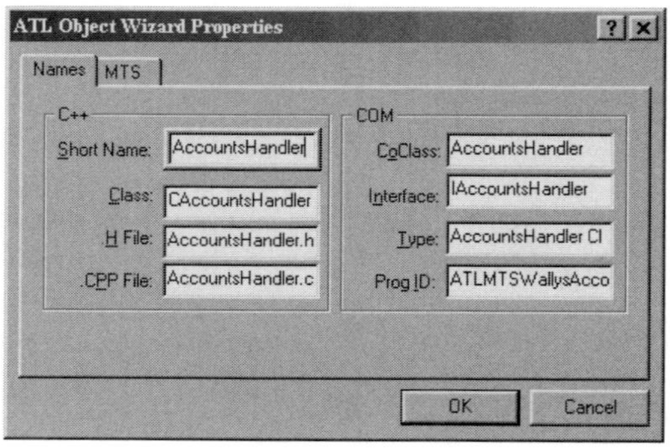


***Figure 6-5** Entering Name information in the ATL Object Wizard*

As illustrated in Figure 6-6, the MTS tab should have the Dual Interface radio button selected and the Support IObjectControl check box checked. Press OK to add the MTS Component Server object to your ATL project.

Move to the Project Explorer window and select the ClassView pane. The IAccountsHandler Interface is displayed; right-click on it to display the shortcut menu. Select the Add Property menu option.

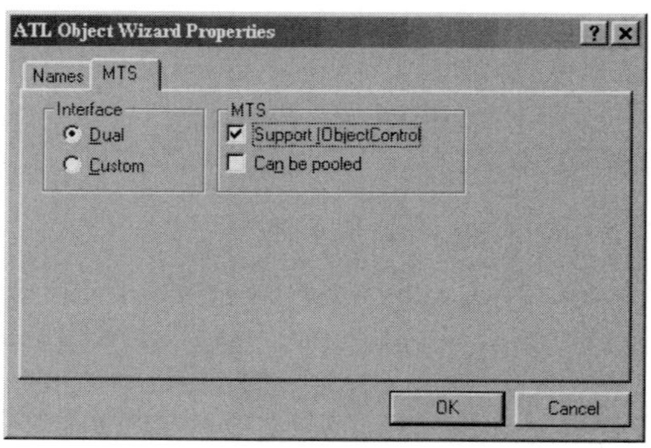


***Figure 6-6** Entering MTS information in the ATL Object Wizard*

The Add Property Wizard dialog box appears; select a Property Type of short. Give it a name of **TotalAccounts**, and check only the Get accessor function to create a read-only property. Figure 6-7 shows how the Add Property dialog should appear when you are done. Press OK to add the property to the MTS COM component.

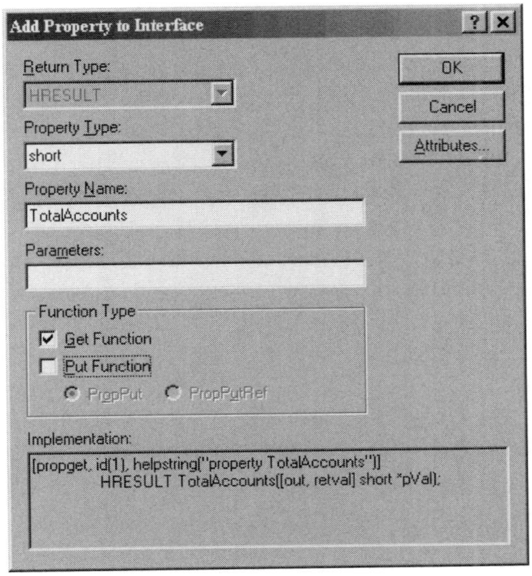


***Figure 6-7*** *Entering the TotalAccounts property with the ATL Add Property Wizard*

Again right-click on the IAccountsHandler Interface in the ClassView pane of the Project Explorer; this time select Add Method from the shortcut menu. The Add Method Wizard dialog box appears; give the method the name of **CreateDatabase**, with no parameters. Figure 6-8 shows how the Add Method dialog should appear when you are done. Press OK to add the method to the MTS COM component.

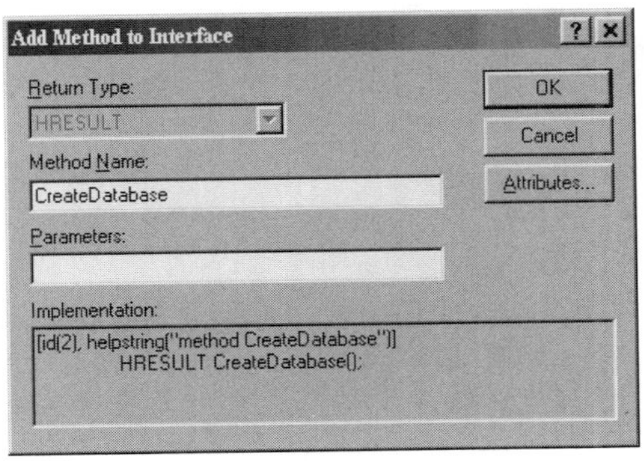


***Figure 6-8*** *Entering the CreateDatabase method with the ATL Add Method Wizard*

Again right-click on the IAccountsHandler Interface in the ClassView pane of the Project Explorer; again select Add Method from the shortcut menu. The Add Method Wizard dialog box appears; give the method the name of **CreateAccount**, with a parameter string of [in] BSTR bstrName, [in] BSTR bstrPassword, [in] long lTotalCredit, [in] long lCharges, [in] BOOL bInUse. Figure 6-9 shows how the Add Method dialog should appear when you are done. Press OK to add the method to the MTS COM component.

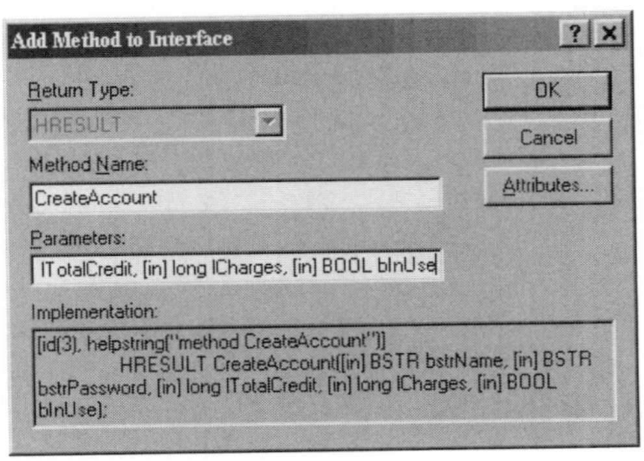


***Figure 6-9*** *Entering the CreateAccount method with the ATL Add Method Wizard*

Again right-click on the IAccountsHandler Interface in the ClassView pane of the Project Explorer; again select Add Method from the shortcut menu. The Add Method Wizard dialog box appears; give the method the name of **DeleteAccount**, with a parameter string of [in] BSTR bstrName, [in] BSTR bstrPassword. Figure 6-10 shows how the Add Method dialog should appear when you are done. Press OK to add the method to the MTS COM component.

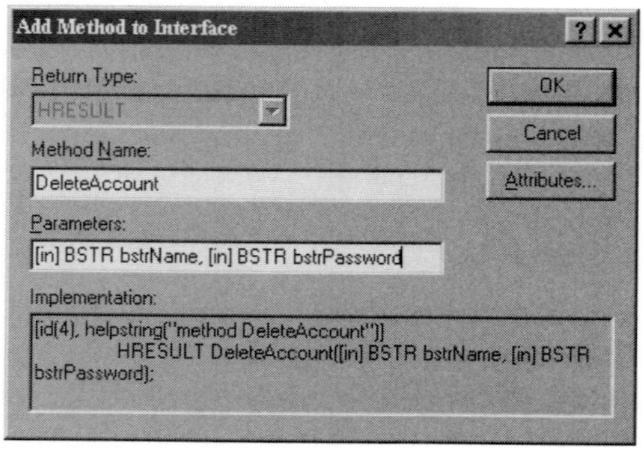


***Figure 6-10*** *Entering the DeleteAccount method with the ATL Add Method Wizard*

Again right-click on the IAccountsHandler Interface in the ClassView pane of the Project Explorer; again select Add Method from the shortcut menu. The Add Method Wizard dialog box appears; give the method the name of **UpdateAccountName**, with a parameter string of [in] BSTR bstrOldName, [in] BSTR bstrNewName. Figure 6-11 shows how the Add Method dialog should appear when you are done. Press OK to add the method to the MTS COM component.

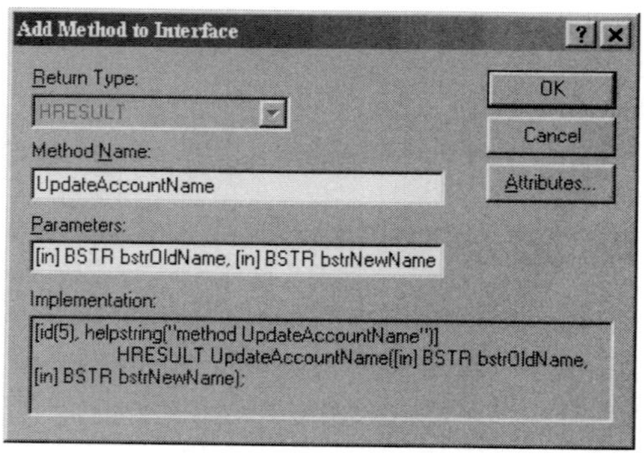


***Figure 6-11*** *Entering the Update-AccountName method with the ATL Add Method Wizard*

Again right-click on the IAccountsHandler Interface in the ClassView pane of the Project Explorer; again select Add Method from the shortcut menu. The Add Method Wizard dialog box appears; give the method the name of **UpdateAccountPassword**, with a parameter string of [in] BSTR bstrName, [in] BSTR bstrOldPassword, [in] BSTR bstrNewPassword. Figure 6-12 shows how the Add Method dialog should appear when you are done. Press OK to add the method to the MTS COM component.

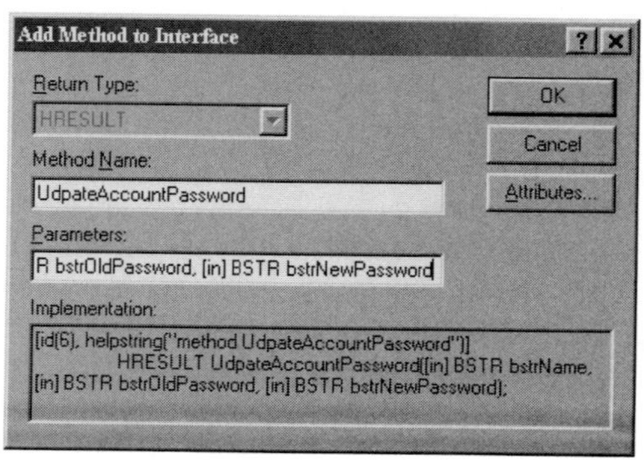


***Figure 6-12*** *Entering the Update-AccountPass-word method with the ATL Add Method Wizard*

Again right-click on the IAccountsHandler Interface in the ClassView pane of the Project Explorer; again select Add Method from the shortcut menu. The Add Method Wizard dialog box appears; give the method the name of **UpdateAccountCredit**, with a parameter string of [in] BSTR bstrName, [in] long lNewCredit. Figure 6-13 shows how the Add Method dialog should appear when you are done. Press OK to add the method to the MTS COM component.

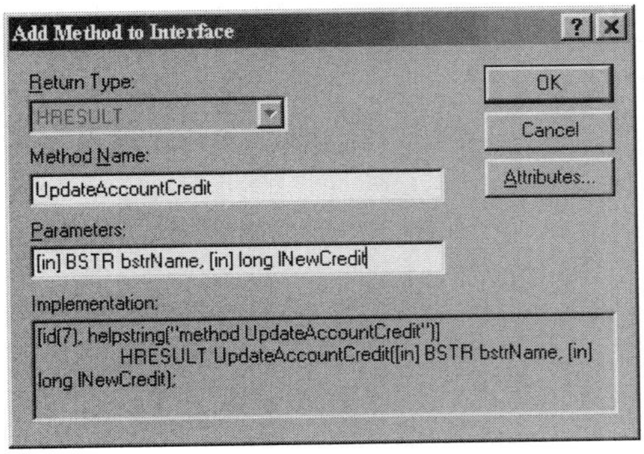


***Figure 6-13*** *Entering the UpdateAccountCredit method with the ATL Add Method Wizard*

Again right-click on the IAccountsHandler Interface in the ClassView pane of the Project Explorer; again select Add Method from the shortcut menu. The Add Method Wizard dialog box appears; give the method the name of **UpdateAccountCharges**, with a parameter string of [in] BSTR bstrName, [in] long lNewCharges. Figure 6-14 shows how the Add Method dialog should appear when you are done. Press OK to add the method to the MTS COM component.

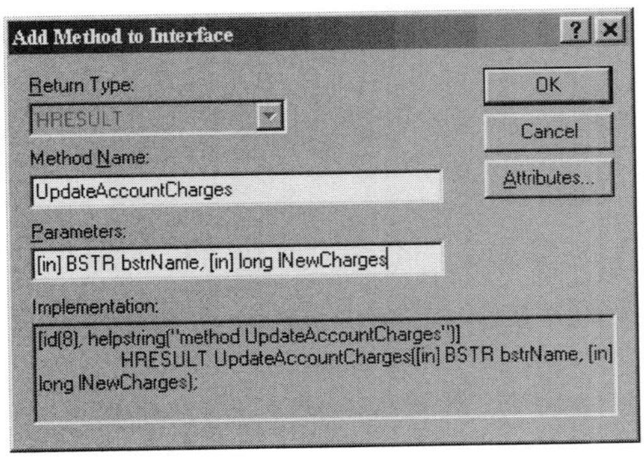


***Figure 6-14*** *Entering the UpdateAccountCharges method with the ATL Add Method Wizard*

Again right-click on the IAccountsHandler Interface in the ClassView pane of the Project Explorer; again select Add Method from the shortcut menu. The Add Method Wizard dialog box appears; give the method the name of **UpdateAccountInUse**, with a parameter string of [in] BSTR bstrName, [in] BOOL bNowInUse. Figure 6-15 shows how the Add Method dialog should appear when you are done. Press OK to add the method to the MTS COM component.

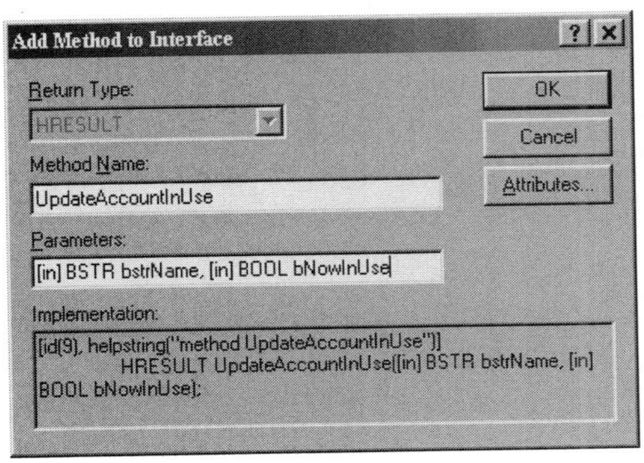


***Figure 6-15*** *Entering the UpdateAccountInUse method with the ATL Add Method Wizard*

Again right-click on the IAccountsHandler Interface in the ClassView pane of the Project Explorer and select Add Property. The Add Property Wizard dialog box appears; select a Property Type of BSTR. Give it a name of **AccountPassword**, enter a parameter string of [in] BSTR bstrName, and leave only the Get accessor function checked to create a read-only property. Figure 6-16 shows how the Add Property dialog should appear when you are done. Press OK to add the property to the MTS COM component.

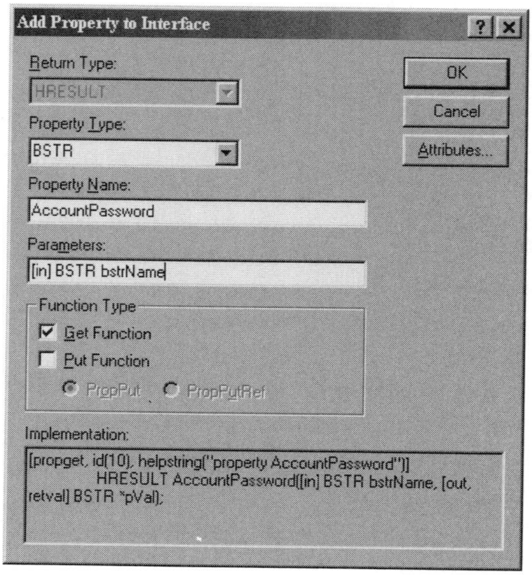


***Figure 6-16** Entering the AccountPassword property with the ATL Add Property Wizard*

Again right-click on the IAccountsHandler Interface in the ClassView pane of the Project Explorer and select Add Property. The Add Property Wizard dialog box appears; select a Property Type of long. Give it a name of **AccountCreditLimit**, enter a parameter string of [in] BSTR bstrName, and leave only the Get accessor function checked to create a read-only property. Figure 6-17 shows how the Add Property dialog should appear when you are done. Press OK to add the property to the MTS COM component.

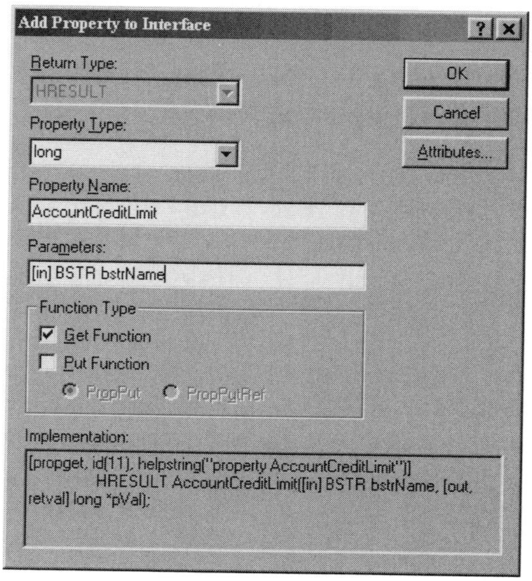


***Figure 6-17** Entering the AccountCreditLimit property with the ATL Add Property Wizard*

Again right-click on the IAccountsHandler Interface in the ClassView pane of the Project Explorer and select Add Property. The Add Property Wizard dialog box appears; select a Property Type of long. Give it a name of **AccountCurrentCharges**, enter a parameter string of [in] BSTR bstrName, and leave only the Get accessor function checked to create a read-only property. Figure 6-18 shows how the Add Property dialog should appear when you are done. Press OK to add the property to the MTS COM component.

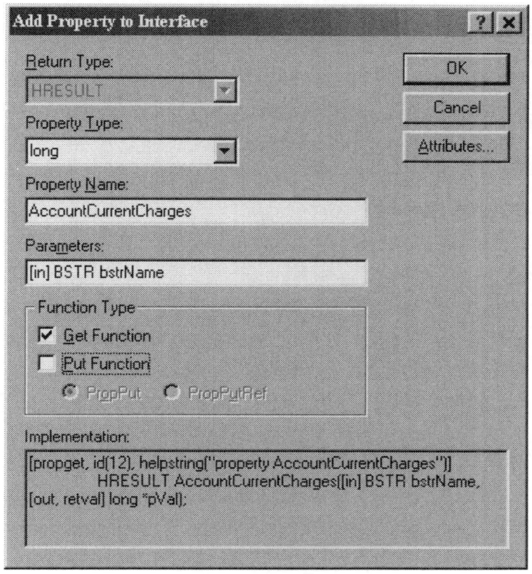


***Figure 6-18***
*Entering the AccountCurrentCharges property with the ATL Add Property Wizard*

Again right-click on the IAccountsHandler Interface in the ClassView pane of the Project Explorer and select Add Property. The Add Property Wizard dialog box appears; select a Property Type of BOOL. Give it a name of **AccountInUse**, enter a parameter string of [in] BSTR bstrName, and leave only the Get accessor function checked to create a read-only property. Figure 6-19 shows how the Add Property dialog should appear when you are done. Press OK to add the property to the MTS COM component.

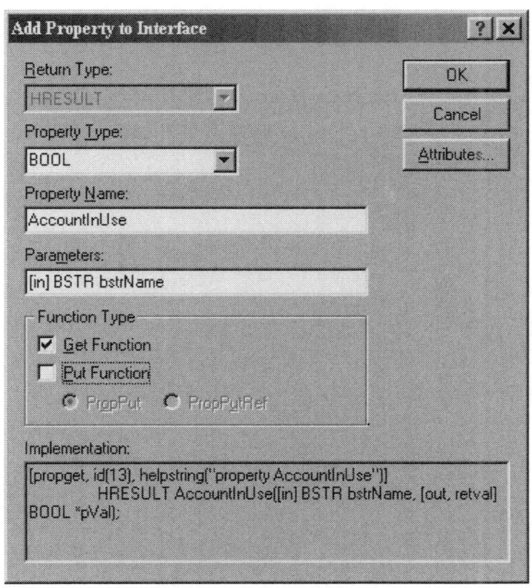


***Figure 6-19***
*Entering the AccountInUse property with the ATL Add Property Wizard*

## Line-By-Line

Next, you need to enter the program code to implement the MTS database functionality that this component implements. Bring up the ACCOUNTSHANDLER.CPP file in the text editor (unlike some ATL projects, we aren't creating a stateful component and thus don't need to modify the .H file). Scan through it and enter or change any bold line of source code in Listing 6-1. Save the project.

```
// AccountsHandler.cpp : Implementation of CAccountsHandler
#include "stdafx.h"
//*** take this out if you get linker errors!!! ***
#include <Initguid.h>
//*** ActiveX Data Objects GUIDs  ***
#include <adoid.h>
//*** ActiveX Data Objects Interfaces ***
#include <adoint.h>
#include "ATLMTSWallysAccount.h"
#include "AccountsHandler.h"

/////////////////////////////////////////////////////////////////////////////
// CAccountsHandler

HRESULT CAccountsHandler::Activate()
{
    HRESULT hr = GetObjectContext(&m_spObjectContext);
    if (SUCCEEDED(hr))
         return S_OK;
    return hr;
}

BOOL CAccountsHandler::CanBePooled()
{
    return FALSE;
}

void CAccountsHandler::Deactivate()
{
    m_spObjectContext.Release();
}


STDMETHODIMP CAccountsHandler::get_TotalAccounts(short *pVal)
{
    AFX_MANAGE_STATE(AfxGetStaticModuleState())

     USES_CONVERSION;
    // TODO: Add your implementation code here
```

```
     //*** define HRESULT holder and set it to OK ***
    HRESULT hr = S_OK;
    //*** Declare our ActiveX Data Object Connection holder and set it to NULL ***
    ADOConnection* adoCoConnection = NULL;
    //*** Declare our ActiveX Data Object Recordset holder and set it to NULL ***
    ADORecordset* adoAccountInfo = NULL;
    //*** Declare our ActiveX Data Object Fields holder and set it to NULL ***
    ADOFields* padoFields = NULL;
    //*** Declare our ActiveX Data Object Field holder and set it to NULL ***
    ADOField* padoField = NULL;
    //*** Attempt to get the ADO Connection IP ***
     hr = CoCreateInstance( CLSID_CADOConnection, NULL, CLSCTX_INPROC_SERVER,
                            IID_IADOConnection, (void **) adoCoConnection );
    //*** If can't get IP abort ***
    if (!SUCCEEDED(hr))
    {
        //*** Inform MTS of failure ***
        m_spObjectContext->SetAbort();
        //*** send back bad HRESULT ***
         return hr;
    }
    //*** Declare a CComBSTR to handle the Sequel Text ***
    CComBSTR ccbstrSQLText;
    //*** Give it the DSN for our samples database ***
    ccbstrSQLText = _T("FILEDSN=WallysAccounts");
    //*** Attempt to open the database ***
    hr = adoCoConnection->Open( ccbstrSQLText.Copy(), NULL, NULL, adCmdUnspecified);
    //*** If can't get database abort ***
    if (!SUCCEEDED(hr))
    {
        //*** Inform MTS of failure ***
        m_spObjectContext->SetAbort();
        //*** Kill the connection IP ***
        adoCoConnection->Release();
        //*** send back bad HRESULT ***
         return hr;
    }
    //*** Declare the wsprintf buffer ***
    TCHAR szSQLBuffer[512];
    wsprintf( szSQLBuffer,
     _T("SELECT TotalAccounts FROM Accounts WHERE AccountName = 'TotalAccounts'"));
    //*** Put it into the CComBSTR via overloaded = operator ***
    ccbstrSQLText = szSQLBuffer;
    //*** Declare a CComVariant to hold returned record count from ADO ***
    CComVariant vRecCount;
    //*** Clear the record count ***
    vRecCount.Clear();
```

```
    //*** Execute the sequel statement on the database ***
     hr = adoCoConnection->Execute( ccbstrSQLText.Copy(), &vRecCount, -1 ,
         &adoAccountInfo );
    //*** If can't reach database abort ***
    if (!SUCCEEDED(hr))
    {
        //*** Inform MTS of failure ***
        m_spObjectContext->SetAbort();
        //*** Kill the connection IP ***
        adoCoConnection->Release();
        //*** send back bad HRESULT ***
        return hr;
    }
    //*** Obtain the fields collection from the recordset ***
      hr = adoAccountInfo->get_Fields( &padoFields );
    //*** If can't reach database abort ***
    if (!SUCCEEDED(hr))
    {
        //*** Inform MTS of failure ***
        m_spObjectContext->SetAbort();
        //*** Kill the connection and recordset IP ***
       adoCoConnection->Release();
       adoAccountInfo->Release();
        //*** send back bad HRESULT ***
       return hr;
    }
    //*** Define a variant to obtain the total accounts field ***
    CComVariant vField = _T("TotalAccounts");
    //*** define a variant to hold the information ***
    CComVariant vAccounts;
    //*** Get the total accounts Field ***
    hr = padoFields->get_Item( vField , &padoField );
    //*** If can't reach database abort ***
    if (!SUCCEEDED(hr))
    {
        //*** Inform MTS of failure ***
        m_spObjectContext->SetAbort();
       //*** Kill the connection, recordset, and fields IP ***
       adoCoConnection->Release();
       adoAccountInfo->Release();
       padoFields->Release();
        //*** send back bad HRESULT ***
       return hr;
    }
    //*** Get the actual total accounts value ***
    hr = padoField->get_Value( &vAccounts );
    //*** If can't reach database abort ***
```

```
    if (!SUCCEEDED(hr))
    {
        //*** Inform MTS of failure ***
        m_spObjectContext->SetAbort();
        //*** Kill the connection, recordset, fields, and field IP ***
        adoCoConnection->Release();
        adoAccountInfo->Release();
        padoFields->Release();
        padoField->Release();
        //*** send back bad HRESULT ***
        return hr;
    }
      //*** return the value from the variant ***
      *pVal = vAccounts.iVal;
    //*** Tell MTS we're OK ***
    m_spObjectContext->SetComplete();
    //*** Kill the connection, recordset, fields, and field IP ***
    adoCoConnection->Release();
    adoAccountInfo->Release();
    padoFields->Release();
    padoField->Release();
    //*** Send back Good Transaction ***
    return S_OK;
}

STDMETHODIMP CAccountsHandler::CreateDatabase()
{
    AFX_MANAGE_STATE(AfxGetStaticModuleState())
      //*** define HRESULT holder and set it to OK ***
    HRESULT hr = S_OK;
    //*** Declare our ActiveX Data Object Connection holder and set it to NULL ***
    ADOConnection* adoCoConnection = NULL;
    //*** Declare our ActiveX Data Object Recordset holder and set it to NULL ***
    ADORecordset* adoAccountInfo = NULL;
    //*** Attempt to get the ADO Connection IP ***
      hr = CoCreateInstance( CLSID_CADOConnection, NULL, CLSCTX_INPROC_SERVER,
                             IID_IADOConnection, (void **) adoCoConnection );
    //*** If can't get IP abort ***
    if (!SUCCEEDED(hr))
    {
        //*** Inform MTS of failure ***
        m_spObjectContext->SetAbort();
        //*** send back bad HRESULT ***
          return hr;
    }
    //*** Declare a CComBSTR to handle the Sequel Text ***
    CComBSTR ccbstrSQLText;
```

```
    //*** Give it the DSN for our samples database ***
    ccbstrSQLText = _T("FILEDSN=WallysAccounts");
    //*** Attempt to open the database ***
    hr = adoCoConnection->Open( ccbstrSQLText.Copy(), NULL, NULL, adCmdUnspecified);
    //*** If can't get database abort ***
    if (!SUCCEEDED(hr))
    {
        //*** Inform MTS of failure ***
        m_spObjectContext->SetAbort();
        //*** Kill the connection IP ***
        adoCoConnection->Release();
        //*** send back bad HRESULT ***
         return hr;
    }
    ccbstrSQLText =
       _T("if not exists (Select name from sysobjects where name = 'Accounts')\n");
    ccbstrSQLText += _T("BEGIN\n");
    ccbstrSQLText += _T("CREATE TABLE Accounts (\n");
    ccbstrSQLText += _T("AccountName varchar(256) NULL ,\n");
    ccbstrSQLText += _T("AccountPassword varchar(256) NULL ,\n");
    ccbstrSQLText += _T("CreditLimit int NULL ,\n");
    ccbstrSQLText += _T("CurrentCharges int NULL ,\n");
    ccbstrSQLText += _T("InUse bit not NULL ,\n");
    ccbstrSQLText += _T("TotalAccounts int NULL ,\n");
    ccbstrSQLText += _T(")\n");
    ccbstrSQLText += _T("END\n");
    //*** Declare a CComVariant to hold returned record count from ADO ***
    CComVariant vRecCount;
    //*** Clear the record count ***
    vRecCount.Clear();
    //*** Execute the sequel statement on the database ***
      hr = adoCoConnection->Execute( ccbstrSQLText.Copy(), &vRecCount, -1 , NULL );
    //*** If can't reach database abort ***
    if (!SUCCEEDED(hr))
    {
        //*** Inform MTS of failure ***
        m_spObjectContext->SetAbort();
        //*** Kill the connection IP ***
        adoCoConnection->Release();
        //*** send back bad HRESULT ***
         return hr;
    }
    //*** Kill the connection, recordset, fields, and field IP ***
    adoCoConnection->Release();
    //*** Send back Good Transaction ***
    return S_OK;
}
```

```

STDMETHODIMP CAccountsHandler::CreateAccount(BSTR bstrName, BSTR bstrPassword,
              long lTotalCredit, long lCharges, BOOL bInUse)
{
  AFX_MANAGE_STATE(AfxGetStaticModuleState())
    //*** Get OLE2T Macro ***
    USES_CONVERSION;
  //*** only use this if you want to use Role-based security ***
  if (m_spObjectContext->IsSecurityEnabled())
  {
       //*** Define a CComBSTR to hold the Role Name
      CComBSTR ccbstrRoleID;
      //*** set it ***
      ccbstrRoleID = _T("WallysMgr");
      //*** Define a Result holder ***
      BOOL bResult;
      //*** make the call ***
      m_spObjectContext->IsCallerInRole( ccbstrRoleID.Copy(), &bResult );
      //*** if not in the role abort ***
      if (!bResult)
      {
         //*** Inform MTS of failure ***
         m_spObjectContext->SetAbort();
         //*** send back bad HRESULT ***
          return E_FAIL;
      }
  }
    //*** define HRESULT holder and set it to OK ***
  HRESULT hr = S_OK;
  //*** Declare our ActiveX Data Object Connection holder and set it to NULL ***
  ADOConnection* adoCoConnection = NULL;
  //*** Declare our ActiveX Data Object Recordset holder and set it to NULL ***
  ADORecordset* adoAccountInfo = NULL;
  //*** Attempt to get the ADO Connection IP ***
    hr = CoCreateInstance( CLSID_CADOConnection, NULL, CLSCTX_INPROC_SERVER,
                           IID_IADOConnection, (void **) adoCoConnection );
  //*** If can't get IP abort ***
  if (!SUCCEEDED(hr))
  {
     //*** Inform MTS of failure ***
     m_spObjectContext->SetAbort();
     //*** send back bad HRESULT ***
      return hr;
  }
  //*** Declare a CComBSTR to handle the Sequel Text ***
  CComBSTR ccbstrSQLText;
  //*** Give it the DSN for our samples database ***
```

```
ccbstrSQLText = _T("FILEDSN=WallysAccounts");
//*** Attempt to open the database ***
hr = adoCoConnection->Open( ccbstrSQLText.Copy(), NULL, NULL, adCmdUnspecified);
//*** If can't get database abort ***
if (!SUCCEEDED(hr))
{
    //*** Inform MTS of failure ***
    m_spObjectContext->SetAbort();
    //*** Kill the connection IP ***
    adoCoConnection->Release();
    //*** send back bad HRESULT ***
     return hr;
}
//*** Declare the wsprintf buffer ***
TCHAR szSQLBuffer[512];
//***Declare CComBSTR for name and password ***
CComBSTR ccbstrName( bstrName );
CComBSTR ccbstrPassword( bstrPassword );
//*** Define TotalAccounts holder
short sTotalAccounts;
//*** call internal method outside COM ***
get_TotalAccounts( &sTotalAccounts );
//*** increment the value ***
sTotalAccounts++;
//*** Create Sequel Statement ***
wsprintf( szSQLBuffer, _T("INSERT INTO Accounts VALUES('%s','%s',%ld,%ld,%b,%d)"),
               OLE2T(ccbstrName.Copy()), OLE2T(ccbstrPassword.Copy()), lTotalCredit,
                     lCharges, bInUse, sTotalAccounts);
//*** Put the buffer in the CComBSTR via overloaded = operator ***
ccbstrSQLText = szSQLBuffer;
//*** Declare a CComVariant to hold returned record count from ADO ***
CComVariant vRecCount;
//*** Clear the record count ***
vRecCount.Clear();
//*** Execute the sequel statement on the database ***
  hr = adoCoConnection->Execute( ccbstrSQLText.Copy(), &vRecCount, -1 , NULL );
//*** If can't reach database abort ***
if (!SUCCEEDED(hr))
{
    //*** Inform MTS of failure ***
    m_spObjectContext->SetAbort();
    //*** Kill the connection IP ***
    adoCoConnection->Release();
    //*** send back bad HRESULT ***
     return hr;
}
//*** Create Sequel Statement ***
```

```
   wsprintf( szSQLBuffer,
    _T("UPDATE Accounts SET TotalAccounts = %d WHERE AccountName = 'TotalAccounts'"),
       sTotalAccounts );
   //*** Put the buffer in the CComBSTR via overloaded = operator ***
   ccbstrSQLText = szSQLBuffer;
   //*** Clear the record count ***
   vRecCount.Clear();
   //*** Execute the sequel statement on the database ***
     hr = adoCoConnection->Execute( ccbstrSQLText.Copy(), &vRecCount, -1 , NULL );
   //*** If can't reach database abort ***
   if (!SUCCEEDED(hr))
   {
       //*** Inform MTS of failure ***
       m_spObjectContext->SetAbort();
      //*** Kill the connection IP ***
      adoCoConnection->Release();
       //*** send back bad HRESULT ***
      return hr;
   }
   //*** if no records updated then account doesn't exist so signal error ***
   if (vRecCount.lVal == 0)
   {
       //*** Inform MTS of failure ***
       m_spObjectContext->SetAbort();
       //*** Kill the connection IP ***
       adoCoConnection->Release();
       //*** send back bad HRESULT ***
       return E_FAIL;
   }
   //*** Tell MTS we're OK ***
   m_spObjectContext->SetComplete();
   //*** Kill the connection ***
   adoCoConnection->Release();
   //*** Send back Good Transaction ***
   return S_OK;
}

STDMETHODIMP CAccountsHandler::DeleteAccount(BSTR bstrName, BSTR bstrPassword)
{
   AFX_MANAGE_STATE(AfxGetStaticModuleState())
     USES_CONVERSION;
   //*** only use this if you want to use Role-based security ***
   if (m_spObjectContext->IsSecurityEnabled())
   {
         //*** Define a CComBSTR to hold the Role Name
        CComBSTR ccbstrRoleID;
        //*** set it ***
```

```
        ccbstrRoleID = _T("WallysMgr");
        //*** Define a Result holder ***
        BOOL bResult;
        //*** make the call ***
        m_spObjectContext->IsCallerInRole( ccbstrRoleID.Copy(), &bResult );
        //*** if not in the role abort ***
        if (!bResult)
        {
           //*** Inform MTS of failure ***
           m_spObjectContext->SetAbort();
           //*** send back bad HRESULT ***
             return E_FAIL;
        }
    }
      //*** define HRESULT holder and set it to OK ***
    HRESULT hr = S_OK;
    //*** Declare our ActiveX Data Object Connection holder and set it to NULL ***
    ADOConnection* adoCoConnection = NULL;
    //*** Declare our ActiveX Data Object Recordset holder and set it to NULL ***
    ADORecordset* adoAccountInfo = NULL;
    //*** Attempt to get the ADO Connection IP ***
      hr = CoCreateInstance( CLSID_CADOConnection, NULL, CLSCTX_INPROC_SERVER,
                             IID_IADOConnection, (void **) adoCoConnection );
    //*** If can't get IP abort ***
    if (!SUCCEEDED(hr))
    {
        //*** Inform MTS of failure ***
        m_spObjectContext->SetAbort();
        //*** send back bad HRESULT ***
         return hr;
    }
    //*** Declare a CComBSTR to handle the Sequel Text ***
    CComBSTR ccbstrSQLText;
    //*** Give it the DSN for our samples database ***
    ccbstrSQLText = _T("FILEDSN=WallysAccounts");
    //*** Attempt to open the database ***
    hr = adoCoConnection->Open( ccbstrSQLText.Copy(), NULL, NULL, adCmdUnspecified);
    //*** If can't get database abort ***
    if (!SUCCEEDED(hr))
    {
        //*** Inform MTS of failure ***
        m_spObjectContext->SetAbort();
        //*** Kill the connection IP ***
        adoCoConnection->Release();
        //*** send back bad HRESULT ***
         return hr;
    }
```

```
    //*** Declare the wsprintf buffer ***
    TCHAR szSQLBuffer[512];
    //***Declare CComBSTR for name  ***
    CComBSTR ccbstrName( bstrName );
    //*** Create Sequel Statement ***
    wsprintf( szSQLBuffer, _T("DELETE Accounts WHERE AccountName = '%s'"),
                OLE2T(ccbstrName.Copy()));
    //*** Put the buffer in the CComBSTR via overloaded = operator ***
    ccbstrSQLText = szSQLBuffer;
    //*** Declare a CComVariant to hold returned record count from ADO ***
    CComVariant vRecCount;
    //*** Clear the record count ***
    vRecCount.Clear();
    //*** Execute the sequel statement on the database ***
      hr = adoCoConnection->Execute( ccbstrSQLText.Copy(), &vRecCount, -1 , NULL );
    //*** If can't reach database abort ***
    if (!SUCCEEDED(hr))
    {
        //*** Inform MTS of failure ***
        m_spObjectContext->SetAbort();
        //*** Kill the connection IP ***
        adoCoConnection->Release();
        //*** send back bad HRESULT ***
          return hr;
    }
    //*** Define TotalAccounts holder
    short sTotalAccounts;
    //*** call internal method outside COM ***
    get_TotalAccounts( &sTotalAccounts );
    //*** increment the value ***
    sTotalAccounts–;
    //*** Create Sequel Statement ***
    wsprintf( szSQLBuffer,
       _T("UPDATE Accounts SET TotalAccounts = %d WHERE AccountName = 'TotalAccounts'"),
          sTotalAccounts);
    //*** Put the buffer in the CComBSTR via overloaded = operator ***
    ccbstrSQLText = szSQLBuffer;
    //*** Clear the record count ***
    vRecCount.Clear();
    //*** Execute the sequel statement on the database ***
      hr = adoCoConnection->Execute( ccbstrSQLText.Copy(), &vRecCount, -1 , NULL );
    //*** If can't reach database abort ***
    if (!SUCCEEDED(hr))
    {
        //*** Inform MTS of failure ***
        m_spObjectContext->SetAbort();
       //*** Kill the connection IP ***
```

```
      adoCoConnection->Release();
       //*** send back bad HRESULT ***
      return hr;
   }
   //*** if no records updated then account doesn't exist so signal error ***
   if (vRecCount.lVal == 0)
   {
       //*** Inform MTS of failure ***
       m_spObjectContext->SetAbort();
       //*** Kill the connection IP ***
       adoCoConnection->Release();
       //*** send back bad HRESULT ***
       return E_FAIL;
   }
   //*** Tell MTS we're OK ***
   m_spObjectContext->SetComplete();
   //*** Kill the connection ***
   adoCoConnection->Release();
   //*** Send back Good Transaction ***
   return S_OK;
}

STDMETHODIMP CAccountsHandler::UpdateAccountName(BSTR bstrOldName, BSTR bstrNewName)
{
   AFX_MANAGE_STATE(AfxGetStaticModuleState())
   // TODO: Add your implementation code here
     USES_CONVERSION;
   //*** only use this if you want to use Role-based security ***
   if (m_spObjectContext->IsSecurityEnabled())
   {
         //*** Define a CComBSTR to hold the Role Name
        CComBSTR ccbstrRoleID;
        //*** set it ***
        ccbstrRoleID = _T("WallysMgr");
        //*** Define a Result holder ***
        BOOL bResult;
        //*** make the call ***
        m_spObjectContext->IsCallerInRole( ccbstrRoleID.Copy(), &bResult );
        //*** if not in the role abort ***
        if (!bResult)
        {
           //*** Inform MTS of failure ***
           m_spObjectContext->SetAbort();
           //*** send back bad HRESULT ***
             return E_FAIL;
        }
   }
```

```
     //*** define HRESULT holder and set it to OK ***
    HRESULT hr = S_OK;
    //*** Declare our ActiveX Data Object Connection holder and set it to NULL ***
    ADOConnection* adoCoConnection = NULL;
    //*** Declare our ActiveX Data Object Recordset holder and set it to NULL ***
    ADORecordset* adoAccountInfo = NULL;
    //*** Attempt to get the ADO Connection IP ***
     hr = CoCreateInstance( CLSID_CADOConnection, NULL CLSCTX_INPROC_SERVER,
                            IID_IADOConnection, (void **) adoCoConnection );
    //*** If can't get IP abort ***
    if (!SUCCEEDED(hr))
    {
        //*** Inform MTS of failure ***
        m_spObjectContext->SetAbort();
        //*** send back bad HRESULT ***
         return hr;
    }
    //*** Declare a CComBSTR to handle the Sequel Text ***
    CComBSTR ccbstrSQLText;
    //*** Give it the DSN for our samples database ***
    ccbstrSQLText = _T("FILEDSN=WallysAccounts");
    //*** Attempt to open the database ***
    hr = adoCoConnection->Open( ccbstrSQLText.Copy(), NULL, NULL, adCmdUnspecified);
    //*** If can't get database abort ***
    if (!SUCCEEDED(hr))
    {
        //*** Inform MTS of failure ***
        m_spObjectContext->SetAbort();
        //*** Kill the connection IP ***
        adoCoConnection->Release();
        //*** send back bad HRESULT ***
        return hr;
    }
    //***Declare CComBSTR for names  ***
    CComBSTR ccbstrNewName( bstrNewName );
    CComBSTR ccbstrOldName( bstrOldName );
    //*** Declare the wsprintf buffer ***
    TCHAR szSQLBuffer[512];
    //*** Create Sequel Statement ***
    wsprintf( szSQLBuffer,
              _T("UPDATE Accounts SET AccountName = '%s' WHERE AccountName = '%s'"),
                             OLE2T(ccbstrNewName.Copy()),
                             OLE2T(ccbstrOldName.Copy()));
    //*** Put the buffer in the CComBSTR via overloaded = operator ***
    ccbstrSQLText = szSQLBuffer;
    //*** Declare a CComVariant to hold returned record count from ADO ***
    CComVariant vRecCount;
```

```
   //*** Clear the record count ***
   vRecCount.Clear();
   //*** Execute the sequel statement on the database ***
     hr = adoCoConnection->Execute( ccbstrSQLText.Copy(), &vRecCount, -1 , NULL );
   //*** If can't reach database abort ***
   if (!SUCCEEDED(hr))
   {
       //*** Inform MTS of failure ***
       m_spObjectContext->SetAbort();
      //*** Kill the connection IP ***
      adoCoConnection->Release();
       //*** send back bad HRESULT ***
      return hr;
   }
   //*** if no records updated then account doesn't exist so signal error ***
   if (vRecCount.lVal == 0)
   {
       //*** Inform MTS of failure ***
       m_spObjectContext->SetAbort();
       //*** Kill the connection IP ***
       adoCoConnection->Release();
       //*** send back bad HRESULT ***
       return E_FAIL;
   }
   //*** Tell MTS we're OK ***
   m_spObjectContext->SetComplete();
   //*** Kill the connection***
   adoCoConnection->Release();
   //*** Send back Good Transaction ***
   return S_OK;
}

STDMETHODIMP CAccountsHandler::UdpateAccountPassword(BSTR bstrName,
             BSTR bstrOldPassword, BSTR bstrNewPassword)
{
   AFX_MANAGE_STATE(AfxGetStaticModuleState())

   // TODO: Add your implementation code here
     USES_CONVERSION;
   //*** only use this if you want to use Role-based security ***
   if (m_spObjectContext->IsSecurityEnabled())
   {
         //*** Define a CComBSTR to hold the Role Name
        CComBSTR ccbstrRoleID;
        //*** set it ***
        ccbstrRoleID = _T("WallysMgr");
        //*** Define a Result holder ***
```

```
        BOOL bResult;
        //*** make the call ***
        m_spObjectContext->IsCallerInRole( ccbstrRoleID.Copy(), &bResult );
        //*** if not in the role abort ***
        if (!bResult)
        {
           //*** Inform MTS of failure ***
           m_spObjectContext->SetAbort();
           //*** send back bad HRESULT ***
            return E_FAIL;
        }
   }
     //*** define HRESULT holder and set it to OK ***
   HRESULT hr = S_OK;
   //*** Declare our ActiveX Data Object Connection holder and set it to NULL ***
   ADOConnection* adoCoConnection = NULL;
   //*** Declare our ActiveX Data Object Recordset holder and set it to NULL ***
   ADORecordset* adoAccountInfo = NULL;
   //*** Attempt to get the ADO Connection IP ***
     hr = CoCreateInstance( CLSID_CADOConnection, NULL, CLSCTX_INPROC_SERVER,
                            IID_IADOConnection, (void **) adoCoConnection );
   //*** If can't get IP abort ***
   if (!SUCCEEDED(hr))
   {
       //*** Inform MTS of failure ***
       m_spObjectContext->SetAbort();
       //*** send back bad HRESULT ***
         return hr;
   }
   //*** Declare a CComBSTR to handle the Sequel Text ***
   CComBSTR ccbstrSQLText;
   //*** Give it the DSN for our samples database ***
   ccbstrSQLText = _T("FILEDSN=WallysAccounts");
   //*** Attempt to open the database ***
   hr = adoCoConnection->Open( ccbstrSQLText.Copy(), NULL, NULL, adCmdUnspecified);
   //*** If can't get database abort ***
   if (!SUCCEEDED(hr))
   {
       //*** Inform MTS of failure ***
       m_spObjectContext->SetAbort();
       //*** Kill the connection IP ***
       adoCoConnection->Release();
       //*** send back bad HRESULT ***
       return hr;
   }
   //***Declare CComBSTR for names  ***
   CComBSTR ccbstrName( bstrName );
```

```
   CComBSTR ccbstrNewPassword( bstrNewPassword );
   CComBSTR ccbstrOldPassword( bstrOldPassword );
   //*** Declare the wsprintf buffer ***
   TCHAR szSQLBuffer[512];
   //*** Create Sequel Statement ***
   wsprintf( szSQLBuffer,
     _T("UPDATE Accounts SET AccountPassword = '%s' WHERE AccountName = '%s' AND
        AccountPassword = '%s'"), OLE2T(ccbstrNewPassword.Copy()),
        OLE2T(ccbstrName.Copy()), OLE2T(ccbstrOldPassword.Copy()));
   //*** Put the buffer in the CComBSTR via overloaded = operator ***
   ccbstrSQLText = szSQLBuffer;
   //*** Declare a CComVariant to hold returned record count from ADO ***
   CComVariant vRecCount;
   //*** Clear the record count ***
   vRecCount.Clear();
   //*** Execute the sequel statement on the database ***
     hr = adoCoConnection->Execute( ccbstrSQLText.Copy(), &vRecCount, -1 , NULL );
   //*** If can't reach database abort ***
   if (!SUCCEEDED(hr))
   {
       //*** Inform MTS of failure ***
       m_spObjectContext->SetAbort();
      //*** Kill the connection IP ***
      adoCoConnection->Release();
       //*** send back bad HRESULT ***
      return hr;
   }
   //*** if no records updated then account doesn't exist so signal error ***
   if (vRecCount.lVal == 0)
   {
       //*** Inform MTS of failure ***
       m_spObjectContext->SetAbort();
       //*** Kill the connection IP ***
       adoCoConnection->Release();
       //*** send back bad HRESULT ***
       return E_FAIL;
   }
   //*** Tell MTS we're OK ***
   m_spObjectContext->SetComplete();
   //*** Kill the connection***
   adoCoConnection->Release();
   //*** Send back Good Transaction ***
   return S_OK;
}

STDMETHODIMP CAccountsHandler::UpdateAccountCredit(BSTR bstrName, long lNewCredit)
{
```

```
AFX_MANAGE_STATE(AfxGetStaticModuleState())
  USES_CONVERSION;
//*** only use this if you want to use Role-based security ***
if (m_spObjectContext->IsSecurityEnabled())
{
      //*** Define a CComBSTR to hold the Role Name
     CComBSTR ccbstrRoleID;
     //*** set it ***
     ccbstrRoleID = _T("WallysMgr");
     //*** Define a Result holder ***
     BOOL bResult;
     //*** make the call ***
     m_spObjectContext->IsCallerInRole( ccbstrRoleID.Copy(), &bResult );
     //*** if not in the role abort ***
     if (!bResult)
     {
        //*** Inform MTS of failure ***
        m_spObjectContext->SetAbort();
        //*** send back bad HRESULT ***
         return E_FAIL;
     }
}
// TODO: Add your implementation code here
  //*** define HRESULT holder and set it to OK ***
HRESULT hr = S_OK;
//*** Declare our ActiveX Data Object Connection holder and set it to NULL ***
ADOConnection* adoCoConnection = NULL;
//*** Declare our ActiveX Data Object Recordset holder and set it to NULL ***
ADORecordset* adoAccountInfo = NULL;
//*** Attempt to get the ADO Connection IP ***
  hr = CoCreateInstance( CLSID_CADOConnection, NULL, CLSCTX_INPROC_SERVER,
                         IID_IADOConnection, (void **) adoCoConnection );
//*** If can't get IP abort ***
if (!SUCCEEDED(hr))
{
    //*** Inform MTS of failure ***
    m_spObjectContext->SetAbort();
    //*** send back bad HRESULT ***
     return hr;
}
//*** Declare a CComBSTR to handle the Sequel Text ***
CComBSTR ccbstrSQLText;
//*** Give it the DSN for our samples database ***
ccbstrSQLText = _T("FILEDSN=WallysAccounts");
//*** Attempt to open the database ***
hr = adoCoConnection->Open( ccbstrSQLText.Copy(), NULL, NULL, adCmdUnspecified);
//*** If can't get database abort ***
```

```
if (!SUCCEEDED(hr))
{
    //*** Inform MTS of failure ***
    m_spObjectContext->SetAbort();
    //*** Kill the connection IP ***
    adoCoConnection->Release();
    //*** send back bad HRESULT ***
     return hr;
}
//***Declare CComBSTR for names  ***
CComBSTR ccbstrName( bstrName );
//*** Declare the wsprintf buffer ***
TCHAR szSQLBuffer[512];
//*** Create Sequel Statement ***
wsprintf( szSQLBuffer,
_T("UPDATE Accounts SET CreditLimit = %ld WHERE AccountName = '%s'"), lNewCredit,
 OLE2T(ccbstrName.Copy()));
//*** Put the buffer in the CComBSTR via overloaded = operator ***
ccbstrSQLText = szSQLBuffer;
//*** Declare a CComVariant to hold returned record count from ADO ***
CComVariant vRecCount;
//*** Clear the record count ***
vRecCount.Clear();
//*** Execute the sequel statement on the database ***
  hr = adoCoConnection->Execute( ccbstrSQLText.Copy(), &vRecCount, -1 , NULL );
//*** If can't reach database abort ***
if (!SUCCEEDED(hr))
{
    //*** Inform MTS of failure ***
    m_spObjectContext->SetAbort();
   //*** Kill the connection IP ***
   adoCoConnection->Release();
    //*** send back bad HRESULT ***
   return hr;
}
//*** if no records updated then account doesn't exist so signal error ***
if (vRecCount.lVal == 0)
{
    //*** Inform MTS of failure ***
    m_spObjectContext->SetAbort();
    //*** Kill the connection IP ***
    adoCoConnection->Release();
    //*** send back bad HRESULT ***
    return E_FAIL;
}
//*** Tell MTS we're OK ***
m_spObjectContext->SetComplete();
```

```
    //*** Kill the connection ***
    adoCoConnection->Release();
    //*** Send back Good Transaction ***
    return S_OK;
}

STDMETHODIMP CAccountsHandler::UpdateAccountCharges(BSTR bstrName, long lNewCharges)
{
    AFX_MANAGE_STATE(AfxGetStaticModuleState())

    // TODO: Add your implementation code here
      USES_CONVERSION;
    // TODO: Add your implementation code here
      //*** define HRESULT holder and set it to OK ***
    HRESULT hr = S_OK;
    //*** Declare our ActiveX Data Object Connection holder and set it to NULL ***
    ADOConnection* adoCoConnection = NULL;
    //*** Declare our ActiveX Data Object Recordset holder and set it to NULL ***
    ADORecordset* adoAccountInfo = NULL;
    //*** Attempt to get the ADO Connection IP ***
      hr = CoCreateInstance( CLSID_CADOConnection, NULL, CLSCTX_INPROC_SERVER,
                             IID_IADOConnection, (void **) adoCoConnection );
    //*** If can't get IP abort ***
    if (!SUCCEEDED(hr))
    {
        //*** Inform MTS of failure ***
        m_spObjectContext->SetAbort();
        //*** send back bad HRESULT ***
         return hr;
    }
    //*** Declare a CComBSTR to handle the Sequel Text ***
    CComBSTR ccbstrSQLText;
    //*** Give it the DSN for our samples database ***
    ccbstrSQLText = _T("FILEDSN=WallysAccounts");
    //*** Attempt to open the database ***
    hr = adoCoConnection->Open( ccbstrSQLText.Copy(), NULL, NULL, adCmdUnspecified);
    //*** If can't get database abort ***
    if (!SUCCEEDED(hr))
    {
        //*** Inform MTS of failure ***
        m_spObjectContext->SetAbort();
        //*** Kill the connection IP ***
        adoCoConnection->Release();
        //*** send back bad HRESULT ***
         return hr;
    }
    //***Declare CComBSTR for names  ***
```

```
    CComBSTR ccbstrName( bstrName );
    //*** Declare the wsprintf buffer ***
    TCHAR szSQLBuffer[512];
    //*** Create Sequel Statement ***
    wsprintf( szSQLBuffer,
      _T("UPDATE Accounts SET CurrentCharges = %ld WHERE AccountName = '%s'"),
        lNewCharges, OLE2T(ccbstrName.Copy()));
    //*** Put the buffer in the CComBSTR via overloaded = operator ***
    ccbstrSQLText = szSQLBuffer;
    //*** Declare a CComVariant to hold returned record count from ADO ***
    CComVariant vRecCount;
    //*** Clear the record count ***
    vRecCount.Clear();
    //*** Execute the sequel statement on the database ***
      hr = adoCoConnection->Execute( ccbstrSQLText.Copy(), &vRecCount, -1 , NULL );
    //*** If can't reach database abort ***
    if (!SUCCEEDED(hr))
    {
        //*** Inform MTS of failure ***
        m_spObjectContext->SetAbort();
       //*** Kill the connection IP ***
       adoCoConnection->Release();
        //*** send back bad HRESULT ***
       return hr;
    }
    //*** if no records updated then account doesn't exist so signal error ***
    if (vRecCount.lVal == 0)
    {
        //*** Inform MTS of failure ***
        m_spObjectContext->SetAbort();
        //*** Kill the connection IP ***
        adoCoConnection->Release();
        //*** send back bad HRESULT ***
        return E_FAIL;
    }
    //*** Tell MTS we're OK ***
    m_spObjectContext->SetComplete();
    //*** Kill the connection ***
    adoCoConnection->Release();
    //*** Send back Good Transaction ***
    return S_OK;
}

STDMETHODIMP CAccountsHandler::UpdateAccountInUse(BSTR bstrName, BOOL bNowInUse)
{
    AFX_MANAGE_STATE(AfxGetStaticModuleState())

```

```
// TODO: Add your implementation code here
  USES_CONVERSION;
// TODO: Add your implementation code here
  //*** define HRESULT holder and set it to OK ***
HRESULT hr = S_OK;
//*** Declare our ActiveX Data Object Connection holder and set it to NULL ***
ADOConnection* adoCoConnection = NULL;
//*** Declare our ActiveX Data Object Recordset holder and set it to NULL ***
ADORecordset* adoAccountInfo = NULL;
//*** Attempt to get the ADO Connection IP ***
  hr = CoCreateInstance( CLSID_CADOConnection, NULL, CLSCTX_INPROC_SERVER,
                         IID_IADOConnection, (void **) adoCoConnection );
//*** If can't get IP abort ***
if (!SUCCEEDED(hr))
{
    //*** Inform MTS of failure ***
    m_spObjectContext->SetAbort();
    //*** send back bad HRESULT ***
     return hr;
}
//*** Declare a CComBSTR to handle the Sequel Text ***
CComBSTR ccbstrSQLText;
//*** Give it the DSN for our samples database ***
ccbstrSQLText = _T("FILEDSN=WallysAccounts");
//*** Attempt to open the database ***
hr = adoCoConnection->Open( ccbstrSQLText.Copy(), NULL, NULL, adCmdUnspecified);
//*** If can't get database abort ***
if (!SUCCEEDED(hr))
{
    //*** Inform MTS of failure ***
    m_spObjectContext->SetAbort();
    //*** Kill the connection IP ***
    adoCoConnection->Release();
    //*** send back bad HRESULT ***
     return hr;
}
//***Declare CComBSTR for names  ***
CComBSTR ccbstrName( bstrName );
//*** Declare the wsprintf buffer ***
TCHAR szSQLBuffer[512];
//*** Create Sequel Statement ***
wsprintf( szSQLBuffer,
  _T("UPDATE Accounts SET InUse = %b WHERE AccountName = '%s'"), bNowInUse,
  OLE2T(ccbstrName.Copy()));
//*** Put the buffer in the CComBSTR via overloaded = operator ***
ccbstrSQLText = szSQLBuffer;
//*** Declare a CComVariant to hold returned record count from ADO ***
```

```
   CComVariant vRecCount;
   //*** Clear the record count ***
   vRecCount.Clear();
   //*** Execute the sequel statement on the database ***
     hr = adoCoConnection->Execute( ccbstrSQLText.Copy(), &vRecCount, -1 , NULL );
   //*** If can't reach database abort ***
   if (!SUCCEEDED(hr))
   {
       //*** Inform MTS of failure ***
       m_spObjectContext->SetAbort();
      //*** Kill the connection IP ***
      adoCoConnection->Release();
       //*** send back bad HRESULT ***
      return hr;
   }
   //*** if no records updated then account doesn't exist so signal error ***
   if (vRecCount.lVal == 0)
   {
       //*** Inform MTS of failure ***
       m_spObjectContext->SetAbort();
       //*** Kill the connection IP ***
       adoCoConnection->Release();
       //*** send back bad HRESULT ***
       return E_FAIL;
   }
   //*** Tell MTS we're OK ***
   m_spObjectContext->SetComplete();
   //*** Kill the connection ***
   adoCoConnection->Release();
   //*** Send back Good Transaction ***
   return S_OK;
}

STDMETHODIMP CAccountsHandler::get_AccountPassword(BSTR bstrName, BSTR *pVal)
{
   AFX_MANAGE_STATE(AfxGetStaticModuleState())
     USES_CONVERSION;
   // TODO: Add your implementation code here
     //*** define HRESULT holder and set it to OK ***
   HRESULT hr = S_OK;
   //*** Declare our ActiveX Data Object Connection holder and set it to NULL ***
   ADOConnection* adoCoConnection = NULL;
   //*** Declare our ActiveX Data Object Recordset holder and set it to NULL ***
   ADORecordset* adoAccountInfo = NULL;
   //*** Declare our ActiveX Data Object Fields holder and set it to NULL ***
   ADOFields* padoFields = NULL;
   //*** Declare our ActiveX Data Object Field holder and set it to NULL ***
```

```
ADOField* padoField = NULL;
//*** Define Error Holder and set it to 0 ***
long lErrorFlags = 0;
//*** Attempt to get the ADO Connection IP ***
  hr = CoCreateInstance( CLSID_CADOConnection, NULL, CLSCTX_INPROC_SERVER,
                         IID_IADOConnection, (void **) adoCoConnection );
//*** If can't get IP abort ***
if (!SUCCEEDED(hr))
{
    //*** Inform MTS of failure ***
    m_spObjectContext->SetAbort();
    //*** send back bad HRESULT ***
     return hr;
}
//*** Declare a CComBSTR to handle the Sequel Text ***
CComBSTR ccbstrSQLText;
//*** Give it the DSN for our samples database ***
ccbstrSQLText = _T("FILEDSN=WallysAccounts");
//*** Attempt to open the database ***
hr = adoCoConnection->Open( ccbstrSQLText.Copy(), NULL, NULL, adCmdUnspecified);
//*** If can't get database abort ***
if (!SUCCEEDED(hr))
{
    //*** Inform MTS of failure ***
    m_spObjectContext->SetAbort();
    //*** Kill the connection IP ***
    adoCoConnection->Release();
    //*** send back bad HRESULT ***
     return hr;
}
//***Declare CComBSTR for names  ***
CComBSTR ccbstrName( bstrName );
//*** Declare the wsprintf buffer ***
TCHAR szSQLBuffer[512];
wsprintf( szSQLBuffer,
  _T("SELECT AccountPassword FROM Accounts WHERE AccountName = '%s'"),
      OLE2T(ccbstrName.Copy()));
//*** Put it into the CComBSTR via overloaded = operator ***
ccbstrSQLText = szSQLBuffer;
//*** Declare a CComVariant to hold returned record count from ADO ***
CComVariant vRecCount;
//*** Clear the record count ***
vRecCount.Clear();
//*** Execute the sequel statement on the database ***
   hr = adoCoConnection->Execute( ccbstrSQLText.Copy(),
          &vRecCount, -1 , &adoAccountInfo );
//*** If can't reach database abort ***
```

```
if (!SUCCEEDED(hr))
{
    //*** Inform MTS of failure ***
    m_spObjectContext->SetAbort();
    //*** Kill the connection IP ***
    adoCoConnection->Release();
    //*** send back bad HRESULT ***
    return hr;
}
//*** Obtain the fields collection from the recordset ***
   hr = adoAccountInfo->get_Fields( &padoFields );
//*** If can't reach database abort ***
if (!SUCCEEDED(hr))
{
    //*** Inform MTS of failure ***
    m_spObjectContext->SetAbort();
    //*** Kill the connection and recordset IP ***
   adoCoConnection->Release();
   adoAccountInfo->Release();
    //*** send back bad HRESULT ***
   return hr;
}
//*** Define a variant to obtain the password field ***
CComVariant vField = _T("AccountPassword");
//*** define a variant to hold the information ***
CComVariant vPassword;
//*** Get the password Field ***
hr = padoFields->get_Item( vField , &padoField );
//*** If can't reach database abort ***
if (!SUCCEEDED(hr))
{
    //*** Inform MTS of failure ***
    m_spObjectContext->SetAbort();
   //*** Kill the connection, recordset, and fields IP ***
   adoCoConnection->Release();
   adoAccountInfo->Release();
   padoFields->Release();
    //*** send back bad HRESULT ***
   return hr;
}
//*** Get the actual password value ***
hr = padoField->get_Value( &vPassword );
//*** If can't reach database abort ***
if (!SUCCEEDED(hr))
{
    //*** Inform MTS of failure ***
    m_spObjectContext->SetAbort();
```

```
        //*** Kill the connection, recordset, fields, and field IP ***
        adoCoConnection->Release();
        adoAccountInfo->Release();
        padoFields->Release();
        padoField->Release();
        //*** send back bad HRESULT ***
        return hr;
    }
       //*** return the value from the variant ***
       *pVal = vPassword.bstrVal;
    //*** Tell MTS we're OK ***
    m_spObjectContext->SetComplete();
    //*** Kill the connection, recordset, fields, and field IP ***
    adoCoConnection->Release();
    adoAccountInfo->Release();
    padoFields->Release();
    padoField->Release();
    //*** Send back Good Transaction ***
    return S_OK;
}

STDMETHODIMP CAccountsHandler::get_AccountCreditLimit(BSTR bstrName, long *pVal)
{
    AFX_MANAGE_STATE(AfxGetStaticModuleState())
       USES_CONVERSION;
    // TODO: Add your implementation code here
       //*** define HRESULT holder and set it to OK ***
    HRESULT hr = S_OK;
    //*** Declare our ActiveX Data Object Connection holder and set it to NULL ***
    ADOConnection* adoCoConnection = NULL;
    //*** Declare our ActiveX Data Object Recordset holder and set it to NULL ***
    ADORecordset* adoAccountInfo = NULL;
    //*** Declare our ActiveX Data Object Fields holder and set it to NULL ***
    ADOFields* padoFields = NULL;
    //*** Declare our ActiveX Data Object Field holder and set it to NULL ***
    ADOField* padoField = NULL;
    //*** Define Error Holder and set it to 0 ***
    long lErrorFlags = 0;
    //*** Attempt to get the ADO Connection IP ***
       hr = CoCreateInstance( CLSID_CADOConnection, NULL, CLSCTX_INPROC_SERVER,
                              IID_IADOConnection, (void **) adoCoConnection );
    //*** If can't get IP abort ***
    if (!SUCCEEDED(hr))
    {
         //*** Inform MTS of failure ***
         m_spObjectContext->SetAbort();
         //*** send back bad HRESULT ***
```

```
       return hr;
  }
  //*** Declare a CComBSTR to handle the Sequel Text ***
  CComBSTR ccbstrSQLText;
  //*** Give it the DSN for our samples database ***
  ccbstrSQLText = _T("FILEDSN=WallysAccounts");
  //*** Attempt to open the database ***
  hr = adoCoConnection->Open( ccbstrSQLText.Copy(), NULL, NULL, adCmdUnspecified);
  //*** If can't get database abort ***
  if (!SUCCEEDED(hr))
  {
      //*** Inform MTS of failure ***
      m_spObjectContext->SetAbort();
      //*** Kill the connection IP ***
      adoCoConnection->Release();
      //*** send back bad HRESULT ***
       return hr;
  }
  //***Declare CComBSTR for names  ***
  CComBSTR ccbstrName( bstrName );
  //*** Declare the wsprintf buffer ***
  TCHAR szSQLBuffer[512];
  wsprintf( szSQLBuffer,
     _T("SELECT CreditLimit FROM Accounts WHERE AccountName = '%s'"),
     OLE2T(ccbstrName.Copy()));
  //*** Put it into the CComBSTR via overloaded = operator ***
  ccbstrSQLText = szSQLBuffer;
  //*** Declare a CComVariant to hold returned record count from ADO ***
  CComVariant vRecCount;
  //*** Clear the record count ***
  vRecCount.Clear();
  //*** Execute the sequel statement on the database ***
     hr = adoCoConnection->Execute( ccbstrSQLText.Copy(), &vRecCount, -1 ,
        &adoAccountInfo );
  //*** If can't reach database abort ***
  if (!SUCCEEDED(hr))
  {
      //*** Inform MTS of failure ***
      m_spObjectContext->SetAbort();
      //*** Kill the connection IP ***
      adoCoConnection->Release();
      //*** send back bad HRESULT ***
      return hr;
  }
  //*** Obtain the fields collection from the recordset ***
     hr = adoAccountInfo->get_Fields( &padoFields );
  //*** If can't reach database abort ***
```

```
if (!SUCCEEDED(hr))
{
    //*** Inform MTS of failure ***
    m_spObjectContext->SetAbort();
    //*** Kill the connection and recordset IP ***
   adoCoConnection->Release();
   adoAccountInfo->Release();
    //*** send back bad HRESULT ***
   return hr;
}
//*** Define a variant to obtain the credit limit field ***
CComVariant vField = _T("CreditLimit");
//*** define a variant to hold the information ***
CComVariant vCreditLimit;
//*** Get the credit limit Field ***
hr = padoFields->get_Item( vField , &padoField );
//*** If can't reach database abort ***
if (!SUCCEEDED(hr))
{
    //*** Inform MTS of failure ***
    m_spObjectContext->SetAbort();
   //*** Kill the connection, recordset, and fields IP ***
   adoCoConnection->Release();
   adoAccountInfo->Release();
   padoFields->Release();
    //*** send back bad HRESULT ***
   return hr;
}
//*** Get the actual credit limit value ***
hr = padoField->get_Value( &vCreditLimit );
//*** If can't reach database abort ***
if (!SUCCEEDED(hr))
{
    //*** Inform MTS of failure ***
    m_spObjectContext->SetAbort();
    //*** Kill the connection, recordset, fields, and field IP ***
    adoCoConnection->Release();
    adoAccountInfo->Release();
    padoFields->Release();
    padoField->Release();
    //*** send back bad HRESULT ***
    return hr;
}
   //*** return the value from the variant ***
   *pVal = vCreditLimit.lVal;
//*** Tell MTS we're OK ***
m_spObjectContext->SetComplete();
```

```
 //*** Kill the connection, recordset, fields, and field IP ***
 adoCoConnection->Release();
 adoAccountInfo->Release();
 padoFields->Release();
 padoField->Release();
 //*** Send back Good Transaction ***
 return S_OK;
}

STDMETHODIMP CAccountsHandler::get_AccountCurrentCharges(BSTR bstrName, long *pVal)
{
 AFX_MANAGE_STATE(AfxGetStaticModuleState())
    USES_CONVERSION;
 // TODO: Add your implementation code here
    //*** define HRESULT holder and set it to OK ***
 HRESULT hr = S_OK;
 //*** Declare our ActiveX Data Object Connection holder and set it to NULL ***
 ADOConnection* adoCoConnection = NULL;
 //*** Declare our ActiveX Data Object Recordset holder and set it to NULL ***
 ADORecordset* adoAccountInfo = NULL;
 //*** Declare our ActiveX Data Object Fields holder and set it to NULL ***
 ADOFields* padoFields = NULL;
 //*** Declare our ActiveX Data Object Field holder and set it to NULL ***
 ADOField* padoField = NULL;
 //*** Define Error Holder and set it to 0 ***
 long lErrorFlags = 0;
 //*** Attempt to get the ADO Connection IP ***
    hr = CoCreateInstance( CLSID_CADOConnection, NULL, CLSCTX_INPROC_SERVER,
                           IID_IADOConnection, (void **) adoCoConnection );
 //*** If can't get IP abort ***
 if (!SUCCEEDED(hr))
 {
     //*** Inform MTS of failure ***
     m_spObjectContext->SetAbort();
     //*** send back bad HRESULT ***
      return hr;
 }
 //*** Declare a CComBSTR to handle the Sequel Text ***
 CComBSTR ccbstrSQLText;
 //*** Give it the DSN for our samples database ***
 ccbstrSQLText = _T("FILEDSN=WallysAccounts");
 //*** Attempt to open the database ***
 hr = adoCoConnection->Open( ccbstrSQLText.Copy(), NULL, NULL, adCmdUnspecified);
 //*** If can't get database abort ***
 if (!SUCCEEDED(hr))
 {
     //*** Inform MTS of failure ***
```

```
        m_spObjectContext->SetAbort();
        //*** Kill the connection IP ***
        adoCoConnection->Release();
        //*** send back bad HRESULT ***
         return hr;
    }
    //***Declare CComBSTR for names  ***
    CComBSTR ccbstrName( bstrName );
    //*** Declare the wsprintf buffer ***
    TCHAR szSQLBuffer[512];
    wsprintf( szSQLBuffer,
    _T("SELECT CurrentCharges FROM Accounts WHERE AccountName = '%s'"),
      OLE2T(ccbstrName.Copy()));
    //*** Put it into the CComBSTR via overloaded = operator ***
    ccbstrSQLText = szSQLBuffer;
    //*** Declare a CComVariant to hold returned record count from ADO ***
    CComVariant vRecCount;
    //*** Clear the record count ***
    vRecCount.Clear();
    //*** Execute the sequel statement on the database ***
       hr = adoCoConnection->Execute( ccbstrSQLText.Copy(), &vRecCount, -1 ,
        &adoAccountInfo );
    //*** If can't reach database abort ***
    if (!SUCCEEDED(hr))
    {
        //*** Inform MTS of failure ***
        m_spObjectContext->SetAbort();
        //*** Kill the connection IP ***
        adoCoConnection->Release();
        //*** send back bad HRESULT ***
        return hr;
    }
    //*** Obtain the fields collection from the recordset ***
       hr = adoAccountInfo->get_Fields( &padoFields );
    //*** If can't reach database abort ***
    if (!SUCCEEDED(hr))
    {
        //*** Inform MTS of failure ***
        m_spObjectContext->SetAbort();
        //*** Kill the connection and recordset IP ***
       adoCoConnection->Release();
       adoAccountInfo->Release();
        //*** send back bad HRESULT ***
       return hr;
    }
    //*** Define a variant to obtain the charges field ***
    CComVariant vField = _T("CurrentCharges");
```

```
  //*** define a variant to hold the information ***
  CComVariant vCurrentCharges;
  //*** Get the charges Field ***
  hr = padoFields->get_Item( vField , &padoField );
  //*** If can't reach database abort ***
  if (!SUCCEEDED(hr))
  {
      //*** Inform MTS of failure ***
      m_spObjectContext->SetAbort();
     //*** Kill the connection, recordset, and fields IP ***
     adoCoConnection->Release();
     adoAccountInfo->Release();
     padoFields->Release();
      //*** send back bad HRESULT ***
     return hr;
  }
  //*** Get the actual charges value ***
  hr = padoField->get_Value( &vCurrentCharges );
  //*** If can't reach database abort ***
  if (!SUCCEEDED(hr))
  {
      //*** Inform MTS of failure ***
      m_spObjectContext->SetAbort();
      //*** Kill the connection, recordset, fields, and field IP ***
      adoCoConnection->Release();
      adoAccountInfo->Release();
      padoFields->Release();
      padoField->Release();
      //*** send back bad HRESULT ***
      return hr;
  }
    //*** return the value from the variant ***
    *pVal = vCurrentCharges.lVal;
  //*** Tell MTS we're OK ***
  m_spObjectContext->SetComplete();
  //*** Kill the connection, recordset, fields, and field IP ***
  adoCoConnection->Release();
  adoAccountInfo->Release();
  padoFields->Release();
  padoField->Release();
  //*** Send back Good Transaction ***
  return S_OK;
}

STDMETHODIMP CAccountsHandler::get_AccountInUse(BSTR bstrName, BOOL *pVal)
{
  AFX_MANAGE_STATE(AfxGetStaticModuleState())
```

```
    USES_CONVERSION;
// TODO: Add your implementation code here
    //*** define HRESULT holder and set it to OK ***
HRESULT hr = S_OK;
//*** Declare our ActiveX Data Object Connection holder and set it to NULL ***
ADOConnection* adoCoConnection = NULL;
//*** Declare our ActiveX Data Object Recordset holder and set it to NULL ***
ADORecordset* adoAccountInfo = NULL;
//*** Declare our ActiveX Data Object Fields holder and set it to NULL ***
ADOFields* padoFields = NULL;
//*** Declare our ActiveX Data Object Field holder and set it to NULL ***
ADOField* padoField = NULL;
//*** Define Error Holder and set it to 0 ***
long lErrorFlags = 0;
//*** Attempt to get the ADO Connection IP ***
   hr = CoCreateInstance( CLSID_CADOConnection, NULL, CLSCTX_INPROC_SERVER,
                          IID_IADOConnection, (void **) adoCoConnection );
//*** If can't get IP abort ***
if (!SUCCEEDED(hr))
{
     //*** Inform MTS of failure ***
     m_spObjectContext->SetAbort();
     //*** send back bad HRESULT ***
       return hr;
}
//*** Declare a CComBSTR to handle the Sequel Text ***
CComBSTR ccbstrSQLText;
//*** Give it the DSN for our samples database ***
ccbstrSQLText = _T("FILEDSN=WallysAccounts");
//*** Attempt to open the database ***
hr = adoCoConnection->Open( ccbstrSQLText.Copy(), NULL, NULL, adCmdUnspecified);
//*** If can't get database abort ***
if (!SUCCEEDED(hr))
{
     //*** Inform MTS of failure ***
     m_spObjectContext->SetAbort();
     //*** Kill the connection IP ***
     adoCoConnection->Release();
     //*** send back bad HRESULT ***
       return hr;
}
//***Declare CComBSTR for names  ***
CComBSTR ccbstrName( bstrName );
//*** Declare the wsprintf buffer ***
TCHAR szSQLBuffer[512];
wsprintf( szSQLBuffer, _T("SELECT InUse FROM Accounts WHERE AccountName = '%s'"),
      OLE2T(ccbstrName.Copy()));
```

```
//*** Put it into the CComBSTR via overloaded = operator ***
ccbstrSQLText = szSQLBuffer;
//*** Declare a CComVariant to hold returned record count from ADO ***
CComVariant vRecCount;
//*** Clear the record count ***
vRecCount.Clear();
//*** Execute the sequel statement on the database ***
   hr = adoCoConnection->Execute( ccbstrSQLText.Copy(), &vRecCount, -1 ,
        &adoAccountInfo );
//*** If can't reach database abort ***
if (!SUCCEEDED(hr))
{
    //*** Inform MTS of failure ***
    m_spObjectContext->SetAbort();
    //*** Kill the connection IP ***
    adoCoConnection->Release();
    //*** send back bad HRESULT ***
    return hr;
}
//*** Obtain the fields collection from the recordset ***
   hr = adoAccountInfo->get_Fields( &padoFields );
//*** If can't reach database abort ***
if (!SUCCEEDED(hr))
{
    //*** Inform MTS of failure ***
    m_spObjectContext->SetAbort();
    //*** Kill the connection and recordset IP ***
   adoCoConnection->Release();
   adoAccountInfo->Release();
    //*** send back bad HRESULT ***
   return hr;
}
//*** Define a variant to obtain the in use field ***
CComVariant vField = _T("InUse");
//*** define a variant to hold the information ***
CComVariant vInUse;
//*** Get the inuse Field ***
hr = padoFields->get_Item( vField , &padoField );
//*** If can't reach database abort ***
if (!SUCCEEDED(hr))
{
    //*** Inform MTS of failure ***
    m_spObjectContext->SetAbort();
   //*** Kill the connection, recordset, and fields IP ***
   adoCoConnection->Release();
   adoAccountInfo->Release();
   padoFields->Release();
```

```
1450.       //*** send back bad HRESULT ***
1451.      return hr;
1452.   }
1453.   //*** Get the actual inuse value ***
1454.   hr = padoField->get_Value( &vInUse );
1455.   //*** If can't reach database abort ***
1456.   if (!SUCCEEDED(hr))
1457.   {
1458.       //*** Inform MTS of failure ***
1459.       m_spObjectContext->SetAbort();
1460.       //*** Kill the connection, recordset, fields, and field IP ***
1461.       adoCoConnection->Release();
1462.       adoAccountInfo->Release();
1463.       padoFields->Release();
1464.       padoField->Release();
1465.       //*** send back bad HRESULT ***
1466.       return hr;
1467.   }
1468.      //*** return the value from the variant ***
1469.      *pVal = vInUse.boolVal;
1470.   //*** Tell MTS we're OK ***
1471.   m_spObjectContext->SetComplete();
1472.   //*** Kill the connection, recordset, fields, and field IP ***
1473.   adoCoConnection->Release();
1474.   adoAccountInfo->Release();
1475.   padoFields->Release();
1476.   padoField->Release();
1477.   //*** Send back Good Transaction ***
1478.   return S_OK;
1479. }
```

***Listing 6-1** ACCOUNTSHANDLER.CPP source code after modifications*

Here's the breakdown (the code is heavily commented and so we'll concentrate on the bigger design issues and some places where the logic may be a bit hard to follow in these comments. Also, since after the first function the code is virtually identical except for single lines calling different database SQL statements, only the first function is detailed below):

- **Lines 3-8** This code brings in the ADO headers so we can access them.
- **Lines 17-20** This code automatically obtains an MTS object context for use in the component's functions. It will be there because in the MTS Explorer (see Chapter 9) we will set this component to Require a Transaction.
- **Lines 38-60** This code initializes the ADO interface pointers needed to interact with the SQL Server database.
- **Lines 61-76** This code contacts the Wallys database and signals an error if it fails. Note that it aborts the transaction for any failure.

- **Lines 77-99** This code executes the SQL text for this particular database interaction and obtains a pRowset interface pointer which contains a set of data that hopefully matches that requested by the command. Note that it aborts the transaction for any failure.
- **Lines 100-112** This code gets a pFields interface pointer from the pRowset IP obtained from executing the SQL statement. This IP contains all the fields of the current rowset so the program can obtain as many as it wants and examine or change their values. Note that it aborts the transaction for any failure.
- **Lines 113-130** This code gets a single pField interface pointer from the pFields IP with the name given. This moves from a collection of all the fields in the current recordset to one single field so its value can be obtained. Note that it aborts the transaction for any failure.
- **Lines 131-145** This code uses the pField interface pointer to obtain the actual value of the field and deal with it as needed (it reads it in this example, but in later examples is used to set it). Note that it aborts the transaction for any failure.
- **Lines 146-156** This code returns the desired value and completes the transaction so any other components will be able to complete successfully as well.
- **Lines 235-254** This code handles using MTS role-based security for a database action. It requires the user to be a member of the WallysMgr role account, which Chapter 9 will show you how to create using the MTS Explorer. Otherwise it will not allow the action to proceed.

Once you are satisfied you've entered the code from the above listing correctly, build the MTS COM Server from the Build menu. If you encounter any errors, please check the code in the listing to find your mistake (it has been exhaustively debugged and is correct). Once you have compiled the component successfully, it is automatically registered on the local machine; if you need to move it to another machine, see Chapter 9. Otherwise, please move on to the next component.

## Creating Another MTS COM Component with ATL

The next step is to use ATL to create an MTS COM server that handles videos in stock for Wally's. The following sections take you through the user interface portions of creating the project in the step-by-step system, then show you the code you need to write and an analysis using the line-by-line approach.

## Step-By-Step

Start Visual C++ 5.0 or 6.0. From the File menu, select New. The New dialog box opens; highlight ATL COM AppWizard. Select an appropriate directory, then enter a project name of **ATLMTSWallysVideos**. Figure 6-20 shows how the New dialog should appear when you are done. Press OK to open the ATL COM AppWizard.

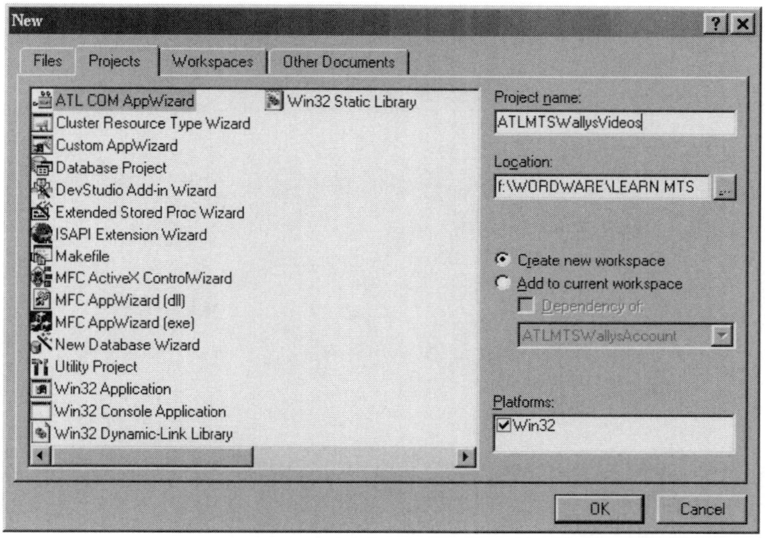


*Figure 6-20*
*The New dialog box creating the ATLMTSWallysVideos ATL project*

In the ATL AppWizard, select the DLL project, and make sure that the Support MFC, Merge Proxy/Stub Code, and Support MTS check boxes are checked. Press Finish.

A confirmation dialog box appears as shown in Figure 6-21; press OK to create the ATL project.

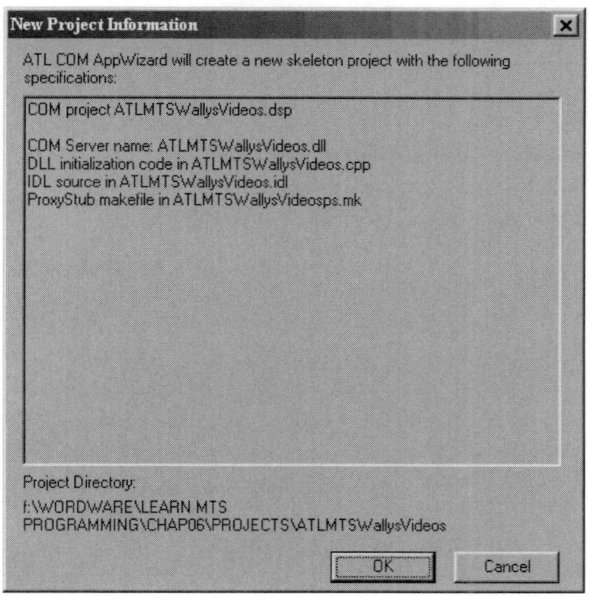


*Figure 6-21*
*The confirmation dialog*

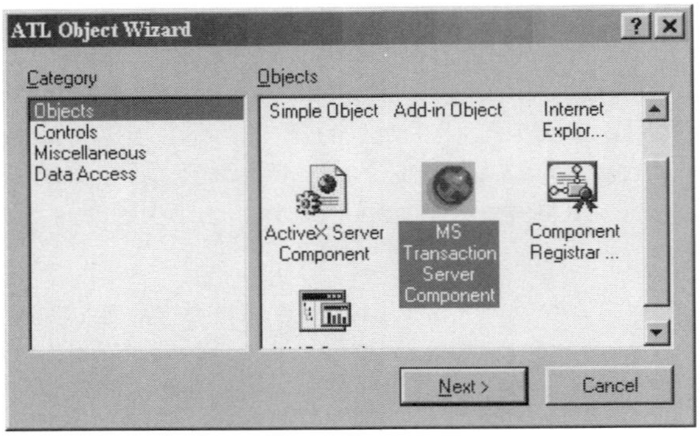


*Figure 6-22* Selecting an MS Transaction Server Component object in the ATL Object Wizard

From the Insert menu, select New ATL Object. The ATL Object Wizard dialog appears, as shown in Figure 6-22. Select the Objects entry in the left-hand list box, and the MS Transaction Server Component entry in the right-hand list box. Press Next to move to the settings pages of the wizard.

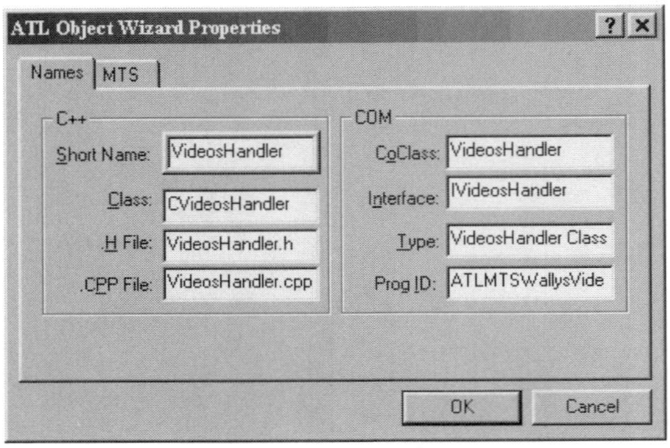


*Figure 6-23* Entering name information in the ATL Object Wizard

Select the Names tab of the next wizard dialog if it is not selected by default. As shown in Figure 6-23, enter **VideosHandler** as the name of the control implementation class; the other boxes will fill in automatically. Accept the default values and select the MTS tab.

As illustrated in Figure 6-24, the MTS tab should have the Dual Interface radio button selected and the Support IObjectControl check box checked. Press OK now to add the MTS Component Server object to your ATL project.

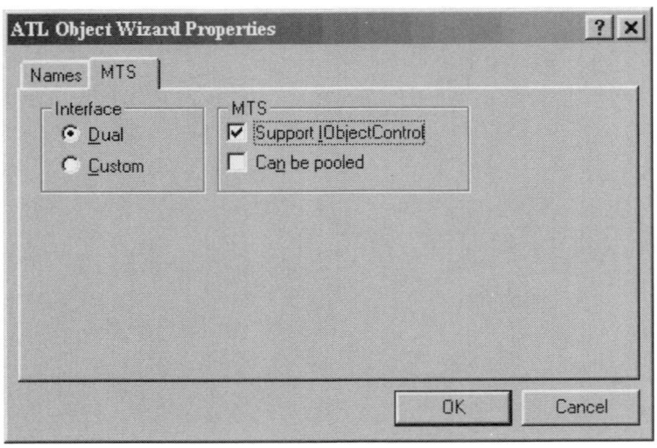


*Figure 6-24* Entering MTS information in the ATL Object Wizard

Move to the Project Explorer window and select the ClassView pane. The IVideosHandler Interface is displayed; right-click on it to display the shortcut menu. Select the Add Property menu option.

The Add Property Wizard dialog box appears; select a Property Type of long. Give it a name of **TotalVideos**, and check only the Get accessor function to create a read-only property. Figure 6-25 shows how the Add Property dialog should appear when you are done. Press OK to add the property to the MTS COM component.

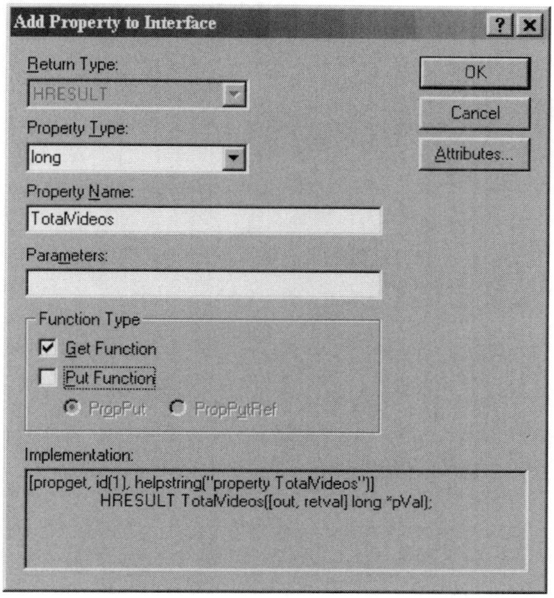


***Figure 6-25*** *Entering the TotalVideos property with the ATL Add Property Wizard*

Again right-click on the IVideosHandler Interface in the ClassView pane of the Project Explorer; this time select Add Method from the shortcut menu. The Add Method Wizard dialog box appears; give the method the name of **CreateDatabase**, with no parameters. Figure 6-26 shows how the Add Method dialog should appear when you are done. Press OK to add the method to the MTS COM component.

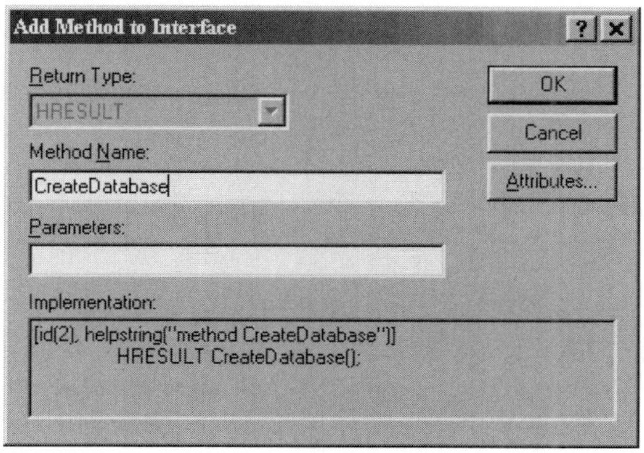


***Figure 6-26*** *Entering the CreateDatabase method with the ATL Add Method Wizard*

Again right-click on the IVideosHandler Interface in the ClassView pane of the Project Explorer; again select Add Method from the shortcut menu. The Add Method Wizard dialog box appears; give the method the name of **AddNewVideo**, with a parameter string of [in] BSTR bstrVideoName, [in] short sPrice, [in] short sTotalCopies, [in] short sAvailableCopies. Figure 6-27 shows how the Add Method dialog should appear when you are done. Press OK to add the method to the MTS COM component.

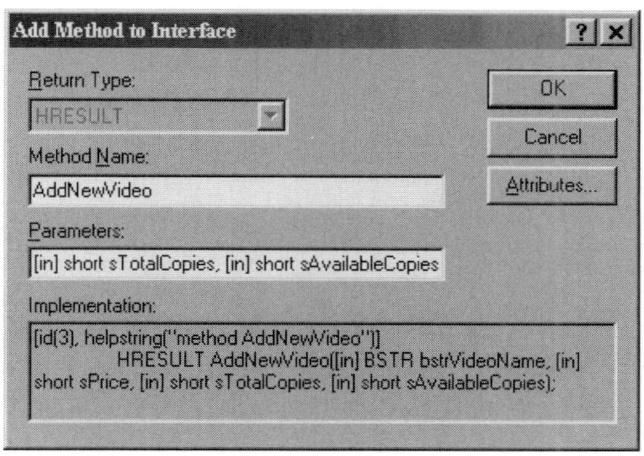


***Figure 6-27*** *Entering the AddNewVideo method with the ATL Add Method Wizard*

Again right-click on the IVideosHandler Interface in the ClassView pane of the Project Explorer; again select Add Method from the shortcut menu. The Add Method Wizard dialog box appears; give the method the name of **DeleteVideo**, with a parameter string of [in] BSTR bstrVideoName. Figure 6-28 shows how the Add Method dialog should appear when you are done. Press OK to add the method to the MTS COM component.

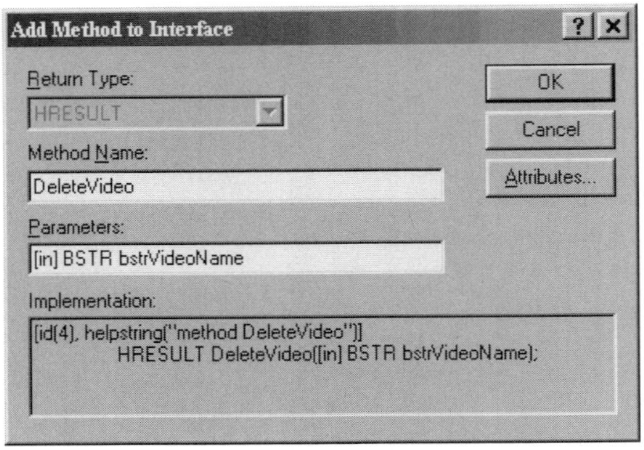


***Figure 6-28*** *Entering the DeleteVideo method with the ATL Add Method Wizard*

Again right-click on the IVideosHandler Interface in the ClassView pane of the Project Explorer; again select Add Method from the shortcut menu. The Add Method Wizard dialog box appears; give the method the name of **UpdateVideoEntryName**, with a parameter string of [in] BSTR bstrOldVideoName, [in] BSTR bstrNewVideoName. Figure 6-29 shows how the Add Method dialog should appear when you are done. Press OK to add the method to the MTS COM component.

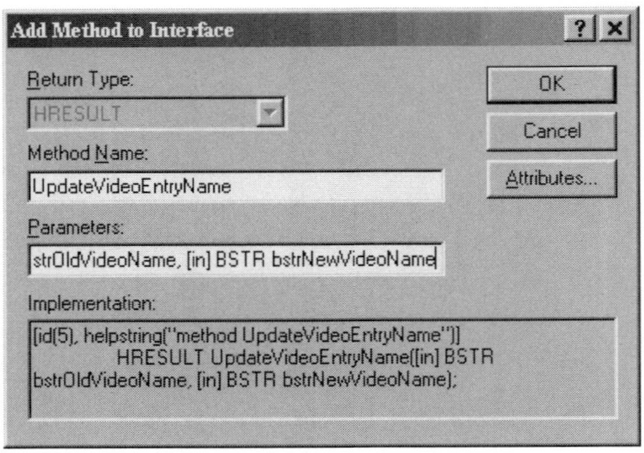


***Figure 6-29*** *Entering the UpdateVideo-EntryName method with the ATL Add Method Wizard*

Again right-click on the IVideosHandler Interface in the ClassView pane of the Project Explorer; again select Add Method from the shortcut menu. The Add Method Wizard dialog box appears; give the method the name of **UpdateVideoEntryPrice**, with a parameter string of [in] BSTR bstrVideoName, [in] short sNewPrice. Figure 6-30 shows how the Add Method dialog should appear when you are done. Press OK to add the method to the MTS COM component.

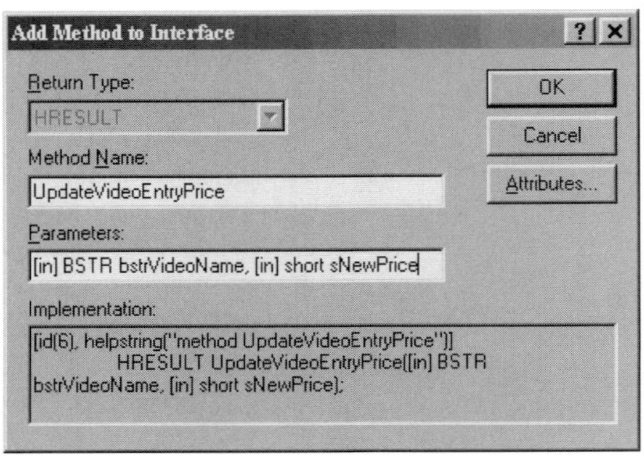


***Figure 6-30*** *Entering the UpdateVideo-EntryPrice method with the ATL Add Method Wizard*

Again right-click on the IVideosHandler Interface in the ClassView pane of the Project Explorer; again select Add Method from the shortcut menu. The Add Method Wizard dialog box appears; give the method the name of **UpdateVideoEntryTotal-Copies**, with a parameter string of [in] BSTR bstrVideoName, [in] short sNewTotalCopies. Figure 6-31 shows how the Add Method dialog should appear when you are done. Press OK to add the method to the MTS COM component.

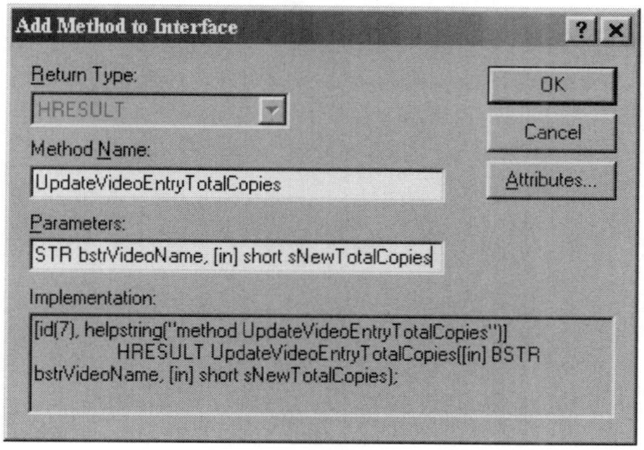


***Figure 6-31*** *Entering the UpdateVideo-EntryTotal-Copies method with the ATL Add Method Wizard*

Again right-click on the IVideosHandler Interface in the ClassView pane of the Project Explorer; again select Add Method from the shortcut menu. The Add Method Wizard dialog box appears; give the method the name of **UpdateVideo-EntryAvailableCopies**, with a parameter string of [in] BSTR bstrVideoName, [in] short sNewAvailableCopies. Figure 6-32 shows how the Add Method dialog should appear when you are done. Press OK to add the method to the MTS COM component.

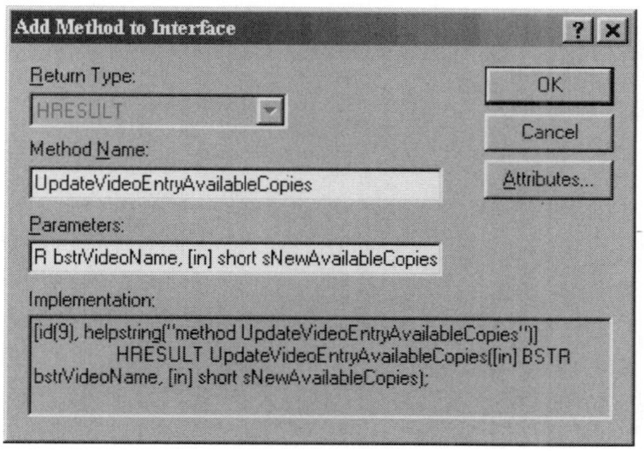


***Figure 6-32*** *Entering the UpdateVideo-EntryAvailable Copies method with the ATL Add Method Wizard*

Again right-click on the IVideosHandler Interface in the ClassView pane of the Project Explorer; this time select Add Property. The Add Property Wizard dialog box appears; select a Property Type of short. Give it a name of **VideoRentalPrice**, enter a parameter string of [in] BSTR bstrVideoName, and leave only the Get accessor function checked to create a read-only property. Figure 6-33 shows how the Add Property dialog should appear when you are done. Press OK to add the property to the MTS COM component.

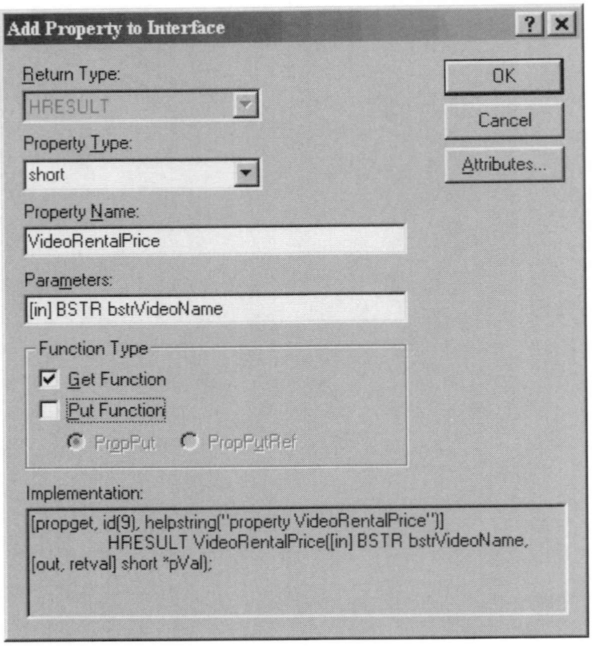


***Figure 6-33***
*Entering the VideoRental-Price property with the ATL Add Property Wizard*

Again right-click on the IVideosHandler Interface in the ClassView pane of the Project Explorer and select Add Property. The Add Property Wizard dialog box appears; select a Property Type of short. Give it a name of **VideoTotal-Copies**, enter a parameter string of [in] BSTR bstrVideoName, and leave only the Get accessor function checked to create a read-only property. Figure 6-34 shows how the Add Property dialog should appear when you are done. Press OK to add the property to the MTS COM component.

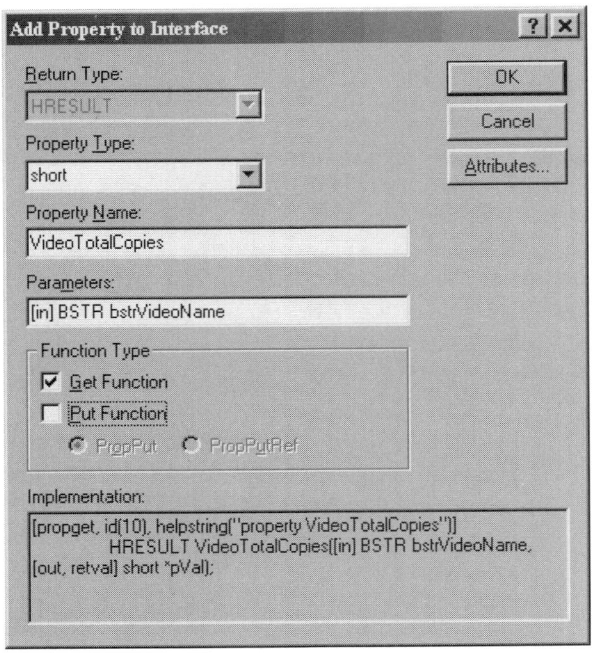


***Figure 6-34***
*Entering the VideoTotal-Copies property with the ATL Add Property Wizard*

Again right-click on the IVideosHandler Interface in the ClassView pane of the Project Explorer and select Add Property. The Add Property Wizard dialog box appears; select a Property Type of short. Give it a name of **VideoAvailableCopies**, enter a parameter string of [in] BSTR bstrVideoName, and leave only the Get accessor function checked to create a read-only property. Figure 6-35 shows how the Add Property dialog should appear when you are done. Press OK to add the property to the MTS COM component.

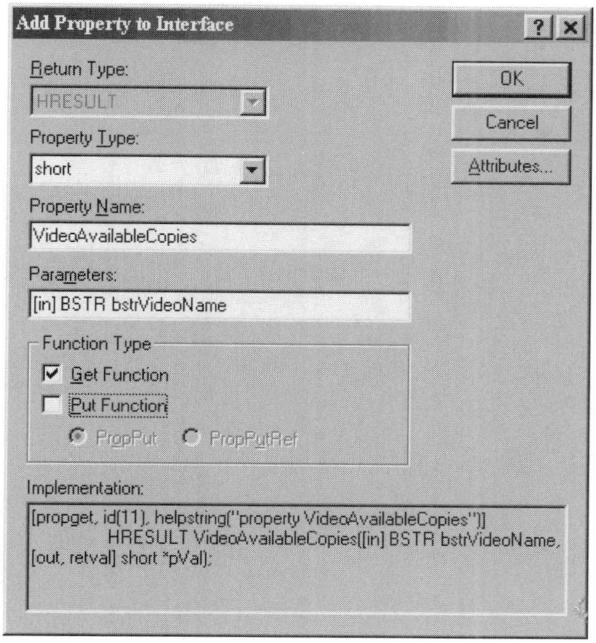


***Figure 6-35*** *Entering the VideoAvailableCopies property with the ATL Add Property Wizard*

Again right-click on the IVideosHandler Interface in the ClassView pane of the Project Explorer; this time select Add Method. The Add Method Wizard dialog box appears; give it a name of **GetVideoNameByNumber**, and enter a parameter string of [in] short sVideoID, [out] BSTR* bstrVideoName. Figure 6-36 shows how the Add Method dialog should appear when you are done. Press OK to add the method to the MTS COM component. Save the project to protect your work.

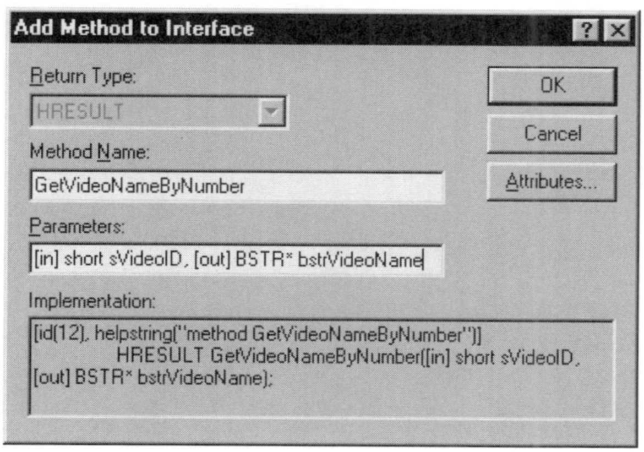


***Figure 6-36*** *Entering the GetVideoNameByNumber method with the ATL Add Method Wizard*

## Line-By-Line

Next, you need to enter the program code to implement the MTS database functionality this component implements. Bring up the VIDEOSHANDLER.CPP file in the text editor. Scan through it and enter or change any boldfaced line of source code in Listing 6-2. Save the project.

```

// VideosHandler.cpp : Implementation of CVideosHandler
#include "stdafx.h"
//*** take this out if you get linker errors!!! ***
#include <Initguid.h>
//*** ActiveX Data Objects GUIDs  ***
#include <adoid.h>
//*** ActiveX Data Objects Interfaces ***
#include <adoint.h>
#include "ATLMTSWallysVideos.h"
#include "VideosHandler.h"

/////////////////////////////////////////////////////////////////////////////
// CVideosHandler

HRESULT CVideosHandler::Activate()
{
   HRESULT hr = GetObjectContext(&m_spObjectContext);
   if (SUCCEEDED(hr))
         return S_OK;
   return hr;
}

BOOL CVideosHandler::CanBePooled()
{
   return FALSE;
}

void CVideosHandler::Deactivate()
{
   m_spObjectContext.Release();
}


STDMETHODIMP CVideosHandler::get_TotalVideos(long *pVal)
{
   AFX_MANAGE_STATE(AfxGetStaticModuleState())
   // TODO: Add your implementation code here
    USES_CONVERSION;
    //*** define HRESULT holder and set it to OK ***
   HRESULT hr = S_OK;
   //*** Declare our ActiveX Data Object Connection holder and set it to NULL ***
   ADOConnection* adoCoConnection = NULL;
   //*** Declare our ActiveX Data Object Recordset holder and set it to NULL ***
   ADORecordset* adoAccountInfo = NULL;
   //*** Declare our ActiveX Data Object Fields holder and set it to NULL ***
   ADOFields* padoFields = NULL;
```

```
    //*** Declare our ActiveX Data Object Field holder and set it to NULL ***
    ADOField* padoField = NULL;
    //*** Attempt to get the ADO Connection IP ***
     hr = CoCreateInstance( CLSID_CADOConnection, NULL, CLSCTX_INPROC_SERVER,
                            IID_IADOConnection, (void **) adoCoConnection );
    //*** If can't get IP abort ***
    if (!SUCCEEDED(hr))
    {
        //*** Inform MTS of failure ***
        m_spObjectContext->SetAbort();
        //*** send back bad HRESULT ***
         return hr;
    }
    //*** Declare a CComBSTR to handle the Sequel Text ***
    CComBSTR ccbstrSQLText;
    //*** Give it the DSN for our samples database ***
    ccbstrSQLText = _T("FILEDSN=WallysVideos");
    //*** Attempt to open the database ***
    hr = adoCoConnection->Open( ccbstrSQLText.Copy(), NULL, NULL, adCmdUnspecified);
    //*** If can't get database abort ***
    if (!SUCCEEDED(hr))
    {
        //*** Inform MTS of failure ***
        m_spObjectContext->SetAbort();
        //*** Kill the connection IP ***
        adoCoConnection->Release();
        //*** send back bad HRESULT ***
         return hr;
    }
    //*** Declare the wsprintf buffer ***
    TCHAR szSQLBuffer[512];
    wsprintf( szSQLBuffer,
     _T("SELECT TotalCopies FROM Videos WHERE VideoName = 'TotalCopies'"));
    //*** Put it into the CComBSTR via overloaded = operator ***
    ccbstrSQLText = szSQLBuffer;
    //*** Declare a CComVariant to hold returned record count from ADO ***
    CComVariant vRecCount;
    //*** Clear the record count ***
    vRecCount.Clear();
    //*** Execute the sequel statement on the database ***
     hr = adoCoConnection->Execute( ccbstrSQLText.Copy(), &vRecCount, -1 ,
      &adoAccountInfo );
    //*** If can't reach database abort ***
    if (!SUCCEEDED(hr))
    {
        //*** Inform MTS of failure ***
        m_spObjectContext->SetAbort();
```

```
        //*** Kill the connection IP ***
        adoCoConnection->Release();
        //*** send back bad HRESULT ***
        return hr;
    }
    //*** Obtain the fields collection from the recordset ***
      hr = adoAccountInfo->get_Fields( &padoFields );
    //*** If can't reach database abort ***
    if (!SUCCEEDED(hr))
    {
        //*** Inform MTS of failure ***
        m_spObjectContext->SetAbort();
        //*** Kill the connection and recordset IP ***
       adoCoConnection->Release();
       adoAccountInfo->Release();
        //*** send back bad HRESULT ***
       return hr;
    }
    //*** Define a variant to obtain the total videos field ***
    CComVariant vField = _T("TotalVideos");
    //*** define a variant to hold the information ***
    CComVariant vVideos;
    //*** Get the total videos Field ***
    hr = padoFields->get_Item( vField , &padoField );
    //*** If can't reach database abort ***
    if (!SUCCEEDED(hr))
    {
        //*** Inform MTS of failure ***
        m_spObjectContext->SetAbort();
       //*** Kill the connection, recordset, and fields IP ***
       adoCoConnection->Release();
       adoAccountInfo->Release();
       padoFields->Release();
        //*** send back bad HRESULT ***
       return hr;
    }
    //*** Get the actual total videos value ***
    hr = padoField->get_Value( &vVideos );
    //*** If can't reach database abort ***
    if (!SUCCEEDED(hr))
    {
        //*** Inform MTS of failure ***
        m_spObjectContext->SetAbort();
        //*** Kill the connection, recordset, fields, and field IP ***
        adoCoConnection->Release();
        adoAccountInfo->Release();
        padoFields->Release();
```

```
        padoField->Release();
        //*** send back bad HRESULT ***
        return hr;
    }
      //*** return the value from the variant ***
      *pVal = vVideos.lVal;
    //*** Tell MTS we're OK ***
    m_spObjectContext->SetComplete();
    //*** Kill the connection, recordset, fields, and field IP ***
    adoCoConnection->Release();
    adoAccountInfo->Release();
    padoFields->Release();
    padoField->Release();
    //*** Send back Good Transaction ***
    return S_OK;
}

STDMETHODIMP CVideosHandler::CreateDatabase()
{
    AFX_MANAGE_STATE(AfxGetStaticModuleState())
      //*** define HRESULT holder and set it to OK ***
    HRESULT hr = S_OK;
    //*** Declare our ActiveX Data Object Connection holder and set it to NULL ***
    ADOConnection* adoCoConnection = NULL;
    //*** Declare our ActiveX Data Object Recordset holder and set it to NULL ***
    ADORecordset* adoAccountInfo = NULL;
    //*** Attempt to get the ADO Connection IP ***
      hr = CoCreateInstance( CLSID_CADOConnection, NULL, CLSCTX_INPROC_SERVER,
                             IID_IADOConnection, (void **) adoCoConnection );
    //*** If can't get IP abort ***
    if (!SUCCEEDED(hr))
    {
        //*** Inform MTS of failure ***
        m_spObjectContext->SetAbort();
        //*** send back bad HRESULT ***
          return hr;
    }
    //*** Declare a CComBSTR to handle the Sequel Text ***
    CComBSTR ccbstrSQLText;
    //*** Give it the DSN for our samples database ***
    ccbstrSQLText = _T("FILEDSN=WallysVideos");
    //*** Attempt to open the database ***
    hr = adoCoConnection->Open( ccbstrSQLText.Copy(), NULL, NULL, adCmdUnspecified);
    //*** If can't get database abort ***
    if (!SUCCEEDED(hr))
    {
        //*** Inform MTS of failure ***
```

```
        m_spObjectContext->SetAbort();
        //*** Kill the connection IP ***
        adoCoConnection->Release();
        //*** send back bad HRESULT ***
          return hr;
    }
    ccbstrSQLText =
       _T("if not exists (Select name from sysobjects where name = 'Videos')\n");
    ccbstrSQLText += _T("BEGIN\n");
    ccbstrSQLText += _T("CREATE TABLE Videos (\n");
    ccbstrSQLText += _T("VideoName varchar(256) NULL ,\n");
    ccbstrSQLText += _T("IDNumber int NULL ,\n");
    ccbstrSQLText += _T("RentalPrice int NULL ,\n");
    ccbstrSQLText += _T("TotalCopies int NULL ,\n");
    ccbstrSQLText += _T("AvailableCopies int NULL ,\n");
    ccbstrSQLText += _T("TotalVideos int NULL ,\n");
    ccbstrSQLText += _T(")\n");
    ccbstrSQLText += _T("END\n");
    //*** Declare a CComVariant to hold returned record count from ADO ***
    CComVariant vRecCount;
    //*** Clear the record count ***
    vRecCount.Clear();
    //*** Execute the sequel statement on the database ***
      hr = adoCoConnection->Execute( ccbstrSQLText.Copy(), &vRecCount, -1 , NULL );
    //*** If can't reach database abort ***
    if (!SUCCEEDED(hr))
    {
        //*** Inform MTS of failure ***
        m_spObjectContext->SetAbort();
        //*** Kill the connection IP ***
        adoCoConnection->Release();
        //*** send back bad HRESULT ***
          return hr;
    }
    //*** Kill the connection, recordset, fields, and field IP ***
    adoCoConnection->Release();
    //*** Send back Good Transaction ***
    return S_OK;
}

STDMETHODIMP CVideosHandler::AddNewVideo(BSTR bstrVideoName, short sPrice, short sTotalCopies, short sAvailableCopies)
{
    AFX_MANAGE_STATE(AfxGetStaticModuleState())
      //*** Get OLE2T Macro ***
      USES_CONVERSION;
    //*** only use this if you want to use Role-based security ***
```

```
  if (m_spObjectContext->IsSecurityEnabled())
  {
       //*** Define a CComBSTR to hold the Role Name
      CComBSTR ccbstrRoleID;
      //*** set it ***
      ccbstrRoleID = _T("WallysMgr");
      //*** Define a Result holder ***
      BOOL bResult;
      //*** make the call ***
      m_spObjectContext->IsCallerInRole( ccbstrRoleID.Copy(), &bResult );
      //*** if not in the role abort ***
      if (!bResult)
      {
         //*** Inform MTS of failure ***
         m_spObjectContext->SetAbort();
         //*** send back bad HRESULT ***
          return E_FAIL;
      }
  }
    //*** define HRESULT holder and set it to OK ***
  HRESULT hr = S_OK;
  //*** Declare our ActiveX Data Object Connection holder and set it to NULL ***
  ADOConnection* adoCoConnection = NULL;
  //*** Declare our ActiveX Data Object Recordset holder and set it to NULL ***
  ADORecordset* adoAccountInfo = NULL;
  //*** Attempt to get the ADO Connection IP ***
    hr = CoCreateInstance( CLSID_CADOConnection, NULL, CLSCTX_INPROC_SERVER,
                           IID_IADOConnection, (void **) adoCoConnection );
  //*** If can't get IP abort ***
  if (!SUCCEEDED(hr))
  {
     //*** Inform MTS of failure ***
     m_spObjectContext->SetAbort();
     //*** send back bad HRESULT ***
      return hr;
  }
  //*** Declare a CComBSTR to handle the Sequel Text ***
  CComBSTR ccbstrSQLText;
  //*** Give it the DSN for our samples database ***
  ccbstrSQLText = _T("FILEDSN=WallysVideos");
  //*** Attempt to open the database ***
  hr = adoCoConnection->Open( ccbstrSQLText.Copy(), NULL, NULL, adCmdUnspecified);
  //*** If can't get database abort ***
  if (!SUCCEEDED(hr))
  {
     //*** Inform MTS of failure ***
     m_spObjectContext->SetAbort();
```

```
        //*** Kill the connection IP ***
        adoCoConnection->Release();
        //*** send back bad HRESULT ***
         return hr;
    }
    //*** define a long holder ***
    long lTotalVideos;
    //*** get current total videos ***
    get_TotalVideos( &lTotalVideos );
    //*** incremententent it );
    lTotalVideos++;
    //*** Declare the wsprintf buffer ***
    TCHAR szSQLBuffer[512];
    //***Declare CComBSTR for name and password ***
    CComBSTR ccbstrVideoName( bstrVideoName );
    //*** Create Sequel Statement ***
    wsprintf( szSQLBuffer, _T("INSERT INTO Videos VALUES('%s',%d,%d,%d,%d)"),
      OLE2T(ccbstrVideoName.Copy()),sPrice, sTotalCopies, sAvailableCopies,
      lTotalVideos);
    //*** Put the buffer in the CComBSTR via overloaded = operator ***
    ccbstrSQLText = szSQLBuffer;
    //*** Declare a CComVariant to hold returned record count from ADO ***
    CComVariant vRecCount;
    //*** Clear the record count ***
    vRecCount.Clear();
    //*** Execute the sequel statement on the database ***
      hr = adoCoConnection->Execute( ccbstrSQLText.Copy(), &vRecCount, -1 , NULL );
    //*** If can't reach database abort ***
    if (!SUCCEEDED(hr))
    {
        //*** Inform MTS of failure ***
        m_spObjectContext->SetAbort();
        //*** Kill the connection IP ***
        adoCoConnection->Release();
        //*** send back bad HRESULT ***
         return hr;
    }
    //*** Create Sequel Statement ***
    wsprintf( szSQLBuffer,
       _T("UPDATE Videos SET TotalVideos = %d WHERE VideoName = 'TotalVideos'"),
       lTotalVideos );
    //*** Put the buffer in the CComBSTR via overloaded = operator ***
    ccbstrSQLText = szSQLBuffer;
    //*** Clear the record count ***
    vRecCount.Clear();
    //*** Execute the sequel statement on the database ***
      hr = adoCoConnection->Execute( ccbstrSQLText.Copy(), &vRecCount, -1 , NULL );
```

```
    //*** If can't reach database abort ***
    if (!SUCCEEDED(hr))
    {
        //*** Inform MTS of failure ***
        m_spObjectContext->SetAbort();
       //*** Kill the connection IP ***
       adoCoConnection->Release();
        //*** send back bad HRESULT ***
       return hr;
    }
    //*** if no records updated then video doesn't exist so signal error ***
    if (vRecCount.lVal == 0)
    {
        //*** Inform MTS of failure ***
        m_spObjectContext->SetAbort();
        //*** Kill the connection IP ***
        adoCoConnection->Release();
        //*** send back bad HRESULT ***
        return E_FAIL;
    }
    //*** Tell MTS we're OK ***
    m_spObjectContext->SetComplete();
    //*** Kill the connection ***
    adoCoConnection->Release();
    //*** Send back Good Transaction ***
    return S_OK;
}

STDMETHODIMP CVideosHandler::DeleteVideo(BSTR bstrVideoName)
{
    AFX_MANAGE_STATE(AfxGetStaticModuleState())
      USES_CONVERSION;
    //*** only use this if you want to use Role-based security ***
    if (m_spObjectContext->IsSecurityEnabled())
    {
          //*** Define a CComBSTR to hold the Role Name
         CComBSTR ccbstrRoleID;
         //*** set it ***
         ccbstrRoleID = _T("WallysMgr");
         //*** Define a Result holder ***
         BOOL bResult;
         //*** make the call ***
         m_spObjectContext->IsCallerInRole( ccbstrRoleID.Copy(), &bResult );
         //*** if not in the role abort ***
         if (!bResult)
         {
            //*** Inform MTS of failure ***
```

```
            m_spObjectContext->SetAbort();
            //*** send back bad HRESULT ***
              return E_FAIL;
        }
    }
      //*** define HRESULT holder and set it to OK ***
    HRESULT hr = S_OK;
    //*** Declare our ActiveX Data Object Connection holder and set it to NULL ***
    ADOConnection* adoCoConnection = NULL;
    //*** Declare our ActiveX Data Object Recordset holder and set it to NULL ***
    ADORecordset* adoAccountInfo = NULL;
    //*** Attempt to get the ADO Connection IP ***
      hr = CoCreateInstance( CLSID_CADOConnection, NULL, CLSCTX_INPROC_SERVER,
                             IID_IADOConnection, (void **) adoCoConnection );
    //*** If can't get IP abort ***
    if (!SUCCEEDED(hr))
    {
        //*** Inform MTS of failure ***
        m_spObjectContext->SetAbort();
        //*** send back bad HRESULT ***
          return hr;
    }
    //*** Declare a CComBSTR to handle the Sequel Text ***
    CComBSTR ccbstrSQLText;
    //*** Give it the DSN for our samples database ***
    ccbstrSQLText = _T("FILEDSN=WallysVideos");
    //*** Attempt to open the database ***
    hr = adoCoConnection->Open( ccbstrSQLText.Copy(), NULL, NULL, adCmdUnspecified);
    //*** If can't get database abort ***
    if (!SUCCEEDED(hr))
    {
        //*** Inform MTS of failure ***
        m_spObjectContext->SetAbort();
        //*** Kill the connection IP ***
        adoCoConnection->Release();
        //*** send back bad HRESULT ***
          return hr;
    }
    //*** Declare the wsprintf buffer ***
    TCHAR szSQLBuffer[512];
    //***Declare CComBSTR for name  ***
    CComBSTR ccbstrVideoName( bstrVideoName );
    //*** Create Sequel Statement ***
    wsprintf( szSQLBuffer, _T("DELETE Videos WHERE VideoName = '%s'"),
               OLE2T(ccbstrVideoName.Copy()));
    //*** Put the buffer in the CComBSTR via overloaded = operator ***
    ccbstrSQLText = szSQLBuffer;
```

```
//*** Declare a CComVariant to hold returned record count from ADO ***
CComVariant vRecCount;
//*** Clear the record count ***
vRecCount.Clear();
//*** Execute the sequel statement on the database ***
  hr = adoCoConnection->Execute( ccbstrSQLText.Copy(), &vRecCount, -1 , NULL );
//*** If can't reach database abort ***
if (!SUCCEEDED(hr))
{
    //*** Inform MTS of failure ***
    m_spObjectContext->SetAbort();
    //*** Kill the connection IP ***
    adoCoConnection->Release();
    //*** send back bad HRESULT ***
     return hr;
}
//*** Define TotalVideos holder
long lTotalVideos;
//*** call internal method outside COM ***
get_TotalVideos( &lTotalVideos );
//*** increment the value ***
lTotalVideos–;
//*** Create Sequel Statement ***
wsprintf( szSQLBuffer,
  _T("UPDATE Videos SET TotalVideoss = %d WHERE VideoName = 'TotalVideos'"),
   lTotalVideos);
//*** Put the buffer in the CComBSTR via overloaded = operator ***
ccbstrSQLText = szSQLBuffer;
//*** Clear the record count ***
vRecCount.Clear();
//*** Execute the sequel statement on the database ***
  hr = adoCoConnection->Execute( ccbstrSQLText.Copy(), &vRecCount, -1 , NULL );
//*** If can't reach database abort ***
if (!SUCCEEDED(hr))
{
    //*** Inform MTS of failure ***
    m_spObjectContext->SetAbort();
   //*** Kill the connection IP ***
   adoCoConnection->Release();
    //*** send back bad HRESULT ***
   return hr;
}
//*** if no records updated then video doesn't exist so signal error ***
if (vRecCount.lVal == 0)
{
    //*** Inform MTS of failure ***
    m_spObjectContext->SetAbort();
```

```
        //*** Kill the connection IP ***
        adoCoConnection->Release();
        //*** send back bad HRESULT ***
        return E_FAIL;
    }
    //*** Tell MTS we're OK ***
    m_spObjectContext->SetComplete();
    //*** Kill the connection ***
    adoCoConnection->Release();
    //*** Send back Good Transaction ***
    return S_OK;
}

STDMETHODIMP CVideosHandler::UpdateVideoEntryName(BSTR bstrOldVideoName,
             BSTR bstrNewVideoName)
{
    AFX_MANAGE_STATE(AfxGetStaticModuleState())
    // TODO: Add your implementation code here
      USES_CONVERSION;
    //*** only use this if you want to use Role-based security ***
    if (m_spObjectContext->IsSecurityEnabled())
    {
           //*** Define a CComBSTR to hold the Role Name
          CComBSTR ccbstrRoleID;
          //*** set it ***
          ccbstrRoleID = _T("WallysMgr");
          //*** Define a Result holder ***
          BOOL bResult;
          //*** make the call ***
          m_spObjectContext->IsCallerInRole( ccbstrRoleID.Copy(), &bResult );
          //*** if not in the role abort ***
          if (!bResult)
          {
             //*** Inform MTS of failure ***
             m_spObjectContext->SetAbort();
             //*** send back bad HRESULT ***
              return E_FAIL;
          }
    }
      //*** define HRESULT holder and set it to OK ***
    HRESULT hr = S_OK;
    //*** Declare our ActiveX Data Object Connection holder and set it to NULL ***
    ADOConnection* adoCoConnection = NULL;
    //*** Declare our ActiveX Data Object Recordset holder and set it to NULL ***
    ADORecordset* adoAccountInfo = NULL;
    //*** Attempt to get the ADO Connection IP ***
      hr = CoCreateInstance( CLSID_CADOConnection, NULL, CLSCTX_INPROC_SERVER,
```

```
                              IID_IADOConnection, (void **) adoCoConnection );
    //*** If can't get IP abort ***
    if (!SUCCEEDED(hr))
    {
        //*** Inform MTS of failure ***
        m_spObjectContext->SetAbort();
        //*** send back bad HRESULT ***
         return hr;
    }
    //*** Declare a CComBSTR to handle the Sequel Text ***
    CComBSTR ccbstrSQLText;
    //*** Give it the DSN for our samples database ***
    ccbstrSQLText = _T("FILEDSN=WallysVideos");
    //*** Attempt to open the database ***
    hr = adoCoConnection->Open( ccbstrSQLText.Copy(), NULL, NULL, adCmdUnspecified);
    //*** If can't get database abort ***
    if (!SUCCEEDED(hr))
    {
        //*** Inform MTS of failure ***
        m_spObjectContext->SetAbort();
        //*** Kill the connection IP ***
        adoCoConnection->Release();
        //*** send back bad HRESULT ***
        return hr;
    }
    //***Declare CComBSTR for names  ***
    CComBSTR ccbstrNewVideoName( bstrNewVideoName );
    CComBSTR ccbstrOldVideoName( bstrOldVideoName );
    //*** Declare the wsprintf buffer ***
    TCHAR szSQLBuffer[512];
    //*** Create Sequel Statement ***
    wsprintf( szSQLBuffer,
      _T("UPDATE Videos SET VideoName = '%s' WHERE VideoName = '%s'"),
      OLE2T(ccbstrNewVideoName.Copy()),
      OLE2T(ccbstrOldVideoName.Copy()) );
    //*** Put the buffer in the CComBSTR via overloaded = operator ***
    ccbstrSQLText = szSQLBuffer;
    //*** Declare a CComVariant to hold returned record count from ADO ***
    CComVariant vRecCount;
    //*** Clear the record count ***
    vRecCount.Clear();
    //*** Execute the sequel statement on the database ***
      hr = adoCoConnection->Execute( ccbstrSQLText.Copy(), &vRecCount, -1 , NULL );
    //*** If can't reach database abort ***
    if (!SUCCEEDED(hr))
    {
        //*** Inform MTS of failure ***
```

```
        m_spObjectContext->SetAbort();
      //*** Kill the connection IP ***
      adoCoConnection->Release();
        //*** send back bad HRESULT ***
      return hr;
   }
   //*** if no records updated then account doesn't exist so signal error ***
   if (vRecCount.lVal == 0)
   {
       //*** Inform MTS of failure ***
       m_spObjectContext->SetAbort();
       //*** Kill the connection IP ***
       adoCoConnection->Release();
       //*** send back bad HRESULT ***
       return E_FAIL;
   }
   //*** Tell MTS we're OK ***
   m_spObjectContext->SetComplete();
   //*** Kill the connection***
   adoCoConnection->Release();
   //*** Send back Good Transaction ***
   return S_OK;
}

STDMETHODIMP CVideosHandler::UpdateVideoEntryPrice(BSTR bstrVideoName,
              short sNewPrice)
{
   AFX_MANAGE_STATE(AfxGetStaticModuleState())
     USES_CONVERSION;
   //*** only use this if you want to use Role-based security ***
   if (m_spObjectContext->IsSecurityEnabled())
   {
         //*** Define a CComBSTR to hold the Role Name
        CComBSTR ccbstrRoleID;
        //*** set it ***
        ccbstrRoleID = _T("WallysMgr");
        //*** Define a Result holder ***
        BOOL bResult;
        //*** make the call ***
        m_spObjectContext->IsCallerInRole( ccbstrRoleID.Copy(), &bResult );
        //*** if not in the role abort ***
        if (!bResult)
        {
           //*** Inform MTS of failure ***
           m_spObjectContext->SetAbort();
           //*** send back bad HRESULT ***
            return E_FAIL;
```

```
        }
    }
    // TODO: Add your implementation code here
      //*** define HRESULT holder and set it to OK ***
    HRESULT hr = S_OK;
    //*** Declare our ActiveX Data Object Connection holder and set it to NULL ***
    ADOConnection* adoCoConnection = NULL;
    //*** Declare our ActiveX Data Object Recordset holder and set it to NULL ***
    ADORecordset* adoAccountInfo = NULL;
    //*** Attempt to get the ADO Connection IP ***
      hr = CoCreateInstance( CLSID_CADOConnection, NULL, CLSCTX_INPROC_SERVER,
                             IID_IADOConnection, (void **) adoCoConnection );
    //*** If can't get IP abort ***
    if (!SUCCEEDED(hr))
    {
        //*** Inform MTS of failure ***
        m_spObjectContext->SetAbort();
        //*** send back bad HRESULT ***
         return hr;
    }
    //*** Declare a CComBSTR to handle the Sequel Text ***
    CComBSTR ccbstrSQLText;
    //*** Give it the DSN for our samples database ***
    ccbstrSQLText = _T("FILEDSN=WallysVideos");
    //*** Attempt to open the database ***
    hr = adoCoConnection->Open( ccbstrSQLText.Copy(), NULL, NULL, adCmdUnspecified);
    //*** If can't get database abort ***
    if (!SUCCEEDED(hr))
    {
        //*** Inform MTS of failure ***
        m_spObjectContext->SetAbort();
        //*** Kill the connection IP ***
        adoCoConnection->Release();
        //*** send back bad HRESULT ***
         return hr;
    }
    //***Declare CComBSTR for names  ***
    CComBSTR ccbstrVideoName( bstrVideoName );
    //*** Declare the wsprintf buffer ***
    TCHAR szSQLBuffer[512];
    //*** Create Sequel Statement ***
    wsprintf( szSQLBuffer,
     _T("UPDATE Videos SET RentalPrice = %d WHERE VideoName = '%s'"), sNewPrice,
      OLE2T(ccbstrVideoName.Copy()) );
    //*** Put the buffer in the CComBSTR via overloaded = operator ***
    ccbstrSQLText = szSQLBuffer;
    //*** Declare a CComVariant to hold returned record count from ADO ***
```

```
   CComVariant vRecCount;
   //*** Clear the record count ***
   vRecCount.Clear();
   //*** Execute the sequel statement on the database ***
     hr = adoCoConnection->Execute( ccbstrSQLText.Copy(), &vRecCount, -1 , NULL );
   //*** If can't reach database abort ***
   if (!SUCCEEDED(hr))
   {
        //*** Inform MTS of failure ***
        m_spObjectContext->SetAbort();
       //*** Kill the connection IP ***
       adoCoConnection->Release();
        //*** send back bad HRESULT ***
       return hr;
   }
   //*** if no records updated then account doesn't exist so signal error ***
   if (vRecCount.lVal == 0)
   {
        //*** Inform MTS of failure ***
        m_spObjectContext->SetAbort();
        //*** Kill the connection IP ***
        adoCoConnection->Release();
        //*** send back bad HRESULT ***
        return E_FAIL;
   }
   //*** Tell MTS we're OK ***
   m_spObjectContext->SetComplete();
   //*** Kill the connection ***
   adoCoConnection->Release();
   //*** Send back Good Transaction ***
   return S_OK;
}

STDMETHODIMP CVideosHandler::UpdateVideoEntryTotalCopies(BSTR bstrVideoName,
             short sNewTotalCopies)
{
   AFX_MANAGE_STATE(AfxGetStaticModuleState())
     USES_CONVERSION;
   //*** only use this if you want to use Role-based security ***
   if (m_spObjectContext->IsSecurityEnabled())
   {
         //*** Define a CComBSTR to hold the Role Name
        CComBSTR ccbstrRoleID;
        //*** set it ***
        ccbstrRoleID = _T("WallysMgr");
        //*** Define a Result holder ***
        BOOL bResult;
```

```
        //*** make the call ***
        m_spObjectContext->IsCallerInRole( ccbstrRoleID.Copy(), &bResult );
        //*** if not in the role abort ***
        if (!bResult)
        {
           //*** Inform MTS of failure ***
           m_spObjectContext->SetAbort();
           //*** send back bad HRESULT ***
            return E_FAIL;
        }
   }
   // TODO: Add your implementation code here
     //*** define HRESULT holder and set it to OK ***
   HRESULT hr = S_OK;
   //*** Declare our ActiveX Data Object Connection holder and set it to NULL ***
   ADOConnection* adoCoConnection = NULL;
   //*** Declare our ActiveX Data Object Recordset holder and set it to NULL ***
   ADORecordset* adoAccountInfo = NULL;
   //*** Attempt to get the ADO Connection IP ***
     hr = CoCreateInstance( CLSID_CADOConnection, NULL, CLSCTX_INPROC_SERVER,
                            IID_IADOConnection, (void **) adoCoConnection );
   //*** If can't get IP abort ***
   if (!SUCCEEDED(hr))
   {
       //*** Inform MTS of failure ***
       m_spObjectContext->SetAbort();
       //*** send back bad HRESULT ***
        return hr;
   }
   //*** Declare a CComBSTR to handle the Sequel Text ***
   CComBSTR ccbstrSQLText;
   //*** Give it the DSN for our samples database ***
   ccbstrSQLText = _T("FILEDSN=WallysVideos");
   //*** Attempt to open the database ***
   hr = adoCoConnection->Open( ccbstrSQLText.Copy(), NULL, NULL, adCmdUnspecified);
   //*** If can't get database abort ***
   if (!SUCCEEDED(hr))
   {
       //*** Inform MTS of failure ***
       m_spObjectContext->SetAbort();
       //*** Kill the connection IP ***
       adoCoConnection->Release();
       //*** send back bad HRESULT ***
        return hr;
   }
   //***Declare CComBSTR for names  ***
   CComBSTR ccbstrVideoName( bstrVideoName );
```

```
   //*** Declare the wsprintf buffer ***
   TCHAR szSQLBuffer[512];
   //*** Create Sequel Statement ***
   wsprintf( szSQLBuffer,
     _T("UPDATE Videos SET TotalCopies = %d WHERE VideoName = '%s'"), sNewTotalCopies,
     OLE2T(ccbstrVideoName.Copy()) );
   //*** Put the buffer in the CComBSTR via overloaded = operator ***
   ccbstrSQLText = szSQLBuffer;
   //*** Declare a CComVariant to hold returned record count from ADO ***
   CComVariant vRecCount;
   //*** Clear the record count ***
   vRecCount.Clear();
   //*** Execute the sequel statement on the database ***
     hr = adoCoConnection->Execute( ccbstrSQLText.Copy(), &vRecCount, -1 , NULL );
   //*** If can't reach database abort ***
   if (!SUCCEEDED(hr))
   {
       //*** Inform MTS of failure ***
       m_spObjectContext->SetAbort();
      //*** Kill the connection IP ***
      adoCoConnection->Release();
       //*** send back bad HRESULT ***
      return hr;
   }
   //*** if no records updated then account doesn't exist so signal error ***
   if (vRecCount.lVal == 0)
   {
       //*** Inform MTS of failure ***
       m_spObjectContext->SetAbort();
       //*** Kill the connection IP ***
       adoCoConnection->Release();
       //*** send back bad HRESULT ***
       return E_FAIL;
   }
   //*** Tell MTS we're OK ***
   m_spObjectContext->SetComplete();
   //*** Kill the connection ***
   adoCoConnection->Release();
   //*** Send back Good Transaction ***
   return S_OK;
}

STDMETHODIMP CVideosHandler::UpdateVideoEntryAvailableCopies(BSTR bstrVideoName,
             short sNewAvailableCopies)
{
   AFX_MANAGE_STATE(AfxGetStaticModuleState())
     USES_CONVERSION;
```

```
// TODO: Add your implementation code here
  //*** define HRESULT holder and set it to OK ***
HRESULT hr = S_OK;
//*** Declare our ActiveX Data Object Connection holder and set it to NULL ***
ADOConnection* adoCoConnection = NULL;
//*** Declare our ActiveX Data Object Recordset holder and set it to NULL ***
ADORecordset* adoAccountInfo = NULL;
//*** Attempt to get the ADO Connection IP ***
  hr = CoCreateInstance( CLSID_CADOConnection, NULL, CLSCTX_INPROC_SERVER,
                         IID_IADOConnection, (void **) adoCoConnection );
//*** If can't get IP abort ***
if (!SUCCEEDED(hr))
{
    //*** Inform MTS of failure ***
    m_spObjectContext->SetAbort();
    //*** send back bad HRESULT ***
     return hr;
}
//*** Declare a CComBSTR to handle the Sequel Text ***
CComBSTR ccbstrSQLText;
//*** Give it the DSN for our samples database ***
ccbstrSQLText = _T("FILEDSN=WallysVideos");
//*** Attempt to open the database ***
hr = adoCoConnection->Open( ccbstrSQLText.Copy(), NULL, NULL, adCmdUnspecified);
//*** If can't get database abort ***
if (!SUCCEEDED(hr))
{
    //*** Inform MTS of failure ***
    m_spObjectContext->SetAbort();
    //*** Kill the connection IP ***
    adoCoConnection->Release();
    //*** send back bad HRESULT ***
     return hr;
}
//***Declare CComBSTR for names  ***
CComBSTR ccbstrVideoName( bstrVideoName );
//*** Declare the wsprintf buffer ***
TCHAR szSQLBuffer[512];
//*** Create Sequel Statement ***
wsprintf( szSQLBuffer,
 _T("UPDATE Videos SET AvailableCopies = %d WHERE VideoName = '%s'"),
     sNewAvailableCopies, OLE2T(ccbstrVideoName.Copy()) );
//*** Put the buffer in the CComBSTR via overloaded = operator ***
ccbstrSQLText = szSQLBuffer;
//*** Declare a CComVariant to hold returned record count from ADO ***
CComVariant vRecCount;
//*** Clear the record count ***
```

```
    vRecCount.Clear();
    //*** Execute the sequel statement on the database ***
      hr = adoCoConnection->Execute( ccbstrSQLText.Copy(), &vRecCount, -1 , NULL );
    //*** If can't reach database abort ***
    if (!SUCCEEDED(hr))
    {
        //*** Inform MTS of failure ***
        m_spObjectContext->SetAbort();
       //*** Kill the connection IP ***
       adoCoConnection->Release();
        //*** send back bad HRESULT ***
       return hr;
    }
    //*** if no records updated then account doesn't exist so signal error ***
    if (vRecCount.lVal == 0)
    {
        //*** Inform MTS of failure ***
        m_spObjectContext->SetAbort();
        //*** Kill the connection IP ***
        adoCoConnection->Release();
        //*** send back bad HRESULT ***
        return E_FAIL;
    }
    //*** Tell MTS we're OK ***
    m_spObjectContext->SetComplete();
    //*** Kill the connection ***
    adoCoConnection->Release();
    //*** Send back Good Transaction ***
    return S_OK;
}

STDMETHODIMP CVideosHandler::get_VideoRentalPrice(BSTR bstrVideoName, short *pVal)
{
    AFX_MANAGE_STATE(AfxGetStaticModuleState())
      USES_CONVERSION;
    // TODO: Add your implementation code here
      //*** define HRESULT holder and set it to OK ***
    HRESULT hr = S_OK;
    //*** Declare our ActiveX Data Object Connection holder and set it to NULL ***
    ADOConnection* adoCoConnection = NULL;
    //*** Declare our ActiveX Data Object Recordset holder and set it to NULL ***
    ADORecordset* adoAccountInfo = NULL;
    //*** Declare our ActiveX Data Object Fields holder and set it to NULL ***
    ADOFields* padoFields = NULL;
    //*** Declare our ActiveX Data Object Field holder and set it to NULL ***
    ADOField* padoField = NULL;
    //*** Define Error Holder and set it to 0 ***
```

```
long lErrorFlags = 0;
//*** Attempt to get the ADO Connection IP ***
  hr = CoCreateInstance( CLSID_CADOConnection, NULL, CLSCTX_INPROC_SERVER,
                         IID_IADOConnection, (void **) adoCoConnection );
//*** If can't get IP abort ***
if (!SUCCEEDED(hr))
{
    //*** Inform MTS of failure ***
    m_spObjectContext->SetAbort();
    //*** send back bad HRESULT ***
     return hr;
}
//*** Declare a CComBSTR to handle the Sequel Text ***
CComBSTR ccbstrSQLText;
//*** Give it the DSN for our samples database ***
ccbstrSQLText = _T("FILEDSN=WallysVideos");
//*** Attempt to open the database ***
hr = adoCoConnection->Open( ccbstrSQLText.Copy(), NULL, NULL, adCmdUnspecified);
//*** If can't get database abort ***
if (!SUCCEEDED(hr))
{
    //*** Inform MTS of failure ***
    m_spObjectContext->SetAbort();
    //*** Kill the connection IP ***
    adoCoConnection->Release();
    //*** send back bad HRESULT ***
     return hr;
}
//***Declare CComBSTR for names  ***
CComBSTR ccbstrVideoName( bstrVideoName );
//*** Declare the wsprintf buffer ***
TCHAR szSQLBuffer[512];
wsprintf( szSQLBuffer,
 _T("SELECT RentalPrice FROM Videos WHERE VideoName = '%s'"),
     OLE2T(ccbstrVideoName.Copy()));
//*** Put it into the CComBSTR via overloaded = operator ***
ccbstrSQLText = szSQLBuffer;
//*** Declare a CComVariant to hold returned record count from ADO ***
CComVariant vRecCount;
//*** Clear the record count ***
vRecCount.Clear();
//*** Execute the sequel statement on the database ***
  hr = adoCoConnection->Execute( ccbstrSQLText.Copy(), &vRecCount, -1 ,
      &adoAccountInfo );
//*** If can't reach database abort ***
if (!SUCCEEDED(hr))
{
```

```
        //*** Inform MTS of failure ***
        m_spObjectContext->SetAbort();
        //*** Kill the connection IP ***
        adoCoConnection->Release();
        //*** send back bad HRESULT ***
        return hr;
    }
    //*** Obtain the fields collection from the recordset ***
      hr = adoAccountInfo->get_Fields( &padoFields );
    //*** If can't reach database abort ***
    if (!SUCCEEDED(hr))
    {
        //*** Inform MTS of failure ***
        m_spObjectContext->SetAbort();
        //*** Kill the connection and recordset IP ***
       adoCoConnection->Release();
       adoAccountInfo->Release();
        //*** send back bad HRESULT ***
       return hr;
    }
    //*** Define a variant to obtain the rental price field ***
    CComVariant vField = _T("RentalPrice");
    //*** define a variant to hold the information ***
    CComVariant vRentalPrice;
    //*** Get the rentalprice Field ***
    hr = padoFields->get_Item( vField , &padoField );
    //*** If can't reach database abort ***
    if (!SUCCEEDED(hr))
    {
        //*** Inform MTS of failure ***
        m_spObjectContext->SetAbort();
       //*** Kill the connection, recordset, and fields IP ***
       adoCoConnection->Release();
       adoAccountInfo->Release();
       padoFields->Release();
        //*** send back bad HRESULT ***
       return hr;
    }
    //*** Get the actual rentalprice value ***
    hr = padoField->get_Value( &vRentalPrice );
    //*** If can't reach database abort ***
    if (!SUCCEEDED(hr))
    {
        //*** Inform MTS of failure ***
        m_spObjectContext->SetAbort();
        //*** Kill the connection, recordset, fields, and field IP ***
        adoCoConnection->Release();
```

```
        adoAccountInfo->Release();
        padoFields->Release();
        padoField->Release();
        //*** send back bad HRESULT ***
        return hr;
    }
      //*** return the value from the variant ***
      *pVal = vRentalPrice.iVal;
    //*** Tell MTS we're OK ***
    m_spObjectContext->SetComplete();
    //*** Kill the connection, recordset, fields, and field IP ***
    adoCoConnection->Release();
    adoAccountInfo->Release();
    padoFields->Release();
    padoField->Release();
    //*** Send back Good Transaction ***
    return S_OK;
}

STDMETHODIMP CVideosHandler::get_VideoTotalCopies(BSTR bstrVideoName, short *pVal)
{
    AFX_MANAGE_STATE(AfxGetStaticModuleState())
        USES_CONVERSION;
    // TODO: Add your implementation code here
        //*** define HRESULT holder and set it to OK ***
    HRESULT hr = S_OK;
    //*** Declare our ActiveX Data Object Connection holder and set it to NULL ***
    ADOConnection* adoCoConnection = NULL;
    //*** Declare our ActiveX Data Object Recordset holder and set it to NULL ***
    ADORecordset* adoAccountInfo = NULL;
    //*** Declare our ActiveX Data Object Fields holder and set it to NULL ***
    ADOFields* padoFields = NULL;
    //*** Declare our ActiveX Data Object Field holder and set it to NULL ***
    ADOField* padoField = NULL;
    //*** Define Error Holder and set it to 0 ***
    long lErrorFlags = 0;
    //*** Attempt to get the ADO Connection IP ***
        hr = CoCreateInstance( CLSID_CADOConnection, NULL, CLSCTX_INPROC_SERVER,
                               IID_IADOConnection, (void **) adoCoConnection );
    //*** If can't get IP abort ***
    if (!SUCCEEDED(hr))
    {
        //*** Inform MTS of failure ***
        m_spObjectContext->SetAbort();
        //*** send back bad HRESULT ***
          return hr;
    }
```

```
//*** Declare a CComBSTR to handle the Sequel Text ***
CComBSTR ccbstrSQLText;
//*** Give it the DSN for our samples database ***
ccbstrSQLText = _T("FILEDSN=WallysVideos");
//*** Attempt to open the database ***
hr = adoCoConnection->Open( ccbstrSQLText.Copy(), NULL, NULL, adCmdUnspecified);
//*** If can't get database abort ***
if (!SUCCEEDED(hr))
{
    //*** Inform MTS of failure ***
    m_spObjectContext->SetAbort();
    //*** Kill the connection IP ***
    adoCoConnection->Release();
    //*** send back bad HRESULT ***
     return hr;
}
//***Declare CComBSTR for names  ***
CComBSTR ccbstrVideoName( bstrVideoName );
//*** Declare the wsprintf buffer ***
TCHAR szSQLBuffer[512];
wsprintf( szSQLBuffer,
   _T("SELECT TotalCopies FROM Videos WHERE VideoName = '%s'"),
   OLE2T(ccbstrVideoName.Copy()));
//*** Put it into the CComBSTR via overloaded = operator ***
ccbstrSQLText = szSQLBuffer;
//*** Declare a CComVariant to hold returned record count from ADO ***
CComVariant vRecCount;
//*** Clear the record count ***
vRecCount.Clear();
//*** Execute the sequel statement on the database ***
   hr = adoCoConnection->Execute( ccbstrSQLText.Copy(), &vRecCount, -1 ,
   &adoAccountInfo );
//*** If can't reach database abort ***
if (!SUCCEEDED(hr))
{
    //*** Inform MTS of failure ***
    m_spObjectContext->SetAbort();
    //*** Kill the connection IP ***
    adoCoConnection->Release();
    //*** send back bad HRESULT ***
    return hr;
}
//*** Obtain the fields collection from the recordset ***
   hr = adoAccountInfo->get_Fields( &padoFields );
//*** If can't reach database abort ***
if (!SUCCEEDED(hr))
{
```

```
        //*** Inform MTS of failure ***
        m_spObjectContext->SetAbort();
        //*** Kill the connection and recordset IP ***
       adoCoConnection->Release();
       adoAccountInfo->Release();
        //*** send back bad HRESULT ***
       return hr;
    }
    //*** Define a variant to obtain the totalcopies field ***
    CComVariant vField = _T("TotalCopies");
    //*** define a variant to hold the information ***
    CComVariant vCopies;
    //*** Get the totalcopies Field ***
    hr = padoFields->get_Item( vField , &padoField );
    //*** If can't reach database abort ***
    if (!SUCCEEDED(hr))
    {
        //*** Inform MTS of failure ***
        m_spObjectContext->SetAbort();
       //*** Kill the connection, recordset, and fields IP ***
       adoCoConnection->Release();
       adoAccountInfo->Release();
       padoFields->Release();
        //*** send back bad HRESULT ***
       return hr;
    }
    //*** Get the actual totalcopies value ***
    hr = padoField->get_Value( &vCopies );
    //*** If can't reach database abort ***
    if (!SUCCEEDED(hr))
    {
        //*** Inform MTS of failure ***
        m_spObjectContext->SetAbort();
        //*** Kill the connection, recordset, fields, and field IP ***
        adoCoConnection->Release();
        adoAccountInfo->Release();
        padoFields->Release();
        padoField->Release();
        //*** send back bad HRESULT ***
        return hr;
    }
       //*** return the value from the variant ***
       *pVal = vCopies.iVal;
    //*** Tell MTS we're OK ***
    m_spObjectContext->SetComplete();
    //*** Kill the connection, recordset, fields, and field IP ***
    adoCoConnection->Release();
```

```
 adoAccountInfo->Release();
 padoFields->Release();
 padoField->Release();
 //*** Send back Good Transaction ***
 return S_OK;
}

STDMETHODIMP CVideosHandler::get_VideoAvailableCopies(BSTR bstrVideoName,
          short *pVal)
{
 AFX_MANAGE_STATE(AfxGetStaticModuleState())
   USES_CONVERSION;
 // TODO: Add your implementation code here
   //*** define HRESULT holder and set it to OK ***
 HRESULT hr = S_OK;
 //*** Declare our ActiveX Data Object Connection holder and set it to NULL ***
 ADOConnection* adoCoConnection = NULL;
 //*** Declare our ActiveX Data Object Recordset holder and set it to NULL ***
 ADORecordset* adoAccountInfo = NULL;
 //*** Declare our ActiveX Data Object Fields holder and set it to NULL ***
 ADOFields* padoFields = NULL;
 //*** Declare our ActiveX Data Object Field holder and set it to NULL ***
 ADOField* padoField = NULL;
 //*** Define Error Holder and set it to 0 ***
 long lErrorFlags = 0;
 //*** Attempt to get the ADO Connection IP ***
   hr = CoCreateInstance( CLSID_CADOConnection, NULL, CLSCTX_INPROC_SERVER,
                  IID_IADOConnection, (void **) adoCoConnection );
 //*** If can't get IP abort ***
 if (!SUCCEEDED(hr))
 {
    //*** Inform MTS of failure ***
    m_spObjectContext->SetAbort();
    //*** send back bad HRESULT ***
     return hr;
 }
 //*** Declare a CComBSTR to handle the Sequel Text ***
 CComBSTR ccbstrSQLText;
 //*** Give it the DSN for our samples database ***
 ccbstrSQLText = _T("FILEDSN=WallysVideos");
 //*** Attempt to open the database ***
 hr = adoCoConnection->Open( ccbstrSQLText.Copy(), NULL, NULL, adCmdUnspecified);
 //*** If can't get database abort ***
 if (!SUCCEEDED(hr))
 {
    //*** Inform MTS of failure ***
    m_spObjectContext->SetAbort();
```

```
      //*** Kill the connection IP ***
      adoCoConnection->Release();
      //*** send back bad HRESULT ***
       return hr;
   }
   //***Declare CComBSTR for names  ***
   CComBSTR ccbstrVideoName( bstrVideoName );
   //*** Declare the wsprintf buffer ***
   TCHAR szSQLBuffer[512];
   wsprintf( szSQLBuffer,
     _T("SELECT AvailableCopies FROM Videos WHERE VideoName = '%s'"),
       OLE2T(ccbstrVideoName.Copy()));
   //*** Put it into the CComBSTR via overloaded = operator ***
   ccbstrSQLText = szSQLBuffer;
   //*** Declare a CComVariant to hold returned record count from ADO ***
   CComVariant vRecCount;
   //*** Clear the record count ***
   vRecCount.Clear();
   //*** Execute the sequel statement on the database ***
     hr = adoCoConnection->Execute( ccbstrSQLText.Copy(), &vRecCount, -1 ,
      &adoAccountInfo );
   //*** If can't reach database abort ***
   if (!SUCCEEDED(hr))
   {
      //*** Inform MTS of failure ***
      m_spObjectContext->SetAbort();
      //*** Kill the connection IP ***
      adoCoConnection->Release();
      //*** send back bad HRESULT ***
      return hr;
   }
   //*** Obtain the fields collection from the recordset ***
     hr = adoAccountInfo->get_Fields( &padoFields );
   //*** If can't reach database abort ***
   if (!SUCCEEDED(hr))
   {
      //*** Inform MTS of failure ***
      m_spObjectContext->SetAbort();
      //*** Kill the connection and recordset IP ***
     adoCoConnection->Release();
     adoAccountInfo->Release();
      //*** send back bad HRESULT ***
     return hr;
   }
   //*** Define a variant to obtain the availablecopies field ***
   CComVariant vField = _T("AvailableCopies");
   //*** define a variant to hold the information ***
```

```
    CComVariant vCopies;
    //*** Get the availablecopies Field ***
    hr = padoFields->get_Item( vField , &padoField );
    //*** If can't reach database abort ***
    if (!SUCCEEDED(hr))
    {
        //*** Inform MTS of failure ***
        m_spObjectContext->SetAbort();
       //*** Kill the connection, recordset, and fields IP ***
       adoCoConnection->Release();
       adoAccountInfo->Release();
       padoFields->Release();
        //*** send back bad HRESULT ***
       return hr;
    }
    //*** Get the actual available value ***
    hr = padoField->get_Value( &vCopies );
    //*** If can't reach database abort ***
    if (!SUCCEEDED(hr))
    {
        //*** Inform MTS of failure ***
        m_spObjectContext->SetAbort();
        //*** Kill the connection, recordset, fields, and field IP ***
        adoCoConnection->Release();
        adoAccountInfo->Release();
        padoFields->Release();
        padoField->Release();
        //*** send back bad HRESULT ***
        return hr;
    }
       //*** return the value from the variant ***
       *pVal = vCopies.iVal;
    //*** Tell MTS we're OK ***
    m_spObjectContext->SetComplete();
    //*** Kill the connection, recordset, fields, and field IP ***
    adoCoConnection->Release();
    adoAccountInfo->Release();
    padoFields->Release();
    padoField->Release();
    //*** Send back Good Transaction ***
    return S_OK;
}

STDMETHODIMP CVideosHandler::GetVideoNameByNumber(short sVideoID,
              BSTR *bstrVideoName)
{
    AFX_MANAGE_STATE(AfxGetStaticModuleState())
```

```
   USES_CONVERSION;
// TODO: Add your implementation code here
   //*** define HRESULT holder and set it to OK ***
HRESULT hr = S_OK;
//*** Declare our ActiveX Data Object Connection holder and set it to NULL ***
ADOConnection* adoCoConnection = NULL;
//*** Declare our ActiveX Data Object Recordset holder and set it to NULL ***
ADORecordset* adoAccountInfo = NULL;
//*** Declare our ActiveX Data Object Fields holder and set it to NULL ***
ADOFields* padoFields = NULL;
//*** Declare our ActiveX Data Object Field holder and set it to NULL ***
ADOField* padoField = NULL;
//*** Define Error Holder and set it to 0 ***
long lErrorFlags = 0;
//*** Attempt to get the ADO Connection IP ***
   hr = CoCreateInstance( CLSID_CADOConnection, NULL, CLSCTX_INPROC_SERVER,
                          IID_IADOConnection, (void **) adoCoConnection );
//*** If can't get IP abort ***
if (!SUCCEEDED(hr))
{
    //*** Inform MTS of failure ***
    m_spObjectContext->SetAbort();
    //*** send back bad HRESULT ***
     return hr;
}
//*** Declare a CComBSTR to handle the Sequel Text ***
CComBSTR ccbstrSQLText;
//*** Give it the DSN for our samples database ***
ccbstrSQLText = _T("FILEDSN=WallysVideos");
//*** Attempt to open the database ***
hr = adoCoConnection->Open( ccbstrSQLText.Copy(), NULL, NULL, adCmdUnspecified);
//*** If can't get database abort ***
if (!SUCCEEDED(hr))
{
    //*** Inform MTS of failure ***
    m_spObjectContext->SetAbort();
    //*** Kill the connection IP ***
    adoCoConnection->Release();
    //*** send back bad HRESULT ***
     return hr;
}
//*** Declare the wsprintf buffer ***
TCHAR szSQLBuffer[512];
wsprintf( szSQLBuffer, _T("SELECT VideoName FROM Videos WHERE IDNumber = %d"),
           sVideoID);
//*** Put it into the CComBSTR via overloaded = operator ***
ccbstrSQLText = szSQLBuffer;
```

```
//*** Declare a CComVariant to hold returned record count from ADO ***
CComVariant vRecCount;
//*** Clear the record count ***
vRecCount.Clear();
//*** Execute the sequel statement on the database ***
   hr = adoCoConnection->Execute( ccbstrSQLText.Copy(), &vRecCount, -1 ,
   &adoAccountInfo );
//*** If can't reach database abort ***
if (!SUCCEEDED(hr))
{
    //*** Inform MTS of failure ***
    m_spObjectContext->SetAbort();
    //*** Kill the connection IP ***
    adoCoConnection->Release();
    //*** send back bad HRESULT ***
    return hr;
}
//*** Obtain the fields collection from the recordset ***
   hr = adoAccountInfo->get_Fields( &padoFields );
//*** If can't reach database abort ***
if (!SUCCEEDED(hr))
{
    //*** Inform MTS of failure ***
    m_spObjectContext->SetAbort();
    //*** Kill the connection and recordset IP ***
   adoCoConnection->Release();
   adoAccountInfo->Release();
    //*** send back bad HRESULT ***
   return hr;
}
//*** Define a variant to obtain the videoname field ***
CComVariant vField = _T("VideoName");
//*** define a variant to hold the information ***
CComVariant vName;
//*** Get the videoname Field ***
hr = padoFields->get_Item( vField , &padoField );
//*** If can't reach database abort ***
if (!SUCCEEDED(hr))
{
    //*** Inform MTS of failure ***
    m_spObjectContext->SetAbort();
   //*** Kill the connection, recordset, and fields IP ***
   adoCoConnection->Release();
   adoAccountInfo->Release();
   padoFields->Release();
    //*** send back bad HRESULT ***
   return hr;
```

```
1363. }
1364. //*** Get the actual videoname value ***
1365. hr = padoField->get_Value( &vName );
1366. //*** If can't reach database abort ***
1367. if (!SUCCEEDED(hr))
1368. {
1369.     //*** Inform MTS of failure ***
1370.     m_spObjectContext->SetAbort();
1371.     //*** Kill the connection, recordset, fields, and field IP ***
1372.     adoCoConnection->Release();
1373.     adoAccountInfo->Release();
1374.     padoFields->Release();
1375.     padoField->Release();
1376.     //*** send back bad HRESULT ***
1377.     return hr;
1378. }
1379.    //*** return the value from the variant ***
1380. CComBSTR bstrName;
1381. bstrName = vName.bstrVal;
1382.    *bstrVideoName = bstrName.Copy();
1383. //*** Kill the connection, recordset, fields, and field IP ***
1384. adoCoConnection->Release();
1385. adoAccountInfo->Release();
1386. padoFields->Release();
1387. padoField->Release();
1388. //*** Send back Good Transaction ***
1389. return S_OK;
1390. }
```

***Listing 6-2** VIDEOSHANDLER.CPP source code after modifications*

Here's the breakdown (the code is heavily commented and so we'll concentrate on the bigger design issues and some places where the logic may be a bit hard to follow in these comments. Also, since after the first function the code is virtually identical except for single lines calling different database SQL statements, only the first function is detailed below):

- **Lines 4-9** This code brings in the ADO headers so we can access them.
- **Lines 17-20** This code automatically obtains an MTS object context for use in the component's functions. It will be there because in the MTS Explorer (see Chapter 9) we will set this component to Require a Transaction.
- **Lines 40-60** This code initializes the ADO interface pointers needed to interact with the SQL Server database.
- **Lines 61-76** This code contacts the Wallys database and signals an error if it fails. Note that it aborts the transaction for any failure.

- **Lines 77-99** This code executes the SQL text for this particular database interaction and obtains a pRowset interface pointer which contains a set of data that hopefully matches that requested by the command. Note that it aborts the transaction for any failure.
- **Lines 100-112** This code gets a pFields interface pointer from the pRowset IP obtained from executing the SQL statement. This IP contains all the fields of the current rowset so the program can obtain as many as it wants and examine or change their values. Note that it aborts the transaction for any failure.
- **Lines 113-130** This code gets a single pField Interface pointer from the pFields IP with the name given. This moves from a collection of all the fields in the current recordset to one single field so its value can be obtained. Note that it aborts the transaction for any failure.
- **Lines 131-145** This code uses the pField Interface pointer to obtain the actual value of the field and deal with it as needed (it reads it in this example, but in later examples is used to set it). Note that it aborts the transaction for any failure.
- **Lines 146-156** This code returns the desired value and completes the transaction so any other components will be able to complete successfully as well.
- **Lines 234-253** This code handles using MTS role-based security for a database action. It requires the user to be a member of the WallysMgr role account, which Chapter 9 will show you how to create using the MTS Explorer. Otherwise it will not allow the action to proceed.

Once you are satisfied you've entered the code from the above listing correctly, build the MTS COM server from the Build menu. If you encounter any errors, please check the code in the listing to find your mistake (it has been exhaustively debugged and is correct). Once you have compiled the component successfully, it is automatically registered on the local machine; if you need to move it to another machine, see Chapter 9. Otherwise, please move on to the next component.

## Creating an MTS ASP Component with ATL

The next step is to use ATL to create an MTS-aware ASP COM Server that handles online video ordering and cancellation for Wally's. The following sections take you through the user interface portions of creating the project in the step-by-step system, then show you the code you need to write and an analysis using the line-by-line approach.

## Step-By-Step

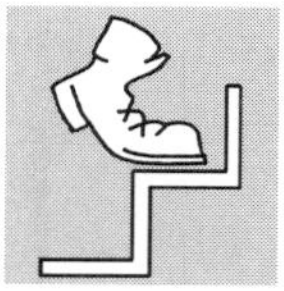

Start Visual C++ 5.0 or 6.0. From the File menu, select New. The New dialog box opens; highlight ATL COM AppWizard. Select an appropriate directory, then enter a project name of **ATLASPWallysVideoManager**. Figure 6-37 shows how the New dialog should appear when you are done. Press OK to open the ATL COM AppWizard.

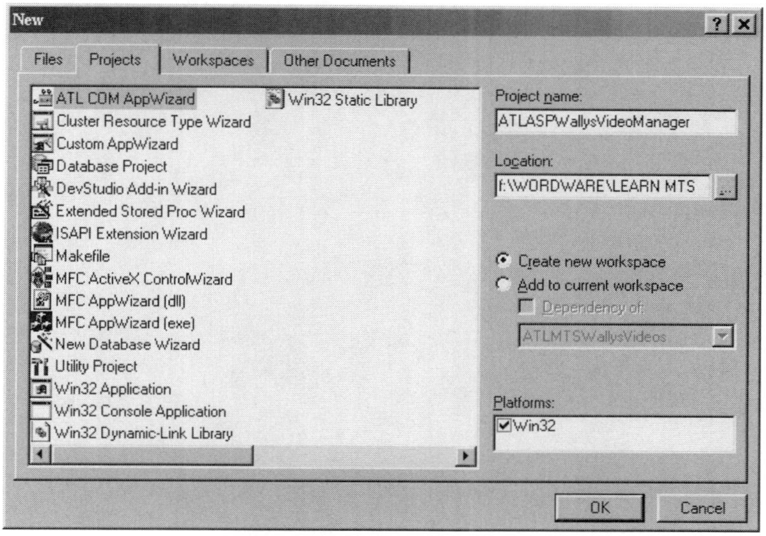


***Figure 6-37*** *The New dialog box creating the ATLASPWallys VideoManager ATL project*

In the ATL AppWizard, select the DLL project, and make sure that the Support MFC, Merge Proxy/Stub Code, and Support MTS check boxes are checked. Press Finish.

A confirmation dialog box appears; press OK to create the ATL project.

From the Insert menu, select New ATL Object. The ATL Object Wizard dialog appears, as shown in Figure 6-38. Select the Objects entry in the left-hand list box, and the ActiveX Server Component entry in the right-hand list box. Press Next to move to the settings pages of the wizard.

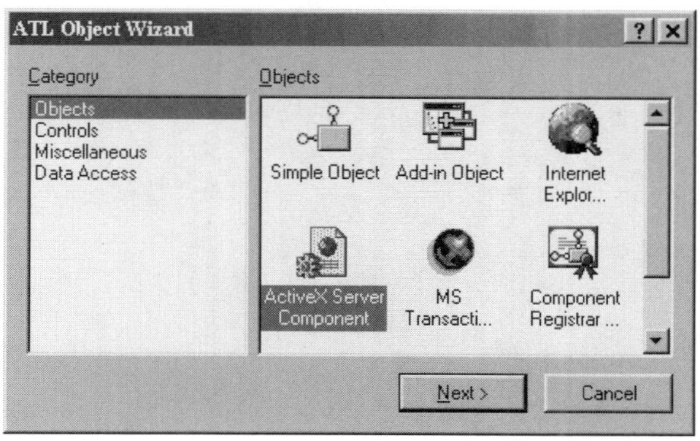


***Figure 6-38*** *Selecting an ActiveX Server Component object in the ATL Object Wizard*

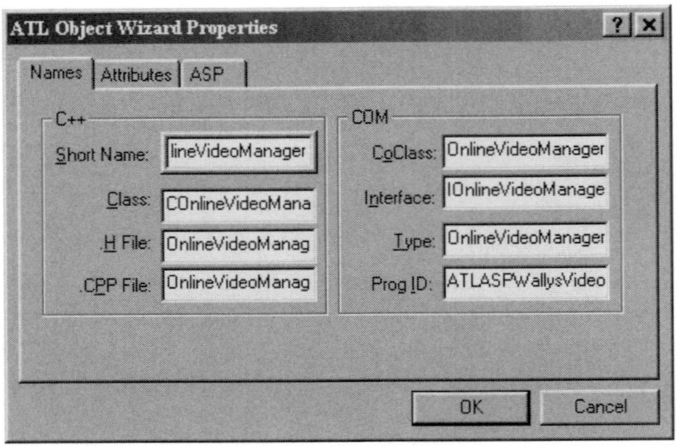


***Figure 6-39*** *Entering name information in the ATL Object Wizard*

Select the Names tab of the next wizard dialog if it is not selected by default. As shown in Figure 6-39, enter **OnlineVideoManager** as the name of the control implementation class; the other boxes will fill in automatically. Accept the default values and select the Attributes tab.

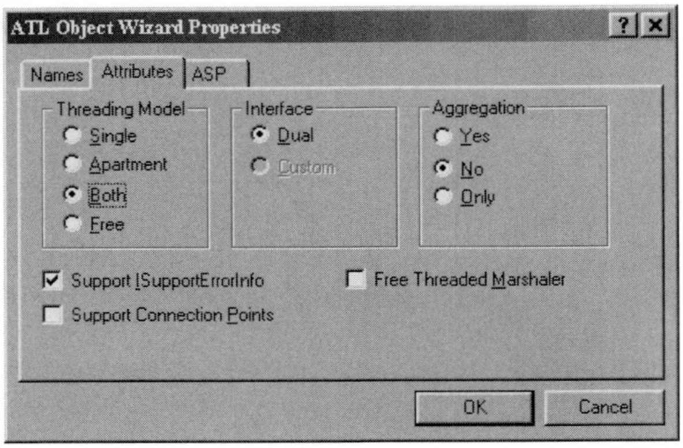


***Figure 6-40*** *Entering attributes information in the ATL Object Wizard*

As shown in Figure 6-40, select the Both Threading Model radio button, the Dual Interface radio button, and the No Aggregation radio button. Check the Support ISupportErrorInfo check box also. Now select the ASP tab.

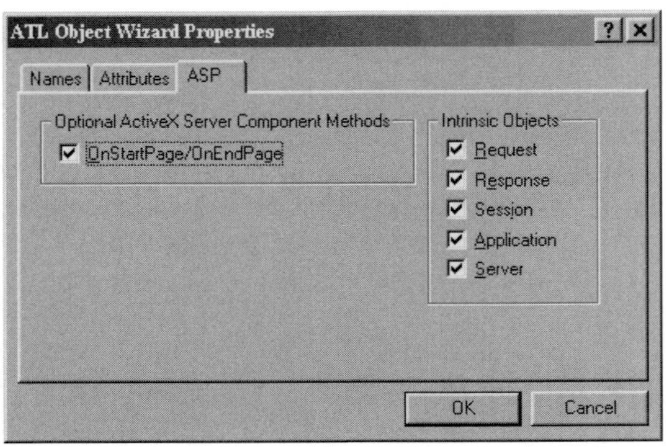


***Figure 6-41*** *Entering ASP information in the ATL Object Wizard*

As illustrated in Figure 6-41, all the check boxes of the ASP tab should be checked to enable all the functionality of ASP for the component. Press OK now to add the ASP Component Server object to your ATL project.

Move to the Project Explorer window and select the ClassView pane. The IOnlineVideoManager Interface is displayed; right-click on it to display the shortcut menu. Select the Add Property menu option.

The Add Property Wizard dialog box appears; select a Property Type of BSTR. Give it a name of **CustomerName**, and check both the Get and Put accessor functions to create a read/write property. Figure 6-42 shows how the Add

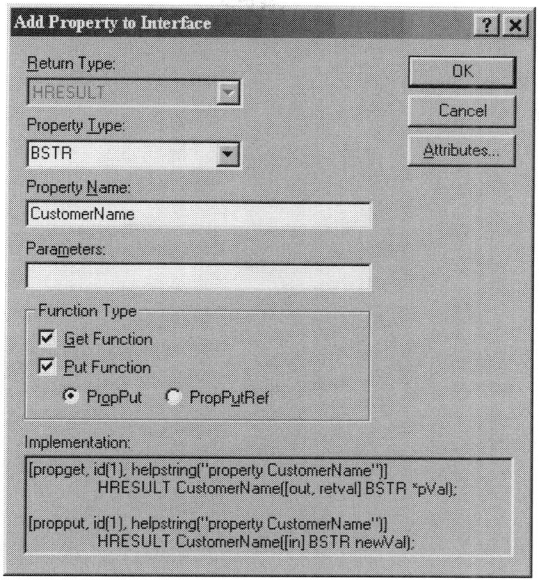


***Figure 6-42*** *Entering the CustomerName property with the ATL Add Property Wizard*

Property dialog should appear when you are done. Press OK to add the property to the ATL COM component.

Again right-click on the IOnlineVideoManager Interface in the ClassView pane of the Project Explorer and select Add Property. The Add Property Wizard dialog box appears; select a Property Type of BSTR. Give it a name of **CustomerPassword**, and check both the Get and Put accessor functions to create a read/write property. Press OK to add the property to the ATL COM component.

Again right-click on the IOnlineVideoManager Interface in the ClassView pane of the Project Explorer and select Add Property. The Add Property Wizard dialog box appears; select a Property Type of BSTR. Give it a name of **VideoName**, and check both the Get and Put accessor functions to create a read/write property. Press OK to add the property to the ATL COM component.

Again right-click on the IOnlineVideoManager Interface in the ClassView pane of the Project Explorer and select Add Property. The Add Property Wizard dialog box appears; select a Property Type of short. Give it a name of **ConnectionType**, and check both the Get and Put accessor functions to create a read/write property. Press OK to add the property to the ATL COM component.

Again right-click on the IOnlineVideoManager Interface in the ClassView pane of the Project Explorer and select Add Property. The Add Property Wizard dialog box appears; select a Property Type of BOOL. Give it a name of **NowPlaying**, and check both the Get and Put accessor functions to create a read/write property. Press OK to add the property to the ATL COM component.

Again right-click on the IOnlineVideoManager Interface in the ClassView pane of the Project Explorer; this time select Add Method from the shortcut menu. The Add Method Wizard dialog box appears; give the method the name of **OrderVideo**, with no parameters. Figure 6-43 shows how the Add Method dialog should appear when you are done. Press OK to add the method to the ATL COM component.

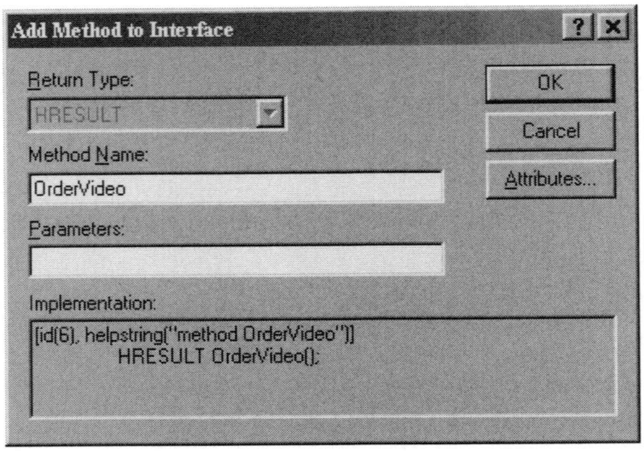


*Figure 6-43 Entering the OrderVideo method with the ATL Add Method Wizard*

Again right-click on the IOnlineVideoManager Interface in the ClassView pane of the Project Explorer; again select Add Method from the shortcut menu. The Add Method Wizard dialog box appears; give the method the name of **TerminateVideo-Play**, with no parameters. Press OK to add the method to the ATL COM component.

Again right-click on the IOnlineVideoManager Interface in the ClassView pane of the Project Explorer; again select Add Method from the shortcut menu. The Add Method Wizard dialog box appears; give the method the name of **GetVideoNameByNumber**, with a parameter string of [in] short sIDNumber, [out] BSTR *bstrVideoName. Press OK to add the method to the ATL COM component. Save the project to protect your work.

## Line-By-Line

Next, you need to enter the program code to implement the MTS database functionality this component implements. Bring up the ONLINEVIDEOMANAGER.H file in the text editor. Scan through it and enter or change any boldfaced line of source code in Listing 6-3. Save the project.

```
// OnlineVideoManager.h : Declaration of the COnlineVideoManager

#ifndef __ONLINEVIDEOMANAGER_H_
#define __ONLINEVIDEOMANAGER_H_

#include "resource.h"       // main symbols
#include <asptlb.h>         // Active Server Pages Definitions

/////////////////////////////////////////////////////////////////////////////
// COnlineVideoManager
class ATL_NO_VTABLE COnlineVideoManager :
    public CComObjectRootEx<CComSingleThreadModel>,
    public CComCoClass<COnlineVideoManager, &CLSID_OnlineVideoManager>,
    public ISupportErrorInfo,
    public IDispatchImpl<IOnlineVideoManager, &IID_IOnlineVideoManager,
           &LIBID_ATLASPWALLYSVIDEOMANAGERLib>
{
public:
    COnlineVideoManager()
    {
        m_bOnStartPageCalled = FALSE;
```

```
    }

public:

DECLARE_REGISTRY_RESOURCEID(IDR_ONLINEVIDEOMANAGER)

DECLARE_PROTECT_FINAL_CONSTRUCT()

BEGIN_COM_MAP(COnlineVideoManager)
    COM_INTERFACE_ENTRY(IOnlineVideoManager)
    COM_INTERFACE_ENTRY(IDispatch)
    COM_INTERFACE_ENTRY(ISupportErrorInfo)
END_COM_MAP()

// ISupportsErrorInfo
    STDMETHOD(InterfaceSupportsErrorInfo)(REFIID riid);

// IOnlineVideoManager
public:
    STDMETHOD(GetVideoNameByNumber)(/*[in]*/ short sIDNumber,
     /*[out]*/ BSTR* bstrVideoName);
    STDMETHOD(TerminateVideoPlay)();
    STDMETHOD(OrderVideo)();
    STDMETHOD(get_NowPlaying)(/*[out, retval]*/ BOOL *pVal);
    STDMETHOD(put_NowPlaying)(/*[in]*/ BOOL newVal);
    STDMETHOD(get_ConnectionType)(/*[out, retval]*/ short *pVal);
    STDMETHOD(put_ConnectionType)(/*[in]*/ short newVal);
    STDMETHOD(get_VideoName)(/*[out, retval]*/ BSTR *pVal);
    STDMETHOD(put_VideoName)(/*[in]*/ BSTR newVal);
    STDMETHOD(get_CustomerPassword)(/*[out, retval]*/ BSTR *pVal);
    STDMETHOD(put_CustomerPassword)(/*[in]*/ BSTR newVal);
    STDMETHOD(get_CustomerName)(/*[out, retval]*/ BSTR *pVal);
    STDMETHOD(put_CustomerName)(/*[in]*/ BSTR newVal);
    //Active Server Pages Methods
    STDMETHOD(OnStartPage)(IUnknown* IUnk);
    STDMETHOD(OnEndPage)();

private:
    CComPtr<IRequest> m_piRequest;                      //Request Object
    CComPtr<IResponse> m_piResponse;                    //Response Object
    CComPtr<ISessionObject> m_piSession;                //Session Object
    CComPtr<IServer> m_piServer;                        //Server Object
    CComPtr<IApplicationObject> m_piApplication;        //Application Object
    BOOL m_bOnStartPageCalled;                          //OnStartPage successful?
    //*** storage for custom properties ***
    CComBSTR bstrCustomerName;
    CComBSTR bstrCustomerPassword;
```

```
69.     CComBSTR bstrVideoName;
70.     short sConnectionType;
71.     BOOL bNowPlaying;
72. };
73.
74. #endif //__ONLINEVIDEOMANAGER_H_
```

***Listing 6-3*** *ONLINEVIDEOMANAGER.H source code after modifications*

Here's the breakdown:

- **Lines 66-71** These lines of code declare the member variables that will hold the underlying data for the component's properties. You'll access them in the CPP file.

Next, bring up the ONLINEVIDEOMANAGER.CPP file in the text editor. Scan through it and enter or change any boldfaced line of source code in Listing 6-4. Save the project.

```

// OnlineVideoManager.cpp : Implementation of COnlineVideoManager
#include "stdafx.h"
#include "ATLASPWallysVideoManager.h"
#include "OnlineVideoManager.h"
#include <mtx.h>
//*** include for ATLMTSWallysAccount Interfaces (assumes CD directory structure) ***
#include "..\ATLMTSWallysAccount\ATLMTSWallysAccount.h"
#include "..\ATLMTSWallysAccount\ATLMTSWallysAccount_i.c"
#include "..\ATLMTSWallysVideos\ATLMTSWallysVideos.h"
#include "..\ATLMTSWallysVideos\ATLMTSWallysVideos_i.c"

////////////////////////////////////////////////////////////////////////////
// COnlineVideoManager

STDMETHODIMP COnlineVideoManager::InterfaceSupportsErrorInfo(REFIID riid)
{
    static const IID* arr[] =
    {
        &IID_IOnlineVideoManager,
    };
    for (int i=0;i<sizeof(arr)/sizeof(arr[0]);i++)
    {
        if (InlineIsEqualGUID(*arr[i],riid))
            return S_OK;
    }
    return S_FALSE;
}

STDMETHODIMP COnlineVideoManager::OnStartPage (IUnknown* pUnk)
{
```

```
    if(!pUnk)
        return E_POINTER;

    CComPtr<IScriptingContext> spContext;
    HRESULT hr;

    // Get the IScriptingContext Interface
    hr = pUnk->QueryInterface(IID_IScriptingContext, (void **)&spContext);
    if(FAILED(hr))
        return hr;

    // Get Request Object Pointer
    hr = spContext->get_Request(&m_piRequest);
    if(FAILED(hr))
    {
        spContext.Release();
        return hr;
    }

    // Get Response Object Pointer
    hr = spContext->get_Response(&m_piResponse);
    if(FAILED(hr))
    {
        m_piRequest.Release();
        return hr;
    }

    // Get Server Object Pointer
    hr = spContext->get_Server(&m_piServer);
    if(FAILED(hr))
    {
        m_piRequest.Release();
        m_piResponse.Release();
        return hr;
    }

    // Get Session Object Pointer
    hr = spContext->get_Session(&m_piSession);
    if(FAILED(hr))
    {
        m_piRequest.Release();
        m_piResponse.Release();
        m_piServer.Release();
        return hr;
    }

    // Get Application Object Pointer
```

```
    hr = spContext->get_Application(&m_piApplication);
    if(FAILED(hr))
    {
         m_piRequest.Release();
         m_piResponse.Release();
         m_piServer.Release();
         m_piSession.Release();
         return hr;
    }
    m_bOnStartPageCalled = TRUE;
    return S_OK;
}

STDMETHODIMP COnlineVideoManager::OnEndPage ()
{
    m_bOnStartPageCalled = FALSE;
    // Release all interfaces
    m_piRequest.Release();
    m_piResponse.Release();
    m_piServer.Release();
    m_piSession.Release();
    m_piApplication.Release();

    return S_OK;
}


STDMETHODIMP COnlineVideoManager::get_CustomerName(BSTR *pVal)
{
    AFX_MANAGE_STATE(AfxGetStaticModuleState())

    // TODO: Add your implementation code here
      *pVal = bstrCustomerName.Copy();
    return S_OK;
}

STDMETHODIMP COnlineVideoManager::put_CustomerName(BSTR newVal)
{
    AFX_MANAGE_STATE(AfxGetStaticModuleState())

    // TODO: Add your implementation code here
      bstrCustomerName = newVal;
    return S_OK;
}

STDMETHODIMP COnlineVideoManager::get_CustomerPassword(BSTR *pVal)
{
```

```
  AFX_MANAGE_STATE(AfxGetStaticModuleState())

  // TODO: Add your implementation code here
    *pVal = bstrCustomerPassword.Copy();
  return S_OK;
}

STDMETHODIMP COnlineVideoManager::put_CustomerPassword(BSTR newVal)
{
  AFX_MANAGE_STATE(AfxGetStaticModuleState())

  // TODO: Add your implementation code here
    bstrCustomerPassword = newVal;
  return S_OK;
}

STDMETHODIMP COnlineVideoManager::get_VideoName(BSTR *pVal)
{
  AFX_MANAGE_STATE(AfxGetStaticModuleState())

  // TODO: Add your implementation code here
    *pVal = bstrVideoName.Copy();
  return S_OK;
}

STDMETHODIMP COnlineVideoManager::put_VideoName(BSTR newVal)
{
  AFX_MANAGE_STATE(AfxGetStaticModuleState())

  // TODO: Add your implementation code here
    bstrVideoName = newVal;
  return S_OK;
}

STDMETHODIMP COnlineVideoManager::get_ConnectionType(short *pVal)
{
  AFX_MANAGE_STATE(AfxGetStaticModuleState())

  // TODO: Add your implementation code here
    *pVal = sConnectionType;
  return S_OK;
}

STDMETHODIMP COnlineVideoManager::put_ConnectionType(short newVal)
{
  AFX_MANAGE_STATE(AfxGetStaticModuleState())

```

```
  // TODO: Add your implementation code here
    sConnectionType = newVal;
  return S_OK;
}

STDMETHODIMP COnlineVideoManager::get_NowPlaying(BOOL *pVal)
{
  AFX_MANAGE_STATE(AfxGetStaticModuleState())

  // TODO: Add your implementation code here
    *pVal = bNowPlaying;
  return S_OK;
}

STDMETHODIMP COnlineVideoManager::put_NowPlaying(BOOL newVal)
{
  AFX_MANAGE_STATE(AfxGetStaticModuleState())

  // TODO: Add your implementation code here
    bNowPlaying = newVal;
  return S_OK;
}

STDMETHODIMP COnlineVideoManager::OrderVideo()
{
  AFX_MANAGE_STATE(AfxGetStaticModuleState())
    //*** define and get an MTS ObjectContext ***
  IObjectContext* pObjectContext;
    HRESULT hr = GetObjectContext( &pObjectContext );
  //*** If we succeed then go ahead and process the request ***
  if (SUCCEEDED(hr))
  {
       //*** Declare IP for WallysAccounts ***
     IAccountsHandler* pAccounts = NULL;
       //*** try to get the IP to the AccountsHandler via MTS ***
     hr = pObjectContext->CreateInstance( CLSID_AccountsHandler ,
                              IID_IAccountsHandler , (void **) pAccounts );
       //*** if bad hresult signal failure and abort call ***
     if (!SUCCEEDED(hr))
      {
          //*** Show Error to User ***
         bstrCustomerName =
             _T("Cannot order video: unable to contact accounts database!");
      return S_OK;
      }
       //*** Declare IP for WallysVideos ***
     IVideosHandler* pVideos = NULL;
```

```
         //*** try to get the IP to the VideoHandler via MTS ***
        hr = pObjectContext->CreateInstance( CLSID_VideosHandler ,
                               IID_IVideosHandler , (void **) pVideos );
         //*** if bad hresult signal failure and abort call ***
        if (!SUCCEEDED(hr))
         {
               //*** Show Error to User ***
              bstrCustomerName =
               _T("Cannot order video: unable to contact videos database!");
            return S_OK;
         }
         //*** turn off committing by default just in case ***
         pObjectContext->DisableCommit();
         //*** Hold the password check string ***
         CComBSTR bstrRealPassword;
         hr = pAccounts->get_AccountPassword( bstrCustomerName ,
                 &bstrRealPassword.m_str );
         //*** if bad hresult signal failure and abort call ***
        if (!SUCCEEDED(hr))
         {
              //*** Show Error to User ***
            bstrCustomerName =
               _T("Cannot order video: unable to contact accounts database!");
            return S_OK;
         }
         //*** if the password isn't right then don't order! ***
         if (bstrCustomerPassword != bstrRealPassword)
         {
            //*** Show Error to User ***
            bstrCustomerName = _T("Cannot Order Video: Password Failure!");
            //*** Tell MTS we goofed and release the pointers ***
              pObjectContext->SetAbort();
              pObjectContext->Release();
              pAccounts->Release();
              pVideos->Release();
            //*** leave ***
            return S_OK;
         }
         //*** obtain the rental price to start things off ***
         short sRentalPrice;
         hr = pVideos->get_VideoRentalPrice( bstrVideoName ,
                         &sRentalPrice );
         //*** if can't get through abort ***
        if (!SUCCEEDED(hr))
         {
            //*** Show Error to User ***
            bstrCustomerName = _T("Cannot order video: video name not found!");
```

```
            //*** Tell MTS we goofed and release the pointers ***
               pObjectContext->SetAbort();
               pObjectContext->Release();
               pAccounts->Release();
               pVideos->Release();
             //*** leave ***
            return S_OK;
        }
        //*** now get the users credit limit and current charges ***
        long lCurrentCharges;
        long lCreditLimit;
        hr = pAccounts->get_AccountCreditLimit( bstrCustomerName , &lCreditLimit );
        hr = pAccounts->get_AccountCurrentCharges( bstrCustomerName ,
                 &lCurrentCharges );
        //*** if we can't get through then abort ***
       if (!SUCCEEDED(hr))
        {
             //*** Show Error to User ***
            bstrCustomerName =
               _T("Cannot order video: unable to contact accounts database!");
            //*** Tell MTS we goofed and release the pointers ***
               pObjectContext->SetAbort();
               pObjectContext->Release();
               pAccounts->Release();
               pVideos->Release();
             //*** leave ***
            return S_OK;
        }
        //*** add the cost of the move to the users's account ***
        lCurrentCharges += sRentalPrice;
        hr = pAccounts->UpdateAccountCharges(bstrCustomerName, lCurrentCharges);
        //*** if can't get through abort ***
       if (!SUCCEEDED(hr))
        {
             //*** Show Error to User ***
            bstrCustomerName =
               _T("Cannot order video: unable to contact accounts database!");
            //*** Tell MTS we goofed and release the pointers ***
               pObjectContext->SetAbort();
               pObjectContext->Release();
               pAccounts->Release();
               pVideos->Release();
             //*** leave ***
            return S_OK;
        }
        //*** oops! if the user has gone over his credit limit blow up! ***
         if (lCurrentCharges > lCreditLimit )
```

```
      {
          //*** Show Error to User ***
         bstrCustomerName =
             _T("Cannot order video: price exceeds credit limit!");
         //*** Tell MTS we goofed and release the pointers ***
           pObjectContext->SetAbort();
           pObjectContext->Release();
           pAccounts->Release();
           pVideos->Release();
          //*** leave ***
         return S_OK;
      }
      //*** if we get this far the user can afford the video so flag it as in use ***
      bNowPlaying = TRUE;
      hr = pAccounts->UpdateAccountInUse(bstrCustomerName,bNowPlaying);
      //*** abort if we can't get through ***
     if (!SUCCEEDED(hr))
      {
          //*** Show Error to User ***
         bstrCustomerName =
             _T("Cannot order video: unable to contact accounts database!");
         //*** Tell MTS we goofed and release the pointers ***
           pObjectContext->SetAbort();
           pObjectContext->Release();
           pAccounts->Release();
           pVideos->Release();
          //*** leave ***
         return S_OK;
      }
      //*** okay now we can commit by default ***
      pObjectContext->EnableCommit();
      pAccounts->Release();
      //*** find out how many copies of the video are available ***
      short sAvailableCopies;
      hr = pVideos->get_VideoAvailableCopies( bstrVideoName ,
                      &sAvailableCopies );
      //*** if we can't get through then abort ***
     if (!SUCCEEDED(hr))
      {
          //*** Show Error to User ***
         bstrCustomerName =
             _T("Cannot order video: unable to contact videos database!");
         //*** Tell MTS we goofed and release the pointers ***
           pObjectContext->SetAbort();
           pObjectContext->Release();
           pVideos->Release();
          //*** leave ***
```

```
            return S_OK;
        }
        //*** oops! if no copies available then abort and roll back everything! ***
        if (sAvailableCopies == 0 )
        {
             //*** Show Error to User ***
            bstrCustomerName =
                _T("Cannot order video: all copies currently rented!");
            //*** Tell MTS we goofed and release the pointers ***
              pObjectContext->SetAbort();
              pObjectContext->Release();
              pVideos->Release();
             //*** leave ***
            return S_OK;
        }
        //*** decrement available copies and update the db ***
        sAvailableCopies–;
        hr = pVideos->UpdateVideoEntryAvailableCopies(bstrVideoName,
                        sAvailableCopies);
        //*** if can't get through then abort ***
       if (!SUCCEEDED(hr))
        {
             //*** Show Error to User ***
            bstrCustomerName =
               _T("Cannot order video: unable to contact videos database!");
            //*** Tell MTS we goofed and release the pointers ***
              pObjectContext->SetAbort();
              pObjectContext->Release();
              pVideos->Release();
             //*** leave ***
            return S_OK;
        }
        //*** signal success and go bye bye ***
        bstrCustomerName =
       _T("Video Ordered! Call 1-800-555-CLAM for fast, hot, clams from Wallys!");
        //*** tell MTS we're good to go ***
        pObjectContext->SetComplete();
        pObjectContext->Release();
        pVideos->Release();
        return S_OK;
    }
    else
    //*** couldn't reach MTS so die
    {
       bstrCustomerName = _T("Cannot order video: unable to contact MTS!");
    }
    //We return S_OK regardless!
```

```
    return S_OK;
}

STDMETHODIMP COnlineVideoManager::TerminateVideoPlay()
{
    AFX_MANAGE_STATE(AfxGetStaticModuleState())

    // TODO: Add your implementation code here
    //*** contact MTS if possible ***
    IObjectContext* pObjectContext;
      HRESULT hr = GetObjectContext( &pObjectContext );
    if (SUCCEEDED(hr))
    {
          //*** Declare IP for WallysAccounts ***
        IAccountsHandler* pAccounts = NULL;
          //*** try to get the IP to the AccountsHandler via MTS ***
        hr = pObjectContext->CreateInstance( CLSID_AccountsHandler ,
                                IID_IAccountsHandler , (void **) pAccounts );
          //*** if bad hresult signal failure and abort call ***
        if (!SUCCEEDED(hr))
         {
             //*** Show Error to User ***
            bstrCustomerName =
           _T("Cannot terminate video: unable to contact accounts database!");
            return S_OK;
         }
          //*** Declare IP for WallysVideos ***
        IVideosHandler* pVideos = NULL;
          //*** try to get the IP to the VideoHandler via MTS ***
        hr = pObjectContext->CreateInstance( CLSID_VideosHandler ,
                                IID_IVideosHandler , (void **) pVideos );
          //*** if bad hresult signal failure and abort call ***
        if (!SUCCEEDED(hr))
         {
             //*** Show Error to User ***
            bstrCustomerName =
              _T("Cannot terminate video: unable to contact videos database!");
            return S_OK;
         }
         //*** turn off default commit ***
         pObjectContext->DisableCommit();
         //*** Hold the password check string ***
         CComBSTR bstrRealPassword;
         hr = pAccounts->get_AccountPassword( bstrCustomerName ,
                 &bstrRealPassword.m_str );
          //*** if bad hresult signal failure and abort call ***
        if (!SUCCEEDED(hr))
```

```
      {
         //*** Show Error to User ***
         bstrCustomerName =
           _T("Cannot terminate video: unable to contact accounts database!");
         return S_OK;
      }
      //*** if we aren't ourselves then blow up! ***
      if (bstrCustomerPassword != bstrRealPassword)
      {
         //*** Show Error to User ***
         bstrCustomerName = _T("Cannot terminate Video: Password Faiure!");
         //*** Tell MTS we goofed and release the pointers ***
           pObjectContext->SetAbort();
           pObjectContext->Release();
           pAccounts->Release();
           pVideos->Release();
         //*** leave ***
         return S_OK;
      }
      //*** check to see if the video really exists ***
      short sRentalPrice;
      hr = pVideos->get_VideoRentalPrice( bstrVideoName ,
                     &sRentalPrice );
      //*** if not then provide raspberry and die ***
     if (!SUCCEEDED(hr))
      {
         //*** Show Error to User ***
         bstrCustomerName = _T("Cannot terminate video: video name not found!");
         //*** Tell MTS we goofed and release the pointers ***
           pObjectContext->SetAbort();
           pObjectContext->Release();
           pAccounts->Release();
           pVideos->Release();
         //*** leave ***
         return S_OK;
      }
      //*** okay now we can shut off the video ***
      bNowPlaying = FALSE;
      hr = pAccounts->UpdateAccountInUse(bstrCustomerName,bNowPlaying);
      //*** unless network fails ***
     if (!SUCCEEDED(hr))
      {
         //*** Show Error to User ***
         bstrCustomerName =
           _T("Cannot terminate video: unable to contact accounts database!");
         //*** Tell MTS we goofed and release the pointers ***
           pObjectContext->SetAbort();
```

```
        pObjectContext->Release();
        pAccounts->Release();
        pVideos->Release();
       //*** leave ***
      return S_OK;
    }
    //*** okay, now we can commit safely by default ***
    pObjectContext->EnableCommit();
    pAccounts->Release();
    //*** get ready to update the video db ***
    short sAvailableCopies;
    short sTotalCopies;
    hr = pVideos->get_VideoAvailableCopies( bstrVideoName ,
              &sAvailableCopies );
    hr = pVideos->get_VideoTotalCopies( bstrVideoName ,
              &sTotalCopies );
    //*** network failure ***
   if (!SUCCEEDED(hr))
    {
       //*** Show Error to User ***
      bstrCustomerName =
        _T("Cannot terminate video: unable to contact videos database!");
      //*** Tell MTS we goofed and release the pointers ***
        pObjectContext->SetAbort();
        pObjectContext->Release();
        pVideos->Release();
       //*** leave ***
      return S_OK;
    }
    //*** bump up available copies ***
    sAvailableCopies++;
    hr = pVideos->UpdateVideoEntryAvailableCopies(bstrVideoName,
             sAvailableCopies);
    //*** network failure ***
   if (!SUCCEEDED(hr))
    {
       //*** Show Error to User ***
      bstrCustomerName =
        _T("Cannot terminate video: unable to contact videos database!");
      //*** Tell MTS we goofed and release the pointers ***
        pObjectContext->SetAbort();
        pObjectContext->Release();
        pVideos->Release();
       //*** leave ***
      return S_OK;
    }
    //*** oops, video wasn't rented after all! ***
```

```
        if (sAvailableCopies > sTotalCopies )
        {
            //*** Show Error to User ***
           bstrCustomerName =
              _T("Cannot terminate video: video not currently playing!");
           //*** Tell MTS we goofed and release the pointers ***
              pObjectContext->SetAbort();
              pObjectContext->Release();
              pVideos->Release();
            //*** leave ***
           return S_OK;
        }
        //*** success message ***
        bstrCustomerName =
              _T("Video Terminated! Wallys thanks you for your patronage!");
        //*** tell MTS we're good to go ***
        pObjectContext->SetComplete();
        pObjectContext->Release();
        pVideos->Release();
        return S_OK;
    }
    else
    {
       bstrCustomerName = _T("Cannot terminate video: unable to contact MTS!");
    }
    return S_OK;
}

STDMETHODIMP COnlineVideoManager::GetVideoNameByNumber(short sIDNumber,
            BSTR *bstrVideoName)
{
    AFX_MANAGE_STATE(AfxGetStaticModuleState())

    // TODO: Add your implementation code here
      //*** Declare IP for WallysVideos ***
    IVideosHandler* pVideos = NULL;
      //*** try to get the IP to the VideoHandler via MTS ***
    HRESULT hr = CoCreateInstance( CLSID_VideosHandler , NULL, CLSCTX_ALL,
                              IID_IVideosHandler , (void **) pVideos );
      //*** if bad hresult signal failure and abort call ***
    if (!SUCCEEDED(hr))
    {
         //*** Show Error to User ***
       bstrCustomerName =
         _T("Cannot update video list: unable to contact videos database!");
       return S_OK;
    }
```

```
596.    //*** get the video name by id number for iterative list box updates ***
597.    hr = pVideos->GetVideoNameByNumber( sIDNumber , bstrVideoName );
598.    //*** network failure ***
599.    if (!SUCCEEDED(hr))
600.    {
601.        //*** Show Error to User ***
602.       bstrCustomerName =
603.        _T("Cannot update video list: unable to contact videos database!");
604.       return S_OK;
605.    }
606.    pVideos->Release();
607.    return S_OK;
608. }
```

***Listing 6-4*** *ONLINEVIDEOMANAGER.CPP source code after modifications*

Here's the breakdown (some of the code is heavily commented and won't be discussed here; also, only the first instance of using a technique is covered to save space):

- **Lines 7-11** This code provides the include files for the video and account manager MTS COM servers. Notice it uses the CD file structure; if you change the location of these projects on your computer, you'll need to change this code to match it.
- **Line 111** This code sets an incoming variable to the internal member variable's value for a component property; it's the same for all such property get functions.
- **Line 120** This code sets an internal member variable to the incoming parameter value for a component property; it's the same for all such property set functions.
- **Lines 199-408** This code to order a video is some of the most important of all the MTS code in this book, so study it carefully! It is heavily commented and it would be redundant to explain it all again here. Instead, notice the way in which except for a beginning password check and video existence check, the code doesn't do its own error checking! Instead, if it encounters a problem (like not enough credit or the video is already rented), it allows MTS to back the database out of the situation; it simply declares an abort and dies.
- **Lines 415-574** This code to terminate a video is some of the most important of all the MTS code in this book, so study it carefully! It is heavily commented and it would be redundant to explain it all again here. Instead, notice the way in which except for a beginning password check and video existence check, the code doesn't do its own error checking!!! Instead, if it encounters a problem (like the video not checked out), it allows MTS to back the database out of the situation; it simply declares an abort and dies.

- **Lines 582-607** This code just calls the underlying video component to get the name of the video via its index number. This allows the ASP component to build a set of values for display, either inside an HTML page or inside a compiled storefront application.

Once you are satisfied you've entered the code from the above two listings correctly, build the ATL COM Server from the Build menu. If you encounter any errors, please check the code in the two listings to find your mistake (it has been exhaustively debugged and is correct). Once you have compiled the component successfully, it is automatically registered on the local machine; if you need to move it to another machine, see Chapter 9. Otherwise, please move on to the next component.

## Creating an MTS-Aware ActiveX Control with ATL

ActiveX controls are the user interface of COM, and can be made MTS-aware just like MTS components and ASP components. The following project will create a full ActiveX control that implements a composite user interface (designed like an MFC dialog box) as well as ActiveX events and standard COM properties and methods. The control serves as the user interface for ordering videos online, either over the Internet or from a storefront application for later online delivery. It connects with the MTS shared properties system as well as the MTS database components created previously.

### *Step-By-Step*

Start Visual C++ 6.0. You can create this project in Visual C++ 5.0, using ATL 2.1; however, you will need to use the older mechanism for adding ActiveX events. (Please see the online documentation for details.) From the File menu, select New. The New dialog box opens; highlight ATL COM AppWizard. Select an appropriate directory, then enter a project name of **ATLAxWallysVideosViewer**. Figure 6-44 shows how the New dialog should appear when you are done. Press OK to open the ATL COM AppWizard.

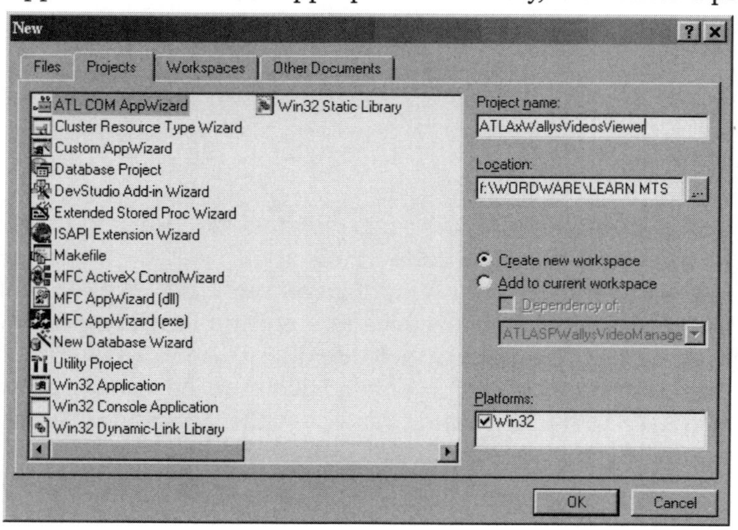


***Figure 6-44** The New dialog box creating the ATLAxWallys-VideosViewer ATL project*

In the ATL AppWizard, select the DLL project, and make sure that the Support MFC, Merge Proxy/Stub Code, and Support MTS check boxes are checked. Press Finish.

A confirmation dialog box appears; press OK to create the ATL project.

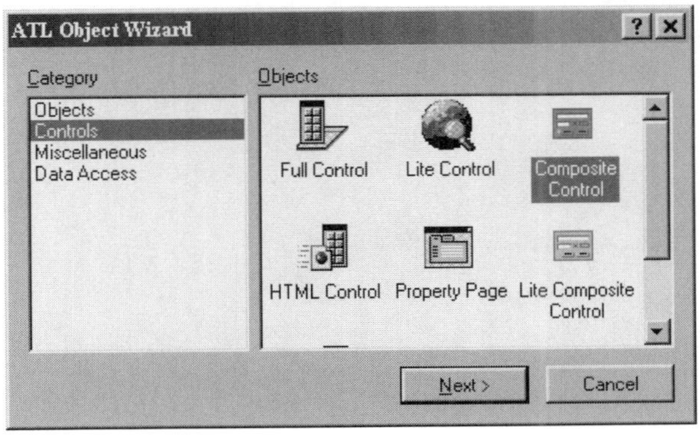


***Figure 6-45*** *Selecting a Composite ActiveX Control object in the ATL Object Wizard*

From the Insert menu, select New ATL Object. The ATL Object Wizard dialog appears, as shown in Figure 6-45. Select the Controls entry in the left-hand list box, and the Composite Control entry in the right-hand list box. Press Next to move to the settings pages of the wizard.

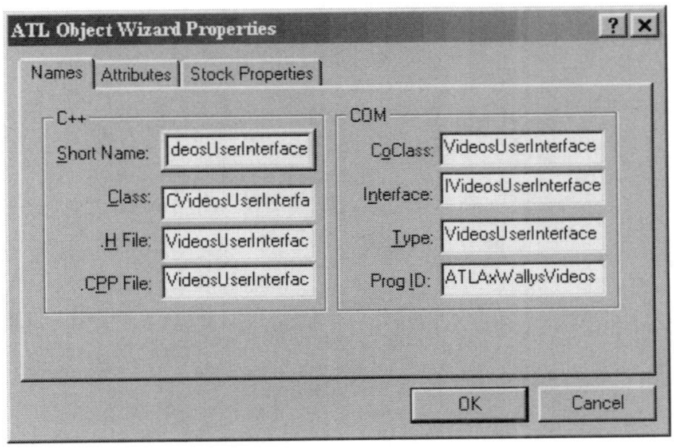


***Figure 6-46*** *Entering name information in the ATL Object Wizard*

Select the Names tab of the next wizard dialog if it is not selected by default. As shown in Figure 6-46, enter **VideosUserInterface** as the name of the control implementation class; the other boxes will fill in automatically. Accept the default values and select the Attributes tab.

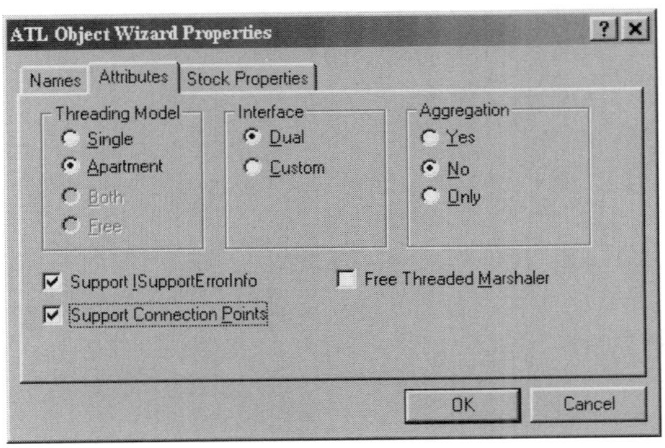


***Figure 6-47*** *Entering attribute information in the ATL Object Wizard*

As illustrated in Figure 6-47, the Attributes tab should have both the Support Connection Points and Support ISupportErrorInfo entries checked, and the Apartment Threading Model, the Dual Interface type, and No Aggregation options selected. Click on the Stock Properties tab next.

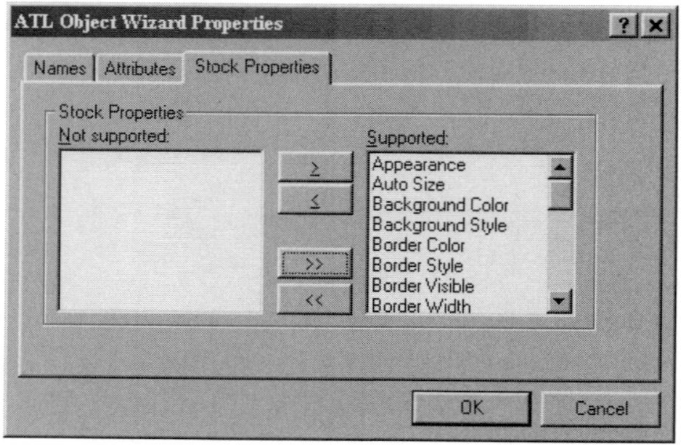


*Figure 6-48*
*Entering stock properties information in the ATL Object Wizard*

The last tab of the Object Wizard dialog has a list box on the left which displays all the available stock properties supported by ATL. Click on the >> button to move all the properties to the right-hand list box, as illustrated in Figure 6-48. Press OK now to add the ActiveX control object to your ATL project.

Move to the Project Explorer window and select the ClassView pane. The IVideosUserInterface Interface is displayed; right-click on it to display the shortcut menu. Select the Add Property menu option.

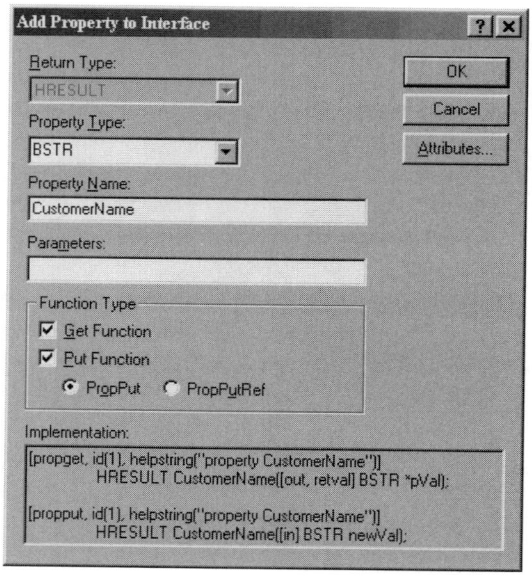


*Figure 6-49*
*Entering the CustomerName property with the ATL Add Property Wizard*

The Add Property Wizard dialog box appears; select a Property Type of BSTR. Give it a name of **CustomerName**, and leave both the Get and Put accessor functions checked. Figure 6-49 shows how the Add Property dialog should appear when you are done. Press OK to add the property to the ActiveX control.

Again right-click on the IVideosUserInterface Interface in the ClassView pane of the Project Explorer and select Add Property. The Add Property Wizard dialog box appears; select a Property Type of BSTR. Give it a name of **CustomerPassword**, and leave both the Get and Put accessor functions checked. Press OK to add the property to the ActiveX control.

Again right-click on the IVideosUserInterface Interface in the ClassView pane of the Project Explorer and select Add Property. The Add Property Wizard dialog box appears; select a Property Type of BSTR. Give it a name of **VideoName**, and leave both the Get and Put accessor functions checked. Press OK to add the property to the ActiveX control.

Again right-click on the IVideosUserInterface Interface in the ClassView pane of the Project Explorer and select Add Property. The Add Property Wizard dialog box appears; select a Property Type of short. Give it a name of

**ConnectionType**, and leave both the Get and Put accessor functions checked. Press OK to add the property to the ActiveX control.

Again right-click on the IVideosUserInterface Interface in the ClassView pane of the Project Explorer and select Add Property. The Add Property Wizard dialog box appears; select a Property Type of BOOL. Give it a name of **VideoPlaying**, and leave both the Get and Put accessor functions checked. Press OK to add the property to the ActiveX control.

Again right-click on the IVideosUserInterface Interface in the ClassView pane of the Project Explorer; this time select Add Method from the shortcut menu. The Add Method Wizard dialog box appears; give the method the name of ClearListbox, with no parameters. Figure 6-50 shows how the Add Method dialog should appear when you are done. Press OK to add the method to the ActiveX control.

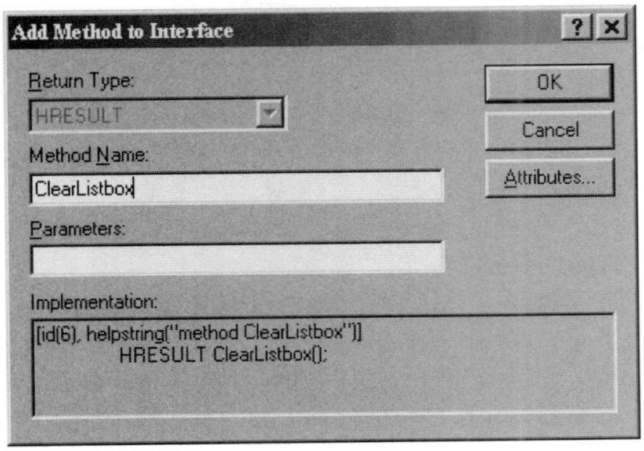


***Figure 6-50*** *Entering the ClearListbox method with the ATL Add Method Wizard*

Again right-click on the IVideosUserInterface Interface in the ClassView pane of the Project Explorer; again select Add Method from the shortcut menu. The Add Method Wizard dialog box appears; give the method the name of **AddListboxItem**, with a parameter of [in] BSTR bstrNewLBItem. Press OK to add the method to the ActiveX control.

Again right-click on the IVideosUserInterface Interface in the ClassView pane of the Project Explorer; again select Add Method from the shortcut menu. The Add Method Wizard dialog box appears; give the method the name of **SetGigabitConnectionAvailability**, with a parameter of [in] BOOL bGigabitConnectionAvailable. Press OK to add the method to the ActiveX control.

Move to the Resources tab of the project window and double-click on the dialog box resource for the control's user interface. Lay out the controls shown in Figure 6-51 using the default names. (The image of a walrus is found on the CD with the book; you can use this image or another as you like.) Save the project.

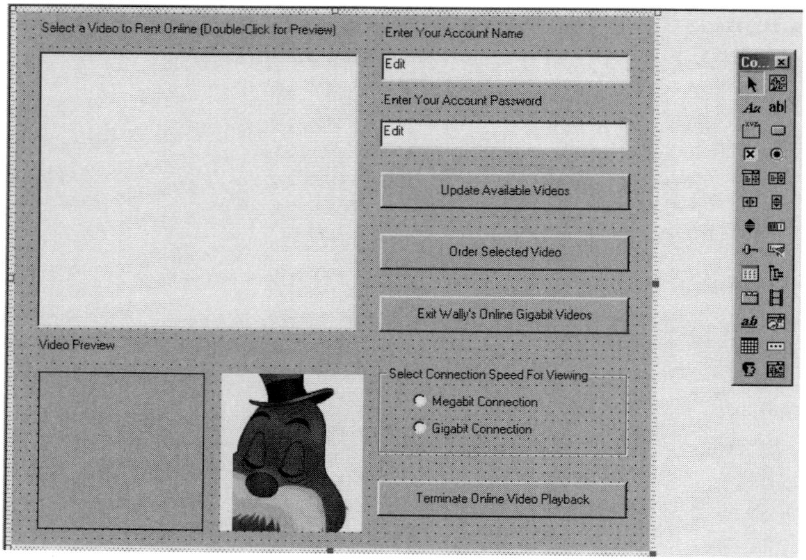


***Figure 6-51*** *Layout of the user interface for the IVideosUser-Interface ActiveX control*

Return to the Classes display in the project window; select the CATLAxWallysVideosViewerAp class and right-click to bring up its shortcut menu. From this menu, select Add Windows Message Handler. The New Windows Message and Event Handlers dialog appears. Select the IDC_BUTTON1 control from the lower right-hand list box, and then select the BN_CLICKED message in the left-hand list box. Click on the Add Handler button to the right; in the dialog that appears, enter **OnClickedButton1** as the event handler function name, as shown in Figure 6-52.

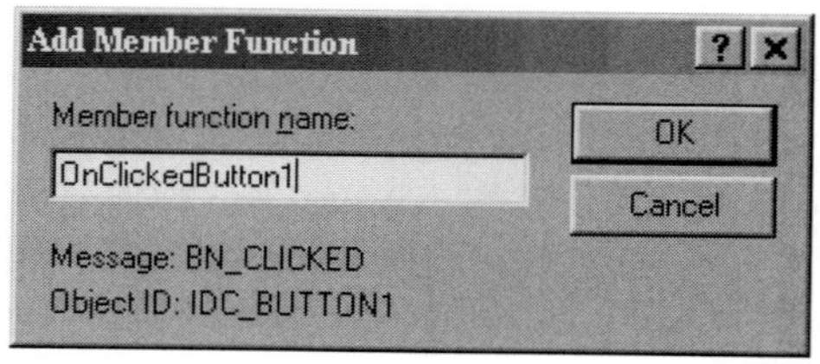


***Figure 6-52*** *Adding a Windows message event handler to the IVideosUserInterface ActiveX control*

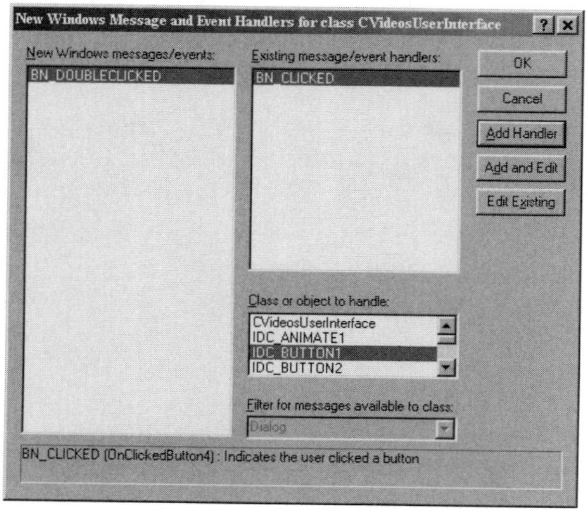


***Figure 6-53*** *The New Windows Message Event Handler dialog for the IVideosUser-Interface ActiveX control*

Figure 6-53 shows how the New Windows Message dialog should appear when this event handler has been added. Repeat the process and add an identical handler for the remaining three buttons.

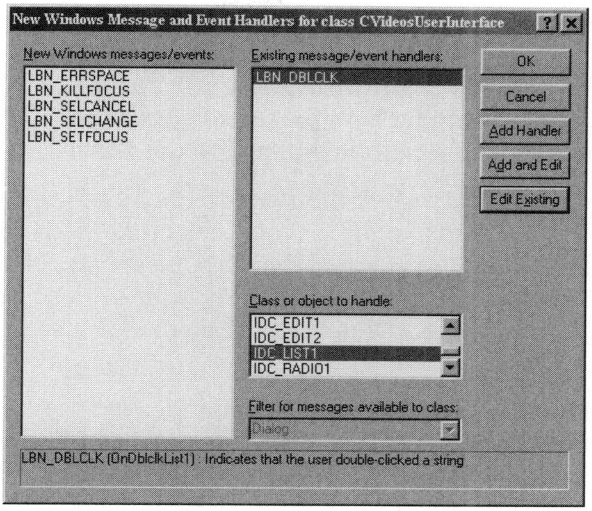


***Figure 6-54***
*Adding the LBN_DBLCLK message*

Next, select the IDC_LIST1 list box entry in the New Windows Message dialog along with the LBN_DBLCLK message and add an event handler for this message following the process described above. Figure 6-54 shows how the New Windows Message dialog should appear when this event handler has been added.

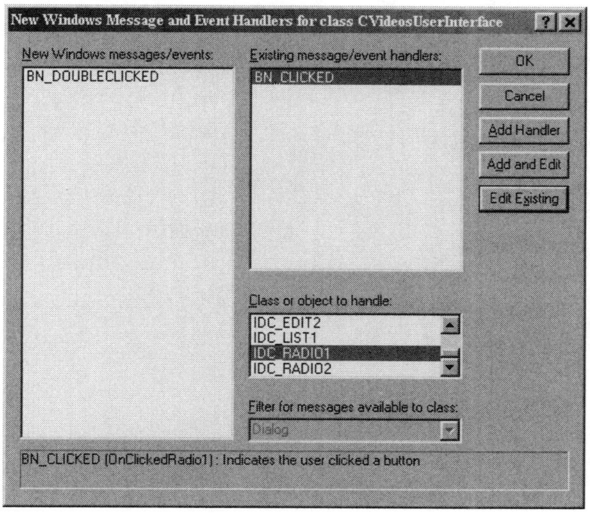


***Figure 6-55***
*Adding the BN_CLICKED message*

Finally, select the IDC_RADIO1 radio button entry in the New Windows Message dialog along with the BN_CLICKED message and add an event handler for this message following the process described above. Figure 6-55 shows how the New Windows Message dialog should appear when this event handler has been added. Repeat this process for the IDC_RADIO2 radio button.

Right-click on the _IVideosUserInterfaceEvents Interface in the ClassView pane of the Project Explorer; select Add Method from the shortcut menu. The Add Method Wizard dialog box appears; give the method the name of **OnUpdateVideoList**, with no parameters (this method will become an ActiveX event). Figure 6-56 shows how the Add Method dialog should appear when you are done. Press OK to add the method to the ActiveX control.

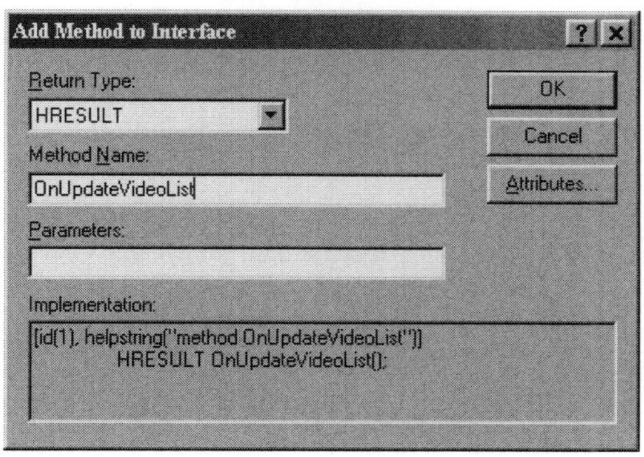


***Figure 6-56***
*Entering the OnUpdate-VideoList method with the ATL Add Method Wizard*

Again right-click on the _IVideosUserInterfaceEvents Interface in the ClassView pane of the Project Explorer; again select Add Method from the shortcut menu. The Add Method Wizard dialog box appears; give the method the name of **OnOrderVideo**, with no parameters (this method will become an ActiveX event). Press OK to add the method to the ActiveX control.

Again right-click on the _IVideosUserInterfaceEvents Interface in the ClassView pane of the Project Explorer; again select Add Method from the shortcut menu. The Add Method Wizard dialog box appears; give the method the name of **OnTerminatePlayback**, with no parameters (this method will become an ActiveX event). Press OK to add the method to the ActiveX control.

Now right-click on the CVideosUserInterface Interface in the ClassView pane of the Project Explorer; select Implement Connection Point from its shortcut menu. The Connection Point Wizard dialog appears as shown in Figure 6-57. Select the single interface listed (the default one ATL provides for events for the ActiveX control) and click on the OK button. The ATL system will create a proxy class to implement the event methods you added earlier and connect them to the control.

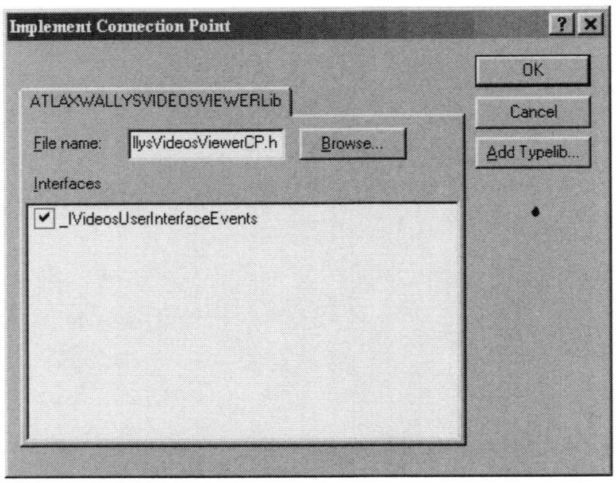


***Figure 6-57** Implementing Connection Points for the ActiveX control*

## Line-By-Line

Now we begin to add the code to create the ActiveX control's MTS and database functionality. Bring up the VIDEOSUSERINTERFACE.H file in the text editor. Scan through it and enter or change any boldfaced line of source code in Listing 6-5. Save the project.

```
// VideosUserInterface.h : Declaration of the CVideosUserInterface

#ifndef __VIDEOSUSERINTERFACE_H_
#define __VIDEOSUSERINTERFACE_H_

#include "resource.h"       // main symbols
#include <atlctl.h>
#include "ATLAxWallysVideosViewerCP.h"
//*** include for SharedProperty Interfaces ***
#include <mtxspm.h>

```

```
/////////////////////////////////////////////////////////////////////////////
// CVideosUserInterface
class ATL_NO_VTABLE CVideosUserInterface :
    public CComObjectRootEx<CComSingleThreadModel>,
    public CStockPropImpl<CVideosUserInterface, IVideosUserInterface,
      &IID_IVideosUserInterface, &LIBID_ATLAXWALLYSVIDEOSVIEWERLib>,
    public CComCompositeControl<CVideosUserInterface>,
    public IPersistStreamInitImpl<CVideosUserInterface>,
    public IOleControlImpl<CVideosUserInterface>,
    public IOleObjectImpl<CVideosUserInterface>,
    public IOleInPlaceActiveObjectImpl<CVideosUserInterface>,
    public IViewObjectExImpl<CVideosUserInterface>,
    public IOleInPlaceObjectWindowlessImpl<CVideosUserInterface>,
    public ISupportErrorInfo,
    public IConnectionPointContainerImpl<CVideosUserInterface>,
    public IPersistStorageImpl<CVideosUserInterface>,
    public ISpecifyPropertyPagesImpl<CVideosUserInterface>,
    public IQuickActivateImpl<CVideosUserInterface>,
    public IDataObjectImpl<CVideosUserInterface>,
    public IProvideClassInfo2Impl<&CLSID_VideosUserInterface,
     &DIID__IVideosUserInterfaceEvents, &LIBID_ATLAXWALLYSVIDEOSVIEWERLib>,
    public IPropertyNotifySinkCP<CVideosUserInterface>,
    public CComCoClass<CVideosUserInterface, &CLSID_VideosUserInterface>,
    public CProxy_IVideosUserInterfaceEvents< CVideosUserInterface >
{
public:
    CVideosUserInterface()
    {
        m_bWindowOnly = TRUE;
        CalcExtent(m_sizeExtent);
    }

DECLARE_REGISTRY_RESOURCEID(IDR_VIDEOSUSERINTERFACE)
DECLARE_NOT_AGGREGATABLE(CVideosUserInterface)

DECLARE_PROTECT_FINAL_CONSTRUCT()

BEGIN_COM_MAP(CVideosUserInterface)
    COM_INTERFACE_ENTRY(IVideosUserInterface)
    COM_INTERFACE_ENTRY(IDispatch)
    COM_INTERFACE_ENTRY(IViewObjectEx)
    COM_INTERFACE_ENTRY(IViewObject2)
    COM_INTERFACE_ENTRY(IViewObject)
    COM_INTERFACE_ENTRY(IOleInPlaceObjectWindowless)
    COM_INTERFACE_ENTRY(IOleInPlaceObject)
    COM_INTERFACE_ENTRY2(IOleWindow, IOleInPlaceObjectWindowless)
    COM_INTERFACE_ENTRY(IOleInPlaceActiveObject)
```

```
    COM_INTERFACE_ENTRY(IOleControl)
    COM_INTERFACE_ENTRY(IOleObject)
    COM_INTERFACE_ENTRY(IPersistStreamInit)
    COM_INTERFACE_ENTRY2(IPersist, IPersistStreamInit)
    COM_INTERFACE_ENTRY(ISupportErrorInfo)
    COM_INTERFACE_ENTRY(IConnectionPointContainer)
    COM_INTERFACE_ENTRY(ISpecifyPropertyPages)
    COM_INTERFACE_ENTRY(IQuickActivate)
    COM_INTERFACE_ENTRY(IPersistStorage)
    COM_INTERFACE_ENTRY(IDataObject)
    COM_INTERFACE_ENTRY(IProvideClassInfo)
    COM_INTERFACE_ENTRY(IProvideClassInfo2)
    COM_INTERFACE_ENTRY_IMPL(IConnectionPointContainer)
END_COM_MAP()

BEGIN_PROP_MAP(CVideosUserInterface)
    PROP_DATA_ENTRY("_cx", m_sizeExtent.cx, VT_UI4)
    PROP_DATA_ENTRY("_cy", m_sizeExtent.cy, VT_UI4)
    PROP_ENTRY("Appearance", DISPID_APPEARANCE, CLSID_NULL)
    PROP_ENTRY("AutoSize", DISPID_AUTOSIZE, CLSID_NULL)
    PROP_ENTRY("BackColor", DISPID_BACKCOLOR, CLSID_StockColorPage)
    PROP_ENTRY("BackStyle", DISPID_BACKSTYLE, CLSID_NULL)
    PROP_ENTRY("BorderColor", DISPID_BORDERCOLOR, CLSID_StockColorPage)
    PROP_ENTRY("BorderStyle", DISPID_BORDERSTYLE, CLSID_NULL)
    PROP_ENTRY("BorderVisible", DISPID_BORDERVISIBLE, CLSID_NULL)
    PROP_ENTRY("BorderWidth", DISPID_BORDERWIDTH, CLSID_NULL)
    PROP_ENTRY("Caption", DISPID_CAPTION, CLSID_NULL)
    PROP_ENTRY("DrawMode", DISPID_DRAWMODE, CLSID_NULL)
    PROP_ENTRY("DrawStyle", DISPID_DRAWSTYLE, CLSID_NULL)
    PROP_ENTRY("DrawWidth", DISPID_DRAWWIDTH, CLSID_NULL)
    PROP_ENTRY("Enabled", DISPID_ENABLED, CLSID_NULL)
    PROP_ENTRY("FillColor", DISPID_FILLCOLOR, CLSID_StockColorPage)
    PROP_ENTRY("FillStyle", DISPID_FILLSTYLE, CLSID_NULL)
    PROP_ENTRY("Font", DISPID_FONT, CLSID_StockFontPage)
    PROP_ENTRY("ForeColor", DISPID_FORECOLOR, CLSID_StockColorPage)
    PROP_ENTRY("HWND", DISPID_HWND, CLSID_NULL)
    PROP_ENTRY("MouseIcon", DISPID_MOUSEICON, CLSID_StockPicturePage)
    PROP_ENTRY("MousePointer", DISPID_MOUSEPOINTER, CLSID_NULL)
    PROP_ENTRY("Picture", DISPID_PICTURE, CLSID_StockPicturePage)
    PROP_ENTRY("TabStop", DISPID_TABSTOP, CLSID_NULL)
    PROP_ENTRY("Text", DISPID_TEXT, CLSID_NULL)
    PROP_ENTRY("Valid", DISPID_VALID, CLSID_NULL)
    // Example entries
    // PROP_ENTRY("Property Description", dispid, clsid)
    // PROP_PAGE(CLSID_StockColorPage)
END_PROP_MAP()

```

```
BEGIN_CONNECTION_POINT_MAP(CVideosUserInterface)
   CONNECTION_POINT_ENTRY(IID_IPropertyNotifySink)
   CONNECTION_POINT_ENTRY(DIID__IVideosUserInterfaceEvents)
END_CONNECTION_POINT_MAP()

BEGIN_MSG_MAP(CVideosUserInterface)
   CHAIN_MSG_MAP(CComCompositeControl<CVideosUserInterface>)
   COMMAND_HANDLER(IDC_BUTTON1, BN_CLICKED, OnClickedButton1)
   COMMAND_HANDLER(IDC_BUTTON2, BN_CLICKED, OnClickedButton2)
   COMMAND_HANDLER(IDC_BUTTON3, BN_CLICKED, OnClickedButton3)
   COMMAND_HANDLER(IDC_BUTTON4, BN_CLICKED, OnClickedButton4)
   COMMAND_HANDLER(IDC_LIST1, LBN_DBLCLK, OnDblclkList1)
   COMMAND_HANDLER(IDC_RADIO1, BN_CLICKED, OnClickedRadio1)
   COMMAND_HANDLER(IDC_RADIO2, BN_CLICKED, OnClickedRadio2)
END_MSG_MAP()
// Handler prototypes:
//  LRESULT MessageHandler(UINT uMsg, WPARAM wParam, LPARAM lParam, BOOL& bHandled);
//  LRESULT CommandHandler(WORD wNotifyCode, WORD wID, HWND hWndCtl, BOOL& bHandled);
//  LRESULT NotifyHandler(int idCtrl, LPNMHDR pnmh, BOOL& bHandled);

BEGIN_SINK_MAP(CVideosUserInterface)
   //Make sure the Event Handlers have __stdcall calling convention
END_SINK_MAP()

   STDMETHOD(OnAmbientPropertyChange)(DISPID dispid)
   {
        if (dispid == DISPID_AMBIENT_BACKCOLOR)
        {
             SetBackgroundColorFromAmbient();
             FireViewChange();
        }
        return IOleControlImpl<
             CVideosUserInterface>::OnAmbientPropertyChange(dispid);
   }



// ISupportsErrorInfo
   STDMETHOD(InterfaceSupportsErrorInfo)(REFIID riid)
   {
        static const IID* arr[] =
        {
             &IID_IVideosUserInterface,
        };
        for (int i=0; i<sizeof(arr)/sizeof(arr[0]); i++)
        {
             if (InlineIsEqualGUID(*arr[i], riid))
```

```
                return S_OK;
        }
        return S_FALSE;
    }

// IViewObjectEx
    DECLARE_VIEW_STATUS(0)

// IVideosUserInterface
public:
    STDMETHOD(SetGigabitConnectionAvailability)(/*[in]*/
       BOOL bGigabitConnectionAvailable);
    STDMETHOD(AddListboxItem)(/*[in]*/ BSTR bstrNewLBItem);
    STDMETHOD(ClearListbox)();
    STDMETHOD(get_VideoPlaying)(/*[out, retval]*/ BOOL *pVal);
    STDMETHOD(put_VideoPlaying)(/*[in]*/ BOOL newVal);
    STDMETHOD(get_ConnectionType)(/*[out, retval]*/ short *pVal);
    STDMETHOD(put_ConnectionType)(/*[in]*/ short newVal);
    STDMETHOD(get_VideoName)(/*[out, retval]*/ BSTR *pVal);
    STDMETHOD(put_VideoName)(/*[in]*/ BSTR newVal);
    STDMETHOD(get_CustomerPassword)(/*[out, retval]*/ BSTR *pVal);
    STDMETHOD(put_CustomerPassword)(/*[in]*/ BSTR newVal);
    STDMETHOD(get_CustomerName)(/*[out, retval]*/ BSTR *pVal);
    STDMETHOD(put_CustomerName)(/*[in]*/ BSTR newVal);
    short m_nAppearance;
    OLE_COLOR m_clrBackColor;
    LONG m_nBackStyle;
    OLE_COLOR m_clrBorderColor;
    LONG m_nBorderStyle;
    BOOL m_bBorderVisible;
    LONG m_nBorderWidth;
    CComBSTR m_bstrCaption;
    LONG m_nDrawMode;
    LONG m_nDrawStyle;
    LONG m_nDrawWidth;
    BOOL m_bEnabled;
    OLE_COLOR m_clrFillColor;
    LONG m_nFillStyle;
    CComPtr<IFontDisp> m_pFont;
    OLE_COLOR m_clrForeColor;
    CComPtr<IPictureDisp> m_pMouseIcon;
    LONG m_nMousePointer;
    CComPtr<IPictureDisp> m_pPicture;
    BOOL m_bTabStop;
    CComBSTR m_bstrText;
    BOOL m_bValid;
      CComBSTR m_bstrCustomerName;
```

```
    CComBSTR m_bstrCustomerPassword;
      CComBSTR m_bstrVideoName;
    short m_sConnectionType;
    BOOL m_bVideoPlaying;
    BOOL m_bGigabitConnectionAvailable;
    enum { IDD = IDD_VIDEOSUSERINTERFACE };
    LRESULT OnClickedButton1(WORD wNotifyCode, WORD wID, HWND hWndCtl, BOOL& bHandled)
    {
        // TODO : Add Code for control notification handler.
        Fire_OnUpdateVideoList();
        return 0;
    }
    LRESULT OnClickedButton2(WORD wNotifyCode, WORD wID, HWND hWndCtl, BOOL& bHandled)
    {
        // TODO : Add Code for control notification handler.
        USES_CONVERSION;
        GetDlgItemText( IDC_EDIT1, m_bstrCustomerName.m_str );
        GetDlgItemText( IDC_EDIT2, m_bstrCustomerPassword.m_str );
        long lSelIndex = SendDlgItemMessage( IDC_LIST1, LB_GETCURSEL,0,0);
        SendDlgItemMessage(IDC_LIST1,LB_GETTEXT,lSelIndex,
            (LONG)OLE2T(m_bstrVideoName.m_str));
        m_sConnectionType = SendDlgItemMessage(IDC_RADIO1, BM_GETCHECK , 0 , 0);
        Fire_OnOrderVideo();
        m_bVideoPlaying = TRUE;
        return 0;
    }
    LRESULT OnClickedButton3(WORD wNotifyCode, WORD wID, HWND hWndCtl, BOOL& bHandled)
    {
        // TODO : Add Code for control notification handler.
        PostQuitMessage( 0 );
        return 0;
    }
    LRESULT OnClickedButton4(WORD wNotifyCode, WORD wID, HWND hWndCtl, BOOL& bHandled)
    {
        // TODO : Add Code for control notification handler.
        if (m_bVideoPlaying)
        {
            Fire_OnTerminatePlayback();
            m_bVideoPlaying = FALSE;
        }
        return 0;
    }
    LRESULT OnDblclkList1(WORD wNotifyCode, WORD wID, HWND hWndCtl, BOOL& bHandled)
    {
        // TODO : Add Code for control notification handler.
        //*** this would download the video and play a sample ***
        return 0;
```

```
    }
    LRESULT OnClickedRadio1(WORD wNotifyCode, WORD wID, HWND hWndCtl, BOOL& bHandled)
    {
         // TODO : Add Code for control notification handler.
         return 0;
    }
    LRESULT OnClickedRadio2(WORD wNotifyCode, WORD wID, HWND hWndCtl, BOOL& bHandled)
    {
         // TODO : Add Code for control notification handler.
         CComVariant varResult;
         BOOL bUseMegabit = TRUE;
         // TODO : Add Code for event handler.
        //*** Define the HRESULT holder and set default value ***
        HRESULT hr = S_OK;
        //*** Define shared property group manager IP ***
        ISharedPropertyGroupManager* spmManager = NULL;
        //*** Define shared property group IP ***
        ISharedPropertyGroup* spmGroup = NULL;
        //*** Define shared property IP for next receipt ***
        ISharedProperty* spmMegabitConnections = NULL;
        //*** Define shared property IP for max receipts ***
        ISharedProperty* spmGigabitConnections = NULL;
        //*** define variant for value of next receipt ***
        CComVariant vMegabitConnex;
        //*** define variant for value of max receipts ***
        CComVariant vGigabitConnex;
        //*** start out getting the SPG manager from MTS ***
        hr = CoCreateInstance(CLSID_SharedPropertyGroupManager, NULL, CLSCTX_ALL,
                  IID_ISharedPropertyGroupManager, (void**) &spmManager );
        if (!SUCCEEDED(hr)) return 0; //not on LAN machine so leave
         //*** define and set isolation mode ***
        LONG lIsolationMode = LockMethod;
        //*** define and set release mode ***
        LONG lReleaseMode = Process;
        //*** define and set existence variable ***
        VARIANT_BOOL bExists = VARIANT_FALSE;
        //*** define BSTR holder for shared property name values ***
        CComBSTR ccbstrPropertyNames;
        //*** start out with WALLYSCONNECTIONS property group ***
        ccbstrPropertyNames = _T("WallysConnections");
        //*** attemt to create or obtain the property group WALLYSCONNECTIONS ***
        hr = spmManager->CreatePropertyGroup(ccbstrPropertyNames.Copy(),
            &lIsolationMode, &lReleaseMode, &bExists, &spmGroup );
        if (!SUCCEEDED(hr))
         {
            //*** release the shared property group manager ***
           spmManager->Release();
```

```
     }
    //*** Define the string for the megabit connections ***
    ccbstrPropertyNames = _T("MegabitConnections");
    //*** Create of obtain the megabitconnections shared property ***
      hr = spmGroup->CreateProperty( ccbstrPropertyNames.Copy(),
           &bExists,&spmMegabitConnections);
    //*** Signal Error ***
    if (!SUCCEEDED(hr))
     {
        //*** Release the shared property group ***
        spmGroup->Release();
        //*** release the shared property group manager ***
        spmManager->Release();
     }
    //*** Define the string for the gigabit connections ***
    ccbstrPropertyNames = _T("GigabitConnections");
    //*** Create or obtain the gigabitconnections shared property ***
      hr = spmGroup->CreateProperty( ccbstrPropertyNames.Copy(),
           &bExists,&spmGigabitConnections);
    //*** Signal Error ***
    if (!SUCCEEDED(hr))
     {
        //*** Release the shared property group ***
        spmGroup->Release();
        //*** release the shared property group manager ***
        spmManager->Release();
     }
    //*** Get the megabit connections value ***
    hr = spmMegabitConnections->get_Value( &vMegabitConnex );
    //*** Signal Error ***
    if (!SUCCEEDED(hr))
     {
        //*** Release the shared property ***
        spmMegabitConnections->Release();
        //*** Release the shared property ***
        spmGigabitConnections->Release();
        //*** Release the shared property group ***
        spmGroup->Release();
        //*** release the shared property group manager ***
        spmManager->Release();
     }
    hr = spmGigabitConnections->get_Value( &vGigabitConnex );
    //*** Signal Error ***
    if (!SUCCEEDED(hr))
     {
        //*** Release the shared property ***
        spmMegabitConnections->Release();
```

```
341.            //*** Release the shared property ***
342.            spmGigabitConnections->Release();
343.            //*** Release the shared property group ***
344.            spmGroup->Release();
345.            //*** release the shared property group manager ***
346.            spmManager->Release();
347.        }
348.        if (vGigabitConnex.intVal == 0)
349.        {
350.            SendDlgItemMessage(IDC_RADIO1,BM_SETCHECK,(WPARAM)BST_CHECKED, 0);
351.        }
352.        return 0;
353.    }
354. };
355.
356. #endif //__VIDEOSUSERINTERFACE_H_
```

***Listing 6-5** VIDEOSUSERINTERFACE.H source code after modifications*

Here's the breakdown (some code is not discussed in detail because it contains exhaustive comments):

- **Lines 9-10** This code declares the header file for the MTS shared property interfaces.
- **Lines 199-204** This code declares the member variables to hold the storage for the ActiveX control's exposed properties. You'll access them in the CPP file.
- **Line 209** This code fires the OnUpdateVideoList ActiveX event for the application or HTML page hosting the control to handle a user request to update the available videos (by calling the ASP component). Notice that the logic is not in the control because then it would need the database to be on the user's system.
- **Lines 215-223** This code fires the OnOrderVideo ActiveX event for the application or HTML page hosting the control to handle a user request to order a video (by calling the ASP component). Notice that it sets the control's internal properties from the user interface controls via old-style Windows API techniques.
- **Line 229** This code posts an exit message to allow users to quit the HTML page if they like or to allow a clerk to close the application on his machine.
- **Lines 235-239** This code fires the OnTerminatePlayback ActiveX event for the application or HTML page hosting the control to handle a user request to terminate a video (by calling the ASP component). Notice that it resets the internal online Boolean member variable.
- **Lines 256-352** This code only executes if the ActiveX control is running inside a compiled application on the server machine at the video

storefront; there it serves to make sure that there are gigabit connections available when the user selects one. On a client machine on the Internet, it exits when it cannot get the MTS shared property group manager interface (it assumes MTS isn't installed on the client computer).

Next, bring up the VIDEOSUSERINTERFACE.CPP file in the text editor. Scan through it and enter or change any boldfaced line of source code in Listing 6-6. Save the project.

```
// VideosUserInterface.cpp : Implementation of CVideosUserInterface

#include "stdafx.h"
#include "ATLAxWallysVideosViewer.h"
#include "VideosUserInterface.h"

/////////////////////////////////////////////////////////////////////////////
// CVideosUserInterface


STDMETHODIMP CVideosUserInterface::get_CustomerName(BSTR *pVal)
{
    AFX_MANAGE_STATE(AfxGetStaticModuleState())

    // TODO: Add your implementation code here
     *pVal = m_bstrCustomerName.Copy();
    return S_OK;
}

STDMETHODIMP CVideosUserInterface::put_CustomerName(BSTR newVal)
{
    AFX_MANAGE_STATE(AfxGetStaticModuleState())

    // TODO: Add your implementation code here
     m_bstrCustomerName = newVal;
    return S_OK;
}

STDMETHODIMP CVideosUserInterface::get_CustomerPassword(BSTR *pVal)
{
    AFX_MANAGE_STATE(AfxGetStaticModuleState())

    // TODO: Add your implementation code here
     *pVal = m_bstrCustomerPassword.Copy();
    return S_OK;
}

STDMETHODIMP CVideosUserInterface::put_CustomerPassword(BSTR newVal)
{
```

```
    AFX_MANAGE_STATE(AfxGetStaticModuleState())

    // TODO: Add your implementation code here
     m_bstrCustomerPassword = newVal;
    return S_OK;
}

STDMETHODIMP CVideosUserInterface::get_VideoName(BSTR *pVal)
{
    AFX_MANAGE_STATE(AfxGetStaticModuleState())

    // TODO: Add your implementation code here
     *pVal = m_bstrVideoName.Copy();
    return S_OK;
}

STDMETHODIMP CVideosUserInterface::put_VideoName(BSTR newVal)
{
    AFX_MANAGE_STATE(AfxGetStaticModuleState())

    // TODO: Add your implementation code here
     m_bstrVideoName = newVal;
    return S_OK;
}

STDMETHODIMP CVideosUserInterface::get_ConnectionType(short *pVal)
{
    AFX_MANAGE_STATE(AfxGetStaticModuleState())

    // TODO: Add your implementation code here
     *pVal = m_sConnectionType;
    return S_OK;
}

STDMETHODIMP CVideosUserInterface::put_ConnectionType(short newVal)
{
    AFX_MANAGE_STATE(AfxGetStaticModuleState())

    // TODO: Add your implementation code here
     m_sConnectionType = newVal;
    return S_OK;
}

STDMETHODIMP CVideosUserInterface::get_VideoPlaying(BOOL *pVal)
{
    AFX_MANAGE_STATE(AfxGetStaticModuleState())

```

```
    // TODO: Add your implementation code here
     *pVal = m_bVideoPlaying;
    return S_OK;
}

STDMETHODIMP CVideosUserInterface::put_VideoPlaying(BOOL newVal)
{
    AFX_MANAGE_STATE(AfxGetStaticModuleState())

    // TODO: Add your implementation code here
     m_bVideoPlaying = newVal;
    return S_OK;
}

STDMETHODIMP CVideosUserInterface::ClearListbox()
{
    AFX_MANAGE_STATE(AfxGetStaticModuleState())

    // TODO: Add your implementation code here
      SendDlgItemMessage( IDC_LIST1,LB_RESETCONTENT, 0 , 0);
    return S_OK;
}

STDMETHODIMP CVideosUserInterface::AddListboxItem(BSTR bstrNewLBItem)
{
    AFX_MANAGE_STATE(AfxGetStaticModuleState())

    // TODO: Add your implementation code here
      USES_CONVERSION;
    SendDlgItemMessage(IDC_LIST1, LB_ADDSTRING, 0,(LPARAM)OLE2T(bstrNewLBItem));
    return S_OK;
}

STDMETHODIMP CVideosUserInterface::SetGigabitConnectionAvailability(
              BOOL bGigabitConnectionAvailable)
{
    AFX_MANAGE_STATE(AfxGetStaticModuleState())

    // TODO: Add your implementation code here
      if (bGigabitConnectionAvailable)
    {
         SendDlgItemMessage(IDC_RADIO2,BM_SETCHECK,(WPARAM)BST_CHECKED, 0);
    }
    else
    {
         SendDlgItemMessage(IDC_RADIO1,BM_SETCHECK,(WPARAM)BST_CHECKED, 0);
    }
```

```
134.    return S_OK;
135. }
```

***Listing 6-6*** *VIDEOSUSERINTERFACE.CPP source code after modifications*

Here's the breakdown of the code (since quite a bit of it is repetitive, only the first use of a technique is covered here):

- **Line 16** This code sets the passed-in [out] parameter to the value of the stored member variable for this particular property. All set methods use this technique.
- **Line 25** This code sets the stored member variable to the value of the passed-in [in] parameter for this particular property. All get methods use this technique.
- **Line 106** This code clears the list box control via old-style Windows programming techniques.
- **Lines 115-116** This code adds a string to the list box using old-style Windows programming techniques.
- **Lines 125-133** This code uses old-style Windows programming techniques to set either the megabit or gigabit connection availability radio button in response to its parameter value.

Once you are satisfied you've entered the code from the above listings correctly, build the ATL ActiveX control from the Build menu. If you encounter any errors, please check the code in the listings to find your mistake (it has been exhaustively debugged and is correct). Once you have compiled the control successfully, it is automatically registered on the local machine; if you need to move it to another machine, see Chapter 9. Otherwise, this completes the ATL MTS components for our book.

## Where We Go From Here

You've completed the ATL versions of the four MTS-aware components for our fictional business application. If you are also interested in MFC development, you can trace the same four elements through Microsoft Foundation Classes in Chapter 7; otherwise, move on to Chapter 8 to see how to create a storefront application for the business as well as the online ordering component in HTML and ASP.

## Chapter Seven

# Creating MFC MTS Components

At this point, you understand how to use COM, ATL, MFC, MTS, and ADO. All these acronyms add up to the most powerful database technology the PC world has ever seen. Now it is time to do some actual programming and put all this information into practice. This chapter will provide you with a set of COM components written in MFC that utilize Microsoft Transaction Server to work with a SQL Server database for a fictitious online video store. In the process, you'll create two MFC MTS components, an MFC ActiveX control with MTS functionality, and an MFC ASP component with MTS features. (For those who prefer to work in ATL, Chapter 6 reproduces these projects in that development framework.) Chapter 8 then provides you with three projects that develop applications using these elements: one in ATL, one in MFC, and one in HTML and Active Server Pages. Chapter 9 then takes you through the steps to install the MTS components and configure them with MTS Explorer, and illustrates running the three applications.

## Uncle Wally's Gigabit Online Video Store and Clam Emporium

For purposes of this book, we'll create a fictional world in which many users of the Internet have access to broadband connections at the megabit or gigabit level, and a service industry has sprung up similar to the "mom and pop" video rental stores of the early 1970s, one which provides access to videos (actually DVDs) online rather than by renting physical tapes. The service exists in two portions: a storefront-based operation where customers come in and set up their accounts and perhaps order videos for later viewing, and an online operation where existing customers connect to the business's web site and order their videos directly online, using their account and password. The business uses MTS to ensure that customers' accounts don't conflict, that videos that are ordered are actually available, and that a given account has the available credit to purchase the video desired.

This arrangement uses four MTS-aware components: two MTS COM servers, one for handling customer accounts and one for handling videos in stock; an ASP COM server to deal with the actual mechanics of ordering online; and an ActiveX control to serve as the front end for the MTS and ASP COM elements, either in a storefront application or via an online HTML page. The storefront applications are compiled and do the same jobs as the ASP component.

# Creating an MTS COM Component with MFC

Our first step will be to use MFC to create an MTS COM server that handles customer accounts for Wally's. The following sections take you through the user interface portions of creating the project in my well-received step-by-step system, then show you the code you need to write and an analysis using the line-by-line approach.

## Step-By-Step

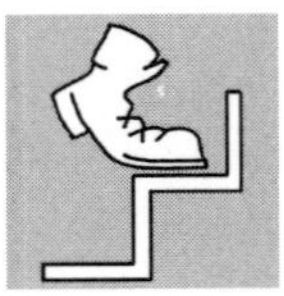

Start Visual C++ 5.0 or 6.0. From the File menu, select New. The New dialog box opens; click on the MFC AppWizard (dll) entry. Next, select an appropriate directory, then enter a project name of **MFCMTSWallysAccounts**. Figure 7-1 shows how the New dialog should appear when you are done. Press OK to open the MFC AppWizard.

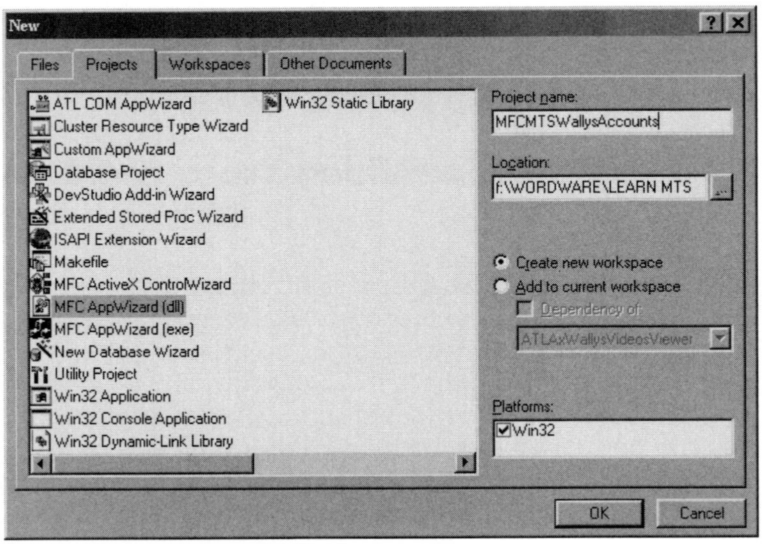


*Figure 7-1 The New dialog box creating the MFCMTSWallysAccounts MFC project*

In the MFC AppWizard, make sure you select a shared MFC DLL, and enable Automation support and source code comments; Figure 7-2 illustrates how the dialog should appear when you are done. Click on the Finish button to create the MTS component project.

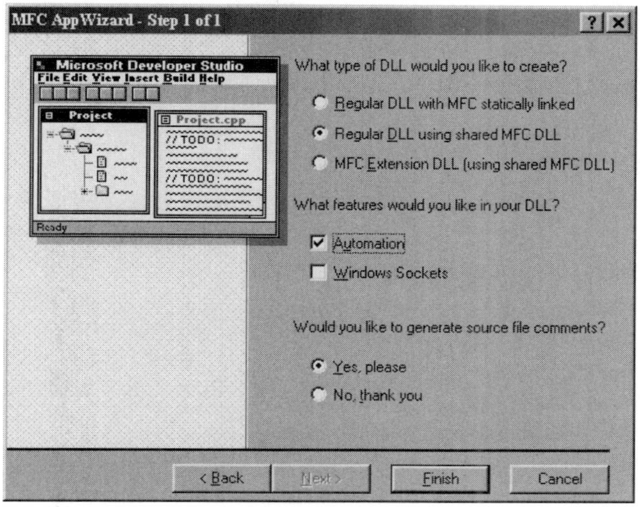


***Figure 7-2*** *Setting the MFC DLL project basic properties*

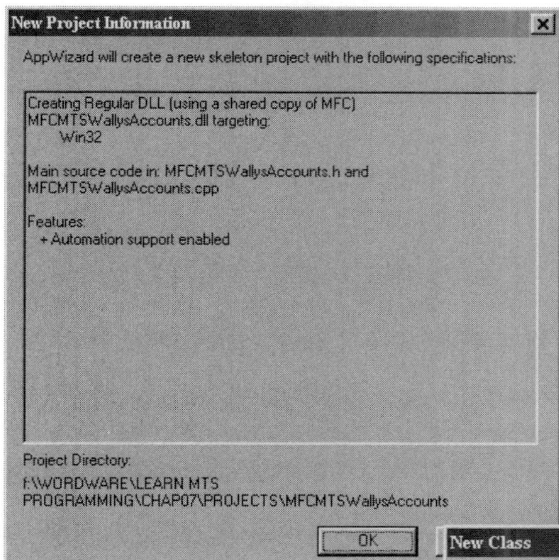


***Figure 7-3*** *The confirmation dialog*

A confirmation dialog box appears as shown in Figure 7-3; press OK to create the MFC project.

When the wizard finishes, you return to the Visual C++ IDE. From the menu, select View|ClassWizard. The MFC ClassWizard dialog appears; move to the Automation tab. At first, there are no enabled controls because the default class does not support Automation. To add an Automation-capable class, click on the Add Class button. A drop-down menu appears; select New Class. The dialog box shown in Figure 7-4 is displayed. Enter a Name of **AccountsHandler**, select a Base Class of CCmdTarget, and make it Createable

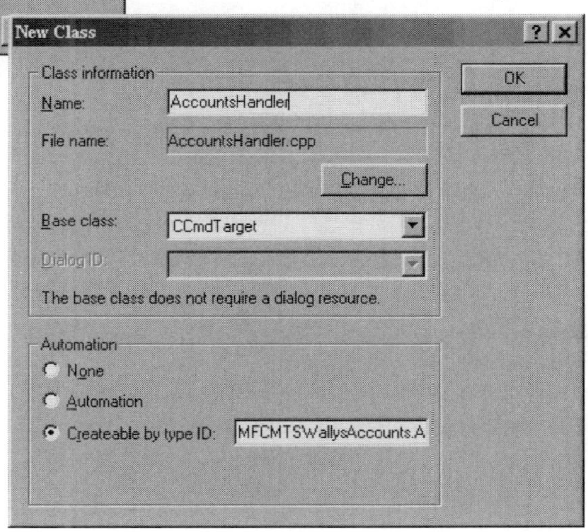


***Figure 7-4*** *Adding an Automation-enabled class to the MFC project*

by Type ID, as shown in the figure. Click on OK to create this class and add it to the project.

Back in ClassWizard, Figure 7-5 shows how it will look with the new Automation-enabled class selected; the various buttons to add methods and properties are now enabled.

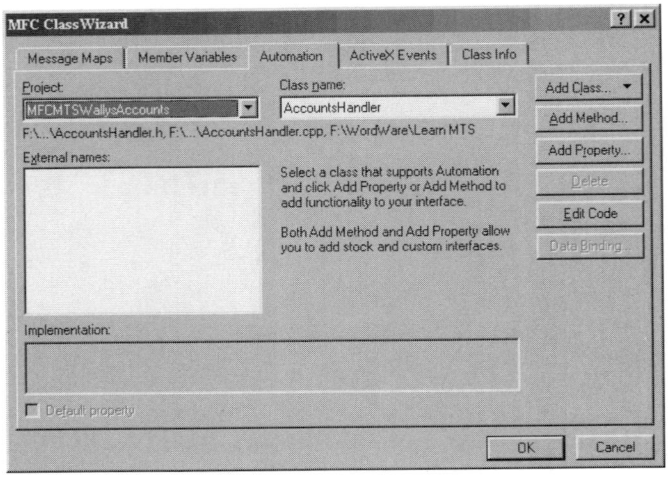


***Figure 7-5***
*The MFC ClassWizard with an Automation-enabled class selected*

Click on the Add Property button to add an Automation property to the MTS Automation COM server. The Add Property dialog box appears, enter a name of **TotalAccounts**. Give it a Type of short, and leave the other default options and values unchanged. Figure 7-6 shows how the Add Property dialog should appear when you are done. Press OK to add the property to the MTS COM server. Figure 7-7 shows how ClassWizard should look with the new property added.

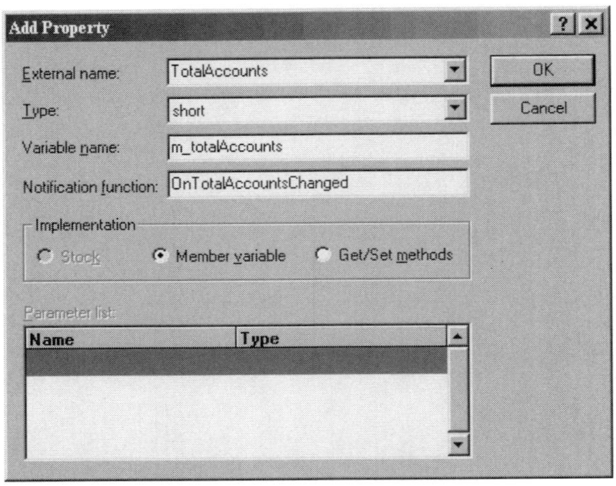


***Figure 7-6***
*Adding the TotalAccounts property*

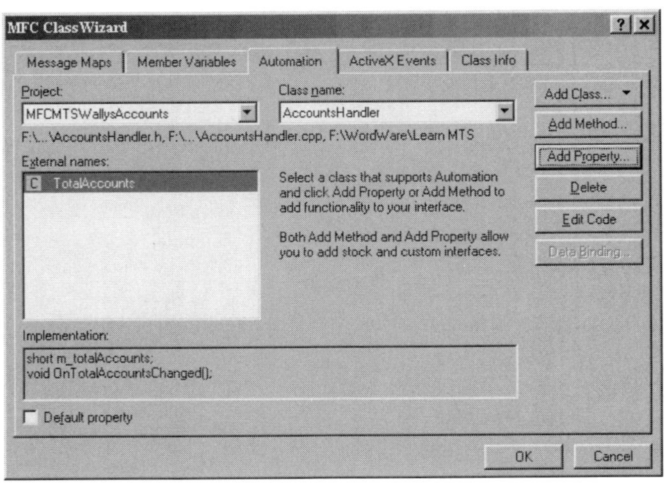


***Figure 7-7***
*The MFC ClassWizard showing the added property*

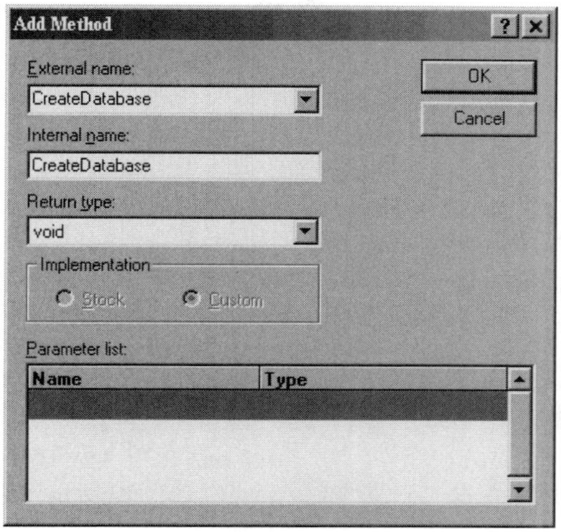


*Figure 7-8*
*Adding the CreateDatabase method*

Next, to add a method function to the MTS COM server, click on the Add Method button of the MFC ClassWizard. In the dialog box that appears, enter a name of **CreateDatabase**. Give it a Return Type of void, and leave the other default options and values unchanged. Figure 7-8 shows how the Add Method dialog should appear when you are done. Press OK to add the method to the MTS COM server. Figure 7-9 shows how the ClassWizard should look with the new method added.

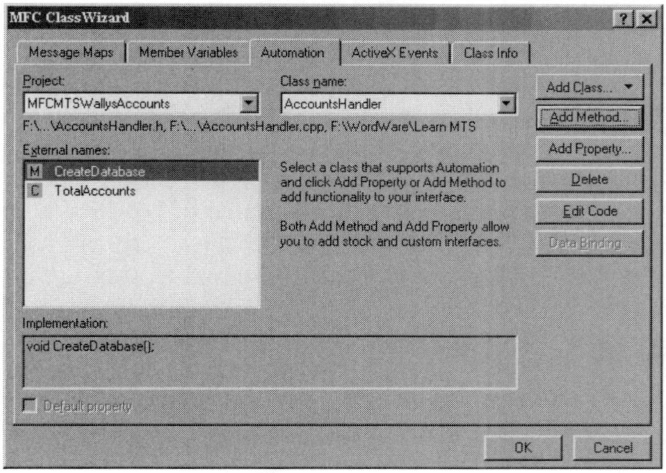


*Figure 7-9*
*The MFC ClassWizard showing the added method*

To add another method function to the MTS COM server, again click on the Add Method button of the MFC ClassWizard. In the dialog box that appears, enter a name of **CreateAccount**. Give it a Return Type of void, and leave the other default options and values unchanged. Then add parameters of strName (type LPCTSTR), strPassword (type LPCTSTR), lTotalCredit (type long), lCharges (type long), and bOnline (type BOOL). Figure 7-10 shows how the Add Method dialog should appear when you are done. Press OK to add the method to the MTS COM server.

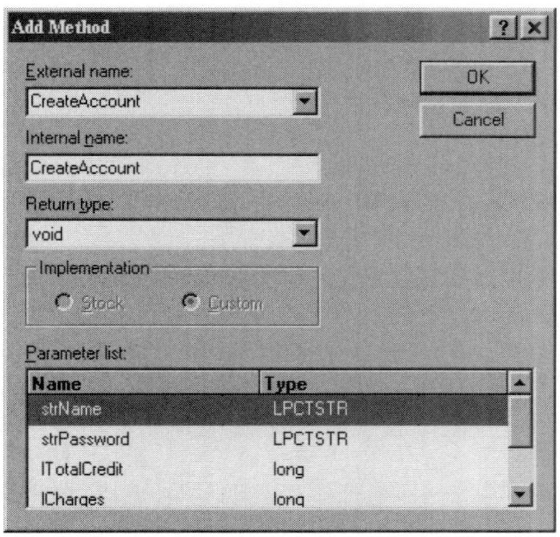


*Figure 7-10*
*Adding the CreateAccount method*

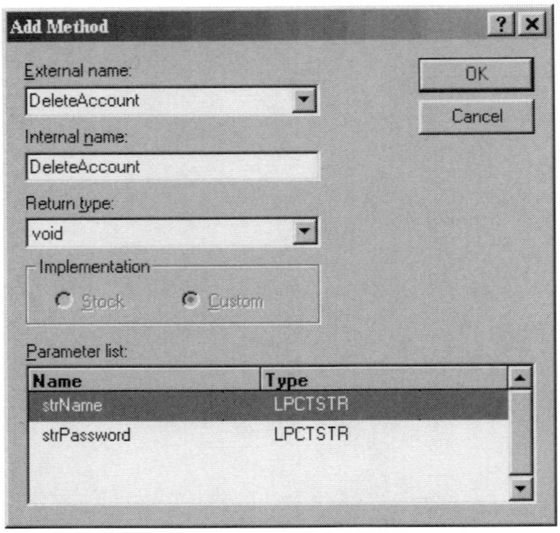


*Figure 7-11 Adding the DeleteAccount method*

To add another method function to the MTS COM server, again click on the Add Method button of the MFC ClassWizard. In the dialog box that appears, enter a name of **DeleteAccount**. Give it a Return Type of void, and leave the other default options and values unchanged. Then add parameters of strName (type LPCTSTR) and strPassword (type LPCTSTR). Figure 7-11 shows how the Add Method dialog should appear when you are done. Press OK to add the method to the MTS COM server.

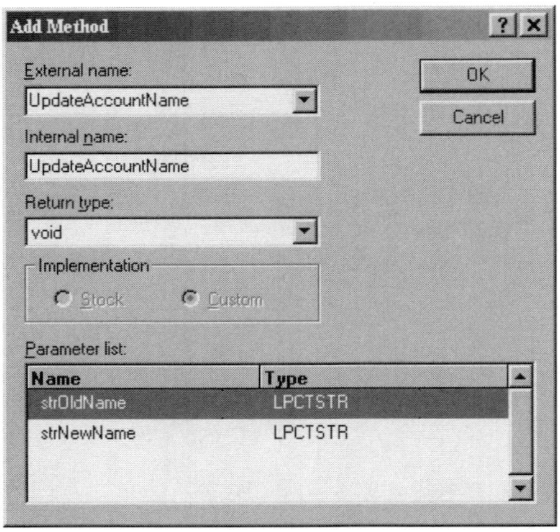


*Figure 7-12 Adding the Update-AccountName method*

To add another method function to the MTS COM server, again click on the Add Method button of the MFC ClassWizard. In the dialog box that appears, enter a name of **UpdateAccountName**. Give it a Return Type of void, and leave the other default options and values unchanged. Then add parameters of strOldName (type LPCTSTR) and strNewName (type LPCTSTR). Figure 7-12 shows how the Add Method dialog should appear when you are done. Press OK to add the method to the MTS COM server.

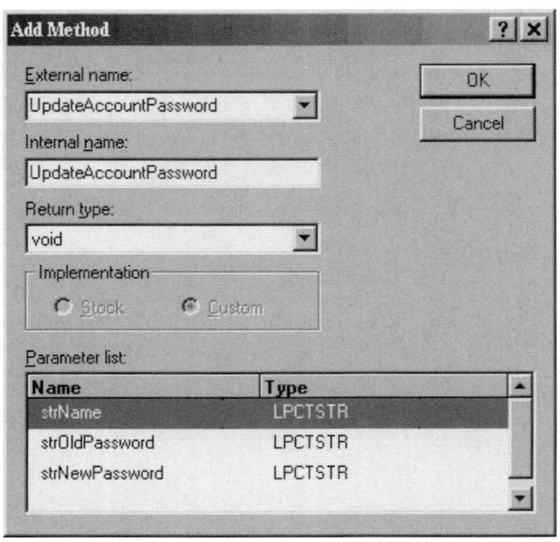


*Figure 7-13 Adding the Update-AccountPass-word method*

To add another method function to the MTS COM server, again click on the Add Method button of the MFC ClassWizard. In the dialog box that appears, enter a name of **UpdateAccountPassword**. Give it a Return Type of void, and leave the other default options and values unchanged. Then add parameters of strName (type LPCTSTR), strOldPassword (type LPCTSTR), and strNewPassword (type LPCTSTR). Figure 7-13 shows how the Add Method dialog should appear when you are done. Press OK to add the method to the MTS COM server.

To add another method function to the MTS COM server, again click on the Add Method button of the MFC ClassWizard. In the dialog box that appears, enter a name of **UpdateAccountCredit**. Give it a Return Type of void, and leave the other default options and values unchanged. Then add parameters of strName (type LPCTSTR) and lNewCredit (type long). Figure 7-14 shows how the Add Method dialog should appear when you are done. Press OK to add the method to the MTS COM server.

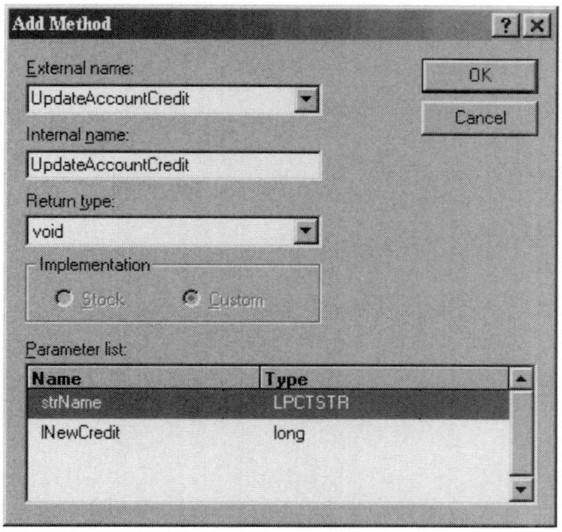


***Figure 7-14*** *Adding the Update-AccountCredit method*

To add another method function to the MTS COM server, again click on the Add Method button of the MFC ClassWizard. In the dialog box that appears, enter a name of **UpdateAccountCharges**. Give it a Return Type of void, and leave the other default options and values unchanged. Then add parameters of strName (type LPCTSTR) and lNewCharges (type long). Figure 7-15 shows how the Add Method dialog should appear when you are done. Press OK to add the method to the MTS COM server.

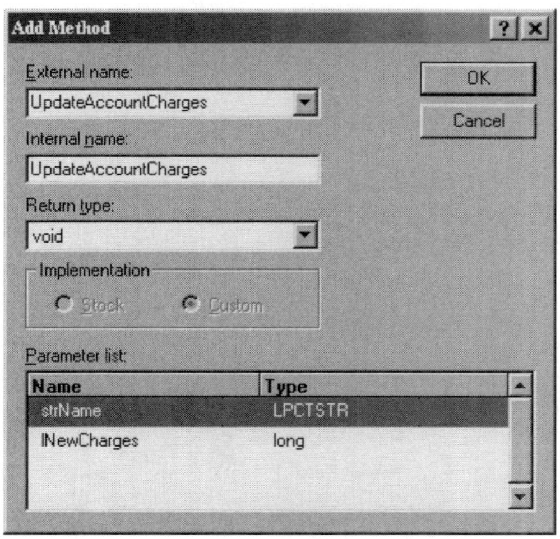


***Figure 7-15*** *Adding the Update-Account-Charges method*

To add another method function to the MTS COM server, again click on the Add Method button of the MFC ClassWizard. In the dialog box that appears, enter a name of **UpdateAccountInUse**. Give it a Return Type of void, and leave the other default options and values unchanged. Then add parameters of strName (type LPCTSTR) and bInUse (type BOOL). Figure 7-16 shows how the Add Method dialog should appear when you are done. Press OK to add the method to the MTS COM server.

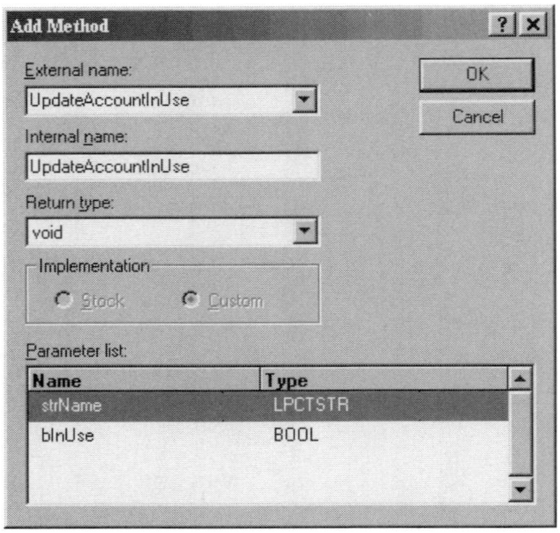


***Figure 7-16*** *Adding the UpdateAccountInUse method*

Now click on the Add Property button to add an Automation property to the MTS Automation COM server. The Add Property dialog box appears; enter a name of **AccountPassword**. Give it a Type of BSTR, and choose Get/Set Methods for the implementation. Add a parameter of strName (type LPCTSTR). Figure 7-17 shows how the Add Property dialog should appear when you are done. Press OK to add the property to the MTS COM server.

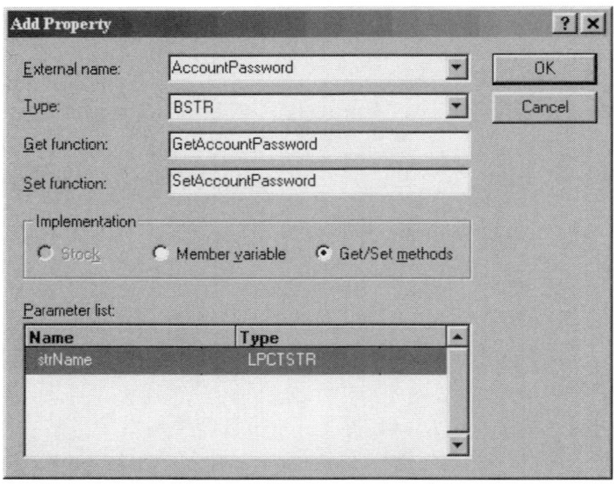


***Figure 7-17*** *Adding the AccountPassword property*

Again click on the Add Property button to add an Automation property to the MTS Automation COM server. The Add Property dialog box appears; enter a name of **AccountCreditLimit**. Give it a Type of long, and choose Get/Set Methods for the implementation. Add a parameter of strName (type **LPCTSTR**). Figure 7-18 shows how the Add Property dialog should appear when you are done. Press OK to add the property to the MTS COM server.

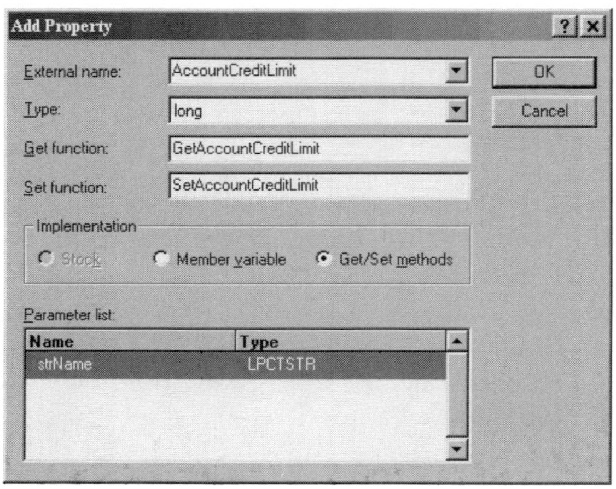


***Figure 7-18*** *Adding the AccountCreditLimit property*

Again click on the Add Property button to add an Automation property to the MTS Automation COM server. The Add Property dialog box appears; enter a name of **AccountCurrentCharges**. Give it a Type of long, and choose Get/Set Methods for the implementation. Add a parameter of strName (type LPCTSTR). Figure 7-19 shows how the Add Property dialog should appear when you are done. Press OK to add the property to the MTS COM server.

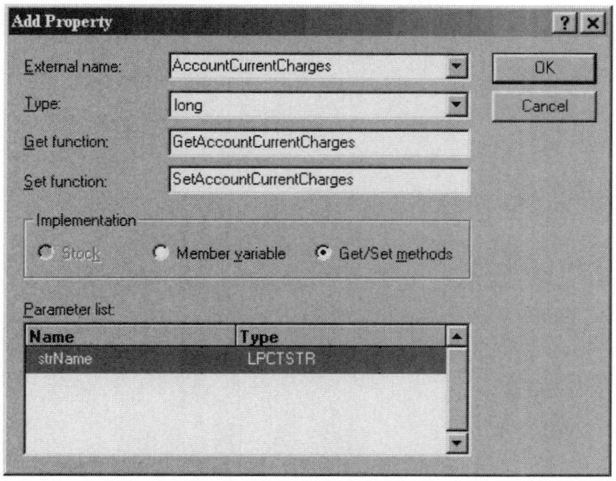


***Figure 7-19*** *Adding the AccountCurrentCharges property*

Again click on the Add Property button to add an Automation property to the MTS Automation COM server. The Add Property dialog box appears; enter a name of **AccountInUse**. Give it a Type of BOOL, and choose Get/Set Methods for the implementation. Add a parameter of strName (type LPCTSTR). Figure 7-20 shows how the Add Property dialog should appear when you are done. Press OK to add the property to the MTS COM server. Then click on OK to close the ClassWizard and write the changes into your MFC project. Save the project to protect your work.

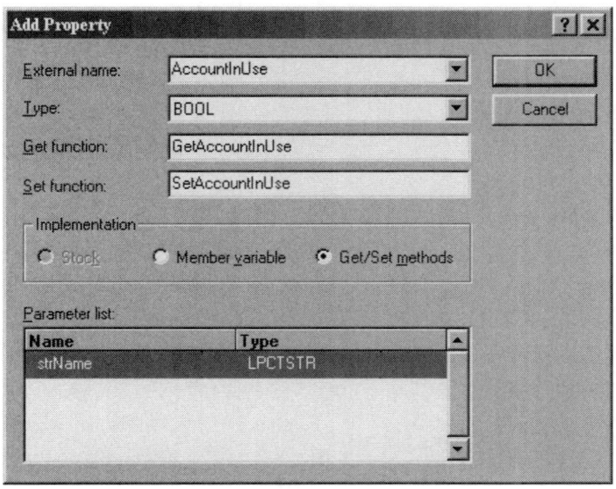


***Figure 7-20*** *Adding AccountInUse property*

## Line-By-Line

Now we begin to add the code to create our MFC COM server! Bring up the ACCOUNTSHANDLER.CPP file in the text editor. Scan through it and enter or change any boldfaced line of source code in Listing 7-1. Save the project.

```
// AccountsHandler.cpp : implementation file
//

#include "stdafx.h"
```

```
//*** take this out if you get linker errors!!! ***
#include <Initguid.h>
//*** MTS headers ***
#include <mtx.h>
//*** ActiveX Data Objects GUIDs  ***
#include <adoid.h>
//*** ActiveX Data Objects Interfaces ***
#include <adoint.h>
#include "MFCMTSWallysAccounts.h"
#include "AccountsHandler.h"

#ifdef _DEBUG
#define new DEBUG_NEW
#undef THIS_FILE
static char THIS_FILE[] = __FILE__;
#endif

/////////////////////////////////////////////////////////////////////////////
// AccountsHandler

IMPLEMENT_DYNCREATE(AccountsHandler, CCmdTarget)

AccountsHandler::AccountsHandler()
{
   EnableAutomation();

   // To keep the application running as long as an OLE automation
   //   object is active, the constructor calls AfxOleLockApp.

   AfxOleLockApp();
}

AccountsHandler::~AccountsHandler()
{
   // To terminate the application when all objects created with
   //   with OLE automation, the destructor calls AfxOleUnlockApp.

   AfxOleUnlockApp();
}


void AccountsHandler::OnFinalRelease()
{
   // When the last reference for an automation object is released
   // OnFinalRelease is called.  The base class will automatically
   // deletes the object.  Add additional cleanup required for your
   // object before calling the base class.
```

```

    CCmdTarget::OnFinalRelease();
}


BEGIN_MESSAGE_MAP(AccountsHandler, CCmdTarget)
    //{{AFX_MSG_MAP(AccountsHandler)
        // NOTE - the ClassWizard will add and remove mapping macros here.
    //}}AFX_MSG_MAP
END_MESSAGE_MAP()

BEGIN_DISPATCH_MAP(AccountsHandler, CCmdTarget)
    //{{AFX_DISPATCH_MAP(AccountsHandler)
    DISP_PROPERTY_NOTIFY(AccountsHandler, "TotalAccounts", m_totalAccounts,
      OnTotalAccountsChanged, VT_I2)
    DISP_FUNCTION(AccountsHandler, "CreateDatabase", CreateDatabase, VT_EMPTY,
      VTS_NONE)
    DISP_FUNCTION(AccountsHandler, "CreateAccount", CreateAccount, VT_EMPTY, VTS_BSTR
       VTS_BSTR VTS_I4 VTS_I4 VTS_BOOL)
    DISP_FUNCTION(AccountsHandler, "DeleteAccount", DeleteAccount, VT_EMPTY, VTS_BSTR
       VTS_BSTR)
    DISP_FUNCTION(AccountsHandler, "UpdateAccountName", UpdateAccountName, VT_EMPTY,
       VTS_BSTR VTS_BSTR)
    DISP_FUNCTION(AccountsHandler, "UpdateAccountPassword", UpdateAccountPassword,
       VT_EMPTY, VTS_BSTR VTS_BSTR VTS_BSTR)
    DISP_FUNCTION(AccountsHandler, "UpdateAccountCredit", UpdateAccountCredit,
       VT_EMPTY, VTS_BSTR VTS_I4)
    DISP_FUNCTION(AccountsHandler, "UpdateAccountCharges", UpdateAccountCharges,
       VT_EMPTY, VTS_BSTR VTS_I4)
    DISP_FUNCTION(AccountsHandler, "UpdateAccountInUse", UpdateAccountInUse, VT_EMPTY,
       VTS_BSTR VTS_BOOL)
    DISP_PROPERTY_PARAM(AccountsHandler, "AccountPassword", GetAccountPassword,
      SetAccountPassword, VT_BSTR, VTS_BSTR)
    DISP_PROPERTY_PARAM(AccountsHandler, "AccountCreditLimit", GetAccountCreditLimit,
      SetAccountCreditLimit, VT_I4, VTS_BSTR)
    DISP_PROPERTY_PARAM(AccountsHandler, "AccountCurrentCharges",
      GetAccountCurrentCharges, SetAccountCurrentCharges, VT_I4, VTS_BSTR)
    DISP_PROPERTY_PARAM(AccountsHandler, "AccountInUse", GetAccountInUse,
      SetAccountInUse, VT_BOOL, VTS_BSTR)
    //}}AFX_DISPATCH_MAP
END_DISPATCH_MAP()

// Note: we add support for IID_IAccountsHandler to support typesafe binding
//  from VBA.  This IID must match the GUID that is attached to the
//  dispinterface in the .ODL file.

// {361BFD79-9A54-11D2-B7EA-00E02916C424}
```

```
static const IID IID_IAccountsHandler =
{ 0x361bfd79, 0x9a54, 0x11d2, { 0xb7, 0xea, 0x0, 0xe0, 0x29, 0x16, 0xc4, 0x24 } };

BEGIN_INTERFACE_MAP(AccountsHandler, CCmdTarget)
  INTERFACE_PART(AccountsHandler, IID_IAccountsHandler, Dispatch)
END_INTERFACE_MAP()

// {361BFD7A-9A54-11D2-B7EA-00E02916C424}
IMPLEMENT_OLECREATE(AccountsHandler, "MFCMTSWallysAccounts.AccountsHandler",
    0x361bfd7a, 0x9a54, 0x11d2, 0xb7, 0xea, 0x0, 0xe0, 0x29, 0x16, 0xc4, 0x24)

/////////////////////////////////////////////////////////////////////////////
// AccountsHandler message handlers

void AccountsHandler::OnTotalAccountsChanged()
{
  // TODO: Add notification handler code
  //*** Declare our ActiveX Data Object Connection holder and set it to NULL ***
  ADOConnection* adoCoConnection = NULL;
  //*** Declare our ActiveX Data Object Recordset holder and set it to NULL ***
  ADORecordset* adoAccountInfo = NULL;
  //*** Declare our ActiveX Data Object Fields holder and set it to NULL ***
  ADOFields* padoFields = NULL;
  //*** Declare our ActiveX Data Object Field holder and set it to NULL ***
  ADOField* padoField = NULL;
  //*** Attempt to get the ADO Connection IP ***
    HRESULT hr = CoCreateInstance( CLSID_CADOConnection, NULL, CLSCTX_INPROC_SERVER,
                              IID_IADOConnection, (void **) adoCoConnection );
  //*** If can't get IP abort ***
  if (!SUCCEEDED(hr))
  {
       AfxThrowOleDispatchException(158,
            _T("MFCMTSWallysAccount Error: ADO Unreachable!"),0);
  }
  //*** Declare a CString to handle the Sequel Text ***
  CString strSQLText;
  //*** Give it the DSN for our samples database ***
  strSQLText = _T("FILEDSN=WallysAccounts");
  //*** Attempt to open the database ***
  hr = adoCoConnection->Open( strSQLText.AllocSysString(), NULL, NULL,
         adCmdUnspecified);
  //*** If can't get database abort ***
  if (!SUCCEEDED(hr))
  {
      //*** Kill the connection and recordset IP ***
     adoCoConnection->Release();
     AfxThrowOleDispatchException(158,
```

```
         _T("MFCMTSWallysAccount Error: Database Unreachable!"),0);
   }
   //*** Declare the wsprintf buffer ***
   TCHAR szSQLBuffer[512];
   wsprintf( szSQLBuffer,
      _T("SELECT TotalAccounts FROM Accounts WHERE AccountName = 'TotalAccounts'"));
   //*** Put it into the CString via overloaded = operator ***
   strSQLText = szSQLBuffer;
   //*** Declare a COleVariant to hold returned record count from ADO ***
   COleVariant vRecCount;
   //*** Clear the record count ***
   vRecCount.Clear();
   //*** Execute the sequel statement on the database ***
     hr = adoCoConnection->Execute( strSQLText.AllocSysString(), &vRecCount, -1 ,
     &adoAccountInfo );
   //*** If can't reach database abort ***
   if (!SUCCEEDED(hr))
   {
       //*** Kill the connection and recordset IP ***
      adoCoConnection->Release();
      AfxThrowOleDispatchException(158,
         _T("MFCMTSWallysAccount Error: Database Unreachable!"),0);
   }
   //*** Obtain the fields collection from the recordset ***
     hr = adoAccountInfo->get_Fields( &padoFields );
   //*** If can't reach database abort ***
   if (!SUCCEEDED(hr))
   {
       //*** Kill the connection and recordset IP ***
      adoCoConnection->Release();
      adoAccountInfo->Release();
      AfxThrowOleDispatchException(158,
         _T("MFCMTSWallysAccount Error: Database Unreachable!"),0);
   }
   //*** Define a variant to obtain the total accounts field ***
   COleVariant vField = _T("TotalAccounts");
   //*** define a variant to hold the information ***
   COleVariant vAccounts;
   //*** Get the TotalAccounts Field ***
   hr = padoFields->get_Item( vField , &padoField );
   //*** If can't reach database abort ***
   if (!SUCCEEDED(hr))
   {
      //*** Kill the connection, recordset, and fields IP ***
      adoCoConnection->Release();
      adoAccountInfo->Release();
      padoFields->Release();
```

```
      AfxThrowOleDispatchException(158,
         _T("MFCMTSWallysAccount Error: Database Unreachable!"),0);
   }
   //*** Get the actual total accounts value ***
   hr = padoField->get_Value( &vAccounts );
   //*** If can't reach database abort ***
   if (!SUCCEEDED(hr))
   {
       //*** Kill the connection, recordset, fields, and field IP ***
       adoCoConnection->Release();
       adoAccountInfo->Release();
       padoFields->Release();
       padoField->Release();
      AfxThrowOleDispatchException(158,
         _T("MFCMTSWallysAccount Error: Database Unreachable!"),0);
   }
     //*** return the value from the variant ***
     m_totalAccounts = vAccounts.iVal;
   //*** Kill the connection, recordset, fields, and field IP ***
   adoCoConnection->Release();
   adoAccountInfo->Release();
   padoFields->Release();
   padoField->Release();
   return;
}

void AccountsHandler::CreateDatabase()
{
   // TODO: Add your dispatch handler code here
     //*** define HRESULT holder and set it to result of CCI ***
   IObjectContext* m_spObjectContext;
   HRESULT hr = GetObjectContext(&m_spObjectContext);
   if (!SUCCEEDED( hr )) AfxThrowOleDispatchException(158,
       _T("MFCMTSWallysAccount Error: MTS Unreachable!"),0);
   //*** Declare our ActiveX Data Object Connection holder and set it to NULL ***
   ADOConnection* adoCoConnection = NULL;
   //*** Declare our ActiveX Data Object Recordset holder and set it to NULL ***
   ADORecordset* adoAccountInfo = NULL;
   //*** Attempt to get the ADO Connection IP ***
     hr = CoCreateInstance( CLSID_CADOConnection, NULL, CLSCTX_INPROC_SERVER,
                            IID_IADOConnection, (void **) adoCoConnection );
   //*** If can't get IP abort ***
   if (!SUCCEEDED(hr))
   {
       //*** Inform MTS of failure ***
       m_spObjectContext->SetAbort();
       m_spObjectContext->Release();
```

```
        AfxThrowOleDispatchException(158,
            _T("MFCMTSWallysAccount Error: ADO Unreachable!"),0);
    }
    //*** Declare a CString to handle the Sequel Text ***
    CString strSQLText;
    //*** Give it the DSN for our samples database ***
    strSQLText = _T("FILEDSN=WallysAccounts");
    //*** Attempt to open the database ***
    hr = adoCoConnection->Open( strSQLText.AllocSysString(), NULL, NULL,
         adCmdUnspecified);
    //*** If can't get database abort ***
    if (!SUCCEEDED(hr))
    {
        //*** Inform MTS of failure ***
        m_spObjectContext->SetAbort();
        m_spObjectContext->Release();
        //*** Kill the connection IP ***
        adoCoConnection->Release();
      AfxThrowOleDispatchException(158,
        _T("MFCMTSWallysAccount Error: Database Unreachable!"),0);
    }
    //*** Create Sequel Statement ***
    strSQLText =
      _T("if not exists (Select name from sysobjects where name = 'Accounts')\n");
    strSQLText += _T("BEGIN\n");
    strSQLText += _T("CREATE TABLE Accounts (\n");
    strSQLText += _T("AccountName varchar(256) NULL ,\n");
    strSQLText += _T("AccountPassword varchar(256) NULL ,\n");
    strSQLText += _T("CreditLimit int NULL ,\n");
    strSQLText += _T("CurrentCharges int NULL ,\n");
    strSQLText += _T("InUse bit NOT NULL ,\n");
    strSQLText += _T("TotalAccounts int NULL ,\n");
    strSQLText += _T(")\n");
    strSQLText +=  _T("END\n");
    //*** Declare a COleVariant to hold returned record count from ADO ***
    COleVariant vRecCount;
    //*** Clear the record count ***
    vRecCount.Clear();
    //*** Execute the sequel statement on the database ***
      hr = adoCoConnection->Execute( strSQLText.AllocSysString(), &vRecCount, -1 , NULL
);
    //*** If can't reach database abort ***
    if (!SUCCEEDED(hr))
    {
        //*** Inform MTS of failure ***
        m_spObjectContext->SetAbort();
        m_spObjectContext->Release();
```

```
        //*** Kill the connection IP ***
        adoCoConnection->Release();
      AfxThrowOleDispatchException(158,
        _T("MFCMTSWallysAccount Error: Database Unreachable!"),0);
   }
   //*** Kill the connection, recordset, fields, and field IP ***
   adoCoConnection->Release();
   //*** Send back Good Transaction ***
   m_spObjectContext->SetComplete();
   m_spObjectContext->Release();
   return;
}

void AccountsHandler::CreateAccount(LPCTSTR strName, LPCTSTR strPassword,
      long lTotalCredit, long lCharges, BOOL bInUse)
{
   // TODO: Add your dispatch handler code here
     //*** define HRESULT holder and set it to result of CCI ***
   IObjectContext* m_spObjectContext;
   HRESULT hr = GetObjectContext(&m_spObjectContext);
   if (!SUCCEEDED( hr )) AfxThrowOleDispatchException(158,
       _T("MFCMTSWallysAccount Error: MTS Unreachable!"),0);
   //*** only use this if you want to use Role-based security ***
   if (m_spObjectContext->IsSecurityEnabled())
   {
         //*** Define a CComBSTR to hold the Role Name
        CString strRoleID;
        //*** set it ***
        strRoleID = _T("WallysMgr");
        //*** Define a Result holder ***
        BOOL bResult;
        //*** make the call ***
        m_spObjectContext->IsCallerInRole( strRoleID.AllocSysString(), &bResult );
        //*** if not in the role abort ***
        if (!bResult) AfxThrowOleDispatchException(158,
            _T("MFCMTSWallysAccount Error: User Not a Manager!"),0);
   }
   //*** Declare our ActiveX Data Object Connection holder and set it to NULL ***
   ADOConnection* adoCoConnection = NULL;
   //*** Declare our ActiveX Data Object Recordset holder and set it to NULL ***
   ADORecordset* adoAccountInfo = NULL;
   //*** Attempt to get the ADO Connection IP ***
     hr = CoCreateInstance( CLSID_CADOConnection, NULL, CLSCTX_INPROC_SERVER,
                           IID_IADOConnection, (void **) adoCoConnection );
   //*** If can't get IP abort ***
   if (!SUCCEEDED(hr))
   {
```

```
        //*** Inform MTS of failure ***
        m_spObjectContext->SetAbort();
        m_spObjectContext->Release();
         AfxThrowOleDispatchException(158,
            _T("MFCMTSWallysAccount Error: ADO Unreachable!"),0);
    }
    //*** Declare a CString to handle the Sequel Text ***
    CString strSQLText;
    //*** Give it the DSN for our samples database ***
    strSQLText = _T("FILEDSN=WallysAccounts");
    //*** Attempt to open the database ***
    hr = adoCoConnection->Open( strSQLText.AllocSysString(), NULL, NULL,
        adCmdUnspecified);
    //*** If can't get database abort ***
    if (!SUCCEEDED(hr))
    {
        //*** Inform MTS of failure ***
        m_spObjectContext->SetAbort();
        m_spObjectContext->Release();
        //*** Kill the connection IP ***
        adoCoConnection->Release();
         AfxThrowOleDispatchException(158,
         _T("MFCMTSWallysAccount Error: Database Unreachable!"),0);
    }
    //*** Declare the wsprintf buffer ***
    TCHAR szSQLBuffer[512];
    //*** Create Sequel Statement ***
    wsprintf( szSQLBuffer, _T("INSERT INTO Accounts VALUES('%s','%s',%ld,%ld,%b,0)"),
                    strName,strPassword,lTotalCredit,lCharges,bInUse);
    //*** Put the buffer in the CString via overloaded = operator ***
    strSQLText = szSQLBuffer;
    //*** Declare a COleVariant to hold returned record count from ADO ***
    COleVariant vRecCount;
    //*** Clear the record count ***
    vRecCount.Clear();
    //*** Execute the sequel statement on the database ***
      hr = adoCoConnection->Execute( strSQLText.AllocSysString(), &vRecCount, -1 ,
         NULL );
    //*** If can't reach database abort ***
    if (!SUCCEEDED(hr))
    {
        //*** Inform MTS of failure ***
        m_spObjectContext->SetAbort();
        m_spObjectContext->Release();
        //*** Kill the connection IP ***
        adoCoConnection->Release();
        //*** send back bad HRESULT ***
```

```
          AfxThrowOleDispatchException(158,
          _T("MFCMTSWallysAccount Error: Database Unreachable!"),0);
    }
    //*** if no records updated then account wasn't created so signal error ***
    if (vRecCount.lVal == 0)
    {
        //*** Inform MTS of failure ***
        m_spObjectContext->SetAbort();
        m_spObjectContext->Release();
        //*** Kill the connection IP ***
        adoCoConnection->Release();
       AfxThrowOleDispatchException(158,
         _T("MFCMTSWallysAccount Error: Database Did Not Accept New Account!"),0);
    }
    //*** Update total accounts ***
    m_totalAccounts++;
    //*** Tell MTS we're OK ***
    m_spObjectContext->SetComplete();
    m_spObjectContext->Release();
    //*** Kill the connection ***
    adoCoConnection->Release();
    return;
}

void AccountsHandler::DeleteAccount(LPCTSTR strName, LPCTSTR strPassword)
{
    // TODO: Add your dispatch handler code here
      //*** define HRESULT holder and set it to result of CCI ***
    IObjectContext* m_spObjectContext;
    HRESULT hr = GetObjectContext(&m_spObjectContext);
    if (!SUCCEEDED( hr )) AfxThrowOleDispatchException(158,
      _T("MFCMTSWallysAccount Error: MTS Unreachable!"),0);
    //*** only use this if you want to use Role-based security ***
    if (m_spObjectContext->IsSecurityEnabled())
    {
         //*** Define a CComBSTR to hold the Role Name
        CString strRoleID;
        //*** set it ***
        strRoleID = _T("WallysMgr");
        //*** Define a Result holder ***
        BOOL bResult;
        //*** make the call ***
        m_spObjectContext->IsCallerInRole( strRoleID.AllocSysString(), &bResult );
        //*** if not in the role abort ***
        if (!bResult) AfxThrowOleDispatchException(158,
            _T("MFCMTSWallysAccount Error: User Not a Manager!"),0);
    }
```

```
//*** Declare our ActiveX Data Object Connection holder and set it to NULL ***
ADOConnection* adoCoConnection = NULL;
//*** Declare our ActiveX Data Object Recordset holder and set it to NULL ***
ADORecordset* adoAccountInfo = NULL;
//*** Attempt to get the ADO Connection IP ***
  hr = CoCreateInstance( CLSID_CADOConnection, NULL, CLSCTX_INPROC_SERVER,
                         IID_IADOConnection, (void **) adoCoConnection );
//*** If can't get IP abort ***
if (!SUCCEEDED(hr))
{
    //*** Inform MTS of failure ***
    m_spObjectContext->SetAbort();
    m_spObjectContext->Release();
     AfxThrowOleDispatchException(158,
        _T("MFCMTSWallysAccount Error: ADO Unreachable!"),0);
}
//*** Declare a CString to handle the Sequel Text ***
CString strSQLText;
//*** Give it the DSN for our samples database ***
strSQLText = _T("FILEDSN=WallysAccounts");
//*** Attempt to open the database ***
hr = adoCoConnection->Open( strSQLText.AllocSysString(), NULL, NULL,
  adCmdUnspecified);
//*** If can't get database abort ***
if (!SUCCEEDED(hr))
{
    //*** Inform MTS of failure ***
    m_spObjectContext->SetAbort();
    m_spObjectContext->Release();
    //*** Kill the connection IP ***
    adoCoConnection->Release();
   AfxThrowOleDispatchException(158,
     _T("MFCMTSWallysAccount Error: Database Unreachable!"),0);
}
//*** Declare the wsprintf buffer ***
TCHAR szSQLBuffer[512];
//*** Create Sequel Statement ***
wsprintf( szSQLBuffer,
 _T("DELETE Accounts WHERE AccountName = '%s' AND AccountPassword = '%s'"),
   strName , strPassword );
//*** Put the buffer in the CSring via overloaded = operator ***
strSQLText = szSQLBuffer;
//*** Declare a COleVariant to hold returned record count from ADO ***
COleVariant vRecCount;
//*** Clear the record count ***
vRecCount.Clear();
//*** Execute the sequel statement on the database ***
```

```
    hr = adoCoConnection->Execute( strSQLText.AllocSysString(), &vRecCount, -1 ,
         NULL );
  //*** If can't reach database abort ***
  if (!SUCCEEDED(hr))
  {
      //*** Inform MTS of failure ***
      m_spObjectContext->SetAbort();
      m_spObjectContext->Release();
      //*** Kill the connection IP ***
      adoCoConnection->Release();
      //*** send back bad HRESULT ***
       AfxThrowOleDispatchException(158,
           _T("MFCMTSWallysAccount Error: Database Unreachable!"),0);
  }
  //*** if no records updated then account doesn't exist or password not matched***
  if (vRecCount.lVal == 0)
  {
      //*** Inform MTS of failure ***
      m_spObjectContext->SetAbort();
      m_spObjectContext->Release();
      //*** Kill the connection IP ***
      adoCoConnection->Release();
     AfxThrowOleDispatchException(158,
       _T("MFCMTSWallysAccount Error: Database did not accept deletion!"),0);
  }
  //*** Update total records ***
  m_totalAccounts–;
  //*** Tell MTS we're OK ***
  m_spObjectContext->SetComplete();
      m_spObjectContext->Release();
  //*** Kill the connection ***
  adoCoConnection->Release();
  //*** Send back Good Transaction ***
  return;
}

void AccountsHandler::UpdateAccountName(LPCTSTR strOldName, LPCTSTR strNewName)
{
  // TODO: Add your implementation code here
    //*** define HRESULT holder and set it to result of CCI ***
  IObjectContext* m_spObjectContext;
  HRESULT hr = GetObjectContext(&m_spObjectContext);
  if (!SUCCEEDED( hr )) AfxThrowOleDispatchException(158,
     _T("MFCMTSWallysAccount Error: MTS Unreachable!"),0);
  //*** only use this if you want to use Role-based security ***
  if (m_spObjectContext->IsSecurityEnabled())
  {
```

```
        //*** Define a CComBSTR to hold the Role Name
        CString strRoleID;
        //*** set it ***
        strRoleID = _T("WallysMgr");
        //*** Define a Result holder ***
        BOOL bResult;
        //*** make the call ***
        m_spObjectContext->IsCallerInRole( strRoleID.AllocSysString(), &bResult );
        //*** if not in the role abort ***
        if (!bResult) AfxThrowOleDispatchException(158,
            _T("MFCMTSWallysAccount Error: User Not a Manager!"),0);
    }
    //*** Declare our ActiveX Data Object Connection holder and set it to NULL ***
    ADOConnection* adoCoConnection = NULL;
    //*** Declare our ActiveX Data Object Recordset holder and set it to NULL ***
    ADORecordset* adoAccountInfo = NULL;
    //*** Attempt to get the ADO Connection IP ***
     hr = CoCreateInstance( CLSID_CADOConnection, NULL, CLSCTX_INPROC_SERVER,
                            IID_IADOConnection, (void **) adoCoConnection );
    //*** If can't get IP abort ***
    if (!SUCCEEDED(hr))
    {
        //*** Inform MTS of failure ***
        m_spObjectContext->SetAbort();
        m_spObjectContext->Release();
         AfxThrowOleDispatchException(158,
            _T("MFCMTSWallysAccount Error: ADO Unreachable!"),0);
    }
    //*** Declare a CString to handle the Sequel Text ***
    CString strSQLText;
    //*** Give it the DSN for our samples database ***
    strSQLText = _T("FILEDSN=WallysAccounts");
    //*** Declare a COleVariant to hold returned record count from ADO ***
    COleVariant vRecCount;
    //*** Clear the record count ***
    vRecCount.Clear();
    //*** Attempt to open the database ***
    hr = adoCoConnection->Open( strSQLText.AllocSysString(), NULL, NULL,
         adCmdUnspecified);
    //*** If can't get database abort ***
    if (!SUCCEEDED(hr))
    {
        //*** Inform MTS of failure ***
        m_spObjectContext->SetAbort();
        m_spObjectContext->Release();
        //*** Kill the connection IP ***
        adoCoConnection->Release();
```

```
        //*** send back bad HRESULT ***
        AfxThrowOleDispatchException(158,
          _T("MFCMTSWallysAccount Error: Database Unreachable!"),0);
    }
    //*** Declare the wsprintf buffer ***
    TCHAR szSQLBuffer[512];
    //*** Create Sequel Statement ***
    wsprintf( szSQLBuffer,
      _T("UPDATE Accounts SET AccountName = '%s' WHERE AccountName = '%s'"),
        strNewName, strOldName );
    //*** Put the buffer in the CString via overloaded = operator ***
    strSQLText = szSQLBuffer;
    //*** Clear the record count ***
    vRecCount.Clear();
    //*** Execute the sequel statement on the database ***
      hr = adoCoConnection->Execute( strSQLText.AllocSysString(), &vRecCount, -1 ,
        NULL );
    //*** If can't reach database abort ***
    if (!SUCCEEDED(hr))
    {
        //*** Inform MTS of failure ***
        m_spObjectContext->SetAbort();
        m_spObjectContext->Release();
       //*** Kill the connection IP ***
       adoCoConnection->Release();
        //*** send back bad HRESULT ***
       AfxThrowOleDispatchException(158,
        _T("MFCMTSWallysAccount Error: Database Unreachable!"),0);
    }
    //*** if no records updated then account doesn't exist so signal error ***
    if (vRecCount.lVal == 0)
    {
        //*** Inform MTS of failure ***
        m_spObjectContext->SetAbort();
        m_spObjectContext->Release();
        //*** Kill the connection IP ***
        adoCoConnection->Release();
        //*** send back bad HRESULT ***
       AfxThrowOleDispatchException(158,
         _T("MFCMTSWallysAccount Error: Account Does Not Exist!"),0);
    }
    //*** Tell MTS we're OK ***
    m_spObjectContext->SetComplete();
        m_spObjectContext->Release();
    //*** Kill the connection***
    adoCoConnection->Release();
    //*** Send back Good Transaction ***
```

```
    return;

}

void AccountsHandler::UpdateAccountPassword(LPCTSTR strName,
        LPCTSTR strOldPassword, LPCTSTR strNewPassword)
{
    // TODO: Add your implementation code here
      //*** define HRESULT holder and set it to result of CCI ***
    IObjectContext* m_spObjectContext;
    HRESULT hr = GetObjectContext(&m_spObjectContext);
    if (!SUCCEEDED( hr )) AfxThrowOleDispatchException(158,
       _T("MFCMTSWallysAccount Error: MTS Unreachable!"),0);
    //*** only use this if you want to use Role-based security ***
    if (m_spObjectContext->IsSecurityEnabled())
    {
          //*** Define a CComBSTR to hold the Role Name
         CString strRoleID;
         //*** set it ***
         strRoleID = _T("WallysMgr");
         //*** Define a Result holder ***
         BOOL bResult;
         //*** make the call ***
         m_spObjectContext->IsCallerInRole( strRoleID.AllocSysString(), &bResult );
         //*** if not in the role abort ***
         if (!bResult) AfxThrowOleDispatchException(158,
              _T("MFCMTSWallysAccount Error: User Not a Manager!"),0);
    }
    //*** Declare our ActiveX Data Object Connection holder and set it to NULL ***
    ADOConnection* adoCoConnection = NULL;
    //*** Declare our ActiveX Data Object Recordset holder and set it to NULL ***
    ADORecordset* adoAccountInfo = NULL;
    //*** Attempt to get the ADO Connection IP ***
      hr = CoCreateInstance( CLSID_CADOConnection, NULL, CLSCTX_INPROC_SERVER,
                          IID_IADOConnection, (void **) adoCoConnection );
    //*** If can't get IP abort ***
    if (!SUCCEEDED(hr))
    {
        //*** Inform MTS of failure ***
        m_spObjectContext->SetAbort();
        m_spObjectContext->Release();
         AfxThrowOleDispatchException(158,
             _T("MFCMTSWallysAccount Error: ADO Unreachable!"),0);
    }
    //*** Declare a CString to handle the Sequel Text ***
    CString strSQLText;
    //*** Give it the DSN for our samples database ***
```

```
strSQLText = _T("FILEDSN=WallysAccounts");
//*** Attempt to open the database ***
hr = adoCoConnection->Open( strSQLText.AllocSysString(), NULL, NULL,
        adCmdUnspecified);
//*** If can't get database abort ***
if (!SUCCEEDED(hr))
{
    //*** Inform MTS of failure ***
    m_spObjectContext->SetAbort();
    //*** Kill the connection IP ***
    m_spObjectContext->Release();
    adoCoConnection->Release();
    //*** send back bad HRESULT ***
    AfxThrowOleDispatchException(158,
      _T("MFCMTSWallysAccount Error: Database Unreachable!"),0);
}
//*** Declare the wsprintf buffer ***
TCHAR szSQLBuffer[512];
//*** Create Sequel Statement ***
wsprintf( szSQLBuffer,
 _T("UPDATE Accounts SET AccountPassword = '%s' WHERE AccountName = '%s' AND
    AccountPassword = '%s'"), strNewPassword, strName,strOldPassword);
//*** Put the buffer in the CString via overloaded = operator ***
strSQLText = szSQLBuffer;
//*** Declare a COleVariant to hold returned record count from ADO ***
COleVariant vRecCount;
//*** Clear the record count ***
vRecCount.Clear();
//*** Execute the sequel statement on the database ***
  hr = adoCoConnection->Execute( strSQLText.AllocSysString(), &vRecCount, -1 ,
    NULL );
//*** If can't reach database abort ***
if (!SUCCEEDED(hr))
{
    //*** Inform MTS of failure ***
    m_spObjectContext->SetAbort();
    m_spObjectContext->Release();
   //*** Kill the connection IP ***
   adoCoConnection->Release();
    //*** send back bad HRESULT ***
   AfxThrowOleDispatchException(158,
     _T("MFCMTSWallysAccount Error: Database Unreachable!"),0);
}
//*** if no records updated then video doesn't exist so signal error ***
if (vRecCount.lVal == 0)
{
    //*** Inform MTS of failure ***
```

```
        m_spObjectContext->SetAbort();
        //*** Kill the connection IP ***
        adoCoConnection->Release();
        //*** send back bad HRESULT ***
       AfxThrowOleDispatchException(158,
         _T("MFCMTSWallysAccount Error: Account Does Not Exist!"),0);
   }
   //*** Tell MTS we're OK ***
   m_spObjectContext->SetComplete();
       m_spObjectContext->Release();
   //*** Kill the connection***
   adoCoConnection->Release();
   //*** Send back Good Transaction ***
   return;
}

void AccountsHandler::UpdateAccountCredit(LPCTSTR strName, long lNewCredit)
{
     //*** define HRESULT holder and set it to result of CCI ***
   IObjectContext* m_spObjectContext;
   HRESULT hr = GetObjectContext(&m_spObjectContext);
   if (!SUCCEEDED( hr )) AfxThrowOleDispatchException(158,
       _T("MFCMTSWallysAccount Error: MTS Unreachable!"),0);
   //*** only use this if you want to use Role-based security ***
   if (m_spObjectContext->IsSecurityEnabled())
   {
         //*** Define a CComBSTR to hold the Role Name
        CString strRoleID;
        //*** set it ***
        strRoleID = _T("WallysMgr");
        //*** Define a Result holder ***
        BOOL bResult;
        //*** make the call ***
        m_spObjectContext->IsCallerInRole( strRoleID.AllocSysString(), &bResult );
        //*** if not in the role abort ***
        if (!bResult) AfxThrowOleDispatchException(158,
            _T("MFCMTSWallysAccount Error: User Not a Manager!"),0);
   }
   //*** Declare our ActiveX Data Object Connection holder and set it to NULL ***
   ADOConnection* adoCoConnection = NULL;
   //*** Declare our ActiveX Data Object Recordset holder and set it to NULL ***
   ADORecordset* adoAccountInfo = NULL;
   //*** Attempt to get the ADO Connection IP ***
     hr = CoCreateInstance( CLSID_CADOConnection, NULL, CLSCTX_INPROC_SERVER,
                         IID_IADOConnection, (void **) adoCoConnection );
   //*** If can't get IP abort ***
   if (!SUCCEEDED(hr))
```

```
{
    //*** Inform MTS of failure ***
    m_spObjectContext->SetAbort();
    m_spObjectContext->Release();
     AfxThrowOleDispatchException(158,
         _T("MFCMTSWallysAccount Error: ADO Unreachable!"),0);
}
//*** Declare a CString to handle the Sequel Text ***
CString strSQLText;
//*** Give it the DSN for our samples database ***
strSQLText = _T("FILEDSN=WallysAccounts");
//*** Attempt to open the database ***
hr = adoCoConnection->Open( strSQLText.AllocSysString(), NULL, NULL,
       adCmdUnspecified);
//*** If can't get database abort ***
if (!SUCCEEDED(hr))
{
    //*** Inform MTS of failure ***
    m_spObjectContext->SetAbort();
    m_spObjectContext->Release();
    //*** Kill the connection IP ***
    adoCoConnection->Release();
    //*** send back bad HRESULT ***
     AfxThrowOleDispatchException(158,
         _T("MFCMTSWallysAccount Error: Database Unreachable!"),0);
}
//*** Declare the wsprintf buffer ***
TCHAR szSQLBuffer[512];
//*** Create Sequel Statement ***
wsprintf( szSQLBuffer,
  _T("UPDATE Accounts SET CreditLimit = %ld WHERE AccountName = '%s'"),
     lNewCredit, strName );
//*** Put the buffer in the CString via overloaded = operator ***
strSQLText = szSQLBuffer;
//*** Declare a COleVariant to hold returned record count from ADO ***
COleVariant vRecCount;
//*** Clear the record count ***
vRecCount.Clear();
//*** Execute the sequel statement on the database ***
  hr = adoCoConnection->Execute( strSQLText.AllocSysString(), &vRecCount, -1 ,
    NULL );
//*** If can't reach database abort ***
if (!SUCCEEDED(hr))
{
    //*** Inform MTS of failure ***
    m_spObjectContext->SetAbort();
    m_spObjectContext->Release();
```

```
        //*** Kill the connection IP ***
        adoCoConnection->Release();
        //*** send back bad HRESULT ***
        AfxThrowOleDispatchException(158,
         _T("MFCMTSWallysAccount Error: Database Unreachable!"),0);
    }
    //*** if no records updated then video doesn't exist so signal error ***
    if (vRecCount.lVal == 0)
    {
        //*** Inform MTS of failure ***
        m_spObjectContext->SetAbort();
        m_spObjectContext->Release();
        //*** Kill the connection IP ***
        adoCoConnection->Release();
        //*** send back bad HRESULT ***
        AfxThrowOleDispatchException(158,
         _T("MFCMTSWallysAccount Error: Account Does Not Exist!"),0);
    }
    //*** Tell MTS we're OK ***
    m_spObjectContext->SetComplete();
    //*** Kill the connection ***
    adoCoConnection->Release();
    //*** Send back Good Transaction ***
    return;
}

void AccountsHandler::UpdateAccountCharges(LPCTSTR strName, long lNewCharges)
{
    // TODO: Add your dispatch handler code here
     //*** define HRESULT holder and set it to result of CCI ***
    IObjectContext* m_spObjectContext;
    HRESULT hr = GetObjectContext(&m_spObjectContext);
    if (!SUCCEEDED( hr )) AfxThrowOleDispatchException(158,
         _T("MFCMTSWallysAccount Error: MTS Unreachable!"),0);
    //*** Declare our ActiveX Data Object Connection holder and set it to NULL ***
    ADOConnection* adoCoConnection = NULL;
    //*** Declare our ActiveX Data Object Recordset holder and set it to NULL ***
    ADORecordset* adoAccountInfo = NULL;
    //*** Attempt to get the ADO Connection IP ***
      hr = CoCreateInstance( CLSID_CADOConnection, NULL, CLSCTX_INPROC_SERVER,
                             IID_IADOConnection, (void **) adoCoConnection );
    //*** If can't get IP abort ***
    if (!SUCCEEDED(hr))
    {
        //*** Inform MTS of failure ***
        m_spObjectContext->SetAbort();
        m_spObjectContext->Release();
```

```
        AfxThrowOleDispatchException(158,
            _T("MFCMTSWallysAccount Error: ADO Unreachable!"),0);
    }
    //*** Declare a CString to handle the Sequel Text ***
    CString strSQLText;
    //*** Give it the DSN for our samples database ***
    strSQLText = _T("FILEDSN=WallysAccounts");
    //*** Attempt to open the database ***
    hr = adoCoConnection->Open( strSQLText.AllocSysString(), NULL, NULL,
          adCmdUnspecified);
    //*** If can't get database abort ***
    if (!SUCCEEDED(hr))
    {
        //*** Inform MTS of failure ***
        m_spObjectContext->SetAbort();
        m_spObjectContext->Release();
        //*** Kill the connection IP ***
        adoCoConnection->Release();
        //*** send back bad HRESULT ***
         AfxThrowOleDispatchException(158,
            _T("MFCMTSWallysAccount Error: Database Unreachable!"),0);
    }
    //*** Declare the wsprintf buffer ***
    TCHAR szSQLBuffer[512];
    //*** Create Sequel Statement ***
    wsprintf( szSQLBuffer,
        _T("UPDATE Accounts SET CurrentCharges = %ld WHERE AccountName = '%s'"),
           lNewCharges, strName );
    //*** Put the buffer in the CString via overloaded = operator ***
    strSQLText = szSQLBuffer;
    //*** Declare a COleVariant to hold returned record count from ADO ***
    COleVariant vRecCount;
    //*** Clear the record count ***
    vRecCount.Clear();
    //*** Execute the sequel statement on the database ***
      hr = adoCoConnection->Execute( strSQLText.AllocSysString(), &vRecCount, -1 ,
       NULL );
    //*** If can't reach database abort ***
    if (!SUCCEEDED(hr))
    {
        //*** Inform MTS of failure ***
        m_spObjectContext->SetAbort();
        m_spObjectContext->Release();
       //*** Kill the connection IP ***
       adoCoConnection->Release();
        //*** send back bad HRESULT ***
       AfxThrowOleDispatchException(158,
```

```
        _T("MFCMTSWallysAccount Error: Database Unreachable!"),0);
   }
   //*** if no records updated then video doesn't exist so signal error ***
   if (vRecCount.lVal == 0)
   {
       //*** Inform MTS of failure ***
       m_spObjectContext->SetAbort();
       m_spObjectContext->Release();
       //*** Kill the connection IP ***
       adoCoConnection->Release();
       //*** send back bad HRESULT ***
      AfxThrowOleDispatchException(158,
        _T("MFCMTSWallysAccount Error: Account Does Not Exist!"),0);
   }
   //*** Tell MTS we're OK ***
   m_spObjectContext->SetComplete();
   //*** Kill the connection ***
   adoCoConnection->Release();
   //*** Send back Good Transaction ***
   return;
}

void AccountsHandler::UpdateAccountInUse(LPCTSTR strName, BOOL bInUse)
{
     //*** define HRESULT holder and set it to result of CCI ***
   IObjectContext* m_spObjectContext;
   HRESULT hr = GetObjectContext(&m_spObjectContext);
   if (!SUCCEEDED( hr )) AfxThrowOleDispatchException(158,
      _T("MFCMTSWallysAccount Error: MTS Unreachable!"),0);
   //*** Declare our ActiveX Data Object Connection holder and set it to NULL ***
   ADOConnection* adoCoConnection = NULL;
   //*** Declare our ActiveX Data Object Recordset holder and set it to NULL ***
   ADORecordset* adoAccountInfo = NULL;
   //*** Attempt to get the ADO Connection IP ***
     hr = CoCreateInstance( CLSID_CADOConnection, NULL, CLSCTX_INPROC_SERVER,
                          IID_IADOConnection, (void **) adoCoConnection );
   //*** If can't get IP abort ***
   if (!SUCCEEDED(hr))
   {
       //*** Inform MTS of failure ***
       m_spObjectContext->SetAbort();
       m_spObjectContext->Release();
        AfxThrowOleDispatchException(158,
            _T("MFCMTSWallysAccount Error: ADO Unreachable!"),0);
   }
   //*** Declare a CString to handle the Sequel Text ***
   CString strSQLText;
```

```
//*** Give it the DSN for our samples database ***
strSQLText = _T("FILEDSN=WallysAccounts");
//*** Attempt to open the database ***
hr = adoCoConnection->Open( strSQLText.AllocSysString(), NULL, NULL,
      adCmdUnspecified);
//*** If can't get database abort ***
if (!SUCCEEDED(hr))
{
    //*** Inform MTS of failure ***
    m_spObjectContext->SetAbort();
    m_spObjectContext->Release();
    //*** Kill the connection IP ***
    adoCoConnection->Release();
    //*** send back bad HRESULT ***
     AfxThrowOleDispatchException(158,
        _T("MFCMTSWallysAccount Error: Database Unreachable!"),0);
}
//*** Declare the wsprintf buffer ***
TCHAR szSQLBuffer[512];
//*** Create Sequel Statement ***
wsprintf( szSQLBuffer,
   _T("UPDATE Videos SET InUse = %b WHERE AccountName = '%s'"), bInUse, strName);
//*** Put the buffer in the CString via overloaded = operator ***
strSQLText = szSQLBuffer;
//*** Declare a COleVariant to hold returned record count from ADO ***
COleVariant vRecCount;
//*** Clear the record count ***
vRecCount.Clear();
//*** Execute the sequel statement on the database ***
  hr = adoCoConnection->Execute( strSQLText.AllocSysString(), &vRecCount, -1 ,
      NULL );
//*** If can't reach database abort ***
if (!SUCCEEDED(hr))
{
    //*** Inform MTS of failure ***
    m_spObjectContext->SetAbort();
    m_spObjectContext->Release();
   //*** Kill the connection IP ***
   adoCoConnection->Release();
    //*** send back bad HRESULT ***
   AfxThrowOleDispatchException(158,
     _T("MFCMTSWallysAccount Error: Database Unreachable!"),0);
}
//*** if no records updated then video doesn't exist so signal error ***
if (vRecCount.lVal == 0)
{
    //*** Inform MTS of failure ***
```

```
        m_spObjectContext->SetAbort();
        m_spObjectContext->Release();
        //*** Kill the connection IP ***
        adoCoConnection->Release();
        //*** send back bad HRESULT ***
       AfxThrowOleDispatchException(158,
          _T("MFCMTSWallysAccount Error: Account Does Not Exist!"),0);
    }
    //*** Tell MTS we're OK ***
    m_spObjectContext->SetComplete();
        m_spObjectContext->Release();
    //*** Kill the connection ***
    adoCoConnection->Release();
    //*** Send back Good Transaction ***
    return;
}

BSTR AccountsHandler::GetAccountPassword(LPCTSTR strName)
{
    CString strResult;
       //*** define HRESULT holder and set it to result of CCI ***
    IObjectContext* m_spObjectContext;
    HRESULT hr = GetObjectContext(&m_spObjectContext);
    if (!SUCCEEDED( hr )) AfxThrowOleDispatchException(158,
        _T("MFCMTSWallysAccount Error: MTS Unreachable!"),0);
    //*** Declare our ActiveX Data Object Connection holder and set it to NULL ***
    ADOConnection* adoCoConnection = NULL;
    //*** Declare our ActiveX Data Object Recordset holder and set it to NULL ***
    ADORecordset* adoAccountInfo = NULL;
    //*** Declare our ActiveX Data Object Fields holder and set it to NULL ***
    ADOFields* padoFields = NULL;
    //*** Declare our ActiveX Data Object Field holder and set it to NULL ***
    ADOField* padoField = NULL;
    //*** Define Error Holder and set it to 0 ***
    long lErrorFlags = 0;
    //*** Attempt to get the ADO Connection IP ***
       hr = CoCreateInstance( CLSID_CADOConnection, NULL, CLSCTX_INPROC_SERVER,
                         IID_IADOConnection, (void **) adoCoConnection );
    //*** If can't get IP abort ***
    if (!SUCCEEDED(hr))
    {
        //*** Inform MTS of failure ***
        m_spObjectContext->SetAbort();
        m_spObjectContext->Release();
         AfxThrowOleDispatchException(158,
            _T("MFCMTSWallysAccount Error: ADO Unreachable!"),0);
    }
```

```
//*** Declare a CString to handle the Sequel Text ***
CString strSQLText;
//*** Give it the DSN for our samples database ***
strSQLText = _T("FILEDSN=WallysVideos");
//*** Attempt to open the database ***
hr = adoCoConnection->Open( strSQLText.AllocSysString(), NULL, NULL,
      adCmdUnspecified);
//*** If can't get database abort ***
if (!SUCCEEDED(hr))
{
    //*** Inform MTS of failure ***
    m_spObjectContext->SetAbort();
    m_spObjectContext->Release();
    //*** Kill the connection IP ***
    adoCoConnection->Release();
    //*** send back bad HRESULT ***
     AfxThrowOleDispatchException(158,
        _T("MFCMTSWallysAccount Error: Database Unreachable!"),0);
}
//*** Declare the wsprintf buffer ***
TCHAR szSQLBuffer[512];
wsprintf( szSQLBuffer,
          _T("SELECT AccountPassword FROM Accounts WHERE AccountName = '%s'"),
      strName);
//*** Put it into the CString via overloaded = operator ***
strSQLText = szSQLBuffer;
//*** Declare a COleVariant to hold returned record count from ADO ***
COleVariant vRecCount;
//*** Clear the record count ***
vRecCount.Clear();
//*** Execute the sequel statement on the database ***
   hr = adoCoConnection->Execute( strSQLText.AllocSysString(), &vRecCount, -1 ,
    &adoAccountInfo );
//*** If can't reach database abort ***
if (!SUCCEEDED(hr))
{
    //*** Inform MTS of failure ***
    m_spObjectContext->SetAbort();
    m_spObjectContext->Release();
    //*** Kill the connection IP ***
    adoCoConnection->Release();
    //*** send back bad HRESULT ***
    AfxThrowOleDispatchException(158,
     _T("MFCMTSWallysAccount Error: Database Unreachable!"),0);
}
//*** Obtain the fields collection from the recordset ***
   hr = adoAccountInfo->get_Fields( &padoFields );
```

```
//*** If can't reach database abort ***
if (!SUCCEEDED(hr))
{
    //*** Inform MTS of failure ***
    m_spObjectContext->SetAbort();
    //*** Kill the connection and recordset IP ***
   adoCoConnection->Release();
   adoAccountInfo->Release();
    //*** send back bad HRESULT ***
   AfxThrowOleDispatchException(158,
    _T("MFCMTSWallysAccount Error: Database Unreachable!"),0);
}
//*** Define a variant to obtain the rental price field ***
COleVariant vField = _T("AccountPassword");
//*** define a variant to hold the information ***
COleVariant vPassword;
//*** Get the RentalPrice Field ***
hr = padoFields->get_Item( vField , &padoField );
//*** If can't reach database abort ***
if (!SUCCEEDED(hr))
{
    //*** Inform MTS of failure ***
    m_spObjectContext->SetAbort();
    m_spObjectContext->Release();
   //*** Kill the connection, recordset, and fields IP ***
   adoCoConnection->Release();
   adoAccountInfo->Release();
   padoFields->Release();
    //*** send back bad HRESULT ***
   AfxThrowOleDispatchException(158,
    _T("MFCMTSWallysAccount Error: Database Unreachable!"),0);
}
//*** Get the actual balance value ***
hr = padoField->get_Value( &vPassword );
//*** If can't reach database abort ***
if (!SUCCEEDED(hr))
{
    //*** Inform MTS of failure ***
    m_spObjectContext->SetAbort();
    m_spObjectContext->Release();
    //*** Kill the connection, recordset, fields, and field IP ***
    adoCoConnection->Release();
    adoAccountInfo->Release();
    padoFields->Release();
    padoField->Release();
    //*** send back bad HRESULT ***
    AfxThrowOleDispatchException(158,
```

```
        _T("MFCMTSWallysAccount Error: Database Unreachable!"),0);
 }
    //*** return the value from the variant ***
    strResult = vPassword.bstrVal;
 //*** Tell MTS we're OK ***
 m_spObjectContext->SetComplete();
     m_spObjectContext->Release();
 //*** Kill the connection, recordset, fields, and field IP ***
 adoCoConnection->Release();
 adoAccountInfo->Release();
 padoFields->Release();
 padoField->Release();
 //*** Send back Good Transaction ***
 return strResult.AllocSysString();
}

void AccountsHandler::SetAccountPassword(LPCTSTR strName, LPCTSTR lpszNewValue)
{
 // TODO: Add your property handler here

}

long AccountsHandler::GetAccountCreditLimit(LPCTSTR strName)
{
 // TODO: Add your property handler here
    //*** define HRESULT holder and set it to result of CCI ***
 IObjectContext* m_spObjectContext;
 HRESULT hr = GetObjectContext(&m_spObjectContext);
 if (!SUCCEEDED( hr )) AfxThrowOleDispatchException(158,
       _T("MFCMTSWallysAccount Error: MTS Unreachable!"),0);
 //*** Declare our ActiveX Data Object Connection holder and set it to NULL ***
 ADOConnection* adoCoConnection = NULL;
 //*** Declare our ActiveX Data Object Recordset holder and set it to NULL ***
 ADORecordset* adoAccountInfo = NULL;
 //*** Declare our ActiveX Data Object Fields holder and set it to NULL ***
 ADOFields* padoFields = NULL;
 //*** Declare our ActiveX Data Object Field holder and set it to NULL ***
 ADOField* padoField = NULL;
 //*** Define Error Holder and set it to 0 ***
 long lErrorFlags = 0;
 //*** Attempt to get the ADO Connection IP ***
    hr = CoCreateInstance( CLSID_CADOConnection, NULL, CLSCTX_INPROC_SERVER,
                        IID_IADOConnection, (void **) adoCoConnection );
 //*** If can't get IP abort ***
 if (!SUCCEEDED(hr))
 {
     //*** Inform MTS of failure ***
```

```
        m_spObjectContext->SetAbort();
        m_spObjectContext->Release();
         AfxThrowOleDispatchException(158,
            _T("MFCMTSWallysAccount Error: ADO Unreachable!"),0);
    }
    //*** Declare a CString to handle the Sequel Text ***
    CString strSQLText;
    //*** Give it the DSN for our samples database ***
    strSQLText = _T("FILEDSN=WallysVideos");
    //*** Attempt to open the database ***
    hr = adoCoConnection->Open( strSQLText.AllocSysString(), NULL, NULL,
          adCmdUnspecified);
    //*** If can't get database abort ***
    if (!SUCCEEDED(hr))
    {
        //*** Inform MTS of failure ***
        m_spObjectContext->SetAbort();
        m_spObjectContext->Release();
        //*** Kill the connection IP ***
        adoCoConnection->Release();
        //*** send back bad HRESULT ***
         AfxThrowOleDispatchException(158,
            _T("MFCMTSWallysAccount Error: Database Unreachable!"),0);
    }
    //*** Declare the wsprintf buffer ***
    TCHAR szSQLBuffer[512];
    wsprintf( szSQLBuffer,
        _T("SELECT CreditLimit FROM Accounts WHERE AccountName = '%s'"),
          strName);
    //*** Put it into the CString via overloaded = operator ***
    strSQLText = szSQLBuffer;
    //*** Declare a COleVariant to hold returned record count from ADO ***
    COleVariant vRecCount;
    //*** Clear the record count ***
    vRecCount.Clear();
    //*** Execute the sequel statement on the database ***
       hr = adoCoConnection->Execute( strSQLText.AllocSysString(), &vRecCount, -1 ,
        &adoAccountInfo );
    //*** If can't reach database abort ***
    if (!SUCCEEDED(hr))
    {
        //*** Inform MTS of failure ***
        m_spObjectContext->SetAbort();
        m_spObjectContext->Release();
        //*** Kill the connection IP ***
        adoCoConnection->Release();
        //*** send back bad HRESULT ***
```

```
        AfxThrowOleDispatchException(158,
            _T("MFCMTSWallysAccount Error: Database Unreachable!"),0);
    }
    //*** Obtain the fields collection from the recordset ***
        hr = adoAccountInfo->get_Fields( &padoFields );
    //*** If can't reach database abort ***
    if (!SUCCEEDED(hr))
    {
        //*** Inform MTS of failure ***
        m_spObjectContext->SetAbort();
        m_spObjectContext->Release();
        //*** Kill the connection and recordset IP ***
       adoCoConnection->Release();
       adoAccountInfo->Release();
        //*** send back bad HRESULT ***
       AfxThrowOleDispatchException(158,
        _T("MFCMTSWallysAccount Error: Database Unreachable!"),0);
    }
    //*** Define a variant to obtain the rental price field ***
    COleVariant vField = _T("CreditLimit");
    //*** define a variant to hold the information ***
    COleVariant vCreditLimit;
    //*** Get the RentalPrice Field ***
    hr = padoFields->get_Item( vField , &padoField );
    //*** If can't reach database abort ***
    if (!SUCCEEDED(hr))
    {
        //*** Inform MTS of failure ***
        m_spObjectContext->SetAbort();
        m_spObjectContext->Release();
       //*** Kill the connection, recordset, and fields IP ***
       adoCoConnection->Release();
       adoAccountInfo->Release();
       padoFields->Release();
        //*** send back bad HRESULT ***
       AfxThrowOleDispatchException(158,
        _T("MFCMTSWallysAccount Error: Database Unreachable!"),0);
    }
    //*** Get the actual balance value ***
    hr = padoField->get_Value( &vCreditLimit );
    //*** If can't reach database abort ***
    if (!SUCCEEDED(hr))
    {
        //*** Inform MTS of failure ***
        m_spObjectContext->SetAbort();
        m_spObjectContext->Release();
        //*** Kill the connection, recordset, fields, and field IP ***
```

```
        adoCoConnection->Release();
        adoAccountInfo->Release();
        padoFields->Release();
        padoField->Release();
        //*** send back bad HRESULT ***
        AfxThrowOleDispatchException(158,
          _T("MFCMTSWallysAccount Error: Database Unreachable!"),0);
  }
      //*** return the value from the variant ***
      long lResult = vCreditLimit.lVal;
  //*** Tell MTS we're OK ***
  m_spObjectContext->SetComplete();
        m_spObjectContext->Release();
  //*** Kill the connection, recordset, fields, and field IP ***
  adoCoConnection->Release();
  adoAccountInfo->Release();
  padoFields->Release();
  padoField->Release();
  //*** Send back Good Transaction ***
  return lResult;
}

void AccountsHandler::SetAccountCreditLimit(LPCTSTR strName, long nNewValue)
{
  // TODO: Add your property handler here

}

long AccountsHandler::GetAccountCurrentCharges(LPCTSTR strName)
{
  // TODO: Add your property handler here
      //*** define HRESULT holder and set it to result of CCI ***
  IObjectContext* m_spObjectContext;
  HRESULT hr = GetObjectContext(&m_spObjectContext);
  if (!SUCCEEDED( hr )) AfxThrowOleDispatchException(158,
      _T("MFCMTSWallysAccount Error: MTS Unreachable!"),0);
  //*** Declare our ActiveX Data Object Connection holder and set it to NULL ***
  ADOConnection* adoCoConnection = NULL;
  //*** Declare our ActiveX Data Object Recordset holder and set it to NULL ***
  ADORecordset* adoAccountInfo = NULL;
  //*** Declare our ActiveX Data Object Fields holder and set it to NULL ***
  ADOFields* padoFields = NULL;
  //*** Declare our ActiveX Data Object Field holder and set it to NULL ***
  ADOField* padoField = NULL;
  //*** Define Error Holder and set it to 0 ***
  long lErrorFlags = 0;
  //*** Attempt to get the ADO Connection IP ***
```

```
   hr = CoCreateInstance( CLSID_CADOConnection, NULL, CLSCTX_INPROC_SERVER,
                          IID_IADOConnection, (void **) adoCoConnection );
//*** If can't get IP abort ***
if (!SUCCEEDED(hr))
{
    //*** Inform MTS of failure ***
    m_spObjectContext->SetAbort();
    m_spObjectContext->Release();
     AfxThrowOleDispatchException(158,
        _T("MFCMTSWallysAccount Error: ADO Unreachable!"),0);
}
//*** Declare a CString to handle the Sequel Text ***
CString strSQLText;
//*** Give it the DSN for our samples database ***
strSQLText = _T("FILEDSN=WallysVideos");
//*** Attempt to open the database ***
hr = adoCoConnection->Open( strSQLText.AllocSysString(), NULL, NULL,
   adCmdUnspecified);
//*** If can't get database abort ***
if (!SUCCEEDED(hr))
{
    //*** Inform MTS of failure ***
    m_spObjectContext->SetAbort();
    m_spObjectContext->Release();
    //*** Kill the connection IP ***
    adoCoConnection->Release();
    //*** send back bad HRESULT ***
     AfxThrowOleDispatchException(158,
      _T("MFCMTSWallysAccount Error: Database Unreachable!"),0);
}
//*** Declare the wsprintf buffer ***
TCHAR szSQLBuffer[512];
wsprintf( szSQLBuffer,
      _T("SELECT CurrentCharges FROM Accounts WHERE AccountName = '%s'"),
       strName);
//*** Put it into the CString via overloaded = operator ***
strSQLText = szSQLBuffer;
//*** Declare a COleVariant to hold returned record count from ADO ***
COleVariant vRecCount;
//*** Clear the record count ***
vRecCount.Clear();
//*** Execute the sequel statement on the database ***
   hr = adoCoConnection->Execute( strSQLText.AllocSysString(), &vRecCount, -1 ,
    &adoAccountInfo );
//*** If can't reach database abort ***
if (!SUCCEEDED(hr))
{
```

```
        //*** Inform MTS of failure ***
        m_spObjectContext->SetAbort();
        m_spObjectContext->Release();
        //*** Kill the connection IP ***
        adoCoConnection->Release();
        //*** send back bad HRESULT ***
        AfxThrowOleDispatchException(158,
          _T("MFCMTSWallysAccount Error: Database Unreachable!"),0);
    }
    //*** Obtain the fields collection from the recordset ***
       hr = adoAccountInfo->get_Fields( &padoFields );
    //*** If can't reach database abort ***
    if (!SUCCEEDED(hr))
    {
        //*** Inform MTS of failure ***
        m_spObjectContext->SetAbort();
        m_spObjectContext->Release();
        //*** Kill the connection and recordset IP ***
       adoCoConnection->Release();
       adoAccountInfo->Release();
        //*** send back bad HRESULT ***
       AfxThrowOleDispatchException(158,
         _T("MFCMTSWallysAccount Error: Database Unreachable!"),0);
    }
    //*** Define a variant to obtain the rental price field ***
    COleVariant vField = _T("CurrentCharges");
    //*** define a variant to hold the information ***
    COleVariant vCurrentCharges;
    //*** Get the RentalPrice Field ***
    hr = padoFields->get_Item( vField , &padoField );
    //*** If can't reach database abort ***
    if (!SUCCEEDED(hr))
    {
        //*** Inform MTS of failure ***
        m_spObjectContext->SetAbort();
        m_spObjectContext->Release();
       //*** Kill the connection, recordset, and fields IP ***
       adoCoConnection->Release();
       adoAccountInfo->Release();
       padoFields->Release();
        //*** send back bad HRESULT ***
       AfxThrowOleDispatchException(158,
          _T("MFCMTSWallysAccount Error: Database Unreachable!"),0);
    }
    //*** Get the actual balance value ***
    hr = padoField->get_Value( &vCurrentCharges );
    //*** If can't reach database abort ***
```

```
 if (!SUCCEEDED(hr))
 {
     //*** Inform MTS of failure ***
     m_spObjectContext->SetAbort();
     m_spObjectContext->Release();
     //*** Kill the connection, recordset, fields, and field IP ***
     adoCoConnection->Release();
     adoAccountInfo->Release();
     padoFields->Release();
     padoField->Release();
     //*** send back bad HRESULT ***
     AfxThrowOleDispatchException(158,
      _T("MFCMTSWallysAccount Error: Database Unreachable!"),0);
 }
    //*** return the value from the variant ***
    long lResult = vCurrentCharges.lVal;
 //*** Tell MTS we're OK ***
 m_spObjectContext->SetComplete();
     m_spObjectContext->Release();
 //*** Kill the connection, recordset, fields, and field IP ***
 adoCoConnection->Release();
 adoAccountInfo->Release();
 padoFields->Release();
 padoField->Release();
 //*** Send back Good Transaction ***
 return lResult;
}

void AccountsHandler::SetAccountCurrentCharges(LPCTSTR strName, long nNewValue)
{
 // TODO: Add your property handler here

}

BOOL AccountsHandler::GetAccountInUse(LPCTSTR strName)
{
 // TODO: Add your property handler here
    //*** define HRESULT holder and set it to result of CCI ***
 IObjectContext* m_spObjectContext;
 HRESULT hr = GetObjectContext(&m_spObjectContext);
 if (!SUCCEEDED( hr )) AfxThrowOleDispatchException(158,
    _T("MFCMTSWallysAccount Error: MTS Unreachable!"),0);
 //*** Declare our ActiveX Data Object Connection holder and set it to NULL ***
 ADOConnection* adoCoConnection = NULL;
 //*** Declare our ActiveX Data Object Recordset holder and set it to NULL ***
 ADORecordset* adoAccountInfo = NULL;
 //*** Declare our ActiveX Data Object Fields holder and set it to NULL ***
```

```
ADOFields* padoFields = NULL;
//*** Declare our ActiveX Data Object Field holder and set it to NULL ***
ADOField* padoField = NULL;
//*** Define Error Holder and set it to 0 ***
long lErrorFlags = 0;
//*** Attempt to get the ADO Connection IP ***
   hr = CoCreateInstance( CLSID_CADOConnection, NULL, CLSCTX_INPROC_SERVER,
                          IID_IADOConnection, (void **) adoCoConnection );
//*** If can't get IP abort ***
if (!SUCCEEDED(hr))
{
    //*** Inform MTS of failure ***
    m_spObjectContext->SetAbort();
    m_spObjectContext->Release();
     AfxThrowOleDispatchException(158,
        _T("MFCMTSWallysAccount Error: ADO Unreachable!"),0);
}
//*** Declare a CString to handle the Sequel Text ***
CString strSQLText;
//*** Give it the DSN for our samples database ***
strSQLText = _T("FILEDSN=WallysVideos");
//*** Attempt to open the database ***
hr = adoCoConnection->Open( strSQLText.AllocSysString(), NULL, NULL,
   adCmdUnspecified);
//*** If can't get database abort ***
if (!SUCCEEDED(hr))
{
    //*** Inform MTS of failure ***
    m_spObjectContext->SetAbort();
    m_spObjectContext->Release();
    //*** Kill the connection IP ***
    adoCoConnection->Release();
    //*** send back bad HRESULT ***
    AfxThrowOleDispatchException(158,
      _T("MFCMTSWallysAccount Error: Database Unreachable!"),0);
}
//*** Declare the wsprintf buffer ***
TCHAR szSQLBuffer[512];
wsprintf( szSQLBuffer, _T("SELECT InUse FROM Accounts WHERE AccountName = '%s'"),
      strName);
//*** Put it into the CString via overloaded = operator ***
strSQLText = szSQLBuffer;
//*** Declare a COleVariant to hold returned record count from ADO ***
COleVariant vRecCount;
//*** Clear the record count ***
vRecCount.Clear();
//*** Execute the sequel statement on the database ***
```

```
    hr = adoCoConnection->Execute( strSQLText.AllocSysString(), &vRecCount, -1 ,
     &adoAccountInfo );
//*** If can't reach database abort ***
if (!SUCCEEDED(hr))
{
     //*** Inform MTS of failure ***
     m_spObjectContext->SetAbort();
     m_spObjectContext->Release();
     //*** Kill the connection IP ***
     adoCoConnection->Release();
     //*** send back bad HRESULT ***
     AfxThrowOleDispatchException(158,
         _T("MFCMTSWallysAccount Error: Database Unreachable!"),0);
}
//*** Obtain the fields collection from the recordset ***
    hr = adoAccountInfo->get_Fields( &padoFields );
//*** If can't reach database abort ***
if (!SUCCEEDED(hr))
{
     //*** Inform MTS of failure ***
     m_spObjectContext->SetAbort();
     m_spObjectContext->Release();
     //*** Kill the connection and recordset IP ***
    adoCoConnection->Release();
    adoAccountInfo->Release();
     //*** send back bad HRESULT ***
    AfxThrowOleDispatchException(158,
        _T("MFCMTSWallysAccount Error: Database Unreachable!"),0);
}
//*** Define a variant to obtain the rental price field ***
COleVariant vField = _T("InUse");
//*** define a variant to hold the information ***
COleVariant vInUse;
//*** Get the RentalPrice Field ***
hr = padoFields->get_Item( vField , &padoField );
//*** If can't reach database abort ***
if (!SUCCEEDED(hr))
{
     //*** Inform MTS of failure ***
     m_spObjectContext->SetAbort();
     m_spObjectContext->Release();
    //*** Kill the connection, recordset, and fields IP ***
    adoCoConnection->Release();
    adoAccountInfo->Release();
    padoFields->Release();
     //*** send back bad HRESULT ***
    AfxThrowOleDispatchException(158,
```

```
1555.          _T("MFCMTSWallysAccount Error: Database Unreachable!"),0);
1556.   }
1557.   //*** Get the actual balance value ***
1558.   hr = padoField->get_Value( &vInUse );
1559.   //*** If can't reach database abort ***
1560.   if (!SUCCEEDED(hr))
1561.   {
1562.       //*** Inform MTS of failure ***
1563.       m_spObjectContext->SetAbort();
1564.       m_spObjectContext->Release();
1565.       //*** Kill the connection, recordset, fields, and field IP ***
1566.       adoCoConnection->Release();
1567.       adoAccountInfo->Release();
1568.       padoFields->Release();
1569.       padoField->Release();
1570.       //*** send back bad HRESULT ***
1571.       AfxThrowOleDispatchException(158,
1572.          _T("MFCMTSWallysAccount Error: Database Unreachable!"),0);
1573.   }
1574.      //*** return the value from the variant ***
1575.      BOOL bResult = vInUse.boolVal;
1576.   //*** Tell MTS we're OK ***
1577.   m_spObjectContext->SetComplete();
1578.       m_spObjectContext->Release();
1579.   //*** Kill the connection, recordset, fields, and field IP ***
1580.   adoCoConnection->Release();
1581.   adoAccountInfo->Release();
1582.   padoFields->Release();
1583.   padoField->Release();
1584.   //*** Send back Good Transaction ***
1585.   return bResult;
1586. }
1587.
1588. void AccountsHandler::SetAccountInUse(LPCTSTR strName, BOOL bNewValue)
1589. {
1590.   // TODO: Add your property handler here
1591.
1592. }
```

***Listing 7-1*** *ACCOUNTSHANDLER.CPP source code after modifications*

Here's the breakdown (the code is heavily commented and so we'll concentrate on the bigger design issues and some places where the logic may be a bit hard to follow in these comments. Also, since after the first function the code is virtually identical except for single lines calling different database SQL statements, only the first function is detailed below):

- **Lines 6-12** This code brings in the ADO and MTS headers so we can access them.

- **Lines 116-132** This code initializes the ADO interface pointers needed to interact with the SQL Server database.
- **Lines 133-168** This code contacts the Wallys database and signals an error if it fails.
- **Lines 169-179** This code executes the SQL text for this particular database interaction and obtains a pRowset interface pointer which contains a set of data that hopefully matches that requested by the command.
- **Lines 180-195** This code gets a pFields interface pointer from the pRowset IP obtained from executing the SQL statement. This IP contains all the fields of the current rowset so the program can obtain as many as it wants and examine or change their values.
- **Lines 196-208** This code gets a single pField interface pointer from the pFields IP with the name given. This moves from a collection of all the fields in the current recordset to one single field so its value can be obtained.
- **Lines 209-216** This code uses the pField interface pointer to obtain the actual value of the field and deal with it as needed (it reads it in this example, but in later examples is used to set it).
- **Lines 222-226** This code obtains an MTS object context for use in the component's functions. It will be there because in the MTS Explorer (see Chapter 9) we will set this component to Require a Transaction. If you also have read the ATL chapter, you will notice that unlike ATL, we have to do this ourselves.
- **Lines 232-242** This code deals with signaling an error to MTS via SetAbort, and then releasing the MTS IObjectContext IP (because unlike the ATL code, we must do this manually). This code will be used whenever an error occurs inside a function that uses an object context. Note also that unlike ATL, it throws MFC exceptions rather than returning error codes.
- **Lines 293-295** This code deals with signaling success to MTS via SetComplete and then releasing the MTS IObjectContext IP (because unlike the ATL code, we must do this manually). This code will be used whenever success occurs inside a function that uses an object context.
- **Lines 308-322** This code deals with using MTS role-based security. It uses properties of the ObjectContext IP to determine if security is enabled, and if so whether the current user is part of the WallysMgr role. If so, it allows the action to proceed; otherwise it throws an exception and aborts the transaction.

Once you are satisfied you've entered the code from the above listing correctly, build the MTS COM server from the Build menu. If you encounter any errors, please check the code to find your mistake (it has been exhaustively debugged and is correct). Once you have compiled the component successfully, it is automatically registered on the local machine; if you need to move it to another machine, see Chapter 9. Otherwise, please move on to the next component.

# Creating Another MTS COM Component with MFC

The next step is to use MFC to create an MTS COM server that handles videos in stock for Wally's. The following sections take you through the user interface portions of creating the project in the step-by-step system, then show you the code you need to write and an analysis using the line-by-line approach.

## *Step By Step*

Start Visual C++ 5.0 or 6.0. From the File menu, select New. The New dialog box opens; click on the MFC AppWizard (dll) entry. Next, select an appropriate directory, then enter a project name of **MFCMTSWallysVideos**. Figure 7-21 shows how the New dialog should appear when you are done. Press OK to open the MFC AppWizard.

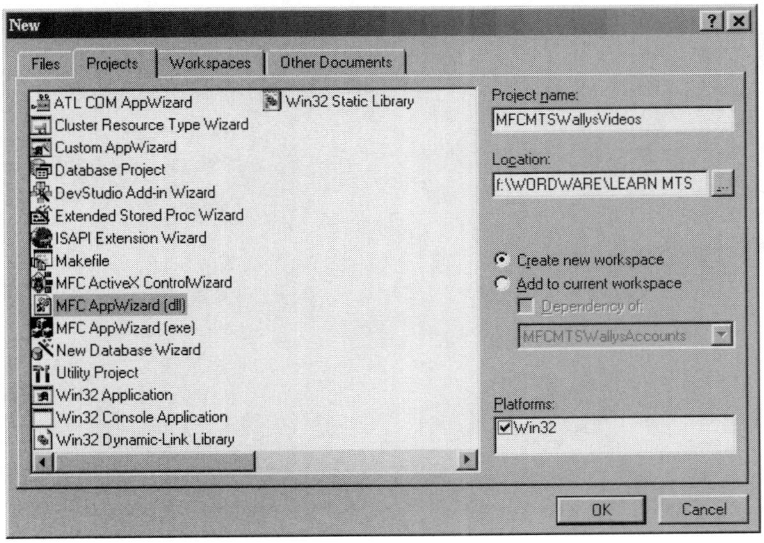


***Figure 7-21*** *The New dialog box creating the MFCMTSWallysVideos MFC project*

In the MFC AppWizard, make sure you select a shared MFC DLL, and enable Automation support and source code comments. Click on the Finish button to create the MTS component project.

A confirmation dialog box appears; press OK to create the MFC project.

When the wizard finishes, you return to the Visual C++ IDE. From the menu, select View|ClassWizard. The MFC ClassWizard dialog appears; move to the Automation tab. At first, there are no enabled controls because the default class does not support Automation. To add an Automation-capable class, click on the Add Class button. A drop-down menu appears; select New Class. The

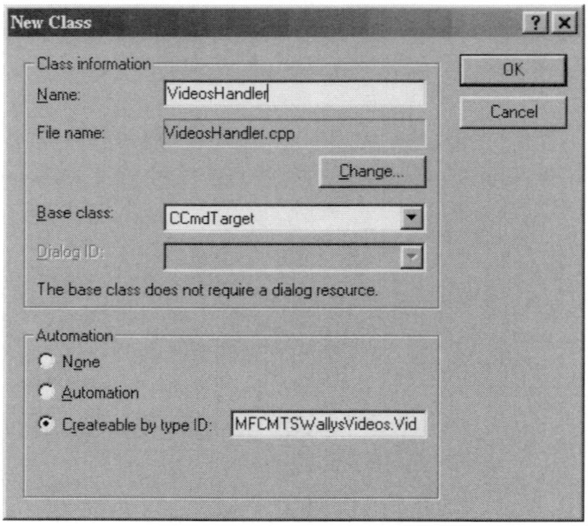


***Figure 7-22** Adding an Automation-enabled class to the MFC project*

dialog box shown in Figure 7-22 is displayed. Enter a name of **VideosHandler**, select a Base Class of CCmdTarget, and make it Createable by Type ID, as shown in the figure. Click on OK to create this class and add it to the project.

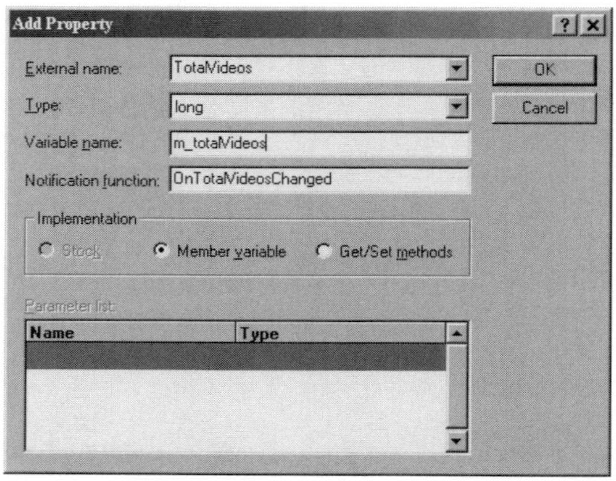


***Figure 7-23** Adding the TotalVideos property*

Back in ClassWizard with the buttons now enabled, click on the Add Property button to add an Automation property to the MTS Automation COM server. The Add Property dialog box appears; enter a name of **TotalVideos**. Give it a Type of long, and leave the other default options and values unchanged. Figure 7-23 shows how the Add Property dialog should appear when you are done. Press OK to add the property to the MTS COM server.

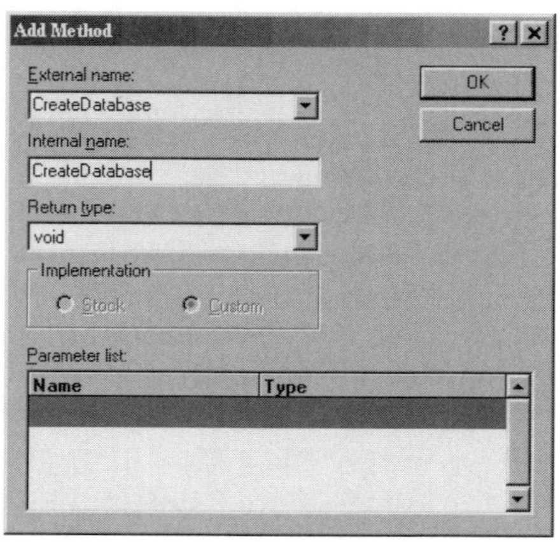


***Figure 7-24** Adding the CreateDatabase method*

Next, to add a method function to the MTS COM server, click on the Add Method button of the MFC ClassWizard. In the dialog box that appears, enter a name of **CreateDatabase**. Give it a Return Type of void, and leave the other default options and values unchanged. Figure 7-24 shows how the Add Method dialog should appear when you are done. Press OK to add the method to the MTS COM server.

To add another method function to the MTS COM server, again click on the Add Method button of the MFC ClassWizard. In the dialog box that appears, enter a name of **AddNewVideo**. Give it a Return Type of void, and leave the other default options and values unchanged. Then add parameters of strVideoName (type LPCTSTR), sPrice (type short), sTotalCopies (type short), and sAvailableCopies (type short) Figure 7-25 shows how the Add Method dialog should appear when you are done. Press OK to add the method to the MTS COM server.

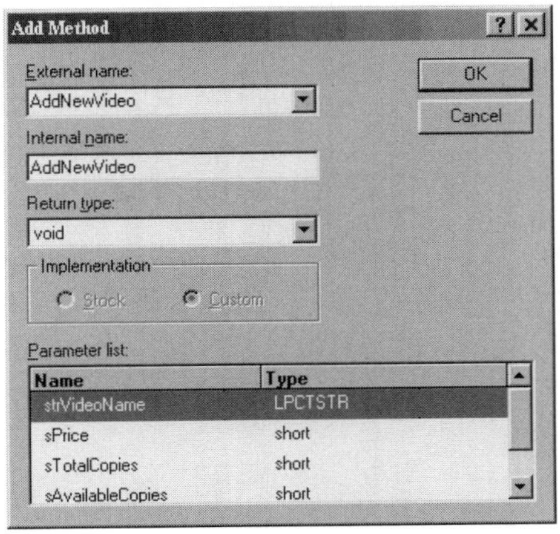


***Figure 7-25*** *Adding the AddNewVideo method*

To add another method function to the MTS COM server, again click on the Add Method button of the MFC ClassWizard. In the dialog box that appears, enter a name of **DeleteVideo**. Give it a Return Type of void, and leave the other default options and values unchanged. Then add a parameter of strVideoName (type LPCTSTR). Press OK to add the method to the MTS COM server.

To add another method function to the MTS COM server, again click on the Add Method button of the MFC ClassWizard. In the dialog box that appears, enter a name of **UpdateVideoEntryName**. Give it a Return Type of void, and leave the other default options and values unchanged. Then add parameters of strOldVideoName (type LPCTSTR) and strNewVideoName (type LPCTSTR). Press OK to add the method to the MTS COM server.

To add another method function to the MTS COM server, again click on the Add Method button of the MFC ClassWizard. In the dialog box that appears, enter a name of **UpdateVideoEntryPrice**. Give it a Return Type of void, and leave the other default options and values unchanged. Then add parameters of strVideoName (type LPCTSTR) and sNewPrice (type short). Press OK to add the method to the MTS COM server.

To add another method function to the MTS COM server, again click on the Add Method button of the MFC ClassWizard. In the dialog box that appears, enter a name of **UpdateVideoEntryTotalCopies**. Give it a Return Type of void, and leave the other default options and values unchanged. Then add parameters of strVideoName (type LPCTSTR) and sNewTotalCopies (type short). Press OK to add the method to the MTS COM server.

To add another method function to the MTS COM server, again click on the Add Method button of the MFC ClassWizard. In the dialog box that appears, enter a name of **UpdateVideoEntryAvailableCopies**. Give it a Return Type of void, and leave the other default options and values unchanged. Then add parameters of strVideoName (type LPCTSTR) and sNewAvailableCopies (type short). Press OK to add the method to the MTS COM server.

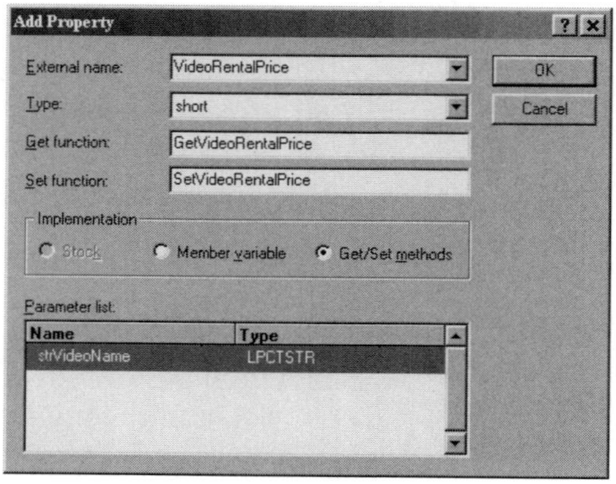


***Figure 7-26*** *Adding the VideoRental-Price property*

Now click on the Add Property button to add an Automation property to the MTS Automation COM server. The Add Property dialog box appears; enter a name of **VideoRentalPrice**. Give it a Type of short, and choose Get/Set Methods for the implementation. Add a parameter of strVideoName (type LPCTSTR). Figure 7-26 shows how the Add Property dialog should appear when you are done. Press OK to add the property to the MTS COM server.

Again click on the Add Property button to add an Automation property to the MTS Automation COM server. The Add Property dialog box appears; enter a name of **VideoTotalCopies**. Give it a Type of short, and choose Get/Set Methods for the implementation. Add a parameter of strVideoName (type LPCTSTR). Press OK to add the property to the MTS COM server.

Again click on the Add Property button to add an Automation property to the MTS Automation COM server. The Add Property dialog box appears; enter a name of **VideoAvailableCopies**. Give it a Type of short, and choose Get/Set Methods for the implementation. Add a parameter of strVideoName (type LPCTSTR). Press OK to add the property to the MTS COM server.

To add another method function to the MTS COM server, again click on the Add Method button of the MFC ClassWizard. In the dialog box that appears, enter a name of **GetVideoNameByNumber**. Give it a Return Type of void, and leave the other default options and values unchanged. Then add parameters of sIDNumber (type short) and strVideoName (type LPCTSTR). Press OK to add the method to the MTS COM server.

## Line-By-Line

Now we begin to add the code to create this MTS COM server! Bring up the VIDEOSHANDLER.CPP file in the text editor. Scan through it and enter or change any boldfaced line of source code in Listing 7-2. Save the project.

```
// VideosHandler.cpp : implementation file
//

#include "stdafx.h"
//*** take this out if you get linker errors!!! ***
```

```
#include <Initguid.h>
//*** ActiveX Data Objects GUIDs  ***
#include <adoid.h>
//*** ActiveX Data Objects Interfaces ***
#include <adoint.h>
//*** MTS headers ***
#include <mtx.h>
#include "MFCMTSWallysVideos.h"
#include "VideosHandler.h"

#ifdef _DEBUG
#define new DEBUG_NEW
#undef THIS_FILE
static char THIS_FILE[] = __FILE__;
#endif

/////////////////////////////////////////////////////////////////////////////
// VideosHandler

IMPLEMENT_DYNCREATE(VideosHandler, CCmdTarget)

VideosHandler::VideosHandler()
{
    EnableAutomation();

    // To keep the application running as long as an OLE automation
    //   object is active, the constructor calls AfxOleLockApp.

    AfxOleLockApp();
}

VideosHandler::~VideosHandler()
{
    // To terminate the application when all objects created with
    //   with OLE automation, the destructor calls AfxOleUnlockApp.

    AfxOleUnlockApp();
}


void VideosHandler::OnFinalRelease()
{
    // When the last reference for an automation object is released
    // OnFinalRelease is called.  The base class will automatically
    // deletes the object.  Add additional cleanup required for your
    // object before calling the base class.

```

```
    CCmdTarget::OnFinalRelease();
}


BEGIN_MESSAGE_MAP(VideosHandler, CCmdTarget)
    //{{AFX_MSG_MAP(VideosHandler)
        // NOTE - the ClassWizard will add and remove mapping macros here.
    //}}AFX_MSG_MAP
END_MESSAGE_MAP()

BEGIN_DISPATCH_MAP(VideosHandler, CCmdTarget)
    //{{AFX_DISPATCH_MAP(VideosHandler)
    DISP_PROPERTY_NOTIFY(VideosHandler, "TotalVideos", m_totalVideos,
      OnTotalVideosChanged, VT_I4)
    DISP_FUNCTION(VideosHandler, "CreateDatabase", CreateDatabase, VT_EMPTY, VTS_NONE)
    DISP_FUNCTION(VideosHandler, "AddNewVideo", AddNewVideo, VT_EMPTY, VTS_BSTR VTS_I2
       VTS_I2 VTS_I2)
    DISP_FUNCTION(VideosHandler, "DeleteVideo", DeleteVideo, VT_EMPTY, VTS_BSTR)
    DISP_FUNCTION(VideosHandler, "UpdateVideoEntryName", UpdateVideoEntryName,
       VT_EMPTY, VTS_BSTR VTS_BSTR)
    DISP_FUNCTION(VideosHandler, "UpdateVideoEntryPrice", UpdateVideoEntryPrice,
       VT_EMPTY, VTS_BSTR VTS_I2)
    DISP_FUNCTION(VideosHandler, "UpdateVideoEntryTotalCopies",
      UpdateVideoEntryTotalCopies, VT_EMPTY, VTS_BSTR VTS_I2)
    DISP_FUNCTION(VideosHandler, "UpdateVideoEntryAvailableCopies",
       UpdateVideoEntryAvailableCopies, VT_EMPTY, VTS_BSTR VTS_I2)
    DISP_FUNCTION(VideosHandler, "GetVideoNameByNumber", GetVideoNameByNumber,
       VT_EMPTY, VTS_I2 VTS_PBSTR)
    DISP_PROPERTY_PARAM(VideosHandler, "VideoRentalPrice", GetVideoRentalPrice,
       SetVideoRentalPrice, VT_I2, VTS_BSTR)
    DISP_PROPERTY_PARAM(VideosHandler, "VideoTotalCopies", GetVideoTotalCopies,
       SetVideoTotalCopies, VT_I2, VTS_BSTR)
    DISP_PROPERTY_PARAM(VideosHandler, "VideoAvailableCopies",
       GetVideoAvailableCopies, SetVideoAvailableCopies, VT_I2, VTS_BSTR)
    //}}AFX_DISPATCH_MAP
END_DISPATCH_MAP()

// Note: we add support for IID_IVideosHandler to support typesafe binding
//  from VBA.  This IID must match the GUID that is attached to the
//  dispinterface in the .ODL file.

// {361BFD8C-9A54-11D2-B7EA-00E02916C424}
static const IID IID_IVideosHandler =
{ 0x361bfd8c, 0x9a54, 0x11d2, { 0xb7, 0xea, 0x0, 0xe0, 0x29, 0x16, 0xc4, 0x24 } };

BEGIN_INTERFACE_MAP(VideosHandler, CCmdTarget)
    INTERFACE_PART(VideosHandler, IID_IVideosHandler, Dispatch)
```

```
END_INTERFACE_MAP()

// {361BFD8D-9A54-11D2-B7EA-00E02916C424}
IMPLEMENT_OLECREATE(VideosHandler, "MFCMTSWallysVideos.VideosHandler", 0x361bfd8d,
   0x9a54, 0x11d2, 0xb7, 0xea, 0x0, 0xe0, 0x29, 0x16, 0xc4, 0x24)

/////////////////////////////////////////////////////////////////////////////
// VideosHandler message handlers

void VideosHandler::OnTotalVideosChanged()
{
  // TODO: Add notification handler code
    //*** define HRESULT holder and set it to OK ***
  HRESULT hr = S_OK;
  //*** Declare our ActiveX Data Object Connection holder and set it to NULL ***
  ADOConnection* adoCoConnection = NULL;
  //*** Declare our ActiveX Data Object Recordset holder and set it to NULL ***
  ADORecordset* adoVideosInfo = NULL;
  //*** Declare our ActiveX Data Object Fields holder and set it to NULL ***
  ADOFields* padoFields = NULL;
  //*** Declare our ActiveX Data Object Field holder and set it to NULL ***
  ADOField* padoField = NULL;
  //*** Attempt to get the ADO Connection IP ***
    hr = CoCreateInstance( CLSID_CADOConnection, NULL, CLSCTX_INPROC_SERVER,
                           IID_IADOConnection, (void **) adoCoConnection );
  //*** If can't get IP abort ***
  if (!SUCCEEDED(hr))
  {
       AfxThrowOleDispatchException(158,
            _T("MFCMTSWallysVideos Error: ADO Unreachable!"),0);
  }
  //*** Declare a CString to handle the Sequel Text ***
  CString strSQLText;
  //*** Give it the DSN for our samples database ***
  strSQLText = _T("FILEDSN=WallysVideos");
  //*** Attempt to open the database ***
  hr = adoCoConnection->Open( strSQLText.AllocSysString(), NULL, NULL,
     adCmdUnspecified);
  //*** If can't get database abort ***
  if (!SUCCEEDED(hr))
  {
      //*** Kill the connection IP ***
      adoCoConnection->Release();
     AfxThrowOleDispatchException(158,
        _T("MFCMTSWallysVideos Error: Database Unreachable!"),0);
  }
  //*** Declare the wsprintf buffer ***
```

```
TCHAR szSQLBuffer[512];
wsprintf( szSQLBuffer,
    _T("SELECT TotalVideos FROM Videos WHERE VideoName = 'TotalVideos'"));
//*** Put it into the CString via overloaded = operator ***
strSQLText = szSQLBuffer;
//*** Declare a COleVariant to hold returned record count from ADO ***
COleVariant vRecCount;
//*** Clear the record count ***
vRecCount.Clear();
//*** Execute the sequel statement on the database ***
  hr = adoCoConnection->Execute( strSQLText.AllocSysString(), &vRecCount, -1 ,
    &adoVideosInfo );
//*** If can't reach database abort ***
if (!SUCCEEDED(hr))
{
    //*** Kill the connection and recordset IP ***
   adoCoConnection->Release();
   AfxThrowOleDispatchException(158,
     _T("MFCMTSWallysVideos Error: Database Unreachable!"),0);
}
//*** Obtain the fields collection from the recordset ***
  hr = adoVideosInfo->get_Fields( &padoFields );
//*** If can't reach database abort ***
if (!SUCCEEDED(hr))
{
    //*** Kill the connection and recordset IP ***
   adoCoConnection->Release();
   adoVideosInfo->Release();
   AfxThrowOleDispatchException(158,
      _T("MFCMTSWallysVideos Error: Database Unreachable!"),0);
}
//*** Define a variant to obtain the total videos field ***
COleVariant vField = _T("TotalVideos");
//*** define a variant to hold the information ***
COleVariant vVideos;
//*** Get the totalvideos Field ***
hr = padoFields->get_Item( vField , &padoField );
//*** If can't reach database abort ***
if (!SUCCEEDED(hr))
{
   //*** Kill the connection, recordset, and fields IP ***
   adoCoConnection->Release();
   adoVideosInfo->Release();
   padoFields->Release();
   AfxThrowOleDispatchException(158,
      _T("MFCMTSWallysVideos Error: Database Unreachable!"),0);
}
```

```
  //*** Get the actual balance value ***
  hr = padoField->get_Value( &vVideos );
  //*** If can't reach database abort ***
  if (!SUCCEEDED(hr))
  {
      //*** Kill the connection, recordset, fields, and field IP ***
      adoCoConnection->Release();
      adoVideosInfo->Release();
      padoFields->Release();
      padoField->Release();
     AfxThrowOleDispatchException(158,
        _T("MFCMTSWallysVideos Error: Database Unreachable!"),0);
  }
    //*** return the value from the variant ***
    m_totalVideos = vVideos.lVal;
  //*** Kill the connection, recordset, fields, and field IP ***
  adoCoConnection->Release();
  adoVideosInfo->Release();
  padoFields->Release();
  padoField->Release();
  return;
}

void VideosHandler::CreateDatabase()
{
  // TODO: Add your dispatch handler code here
    //*** define HRESULT holder and set it to result of CCI ***
  IObjectContext* m_spObjectContext;
  HRESULT hr = GetObjectContext(&m_spObjectContext);
  if (!SUCCEEDED( hr )) AfxThrowOleDispatchException(158,
      _T("MFCMTSWallysVideos Error: MTS Unreachable!"),0);
  //*** Declare our ActiveX Data Object Connection holder and set it to NULL ***
  ADOConnection* adoCoConnection = NULL;
  //*** Declare our ActiveX Data Object Recordset holder and set it to NULL ***
  ADORecordset* adoVideosInfo = NULL;
  //*** Attempt to get the ADO Connection IP ***
    hr = CoCreateInstance( CLSID_CADOConnection, NULL, CLSCTX_INPROC_SERVER,
                           IID_IADOConnection, (void **) adoCoConnection );
  //*** If can't get IP abort ***
  if (!SUCCEEDED(hr))
  {
      //*** Inform MTS of failure ***
      m_spObjectContext->SetAbort();
      m_spObjectContext->Release();
        AfxThrowOleDispatchException(158,
           _T("MFCMTSWallysVideos Error: ADO Unreachable!"),0);
  }
```

```
//*** Declare a CString to handle the Sequel Text ***
CString strSQLText;
//*** Give it the DSN for our samples database ***
strSQLText = _T("FILEDSN=WallysVideos");
//*** Attempt to open the database ***
hr = adoCoConnection->Open( strSQLText.AllocSysString(), NULL, NULL,
    adCmdUnspecified);
//*** If can't get database abort ***
if (!SUCCEEDED(hr))
{
    //*** Inform MTS of failure ***
    m_spObjectContext->SetAbort();
    //*** Kill the connection IP ***
    adoCoConnection->Release();
    m_spObjectContext->Release();
   AfxThrowOleDispatchException(158,
      _T("MFCMTSWallysVideos Error: Database Unreachable!"),0);
}
//*** Create Sequel Statement ***
strSQLText =
  _T("if not exists (Select name from sysobjects where name = 'Videos')\n");
strSQLText += _T("BEGIN\n");
strSQLText += _T("CREATE TABLE Videos (\n");
strSQLText += _T("VideoName varchar(256) NULL ,\n");
strSQLText += _T("IDNumber int NULL ,\n");
strSQLText += _T("RentalPrice int NULL ,\n");
strSQLText += _T("TotalCopies int NULL ,\n");
strSQLText += _T("AvailableCopies int NULL ,\n");
strSQLText += _T("TotalVideos int NULL ,\n");
strSQLText += _T(")\n");
strSQLText += _T("END\n");
//*** Declare a COleVariant to hold returned record count from ADO ***
COleVariant vRecCount;
//*** Clear the record count ***
vRecCount.Clear();
//*** Execute the sequel statement on the database ***
  hr = adoCoConnection->Execute( strSQLText.AllocSysString(), &vRecCount, -1 ,
   NULL );
//*** If can't reach database abort ***
if (!SUCCEEDED(hr))
{
    //*** Inform MTS of failure ***
    m_spObjectContext->SetAbort();
    //*** Kill the connection IP ***
    adoCoConnection->Release();
    m_spObjectContext->Release();
    AfxThrowOleDispatchException(158,
```

```
        _T("MFCMTSWallysVideos Error: Database Unreachable!"),0);
  } //*** Kill the connection, recordset, fields, and field IP ***
  adoCoConnection->Release();
  m_spObjectContext->SetComplete();
  m_spObjectContext->Release();
  //*** Send back Good Transaction ***
  return;
}

void VideosHandler::AddNewVideo(LPCTSTR strVideoName, short sPrice,
     short sTotalCopies, short sAvailableCopies)
{
  // TODO: Add your dispatch handler code here
   //*** define HRESULT holder and set it to result of CCI ***
  IObjectContext* m_spObjectContext;
  HRESULT hr = GetObjectContext(&m_spObjectContext);
  if (!SUCCEEDED( hr )) AfxThrowOleDispatchException(158,
       _T("MFCMTSWallysVideos Error: MTS Unreachable!"),0);
  //*** only use this if you want to use Role-based security ***
  if (m_spObjectContext->IsSecurityEnabled())
  {
        //*** Define a CString to hold the Role Name
       CString strRoleID;
       //*** set it ***
       strRoleID = _T("WallysMgr");
       //*** Define a Result holder ***
       BOOL bResult;
       //*** make the call ***
       m_spObjectContext->IsCallerInRole( strRoleID.AllocSysString(), &bResult );
       //*** if not in the role abort ***
       if (!bResult) AfxThrowOleDispatchException(158,
           _T("MFCMTSWallysVideos Error: User not in Manager Role!"),0);
  }
  //*** Declare our ActiveX Data Object Connection holder and set it to NULL ***
  ADOConnection* adoCoConnection = NULL;
  //*** Declare our ActiveX Data Object Recordset holder and set it to NULL ***
  ADORecordset* adoVideosInfo = NULL;
  //*** Attempt to get the ADO Connection IP ***
    hr = CoCreateInstance( CLSID_CADOConnection, NULL, CLSCTX_INPROC_SERVER,
                          IID_IADOConnection, (void **) adoCoConnection );
  //*** If can't get IP abort ***
  if (!SUCCEEDED(hr))
  {
      //*** Inform MTS of failure ***
      m_spObjectContext->SetAbort();
      m_spObjectContext->Release();
       AfxThrowOleDispatchException(158,
```

```
        _T("MFCMTSWallysVideos Error: ADO Unreachable!"),0);
}
//*** Declare a CString to handle the Sequel Text ***
CString strSQLText;
//*** Give it the DSN for our samples database ***
strSQLText = _T("FILEDSN=WallysVideos");
//*** Attempt to open the database ***
hr = adoCoConnection->Open( strSQLText.AllocSysString(), NULL, NULL,
     adCmdUnspecified);
//*** If can't get database abort ***
if (!SUCCEEDED(hr))
{
    //*** Inform MTS of failure ***
    m_spObjectContext->SetAbort();
    m_spObjectContext->Release();
    //*** Kill the connection IP ***
    adoCoConnection->Release();
   AfxThrowOleDispatchException(158,
      _T("MFCMTSWallysVideos Error: Database Unreachable!"),0);
}
//*** Declare the wsprintf buffer ***
TCHAR szSQLBuffer[512];
//*** Create Sequel Statement ***
wsprintf( szSQLBuffer, _T("INSERT INTO Videos VALUES('%s',%d,%d,%d,0)"),
               strVideoName,sPrice,sTotalCopies,sAvailableCopies);
//*** Put the buffer in the CString via overloaded = operator ***
strSQLText = szSQLBuffer;
//*** Declare a COleVariant to hold returned record count from ADO ***
COleVariant vRecCount;
//*** Clear the record count ***
vRecCount.Clear();
//*** Execute the sequel statement on the database ***
  hr = adoCoConnection->Execute( strSQLText.AllocSysString(), &vRecCount, -1 ,
    NULL );
//*** If can't reach database abort ***
if (!SUCCEEDED(hr))
{
    //*** Inform MTS of failure ***
    m_spObjectContext->SetAbort();
    //*** Kill the connection IP ***
    adoCoConnection->Release();
    m_spObjectContext->Release();
    AfxThrowOleDispatchException(158,
      _T("MFCMTSWallysVideos Error: Database Unreachable!"),0);
}
//*** if no records updated then video doesn't exist so signal error ***
if (vRecCount.lVal == 0)
```

```
    {
        //*** Inform MTS of failure ***
        m_spObjectContext->SetAbort();
        //*** Kill the connection IP ***
        adoCoConnection->Release();
        m_spObjectContext->Release();
       AfxThrowOleDispatchException(158,
          _T("MFCMTSWallysVideos Error: Database Did Not Accept New Video!"),0);
    }
    //*** Increment total videos ***
    m_totalVideos++;
    //*** Tell MTS we're OK ***
    m_spObjectContext->SetComplete();
    //*** Kill the connection ***
    adoCoConnection->Release();
    m_spObjectContext->Release();
    //*** Send back Good Transaction ***
    return;
}

void VideosHandler::DeleteVideo(LPCTSTR strVideoName)
{
      //*** define HRESULT holder and set it to result of CCI ***
    IObjectContext* m_spObjectContext;
    HRESULT hr = GetObjectContext(&m_spObjectContext);
    if (!SUCCEEDED( hr )) AfxThrowOleDispatchException(158,
         _T("MFCMTSWallysVideos Error: MTS Unreachable!"),0);
    //*** only use this if you want to use Role-based security ***
    if (m_spObjectContext->IsSecurityEnabled())
    {
         //*** Define a CString to hold the Role Name
        CString strRoleID;
        //*** set it ***
        strRoleID = _T("WallysMgr");
        //*** Define a Result holder ***
        BOOL bResult;
        //*** make the call ***
        m_spObjectContext->IsCallerInRole( strRoleID.AllocSysString(), &bResult );
        //*** if not in the role abort ***
        if (!bResult) AfxThrowOleDispatchException(158,
            _T("MFCMTSWallysVideos Error: User not in Manager Role!"),0);
    }
    //*** Declare our ActiveX Data Object Connection holder and set it to NULL ***
    ADOConnection* adoCoConnection = NULL;
    //*** Declare our ActiveX Data Object Recordset holder and set it to NULL ***
    ADORecordset* adoVideosInfo = NULL;
    //*** Attempt to get the ADO Connection IP ***
```

```
    hr = CoCreateInstance( CLSID_CADOConnection, NULL, CLSCTX_INPROC_SERVER,
                          IID_IADOConnection, (void **) adoCoConnection );
   //*** If can't get IP abort ***
   if (!SUCCEEDED(hr))
   {
       //*** Inform MTS of failure ***
       m_spObjectContext->SetAbort();
       m_spObjectContext->Release();
        AfxThrowOleDispatchException(158,
            _T("MFCMTSWallysVideos Error: ADO Unreachable!"),0);
   }
   //*** Declare a CString to handle the Sequel Text ***
   CString strSQLText;
   //*** Give it the DSN for our samples database ***
   strSQLText = _T("FILEDSN=WallysVideos");
   //*** Attempt to open the database ***
   hr = adoCoConnection->Open( strSQLText.AllocSysString(), NULL, NULL,
        adCmdUnspecified);
   //*** If can't get database abort ***
   if (!SUCCEEDED(hr))
   {
       //*** Inform MTS of failure ***
       m_spObjectContext->SetAbort();
       m_spObjectContext->Release();
       //*** Kill the connection IP ***
       adoCoConnection->Release();
      AfxThrowOleDispatchException(158,
          _T("MFCMTSWallysVideos Error: Database Unreachable!"),0);
   }
   //*** Declare the wsprintf buffer ***
   TCHAR szSQLBuffer[512];
   //*** Create Sequel Statement ***
   wsprintf( szSQLBuffer, _T("DELETE Videos WHERE VideoName = '%s'"),
                 strVideoName);
   //*** Put the buffer in the CString via overloaded = operator ***
   strSQLText = szSQLBuffer;
   //*** Declare a COleVariant to hold returned record count from ADO ***
   COleVariant vRecCount;
   //*** Clear the record count ***
   vRecCount.Clear();
   //*** Execute the sequel statement on the database ***
     hr = adoCoConnection->Execute( strSQLText.AllocSysString(), &vRecCount, -1 ,
         NULL );
   //*** If can't reach database abort ***
   if (!SUCCEEDED(hr))
   {
       //*** Inform MTS of failure ***
```

```
        m_spObjectContext->SetAbort();
        //*** Kill the connection IP ***
        adoCoConnection->Release();
        m_spObjectContext->Release();
        AfxThrowOleDispatchException(158,
         _T("MFCMTSWallysVideos Error: Database Unreachable!"),0);
    }
    //*** Decrement total videos ***
    m_totalVideos–;
    //*** if no records updated then video doesn't exist so signal error ***
    if (vRecCount.lVal == 0)
    {
        //*** Inform MTS of failure ***
        m_spObjectContext->SetAbort();
        //*** Kill the connection IP ***
        adoCoConnection->Release();
        m_spObjectContext->Release();
       AfxThrowOleDispatchException(158,
         _T("MFCMTSWallysVideos Error: Database Did Not Accept Deletion!"),0);
    }
    //*** Tell MTS we're OK ***
    m_spObjectContext->SetComplete();
    //*** Kill the connection ***
    adoCoConnection->Release();
    m_spObjectContext->Release();
    //*** Send back Good Transaction ***
    return;
}

void VideosHandler::UpdateVideoEntryName(LPCTSTR strOldVideoName,
     LPCTSTR strNewVideoName)
{
      //*** define HRESULT holder and set it to result of CCI ***
    IObjectContext* m_spObjectContext;
    HRESULT hr = GetObjectContext(&m_spObjectContext);
    if (!SUCCEEDED( hr )) AfxThrowOleDispatchException(158,
       _T("MFCMTSWallysVideos Error: MTS Unreachable!"),0);
    //*** only use this if you want to use Role-based security ***
    if (m_spObjectContext->IsSecurityEnabled())
    {
         //*** Define a CString to hold the Role Name
        CString strRoleID;
        //*** set it ***
        strRoleID = _T("WallysMgr");
        //*** Define a Result holder ***
        BOOL bResult;
        //*** make the call ***
```

```
        m_spObjectContext->IsCallerInRole( strRoleID.AllocSysString(), &bResult );
        //*** if not in the role abort ***
        if (!bResult) AfxThrowOleDispatchException(158,
            _T("MFCMTSWallysVideos Error: User not in Manager Role!"),0);
    }
    //*** Declare our ActiveX Data Object Connection holder and set it to NULL ***
    ADOConnection* adoCoConnection = NULL;
    //*** Declare our ActiveX Data Object Recordset holder and set it to NULL ***
    ADORecordset* adoVideosInfo = NULL;
    //*** Attempt to get the ADO Connection IP ***
      hr = CoCreateInstance( CLSID_CADOConnection, NULL, CLSCTX_INPROC_SERVER,
                            IID_IADOConnection, (void **) adoCoConnection );
    //*** If can't get IP abort ***
    if (!SUCCEEDED(hr))
    {
        //*** Inform MTS of failure ***
        m_spObjectContext->SetAbort();
        m_spObjectContext->Release();
         AfxThrowOleDispatchException(158,
             _T("MFCMTSWallysVideos Error: ADO Unreachable!"),0);
    }
    //*** Declare a CString to handle the Sequel Text ***
    CString strSQLText;
    //*** Give it the DSN for our samples database ***
    strSQLText = _T("FILEDSN=WallysVideos");
    //*** Attempt to open the database ***
    hr = adoCoConnection->Open( strSQLText.AllocSysString(), NULL, NULL,
          adCmdUnspecified);
    //*** If can't get database abort ***
    if (!SUCCEEDED(hr))
    {
        //*** Inform MTS of failure ***
        m_spObjectContext->SetAbort();
        m_spObjectContext->Release();
        //*** Kill the connection IP ***
        adoCoConnection->Release();
       AfxThrowOleDispatchException(158,
          _T("MFCMTSWallysVideos Error: Database Unreachable!"),0);
    }
    //*** Declare the wsprintf buffer ***
    TCHAR szSQLBuffer[512];
    //*** Create Sequel Statement ***
    wsprintf( szSQLBuffer,
      _T("UPDATE Videos SET VideoName = '%s' WHERE VideoName = '%s'"),
         strNewVideoName, strOldVideoName );
    //*** Put the buffer in the CString via overloaded = operator ***
    strSQLText = szSQLBuffer;
```

```
    //*** Declare a COleVariant to hold returned record count from ADO ***
    COleVariant vRecCount;
    //*** Clear the record count ***
    vRecCount.Clear();
    //*** Execute the sequel statement on the database ***
      hr = adoCoConnection->Execute( strSQLText.AllocSysString(), &vRecCount, -1 ,
           NULL );
    //*** If can't reach database abort ***
    if (!SUCCEEDED(hr))
    {
        //*** Inform MTS of failure ***
        m_spObjectContext->SetAbort();
       //*** Kill the connection IP ***
       adoCoConnection->Release();
        m_spObjectContext->Release();
        AfxThrowOleDispatchException(158,
          _T("MFCMTSWallysVideos Error: Database Unreachable!"),0);
    }
    //*** if no records updated then video doesn't exist so signal error ***
    if (vRecCount.lVal == 0)
    {
        //*** Inform MTS of failure ***
        m_spObjectContext->SetAbort();
        //*** Kill the connection IP ***
        adoCoConnection->Release();
        m_spObjectContext->Release();
       AfxThrowOleDispatchException(158,
         _T("MFCMTSWallysVideos Error: Videos Does Not Exist!"),0);
    }
    //*** Tell MTS we're OK ***
    m_spObjectContext->SetComplete();
    //*** Kill the connection***
    adoCoConnection->Release();
    m_spObjectContext->Release();
    //*** Send back Good Transaction ***
    return;
}

void VideosHandler::UpdateVideoEntryPrice(LPCTSTR strVideoName, short sNewPrice)
{
      //*** define HRESULT holder and set it to result of CCI ***
    IObjectContext* m_spObjectContext;
    HRESULT hr = GetObjectContext(&m_spObjectContext);
    if (!SUCCEEDED( hr )) AfxThrowOleDispatchException(158,
        _T("MFCMTSWallysVideos Error: MTS Unreachable!"),0);
    //*** only use this if you want to use Role-based security ***
    if (m_spObjectContext->IsSecurityEnabled())
```

```
{
      //*** Define a CString to hold the Role Name
     CString strRoleID;
     //*** set it ***
     strRoleID = _T("WallysMgr");
     //*** Define a Result holder ***
     BOOL bResult;
     //*** make the call ***
     m_spObjectContext->IsCallerInRole( strRoleID.AllocSysString(), &bResult );
     //*** if not in the role abort ***
     if (!bResult) AfxThrowOleDispatchException(158,
         _T("MFCMTSWallysVideos Error: User not in Manager Role!"),0);
}
//*** Declare our ActiveX Data Object Connection holder and set it to NULL ***
ADOConnection* adoCoConnection = NULL;
//*** Declare our ActiveX Data Object Recordset holder and set it to NULL ***
ADORecordset* adoVideosInfo = NULL;
//*** Attempt to get the ADO Connection IP ***
  hr = CoCreateInstance( CLSID_CADOConnection, NULL, CLSCTX_INPROC_SERVER,
                         IID_IADOConnection, (void **) adoCoConnection );
//*** If can't get IP abort ***
if (!SUCCEEDED(hr))
{
    //*** Inform MTS of failure ***
    m_spObjectContext->SetAbort();
    m_spObjectContext->Release();
     AfxThrowOleDispatchException(158,
         _T("MFCMTSWallysVideos Error: ADO Unreachable!"),0);
}
//*** Declare a CString to handle the Sequel Text ***
CString strSQLText;
//*** Give it the DSN for our samples database ***
strSQLText = _T("FILEDSN=WallysVideos");
//*** Attempt to open the database ***
hr = adoCoConnection->Open( strSQLText.AllocSysString(), NULL, NULL,
    adCmdUnspecified);
//*** If can't get database abort ***
if (!SUCCEEDED(hr))
{
    //*** Inform MTS of failure ***
    m_spObjectContext->SetAbort();
    m_spObjectContext->Release();
    //*** Kill the connection IP ***
    adoCoConnection->Release();
   AfxThrowOleDispatchException(158,
      _T("MFCMTSWallysVideos Error: Database Unreachable!"),0);
}
```

```
    //*** Declare the wsprintf buffer ***
    TCHAR szSQLBuffer[512];
    //*** Create Sequel Statement ***
    wsprintf( szSQLBuffer,
      _T("UPDATE Videos SET RentalPrice = %d WHERE VideoName = '%s'"),
        sNewPrice,  strVideoName );
    //*** Put the buffer in the CString via overloaded = operator ***
    strSQLText = szSQLBuffer;
    //*** Declare a COleVariant to hold returned record count from ADO ***
    COleVariant vRecCount;
    //*** Clear the record count ***
    vRecCount.Clear();
    //*** Execute the sequel statement on the database ***
      hr = adoCoConnection->Execute( strSQLText.AllocSysString(), &vRecCount, -1 ,
            NULL );
    //*** If can't reach database abort ***
    if (!SUCCEEDED(hr))
    {
        //*** Inform MTS of failure ***
        m_spObjectContext->SetAbort();
       //*** Kill the connection IP ***
       adoCoConnection->Release();
        m_spObjectContext->Release();
        AfxThrowOleDispatchException(158,
           _T("MFCMTSWallysVideos Error: Database Unreachable!"),0);
    }
    //*** if no records updated then video doesn't exist so signal error ***
    if (vRecCount.lVal == 0)
    {
        //*** Inform MTS of failure ***
        m_spObjectContext->SetAbort();
        //*** Kill the connection IP ***
        adoCoConnection->Release();
        m_spObjectContext->Release();
       AfxThrowOleDispatchException(158,
          _T("MFCMTSWallysVideos Error: Videos Does Not Exist!"),0);
    }
    //*** Tell MTS we're OK ***
    m_spObjectContext->SetComplete();
    //*** Kill the connection ***
    adoCoConnection->Release();
    m_spObjectContext->Release();
    //*** Send back Good Transaction ***
    return;
}

void VideosHandler::UpdateVideoEntryTotalCopies(LPCTSTR strVideoName,
```

```
        short sNewTotalCopies)
{
     //*** define HRESULT holder and set it to result of CCI ***
   IObjectContext* m_spObjectContext;
   HRESULT hr = GetObjectContext(&m_spObjectContext);
   if (!SUCCEEDED( hr )) AfxThrowOleDispatchException(158,
       _T("MFCMTSWallysVideos Error: MTS Unreachable!"),0);
   //*** only use this if you want to use Role-based security ***
   if (m_spObjectContext->IsSecurityEnabled())
   {
        //*** Define a CString to hold the Role Name
       CString strRoleID;
       //*** set it ***
       strRoleID = _T("WallysMgr");
       //*** Define a Result holder ***
       BOOL bResult;
       //*** make the call ***
       m_spObjectContext->IsCallerInRole( strRoleID.AllocSysString(), &bResult );
       //*** if not in the role abort ***
       if (!bResult) AfxThrowOleDispatchException(158,
           _T("MFCMTSWallysVideos Error: User not in Manager Role!"),0);
   }
   //*** Declare our ActiveX Data Object Connection holder and set it to NULL ***
   ADOConnection* adoCoConnection = NULL;
   //*** Declare our ActiveX Data Object Recordset holder and set it to NULL ***
   ADORecordset* adoVideosInfo = NULL;
   //*** Attempt to get the ADO Connection IP ***
     hr = CoCreateInstance( CLSID_CADOConnection, NULL, CLSCTX_INPROC_SERVER,
                            IID_IADOConnection, (void **) adoCoConnection );
   //*** If can't get IP abort ***
   if (!SUCCEEDED(hr))
   {
       //*** Inform MTS of failure ***
       m_spObjectContext->SetAbort();
       m_spObjectContext->Release();
        AfxThrowOleDispatchException(158,
            _T("MFCMTSWallysVideos Error: ADO Unreachable!"),0);
   }
   //*** Declare a CString to handle the Sequel Text ***
   CString strSQLText;
   //*** Give it the DSN for our samples database ***
   strSQLText = _T("FILEDSN=WallysVideos");
   //*** Attempt to open the database ***
   hr = adoCoConnection->Open( strSQLText.AllocSysString(), NULL, NULL,
         adCmdUnspecified);
   //*** If can't get database abort ***
   if (!SUCCEEDED(hr))
```

```
{
    //*** Inform MTS of failure ***
    m_spObjectContext->SetAbort();
    m_spObjectContext->Release();
    //*** Kill the connection IP ***
    adoCoConnection->Release();
   AfxThrowOleDispatchException(158,
       _T("MFCMTSWallysVideos Error: Database Unreachable!"),0);
}
//*** Declare the wsprintf buffer ***
TCHAR szSQLBuffer[512];
//*** Create Sequel Statement ***
wsprintf( szSQLBuffer,
   _T("UPDATE Videos SET TotalCopies = %d WHERE VideoName = '%s'"),
      sNewTotalCopies, strVideoName );
//*** Put the buffer in the CString via overloaded = operator ***
strSQLText = szSQLBuffer;
//*** Declare a COleVariant to hold returned record count from ADO ***
COleVariant vRecCount;
//*** Clear the record count ***
vRecCount.Clear();
//*** Execute the sequel statement on the database ***
  hr = adoCoConnection->Execute( strSQLText.AllocSysString(), &vRecCount, -1 ,
   NULL );
//*** If can't reach database abort ***
if (!SUCCEEDED(hr))
{
    //*** Inform MTS of failure ***
    m_spObjectContext->SetAbort();
   //*** Kill the connection IP ***
   adoCoConnection->Release();
    m_spObjectContext->Release();
    AfxThrowOleDispatchException(158,
     _T("MFCMTSWallysVideos Error: Database Unreachable!"),0);
}
//*** if no records updated then video doesn't exist so signal error ***
if (vRecCount.lVal == 0)
{
    //*** Inform MTS of failure ***
    m_spObjectContext->SetAbort();
    //*** Kill the connection IP ***
    adoCoConnection->Release();
    m_spObjectContext->Release();
   AfxThrowOleDispatchException(158,
      _T("MFCMTSWallysVideos Error: Videos Does Not Exist!"),0);
}
//*** Tell MTS we're OK ***
```

```
    m_spObjectContext->SetComplete();
    //*** Kill the connection ***
    adoCoConnection->Release();
    m_spObjectContext->Release();
    //*** Send back Good Transaction ***
    return;
}

void VideosHandler::UpdateVideoEntryAvailableCopies(LPCTSTR strVideoName,
      short sNewAvailableCopies)
{
      //*** define HRESULT holder and set it to result of CCI ***
    IObjectContext* m_spObjectContext;
    HRESULT hr = GetObjectContext(&m_spObjectContext);
    if (!SUCCEEDED( hr )) AfxThrowOleDispatchException(158,
        _T("MFCMTSWallysVideos Error: MTS Unreachable!"),0);
    //*** only use this if you want to use Role-based security ***
    if (m_spObjectContext->IsSecurityEnabled())
    {
          //*** Define a CString to hold the Role Name
         CString strRoleID;
         //*** set it ***
         strRoleID = _T("WallysMgr");
         //*** Define a Result holder ***
         BOOL bResult;
         //*** make the call ***
         m_spObjectContext->IsCallerInRole( strRoleID.AllocSysString(), &bResult );
         //*** if not in the role abort ***
         if (!bResult) AfxThrowOleDispatchException(158,
             _T("MFCMTSWallysVideos Error: User not in Manager Role!"),0);
    }
    //*** Declare our ActiveX Data Object Connection holder and set it to NULL ***
    ADOConnection* adoCoConnection = NULL;
    //*** Declare our ActiveX Data Object Recordset holder and set it to NULL ***
    ADORecordset* adoVideosInfo = NULL;
    //*** Attempt to get the ADO Connection IP ***
      hr = CoCreateInstance( CLSID_CADOConnection, NULL, CLSCTX_INPROC_SERVER,
                             IID_IADOConnection, (void **) adoCoConnection );
    //*** If can't get IP abort ***
    if (!SUCCEEDED(hr))
    {
        //*** Inform MTS of failure ***
        m_spObjectContext->SetAbort();
        m_spObjectContext->Release();
         AfxThrowOleDispatchException(158,
             _T("MFCMTSWallysVideos Error: ADO Unreachable!"),0);
    }
```

```
//*** Declare a CString to handle the Sequel Text ***
CString strSQLText;
//*** Give it the DSN for our samples database ***
strSQLText = _T("FILEDSN=WallysVideos");
//*** Attempt to open the database ***
hr = adoCoConnection->Open( strSQLText.AllocSysString(), NULL, NULL,
       adCmdUnspecified);
//*** If can't get database abort ***
if (!SUCCEEDED(hr))
{
    //*** Inform MTS of failure ***
    m_spObjectContext->SetAbort();
    m_spObjectContext->Release();
    //*** Kill the connection IP ***
    adoCoConnection->Release();
   AfxThrowOleDispatchException(158,
      _T("MFCMTSWallysVideos Error: Database Unreachable!"),0);
}
//*** Declare the wsprintf buffer ***
TCHAR szSQLBuffer[512];
//*** Create Sequel Statement ***
wsprintf( szSQLBuffer,
   _T("UPDATE Videos SET AvailableCopies = %d WHERE VideoName = '%s'"),
    sNewAvailableCopies, strVideoName );
//*** Put the buffer in the CString via overloaded = operator ***
strSQLText = szSQLBuffer;
//*** Declare a COleVariant to hold returned record count from ADO ***
COleVariant vRecCount;
//*** Clear the record count ***
vRecCount.Clear();
//*** Execute the sequel statement on the database ***
  hr = adoCoConnection->Execute( strSQLText.AllocSysString(), &vRecCount, -1 ,
       NULL );
//*** If can't reach database abort ***
if (!SUCCEEDED(hr))
{
    //*** Inform MTS of failure ***
    m_spObjectContext->SetAbort();
   //*** Kill the connection IP ***
   adoCoConnection->Release();
    m_spObjectContext->Release();
    AfxThrowOleDispatchException(158,
       _T("MFCMTSWallysVideos Error: Database Unreachable!"),0);
}
//*** if no records updated then video doesn't exist so signal error ***
if (vRecCount.lVal == 0)
{
```

```
        //*** Inform MTS of failure ***
        m_spObjectContext->SetAbort();
        //*** Kill the connection IP ***
        adoCoConnection->Release();
        m_spObjectContext->Release();
      AfxThrowOleDispatchException(158,
        _T("MFCMTSWallysVideos Error: Videos Does Not Exist!"),0);
    }
    //*** Tell MTS we're OK ***
    m_spObjectContext->SetComplete();
    //*** Kill the connection ***
    adoCoConnection->Release();
    m_spObjectContext->Release();
    //*** Send back Good Transaction ***
    return;
}

short VideosHandler::GetVideoRentalPrice(LPCTSTR strVideoName)
{
    // TODO: Add your property handler here
      //*** define HRESULT holder and set it to result of CCI ***
    IObjectContext* m_spObjectContext;
    HRESULT hr = GetObjectContext(&m_spObjectContext);
    if (!SUCCEEDED( hr )) AfxThrowOleDispatchException(158,
          _T("MFCMTSWallysVideos Error: MTS Unreachable!"),0);
    //*** Declare our ActiveX Data Object Connection holder and set it to NULL ***
    ADOConnection* adoCoConnection = NULL;
    //*** Declare our ActiveX Data Object Recordset holder and set it to NULL ***
    ADORecordset* adoVideosInfo = NULL;
    //*** Declare our ActiveX Data Object Fields holder and set it to NULL ***
    ADOFields* padoFields = NULL;
    //*** Declare our ActiveX Data Object Field holder and set it to NULL ***
    ADOField* padoField = NULL;
    //*** Define Error Holder and set it to 0 ***
    long lErrorFlags = 0;
    //*** Attempt to get the ADO Connection IP ***
      hr = CoCreateInstance( CLSID_CADOConnection, NULL, CLSCTX_INPROC_SERVER,
                             IID_IADOConnection, (void **) adoCoConnection );
    //*** If can't get IP abort ***
    if (!SUCCEEDED(hr))
    {
        //*** Inform MTS of failure ***
        m_spObjectContext->SetAbort();
        m_spObjectContext->Release();
         AfxThrowOleDispatchException(158,
             _T("MFCMTSWallysVideos Error: ADO Unreachable!"),0);
    }
```

```
//*** Declare a CString to handle the Sequel Text ***
CString strSQLText;
//*** Give it the DSN for our samples database ***
strSQLText = _T("FILEDSN=WallysVideos");
//*** Attempt to open the database ***
hr = adoCoConnection->Open( strSQLText.AllocSysString(), NULL, NULL,
     adCmdUnspecified);
//*** If can't get database abort ***
if (!SUCCEEDED(hr))
{
    //*** Inform MTS of failure ***
    m_spObjectContext->SetAbort();
    m_spObjectContext->Release();
    //*** Kill the connection IP ***
    adoCoConnection->Release();
   AfxThrowOleDispatchException(158,
      _T("MFCMTSWallysVideos Error: Database Unreachable!"),0);
}
//*** Declare the wsprintf buffer ***
TCHAR szSQLBuffer[512];
wsprintf( szSQLBuffer,
   _T("SELECT RentalPrice FROM Videos WHERE VideoName = '%s'"),
   strVideoName);
//*** Put it into the CString via overloaded = operator ***
strSQLText = szSQLBuffer;
//*** Declare a COleVariant to hold returned record count from ADO ***
COleVariant vRecCount;
//*** Clear the record count ***
vRecCount.Clear();
//*** Execute the sequel statement on the database ***
  hr = adoCoConnection->Execute( strSQLText.AllocSysString(), &vRecCount, -1 ,
     &adoVideosInfo );
//*** If can't reach database abort ***
if (!SUCCEEDED(hr))
{
    //*** Inform MTS of failure ***
    m_spObjectContext->SetAbort();
    //*** Kill the connection IP ***
    adoCoConnection->Release();
    m_spObjectContext->Release();
    AfxThrowOleDispatchException(158,
      _T("MFCMTSWallysVideos Error: Database Unreachable!"),0);
}
//*** Obtain the fields collection from the recordset ***
  hr = adoVideosInfo->get_Fields( &padoFields );
//*** If can't reach database abort ***
if (!SUCCEEDED(hr))
```

```
{
    //*** Inform MTS of failure ***
    m_spObjectContext->SetAbort();
    //*** Kill the connection and recordset IP ***
   adoCoConnection->Release();
   adoVideosInfo->Release();
    m_spObjectContext->Release();
   AfxThrowOleDispatchException(158,
     _T("MFCMTSWallysVideos Error: Database Unreachable!"),0);
}
//*** Define a variant to obtain the rental price field ***
COleVariant vField = _T("RentalPrice");
//*** define a variant to hold the information ***
COleVariant vPrice;
//*** Get the RentalPrice Field ***
hr = padoFields->get_Item( vField , &padoField );
//*** If can't reach database abort ***
if (!SUCCEEDED(hr))
{
    //*** Inform MTS of failure ***
    m_spObjectContext->SetAbort();
   //*** Kill the connection, recordset, and fields IP ***
   adoCoConnection->Release();
   adoVideosInfo->Release();
   padoFields->Release();
    m_spObjectContext->Release();
   AfxThrowOleDispatchException(158,
     _T("MFCMTSWallysVideos Error: Database Unreachable!"),0);
}
//*** Get the actual rentalprice value ***
hr = padoField->get_Value( &vPrice );
//*** If can't reach database abort ***
if (!SUCCEEDED(hr))
{
    //*** Inform MTS of failure ***
    m_spObjectContext->SetAbort();
    //*** Kill the connection, recordset, fields, and field IP ***
    adoCoConnection->Release();
    adoVideosInfo->Release();
    padoFields->Release();
    padoField->Release();
    m_spObjectContext->Release();
    AfxThrowOleDispatchException(158,
      _T("MFCMTSWallysVideos Error: Database Unreachable!"),0);
}
   //*** return the value from the variant ***
   short sResult = vPrice.iVal;
```

```
 //*** Tell MTS we're OK ***
 m_spObjectContext->SetComplete();
 //*** Kill the connection, recordset, fields, and field IP ***
 adoCoConnection->Release();
 adoVideosInfo->Release();
 padoFields->Release();
 padoField->Release();
 m_spObjectContext->Release();
 //*** Send back Good Transaction ***
 return sResult;
}

void VideosHandler::SetVideoRentalPrice(LPCTSTR strVideoName, short nNewValue)
{
 // TODO: Add your property handler here

}

short VideosHandler::GetVideoTotalCopies(LPCTSTR strVideoName)
{
 // TODO: Add your property handler here
    //*** define HRESULT holder and set it to result of CCI ***
 IObjectContext* m_spObjectContext;
 HRESULT hr = GetObjectContext(&m_spObjectContext);
 if (!SUCCEEDED( hr )) AfxThrowOleDispatchException(158,
     _T("MFCMTSWallysVideos Error: MTS Unreachable!"),0);
 //*** Declare our ActiveX Data Object Connection holder and set it to NULL ***
 ADOConnection* adoCoConnection = NULL;
 //*** Declare our ActiveX Data Object Recordset holder and set it to NULL ***
 ADORecordset* adoVideosInfo = NULL;
 //*** Declare our ActiveX Data Object Fields holder and set it to NULL ***
 ADOFields* padoFields = NULL;
 //*** Declare our ActiveX Data Object Field holder and set it to NULL ***
 ADOField* padoField = NULL;
 //*** Attempt to get the ADO Connection IP ***
    hr = CoCreateInstance( CLSID_CADOConnection, NULL, CLSCTX_INPROC_SERVER,
                           IID_IADOConnection, (void **) adoCoConnection );
 //*** If can't get IP abort ***
 if (!SUCCEEDED(hr))
 {
     //*** Inform MTS of failure ***
     m_spObjectContext->SetAbort();
     m_spObjectContext->Release();
      AfxThrowOleDispatchException(158,
          _T("MFCMTSWallysVideos Error: ADO Unreachable!"),0);
 }
 //*** Declare a CString to handle the Sequel Text ***
```

```
CString strSQLText;
//*** Give it the DSN for our samples database ***
strSQLText = _T("FILEDSN=WallysVideos");
//*** Attempt to open the database ***
hr = adoCoConnection->Open( strSQLText.AllocSysString(), NULL, NULL,
     adCmdUnspecified);
//*** If can't get database abort ***
if (!SUCCEEDED(hr))
{
    //*** Inform MTS of failure ***
    m_spObjectContext->SetAbort();
    m_spObjectContext->Release();
    //*** Kill the connection IP ***
    adoCoConnection->Release();
   AfxThrowOleDispatchException(158,
       _T("MFCMTSWallysVideos Error: Database Unreachable!"),0);
}
//*** Declare the wsprintf buffer ***
TCHAR szSQLBuffer[512];
wsprintf( szSQLBuffer,
    _T("SELECT TotalCopies FROM Videos WHERE VideoName = '%s'"),
       strVideoName);
//*** Put it into the CString via overloaded = operator ***
strSQLText = szSQLBuffer;
//*** Declare a COleVariant to hold returned record count from ADO ***
COleVariant vRecCount;
//*** Clear the record count ***
vRecCount.Clear();
//*** Execute the sequel statement on the database ***
   hr = adoCoConnection->Execute( strSQLText.AllocSysString(), &vRecCount, -1 ,
       &adoVideosInfo );
//*** If can't reach database abort ***
if (!SUCCEEDED(hr))
{
    //*** Inform MTS of failure ***
    m_spObjectContext->SetAbort();
    //*** Kill the connection IP ***
    adoCoConnection->Release();
    m_spObjectContext->Release();
    AfxThrowOleDispatchException(158,
       _T("MFCMTSWallysVideos Error: Database Unreachable!"),0);
}
//*** Obtain the fields collection from the recordset ***
   hr = adoVideosInfo->get_Fields( &padoFields );
//*** If can't reach database abort ***
if (!SUCCEEDED(hr))
{
```

```
    //*** Inform MTS of failure ***
    m_spObjectContext->SetAbort();
    //*** Kill the connection and recordset IP ***
   adoCoConnection->Release();
   adoVideosInfo->Release();
    m_spObjectContext->Release();
    AfxThrowOleDispatchException(158,
       _T("MFCMTSWallysVideos Error: Database Unreachable!"),0);
}
//*** Define a variant to obtain the totalcopies field ***
COleVariant vField = _T("TotalCopies");
//*** define a variant to hold the information ***
COleVariant vCopies;
//*** Get the totalcopies Field ***
hr = padoFields->get_Item( vField , &padoField );
//*** If can't reach database abort ***
if (!SUCCEEDED(hr))
{
    //*** Inform MTS of failure ***
    m_spObjectContext->SetAbort();
   //*** Kill the connection, recordset, and fields IP ***
   adoCoConnection->Release();
   adoVideosInfo->Release();
   padoFields->Release();
    m_spObjectContext->Release();
    AfxThrowOleDispatchException(158,
      _T("MFCMTSWallysVideos Error: Database Unreachable!"),0);
}
//*** Get the actual totalcopies value ***
hr = padoField->get_Value( &vCopies );
//*** If can't reach database abort ***
if (!SUCCEEDED(hr))
{
    //*** Inform MTS of failure ***
    m_spObjectContext->SetAbort();
    //*** Kill the connection, recordset, fields, and field IP ***
    adoCoConnection->Release();
    adoVideosInfo->Release();
    padoFields->Release();
    padoField->Release();
    m_spObjectContext->Release();
    AfxThrowOleDispatchException(158,
      _T("MFCMTSWallysVideos Error: Database Unreachable!"),0);
}
   //*** return the value from the variant ***
   short sResult = vCopies.iVal;
//*** Tell MTS we're OK ***
```

```
 m_spObjectContext->SetComplete();
 //*** Kill the connection, recordset, fields, and field IP ***
 adoCoConnection->Release();
 adoVideosInfo->Release();
 padoFields->Release();
 padoField->Release();
 m_spObjectContext->Release();
 //*** Send back Good Transaction ***
 return sResult;
}

void VideosHandler::SetVideoTotalCopies(LPCTSTR strVideoName, short nNewValue)
{
 // TODO: Add your property handler here

}

short VideosHandler::GetVideoAvailableCopies(LPCTSTR strVideoName)
{
 // TODO: Add your property handler here
    //*** define HRESULT holder and set it to result of CCI ***
 IObjectContext* m_spObjectContext;
 HRESULT hr = GetObjectContext(&m_spObjectContext);
 if (!SUCCEEDED( hr )) AfxThrowOleDispatchException(158,
      _T("MFCMTSWallysVideos Error: MTS Unreachable!"),0);
 //*** Declare our ActiveX Data Object Connection holder and set it to NULL ***
 ADOConnection* adoCoConnection = NULL;
 //*** Declare our ActiveX Data Object Recordset holder and set it to NULL ***
 ADORecordset* adoVideosInfo = NULL;
 //*** Declare our ActiveX Data Object Fields holder and set it to NULL ***
 ADOFields* padoFields = NULL;
 //*** Declare our ActiveX Data Object Field holder and set it to NULL ***
 ADOField* padoField = NULL;
 //*** Attempt to get the ADO Connection IP ***
    hr = CoCreateInstance( CLSID_CADOConnection, NULL, CLSCTX_INPROC_SERVER,
                          IID_IADOConnection, (void **) adoCoConnection );
 //*** If can't get IP abort ***
 if (!SUCCEEDED(hr))
 {
     //*** Inform MTS of failure ***
     m_spObjectContext->SetAbort();
     m_spObjectContext->Release();
      AfxThrowOleDispatchException(158,
          _T("MFCMTSWallysVideos Error: ADO Unreachable!"),0);
 }
 //*** Declare a CString to handle the Sequel Text ***
 CString strSQLText;
```

```
//*** Give it the DSN for our samples database ***
strSQLText = _T("FILEDSN=WallysVideos");
//*** Attempt to open the database ***
hr = adoCoConnection->Open( strSQLText.AllocSysString(), NULL, NULL,
      adCmdUnspecified);
//*** If can't get database abort ***
if (!SUCCEEDED(hr))
{
     //*** Inform MTS of failure ***
     m_spObjectContext->SetAbort();
     m_spObjectContext->Release();
     //*** Kill the connection IP ***
     adoCoConnection->Release();
    AfxThrowOleDispatchException(158,
       _T("MFCMTSWallysVideos Error: Database Unreachable!"),0);
}
//*** Declare the wsprintf buffer ***
TCHAR szSQLBuffer[512];
wsprintf( szSQLBuffer,
  _T("SELECT AvailableCopies FROM Videos WHERE VideoName = '%s'"), strVideoName);
//*** Declare a COleVariant to hold returned record count from ADO ***
COleVariant vRecCount;
//*** Clear the record count ***
vRecCount.Clear();
//*** Put it into the CString via overloaded = operator ***
strSQLText = szSQLBuffer;
//*** Execute the sequel statement on the database ***
    hr = adoCoConnection->Execute( strSQLText.AllocSysString(), &vRecCount, -1 ,
     &adoVideosInfo );
//*** If can't reach database abort ***
if (!SUCCEEDED(hr))
{
     //*** Inform MTS of failure ***
     m_spObjectContext->SetAbort();
     //*** Kill the connection IP ***
     adoCoConnection->Release();
     m_spObjectContext->Release();
     AfxThrowOleDispatchException(158,
        _T("MFCMTSWallysVideos Error: Database Unreachable!"),0);
}
//*** Obtain the fields collection from the recordset ***
    hr = adoVideosInfo->get_Fields( &padoFields );
//*** If can't reach database abort ***
if (!SUCCEEDED(hr))
{
     //*** Inform MTS of failure ***
     m_spObjectContext->SetAbort();
```

```
      //*** Kill the connection and recordset IP ***
     adoCoConnection->Release();
     adoVideosInfo->Release();
      m_spObjectContext->Release();
      AfxThrowOleDispatchException(158,
         _T("MFCMTSWallysVideos Error: Database Unreachable!"),0);
  }
  //*** Define a variant to obtain the availablecopies field ***
  COleVariant vField = _T("AvailableCopies");
  //*** define a variant to hold the information ***
  COleVariant vCopies;
  //*** Get the availablecopies Field ***
  hr = padoFields->get_Item( vField , &padoField );
  //*** If can't reach database abort ***
  if (!SUCCEEDED(hr))
  {
      //*** Inform MTS of failure ***
      m_spObjectContext->SetAbort();
     //*** Kill the connection, recordset, and fields IP ***
     adoCoConnection->Release();
     adoVideosInfo->Release();
     padoFields->Release();
      m_spObjectContext->Release();
      AfxThrowOleDispatchException(158,
        _T("MFCMTSWallysVideos Error: Database Unreachable!"),0);
  }
  //*** Get the actual availablecopies value ***
  hr = padoField->get_Value( &vCopies );
  //*** If can't reach database abort ***
  if (!SUCCEEDED(hr))
  {
      //*** Inform MTS of failure ***
      m_spObjectContext->SetAbort();
      //*** Kill the connection, recordset, fields, and field IP ***
      adoCoConnection->Release();
      adoVideosInfo->Release();
      padoFields->Release();
      padoField->Release();
      m_spObjectContext->Release();
      AfxThrowOleDispatchException(158,
          _T("MFCMTSWallysVideos Error: Database Unreachable!"),0);
  }
     //*** return the value from the variant ***
     short sResult = vCopies.iVal;
  //*** Tell MTS we're OK ***
  m_spObjectContext->SetComplete();
  //*** Kill the connection, recordset, fields, and field IP ***
```

```
 adoCoConnection->Release();
 adoVideosInfo->Release();
 padoFields->Release();
 padoField->Release();
 m_spObjectContext->Release();
 //*** Send back Good Transaction ***
 return sResult;
}

void VideosHandler::SetVideoAvailableCopies(LPCTSTR strVideoName, short nNewValue)
{
 // TODO: Add your property handler here

}


void VideosHandler::GetVideoNameByNumber(short sVideoID, BSTR FAR* bstrVideoName)
{
    //*** define HRESULT holder and set it to result of CCI ***
 IObjectContext* m_spObjectContext;
 HRESULT hr = GetObjectContext(&m_spObjectContext);
 if (!SUCCEEDED( hr )) AfxThrowOleDispatchException(158,
     _T("MFCMTSWallysVideos Error: MTS Unreachable!"),0);
 //*** Declare our ActiveX Data Object Connection holder and set it to NULL ***
 ADOConnection* adoCoConnection = NULL;
 //*** Declare our ActiveX Data Object Recordset holder and set it to NULL ***
 ADORecordset* adoVideosInfo = NULL;
 //*** Declare our ActiveX Data Object Fields holder and set it to NULL ***
 ADOFields* padoFields = NULL;
 //*** Declare our ActiveX Data Object Field holder and set it to NULL ***
 ADOField* padoField = NULL;
 //*** Attempt to get the ADO Connection IP ***
    hr = CoCreateInstance( CLSID_CADOConnection, NULL, CLSCTX_INPROC_SERVER,
                         IID_IADOConnection, (void **) adoCoConnection );
 //*** If can't get IP abort ***
 if (!SUCCEEDED(hr))
 {
     //*** Inform MTS of failure ***
     m_spObjectContext->SetAbort();
     m_spObjectContext->Release();
      AfxThrowOleDispatchException(158,
          _T("MFCMTSWallysVideos Error: ADO Unreachable!"),0);
 }
 //*** Declare a CString to handle the Sequel Text ***
 CString strSQLText;
 //*** Give it the DSN for our samples database ***
 strSQLText = _T("FILEDSN=WallysVideos");
```

```
//*** Attempt to open the database ***
hr = adoCoConnection->Open( strSQLText.AllocSysString(), NULL, NULL,
       adCmdUnspecified);
//*** If can't get database abort ***
if (!SUCCEEDED(hr))
{
    //*** Inform MTS of failure ***
    m_spObjectContext->SetAbort();
    m_spObjectContext->Release();
    //*** Kill the connection IP ***
    adoCoConnection->Release();
   AfxThrowOleDispatchException(158,
       _T("MFCMTSWallysVideos Error: Database Unreachable!"),0);
}
//*** Declare the wsprintf buffer ***
TCHAR szSQLBuffer[512];
wsprintf( szSQLBuffer,
      _T("SELECT VideoName FROM Videos WHERE IDNumber = %d"), sVideoID);
//*** Put it into the CString via overloaded = operator ***
strSQLText = szSQLBuffer;
//*** Declare a COleVariant to hold returned record count from ADO ***
COleVariant vRecCount;
//*** Clear the record count ***
vRecCount.Clear();
//*** Execute the sequel statement on the database ***
   hr = adoCoConnection->Execute( strSQLText.AllocSysString(), &vRecCount, -1 ,
      &adoVideosInfo );
//*** If can't reach database abort ***
if (!SUCCEEDED(hr))
{
    //*** Inform MTS of failure ***
    m_spObjectContext->SetAbort();
    //*** Kill the connection IP ***
    adoCoConnection->Release();
    m_spObjectContext->Release();
    AfxThrowOleDispatchException(158,
      _T("MFCMTSWallysVideos Error: Database Unreachable!"),0);
}
//*** Obtain the fields collection from the recordset ***
   hr = adoVideosInfo->get_Fields( &padoFields );
//*** If can't reach database abort ***
if (!SUCCEEDED(hr))
{
    //*** Inform MTS of failure ***
    m_spObjectContext->SetAbort();
    //*** Kill the connection and recordset IP ***
   adoCoConnection->Release();
```

```
    adoVideosInfo->Release();
    m_spObjectContext->Release();
    AfxThrowOleDispatchException(158,
      _T("MFCMTSWallysVideos Error: Database Unreachable!"),0);
}
//*** Define a variant to obtain the videoname field ***
COleVariant vField = _T("VideoName");
//*** define a variant to hold the information ***
COleVariant vName;
//*** Get the videoname Field ***
hr = padoFields->get_Item( vField , &padoField );
//*** If can't reach database abort ***
if (!SUCCEEDED(hr))
{
    //*** Inform MTS of failure ***
    m_spObjectContext->SetAbort();
    //*** Kill the connection, recordset, and fields IP ***
    adoCoConnection->Release();
    adoVideosInfo->Release();
    padoFields->Release();
    m_spObjectContext->Release();
    AfxThrowOleDispatchException(158,
      _T("MFCMTSWallysVideos Error: Database Unreachable!"),0);
}
//*** Get the actual videoname value ***
hr = padoField->get_Value( &vName );
//*** If can't reach database abort ***
if (!SUCCEEDED(hr))
{
    //*** Inform MTS of failure ***
    m_spObjectContext->SetAbort();
    //*** Kill the connection, recordset, fields, and field IP ***
    adoCoConnection->Release();
    adoVideosInfo->Release();
    padoFields->Release();
    padoField->Release();
    m_spObjectContext->Release();
    AfxThrowOleDispatchException(158,
      _T("MFCMTSWallysVideos Error: Database Unreachable!"),0);
}
    //*** return the value from the variant ***
    *bstrVideoName = vName.bstrVal;
//*** Tell MTS we're OK ***
m_spObjectContext->SetComplete();
//*** Kill the connection, recordset, fields, and field IP ***
adoCoConnection->Release();
adoVideosInfo->Release();
```

```
1463.   padoFields->Release();
1464.   padoField->Release();
1465.   m_spObjectContext->Release();
1466.   //*** Send back Good Transaction ***
1467.   return;
1468.
1469. }
```

***Listing 7-2*** *VIDEOSHANDLER.CPP source code after modifications*

Here's the breakdown (the code is heavily commented and so we'll concentrate on the bigger design issues and some places where the logic may be a bit hard to follow in these comments. Also, since after the first function the code is virtually identical except for single lines calling different database SQL statements, only the first function is detailed below):

- **Lines 6-12** This code brings in the ADO and MTS headers so we can access them.
- **Lines 112-130** This code initializes the ADO interface pointers needed to interact with the SQL Server database.
- **Lines 131-166** This code contacts the Wallys database and signals an error if it fails.
- **Lines 167-177** This code executes the SQL text for this particular database interaction and obtains a pRowset interface pointer which contains a set of data that hopefully matches that requested by the command.
- **Lines 178-193** This code gets a pFields interface pointer from the pRowset IP obtained from executing the SQL statement. This IP contains all the fields of the current rowset so the program can obtain as many as it wants and examine or change their values.
- **Lines 194-206** This code gets a single pField interface pointer from the pFields IP with the name given. This moves from a collection of all the fields in the current recordset to one single field so its value can be obtained.
- **Lines 207-214** This code uses the pField interface pointer to obtain the actual value of the field and deal with it as needed (it reads it in this example, but in later examples is used to set it).
- **Lines 220-224** This code obtains an MTS object context for use in the component's functions. It will be there because in the MTS Explorer (see Chapter 9) we will set this component to Require a Transaction. If you also have read the ATL chapter, you will notice that unlike ATL, we have to do this ourselves.
- **Lines 232-240** This code deals with signaling an error to MTS via SetAbort, and then releasing the MTS IObjectContext IP (because unlike the ATL code, we must do this manually). This code will be used whenever an error occurs inside a function that uses an object context. Note also that unlike ATL, it throws MFC exceptions rather than returning error codes.

- **Lines 290-293** This code deals with signaling success to MTS via SetComplete and then releasing the MTS IObjectContext IP (because unlike the ATL code, we must do this manually). This code will be used whenever success occurs inside a function that uses an object context.
- **Lines 306-320** This code deals with using MTS role-based security. It uses properties of the ObjectContext IP to determine if security is enabled, and if so whether the current user is part of the WallysMgr role. If so, it allows the action to proceed; otherwise it throws an exception and aborts the transaction.

Once you are satisfied you've entered the code from the above listing correctly, build the MTS COM server from the Build menu. If you encounter any errors, please check the code to find your mistake (it has been exhaustively debugged and is correct). Once you have compiled the component successfully, it is automatically registered on the local machine; if you need to move it to another machine, see Chapter 9. Otherwise, please move on to the next component.

# Creating an MTS ASP Component with MFC

The next step is to use MFC to create an MTS-aware ASP COM server that handles online video ordering and cancellation for Wally's. The following sections take you through the user interface portions of creating the project in the step-by-step system, then show you the code you need to write and an analysis using the line-by-line approach.

## Step-By-Step

Start Visual C++ 5.0 or 6.0. From the File menu, select New. The New dialog box opens; click on the MFC AppWizard (dll) entry. Next, select an appropriate directory, then enter a project name of **MFCASPWallysVideoManager**. Figure 7-27 shows how the New dialog should appear when you are done. Press OK to open the MFC AppWizard.

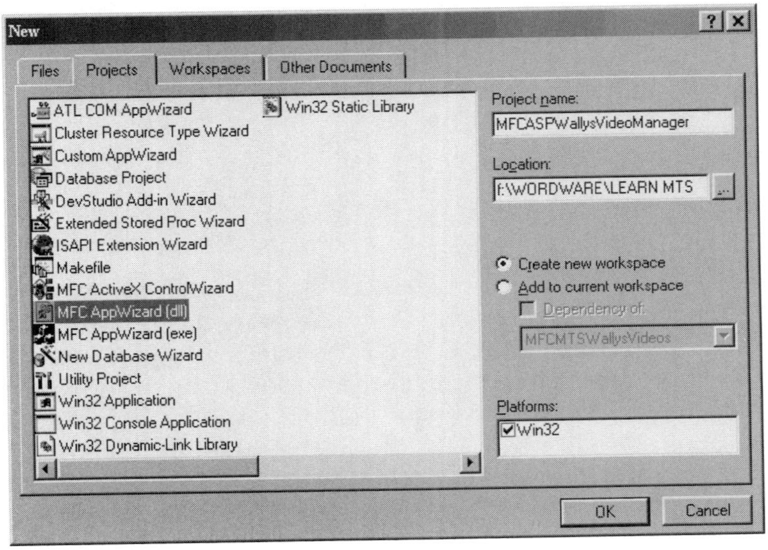


*Figure 7-27 The New dialog box creating the MFCASPWallysVideos MFC Project*

In the MFC AppWizard, make sure you select a shared MFC DLL, and enable Automation support and source code comments. Click on the Finish button to create the MTS component project.

A confirmation dialog box appears; press OK to create the MFC project.

When the wizard finishes, you return to the Visual C++ IDE. From the menu, select View|ClassWizard. The MFC ClassWizard dialog appears; move to the Automation tab. At first, there are no enabled controls because the default class does not support Automation. To add an Automation-capable class, click on the Add Class button. A drop-down menu appears; select New Class. The dialog box shown in Figure 7-28 is displayed. Enter a name of **OnlineVideoManager**, select a Base Class of CCmdTarget, and make it Createable by Type ID, as shown in the figure. Click on OK to create this class and add it to the project.

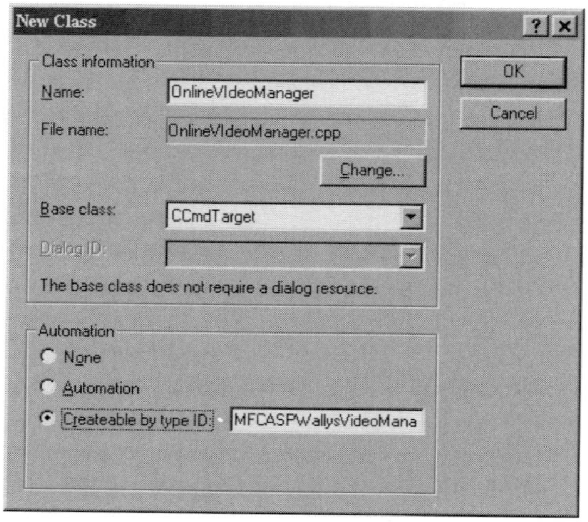


*Figure 7-28*
*Adding an Automation-enabled class to the MFC project*

Next, to add a method function to the MTS COM server, click on the Add Method button of the MFC ClassWizard. In the dialog box that appears, enter a name of **OnStartPage**. Give it a Return Type of void, and leave the other default options and values unchanged. Enter a parameter value of pUnk of type LPUNKNOWN*. Figure 7-29 shows how the Add Method dialog should appear when you are done. Press OK to add the method to the MTS COM server.

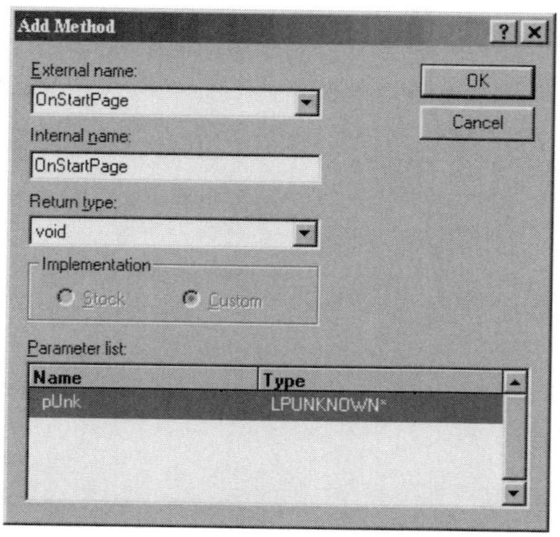


*Figure 7-29*
*Adding the OnStartPage method*

Now click on the Add Property button to add an Automation property to the MTS Automation COM server. The Add Property dialog box appears; enter a name of **CustomerName**. Give it a Type of CString, and choose Member Variable for the implementation. Figure 7-30 shows how the Add Property dialog should appear when you are done. Press OK to add the property to the MTS COM server.

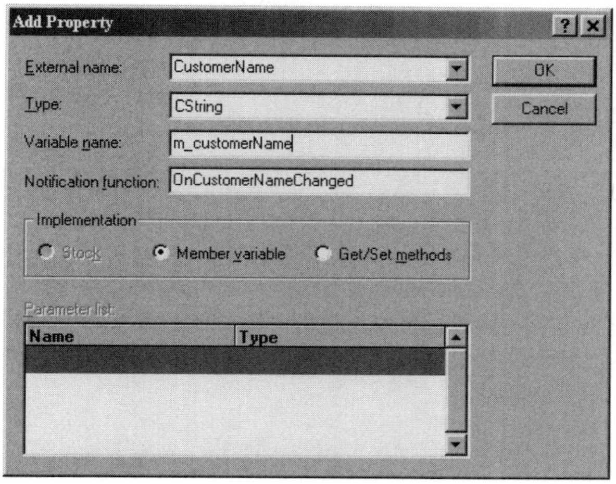


***Figure 7-30***
*Adding the CustomerName property*

Again click on the Add Property button to add an Automation property to the MTS Automation COM server. The Add Property dialog box appears; enter a name of **CustomerPassword**. Give it a Type of CString, and choose Member Variable for the implementation. Press OK to add the property to the MTS COM server.

Again click on the Add Property button to add an Automation property to the MTS Automation COM server. The Add Property dialog box appears; enter a name of **VideoName**. Give it a Type of CString, and choose Member Variable for the implementation. Press OK to add the property to the MTS COM server.

Again click on the Add Property button to add an Automation property to the MTS Automation COM server. The Add Property dialog box appears; enter a name of **ConnectionType**. Give it a Type of short, and choose Member Variable for the implementation. Press OK to add the property to the MTS COM server.

Again click on the Add Property button to add an Automation property to the MTS Automation COM server. The Add Property dialog box appears; enter a name of **NowPlaying**. Give it a Type of BOOL, and choose Member Variable for the implementation. Press OK to add the property to the MTS COM server.

To add another method function to the MTS COM server, click on the Add Method button of the MFC ClassWizard. In the dialog box that appears, enter a name of **OrderVideo**. Give it a Return Type of void, and leave the other default options and values unchanged. Figure 7-31 shows how the Add Method dialog should appear when you are done. Press OK to add the method to the MTS COM server.

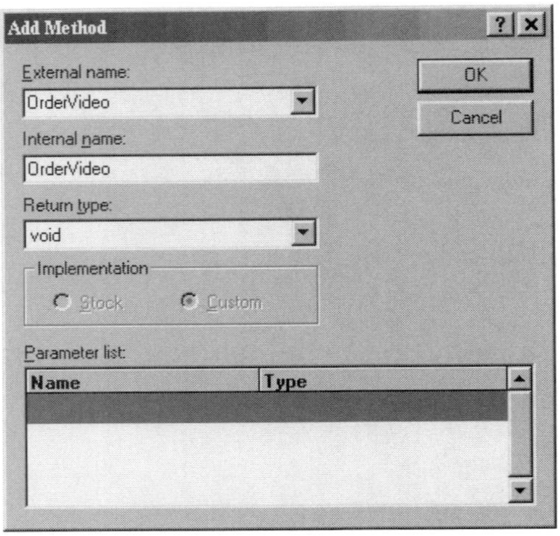


*Figure 7-31*
*Adding the OrderVideo method*

To add another method function to the MTS COM server, again click on the Add Method button of the MFC ClassWizard. In the dialog box that appears; enter a name of **TerminateVideoPlay**. Give it a Return Type of void, and leave the other default options and values unchanged. Press OK to add the method to the MTS COM server.

To add another method function to the MTS COM server, again click on the Add Method button of the MFC ClassWizard. In the dialog box that appears; enter a name of **GetVideoNameByNumber**. Give it a Return Type of void, and leave the other default options and values unchanged. Then add parameters of sIDNumber (type short) and strVideoName (type LPCTSTR). Press OK to add the method to the MTS COM server. Then click on OK to close the ClassWizard and add the changes to the project. Save the project to protect your work.

## Line-By-Line

Next, you need to enter the program code to add the MTS database functionality this component implements. Bring up the ONLINEVIDEOMANAGER.CPP file in the text editor. Scan through it and enter or change any boldfaced line of source code in Listing 7-3. Save the project.

```
// OnlineVideoManager.cpp : implementation file
//

#include "stdafx.h"
#include "MFCASPWallysVideoManager.h"
#include "OnlineVIdeoManager.h"

#ifdef _DEBUG
#define new DEBUG_NEW
#undef THIS_FILE
```

```
static char THIS_FILE[] = __FILE__;
#endif
//*** add mts headers ***
#include <mtx.h>
//*** bring in the MFC wrappers ***
#include "mfcmtswallysaccounts.h"
#include "mfcmtswallysvideos.h"

/////////////////////////////////////////////////////////////////////////////
// OnlineVIdeoManager

IMPLEMENT_DYNCREATE(OnlineVIdeoManager, CCmdTarget)

OnlineVIdeoManager::OnlineVIdeoManager()
{
    EnableAutomation();

    // To keep the application running as long as an OLE automation
    //   object is active, the constructor calls AfxOleLockApp.

    AfxOleLockApp();
}

OnlineVIdeoManager::~OnlineVIdeoManager()
{
    // To terminate the application when all objects created with
    //   with OLE automation, the destructor calls AfxOleUnlockApp.

    AfxOleUnlockApp();
}


void OnlineVIdeoManager::OnFinalRelease()
{
    // When the last reference for an automation object is released
    // OnFinalRelease is called.  The base class will automatically
    // deletes the object.  Add additional cleanup required for your
    // object before calling the base class.

    CCmdTarget::OnFinalRelease();
}


BEGIN_MESSAGE_MAP(OnlineVIdeoManager, CCmdTarget)
    //{{AFX_MSG_MAP(OnlineVIdeoManager)
        // NOTE - the ClassWizard will add and remove mapping macros here.
    //}}AFX_MSG_MAP
```

```
END_MESSAGE_MAP()

BEGIN_DISPATCH_MAP(OnlineVIdeoManager, CCmdTarget)
   //{{AFX_DISPATCH_MAP(OnlineVIdeoManager)
   DISP_PROPERTY_NOTIFY(OnlineVIdeoManager, "CustomerName", m_customerName,
       OnCustomerNameChanged, VT_BSTR)
   DISP_PROPERTY_NOTIFY(OnlineVIdeoManager, "CustomerPassword", m_customerPassword,
       OnCustomerPasswordChanged, VT_BSTR)
   DISP_PROPERTY_NOTIFY(OnlineVIdeoManager, "VideoName", m_videoName,
      OnVideoNameChanged, VT_BSTR)
   DISP_PROPERTY_NOTIFY(OnlineVIdeoManager, "ConnectionType", m_connectionType,
      OnConnectionTypeChanged, VT_I2)
   DISP_PROPERTY_NOTIFY(OnlineVIdeoManager, "NowPlaying", m_nowPlaying,
      OnNowPlayingChanged, VT_BOOL)
   DISP_FUNCTION(OnlineVIdeoManager, "OnStartPage", OnStartPage, VT_EMPTY,
      VTS_PUNKNOWN)
   DISP_FUNCTION(OnlineVIdeoManager, "OrderVideo", OrderVideo, VT_EMPTY, VTS_NONE)
   DISP_FUNCTION(OnlineVIdeoManager, "TerminateVideoPlay", TerminateVideoPlay,
     VT_EMPTY, VTS_NONE)
   DISP_FUNCTION(OnlineVIdeoManager, "GetVideoNameByNumber", GetVideoNameByNumber,
      VT_EMPTY, VTS_I2 VTS_BSTR)
   //}}AFX_DISPATCH_MAP
END_DISPATCH_MAP()

// Note: we add support for IID_IOnlineVIdeoManager to support typesafe binding
//  from VBA.  This IID must match the GUID that is attached to the
//  dispinterface in the .ODL file.

// {361BFDA0-9A54-11D2-B7EA-00E02916C424}
static const IID IID_IOnlineVIdeoManager =
{ 0x361bfda0, 0x9a54, 0x11d2, { 0xb7, 0xea, 0x0, 0xe0, 0x29, 0x16, 0xc4, 0x24 } };

BEGIN_INTERFACE_MAP(OnlineVIdeoManager, CCmdTarget)
   INTERFACE_PART(OnlineVIdeoManager, IID_IOnlineVIdeoManager, Dispatch)
END_INTERFACE_MAP()

// {361BFDA1-9A54-11D2-B7EA-00E02916C424}
IMPLEMENT_OLECREATE(OnlineVIdeoManager, "MFCASPWallysVideoManager.OnlineVIdeoMan",
  0x361bfda1, 0x9a54, 0x11d2, 0xb7, 0xea, 0x0, 0xe0, 0x29, 0x16, 0xc4, 0x24)

/////////////////////////////////////////////////////////////////////////////
// OnlineVIdeoManager message handlers

void OnlineVIdeoManager::OnStartPage(LPUNKNOWN FAR* pUnk)
{
   // TODO: Add your dispatch handler code here

```

```
}

void OnlineVIdeoManager::OnCustomerNameChanged()
{
  // TODO: Add notification handler code

}

void OnlineVIdeoManager::OnCustomerPasswordChanged()
{
  // TODO: Add notification handler code

}

void OnlineVIdeoManager::OnVideoNameChanged()
{
  // TODO: Add notification handler code

}

void OnlineVIdeoManager::OnConnectionTypeChanged()
{
  // TODO: Add notification handler code

}

void OnlineVIdeoManager::OnNowPlayingChanged()
{
  // TODO: Add notification handler code

}

void OnlineVIdeoManager::OrderVideo()
{
  // TODO: Add your dispatch handler code here
  IObjectContext* pObjectContext;
   HRESULT hr = GetObjectContext( &pObjectContext );
  if (SUCCEEDED(hr))
  {
      //*** Declare Accounts IP ***
      IAccountsHandler* pAccounts = NULL;
       //*** hold the GUID ***
       LPCLSID pID = NULL;
       //*** hold the CLSID in Registry format ***
       CString cstrCLSID;
      //*** We have to use this to get our IP ***
      IDispatch* pDispatch = NULL;
```

```
        //*** Set the class ID value again ***
        cstrCLSID = _T("361BFD7A-9A54-11D2-B7EA-00E02916C424");
        //*** get the GUID ***
        CLSIDFromString( cstrCLSID.AllocSysString() ,pID);
         //*** try to get the IP to the Account via MTS; don't engage error handler!***
       hr = pObjectContext->CreateInstance( *pID ,
            IID_IDispatch , (void **) pDispatch );
         //*** only do this if succeed ***
       if (SUCCEEDED(hr))
        {
            //*** Set class to acquired IDispatch pointer ***
             pAccounts->AttachDispatch( pDispatch );
        }
        else
        {
            //*** Show Error to User ***
           m_customerName =
               _T("Cannot order video: unable to contact accounts database!");
           return;
        }
       //*** Declare Videos IP ***
       IVideosHandler* pVideos = NULL;
        //*** hold the GUID ***
        LPCLSID pID2 = NULL;
        //*** hold the CLSID in Registry format ***
        CString cstrCLSID2;
       //*** We have to use this to get our IP ***
       IDispatch* pDispatch2 = NULL;
        //*** Set the class ID value again ***
        cstrCLSID2 = _T("361BFD8D-9A54-11D2-B7EA-00E02916C424");
        //*** get the GUID ***
        CLSIDFromString( cstrCLSID2.AllocSysString() ,pID2);
         //*** try to get the IP to the Account via MTS; don't engage error handler!***
       hr = pObjectContext->CreateInstance( *pID2 ,
            IID_IDispatch , (void **) pDispatch2 );
         //*** only do this if succeed ***
       if (SUCCEEDED(hr))
        {
            //*** Set class to acquired IDispatch pointer ***
             pVideos->AttachDispatch( pDispatch2 );
        }
        else
        {
            //*** Show Error to User ***
           m_customerName =
               _T("Cannot order video: unable to contact videos database!");
           return;
```

```
    }
    //*** turn off delayed commits ***
    pObjectContext->DisableCommit();
    try
    {
         //*** Hold the password check string ***
         CString strRealPassword =
              pAccounts->GetAccountPassword( m_customerName );
         if (m_customerPassword != strRealPassword)
         {
            //*** Show Error to User ***
            m_customerName = _T("Cannot Order Video: Password Faiure!");
            //*** Tell MTS we goofed and release the pointers ***
              pObjectContext->SetAbort();
              pObjectContext->Release();
              //*** release the IP **
              pAccounts->ReleaseDispatch();
              pVideos->ReleaseDispatch();
            //*** leave ***
            return;
         }
         //*** get price of video ***
         short sRentalPrice = pVideos->GetVideoRentalPrice( m_videoName );
         //*** get credit limit ***
         long lCreditLimit =
               pAccounts->GetAccountCreditLimit( m_customerName );
         //*** get current bill ***
         long lCurrentCharges =
                  pAccounts->GetAccountCurrentCharges( m_customerName );
         //*** add price to bill ***
         lCurrentCharges += sRentalPrice;
         //*** bill customer ***
         pAccounts->UpdateAccountCharges(m_customerName ,lCurrentCharges );
         //*** if use can't afford it abort transaction ***
         if (lCurrentCharges > lCreditLimit )
         {
            //*** Show Error to User ***
            m_customerName =
                 _T("Cannot order video: price exceeds credit limit!");
            //*** Tell MTS we goofed and release the pointers ***
              pObjectContext->SetAbort();
              pObjectContext->Release();
              //*** release IPs ***
              pAccounts->ReleaseDispatch();
              pVideos->ReleaseDispatch();
            //*** leave ***
            return;
```

```
            }
            //*** set variable ***
            m_nowPlaying = TRUE;
            //*** turn on the account;
            pAccounts->UpdateAccountInUse(m_customerName , m_nowPlaying );
            //*** allow delayed commits ***
            pObjectContext->EnableCommit();
            //*** release this IP since we're done with it ***
            pAccounts->ReleaseDispatch();
            //*** get available copies ***
            short sAvailableCopies =
                 pVideos->GetVideoAvailableCopies( m_videoName );
            //*** if no available copies then abort transaction ***
            if (sAvailableCopies == 0 )
            {
               //*** Show Error to User ***
               m_customerName =
                     _T("Cannot order video: all copies currently rented!");
               //*** Tell MTS we goofed and release the pointers ***
                 pObjectContext->SetAbort();
                 pObjectContext->Release();
                 //*** release the IP ***
                 pVideos->ReleaseDispatch();
               //*** leave ***
               return;
            }
            //*** reduce available copies ***
            sAvailableCopies–;
            //*** remove an available copy since in use ***
            pVideos->UpdateVideoEntryAvailableCopies(m_videoName ,
                   sAvailableCopies);
            //*** success message ***
            m_customerName =
          _T("Video Ordered! Call 1-800-555-CLAM for fast, hot, clams from Wallys!");
            //*** tell MTS we're good to go ***
            pObjectContext->SetComplete();
            pObjectContext->Release();
            //*** release the IP ***
            pVideos->ReleaseDispatch();
            //*** leave **
            return;
        }
        //*** catch OLE error from wrappers ***
        catch( COleDispatchException* e)
        {
            //*** error message ***
            m_customerName = _T("Cannot terminate video: network failure!");
```

```

        }
    }
    else
    {
        //*** indicate MTS failure ***
       m_customerName = _T("Cannot order video: unable to contact MTS!");
    }
    //*** go bye bye ***
      return;
}

void OnlineVIdeoManager::TerminateVideoPlay()
{
   // TODO: Add your dispatch handler code here
   IObjectContext* pObjectContext;
     HRESULT hr = GetObjectContext( &pObjectContext );
   if (SUCCEEDED(hr))
   {
       //*** Declare Accounts IP ***
       IAccountsHandler* pAccounts = NULL;
        //*** hold the GUID ***
        LPCLSID pID = NULL;
        //*** hold the CLSID in Registry format ***
        CString cstrCLSID;
       //*** We have to use this to get our IP ***
       IDispatch* pDispatch = NULL;
        //*** Set the class ID value again ***
        cstrCLSID = _T("361BFD7A-9A54-11D2-B7EA-00E02916C424");
        //*** get the GUID ***
        CLSIDFromString( cstrCLSID.AllocSysString() ,pID);
         //*** try to get the IP to the Account via MTS; don't engage error handler!***
       hr = pObjectContext->CreateInstance( *pID ,
            IID_IDispatch , (void **) pDispatch );
         //*** only do this if succeed ***
       if (SUCCEEDED(hr))
        {
             //*** Set class to acquired IDispatch pointer ***
              pAccounts->AttachDispatch( pDispatch );
        }
        else
        {
            //*** Show Error to User ***
           m_customerName =
              _T("Cannot terminate video: unable to contact accounts database!");
           return;
        }
```

```
    //*** Declare Videos IP ***
    IVideosHandler* pVideos = NULL;
     //*** hold the GUID ***
     LPCLSID pID2 = NULL;
     //*** hold the CLSID in Registry format ***
     CString cstrCLSID2;
    //*** We have to use this to get our IP ***
    IDispatch* pDispatch2 = NULL;
     //*** Set the class ID value again ***
     cstrCLSID2 = _T("361BFD8D-9A54-11D2-B7EA-00E02916C424");
     //*** get the GUID ***
     CLSIDFromString( cstrCLSID2.AllocSysString() ,pID2);
      //*** try to get the IP to the Account via MTS; don't engage error handler!***
    hr = pObjectContext->CreateInstance( *pID2 ,
         IID_IDispatch , (void **) pDispatch2 );
      //*** only do this if succeed ***
    if (SUCCEEDED(hr))
     {
         //*** Set class to acquired IDispatch pointer ***
         pVideos->AttachDispatch( pDispatch2 );
     }
     else
     {
         //*** Show Error to User ***
        m_customerName =
            _T("Cannot terminate video: unable to contact videos database!");
        return;
     }
     //*** turn off delayed commits ***
     pObjectContext->DisableCommit();
     //*** error handler ***
     try
     {
          //*** Hold the password check string ***
          CString strRealPassword =
                 pAccounts->GetAccountPassword( m_customerName );
          //*** if not right password then abort! ***
          if (m_customerPassword != strRealPassword)
          {
             //*** Show Error to User ***
             m_customerName = _T("Cannot terminate Video: Password Faiure!");
             //*** Tell MTS we goofed and release the pointers ***
               pObjectContext->SetAbort();
               pObjectContext->Release();
               //*** release the IPs ***
               pAccounts->ReleaseDispatch();
               pVideos->ReleaseDispatch();
```

```
            //*** leave ***
            return;
        }
        //*** inner error handler ***
        try
        {
              //*** test to see if videoname in db ***
             short sRentalPrice = pVideos->GetVideoRentalPrice( m_videoName);
        }
        //*** handle the lack of video in db ***
        catch( COleDispatchException* e )
        {
            //*** Show Error to User ***
            m_customerName = _T("Cannot terminate Video: Video not in DB!");
            //*** Tell MTS we goofed and release the pointers ***
              pObjectContext->SetAbort();
              pObjectContext->Release();
              //*** release the IPs ***
              pAccounts->ReleaseDispatch();
              pVideos->ReleaseDispatch();
            //*** leave ***
            return;
        }
        //*** update the account as no longer in use ***
        m_nowPlaying = FALSE;
        pAccounts->UpdateAccountInUse(m_customerName , m_nowPlaying);
        //*** allow delayed commit ***
        pObjectContext->EnableCommit();
        //*** release IP since we don't need it anymore ***
        pAccounts->ReleaseDispatch();
        //*** get the total copies ***
        short sTotalCopies = pVideos->GetVideoTotalCopies( m_videoName );
        //*** get the available copies **
        short sAvailableCopies =
                pVideos->GetVideoAvailableCopies( m_videoName );
        //*** increment available copies since one not in use now ***
        sAvailableCopies++;
        //** if too many copies then video somehow released previously ***
        if (sAvailableCopies > sTotalCopies)
        {
            //*** Show Error to User ***
            m_customerName =
                    _T("Cannot terminate Video: Video not in use!");
            //*** Tell MTS we goofed and release the pointers ***
              pObjectContext->SetAbort();
              pObjectContext->Release();
              //*** release the IPs ***
```

```
                    pVideos->ReleaseDispatch();
                  //*** leave ***
                  return;
               }
               //*** update available copies ***
               pVideos->UpdateVideoEntryAvailableCopies(m_videoName ,
                    sAvailableCopies);
               //*** success message ***
               m_customerName =
                    _T("Video Terminated! Wallys thanks you for your business!");
               //*** tell MTS we're good to go ***
               pObjectContext->SetComplete();
               //*** release the IP ***
               pObjectContext->Release();
               //*** release the IP ***
               pVideos->ReleaseDispatch();
               //*** go bye bye ***
               return;
          }
          //*** catch OLE error from wrappers ***
          catch( COleDispatchException* e)
          {
               //*** error message ***
               m_customerName = _T("Cannot terminate video: network failure!");

          }
     }
     else
     {
          //*** indicate MTS failure ***
         m_customerName = _T("Cannot order video: unable to contact MTS!");
     }
     //*** go bye bye ***
     return;
}

void OnlineVIdeoManager::GetVideoNameByNumber(short sIDNumber, LPCTSTR strVideoName)
{
     // TODO: Add your dispatch handler code here
     //*** Declare Videos IP ***
     IVideosHandler* pVideos = NULL;
     //*** hold the GUID ***
     LPCLSID pID2 = NULL;
     //*** hold the CLSID in Registry format ***
     CString cstrCLSID2;
     //*** We have to use this to get our IP ***
     IDispatch* pDispatch2 = NULL;
```

```
//*** Set the class ID value again ***
cstrCLSID2 = _T("361BFD8D-9A54-11D2-B7EA-00E02916C424");
//*** get the GUID ***
CLSIDFromString( cstrCLSID2.AllocSysString() ,pID2);
  //*** try to get the IP to the Account; don't engage error handler! ***
HRESULT hr = CoCreateInstance( *pID2 , NULL, CLSCTX_ALL,
   IID_IDispatch , (void **) pDispatch2 );
  //*** only do this if succeed ***
if (SUCCEEDED(hr))
{
     //*** Set class to acquired IDispatch pointer ***
      pVideos->AttachDispatch( pDispatch2 );
}
else
{
     //*** Show Error to User ***
   m_customerName =
     _T("Cannot update video list: unable to contact videos database!");
   //*** go bye bye ***
   return;
}
//*** Define a CString ***
CString strHolder;
//*** define a BSTR holder ***
BSTR bstrHolder;
//*** error handler ***
try
{
     //*** get the name to go with the iteration number ***
    pVideos->GetVideoNameByNumber( sIDNumber , &bstrHolder );
}
//*** deal with screwups ***
catch( COleDispatchException* e )
{
     //*** Show Error to User ***
   m_customerName =
     _T("Cannot update video list: unable to contact videos database!");
   return;
}
//*** Move the BSTR into the CString ***
strHolder = bstrHolder;
//*** Move the CString into the LPCTSTR ***
strVideoName = strHolder;
//*** release the IP ***
pVideos->ReleaseDispatch();
//*** Go bye bye ***
return;
```

```
528.
529. }
```

***Listing 7-3** ONLINEVIDEOMANAGER.CPP source code after modifications*

Here's the breakdown (some of the code is heavily commented and won't be discussed here; also, only the first instance of using a technique is covered to save space):

- **Lines 13-14** This code provides the include files for the MTS calls.
- **Lines 15-17** This code provides the include files for the video and account manager MTS COM servers. You created them previously via the MFC ClassWizard.
- **Lines 140-302** This code to order a video is some of the most important of all the MTS code in this book, so study it carefully! It is heavily commented and it would be redundant to explain it all again here. Instead, notice the way in which except for a beginning password check and video existence check, the code doesn't do its own error checking! Instead, if it encounters a problem (like not enough credit or the video is already rented), it allows MTS to back the database out of the situation; it simply declares an abort and dies. Also note the way that the MFC wrapper code is used after MTS is used to obtain the basic IP; if the MFC wrappers are used directly, then the components won't be part of the MTS transactions.
- **Lines 308-467** This code to terminate a video is some of the most important of all the MTS code in this book, so study it carefully! It is heavily commented and it would be redundant to explain it all again here. Instead, notice the way in which except for a beginning password check and video existence check, the code doesn't do its own error checking! Instead, if it encounters a problem (like not enough credit or the video is already rented), it allows MTS to back the database out of the situation; it simply declares an abort and dies. Also note the way that the MFC wrapper code is used after MTS is used to obtain the basic IP; if the MFC wrappers are used directly, then the components won't be part of the MTS transactions.
- **Lines 473-527** This code just calls the underlying video component to get the name of the video via its index number. This allows the ASP component to build a set of values for display, either inside an HTML page or inside a compiled storefront application.

Once you are satisfied you've entered the code from the above listing correctly, build the MFC COM server from the Build menu. If you encounter any errors, please check the code in the listing to find your mistake (it has been exhaustively debugged and is correct). Once you have compiled the component successfully, it is automatically registered on the local machine; if you need to move it to another machine, see Chapter 9. Otherwise, please move on to the next component.

# Creating an MTS-Aware ActiveX Control with MFC

ActiveX controls are the user interface of COM, and can be made MTS-aware just like MTS components and ASP components. The following project will create a Full ActiveX control using MFC code-based techniques that parallel the ATL Composite control from Chapter 6 and provides support for ActiveX events and standard COM properties and methods. The control serves as the user interface for ordering videos online, either over the Internet or from a storefront application for later online delivery. It connects with the MTS shared properties system as well as the MTS database components created previously.

## *Step-By-Step*

Start Visual C++ 5.0 or 6.0 (you can do this project in either version). From the File menu, select New. The New dialog box opens; click on the MFC ActiveX ControlWizard entry. Next, select an appropriate directory, then enter a project name of **MFCAxWallysVideosViewer**. Figure 7-32 shows how the New dialog should appear when you are done. Press OK to open the MFC ActiveX ControlWizard.

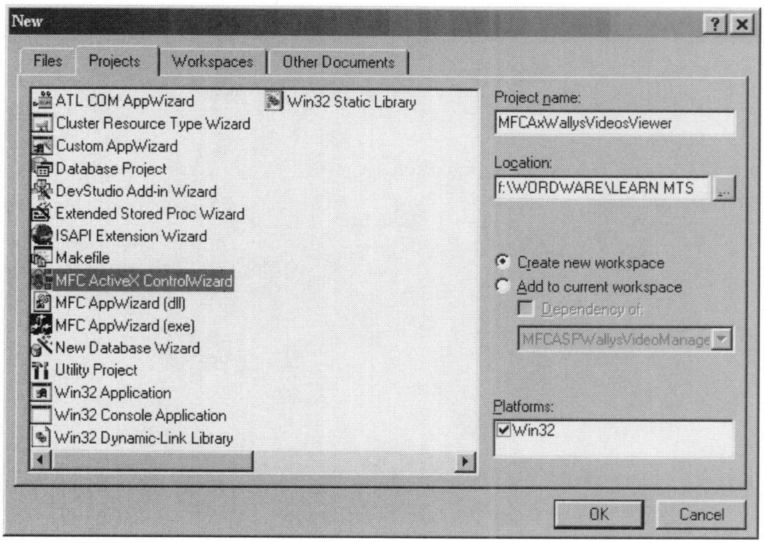


***Figure 7-32** The New dialog box creating the MFCAxWallys-VideosViewer MFC project*

In the MFC ActiveX ControlWizard, make sure only 1 control is entered, then select no runtime license, automatic generation of comments, and no help file generation; Figure 7-33 illustrates how the dialog should appear when you are done. Click on the Next button to move to the additional ActiveX control properties for the wizard.

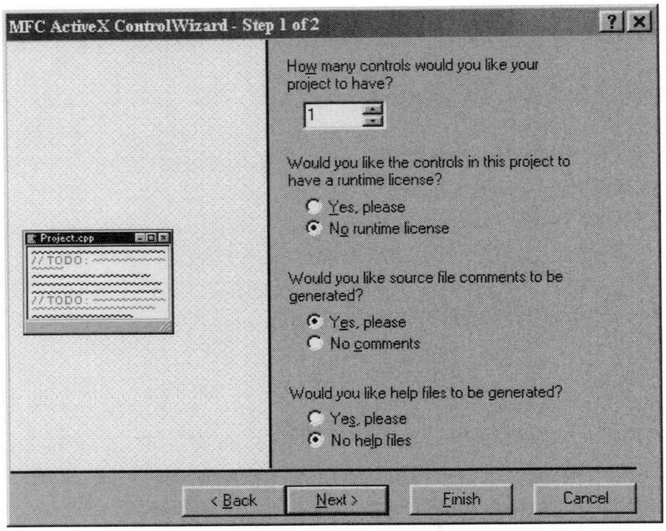


***Figure 7-33***
*Setting the ActiveX control project basic properties*

On the second page of the MFC ActiveX ControlWizard, you have a number of options that control the behavior of the control. For this control project, uncheck all of them except Activates When Visible; Figure 7-34 illustrates how the dialog should appear when you are done. Click on the Finish button to create the ActiveX control project.

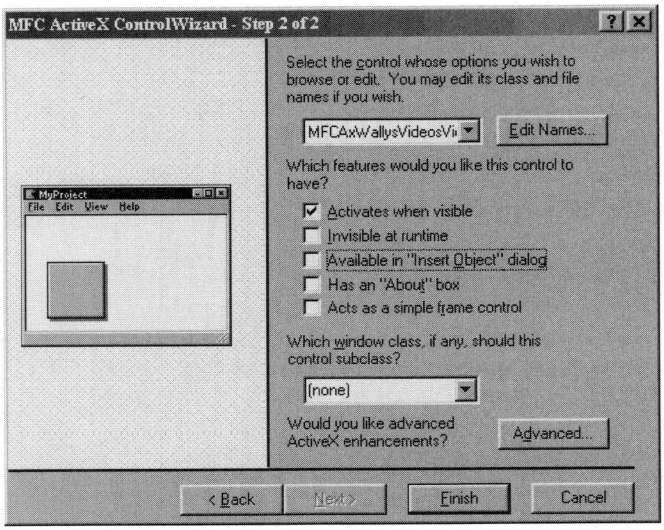


***Figure 7-34***
*Setting the ActiveX control project additional properties*

A confirmation dialog box appears as shown in Figure 7-35; press OK to create the MFC project.

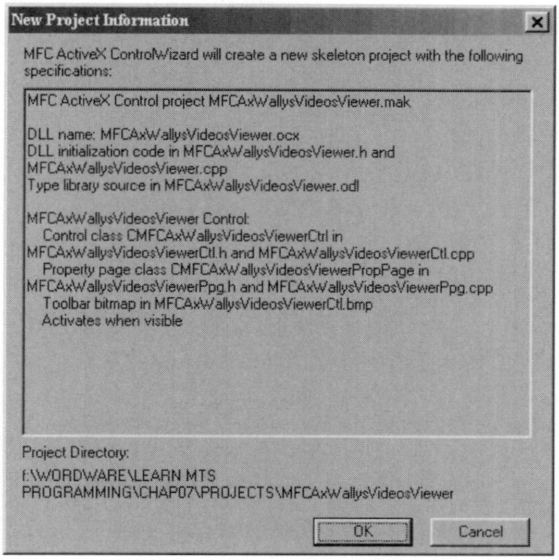


***Figure 7-35*** *The confirmation dialog*

From the menu, select View|ClassWizard. The MFC ClassWizard dialog appears. The CMFCActiveXEncryptorCtl class is already selected, with no current Automation properties or methods available. Your task is now to add these properties and methods for the control.

To add a data property to the ActiveX control, click on the Add Property button of the MFC ClassWizard. In the dialog box that appears, enter a name of **CustomerName**. Give it a Type of CString, and leave the other default options and values unchanged. Figure 7-36 shows how the Add Property dialog should appear when you are done. Press OK to add the property to the ActiveX control.

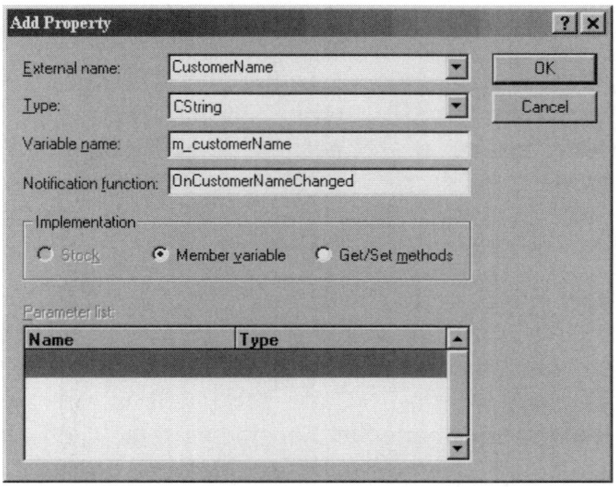


***Figure 7-36*** *Adding the CustomerName property*

To add another data property to the ActiveX control, again click on the Add Property button of the MFC ClassWizard. In the dialog box that appears, enter a name of **CustomerPassword**. Give it a Type of CString, and leave the other default options and values unchanged. Press OK to add the property to the ActiveX control.

Again click on the Add Property button of the MFC ClassWizard. In the dialog box that appears, enter a name of **VideoName**. Give it a Type of CString, and leave the other default options and values unchanged. Press OK to add the property to the ActiveX control.

Again click on the Add Property button of the MFC ClassWizard. In the dialog box that appears, enter a name of **ConnectionType**. Give it a Type of short, and leave the other default options and values unchanged. Press OK to add the property to the ActiveX control.

For the last property for this control, again click on the Add Property button of the MFC ClassWizard. In the dialog box that appears, enter a name of **VideoPlaying**. Give it a Type of BOOL, and leave the other default options and values unchanged. Press OK to add the property to the ActiveX control.

Next, to add a method function to the ActiveX control, click on the Add Method button of the MFC ClassWizard. In the dialog box that appears, enter a name of **ClearListbox**. Give it a Return Type of void, and leave the other default options and values unchanged. Press OK to add the method to the ActiveX control.

To add another method function to the ActiveX control, again click on the Add Method button of the MFC ClassWizard. In the dialog box that appears, enter a name of **AddListboxItem**. Give it a Return Type of void, and leave the other default options and values unchanged. Add a parameter named strNewLBItem (type LPCTSTR). Press OK to add the method to the ActiveX control.

To add a final method function to the ActiveX control, again click on the Add Method button of the MFC ClassWizard. In the dialog box that appears, enter a name of **SetGigabitConnAvailability**. Give it a Return Type of void, and leave the other default options and values unchanged. Add a parameter named bGigabitConnAvailable (type BOOL). Press OK to add the method to the ActiveX control. Then click on OK again to close ClassWizard and write the changes into your project. Save the project to protect your work.

Unlike ATL, MFC does not currently have a visual editor for its ActiveX control user interface. Instead, you will need to add the controls for the display in code. For this to connect correctly in the MFC system, you must manually add resource identifiers for all the MFC controls you'll use on the control's UI display. Click on the View|Resource Symbols menu item. The Resource Symbols dialog box appears; it will currently have only one identifier automatically created. To add another one, click on the New button. A dialog box appears similar to that shown in Figure 7-37. Enter a name of **IDC_STATIC1** and a value

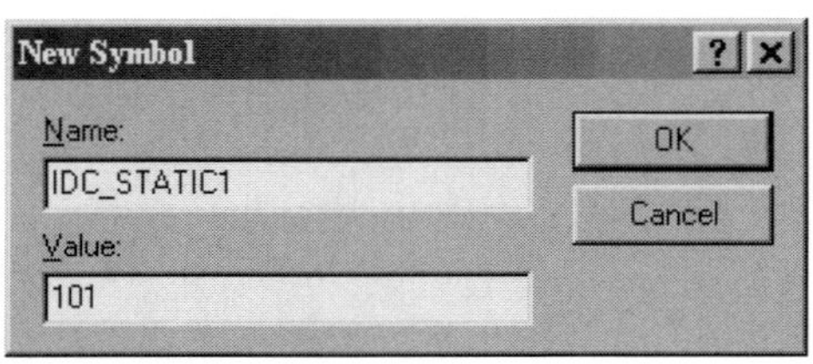


*Figure 7-37 Adding a Resource ID with the New Symbol dialog*

of **101**. Then click on OK to add this to the Resource ID list for the project.

Repeat this process for identifiers of IDC_STATIC2, IDC_STATIC3, IDC_STATIC4, IDC_STATIC5, and IDC_STATIC6. Add identifiers for IDC_EDIT1, IDC_EDIT2, and IDC_LIST1. Finally, add identifiers for IDC_BUTTON1, IDC_BUTTON2, IDC_BUTTON3, IDC_BUTTON4, IDC_RADIO1, and IDC_RADIO2. Give them sequential number values starting with 102. Figure 7-38 shows how the Resource Symbols dialog box might appear when you are done (depending on the order in which you enter the symbols). Click on OK to add the identifiers to the project. Save the project to protect your work.

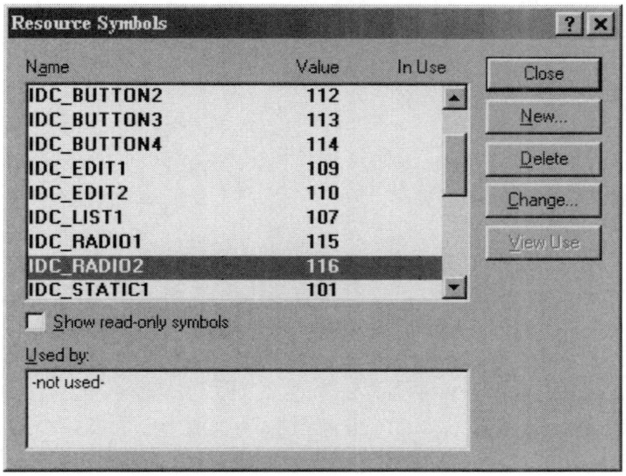


***Figure 7-38*** *The MFC Resource Symbols dialog*

Next, you need to add three ActiveX events to the ActiveX control so that it can trigger actions in its container (the control will not implement this functionality itself since it is designed to run on a client without MTS capabilities). Use the View|ClassWizard menu option to bring up the ClassWizard dialog again. Click on the ActiveX Events tab; no events should currently exist. Click on the Add Event button. A display similar to that shown in Figure 7-39 should appear. Enter a name of **OnUpdateVideoList**; leave the remaining information as created by ClassWizard and click on OK to add the ActiveX event to the control.

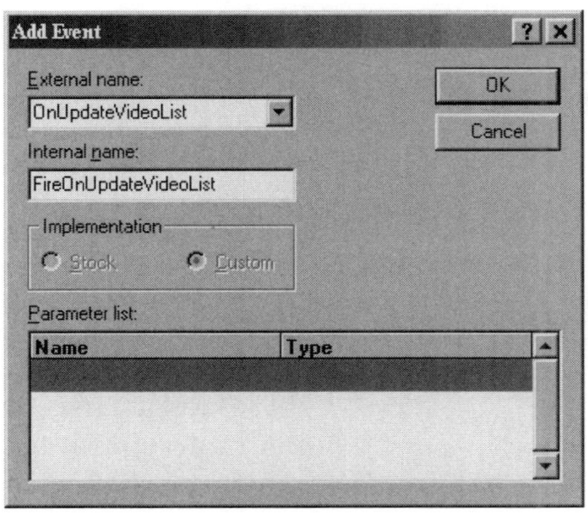


***Figure 7-39*** *Adding the OnUpdate-VideoList event with the MFC ClassWizard*

Repeat the previous step, this time giving the new ActiveX event a name of **OnOrderVideo**. Figure 7-40 shows how the Add Event dialog box should look when you are done. Click on OK to add this new ActiveX event to the control.

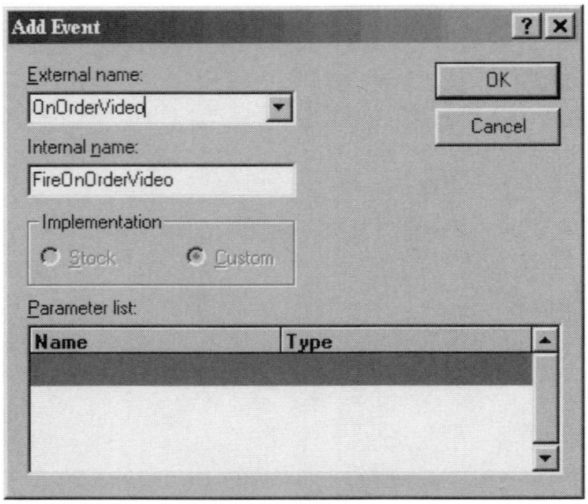


*Figure 7-40*
*Adding the OnOrderVideo event with the MFC ClassWizard*

Repeat the previous step a final time, giving the event a name of **OnTerminatePlayback**. Figure 7-41 shows how the dialog box should look when you are done. Click on OK to add this new ActiveX event to the control. Then click on OK to close ClassWizard and write the changes into the project. Save the project to protect your work.

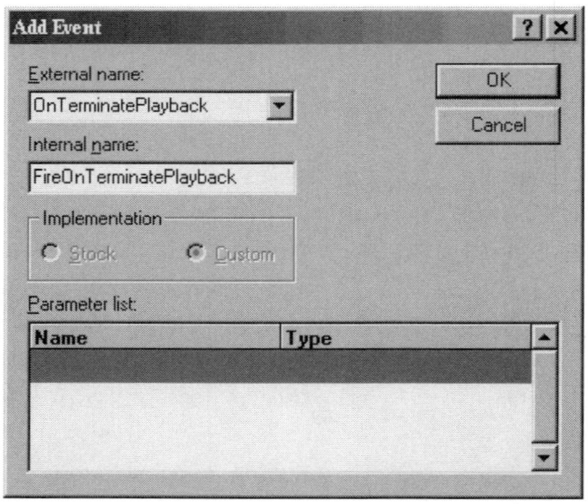


*Figure 7-41*
*Adding the OnTerminate-VideoPlayback event with the MFC ClassWizard*

The last steps you need to take before entering code are making the shared property interfaces from MTS available. To do this, bring up ClassWizard and select the Automation tab. Click on the Add Class button and choose From A Type Library in the drop-down menu. Browse to the C:\WINDOWS\SYSTEM\MTS\ directory (or equivalent on your system) and locate the MTXSPM.DLL file; click on OK. A dialog box similar to that shown in Figure 7-42 will appear, showing the three interfaces for the shared property manager. Click on OK twice to bring them into the project. Save the project to protect your work.

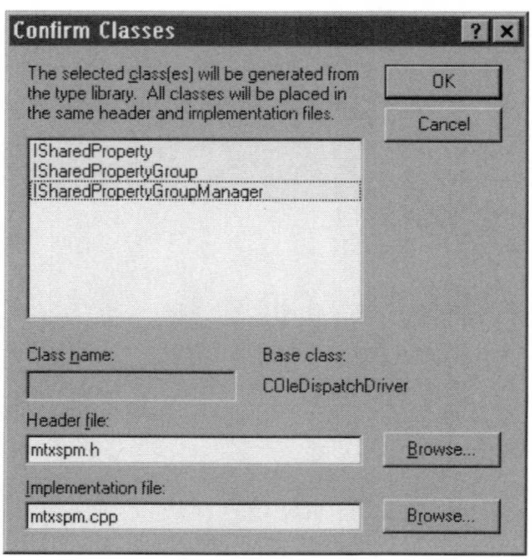


*Figure 7-42*
*The MFC ClassWizard bringing in the MFC shared property interfaces*

## Line-By-Line

Now we begin to add the code to create our MFC ActiveX control! Bring up the MFCAXWALLYSVIDEOSVIEWERCTL.H file in the text editor. Scan through it and enter or change any boldfaced line of source code in Listing 7-4. Save the project.

```
#if !defined(
AFX_MFCAXWALLYSVIDEOSVIEWERCTL_H__361BFDB5_9A54_11D2_B7EA_00E02916C424__INCLUDED_)
#define
AFX_MFCAXWALLYSVIDEOSVIEWERCTL_H__361BFDB5_9A54_11D2_B7EA_00E02916C424__INCLUDED_

#if _MSC_VER > 1000
#pragma once
#endif // _MSC_VER > 1000

// MFCAxWallysVideosViewerCtl.h :
// Declaration of the CMFCAxWallysVideosViewerCtrl ActiveX Control class.

///////////////////////////////////////////////////////////////////////////
// CMFCAxWallysVideosViewerCtrl : See MFCAxWallysVideosViewerCtl.cpp for
// implementation.

class CMFCAxWallysVideosViewerCtrl : public COleControl
{
    DECLARE_DYNCREATE(CMFCAxWallysVideosViewerCtrl)

// Constructor
public:
    CMFCAxWallysVideosViewerCtrl();

// Overrides
    // ClassWizard generated virtual function overrides
    //{{AFX_VIRTUAL(CMFCAxWallysVideosViewerCtrl)
    public:
    virtual void OnDraw(CDC* pdc, const CRect& rcBounds, const CRect& rcInvalid);
    virtual void DoPropExchange(CPropExchange* pPX);
    virtual void OnResetState();
    //}}AFX_VIRTUAL

// Implementation
protected:
    ~CMFCAxWallysVideosViewerCtrl();

    DECLARE_OLECREATE_EX(CMFCAxWallysVideosViewerCtrl)    // Class factory and guid
    DECLARE_OLETYPELIB(CMFCAxWallysVideosViewerCtrl)      // GetTypeInfo
    DECLARE_PROPPAGEIDS(CMFCAxWallysVideosViewerCtrl)     // Property page IDs
    DECLARE_OLECTLTYPE(CMFCAxWallysVideosViewerCtrl)      // Type name and misc status
```

```

// Message maps
    //{{AFX_MSG(CMFCAxWallysVideosViewerCtrl)
    afx_msg int OnCreate(LPCREATESTRUCT lpCreateStruct);
    //}}AFX_MSG
    afx_msg void OnClickedButton1();
    afx_msg void OnClickedButton2();
    afx_msg void OnClickedButton3();
    afx_msg void OnClickedButton4();
    afx_msg void OnClickedRadio1();
    afx_msg void OnClickedRadio2();
    afx_msg void OnDblclkList1();
    DECLARE_MESSAGE_MAP()

// Dispatch maps
    //{{AFX_DISPATCH(CMFCAxWallysVideosViewerCtrl)
    CString m_customerName;
    afx_msg void OnCustomerNameChanged();
    CString m_customerPassword;
    afx_msg void OnCustomerPasswordChanged();
    CString m_videoName;
    afx_msg void OnVideoNameChanged();
    short m_connectionType;
    afx_msg void OnConnectionTypeChanged();
    BOOL m_videoPlaying;
    afx_msg void OnVideoPlayingChanged();
    afx_msg void ClearListbox();
    afx_msg void AddListboxItem(LPCTSTR strNewLBItem);
    afx_msg void SetGigabitConnAvailability(BOOL bGigabitConnAvailable);
    //}}AFX_DISPATCH
    DECLARE_DISPATCH_MAP()

// Event maps
    //{{AFX_EVENT(CMFCAxWallysVideosViewerCtrl)
    void FireOnUpdateVideoList()
        {FireEvent(eventidOnUpdateVideoList,EVENT_PARAM(VTS_NONE));}
    void FireOnOrderVideo()
        {FireEvent(eventidOnOrderVideo,EVENT_PARAM(VTS_NONE));}
    void FireOnTerminatePlayback()
        {FireEvent(eventidOnTerminatePlayback,EVENT_PARAM(VTS_NONE));}
    //}}AFX_EVENT
    DECLARE_EVENT_MAP()

// Dispatch and event IDs
public:
    CEdit m_Edit1;
    CEdit m_Edit2;
```

```
89.     CStatic m_Static1;
90.     CStatic m_Static2;
91.     CStatic m_Static3;
92.     CStatic m_Static4;
93.     CStatic m_Static5;
94.     CStatic m_Static6;
95.     CButton m_Button1;
96.     CButton m_Button2;
97.     CButton m_Button3;
98.     CButton m_Button4;
99.     CButton m_Button5;
100.    CButton m_Button6;
101.    CListBox m_Listbox1;
102.    enum {
103.    //{{AFX_DISP_ID(CMFCAxWallysVideosViewerCtrl)
104.    dispidCustomerName = 1L,
105.    dispidCustomerPassword = 2L,
106.    dispidVideoName = 3L,
107.    dispidConnectionType = 4L,
108.    dispidVideoPlaying = 5L,
109.    dispidClearListbox = 6L,
110.    dispidAddListboxItem = 7L,
111.    dispidSetGigabitConnAvailability = 8L,
112.    eventidOnUpdateVideoList = 1L,
113.    eventidOnOrderVideo = 2L,
114.    eventidOnTerminatePlayback = 3L,
115.    //}}AFX_DISP_ID
116.    };
117. };
118.
119. //{{AFX_INSERT_LOCATION}}
120. // Microsoft Visual C++ will insert additional declarations immediately before the
121. //  previous line.
122.
123. #endif
124. //!defined(
125. AFX_MFCAXWALLYSVIDEOSVIEWERCTL_H__361BFDB5_9A54_11D2_B7EA_00E02916C424__INCLUDED)
```

***Listing 7-4** MFCAXWALLYSVIDEOSVIEWERCTL.H source code after modifications*

Here's the breakdown (some code is not discussed in detail because it contains exhaustive comments):

- **Lines 47-53** This code declares the event handlers for user clicks on the buttons, list box, and radio buttons (you cannot do this visually in MFC).
- **Lines 87-101** This code declares the member variables to hold the user interface for the ActiveX control; they'll be initialized in the CPP file.

Next, bring up the MFCAXWALLYSVIDEOSVIEWERCTL.CPP file in the text editor. Scan through it and enter or change any boldfaced line of source code in Listing 7-5. Save the project.

```
// MFCAxWallysVideosViewerCtl.cpp :
// Implementation of the CMFCAxWallysVideosViewerCtrl ActiveX Control class.

#include "stdafx.h"
#include "MFCAxWallysVideosViewer.h"
#include "MFCAxWallysVideosViewerCtl.h"
#include "MFCAxWallysVideosViewerPpg.h"
#include "mtxspm.h"

#ifdef _DEBUG
#define new DEBUG_NEW
#undef THIS_FILE
static char THIS_FILE[] = __FILE__;
#endif


IMPLEMENT_DYNCREATE(CMFCAxWallysVideosViewerCtrl, COleControl)


/////////////////////////////////////////////////////////////////////////////
// Message map

BEGIN_MESSAGE_MAP(CMFCAxWallysVideosViewerCtrl, COleControl)
   //{{AFX_MSG_MAP(CMFCAxWallysVideosViewerCtrl)
   ON_WM_CREATE()
   //}}AFX_MSG_MAP
   ON_OLEVERB(AFX_IDS_VERB_PROPERTIES, OnProperties)
   ON_BN_CLICKED( IDC_BUTTON1, OnClickedButton1 )
   ON_BN_CLICKED( IDC_BUTTON2, OnClickedButton2 )
   ON_BN_CLICKED( IDC_BUTTON3, OnClickedButton3 )
   ON_BN_CLICKED( IDC_BUTTON4, OnClickedButton4 )
   ON_BN_CLICKED( IDC_RADIO1, OnClickedRadio1 )
   ON_BN_CLICKED( IDC_RADIO2, OnClickedRadio2 )
   ON_LBN_DBLCLK( IDC_LIST1, OnDblclkList1 )
END_MESSAGE_MAP()


/////////////////////////////////////////////////////////////////////////////
// Dispatch map

BEGIN_DISPATCH_MAP(CMFCAxWallysVideosViewerCtrl, COleControl)
   //{{AFX_DISPATCH_MAP(CMFCAxWallysVideosViewerCtrl)
   DISP_PROPERTY_NOTIFY(CMFCAxWallysVideosViewerCtrl, "CustomerName", m_customerName,
      OnCustomerNameChanged, VT_BSTR)
```

```
    DISP_PROPERTY_NOTIFY(CMFCAxWallysVideosViewerCtrl, "CustomerPassword",
        m_customerPassword, OnCustomerPasswordChanged, VT_BSTR)
    DISP_PROPERTY_NOTIFY(CMFCAxWallysVideosViewerCtrl, "VideoName", m_videoName,
       OnVideoNameChanged, VT_BSTR)
    DISP_PROPERTY_NOTIFY(CMFCAxWallysVideosViewerCtrl, "ConnectionType",
       m_connectionType, OnConnectionTypeChanged, VT_I2)
    DISP_PROPERTY_NOTIFY(CMFCAxWallysVideosViewerCtrl, "VideoPlaying", m_videoPlaying,
       OnVideoPlayingChanged, VT_BOOL)
    DISP_FUNCTION(CMFCAxWallysVideosViewerCtrl, "ClearListbox", ClearListbox,
      VT_EMPTY, VTS_NONE)
    DISP_FUNCTION(CMFCAxWallysVideosViewerCtrl, "AddListboxItem", AddListboxItem,
      VT_EMPTY, VTS_BSTR)
    DISP_FUNCTION(CMFCAxWallysVideosViewerCtrl, "SetGigabitConnAvailability",
      SetGigabitConnAvailability, VT_EMPTY, VTS_BOOL)
    //}}AFX_DISPATCH_MAP
END_DISPATCH_MAP()


/////////////////////////////////////////////////////////////////////////////
// Event map

BEGIN_EVENT_MAP(CMFCAxWallysVideosViewerCtrl, COleControl)
    //{{AFX_EVENT_MAP(CMFCAxWallysVideosViewerCtrl)
    EVENT_CUSTOM("OnUpdateVideoList", FireOnUpdateVideoList, VTS_NONE)
    EVENT_CUSTOM("OnOrderVideo", FireOnOrderVideo, VTS_NONE)
    EVENT_CUSTOM("OnTerminatePlayback", FireOnTerminatePlayback, VTS_NONE)
    //}}AFX_EVENT_MAP
END_EVENT_MAP()


/////////////////////////////////////////////////////////////////////////////
// Property pages

// TODO: Add more property pages as needed.  Remember to increase the count!
BEGIN_PROPPAGEIDS(CMFCAxWallysVideosViewerCtrl, 1)
    PROPPAGEID(CMFCAxWallysVideosViewerPropPage::guid)
END_PROPPAGEIDS(CMFCAxWallysVideosViewerCtrl)


/////////////////////////////////////////////////////////////////////////////
// Initialize class factory and guid

IMPLEMENT_OLECREATE_EX(CMFCAxWallysVideosViewerCtrl,
    "MFCAXWALLYSVIDEOSVIEWER.MFCAxWallysVideosViewerCtrl.1",
    0x361bfda8, 0x9a54, 0x11d2, 0xb7, 0xea, 0, 0xe0, 0x29, 0x16, 0xc4, 0x24)


```

```
/////////////////////////////////////////////////////////////////////////////
// Type library ID and version

IMPLEMENT_OLETYPELIB(CMFCAxWallysVideosViewerCtrl, _tlid, _wVerMajor, _wVerMinor)


/////////////////////////////////////////////////////////////////////////////
// Interface IDs

const IID BASED_CODE IID_DMFCAxWallysVideosViewer =
        { 0x361bfda6, 0x9a54, 0x11d2, { 0xb7, 0xea, 0, 0xe0, 0x29, 0x16, 0xc4, 0x24
            } };
const IID BASED_CODE IID_DMFCAxWallysVideosViewerEvents =
        { 0x361bfda7, 0x9a54, 0x11d2, { 0xb7, 0xea, 0, 0xe0, 0x29, 0x16, 0xc4, 0x24
            } };


/////////////////////////////////////////////////////////////////////////////
// Control type information

static const DWORD BASED_CODE _dwMFCAxWallysVideosViewerOleMisc =
  OLEMISC_ACTIVATEWHENVISIBLE |
  OLEMISC_SETCLIENTSITEFIRST |
  OLEMISC_INSIDEOUT |
  OLEMISC_CANTLINKINSIDE |
  OLEMISC_RECOMPOSEONRESIZE;

IMPLEMENT_OLECTLTYPE(CMFCAxWallysVideosViewerCtrl, IDS_MFCAXWALLYSVIDEOSVIEWER,
                     _dwMFCAxWallysVideosViewerOleMisc)


/////////////////////////////////////////////////////////////////////////////
// CMFCAxWallysVideosViewerCtrl::CMFCAxWallysVideosViewerCtrlFactory::UpdateRegistry-
// Adds or removes system registry entries for CMFCAxWallysVideosViewerCtrl

BOOL
 CMFCAxWallysVideosViewerCtrl::CMFCAxWallysVideosViewerCtrlFactory::UpdateRegistry(
     BOOL bRegister)
{
  // TODO: Verify that your control follows apartment-model threading rules.
  // Refer to MFC TechNote 64 for more information.
  // If your control does not conform to the apartment-model rules, then
  // you must modify the code below, changing the 6th parameter from
  // afxRegApartmentThreading to 0.

  if (bRegister)
      return AfxOleRegisterControlClass(
```

```
            AfxGetInstanceHandle(),
            m_clsid,
            m_lpszProgID,
            IDS_MFCAXWALLYSVIDEOSVIEWER,
            IDB_MFCAXWALLYSVIDEOSVIEWER,
            afxRegApartmentThreading,
            _dwMFCAxWallysVideosViewerOleMisc,
            _tlid,
            _wVerMajor,
            _wVerMinor);
  else
        return AfxOleUnregisterClass(m_clsid, m_lpszProgID);
}


/////////////////////////////////////////////////////////////////////////////
// CMFCAxWallysVideosViewerCtrl::CMFCAxWallysVideosViewerCtrl - Constructor

CMFCAxWallysVideosViewerCtrl::CMFCAxWallysVideosViewerCtrl()
{
  InitializeIIDs(&IID_DMFCAxWallysVideosViewer,
       &IID_DMFCAxWallysVideosViewerEvents);

  // TODO: Initialize your control's instance data here.
  //*** set control to proper size ***
  SetInitialSize( 380 , 305 );
}


/////////////////////////////////////////////////////////////////////////////
// CMFCAxWallysVideosViewerCtrl::~CMFCAxWallysVideosViewerCtrl - Destructor

CMFCAxWallysVideosViewerCtrl::~CMFCAxWallysVideosViewerCtrl()
{
  // TODO: Cleanup your control's instance data here.
}


/////////////////////////////////////////////////////////////////////////////
// CMFCAxWallysVideosViewerCtrl::OnDraw - Drawing function

void CMFCAxWallysVideosViewerCtrl::OnDraw(
            CDC* pdc, const CRect& rcBounds, const CRect& rcInvalid)
{
  // TODO: Replace the following code with your own drawing code.
  //*** set background to button color for static controls ***
  CBrush* pBrush = new CBrush(); //*** create brush ***
```

```
   pBrush->CreateSolidBrush(GetSysColor( COLOR_BTNFACE ) ); //*** get color ***
   pdc->FillRect(rcBounds, pBrush ); //*** draw background ***
   delete pBrush; //*** delete to avoid memory leak ***
}


/////////////////////////////////////////////////////////////////////////////
// CMFCAxWallysVideosViewerCtrl::DoPropExchange - Persistence support

void CMFCAxWallysVideosViewerCtrl::DoPropExchange(CPropExchange* pPX)
{
   ExchangeVersion(pPX, MAKELONG(_wVerMinor, _wVerMajor));
   COleControl::DoPropExchange(pPX);

   // TODO: Call PX_ functions for each persistent custom property.

}


/////////////////////////////////////////////////////////////////////////////
// CMFCAxWallysVideosViewerCtrl::OnResetState - Reset control to default state

void CMFCAxWallysVideosViewerCtrl::OnResetState()
{
   COleControl::OnResetState();  // Resets defaults found in DoPropExchange

   // TODO: Reset any other control state here.
}


/////////////////////////////////////////////////////////////////////////////
// CMFCAxWallysVideosViewerCtrl message handlers

void CMFCAxWallysVideosViewerCtrl::OnCustomerNameChanged()
{
   // TODO: Add notification handler code

   SetModifiedFlag();
}

void CMFCAxWallysVideosViewerCtrl::OnCustomerPasswordChanged()
{
   // TODO: Add notification handler code

   SetModifiedFlag();
}

```

```
void CMFCAxWallysVideosViewerCtrl::OnVideoNameChanged()
{
  // TODO: Add notification handler code

  SetModifiedFlag();
}

void CMFCAxWallysVideosViewerCtrl::OnConnectionTypeChanged()
{
  // TODO: Add notification handler code

  SetModifiedFlag();
}

void CMFCAxWallysVideosViewerCtrl::OnVideoPlayingChanged()
{
  // TODO: Add notification handler code

  SetModifiedFlag();
}

void CMFCAxWallysVideosViewerCtrl::ClearListbox()
{
  // TODO: Add your dispatch handler code here
    SendDlgItemMessage( IDC_LIST1,LB_RESETCONTENT, 0 , 0);
}

void CMFCAxWallysVideosViewerCtrl::AddListboxItem(LPCTSTR strNewLBItem)
{
  // TODO: Add your dispatch handler code here
  SendDlgItemMessage(IDC_LIST1, LB_ADDSTRING, 0,(LPARAM)strNewLBItem);
}

void CMFCAxWallysVideosViewerCtrl::SetGigabitConnAvailability(
      BOOL bGigabitConnAvailable)
{
  // TODO: Add your dispatch handler code here
    if (bGigabitConnAvailable)
  {
        SendDlgItemMessage(IDC_RADIO2,BM_SETCHECK,(WPARAM)BST_CHECKED, 0);
  }
  else
  {
        SendDlgItemMessage(IDC_RADIO1,BM_SETCHECK,(WPARAM)BST_CHECKED, 0);
  }
}

```

```
int CMFCAxWallysVideosViewerCtrl::OnCreate(LPCREATESTRUCT lpCreateStruct)
{
    if (COleControl::OnCreate(lpCreateStruct) == -1)
        return -1;

    // TODO: Add your specialized creation code here
    CRect rect1(15,5,208,26);
    m_Static1.Create( _T("Select a video"),
                        WS_CHILD | WS_VISIBLE, rect1, this, IDC_STATIC1);
    CRect rect2(222,6,368,25);
    m_Static2.Create( _T("Account name"),
                        WS_CHILD | WS_VISIBLE, rect2, this, IDC_STATIC2);
    CRect rect3(221,54,367,73);
    m_Static3.Create( _T("Account password"),
                         WS_CHILD | WS_VISIBLE, rect3, this, IDC_STATIC3);
    CRect rect4(15,185,208,206);
    m_Static4.Create( _T("Video Preview"),
                        WS_CHILD | WS_VISIBLE, rect4, this, IDC_STATIC4);
    CRect rect5(15,205,210,295);
    m_Static5.Create( _T(""),
                        WS_CHILD | WS_VISIBLE | SS_BITMAP, rect5, this,
                          IDC_STATIC5);
    CRect rect6(220,200,370,270);
    m_Static6.Create( _T("Select Connection Speed"),
                        WS_CHILD | WS_VISIBLE | WS_GROUP, rect6, this,
                          IDC_STATIC6);
    CRect rect7(220,32,369,48);
    m_Edit1.Create( WS_CHILD | WS_VISIBLE | WS_BORDER | ES_AUTOHSCROLL , rect7,
                      this, IDC_EDIT1);
    CRect rect8(219,80,368,96);
    m_Edit2.Create( WS_CHILD | WS_VISIBLE | WS_BORDER | ES_AUTOHSCROLL, rect8,
                     this, IDC_EDIT2);
    CRect rect9(220,100,370,120);
    m_Button1.Create( _T("Update Videos"),
                        WS_CHILD | WS_VISIBLE |BS_PUSHBUTTON, rect9, this,
                           IDC_BUTTON1);
    CRect rect10(220,135,370,155);
    m_Button2.Create( _T("Order Video"),
                        WS_CHILD | WS_VISIBLE | BS_PUSHBUTTON, rect10, this,
                           IDC_BUTTON2);
    CRect rect11(220,170,370,190);
    m_Button3.Create( _T("Exit Wally's"),
                        WS_CHILD | WS_VISIBLE |BS_PUSHBUTTON, rect11, this,
                         IDC_BUTTON3);
    CRect rect12(220,275,370,295);
    m_Button4.Create( _T("Terminate Playback"),
                        WS_CHILD | WS_VISIBLE | BS_PUSHBUTTON, rect12, this,
```

```
                         IDC_BUTTON4);
   CRect rect13(240,235,350,247);
   m_Button5.Create( _T("Megabit Conn"),
                       WS_CHILD | WS_VISIBLE | BS_RADIOBUTTON, rect13, this,
                         IDC_RADIO1);
   CRect rect14(240,252,350,265);
   m_Button6.Create( _T("Gigabit Conn"),
                       WS_CHILD | WS_VISIBLE | BS_RADIOBUTTON, rect14, this,
                         IDC_RADIO2);
   CRect rect16(14,27,206,180);
   m_Listbox1.Create( WS_CHILD | WS_VISIBLE  | WS_BORDER | WS_VSCROLL |
                       WS_HSCROLL, rect16, this, IDC_LIST1);

   return 0;
}

void CMFCAxWallysVideosViewerCtrl::OnClickedButton1( )
{
   // TODO : Add Code for control notification handler.
   FireOnUpdateVideoList();
}
void CMFCAxWallysVideosViewerCtrl::OnClickedButton2( )
{
   // TODO : Add Code for control notification handler.
   GetDlgItemText( IDC_EDIT1, m_customerName );
   GetDlgItemText( IDC_EDIT2, m_customerPassword );
   long lSelIndex = SendDlgItemMessage( IDC_LIST1, LB_GETCURSEL,0,0);
   SendDlgItemMessage(IDC_LIST1,LB_GETTEXT,lSelIndex,(LONG)&m_videoName);
   m_connectionType = SendDlgItemMessage(IDC_RADIO1, BM_GETCHECK , 0 , 0);
   FireOnOrderVideo();
   m_videoPlaying = TRUE;
}
void CMFCAxWallysVideosViewerCtrl::OnClickedButton3( )
{
   // TODO : Add Code for control notification handler.
   PostQuitMessage( 0 );
}
void CMFCAxWallysVideosViewerCtrl::OnClickedButton4( )
{
   // TODO : Add Code for control notification handler.
   if (m_videoPlaying)
   {
        FireOnTerminatePlayback();
        m_videoPlaying = FALSE;
   }
}
void CMFCAxWallysVideosViewerCtrl::OnDblclkList1()
```

```
{
    // TODO : Add Code for control notification handler.
    //*** this would download the video and play a sample ***
}
void CMFCAxWallysVideosViewerCtrl::OnClickedRadio1()
{
    // TODO : Add Code for control notification handler.
    SendDlgItemMessage(IDC_RADIO1,BM_SETCHECK,(WPARAM)BST_CHECKED, 0);
    SendDlgItemMessage(IDC_RADIO2,BM_SETCHECK,(WPARAM)BST_UNCHECKED, 0);
}
void CMFCAxWallysVideosViewerCtrl::OnClickedRadio2()
{
    SendDlgItemMessage(IDC_RADIO2,BM_SETCHECK,(WPARAM)BST_CHECKED, 0);
    SendDlgItemMessage(IDC_RADIO1,BM_SETCHECK,(WPARAM)BST_UNCHECKED, 0);
    // TODO : Add Code for control notification handler.
    ISharedPropertyGroupManager* spmManager = NULL;
    //*** Define shared property group IP ***
    ISharedPropertyGroup* spmGroup = NULL;
    //*** Define shared property IP for next receipt ***
    ISharedProperty* spmMegabitConnections = NULL;
    //*** Define shared property IP for max receipts ***
    ISharedProperty* spmGigabitConnections = NULL;
    //*** define variant for value of next receipt ***
    COleVariant vMegabitConnex;
    //*** define variant for value of max receipts ***
    COleVariant vGigabitConnex;
    //*** start out getting the SPG manager from MTS ***
    if (!spmManager->CreateDispatch(_T("MTxSpm.SharedPropertyGroupManager.1")))
    {
         //*** Show Error to User ***
        MessageBox(_T("MTS SPM Currently Off-Line; Please Try Again Later!"),
                        "MFCAxWallysideoViewerCtl", MB_OK);
    }

    //*** define and set isolation mode ***
    LONG lIsolationMode = 1; //Lockmethod
    //*** define and set release mode ***
    LONG lReleaseMode = 1; //Process
    //*** define and set existence variable ***
    int bExists;
    //*** define BSTR holder for shared property name values ***
    CString strPropertyNames;
    //*** start out with WALLYSCONNECTIONS property group ***
    strPropertyNames = _T("WallysConnections");
    //*** attemt to create or obtain the property group WALLYSCONNECTIONS ***
    spmGroup->AttachDispatch( spmManager->CreatePropertyGroup(strPropertyNames,
        &lIsolationMode, &lReleaseMode, &bExists ));
```

```
if (spmGroup->m_lpDispatch == NULL)
{
      //*** Show Error to User ***
      MessageBox(_T("MTS SPM Currently Off-Line; Please Try Again Later!"),
                    "MFCAxWallysideoViewerCtl", MB_OK);
     //*** release the shared property group manager ***
    spmManager->ReleaseDispatch();
}
//*** Define the string for the megabit connections ***
strPropertyNames = _T("MegabitConnections");
//*** Create of obtain the megabitconnections shared property ***
  spmMegabitConnections->AttachDispatch(
    spmGroup->CreateProperty( strPropertyNames,
       &bExists));
//*** Signal Error ***
if (spmMegabitConnections->m_lpDispatch == NULL)
{
      //*** Show Error to User ***
      MessageBox(_T("MTS SPM Currently Off-Line; Please Try Again Later!"),
                    "MFCAxWallysideoViewerCtl", MB_OK);
    //*** Release the shared property group ***
    spmGroup->ReleaseDispatch();
    //*** release the shared property group manager ***
    spmManager->ReleaseDispatch();
}
//*** Define the string for the gigabit connections ***
strPropertyNames = _T("GigabitConnections");
//*** Create or obtain the gigabitconnections shared property ***
  spmGigabitConnections->AttachDispatch(
    spmGroup->CreateProperty( strPropertyNames,
      &bExists ));
//*** Signal Error ***
if (spmGigabitConnections->m_lpDispatch == NULL)
{
      //*** Show Error to User ***
      MessageBox(_T("MTS SPM Currently Off-Line; Please Try Again Later!"),
                    "MFCAxWallysideoViewerCtl", MB_OK);
    //*** Release the shared property group ***
    spmGroup->ReleaseDispatch();
    //*** release the shared property group manager ***
    spmManager->ReleaseDispatch();
}
//*** Get the megabit connections value ***
  vMegabitConnex = spmMegabitConnections->GetValue(  );
vGigabitConnex = spmGigabitConnections->GetValue(  );
//*** if no data then initialized so set it ***
if (vMegabitConnex.intVal == 0)
```

```
468.    {
469.         vMegabitConnex.intVal = 100;
470.         vGigabitConnex.intVal = 2;
471.         //** send data back to SPM ***
472.        spmGigabitConnections->SetValue( vGigabitConnex );
473.        spmMegabitConnections->SetValue( vMegabitConnex );
474.    }
475.    //*** Release the shared property ***
476.    spmMegabitConnections->ReleaseDispatch();
477.    //*** Release the shared property ***
478.    spmGigabitConnections->ReleaseDispatch();
479.    //*** Release the shared property group ***
480.    spmGroup->ReleaseDispatch();
481.    //*** release the shared property group manager ***
482.    spmManager->ReleaseDispatch();
483.    //*** handle the UI ***
484.    if (vGigabitConnex.intVal == 0)
485.    {
486.       SendDlgItemMessage(IDC_RADIO2,BM_SETCHECK,(WPARAM)BST_UNCHECKED, 0);
487.       SendDlgItemMessage(IDC_RADIO1,BM_SETCHECK,(WPARAM)BST_CHECKED, 0);
488.    }
489. }
```

***Listing 7-5*** *MFCAXWALLYSVIDEOSVIEWERCTL.CPP source code after modifications*

Here's the breakdown of the code:

- **Line 8** This code brings in the MTXSPM wrappers created earlier to use the MTS Shared Property system.
- **Lines 28-34** This code attaches the event handlers for user interface controls to the message pump for MFC (you don't use ClassWizard due to the lack of a visual designer).
- **Lines 184-188** This code draws the background of the control (the controls for the UI draw themselves). Notice that it sets the background color to match that of the static controls for aesthetics.
- **Line 257** This code clears the list box control via old-style Windows programming techniques.
- **Line 263** This code adds a string to the list box using old-style Windows programming techniques.
- **Lines 270-277** This code uses old-style Windows programming techniques to set either the megabit or gigabit connection availability radio button in response to its parameter value.
- **Lines 286-338** This code creates the user interface for the ActiveX control. Unlike ATL or Visual Basic, MFC does not support using a visual control designer. Notice that it must be put in the OnCreate handler rather than the class initialization code!

- **Lines 343-347** This code fires the OnUpdateVideoList ActiveX event for the application or HTML page hosting the control to handle (by calling the ASP component).
- **Lines 348-358** This code fires the OnOrderVideo ActiveX event for the application or HTML page hosting the control to handle (by calling the ASP component). Notice that it sets the control's internal properties from the user interface controls via old-style Windows API techniques.
- **Lines 359-363** This code posts an exit message to allow users to quit the HTML page if they like or to allow a clerk to close the application on his machine.
- **Lines 364-372** This code fires the OnTerminatePlayback ActiveX event for the application or HTML page hosting the control to handle (by calling the ASP component). Notice that it resets the internal online Boolean member variable.
- **Lines 373-377** This code is a placeholder to allow playing a sample video if desired when the user double-clicks a video name entry.
- **Lines 378-383** This code responds to user interface actions to set the radio buttons correctly.
- **Lines 384-489** This code only executes if the ActiveX control is running inside a compiled application on the server machine at the video storefront; there it serves to make sure that there are gigabit connections available when the user selects one. On a client machine on the Internet, it exits when it cannot get the MTS shared property group manager interface (it assumes MTS isn't installed on the client computer).

Once you are satisfied you've entered the code from the above listing correctly, build the MFC ActiveX control from the Build menu. If you encounter any errors, please check the code in the listing to find your mistake (it has been exhaustively debugged and is correct). Once you have compiled the control successfully, it is automatically registered on the local machine; if you need to move it to another machine, the directions are in Chapter 9. Otherwise, this completes the MFC MTS components for our book.

## Where We Go From Here

You've completed the MFC versions of the four MTS-aware components for our fictional business application. If you are also interested in ATL development, you can trace the same four elements through Active Template Library in Chapter 6; otherwise, move on to Chapter 8 to see how to create an ATL storefront application for the business as well as the online ordering component in HTML and ASP.

## Chapter Eight

# Creating MTS Applications in ATL and MFC

At this point, if you've been working your way through the book one chapter at a time, you have created either four ATL or four MFC MTS components (or both) to access a SQL Server 6 or 7 database group representing the customers and videos of a fictitious broadband Internet online video store. What remains to do is to create applications that use these components. This chapter will present three different versions of such an application: one each in MFC and ATL that represents the storefront's access to the customers and video databases, as well as an ability to process a phone order for a video. Also, for those who have access to Internet Information Server (IIS) and Active Server Pages (ASP), an additional application written in HTML and ASP using the ActiveX control to simulate online Internet ordering is presented as well. Chapter 9 will guide you through setting up the MTS-aware components in MTS Explorer and show you how to run the applications and test their MTS functionality. Chapter 10 will then show you how to support and deploy the components over the Internet.

## Uncle Wally's Gigabit Online Video Store and Clam Emporium Storefront Application

For purposes of this book, we'll create a fictional world in which many users of the Internet have access to broadband connections at the megabit or gigabit level, and a service industry has sprung up similar to the "mom and pop" video rental stores of the early 1980s, one which provides access to videos (actually DVDs) online rather than by renting physical tapes. The service exists in two portions: a storefront-based operation where customers come in and set up their accounts and perhaps order videos for later viewing, and an online operation where existing customers connect to the business's web site and order their videos directly online, using their account and password. The business uses MTS to ensure that customers' accounts don't conflict, that videos that are ordered are actually available, and that a given account has the available credit to purchase the video desired.

This arrangement uses four MTS-aware components: two MTS COM servers, one for handling customer accounts and one for handling videos in stock; an ASP COM server to deal with the actual mechanics of ordering online; and an ActiveX control to serve as the front end for the MTS and ASP COM elements, either in a storefront application or via an online HTML page. The storefront applications are compiled and do the same jobs as the ASP component.

# Creating an MTS Application with ATL

In the final analysis, even the most sophisticated MTS component needs a home, and that means an application. The following project demonstrates an ATL-based application that uses the MTS ATL components we created in Chapter 6 to allow a fictional store clerk to interact with the videos and accounts databases as well as order a video for a customer over the phone (for the low-tech crowd...). If you prefer MFC instead of ATL, please skip down to that section where this application will be reproduced. If you work exclusively in the HTML/ASP environment, skip to the last section for an example of doing the online ordering of videos in an ASP application.

## Step-By-Step

Start Visual C++ 6.0. From the File menu, select New. The New dialog box opens; click on the ATL COM AppWizard entry. Next, select an appropriate directory, then enter a project name of ATLWallysVideoStore. Figure 8-1 shows how the New dialog should appear when you are done.

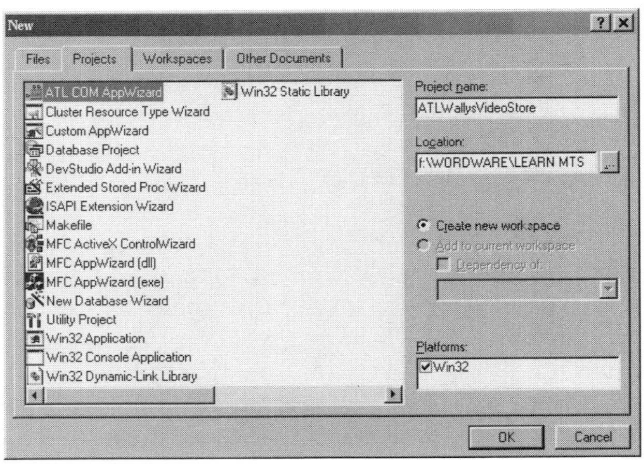


*Figure 8-1*
*The New dialog box creating the ATLWallys-VideoStore ATL project*

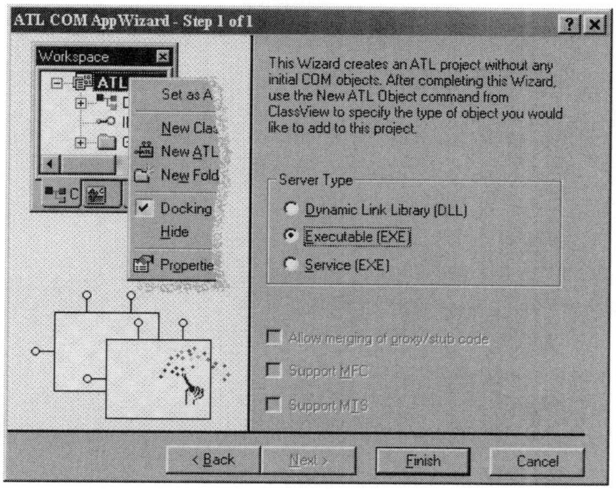


***Figure 8-2*** *Setting the ATL COM AppWizard properties*

As shown in Figure 8-2, make sure the EXE option is selected in the ATL COM AppWizard. All the other options will gray out since they don't apply to EXE projects. Click on Finish to generate the ATL EXE project.

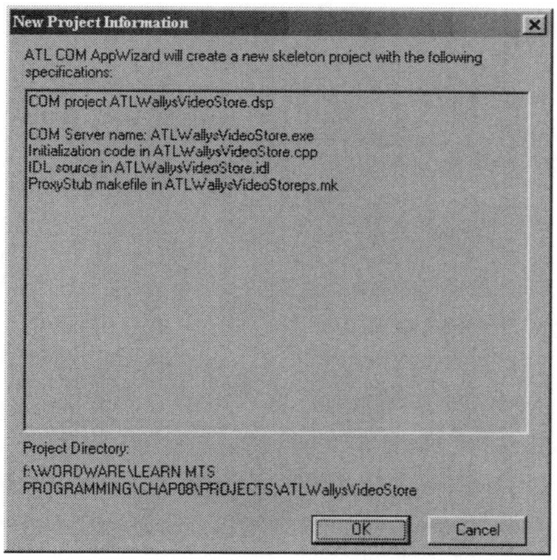


***Figure 8-3*** *The confirmation dialog*

A confirmation dialog box appears as shown in Figure 8-3; press OK to create the ATL project.

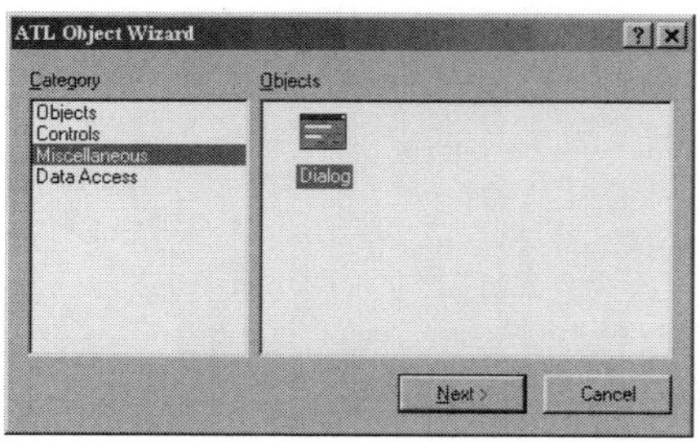


***Figure 8-4*** *Selecting a Dialog Box object in the ATL Object Wizard*

Once the IDE returns to life, select the Insert|New ATL Object menu option. In the ATL Object Wizard, choose the Miscellaneous entry in the left-hand list box, and then select the Dialog entry on the right, as shown in Figure 8-4. Click on Next to set the properties of the dialog box that will be the main display of the application.

Click on the Names tab of the next dialog box; enter a name of **StoreUI** for the Dialog Box object. As illustrated in Figure 8-5, this name will be reflected in all the other edit controls in an appropriate fashion. Click on the OK button to add the Dialog Box object to your application. Save the project to protect your work.

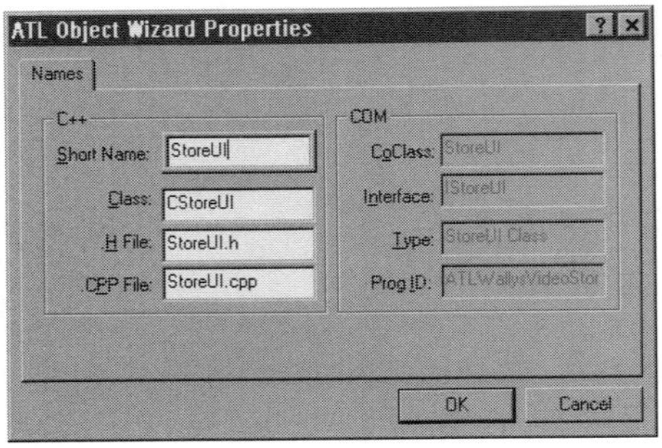


*Figure 8-5* *Entering name information in the ATL Object Wizard dialog*

In the IDE again, click on the workspace viewer ResourceView tab and open the dialog box entry in the tree control. Double-click on the IDD_STOREUIDLG dialog box entry. It will come up in a dialog box editor window. Remove the default static text control and button controls. Figure 8-6 shows the layout of the StoreUI dialog box as it exists in the project supplied on the companion CD. Rather than spend a page telling you how to lay out your own version of this dialog, we'll assume you either are using the one on the CD or can figure out how to duplicate the display yourself. Save the project when you've finished laying out the dialog box.

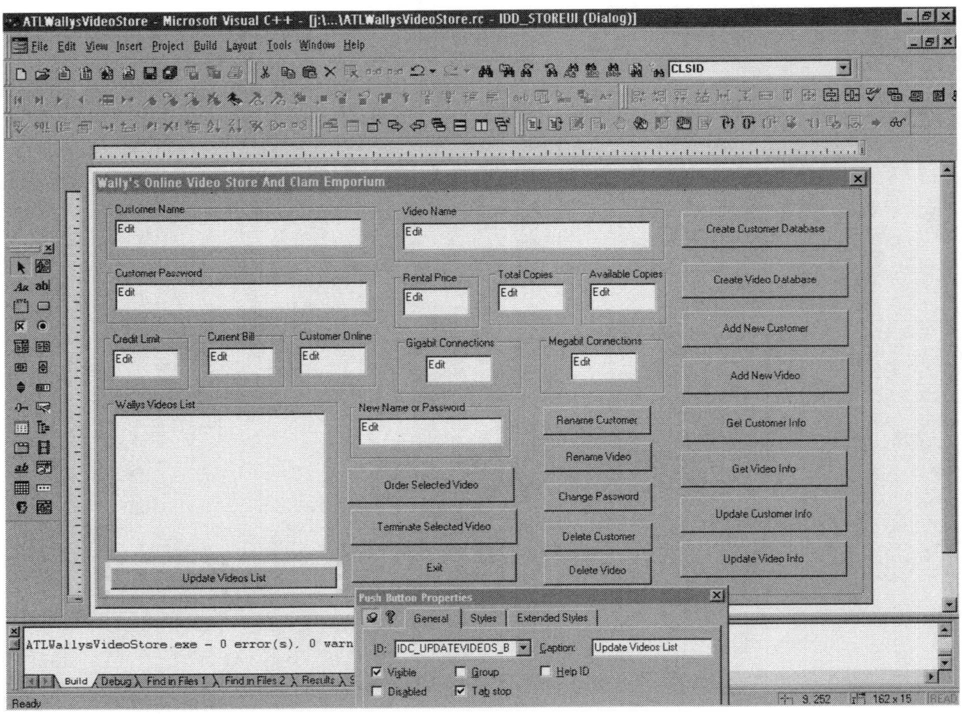


*Figure 8-6* *Visual layout of the StoreUI dialog*

The next IDE work you need to do on the ATL application prior to code entry is to connect the various user interface controls to underlying code functions.

In ATL 2.1, you would have been required to do this by hand. In ATL 3.0, however, some automation has been added. In the WallysVideosDlg dialog box resource, double-click on the Add New Customer pushbutton control. A dialog box will appear, showing you all the various control identifiers and associated messages for the dialog box. Select the button's entry in the lower right-hand list box, then click on the BN_CLICKED message ID in the left-hand list box. Finally, click on the Add Handler button to the upper right. A dialog box similar to that shown in Figure 8-7 appears, giving a default name for the message handler function. Accept it by clicking on the OK button.

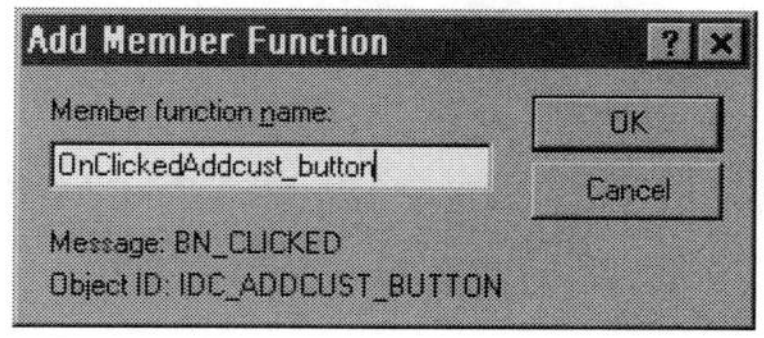


***Figure 8-7***
*Adding a message handler function for button click messages*

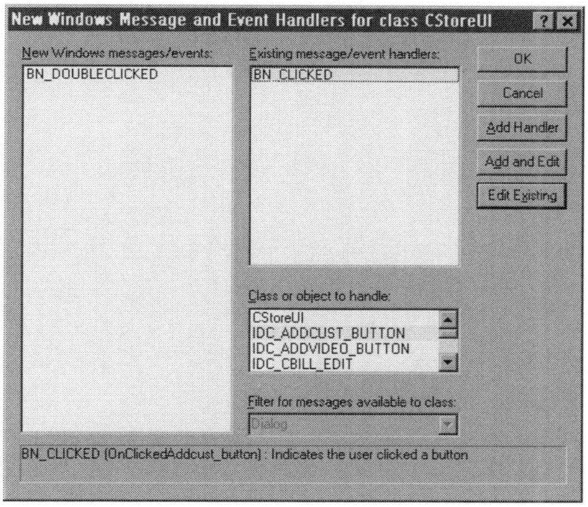


***Figure 8-8***
*The New Windows Message dialog showing an added message handler*

Figure 8-8 shows you how the dialog box will appear afterwards, reflecting the added message handler. Repeat these steps for all the button controls on the dialog box. Save the project.

## Line-By-Line

Now we are ready to enter the program code for the ATL WallysVideoStore application. The first file that needs to be changed is the main one for the project because ATL assumed we are creating an EXE COM server application when we used the ATL COM AppWizard. We aren't, and so we need to rip out some code and replace it with some of our own to make this a real application. Bring up the ATLWALLYSVIDEOSTORE.CPP file in the text editor. Scan through it and enter or change any boldfaced line of source code in Listing 8-1; notice that quite a bit of code has been removed, but some has been left. Be sure you don't delete anything that isn't deleted in the listing! Save the project.

```
// ATLWallysVideoStore.cpp : Implementation of WinMain

// Note: Proxy/Stub Information
//      To build a separate proxy/stub DLL,
//      run nmake -f ATLWallysVideoStoreps.mk in the project directory.
```

```

#include "stdafx.h"
#include "resource.h"
#include <initguid.h>
#include "ATLWallysVideoStore.h"
#include "ATLWallysVideoStore_i.c"
//*** online video manager externs ***
#include "ATLASPWallysVideoManager_i.c"
//*** include dialog box ***
#include "StoreUI.h"

const DWORD dwTimeOut = 5000;      // time for EXE to be idle before shutting down
const DWORD dwPause = 1000;        // time to wait for threads to finish up

// Passed to CreateThread to monitor the shutdown event
static DWORD WINAPI MonitorProc(void* pv)
{
    CExeModule* p = (CExeModule*)pv;
    p->MonitorShutdown();
    return 0;
}

LONG CExeModule::Unlock()
{
    LONG l = CComModule::Unlock();
    if (l == 0)
    {
        bActivity = true;
        SetEvent(hEventShutdown); // tell monitor that we transitioned to zero
    }
    return l;
}

//Monitors the shutdown event
void CExeModule::MonitorShutdown()
{
    while (1)
    {
        WaitForSingleObject(hEventShutdown, INFINITE);
        DWORD dwWait=0;
        do
        {
            bActivity = false;
            dwWait = WaitForSingleObject(hEventShutdown, dwTimeOut);
        } while (dwWait == WAIT_OBJECT_0);
        // timed out
        if (!bActivity && m_nLockCnt == 0) // if no activity let's really bail
```

```
        {
#if _WIN32_WINNT >= 0x0400 & defined(_ATL_FREE_THREADED)
            CoSuspendClassObjects();
            if (!bActivity && m_nLockCnt == 0)
#endif
                break;
        }
    }
    CloseHandle(hEventShutdown);
    PostThreadMessage(dwThreadID, WM_QUIT, 0, 0);
}

bool CExeModule::StartMonitor()
{
    hEventShutdown = CreateEvent(NULL, false, false, NULL);
    if (hEventShutdown == NULL)
        return false;
    DWORD dwThreadID;
    HANDLE h = CreateThread(NULL, 0, MonitorProc, this, 0, &dwThreadID);
    return (h != NULL);
}

CExeModule _Module;

BEGIN_OBJECT_MAP(ObjectMap)
END_OBJECT_MAP()


LPCTSTR FindOneOf(LPCTSTR p1, LPCTSTR p2)
{
    while (p1 != NULL && *p1 != NULL)
    {
        LPCTSTR p = p2;
        while (p != NULL && *p != NULL)
        {
            if (*p1 == *p)
                return CharNext(p1);
            p = CharNext(p);
        }
        p1 = CharNext(p1);
    }
    return NULL;
}

/////////////////////////////////////////////////////////////////////////////
//
extern "C" int WINAPI _tWinMain(HINSTANCE hInstance,
```

```
100.     HINSTANCE /*hPrevInstance*/, LPTSTR lpCmdLine, int /*nShowCmd*/)
101. {
102.
103. #if _WIN32_WINNT >= 0x0400 & defined(_ATL_FREE_THREADED)
104.     HRESULT hRes = CoInitializeEx(NULL, COINIT_MULTITHREADED);
105. #else
106.     HRESULT hRes = CoInitialize(NULL);
107. #endif
108.     _ASSERTE(SUCCEEDED(hRes));
109.     _Module.Init(ObjectMap, hInstance, &LIBID_ATLWALLYSVIDEOSTORELib);
110.     _Module.dwThreadID = GetCurrentThreadId();
111.
112.    //*** define dialog ***
113.    CStoreUI WallysStoreDlg;
114.    // *** create it ***
115.    WallysStoreDlg.Create(NULL);
116.    //*** show it ***
117.    WallysStoreDlg.ShowWindow(SW_SHOWNORMAL);
118.    //*** fun with messages ***
119.     MSG msg;
120.     while (GetMessage(&msg, 0, 0, 0))
121.    {
122.       TranslateMessage(&msg);
123.       DispatchMessage(&msg);
124.     }
125.    //** go bye bye ***
126.     _Module.Term();
127.     CoUninitialize();
128.     return 0;
129. }
130.
```

***Listing 8-1*** *ATLWALLYSVIDEOSTORE.CPP source code after modifications*

Here's the breakdown:

- **Lines 12-13** This code allows us to declare and use the IOnlineVideoManager interface pointer and its associated methods. (The CD code has a copy of this file; if you are creating the projects from scratch, you need to move a copy of the file into the current directory.)
- **Lines 14-15** This code puts in the header files so that we can interact with the dialog box.
- **Lines 99-107** A lot of stuff has been taken out here that would normally deal with setting up an EXE COM server. The really important part is the CoInitialize call that turns on COM for us, make sure it is there or the entire project won't work!

- **Lines 108-117** Some stuff has been removed here that handles EXE COM Server setup. More importantly, we declare and create the dialog box class object. We show the customer dialog box at startup.
- **Lines 118-125** The changes here are twofold: First, we make the message handler into a block by adding a curly brace, and also put in a TranslateMessage call so that our dialog box gets the right message ID values. Also, we pulled out a lot of EXE COM server code, but left the vital CoUninitialize call to shut down COM when we're done.

All the other code for our ATL application lives in the header files for the dialog box. To start entering it, bring up the STOREUI.H file in the text editor. Scan through it and enter or change any boldfaced line of source code in Listing 8-2. Save the project.

```
// StoreUI.h : Declaration of the CStoreUI

#ifndef __STOREUI_H_
#define __STOREUI_H_

#include "resource.h"       // main symbols
#include <atlhost.h>
//*** Accounts MTS component ***
#include "ATLMTSWallysAccount.h"
//*** Videos MTS component ***
#include "ATLMTSWallysVideos.h"
//*** Ordering Component ***
#include "ATLASPWallysVideoManager.h"
//*** MTS Shared Properties ***
#include <mtx.h>
#include <mtxspm.h>
/////////////////////////////////////////////////////////////////////////////
// CStoreUI
class CStoreUI :
    public CAxDialogImpl<CStoreUI>
{
public:
    CStoreUI()
    {
          //*** talk to the shared property system when we initialize ***
          CComVariant varResult;
          BOOL bUseMegabit = TRUE;
        //*** Define the HRESULT holder and set default value ***
        HRESULT hr = S_OK;
        //*** Define shared property group manager IP ***
        ISharedPropertyGroupManager* spmManager = NULL;
        //*** Define shared property group IP ***
        ISharedPropertyGroup* spmGroup = NULL;
        //*** Define shared property IP for next receipt ***
```

```
        ISharedProperty* spmMegabitConnections = NULL;
        //*** Define shared property IP for max receipts ***
        ISharedProperty* spmGigabitConnections = NULL;
        //*** define variant for value of next receipt ***
        CComVariant vMegabitConnex;
        //*** define variant for value of max receipts ***
        CComVariant vGigabitConnex;
        //*** start out getting the SPG manager from MTS ***
        hr = CoCreateInstance(CLSID_SharedPropertyGroupManager, NULL, CLSCTX_ALL,
                  IID_ISharedPropertyGroupManager, (void**) &spmManager );
        if (!SUCCEEDED(hr))
         {
             //*** Show Error to User ***
             MessageBox(
               _T("MTS SPM Currently Off-Line; Please Try Again Later!"),
             "ATLWallysVideoStore", MB_OK);
             //*** release the shared property group manager ***
            spmManager->Release();
         }
        //*** define and set isolation mode ***
        LONG lIsolationMode = LockMethod;
        //*** define and set release mode ***
        LONG lReleaseMode = Process;
        //*** define and set existence variable ***
        VARIANT_BOOL bExists = VARIANT_FALSE;
        //*** define BSTR holder for shared property name values ***
        CComBSTR ccbstrPropertyNames;
        //*** start out with WALLYSCONNECTIONS property group ***
        ccbstrPropertyNames = _T("WallysConnections");
        //*** attemt to create or obtain the property group WALLYSCONNECTIONS ***
        hr = spmManager->CreatePropertyGroup(ccbstrPropertyNames.Copy(),
             &lIsolationMode, &lReleaseMode, &bExists, &spmGroup );
        if (!SUCCEEDED(hr))
         {
             //*** Show Error to User ***
             MessageBox(
               _T("MTS SPM Currently Off-Line; Please Try Again Later!"),
             "ATLWallysVideoStore", MB_OK);
             //*** release the shared property group manager ***
            spmManager->Release();
         }
        //*** Define the string for the megabit connections ***
        ccbstrPropertyNames = _T("MegabitConnections");
        //*** Create of obtain the megabitconnections shared property ***
         hr = spmGroup->CreateProperty( ccbstrPropertyNames.Copy(),
                &bExists,&spmMegabitConnections);
        //*** Signal Error ***
```

```
        if (!SUCCEEDED(hr))
         {
             //*** Show Error to User ***
             MessageBox(
                 _T("MTS SPM Currently Off-Line; Please Try Again Later!"),
          "ATLWallysVideoStore", MB_OK);
            //*** Release the shared property group ***
            spmGroup->Release();
            //*** release the shared property group manager ***
            spmManager->Release();
         }
        //*** Define the string for the gigabit connections ***
        ccbstrPropertyNames = _T("GigabitConnections");
        //*** Create or obtain the gigabitconnections shared property ***
         hr = spmGroup->CreateProperty( ccbstrPropertyNames.Copy(),
                &bExists,&spmGigabitConnections);
        //*** Signal Error ***
        if (!SUCCEEDED(hr))
         {
             //*** Show Error to User ***
             MessageBox(
                 _T("MTS SPM Currently Off-Line; Please Try Again Later!"),
             "ATLWallysVideoStore", MB_OK);
            //*** Release the shared property group ***
            spmGroup->Release();
            //*** release the shared property group manager ***
            spmManager->Release();
         }
        //*** Get the megabit connections value ***
        hr = spmMegabitConnections->get_Value( &vMegabitConnex );
        //*** Signal Error ***
        if (!SUCCEEDED(hr))
         {
             //*** Show Error to User ***
             MessageBox(
                 _T("MTS SPM Currently Off-Line; Please Try Again Later!"),
            "ATLWallysVideoStore", MB_OK);
            //*** Release the shared property ***
            spmMegabitConnections->Release();
            //*** Release the shared property ***
            spmGigabitConnections->Release();
            //*** Release the shared property group ***
            spmGroup->Release();
            //*** release the shared property group manager ***
            spmManager->Release();
         }
        hr = spmGigabitConnections->get_Value( &vGigabitConnex );
```

```
        //*** Signal Error ***
        if (!SUCCEEDED(hr))
         {
              //*** Show Error to User ***
             MessageBox(
              _T("MTS SPM Currently Off-Line; Please Try Again Later!"),
           "ATLWallysVideoStore", MB_OK);
            //*** Release the shared property ***
            spmMegabitConnections->Release();
            //*** Release the shared property ***
            spmGigabitConnections->Release();
            //*** Release the shared property group ***
            spmGroup->Release();
            //*** release the shared property group manager ***
            spmManager->Release();
         }
         //*** if no data then initialized so set it ***
         if (vMegabitConnex.intVal == 0)
         {
               vMegabitConnex.intVal = 100;
               vGigabitConnex.intVal = 2;
               //** send data back to SPM ***
            hr = spmGigabitConnections->put_Value( vGigabitConnex );
            hr = spmMegabitConnections->put_Value( vMegabitConnex );
         }
         //*** set our UI ***
         SetDlgItemInt(IDC_GIGABITCONNEX_EDIT, vGigabitConnex.intVal, FALSE );
         SetDlgItemInt(IDC_MEGABITCONNEX_EDIT, vMegabitConnex.intVal, FALSE );
        //*** Release the shared property ***
        spmMegabitConnections->Release();
        //*** Release the shared property ***
        spmGigabitConnections->Release();
        //*** Release the shared property group ***
        spmGroup->Release();
        //*** release the shared property group manager ***
        spmManager->Release();
    }

    ~CStoreUI()
    {
    }

    enum { IDD = IDD_STOREUI };

BEGIN_MSG_MAP(CStoreUI)
    MESSAGE_HANDLER(WM_INITDIALOG, OnInitDialog)
    COMMAND_HANDLER(IDC_ADDCUST_BUTTON, BN_CLICKED, OnClickedAddcust_button)
```

```
    COMMAND_HANDLER(IDC_ADDVIDEO_BUTTON, BN_CLICKED, OnClickedAddvideo_button)
    COMMAND_HANDLER(IDC_CREATECUSTDB_BUTTON, BN_CLICKED, OnClickedCreatecustdb_button)
    COMMAND_HANDLER(IDC_CREATEVIDEODB_BUTTON, BN_CLICKED,
       OnClickedCreatevideodb_button)
    COMMAND_HANDLER(IDC_GETCUSTINFO_BUTTON, BN_CLICKED, OnClickedGetcustinfo_button)
    COMMAND_HANDLER(IDC_GETVIDEOINFO_BUTTON, BN_CLICKED, OnClickedGetvideoinfo_button)
    COMMAND_HANDLER(IDC_ORDERVIDEO_BUTTON, BN_CLICKED, OnClickedOrdervideo_button)
    COMMAND_HANDLER(IDC_TERMVIDEO_BUTTON, BN_CLICKED, OnClickedTermvideo_button)
    COMMAND_HANDLER(IDC_UPDATECUST_BUTTON, BN_CLICKED, OnClickedUpdatecust_button)
    COMMAND_HANDLER(IDC_UPDATEVIDEOINFO_BUTTON, BN_CLICKED,
       OnClickedUpdatevideoinfo_button)
    COMMAND_HANDLER(IDC_EXIT_BUTTON, BN_CLICKED, OnClickedExit_button)
    MESSAGE_HANDLER(WM_CLOSE, OnClose)
    COMMAND_HANDLER(IDC_DELETECUST_BUTTON, BN_CLICKED, OnClickedDeletecust_button)
    COMMAND_HANDLER(IDC_DELETEVIDEO_BUTTON, BN_CLICKED, OnClickedDeletevideo_button)
    COMMAND_HANDLER(IDC_CHANGEPW_BUTTON2, BN_CLICKED, OnClickedChangepw_button2)
    COMMAND_HANDLER(IDC_RENAMECUST_BUTTON, BN_CLICKED, OnClickedRenamecust_button)
    COMMAND_HANDLER(IDC_RENAMEVIDEO_BUTTON, BN_CLICKED, OnClickedRenamevideo_button)
    COMMAND_HANDLER(IDC_UPDATEVIDEOS_BUTTON, BN_CLICKED, OnClickedUpdatevideos_button)
END_MSG_MAP()
// Handler prototypes:
//  LRESULT MessageHandler(UINT uMsg, WPARAM wParam, LPARAM lParam, BOOL& bHandled);
//  LRESULT CommandHandler(WORD wNotifyCode, WORD wID, HWND hWndCtl, BOOL& bHandled);
//  LRESULT NotifyHandler(int idCtrl, LPNMHDR pnmh, BOOL& bHandled);

    LRESULT OnInitDialog(UINT uMsg, WPARAM wParam, LPARAM lParam, BOOL& bHandled)
    {
        return 1;  // Let the system set the focus
    }

    LRESULT OnClickedAddcust_button(WORD wNotifyCode, WORD wID, HWND hWndCtl,
      BOOL& bHandled)
    {
        // TODO : Add Code for control notification handler.
        //*** define holders for customer data
        CComBSTR ccbstrCustomerName;
        CComBSTR ccbstrCustomerPassword;
        int iCreditLimit;
        int iCurrentCharges;
        bool bOnLine = FALSE;
        //*** get the data from the UI ***
        GetDlgItemText( IDC_CNAME_EDIT, ccbstrCustomerName.m_str );
        GetDlgItemText( IDC_CPW_EDIT, ccbstrCustomerPassword.m_str );
        GetDlgItemInt( IDC_CBILL_EDIT, &iCurrentCharges , FALSE);
        GetDlgItemInt(IDC_CCREDIT_EDIT,&iCreditLimit,FALSE);
         //*** Declare IP for WallysAccounts ***
      IAccountsHandler* pAccounts = NULL;
```

```
        //*** Declare generic HRESULT holder ***
      HRESULT hr = S_OK;
        //*** try to get the IP to the AccountsHandler via MTS ***
      hr = CoCreateInstance( CLSID_AccountsHandler , NULL, CLSCTX_INPROC_SERVER,
                             IID_IAccountsHandler , (void **) pAccounts );
        //*** if bad hresult signal failure and abort call ***
      if (!SUCCEEDED(hr))
        {
          //*** Show Error to User ***
          MessageBox(
               _T("Wally's Currently Off-Line; Please Try Again Later!"),
             "ATLWallysVideoStore", MB_OK);
          return 0;
        }
  //*** Find out if the account exists and if so abort account creation ***
        int iOnLine;
  hr = pAccounts->get_AccountInUse( ccbstrCustomerName.Copy() , &iOnLine );
        if (SUCCEEDED(hr))
        {
          //*** Show Error to User ***
          MessageBox(
              _T("Cannot Add Account: Name already in use!"),
                "ATLWallysVideoStore", MB_OK);
          //*** release the pointer ***
          pAccounts->Release();
           //*** leave ***
          return 0;
        }
        //*** since account didn't exist we can try to create it ***
        hr = pAccounts->CreateAccount( ccbstrCustomerName.Copy(),
           ccbstrCustomerPassword.Copy(), iCreditLimit, iCurrentCharges,bOnLine);
       if (!SUCCEEDED(hr))
        {
          //*** Show Error to User ***
          MessageBox(
              _T("Could Not Create Account; Please Try Again Later!"),
                 "ATLWallysVideoStore", MB_OK);
          //*** release the pointer ***
          pAccounts->Release();
           //*** leave ***
          return 0;
        }
        //*** Release the IP ***
        pAccounts->Release();
         //*** Show Success to User ***
        MessageBox(
            _T("Customer Added!"),"ATLWallysVideoStore", MB_OK);
```

```
      //*** leave ***
        return 0;
  }
  LRESULT OnClickedAddvideo_button(WORD wNotifyCode, WORD wID, HWND hWndCtl,
    BOOL& bHandled)
  {
        // TODO : Add Code for control notification handler.
        CComBSTR ccbstrVideoName;
        int sVideoPrice;
        int sTotalVideos;
        int sAvailableVideos;
        GetDlgItemText( IDC_VNAME_EDIT, ccbstrVideoName.m_str );
        GetDlgItemInt( IDC_VRENTPRICE_EDIT, &sVideoPrice , FALSE);
        GetDlgItemInt(IDC_VTOTCOPIES_EDIT,&sTotalVideos,FALSE);
        GetDlgItemInt(IDC_VAVAILCOPIES_EDIT,&sAvailableVideos,FALSE);
         //*** Declare IP for WallysVideos ***
      IVideosHandler* pVideos = NULL;
         //*** Declare generic HRESULT holder ***
      HRESULT hr = S_OK;
         //*** try to get the IP to the VideoHandler via MTS ***
      hr = CoCreateInstance( CLSID_VideosHandler , NULL, CLSCTX_INPROC_SERVER,
                             IID_IVideosHandler , (void **) pVideos );
         //*** if bad hresult signal failure and abort call ***
      if (!SUCCEEDED(hr))
        {
            //*** Show Error to User ***
           MessageBox(_T("Wally's Currently Off-Line; Please Try Again Later!"),
                              "ATLWallysVideoStore", MB_OK);
           return 0;
        }
        //*** Find out if the video exists ***
        short sVideoPrice2;
        hr = pVideos->get_VideoRentalPrice( ccbstrVideoName.Copy() ,
                        &sVideoPrice2 );
        if (SUCCEEDED(hr))
        {
            //*** Show Error to User ***
           MessageBox(_T("Cannot Add Video: Name already in use!"),
                              "ATLWallysVideoStore", MB_OK);
           //*** release the pointer ***
           pVideos->Release();
            //*** leave ***
           return 0;
        }
        //*** since video didn't exist we can try to create it ***
        hr = pVideos->AddNewVideo(ccbstrVideoName.Copy(),
                                     sVideoPrice,
```

```
                                                sTotalVideos,
                                                sAvailableVideos);
        if (!SUCCEEDED(hr))
         {
             //*** Show Error to User ***
            MessageBox(_T("Could Not Add Video; Please Try Again Later!"),
                                   "ATLWallysVideoStore", MB_OK);
            //*** release the pointer ***
            pVideos->Release();
             //*** leave ***
            return 0;
         }
         //*** Release the IP ***
         pVideos->Release();
          //*** Show Success to User ***
         MessageBox(_T("Video Added!"),"ATLWallysVideoStore", MB_OK);
        //*** leave ***
         return 0;
    }
    LRESULT OnClickedCreatecustdb_button(WORD wNotifyCode, WORD wID, HWND hWndCtl,
       BOOL& bHandled)
    {
         // TODO : Add Code for control notification handler.
          //*** Declare IP for WallysAccounts ***
        IAccountsHandler* pAccounts = NULL;
          //*** Declare generic HRESULT holder ***
        HRESULT hr = S_OK;
          //*** try to get the IP to the AccountsHandler via MTS ***
        hr = CoCreateInstance( CLSID_AccountsHandler , NULL, CLSCTX_INPROC_SERVER,
                               IID_IAccountsHandler , (void **) pAccounts );
          //*** if bad hresult signal failure and abort call ***
        if (!SUCCEEDED(hr))
         {
             //*** Show Error to User ***
            MessageBox(
                 _T("Wally's Currently Off-Line; Please Try Again Later!"),
                 "ATLWallysVideoStore", MB_OK);
            return 0;
         }
         //*** create database ***
         hr = pAccounts->CreateDatabase();
        if (!SUCCEEDED(hr))
         {
             //*** Show Error to User ***
            MessageBox(
               _T("Could Not Create Database; Please Try Again Later!"),
                  "ATLWallysVideoStore", MB_OK);
```

```
            //*** release the pointer ***
            pAccounts->Release();
             //*** leave ***
            return 0;
        }
        //*** Release the IP ***
        pAccounts->Release();
         //*** Show Success to User ***
        MessageBox(_T("Customer Database Created!"),
            "ATLWallysVideoStore", MB_OK);
      //*** leave ***
        return 0;
}
LRESULT OnClickedCreatevideodb_button(WORD wNotifyCode, WORD wID, HWND hWndCtl,
      BOOL& bHandled)
{
        // TODO : Add Code for control notification handler.
         //*** Declare IP for WallysVideos ***
      IVideosHandler* pVideos = NULL;
         //*** Declare generic HRESULT holder ***
      HRESULT hr = S_OK;
         //*** try to get the IP to the VideoHandler via MTS ***
      hr = CoCreateInstance( CLSID_VideosHandler , NULL, CLSCTX_INPROC_SERVER,
                           IID_IVideosHandler , (void **) pVideos );
         //*** if bad hresult signal failure and abort call ***
      if (!SUCCEEDED(hr))
        {
             //*** Show Error to User ***
            MessageBox(_T("Wally's Currently Off-Line; Please Try Again Later!"),
                                   "ATLWallysVideoStore", MB_OK);
            return 0;
        }
        //*** Create the database ***
        hr = pVideos->CreateDatabase();
      if (!SUCCEEDED(hr))
        {
             //*** Show Error to User ***
            MessageBox(_T("Could Not Create Database; Please Try Again Later!"),
                                   "ATLWallysVideoStore", MB_OK);
            //*** release the pointer ***
            pVideos->Release();
             //*** leave ***
            return 0;
        }
        //*** Release the IP ***
        pVideos->Release();
         //*** Show Success to User ***
```

```
        MessageBox(_T("Video Database Created!"),"ATLWallysVideoStore", MB_OK);
      //*** leave ***
        return 0;
  }
  LRESULT OnClickedGetcustinfo_button(WORD wNotifyCode, WORD wID, HWND hWndCtl,
      BOOL& bHandled)
  {
        // TODO : Add Code for control notification handler.
        //*** bring in string macros ***
        USES_CONVERSION;
        //*** define holders for customer data
        CComBSTR ccbstrCustomerName;
        CComBSTR ccbstrCustomerPassword;
        CComBSTR ccbstrCustomerOnline;
        long lCreditLimit;
        long lCurrentCharges;
        BOOL bOnLine;
        //*** get the customer name ***
        GetDlgItemText( IDC_CNAME_EDIT, ccbstrCustomerName.m_str );
         //*** Declare IP for WallysAccounts ***
      IAccountsHandler* pAccounts = NULL;
         //*** Declare generic HRESULT holder ***
      HRESULT hr = S_OK;
         //*** try to get the IP to the AccountsHandler via MTS ***
      hr = CoCreateInstance( CLSID_AccountsHandler , NULL, CLSCTX_INPROC_SERVER,
                              IID_IAccountsHandler , (void **) pAccounts );
         //*** if bad hresult signal failure and abort call ***
      if (!SUCCEEDED(hr))
        {
            //*** Show Error to User ***
           MessageBox(
               _T("Wally's Currently Off-Line; Please Try Again Later!"),
                 "ATLWallysVideoStore", MB_OK);
           return 0;
        }
        //*** get account info except for password ***
        hr = pAccounts->get_AccountCreditLimit(
               ccbstrCustomerName.Copy(), &lCreditLimit );
        hr = pAccounts->get_AccountCurrentCharges(
               ccbstrCustomerName.Copy(), &lCurrentCharges );
        hr = pAccounts->get_AccountInUse(
               ccbstrCustomerName.Copy(), &bOnLine );
      if (!SUCCEEDED(hr))
        {
            //*** Show Error to User ***
           MessageBox(
               _T("Could Not Obtain Account; Please Try Again Later!"),
```

```
                    "ATLWallysVideoStore", MB_OK);
            //*** release the pointer ***
            pAccounts->Release();
             //*** leave ***
            return 0;
        }
        //*** data conversions ***
        int iCurrentCharges = (int) lCurrentCharges;
        int iCreditLimit = (int) lCreditLimit;
        //*** set the data from the UI ***
        SetDlgItemInt( IDC_CBILL_EDIT, iCurrentCharges , FALSE);
        SetDlgItemInt(IDC_CCREDIT_EDIT,iCreditLimit,FALSE);
        //*** do the text display of boolean ***
        if (bOnLine)
        {
              ccbstrCustomerOnline = _T("Yes");
            SetDlgItemText( IDC_CONLINE_EDIT,
               OLE2T(ccbstrCustomerOnline.m_str));
        }
        else
        {
              ccbstrCustomerOnline = _T("No");
            SetDlgItemText( IDC_CONLINE_EDIT,
              OLE2T(ccbstrCustomerOnline.m_str));
        }
        //*** Release the IP ***
        pAccounts->Release();
         //*** Show Success to User ***
        MessageBox(_T("Account Info Acquired!"),"ATLWallysVideoStore", MB_OK);
       //*** leave ***
        return 0;
    }
    LRESULT OnClickedGetvideoinfo_button(WORD wNotifyCode, WORD wID, HWND hWndCtl,
      BOOL& bHandled)
    {
        // TODO : Add Code for control notification handler.
        //*** bring in macros ***
        USES_CONVERSION;//*** define vars to get info
        CComBSTR ccbstrVideoName;
        short sVideoPrice;
        short sTotalVideos;
        short sAvailableVideos;
        //*** get the video name ***
        GetDlgItemText( IDC_VNAME_EDIT, ccbstrVideoName.m_str );
         //*** Declare IP for WallysVideos ***
       IVideosHandler* pVideos = NULL;
         //*** Declare generic HRESULT holder ***
```

```
        HRESULT hr = S_OK;
          //*** try to get the IP to the VideoHandler via MTS ***
        hr = CoCreateInstance( CLSID_VideosHandler , NULL, CLSCTX_INPROC_SERVER,
                               IID_IVideosHandler , (void **) pVideos );
          //*** if bad hresult signal failure and abort call ***
        if (!SUCCEEDED(hr))
         {
            //*** Show Error to User ***
           MessageBox(_T("Wally's Currently Off-Line; Please Try Again Later!"),
                              "ATLWallysVideoStore", MB_OK);
           return 0;
         }
         //*** get video data ***
         hr = pVideos->get_VideoRentalPrice( ccbstrVideoName.Copy() ,
                     &sVideoPrice );
         hr = pVideos->get_VideoTotalCopies( ccbstrVideoName.Copy() ,
                     &sTotalVideos );
         hr = pVideos->get_VideoAvailableCopies( ccbstrVideoName.Copy() ,
                     &sAvailableVideos );
        if (!SUCCEEDED(hr))
         {
            //*** Show Error to User ***
           MessageBox(_T("Could Not Obtain Video; Please Try Again Later!"),
                              "ATLWallysVideoStore", MB_OK);
           //*** release the pointer ***
           pVideos->Release();
            //*** leave ***
           return 0;
         }
         //*** display the info ***
         SetDlgItemInt( IDC_VRENTPRICE_EDIT, sVideoPrice , FALSE);
         SetDlgItemInt(IDC_VTOTCOPIES_EDIT , sTotalVideos,FALSE);
         SetDlgItemInt(IDC_VAVAILCOPIES_EDIT, sAvailableVideos,FALSE);
         //*** Release the IP ***
         pVideos->Release();
          //*** Show Success to User ***
         MessageBox(_T("Video Info Acquired!"),"ATLWallysVideoStore", MB_OK);
        //*** leave ***
         return 0;
    }
    LRESULT OnClickedOrdervideo_button(WORD wNotifyCode, WORD wID, HWND hWndCtl,
        BOOL& bHandled)
    {
         // TODO : Add Code for control notification handler.
         //*** OLE2T Macro ***
         USES_CONVERSION;
         CComVariant varResult;
```

```
         BOOL bUseMegabit = TRUE;
        //*** Define the HRESULT holder and set default value ***
        HRESULT hr = S_OK;
         /* uncomment to turn on shared property support
        //*** Define shared property group manager IP ***
        ISharedPropertyGroupManager* spmManager = NULL;
        //*** Define shared property group IP ***
        ISharedPropertyGroup* spmGroup = NULL;
        //*** Define shared property IP for next receipt ***
        ISharedProperty* spmMegabitConnections = NULL;
        //*** Define shared property IP for max receipts ***
        ISharedProperty* spmGigabitConnections = NULL;
        //*** define variant for value of next receipt ***
        CComVariant vMegabitConnex;
        //*** define variant for value of max receipts ***
        CComVariant vGigabitConnex;
        //*** start out getting the SPG manager from MTS ***
        hr = CoCreateInstance(CLSID_SharedPropertyGroupManager, NULL, CLSCTX_ALL,
                IID_ISharedPropertyGroupManager, (void**) &spmManager );
        if (!SUCCEEDED(hr))
         {
             //*** Show Error to User ***
            MessageBox(
              _T("MTS SPM Currently Off-Line; Please Try Again Later!"),
                                "ATLWallysVideoStore", MB_OK);
            //*** release the shared property group manager ***
           spmManager->Release();
         }
        //*** define and set isolation mode ***
        LONG lIsolationMode = LockMethod;
        //*** define and set release mode ***
        LONG lReleaseMode = Process;
        //*** define and set existence variable ***
        VARIANT_BOOL bExists = VARIANT_FALSE;
        //*** define BSTR holder for shared property name values ***
        CComBSTR ccbstrPropertyNames;
        //*** start out with WALLYSCONNECTIONS property group ***
        ccbstrPropertyNames = _T("WallysConnections");
        //*** attemt to create or obtain the property group WALLYSCONNECTIONS ***
        hr = spmManager->CreatePropertyGroup(ccbstrPropertyNames.Copy(),
             &lIsolationMode, &lReleaseMode, &bExists, &spmGroup );
        if (!SUCCEEDED(hr))
         {
             //*** Show Error to User ***
            MessageBox(
              _T("MTS SPM Currently Off-Line; Please Try Again Later!"),
                                "ATLWallysVideoStore", MB_OK);
```

```
            //*** release the shared property group manager ***
           spmManager->Release();
        }
       //*** Define the string for the megabit connections ***
       ccbstrPropertyNames = _T("MegabitConnections");
       //*** Create of obtain the megabitconnections shared property ***
         hr = spmGroup->CreateProperty( ccbstrPropertyNames.Copy(),
               &bExists,&spmMegabitConnections);
       //*** Signal Error ***
       if (!SUCCEEDED(hr))
        {
            //*** Show Error to User ***
            MessageBox(
                _T("MTS SPM Currently Off-Line; Please Try Again Later!"),
                                  "ATLWallysVideoStore", MB_OK);
           //*** Release the shared property group ***
           spmGroup->Release();
           //*** release the shared property group manager ***
           spmManager->Release();
        }
       //*** Define the string for the gigabit connections ***
       ccbstrPropertyNames = _T("GigabitConnections");
       //*** Create or obtain the gigabitconnections shared property ***
         hr = spmGroup->CreateProperty( ccbstrPropertyNames.Copy(),
              &bExists,&spmGigabitConnections);
       //*** Signal Error ***
       if (!SUCCEEDED(hr))
        {
            //*** Show Error to User ***
            MessageBox(
               _T("MTS SPM Currently Off-Line; Please Try Again Later!"),
                                  "ATLWallysVideoStore", MB_OK);
           //*** Release the shared property group ***
           spmGroup->Release();
           //*** release the shared property group manager ***
           spmManager->Release();
        }
       //*** Get the megabit connections value ***
       hr = spmMegabitConnections->get_Value( &vMegabitConnex );
       //*** Signal Error ***
       if (!SUCCEEDED(hr))
        {
            //*** Show Error to User ***
            MessageBox(
           _T("MTS SPM Currently Off-Line; Please Try Again Later!"),
                                  "ATLWallysVideoStore", MB_OK);
           //*** Release the shared property ***
```

```
            spmMegabitConnections->Release();
            //*** Release the shared property ***
            spmGigabitConnections->Release();
            //*** Release the shared property group ***
            spmGroup->Release();
            //*** release the shared property group manager ***
            spmManager->Release();
         }
        hr = spmGigabitConnections->get_Value( &vGigabitConnex );
        //*** Signal Error ***
        if (!SUCCEEDED(hr))
         {
             //*** Show Error to User ***
             MessageBox(
               _T("MTS SPM Currently Off-Line; Please Try Again Later!"),
                                  "ATLWallysVideoStore", MB_OK);
            //*** Release the shared property ***
            spmMegabitConnections->Release();
            //*** Release the shared property ***
            spmGigabitConnections->Release();
            //*** Release the shared property group ***
            spmGroup->Release();
            //*** release the shared property group manager ***
            spmManager->Release();
         }
         //*** if no data then uninitialized (should never happen) ***
         if (vMegabitConnex.intVal == 0)
         {
              vMegabitConnex.intVal = 100;
              vGigabitConnex.intVal = 2;
         }
         else
         {
              if (vGigabitConnex.intVal == 0)
              {
                   bUseMegabit = TRUE;
                   vMegabitConnex.intVal-;
              }
              else
              {
                   bUseMegabit = FALSE;
                   vGigabitConnex.intVal-;
              }
         }
         //*** put in the changed shared property values ***
        hr = spmGigabitConnections->put_Value( vGigabitConnex );
        hr = spmMegabitConnections->put_Value( vMegabitConnex );
```

```
        //*** Set the display UI ***
        SetDlgItemInt(IDC_GIGABITCONNEX_EDIT, vGigabitConnex.intVal, FALSE );
        SetDlgItemInt(IDC_MEGABITCONNEX_EDIT, vMegabitConnex.intVal, FALSE );
       //*** Release the shared property ***
       spmMegabitConnections->Release();
       //*** Release the shared property ***
       spmGigabitConnections->Release();
       //*** Release the shared property group ***
       spmGroup->Release();
       //*** release the shared property group manager ***
       spmManager->Release();
        remove to turn on shared property support */
        //*** Get the ordering info ***
        CComBSTR bstrCustomerName;
        CComBSTR bstrCustomerPassword;
        CComBSTR bstrVideoName;
        GetDlgItemText( IDC_CNAME_EDIT, bstrCustomerName.m_str );
        GetDlgItemText( IDC_CPW_EDIT, bstrCustomerPassword.m_str );
        long lSelIndex = SendDlgItemMessage( IDC_VIDEOLIST, LB_GETCURSEL,0,0);
        SendDlgItemMessage(IDC_VIDEOLIST,LB_GETTEXT,lSelIndex,
            (LONG)OLE2T(bstrVideoName.m_str));
        //*** Declare IP for WallysAccounts ***
       IOnlineVideoManager* pManager = NULL;
        //*** Declare generic HRESULT holder ***
       hr = S_OK;
        //*** try to get the IP to the AccountsHandler via MTS ***
       hr = CoCreateInstance( CLSID_OnlineVideoManager ,
                              NULL, CLSCTX_INPROC_SERVER,
                             IID_IOnlineVideoManager , (void **) pManager );
        //*** if bad hresult signal failure and abort call ***
       if (!SUCCEEDED(hr))
        {
           //*** Show Error to User ***
          MessageBox(_T("Wally's Currently Off-Line; Please Try Again Later!"),
                              "ATLWallysVideoStore", MB_OK);
          return 0;
        }
        //*** set up the properties with the info from our UI ***
        hr = pManager->put_CustomerName( bstrCustomerName );
        hr = pManager->put_CustomerPassword( bstrCustomerPassword );
        hr = pManager->put_VideoName( bstrVideoName );
        //*** call the order method ***
        hr = pManager->OrderVideo();
        //*** obtain the result from the component ***
        CComBSTR ccbstrOutputMsg;
        hr = pManager->get_CustomerName( &ccbstrOutputMsg.m_str );
        //*** display it ***
```

```
        MessageBox( OLE2T( ccbstrOutputMsg ),"ATLWallysVideoStore",MB_OK);
        //*** release the component ***
        pManager->Release();
        //*** say we're okay either way cause we are! ***
        return 0;
    }
    LRESULT OnClickedTermvideo_button(WORD wNotifyCode, WORD wID, HWND hWndCtl,
       BOOL& bHandled)
    {
        // TODO : Add Code for event handler.
         //*** Declare IP for WallysVideos ***
       IVideosHandler* pVideos = NULL;
         //*** Declare generic HRESULT holder ***
       HRESULT hr = S_OK;
         //*** try to get the IP to the VideoHandler via MTS ***
       hr = CoCreateInstance( CLSID_VideosHandler ,
                               NULL, CLSCTX_INPROC_SERVER,
                              IID_IVideosHandler , (void **) pVideos );
         //*** if bad hresult signal failure and abort call ***
       if (!SUCCEEDED(hr))
        {
           //*** Show Error to User ***
          MessageBox(_T("Wally's Currently Off-Line; Please Try Again Later!"),
                               "ATLWallysVideoStore", MB_OK);
          return 0;
        }
         //*** Declare IP for WallysAccounts ***
       IAccountsHandler* pAccounts = NULL;
         //*** Declare generic HRESULT holder ***
       hr = S_OK;
         //*** try to get the IP to the AccountsHandler via MTS ***
       hr = CoCreateInstance( CLSID_AccountsHandler ,
                               NULL, CLSCTX_INPROC_SERVER,
                              IID_IAccountsHandler , (void **) pAccounts );
         //*** if bad hresult signal failure and abort call ***
       if (!SUCCEEDED(hr))
        {
           //*** Show Error to User ***
          MessageBox(_T("Wally's Currently Off-Line; Please Try Again Later!"),
                               "ATLWallysVideoStore", MB_OK);
          return 0;
        }
         //*** declare vars for data holding ***
         CComBSTR bstrCustomerName;
         CComBSTR bstrVideoName;
         //*** get customer and video names ***
         GetDlgItemText( IDC_CNAME_EDIT, bstrCustomerName.m_str );
```

```
        GetDlgItemText( IDC_VNAME_EDIT, bstrVideoName.m_str );
        //*** declare avail copies var and fill it ***
        short sAvailableCopies;
        hr = pVideos->get_VideoAvailableCopies( bstrVideoName.Copy() ,
                                &sAvailableCopies );
        //*** bump it up by one ***
        sAvailableCopies++;
        //*** update the db ***
        hr = pVideos->UpdateVideoEntryAvailableCopies(bstrVideoName.Copy(),
                           sAvailableCopies);
        //*** handle failure ***
       if (!SUCCEEDED(hr))
        {
            //*** Show Error to User ***
           MessageBox(
               _T("Unable to terminate video playback; Please Try Again Later!"),
                                "ATLWallysVideoStore", MB_OK);
           //*** release the pointer ***
           pVideos->Release();
            //*** leave ***
           return 0;
        }
        //*** update customer not online ***
        BOOL bOnLine = FALSE;
        hr = pAccounts->UpdateAccountInUse(bstrCustomerName.Copy(),bOnLine);
        //*** handle failure ***
       if (!SUCCEEDED(hr))
        {
                //*** Show Error to User ***
                MessageBox(
                 _T("Unable to terminate video playback; Please Try Again Later!"),
                                "ATLWallysVideoStore", MB_OK);
                //*** release the pointer ***
                 pAccounts->Release();
                //*** leave ***
                return 0;
        }
        //*** Release the IPs ***
        pVideos->Release();
        pAccounts->Release();
        //*** Show Success to User ***
        MessageBox(
           _T("Video Playback Terminated! Wallys thanks you for your business!"),
                         "ATLWallysVideoStore", MB_OK);
        return 0;
    }
    LRESULT OnClickedUpdatecust_button(WORD wNotifyCode, WORD wID, HWND hWndCtl,
```

```
    BOOL& bHandled)
{
    // TODO : Add Code for control notification handler.
    //*** define holders for customer data
    CComBSTR ccbstrCustomerName;
    CComBSTR ccbstrCustomerPassword;
    CComBSTR ccbstrCustomerOnline;
    long lCreditLimit;
    long lCurrentCharges;
    int iCreditLimit;
    int iCurrentCharges;
    BOOL bOnLine;
    //*** get the customer info for update ***
    GetDlgItemText( IDC_CNAME_EDIT, ccbstrCustomerName.m_str );
    GetDlgItemText( IDC_CPW_EDIT, ccbstrCustomerPassword.m_str );
    GetDlgItemText( IDC_CONLINE_EDIT, ccbstrCustomerOnline.m_str );
    //*** convert string to boolean ***
    if (ccbstrCustomerOnline == "Yes")
    {
        bOnLine = TRUE;
    }
    else
    {
        bOnLine = FALSE;
    }
    GetDlgItemInt( IDC_CBILL_EDIT, &iCurrentCharges , FALSE);
    GetDlgItemInt(IDC_CCREDIT_EDIT,&iCreditLimit,FALSE);
    //*** convert short to long ***
    lCreditLimit = iCreditLimit;
    lCurrentCharges = iCurrentCharges;
    //*** Declare IP for WallysAccounts ***
    IAccountsHandler* pAccounts = NULL;
    //*** Declare generic HRESULT holder ***
    HRESULT hr = S_OK;
    //*** try to get the IP to the AccountsHandler via MTS ***
    hr = CoCreateInstance( CLSID_AccountsHandler , NULL, CLSCTX_INPROC_SERVER,
                           IID_IAccountsHandler , (void **) pAccounts );
    //*** if bad hresult signal failure and abort call ***
    if (!SUCCEEDED(hr))
    {
        //*** Show Error to User ***
        MessageBox(
            _T("Wally's Currently Off-Line; Please Try Again Later!"),
            "ATLWallysVideoStore", MB_OK);
        return 0;
    }
    //*** update account info except for password and name ***
```

```
        hr = pAccounts->UpdateAccountCredit( ccbstrCustomerName.Copy(),
                lCreditLimit );
        hr = pAccounts->UpdateAccountCharges( ccbstrCustomerName.Copy(),
                lCurrentCharges );
        hr = pAccounts->UpdateAccountInUse( ccbstrCustomerName.Copy(),
                bOnLine );
      if (!SUCCEEDED(hr))
        {
            //*** Show Error to User ***
            MessageBox(
               _T("Could Not Update Account; Please Try Again Later!"),
                 "ATLWallysVideoStore", MB_OK);
            //*** release the pointer ***
            pAccounts->Release();
            //*** leave ***
            return 0;
        }
        //*** Release the IP ***
        pAccounts->Release();
        //*** Show Success to User ***
        MessageBox(_T("Account Updated!"),"ATLWallysVideoStore", MB_OK);
      //*** leave ***
        return 0;
}
LRESULT OnClickedUpdatevideoinfo_button(WORD wNotifyCode, WORD wID, HWND hWndCtl,
   BOOL& bHandled)
{
        // TODO : Add Code for control notification handler.
        //*** declare variables for video data
        CComBSTR ccbstrVideoName;
        int sVideoPrice;
        int sTotalVideos;
        int sAvailableVideos;
        //*** get data from the UI ***
        GetDlgItemText( IDC_VNAME_EDIT, ccbstrVideoName.m_str );
        GetDlgItemInt( IDC_VRENTPRICE_EDIT, &sVideoPrice , FALSE);
        GetDlgItemInt(IDC_VTOTCOPIES_EDIT,&sTotalVideos,FALSE);
        GetDlgItemInt(IDC_VAVAILCOPIES_EDIT,&sAvailableVideos,FALSE);
        //*** Declare IP for WallysVideos ***
      IVideosHandler* pVideos = NULL;
        //*** Declare generic HRESULT holder ***
      HRESULT hr = S_OK;
        //*** try to get the IP to the VideoHandler via MTS ***
      hr = CoCreateInstance( CLSID_VideosHandler , NULL, CLSCTX_INPROC_SERVER,
                              IID_IVideosHandler , (void **) pVideos );
        //*** if bad hresult signal failure and abort call ***
      if (!SUCCEEDED(hr))
```

```
        {
            //*** Show Error to User ***
            MessageBox(_T("Wally's Currently Off-Line; Please Try Again Later!"),
                                "ATLWallysVideoStore", MB_OK);
            return 0;
        }
        //*** update video information except name ***
        hr = pVideos->UpdateVideoEntryPrice(ccbstrVideoName.Copy(),
                                sVideoPrice);
        hr = pVideos->UpdateVideoEntryTotalCopies(ccbstrVideoName.Copy(),
                                sTotalVideos);
        hr = pVideos->UpdateVideoEntryAvailableCopies(ccbstrVideoName.Copy(),
                                sAvailableVideos);
        //*** handle failures ***
       if (!SUCCEEDED(hr))
        {
            //*** Show Error to User ***
            MessageBox(_T("Could Not Update Video; Please Try Again Later!"),
                                "ATLWallysVideoStore", MB_OK);
            //*** release the pointer ***
            pVideos->Release();
            //*** leave ***
            return 0;
        }
        //*** Release the IP ***
        pVideos->Release();
        //*** Show Success to User ***
        MessageBox(_T("Video Updated!"),"ATLWallysVideoStore", MB_OK);
       //*** leave ***
        return 0;
    }
    LRESULT OnClickedExit_button(WORD wNotifyCode, WORD wID, HWND hWndCtl,
            BOOL& bHandled)
    {
        // TODO : Add Code for control notification handler.
        //*** tell application to close ***
        PostQuitMessage(0);
        //*** do this to shut down the window correctly ***
        DestroyWindow();
        //*** be nice ***
        return 0;
    }
    LRESULT OnClose(UINT uMsg, WPARAM wParam, LPARAM lParam, BOOL& bHandled)
    {
        // TODO : Add Code for message handler. Call DefWindowProc if necessary.
        //*** tell application to close ***
        PostQuitMessage(0);
```

```
        //*** do this to shut down the window correctly ***
        DestroyWindow();
        //*** be nice ***
        return 0;
}
LRESULT OnClickedDeletecust_button(WORD wNotifyCode, WORD wID, HWND hWndCtl,
    BOOL& bHandled)
{
        // TODO : Add Code for control notification handler.
        //*** define vars to hold data ***
        CComBSTR ccbstrCustomerName;
        CComBSTR ccbstrCustomerPassword;
        GetDlgItemText( IDC_CNAME_EDIT, ccbstrCustomerName.m_str );
        GetDlgItemText( IDC_CPW_EDIT, ccbstrCustomerPassword.m_str );
         //*** Declare IP for WallysAccounts ***
       IAccountsHandler* pAccounts = NULL;
         //*** Declare generic HRESULT holder ***
       HRESULT hr = S_OK;
         //*** try to get the IP to the AccountsHandler via MTS ***
       hr = CoCreateInstance( CLSID_AccountsHandler , NULL, CLSCTX_INPROC_SERVER,
                              IID_IAccountsHandler , (void **) pAccounts );
         //*** if bad hresult signal failure and abort call ***
       if (!SUCCEEDED(hr))
        {
            //*** Show Error to User ***
           MessageBox(
               _T("Wally's Currently Off-Line; Please Try Again Later!"),
                "ATLWallysVideoStore", MB_OK);
           return 0;
        }
        //*** Find out if the account password matches
            //*** and if not abort account change ***
        CComBSTR ccbstrRealPassword;
        hr = pAccounts->get_AccountPassword( ccbstrCustomerName.Copy() ,
               &ccbstrRealPassword.m_str );
          //*** if bad hresult signal failure and abort call ***
       if (!SUCCEEDED(hr))
        {
             //*** Show Error to User ***
           MessageBox(_T("Wally's Currently Off-Line; Please Try Again Later!"),
               "ATLWallysVideoStore", MB_OK);
           return 0;
        }
        if (ccbstrCustomerPassword != ccbstrRealPassword)
        {
             //*** Show Error to User ***
           MessageBox(_T("Cannot Change Account: Password Faiure!"),
```

```
                "ATLWallysVideoStore", MB_OK);
            //*** release the pointer ***
            pAccounts->Release();
              //*** leave ***
            return 0;
        }
        //*** do the deletion ***
        hr = pAccounts->DeleteAccount( ccbstrCustomerName.Copy(),
               ccbstrCustomerPassword.Copy());
      if (!SUCCEEDED(hr))
        {
              //*** Show Error to User ***
            MessageBox(
            _T("Unable to delete account; Please Try Again Later!"),
               "ATLWallysVideoStore", MB_OK);
            //*** release the pointer ***
            pAccounts->Release();
              //*** leave ***
            return 0;
        }
        //*** Release the IP ***
        pAccounts->Release();
          //*** Show Success to User ***
        MessageBox(_T("Customer Deleted!"),"ATLWallysVideoStore", MB_OK);
      //*** leave ***
        return 0;
}
LRESULT OnClickedDeletevideo_button(WORD wNotifyCode, WORD wID, HWND hWndCtl,
     BOOL& bHandled)
{
        // TODO : Add Code for control notification handler.
        CComBSTR ccbstrVideoName;
        GetDlgItemText( IDC_VNAME_EDIT, ccbstrVideoName.m_str );
          //*** Declare IP for WallysVideos ***
      IVideosHandler* pVideos = NULL;
          //*** Declare generic HRESULT holder ***
      HRESULT hr = S_OK;
          //*** try to get the IP to the VideoHandler via MTS ***
      hr = CoCreateInstance( CLSID_VideosHandler ,
                              NULL, CLSCTX_INPROC_SERVER,
                            IID_IVideosHandler , (void **) pVideos );
          //*** if bad hresult signal failure and abort call ***
      if (!SUCCEEDED(hr))
        {
              //*** Show Error to User ***
            MessageBox(_T("Wally's Currently Off-Line; Please Try Again Later!"),
                              "ATLWallysVideoStore", MB_OK);
```

```
            return 0;
        }
        //*** Find out if the video exists ***
        short sVideoPrice2;
        hr = pVideos->get_VideoRentalPrice( ccbstrVideoName.Copy() ,
                                &sVideoPrice2 );
        if (!SUCCEEDED(hr))
        {
              //*** Show Error to User ***
            MessageBox(_T("Cannot Delete Video: Name not in database!"),
                                    "ATLWallysVideoStore", MB_OK);
            //*** release the pointer ***
            pVideos->Release();
              //*** leave ***
            return 0;
        }
        //*** since video exists we can try to delete it ***
        hr = pVideos->DeleteVideo(ccbstrVideoName.Copy());
      if (!SUCCEEDED(hr))
        {
              //*** Show Error to User ***
            MessageBox(_T("Could Not Delete Video; Please Try Again Later!"),
                                    "ATLWallysVideoStore", MB_OK);
            //*** release the pointer ***
            pVideos->Release();
              //*** leave ***
            return 0;
        }
        //*** Release the IP ***
        pVideos->Release();
          //*** Show Success to User ***
        MessageBox(_T("Video Deleted!"),"ATLWallysVideoStore", MB_OK);
      //*** leave ***
        return 0;
}
LRESULT OnClickedChangepw_button2(WORD wNotifyCode, WORD wID, HWND hWndCtl,
      BOOL& bHandled)
{
        // TODO : Add Code for control notification handler.
        //*** define vars to hold data ***
        CComBSTR ccbstrCustomerName;
        CComBSTR ccbstrCustomerPassword;
        CComBSTR ccbstrCustomerNewPassword;
        GetDlgItemText( IDC_CNAME_EDIT, ccbstrCustomerName.m_str );
        GetDlgItemText( IDC_CPW_EDIT, ccbstrCustomerPassword.m_str );
        GetDlgItemText( IDC_NEWNAME_EDIT, ccbstrCustomerNewPassword.m_str );
          //*** Declare IP for WallysAccounts ***
```

```
    IAccountsHandler* pAccounts = NULL;
      //*** Declare generic HRESULT holder ***
    HRESULT hr = S_OK;
      //*** try to get the IP to the AccountsHandler via MTS ***
    hr = CoCreateInstance( CLSID_AccountsHandler , NULL, CLSCTX_INPROC_SERVER,
                           IID_IAccountsHandler , (void **) pAccounts );
      //*** if bad hresult signal failure and abort call ***
    if (!SUCCEEDED(hr))
     {
        //*** Show Error to User ***
       MessageBox(
           _T("Wally's Currently Off-Line; Please Try Again Later!"),
             "ATLWallysVideoStore", MB_OK);
       return 0;
     }
     //*** do the password change ***
     hr = pAccounts->UdpateAccountPassword( ccbstrCustomerName.Copy(),
         ccbstrCustomerPassword.Copy(), ccbstrCustomerNewPassword.Copy() );
     //*** handle failure ***
    if (!SUCCEEDED(hr))
     {
        //*** Show Error to User ***
       MessageBox(
  _T("Unable to change password; Please check old password and try Again!"),
     "ATLWallysVideoStore", MB_OK);
       //*** release the pointer ***
       pAccounts->Release();
         //*** leave ***
       return 0;
     }
     //*** Release the IP ***
     pAccounts->Release();
       //*** Show Success to User ***
     MessageBox(
        _T("Customer Password changed!"),"ATLWallysVideoStore", MB_OK);
    //*** leave ***
     return 0;
}
LRESULT OnClickedRenamecust_button(WORD wNotifyCode, WORD wID, HWND hWndCtl,
  BOOL& bHandled)
{
     // TODO : Add Code for control notification handler.
     //*** define vars to hold data ***
     CComBSTR ccbstrCustomerName;
     CComBSTR ccbstrCustomerPassword;
     CComBSTR ccbstrCustomerNewName;
     GetDlgItemText( IDC_NEWNAME_EDIT, ccbstrCustomerNewName.m_str );
```

```
    GetDlgItemText( IDC_CNAME_EDIT, ccbstrCustomerName.m_str );
    GetDlgItemText( IDC_CPW_EDIT, ccbstrCustomerPassword.m_str );
     //*** Declare IP for WallysAccounts ***
   IAccountsHandler* pAccounts = NULL;
     //*** Declare generic HRESULT holder ***
   HRESULT hr = S_OK;
     //*** try to get the IP to the AccountsHandler via MTS ***
   hr = CoCreateInstance( CLSID_AccountsHandler , NULL, CLSCTX_INPROC_SERVER,
                          IID_IAccountsHandler , (void **) pAccounts );
     //*** if bad hresult signal failure and abort call ***
   if (!SUCCEEDED(hr))
    {
        //*** Show Error to User ***
      MessageBox(
        _T("Wally's Currently Off-Line; Please Try Again Later!"),
          "ATLWallysVideoStore", MB_OK);
      return 0;
    }
    //*** do password verification ***
    CComBSTR ccbstrRealPassword;
    hr = pAccounts->get_AccountPassword( ccbstrCustomerName.Copy() ,
         &ccbstrRealPassword.m_str );
     //*** if bad hresult signal failure and abort call ***
   if (!SUCCEEDED(hr))
    {
        //*** Show Error to User ***
      MessageBox(
          _T("Wally's Currently Off-Line; Please Try Again Later!"),
          "ATLWallysVideoStore", MB_OK);
      return 0;
    }
    if (ccbstrCustomerPassword != ccbstrRealPassword)
    {
        //*** Show Error to User ***
      MessageBox(
          _T("Cannot Change Account: Password Faiure!"),
            "ATLWallysVideoStore", MB_OK);
      //*** release the pointer ***
      pAccounts->Release();
        //*** leave ***
      return 0;
    }
    //*** do the password change ***
    hr = pAccounts->UpdateAccountName( ccbstrCustomerName.Copy(),
            ccbstrCustomerNewName.Copy() );
    //*** handle failure ***
   if (!SUCCEEDED(hr))
```

```
        {
            //*** Show Error to User ***
          MessageBox(
              _T("Unable to change account name; Please try again later!"),
               "ATLWallysVideoStore", MB_OK);
          //*** release the pointer ***
          pAccounts->Release();
            //*** leave ***
          return 0;
        }
        //*** Release the IP ***
        pAccounts->Release();
          //*** Show Success to User ***
        MessageBox(_T("Customer Name changed!"),"ATLWallysVideoStore", MB_OK);
      //*** leave ***
        return 0;
}
LRESULT OnClickedRenamevideo_button(WORD wNotifyCode, WORD wID, HWND hWndCtl,
    BOOL& bHandled)
{
        // TODO : Add Code for control notification handler.
        CComBSTR ccbstrVideoName;
        CComBSTR ccbstrVideoNewName;
        GetDlgItemText( IDC_NEWNAME_EDIT, ccbstrVideoNewName.m_str );
        GetDlgItemText( IDC_VNAME_EDIT, ccbstrVideoName.m_str );
          //*** Declare IP for WallysVideos ***
      IVideosHandler* pVideos = NULL;
          //*** Declare generic HRESULT holder ***
      HRESULT hr = S_OK;
          //*** try to get the IP to the VideoHandler via MTS ***
      hr = CoCreateInstance( CLSID_VideosHandler ,
                                  NULL, CLSCTX_INPROC_SERVER,
                                IID_IVideosHandler , (void **) pVideos );
          //*** if bad hresult signal failure and abort call ***
      if (!SUCCEEDED(hr))
        {
            //*** Show Error to User ***
          MessageBox(_T("Wally's Currently Off-Line; Please Try Again Later!"),
                                  "ATLWallysVideoStore", MB_OK);
          return 0;
        }
        //*** Find out if the video exists ***
        short sVideoPrice2;
        hr = pVideos->get_VideoRentalPrice( ccbstrVideoName.Copy() ,
                         &sVideoPrice2 );
        if (!SUCCEEDED(hr))
        {
```

```
            //*** Show Error to User ***
          MessageBox(_T("Cannot Rename Video: Name not in database!"),
                              "ATLWallysVideoStore", MB_OK);
          //*** release the pointer ***
          pVideos->Release();
            //*** leave ***
          return 0;
      }
      //*** since video exists we can try to rename it ***
      hr = pVideos->UpdateVideoEntryName(ccbstrVideoName.Copy(),
           ccbstrVideoNewName.Copy());
     if (!SUCCEEDED(hr))
      {
            //*** Show Error to User ***
          MessageBox(_T("Could Not Rename Video; Please Try Again Later!"),
                              "ATLWallysVideoStore", MB_OK);
          //*** release the pointer ***
          pVideos->Release();
            //*** leave ***
          return 0;
      }
      //*** Release the IP ***
      pVideos->Release();
        //*** Show Success to User ***
      MessageBox(_T("Video Renamed!"),"ATLWallysVideoStore", MB_OK);
     //*** leave ***
      return 0;
}
LRESULT OnClickedUpdatevideos_button(WORD wNotifyCode, WORD wID, HWND hWndCtl,
     BOOL& bHandled)
{
      // TODO : Add Code for event handler.
      //*** OLE2T Macro ***
        USES_CONVERSION;
        //*** Declare IP for WallysVideos ***
     IVideosHandler* pVideos = NULL;
        //*** Declare generic HRESULT holder ***
     HRESULT hr = S_OK;
        //*** try to get the IP to the VideoHandler via MTS ***
     hr = CoCreateInstance( CLSID_VideosHandler , NULL, CLSCTX_INPROC_SERVER,
                              IID_IVideosHandler , (void **) pVideos );
        //*** if bad hresult signal failure and abort call ***
     if (!SUCCEEDED(hr))
      {
            //*** Show Error to User ***
          MessageBox(_T("Wally's Currently Off-Line Please Try Again Later!"),
                              "ATLWallysVideoStore", MB_OK);
```

```
1304.             return 0;
1305.         }
1306.         //*** hold total videos ***
1307.         long lTotalVideos;
1308.         hr = pVideos->get_TotalVideos( &lTotalVideos );
1309.         //*** handle failure ***
1310.        if (!SUCCEEDED(hr))
1311.         {
1312.              //*** Show Error to User ***
1313.             MessageBox(_T("Wally's Currently Off-Line; Please Try Again Later!"),
1314.                                  "ATLWallysVideoStore", MB_OK);
1315.             return 0;
1316.         }
1317.         //*** hold video name sent back ***
1318.         CComBSTR bstrVideoName;
1319.         //*** note that we have x + 1 records but 0th record
1320.             //*** is holder for total videos ***
1321.         for (int i=1;i<=lTotalVideos;i++)
1322.         {
1323.              //*** get the name by number ***
1324.              pVideos->GetVideoNameByNumber( i, &bstrVideoName.m_str );
1325.              //*** put it in the list ***
1326.            SendDlgItemMessage(IDC_VIDEOLIST, LB_ADDSTRING,
1327.               0,(LPARAM)OLE2T(bstrVideoName.m_str));
1328.         }
1329.         //*** Release the IPs ***
1330.         pVideos->Release();
1331.         //*** leave ***
1332.         return 0;
1333.   }
1334. };
1335.
1336. #endif //__STOREUI_H_
```

***Listing 8-2** STOREUI.H source code after modifications*

Here's the breakdown (since much of the code duplicates itself, only the first example of a type of code is covered here):

- **Lines 8-16** These lines bring in header files for the Accounts, Videos, and OnlineVideoManager components, plus the MTS Shared Property system.
- **Lines 210-236** This code does the grunge work of connecting the application with the MTS-aware component that interacts with its database using COM techniques.
- **Lines 237-250** This code demonstrates a vital part of MTS programming, namely that MTS can't do everything! You must check for such

things as pre-existing account names when adding a new account, which this code does. Notice that it works outside of MTS.

- **Lines 251-270** Once you've decided it is okay to create the account, the program makes the creation call. The key point to pick up on here is the absolute lack of MTS functionality at the client end! Although the MTS component checks the security role of the person making the request (i.e., it must be a manager rather than a clerk) and invokes a required transaction for the adding of the account, none of that is seen at the application end. It all takes place inside MTS when the component instance was created, and inside the MTS-aware component itself.

Now that you've completed the code entry, you need to compile the application. Use the Build|Build menu option to do this; if you encounter errors, check your code against these listings or the code on the CD. Once you have a successful compilation and registration, you're ready to move on to reproducing the application in MFC, creating an ASP application for the MTS components, or using MTS Explorer to set up the MTS-aware components and then running them to observe MTS in action.

## Creating an MTS Application with MFC

In the final analysis, even the most sophisticated MTS component needs a home, and that means an application. The following project demonstrates an MFC-based application that uses the MTS MFC components we created in Chapter 7 to allow a fictional store clerk to interact with videos and accounts databases as well as order a video for a customer over the phone (for the low-tech crowd...). If you prefer ATL instead of MFC, please skip back to that section where this application will be reproduced. If you work exclusively in the HTML/ASP environment, skip to the last section for an example of doing the online ordering of videos in an ASP application.

### *Step By Step*

Start Visual C++ 6.0. From the File menu, select New. The New dialog box opens; click on the MFC AppWizard (exe) entry. Next, select an appropriate directory, then enter a project name of **MFCWallysVideoStore**. Figure 8-9 shows how the New dialog should appear when you are done.

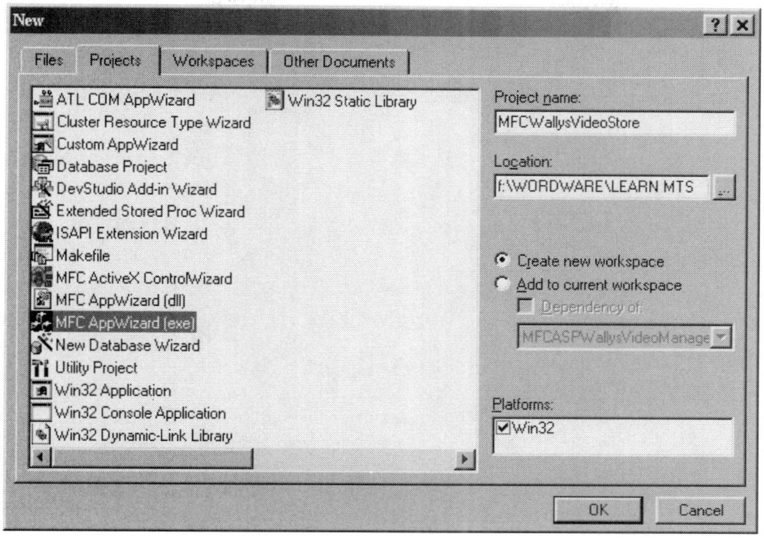


***Figure 8-9***
*The New dialog box creating the MFCWallysVideoStore MFC project*

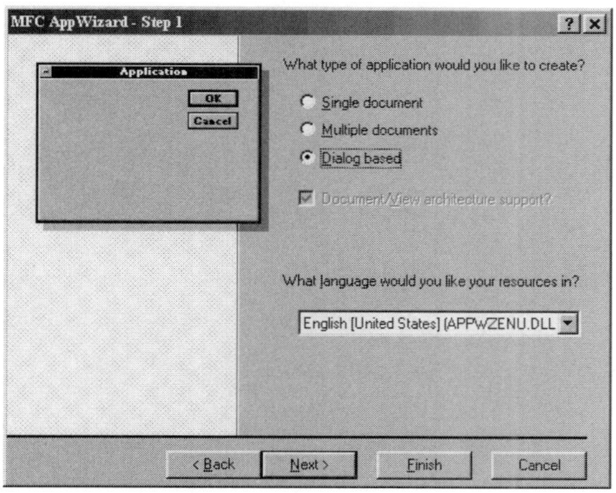


***Figure 8-10***
*Setting the MFC application project basic properties*

In the MFC AppWizard's first dialog page, make sure the Dialog Based radio button is selected, as indicated in Figure 8-10. Click on the Next button to move to the next page of the wizard.

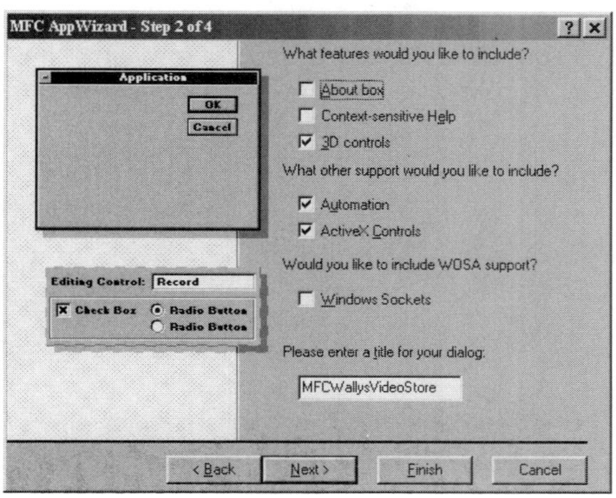


***Figure 8-11***
*Setting the MFC application project COM properties*

On the second page of the MFC AppWizard, you have a number of options that control the behavior of the application. Make sure that both Automation and ActiveX Control support is checked, and enter a title of **MFCWallysVideoStore**. Figure 8-11 illustrates how the dialog should appear when you are done. Click on the Next button to move to the next page of the AppWizard.

On the third page of the MFC AppWizard, select the only available option for the user interface (MFC Standard), and enable source file comments and use of MFC as a shared DLL (to save executable size). Figure 8-12 illustrates how the dialog should appear when you are done. Click on the Next button to move to the next page of the AppWizard.

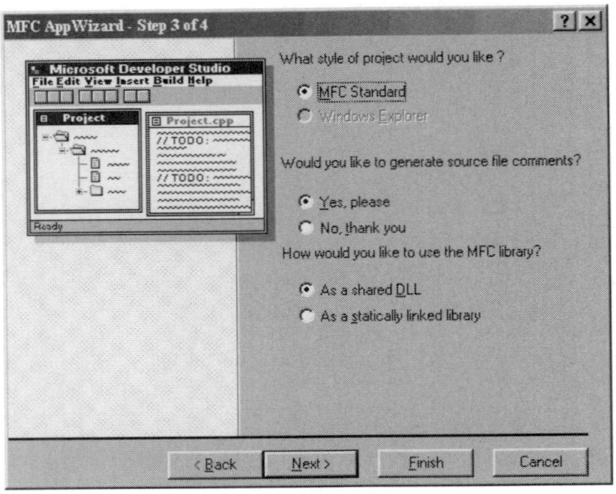


***Figure 8-12***
*Setting the MFC application project user interface properties*

On the fourth page of the MFC AppWizard, you see the results of the choices you made in the previous dialogs. Figure 8-13 illustrates how the dialog should appear when you are done. Click on the Finish button to create the MFC application.

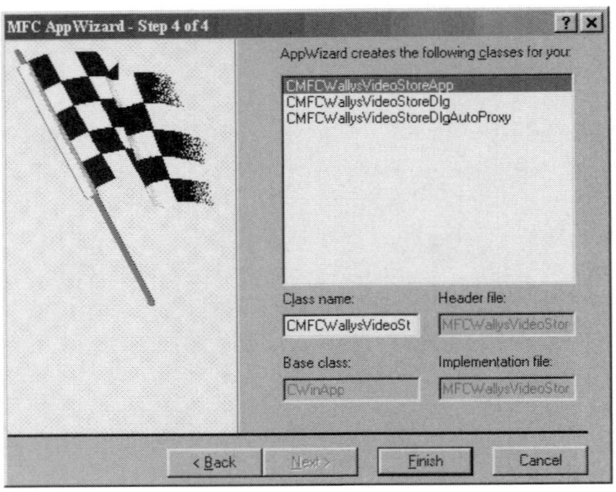


***Figure 8-13***
*The final MFC AppWizard page*

A confirmation dialog box appears as shown in Figure 8-14; press OK to create the MFC project.

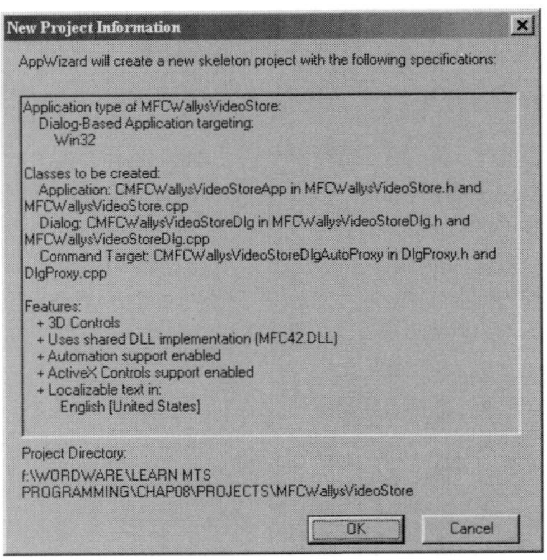


***Figure 8-14***
*The confirmation dialog*

Back in the Visual C++ IDE, bring up the workspace viewer, and select the ResourceView tab. Expand the dialogs entry and double-click on its only element, which is the main dialog resource for the application. Using Figure 8-15 as your guide, lay out the controls as shown on the figure, accepting the default ID values generated by Visual C++ (you can change them to match those in the CD project if you wish later). Save the project to protect your work.

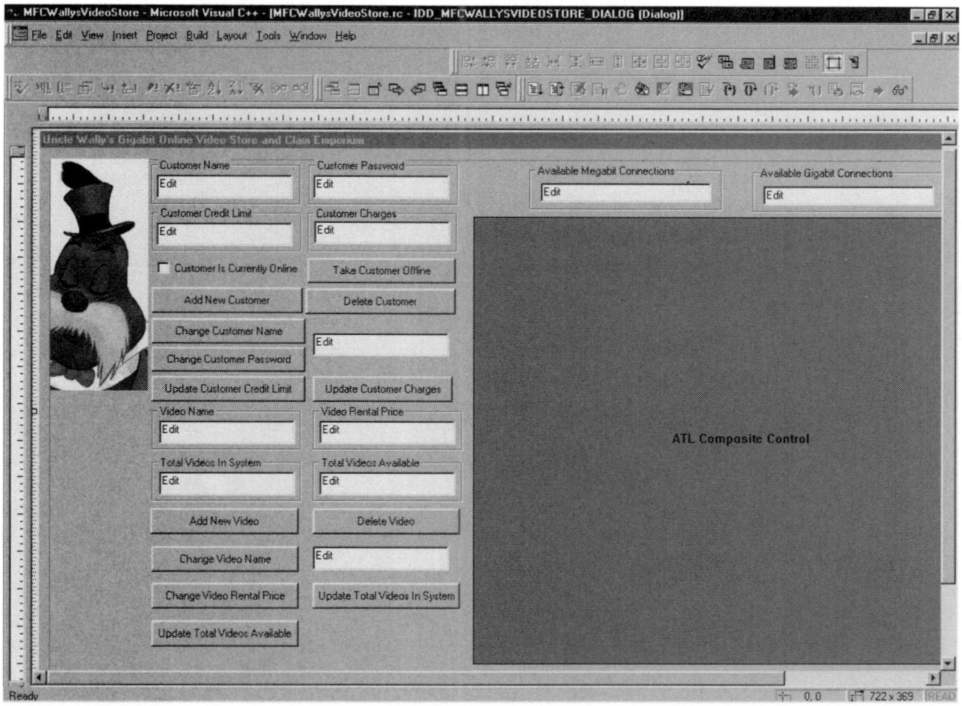


***Figure 8-15*** *The main dialog display of the MFC application in the Resource Editor*

The next step in developing the MFC application is to add the button event handlers. To do this, simply double-click on one of the button controls; the New Windows Message dialog will appear as shown in Figure 8-16. Select the BN_CLICKED event from the left-hand list box for each button control, and click on the Add Handler button for each one, accepting the default name each time. Click on OK to add the event handlers to the project. Save the project to protect your work. Figure 8-17 shows how the dialog will appear afterwards.

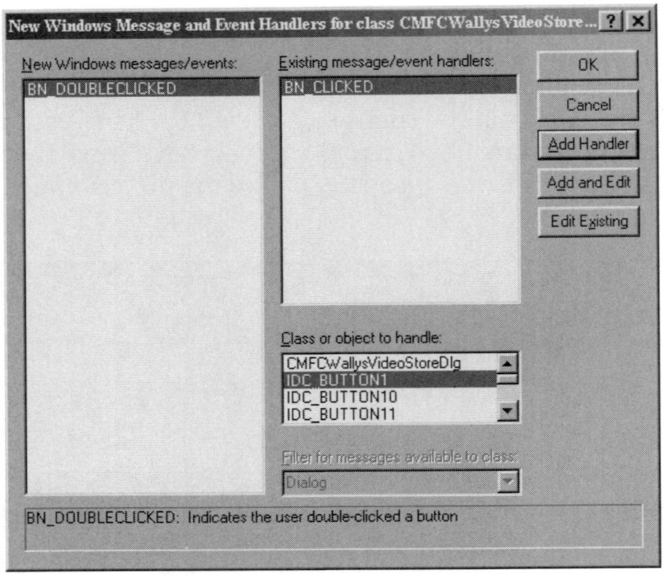


*Figure 8-16*
*Adding button click event handlers in MFC*

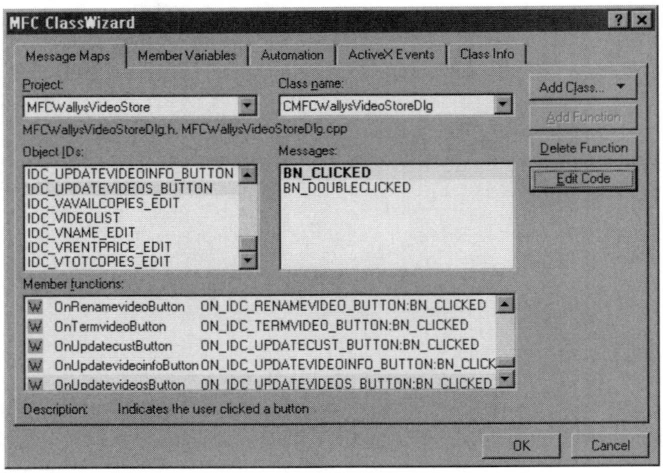


*Figure 8-17*
*MFC ClassWizard showing added event handlers*

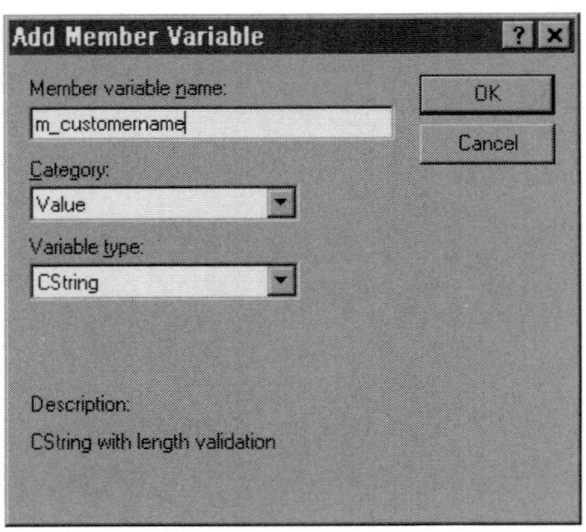


*Figure 8-18*
*Adding the m_customername variable in MFC*

Next you need to set up member variables to translate the data in the edit controls and other controls for use by the MFC application. Hold down the Ctrl key and double-click on the edit control inside the Customer Name groupbox. The Add Member Variable Wizard dialog appears as shown in Figure 8-18. Enter **m_customername** as the name of the member variable, set its Category to Value and its Type to CString, and click on the OK button.

Repeat this process for the appropriate edit controls for the m_customerpassword, m_customercredit, m_customerbill, m_customeronline, m_videoname, m_videorentalprice, m_videototalcopies, m_videoavailablecopies, and m_newname member variables. Close the ClassWizard by clicking on OK.

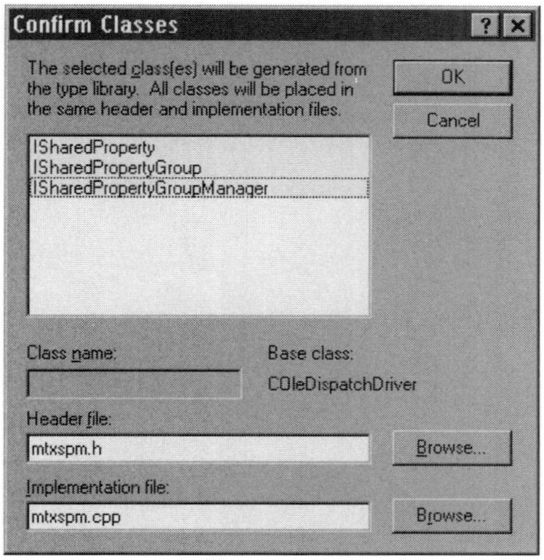


***Figure 8-19*** *Adding support for MTS shared properties*

Next, use ClassWizard to import the MTS Shared Property DLL via the Add Class From A Type Library button menu. Locate the MTXSPM.DLL in the C:\WINDOWS\SYSTEM\MTS\ directory. When you select it you'll see the dialog in Figure 8-19. Click on OK to add support for the MTS Shared Property system to the application.

Finally, use ClassWizard to import the three DLLs for the MFC versions of the AccountsHandler, VideosHandler, and OnlineVideoManager components via the Add Class From A Type Library button menu. Locate the MTXSPM.DLL in the directories where they were created in Chapter 7.

## Line-By-Line

At this point you are ready to begin entering the code to support the user interface for this MTS application. Bring up the MFCWALLYSVIDEOSTOREDLG.CPP file in the text editor. Scan through it and enter or change any boldfaced line of source code in Listing 8-3. Save the project.

```
// MFCWallysVideoStoreDlg.cpp : implementation file
//

#include "stdafx.h"
#include "MFCWallysVideoStore.h"
#include "MFCWallysVideoStoreDlg.h"
#include "DlgProxy.h"
#include "mtxspm.h"
#include "mfcaspwallysvideomanager.h"
#include "mfcmtswallysaccounts.h"
#include "mfcmtswallysvideos.h"
#ifdef _DEBUG
```

```
#define new DEBUG_NEW
#undef THIS_FILE
static char THIS_FILE[] = __FILE__;
#endif

/////////////////////////////////////////////////////////////////////////////
// CMFCWallysVideoStoreDlg dialog

IMPLEMENT_DYNAMIC(CMFCWallysVideoStoreDlg, CDialog);

CMFCWallysVideoStoreDlg::CMFCWallysVideoStoreDlg(CWnd* pParent /*=NULL*/)
    : CDialog(CMFCWallysVideoStoreDlg::IDD, pParent)
{
    //{{AFX_DATA_INIT(CMFCWallysVideoStoreDlg)
    m_customername = _T("");
    m_customerpassword = _T("");
    m_customercredit = 0;
    m_customerbill = 0;
    m_customeronline = FALSE;
    m_videoname = _T("");
    m_videorentalprice = 0;
    m_videototalcopies = 0;
    m_videoavailablecopies = 0;
    m_gigabitconnectionsavailable = 0;
    m_megabitconnectionsavailable = 0;
    m_newname = _T("");
    //}}AFX_DATA_INIT
    // Note that LoadIcon does not require a subsequent DestroyIcon in Win32
    m_hIcon = AfxGetApp()->LoadIcon(IDR_MAINFRAME);
    m_pAutoProxy = NULL;
}

CMFCWallysVideoStoreDlg::~CMFCWallysVideoStoreDlg()
{
    // If there is an automation proxy for this dialog, set
    //  its back pointer to this dialog to NULL, so it knows
    //  the dialog has been deleted.
    if (m_pAutoProxy != NULL)
        m_pAutoProxy->m_pDialog = NULL;
}

void CMFCWallysVideoStoreDlg::DoDataExchange(CDataExchange* pDX)
{
    CDialog::DoDataExchange(pDX);
    //{{AFX_DATA_MAP(CMFCWallysVideoStoreDlg)
    DDX_Text(pDX, IDC_CNAME_EDIT, m_customername);
    DDX_Text(pDX, IDC_CPW_EDIT, m_customerpassword);
```

```
    DDX_Text(pDX, IDC_CCREDIT_EDIT, m_customercredit);
    DDX_Text(pDX, IDC_CBILL_EDIT, m_customerbill);
    DDX_Text(pDX, IDC_CONLINE_EDIT, m_customeronline);
    DDX_Text(pDX, IDC_VNAME_EDIT, m_videoname);
    DDX_Text(pDX, IDC_VRENTPRICE_EDIT, m_videorentalprice);
    DDX_Text(pDX, IDC_VTOTCOPIES_EDIT, m_videototalcopies);
    DDX_Text(pDX, IDC_VAVAILCOPIES_EDIT, m_videoavailablecopies);
    DDX_Text(pDX, IDC_GIGABITCONNEX_EDIT, m_gigabitconnectionsavailable);
    DDX_Text(pDX, IDC_MEGABITCONNEX_EDIT, m_megabitconnectionsavailable);
    DDX_Text(pDX, IDC_NEWNAME_EDIT, m_newname);
    //}}AFX_DATA_MAP
}

BEGIN_MESSAGE_MAP(CMFCWallysVideoStoreDlg, CDialog)
    //{{AFX_MSG_MAP(CMFCWallysVideoStoreDlg)
    ON_WM_PAINT()
    ON_WM_QUERYDRAGICON()
    ON_WM_CLOSE()
    ON_BN_CLICKED(IDC_ADDCUST_BUTTON, OnAddcustButton)
    ON_BN_CLICKED(IDC_ADDVIDEO_BUTTON, OnAddvideoButton)
    ON_BN_CLICKED(IDC_CHANGEPW_BUTTON2, OnChangepwButton2)
    ON_BN_CLICKED(IDC_CREATECUSTDB_BUTTON, OnCreatecustdbButton)
    ON_BN_CLICKED(IDC_CREATEVIDEODB_BUTTON, OnCreatevideodbButton)
    ON_BN_CLICKED(IDC_DELETECUST_BUTTON, OnDeletecustButton)
    ON_BN_CLICKED(IDC_DELETEVIDEO_BUTTON, OnDeletevideoButton)
    ON_BN_CLICKED(IDC_EXIT_BUTTON, OnExitButton)
    ON_BN_CLICKED(IDC_GETCUSTINFO_BUTTON, OnGetcustinfoButton)
    ON_BN_CLICKED(IDC_GETVIDEOINFO_BUTTON, OnGetvideoinfoButton)
    ON_BN_CLICKED(IDC_ORDERVIDEO_BUTTON, OnOrdervideoButton)
    ON_BN_CLICKED(IDC_RENAMECUST_BUTTON, OnRenamecustButton)
    ON_BN_CLICKED(IDC_RENAMEVIDEO_BUTTON, OnRenamevideoButton)
    ON_BN_CLICKED(IDC_TERMVIDEO_BUTTON, OnTermvideoButton)
    ON_BN_CLICKED(IDC_UPDATECUST_BUTTON, OnUpdatecustButton)
    ON_BN_CLICKED(IDC_UPDATEVIDEOINFO_BUTTON, OnUpdatevideoinfoButton)
    ON_BN_CLICKED(IDC_UPDATEVIDEOS_BUTTON, OnUpdatevideosButton)
    //}}AFX_MSG_MAP
END_MESSAGE_MAP()

/////////////////////////////////////////////////////////////////////////////
// CMFCWallysVideoStoreDlg message handlers

BOOL CMFCWallysVideoStoreDlg::OnInitDialog()
{
   CDialog::OnInitDialog();

   // Set the icon for this dialog.  The framework does this automatically
   //  when the application's main window is not a dialog
```

```
SetIcon(m_hIcon, TRUE);              // Set big icon
SetIcon(m_hIcon, FALSE);        // Set small icon

// TODO: Add extra initialization here
//*** talk to the shared property system when we initialize ***
//*** Define shared property group manager IP ***
ISharedPropertyGroupManager* spmManager = NULL;
//*** Define shared property group IP ***
ISharedPropertyGroup* spmGroup = NULL;
//*** Define shared property IP for next receipt ***
ISharedProperty* spmMegabitConnections = NULL;
//*** Define shared property IP for max receipts ***
ISharedProperty* spmGigabitConnections = NULL;
//*** define variant for value of next receipt ***
COleVariant vMegabitConnex;
//*** define variant for value of max receipts ***
COleVariant vGigabitConnex;
//*** start out getting the SPG manager from MTS ***
if (!spmManager->CreateDispatch(_T("MTxSpm.SharedPropertyGroupManager.1")))
{
      //*** Show Error to User ***
     MessageBox(_T("MTS SPM Currently Off-Line; Please Try Again Later!"),
                        "MFCWallysVideoStore", MB_OK);
}

//*** define and set isolation mode ***
LONG lIsolationMode = 1; //Lockmethod
//*** define and set release mode ***
LONG lReleaseMode = 1; //Process
//*** define and set existence variable ***
int bExists;
//*** define BSTR holder for shared property name values ***
CString strPropertyNames;
//*** start out with WALLYSCONNECTIONS property group ***
strPropertyNames = _T("WallysConnections");
//*** attemt to create or obtain the property group WALLYSCONNECTIONS ***
spmGroup->AttachDispatch( spmManager->CreatePropertyGroup(strPropertyNames,
     &lIsolationMode, &lReleaseMode, &bExists ));
if (spmGroup->m_lpDispatch == NULL)
{
      //*** Show Error to User ***
     MessageBox(_T("MTS SPM Currently Off-Line; Please Try Again Later!"),
                        "MFCWallysVideoStore", MB_OK);
     //*** release the shared property group manager ***
    spmManager->ReleaseDispatch();
}
//*** Define the string for the megabit connections ***
```

```
strPropertyNames = _T("MegabitConnections");
//*** Create of obtain the megabitconnections shared property ***
  spmMegabitConnections->AttachDispatch(
    spmGroup->CreateProperty( strPropertyNames,
        &bExists));
//*** Signal Error ***
if (spmMegabitConnections->m_lpDispatch == NULL)
{
      //*** Show Error to User ***
      MessageBox(_T("MTS SPM Currently Off-Line; Please Try Again Later!"),
                          "MFCWallysVideoStore", MB_OK);
    //*** Release the shared property group ***
    spmGroup->ReleaseDispatch();
    //*** release the shared property group manager ***
    spmManager->ReleaseDispatch();
}
//*** Define the string for the gigabit connections ***
strPropertyNames = _T("GigabitConnections");
//*** Create or obtain the gigabitconnections shared property ***
  spmGigabitConnections->AttachDispatch(
    spmGroup->CreateProperty( strPropertyNames,
      &bExists ));
//*** Signal Error ***
if (spmGigabitConnections->m_lpDispatch == NULL)
{
      //*** Show Error to User ***
      MessageBox(_T("MTS SPM Currently Off-Line; Please Try Again Later!"),
                          "MFCWallysVideoStore", MB_OK);
    //*** Release the shared property group ***
    spmGroup->ReleaseDispatch();
    //*** release the shared property group manager ***
    spmManager->ReleaseDispatch();
}
//*** Get the megabit connections value ***
  vMegabitConnex = spmMegabitConnections->GetValue(  );
vGigabitConnex = spmGigabitConnections->GetValue(  );
//*** if no data then initialized so set it ***
if (vMegabitConnex.intVal == 0)
{
      vMegabitConnex.intVal = 100;
      vGigabitConnex.intVal = 2;
      //** send data back to SPM ***
    spmGigabitConnections->SetValue( vGigabitConnex );
    spmMegabitConnections->SetValue( vMegabitConnex );
}
//*** set our UI ***
m_gigabitconnectionsavailable = vGigabitConnex.intVal;
```

```
    m_megabitconnectionsavailable = vMegabitConnex.intVal;
    //*** Release the shared property ***
    spmMegabitConnections->ReleaseDispatch();
    //*** Release the shared property ***
    spmGigabitConnections->ReleaseDispatch();
    //*** Release the shared property group ***
    spmGroup->ReleaseDispatch();
    //*** release the shared property group manager ***
    spmManager->ReleaseDispatch();
    return TRUE;  // return TRUE  unless you set the focus to a control
}

// If you add a minimize button to your dialog, you will need the code below
//  to draw the icon.  For MFC applications using the document/view model,
//  this is automatically done for you by the framework.

void CMFCWallysVideoStoreDlg::OnPaint()
{
    if (IsIconic())
    {
         CPaintDC dc(this); // device context for painting

         SendMessage(WM_ICONERASEBKGND, (WPARAM) dc.GetSafeHdc(), 0);

         // Center icon in client rectangle
         int cxIcon = GetSystemMetrics(SM_CXICON);
         int cyIcon = GetSystemMetrics(SM_CYICON);
         CRect rect;
         GetClientRect(&rect);
         int x = (rect.Width() - cxIcon + 1) / 2;
         int y = (rect.Height() - cyIcon + 1) / 2;

         // Draw the icon
         dc.DrawIcon(x, y, m_hIcon);
    }
    else
    {
         CDialog::OnPaint();
    }
}

// The system calls this to obtain the cursor to display while the user drags
//  the minimized window.
HCURSOR CMFCWallysVideoStoreDlg::OnQueryDragIcon()
{
    return (HCURSOR) m_hIcon;
}
```

```

// Automation servers should not exit when a user closes the UI
//  if a controller still holds on to one of its objects.  These
//  message handlers make sure that if the proxy is still in use,
//  then the UI is hidden but the dialog remains around if it
//  is dismissed.

void CMFCWallysVideoStoreDlg::OnClose()
{
  if (CanExit())
       CDialog::OnClose();
}


BOOL CMFCWallysVideoStoreDlg::CanExit()
{
  // If the proxy object is still around, then the automation
  //  controller is still holding on to this application.  Leave
  //  the dialog around, but hide its UI.
  if (m_pAutoProxy != NULL)
  {
       ShowWindow(SW_HIDE);
       return FALSE;
  }

  return TRUE;
}


void CMFCWallysVideoStoreDlg::OnAddcustButton()
{
  // TODO: Add your control notification handler code here
  IAccountsHandler* pAccounts = NULL;
  //*** attempt to contact MFC Accounts Handler and signal error if fail ***
  if (!pAccounts->CreateDispatch("MFCMTSWallysAccounts.AccountsHandler.1"))
  {
      //*** Show Error to User ***
     MessageBox(
         _T("Wally's Currently Off-Line; Please Try Again Later!"),
         "MFCWallysVideoStore", MB_OK);
     //*** leave ***
     return;
  }
  //*** Create Account ***
  try
  {
       pAccounts->CreateAccount( m_customername, m_customerpassword,
```

```
            m_customercredit, m_customerbill, m_customeronline );
        //*** Release the IP ***
        pAccounts->ReleaseDispatch();
        //*** Show Success to User ***
        MessageBox(_T("Customer Added!"),"MFCWallysVideoStore", MB_OK);
    }
    catch( COleDispatchException* e )
    {
        //*** Show Error to User ***
        CString strError;
        strError = _T("Cannot Add Account due to error: ");
        strError += e->m_strDescription;
        strError += _T(" Please Try Again Later!");
        MessageBox( strError ,"MFCWallysVideoStore", MB_OK);
        //*** release the pointer ***
        pAccounts->ReleaseDispatch();
        //*** leave ***
        return;
    }
}

void CMFCWallysVideoStoreDlg::OnAddvideoButton()
{
    // TODO: Add your control notification handler code here
    IVideosHandler* pVideos = NULL;
    //*** attempt to contact MFC Videos Handler and signal error if fail ***
    if (!pVideos->CreateDispatch("MFCMTSWallysVideos.VideosHandler.1"))
    {
        //*** Show Error to User ***
        MessageBox(
            _T("Wally's Currently Off-Line; Please Try Again Later!"),
             "MFCWallysVideoStore", MB_OK);
        //*** leave ***
        return;
    }
    //*** Create New Video ***
    try
    {
        pVideos->AddNewVideo( m_videoname, m_videorentalprice,
          m_videototalcopies,
             m_videoavailablecopies );
        //*** Release the IP ***
        pVideos->ReleaseDispatch();
        //*** Show Success to User ***
        MessageBox(_T("Video Added!"),"MFCWallysVideoStore", MB_OK);
    }
    catch( COleDispatchException* e )
```

```
  {
      //*** Show Error to User ***
     CString strError;
     strError = _T("Cannot Add Video due to error: ");
     strError += e->m_strDescription;
     strError += _T(" Please Try Again Later!");
     MessageBox( strError ,"MFCWallysVideoStore", MB_OK);
     //*** release the pointer ***
     pVideos->ReleaseDispatch();
      //*** leave ***
     return;
  }
}

void CMFCWallysVideoStoreDlg::OnChangepwButton2()
{
  // TODO: Add your control notification handler code here
  IAccountsHandler* pAccounts = NULL;
  //*** attempt to contact MFC Accounts Handler and signal error if fail ***
  if (!pAccounts->CreateDispatch("MFCMTSWallysAccounts.AccountsHandler.1"))
  {
      //*** Show Error to User ***
     MessageBox(
        _T("Wally's Currently Off-Line; Please Try Again Later!"),
        "MFCWallysVideoStore", MB_OK);
     //*** leave ***
     return;
  }
  //*** Change Password ***
  try
  {
      pAccounts->UpdateAccountPassword(
          m_customername,m_customerpassword,m_newname);
      //*** Release the IP ***
      pAccounts->ReleaseDispatch();
      //*** Show Success to User ***
      MessageBox(_T("Customer Password Changed!"),
        "MFCWallysVideoStore", MB_OK);
  }
  catch( COleDispatchException* e )
  {
      //*** Show Error to User ***
     CString strError;
     strError = _T("Cannot Change Password due to error: ");
     strError += e->m_strDescription;
     strError += _T(" Please Try Again Later!");
     MessageBox( strError ,"MFCWallysVideoStore", MB_OK);
```

```
        //*** release the pointer ***
        pAccounts->ReleaseDispatch();
          //*** leave ***
        return;
    }

}

void CMFCWallysVideoStoreDlg::OnCreatecustdbButton()
{
    // TODO: Add your control notification handler code here
    IAccountsHandler* pAccounts = NULL;
    //*** attempt to contact MFC Accounts Handler and signal error if fail ***
    if (!pAccounts->CreateDispatch("MFCMTSWallysAccounts.AccountsHandler.1"))
    {
          //*** Show Error to User ***
        MessageBox(
           _T("Wally's Currently Off-Line; Please Try Again Later!"),
            "MFCWallysVideoStore", MB_OK);
        //*** leave ***
        return;
    }
    //*** Create Database ***
    try
    {
         pAccounts->CreateDatabase();
         //*** Release the IP ***
         pAccounts->ReleaseDispatch();
         //*** Show Success to User ***
         MessageBox(_T("Customer Database Created!"),
            "MFCWallysVideoStore", MB_OK);
    }
    catch( COleDispatchException* e )
    {
          //*** Show Error to User ***
        CString strError;
        strError = _T("Cannot Create Database due to error: ");
        strError += e->m_strDescription;
        strError += _T(" Please Try Again Later!");
        MessageBox( strError ,"MFCWallysVideoStore", MB_OK);
        //*** release the pointer ***
        pAccounts->ReleaseDispatch();
          //*** leave ***
        return;
    }

}
```

```

void CMFCWallysVideoStoreDlg::OnCreatevideodbButton()
{
   // TODO: Add your control notification handler code here
   IVideosHandler* pVideos = NULL;
   //*** attempt to contact MFC Videos Handler and signal error if fail ***
   if (!pVideos->CreateDispatch("MFCMTSWallysVideos.VideosHandler.1"))
   {
        //*** Show Error to User ***
      MessageBox(
       _T("Wally's Currently Off-Line; Please Try Again Later!"),
       "MFCWallysVideoStore", MB_OK);
      //*** leave ***
      return;
   }
   //*** Create Video database ***
   try
   {
        pVideos->CreateDatabase();
        //*** Release the IP ***
        pVideos->ReleaseDispatch();
        //*** Show Success to User ***
        MessageBox(_T("Video Database Created!"),"MFCWallysVideoStore", MB_OK);
   }
   catch( COleDispatchException* e )
   {
        //*** Show Error to User ***
      CString strError;
      strError = _T("Cannot Create Video Database due to error: ");
      strError += e->m_strDescription;
      strError += _T(" Please Try Again Later!");
      MessageBox( strError ,"MFCWallysVideoStore", MB_OK);
      //*** release the pointer ***
      pVideos->ReleaseDispatch();
        //*** leave ***
      return;
   }

}

void CMFCWallysVideoStoreDlg::OnDeletecustButton()
{
   // TODO: Add your control notification handler code here
   IAccountsHandler* pAccounts = NULL;
   //*** attempt to contact MFC Accounts Handler and signal error if fail ***
   if (!pAccounts->CreateDispatch("MFCMTSWallysAccounts.AccountsHandler.1"))
   {
```

```
        //*** Show Error to User ***
      MessageBox(
         _T("Wally's Currently Off-Line; Please Try Again Later!"),
            "MFCWallysVideoStore", MB_OK);
      //*** leave ***
      return;
   }
   //*** delete customer ***
   try
   {
         pAccounts->DeleteAccount( m_customername, m_customerpassword );
         //*** Release the IP ***
         pAccounts->ReleaseDispatch();
         //*** Show Success to User ***
         MessageBox(_T("Customer Deleted!"),"MFCWallysVideoStore", MB_OK);
   }
   catch( COleDispatchException* e )
   {
        //*** Show Error to User ***
      CString strError;
      strError = _T("Cannot Delete Customer due to error: ");
      strError += e->m_strDescription;
      strError += _T(" Please Try Again Later!");
      MessageBox( strError ,"MFCWallysVideoStore", MB_OK);
      //*** release the pointer ***
      pAccounts->ReleaseDispatch();
        //*** leave ***
      return;
   }

}

void CMFCWallysVideoStoreDlg::OnDeletevideoButton()
{
   // TODO: Add your control notification handler code here
   IVideosHandler* pVideos = NULL;
   //*** attempt to contact MFC Videos Handler and signal error if fail ***
   if (!pVideos->CreateDispatch("MFCMTSWallysVideos.VideosHandler.1"))
   {
        //*** Show Error to User ***
      MessageBox(
         _T("Wally's Currently Off-Line; Please Try Again Later!"),
          "MFCWallysVideoStore", MB_OK);
      //*** leave ***
      return;
   }
   //*** Delete Video ***
```

```
  try
  {
       pVideos->DeleteVideo( m_videoname );
       //*** Release the IP ***
       pVideos->ReleaseDispatch();
       //*** Show Success to User ***
       MessageBox(_T("Video Deleted!"),"MFCWallysVideoStore", MB_OK);
  }
  catch( COleDispatchException* e )
  {
      //*** Show Error to User ***
     CString strError;
     strError = _T("Cannot Delete Video due to error: ");
     strError += e->m_strDescription;
     strError += _T(" Please Try Again Later!");
     MessageBox( strError ,"MFCWallysVideoStore", MB_OK);
     //*** release the pointer ***
     pVideos->ReleaseDispatch();
       //*** leave ***
     return;
  }
}

void CMFCWallysVideoStoreDlg::OnExitButton()
{
  // TODO: Add your control notification handler code here
  PostQuitMessage( 0 );
  DestroyWindow();
}

void CMFCWallysVideoStoreDlg::OnGetcustinfoButton()
{
  // TODO: Add your control notification handler code here
  IAccountsHandler* pAccounts = NULL;
  //*** attempt to contact MFC Accounts Handler and signal error if fail ***
  if (!pAccounts->CreateDispatch("MFCMTSWallysAccounts.AccountsHandler.1"))
  {
      //*** Show Error to User ***
     MessageBox(
        _T("Wally's Currently Off-Line; Please Try Again Later!"),
          "MFCWallysVideoStore", MB_OK);
     //*** leave ***
     return;
  }
  //*** get customer info ***
  try
  {
```

```
        m_customercredit = pAccounts->GetAccountCreditLimit( m_customername );
        m_customerbill = pAccounts->GetAccountCurrentCharges( m_customername );
        m_customeronline = pAccounts->GetAccountInUse( m_customername );
        //*** Release the IP ***
        pAccounts->ReleaseDispatch();
        //*** Show Success to User ***
        MessageBox(_T("Customer Info Acquired!"),"MFCWallysVideoStore", MB_OK);
    }
    catch( COleDispatchException* e )
    {
        //*** Show Error to User ***
      CString strError;
      strError = _T("Cannot Acquire Customer Info due to error: ");
      strError += e->m_strDescription;
      strError += _T(" Please Try Again Later!");
      MessageBox( strError ,"MFCWallysVideoStore", MB_OK);
      //*** release the pointer ***
      pAccounts->ReleaseDispatch();
        //*** leave ***
      return;
    }
}

void CMFCWallysVideoStoreDlg::OnGetvideoinfoButton()
{
    // TODO: Add your control notification handler code here
    IVideosHandler* pVideos = NULL;
    //*** attempt to contact MFC Videos Handler and signal error if fail ***
    if (!pVideos->CreateDispatch("MFCMTSWallysVideos.VideosHandler.1"))
    {
        //*** Show Error to User ***
      MessageBox(
        _T("Wally's Currently Off-Line; Please Try Again Later!"),
          "MFCWallysVideoStore", MB_OK);
      //*** leave ***
      return;
    }
    //*** Get video info ***
    try
    {
        m_videorentalprice = pVideos->GetVideoRentalPrice( m_videoname );
        m_videototalcopies = pVideos->GetVideoTotalCopies( m_videoname );
        m_videoavailablecopies = pVideos->GetVideoAvailableCopies(
            m_videoname );
        //*** Release the IP ***
        pVideos->ReleaseDispatch();
        //*** Show Success to User ***
```

```
        MessageBox(_T("Video Info Acquired!"),"MFCWallysVideoStore", MB_OK);
  }
  catch( COleDispatchException* e )
  {
       //*** Show Error to User ***
     CString strError;
     strError = _T("Cannot Acquire Video Info due to error: ");
     strError += e->m_strDescription;
     strError += _T(" Please Try Again Later!");
     MessageBox( strError ,"MFCWallysVideoStore", MB_OK);
     //*** release the pointer ***
     pVideos->ReleaseDispatch();
       //*** leave ***
     return;
  }
}

void CMFCWallysVideoStoreDlg::OnOrdervideoButton()
{
  // TODO: Add your control notification handler code here
  //*** define megabit connection holder
  BOOL bUseMegabit;
  //*** Define shared property group manager IP ***
  ISharedPropertyGroupManager* spmManager = NULL;
  //*** Define shared property group IP ***
  ISharedPropertyGroup* spmGroup = NULL;
  //*** Define shared property IP for next receipt ***
  ISharedProperty* spmMegabitConnections = NULL;
  //*** Define shared property IP for max receipts ***
  ISharedProperty* spmGigabitConnections = NULL;
  //*** define variant for value of next receipt ***
  COleVariant vMegabitConnex;
  //*** define variant for value of max receipts ***
  COleVariant vGigabitConnex;
  //*** start out getting the SPG manager from MTS ***
  if (!spmManager->CreateDispatch(_T("MTxSpm.SharedPropertyGroupManager.1")))
  {
       //*** Show Error to User ***
      MessageBox(_T("MTS SPM Currently Off-Line; Please Try Again Later!"),
                         "MFCWallysVideoStore", MB_OK);
  }
  //*** define and set isolation mode ***
  LONG lIsolationMode = 1; //Lockmethod
  //*** define and set release mode ***
  LONG lReleaseMode = 1; //Process
  //*** define and set existence variable ***
  int bExists;
```

```
//*** define BSTR holder for shared property name values ***
CString strPropertyNames;
//*** start out with WALLYSCONNECTIONS property group ***
strPropertyNames = _T("WallysConnections");
//*** attemt to create or obtain the property group WALLYSCONNECTIONS ***
spmGroup->AttachDispatch( spmManager->CreatePropertyGroup(strPropertyNames,
     &lIsolationMode, &lReleaseMode, &bExists ));
if (spmGroup->m_lpDispatch == NULL)
{
      //*** Show Error to User ***
     MessageBox(_T("MTS SPM Currently Off-Line; Please Try Again Later!"),
                         "MFCWallysVideoStore", MB_OK);
     //*** release the shared property group manager ***
    spmManager->ReleaseDispatch();
}
//*** Define the string for the megabit connections ***
strPropertyNames = _T("MegabitConnections");
//*** Create of obtain the megabitconnections shared property ***
  spmMegabitConnections->AttachDispatch(
   spmGroup->CreateProperty( strPropertyNames,
        &bExists));
//*** Signal Error ***
if (spmMegabitConnections->m_lpDispatch == NULL)
{
      //*** Show Error to User ***
     MessageBox(_T("MTS SPM Currently Off-Line; Please Try Again Later!"),
                         "MFCWallysVideoStore", MB_OK);
    //*** Release the shared property group ***
    spmGroup->ReleaseDispatch();
    //*** release the shared property group manager ***
    spmManager->ReleaseDispatch();
}
//*** Define the string for the gigabit connections ***
strPropertyNames = _T("GigabitConnections");
//*** Create or obtain the gigabitconnections shared property ***
  spmGigabitConnections->AttachDispatch(
    spmGroup->CreateProperty( strPropertyNames,
      &bExists ));
//*** Signal Error ***
if (spmGigabitConnections->m_lpDispatch == NULL)
{
      //*** Show Error to User ***
     MessageBox(_T("MTS SPM Currently Off-Line; Please Try Again Later!"),
                         "MFCWallysVideoStore", MB_OK);
    //*** Release the shared property group ***
    spmGroup->ReleaseDispatch();
    //*** release the shared property group manager ***
```

```
        spmManager->ReleaseDispatch();
    }
    //*** Get the megabit connections value ***
      vMegabitConnex = spmMegabitConnections->GetValue(  );
    vGigabitConnex = spmGigabitConnections->GetValue(  );
    //*** if no data then initialized so set it ***
    if (vMegabitConnex.intVal == 0)
    {
          vMegabitConnex.intVal = 100;
          vGigabitConnex.intVal = 2;
          //** send data back to SPM ***
         spmGigabitConnections->SetValue( vGigabitConnex );
         spmMegabitConnections->SetValue( vMegabitConnex );
    }
    else
    {
          if (vGigabitConnex.intVal == 0)
          {
                bUseMegabit = TRUE;
                vMegabitConnex.intVal-;
          }
          else
          {
                bUseMegabit = FALSE;
                vGigabitConnex.intVal-;
          }
          //*** update the spm ***
         spmGigabitConnections->SetValue( vGigabitConnex );
         spmMegabitConnections->SetValue( vMegabitConnex );
    }
    //*** set our UI ***
    m_gigabitconnectionsavailable = vGigabitConnex.intVal;
    m_megabitconnectionsavailable = vMegabitConnex.intVal;
    //*** Release the shared property ***
    spmMegabitConnections->ReleaseDispatch();
    //*** Release the shared property ***
    spmGigabitConnections->ReleaseDispatch();
    //*** Release the shared property group ***
    spmGroup->ReleaseDispatch();
    //*** release the shared property group manager ***
    spmManager->ReleaseDispatch();
    //*** Get the ordering info ***
    long lSelIndex = SendDlgItemMessage( IDC_VIDEOLIST, LB_GETCURSEL,0,0);
    SendDlgItemMessage(IDC_VIDEOLIST,LB_GETTEXT,lSelIndex,(LONG)&m_videoname);
      //*** Declare IP for MFCASPWallysVideoManager and get it ***
    IOnlineVIdeoManager* pManager = NULL;
    if (!pManager->CreateDispatch(
```

```
        "MFCAspWallysVideoManager.OnlineVIdeoManager.1" ))
   {
        //*** Show Error to User ***
      MessageBox(_T("Wally's Currently Off-Line; Please Try Again Later!"),
                            "MFCWallysVideoStore", MB_OK);
      //*** leave ***
      return;
   }
   //*** set up the properties with the info from our UI ***
   pManager->SetCustomerName( m_customername );
   pManager->SetCustomerPassword( m_customerpassword );
   pManager->SetVideoName( m_videoname );
   //*** order video ***
   pManager->OrderVideo();
   //*** obtain the result from the component ***
   CString strOutputMsg;
   strOutputMsg = pManager->GetCustomerName();
   //*** display it ***
   MessageBox( strOutputMsg ,"MFCWallysVideoStore",MB_OK);
   //*** release the component ***
   pManager->ReleaseDispatch();

}

void CMFCWallysVideoStoreDlg::OnRenamecustButton()
{
   // TODO: Add your control notification handler code here
   IAccountsHandler* pAccounts = NULL;
   //*** attempt to contact MFC Accounts Handler and signal error if fail ***
   if (!pAccounts->CreateDispatch("MFCMTSWallysAccounts.AccountsHandler.1"))
   {
        //*** Show Error to User ***
      MessageBox(
         _T("Wally's Currently Off-Line; Please Try Again Later!"),
         "MFCWallysVideoStore", MB_OK);
      //*** leave ***
      return;
   }
   //*** change customer name ***
   try
   {
        pAccounts->UpdateAccountName( m_customername, m_newname );
        //*** Release the IP ***
        pAccounts->ReleaseDispatch();
        //*** Show Success to User ***
        MessageBox(_T("Customer Name Changed!"),"MFCWallysVideoStore", MB_OK);
   }
```

```
    catch( COleDispatchException* e )
    {
         //*** Show Error to User ***
       CString strError;
       strError = _T("Cannot Change Customer Name due to error: ");
       strError += e->m_strDescription;
       strError += _T(" Please Try Again Later!");
       MessageBox( strError ,"MFCWallysVideoStore", MB_OK);
       //*** release the pointer ***
       pAccounts->ReleaseDispatch();
         //*** leave ***
       return;
    }
}

void CMFCWallysVideoStoreDlg::OnRenamevideoButton()
{
    // TODO: Add your control notification handler code here
    IVideosHandler* pVideos = NULL;
    //*** attempt to contact MFC Videos Handler and signal error if fail ***
    if (!pVideos->CreateDispatch("MFCMTSWallysVideos.VideosHandler.1"))
    {
         //*** Show Error to User ***
       MessageBox(
          _T("Wally's Currently Off-Line; Please Try Again Later!"),
           "MFCWallysVideoStore", MB_OK);
       //*** leave ***
       return;
    }
    //*** Change video name ***
    try
    {
         pVideos->UpdateVideoEntryName( m_videoname, m_newname );
         //*** Release the IP ***
         pVideos->ReleaseDispatch();
         //*** Show Success to User ***
         MessageBox(_T("Video Name Changed!"),"MFCWallysVideoStore", MB_OK);
    }
    catch( COleDispatchException* e )
    {
         //*** Show Error to User ***
       CString strError;
       strError = _T("Cannot Change Video Name due to error: ");
       strError += e->m_strDescription;
       strError += _T(" Please Try Again Later!");
       MessageBox( strError ,"MFCWallysVideoStore", MB_OK);
       //*** release the pointer ***
```

```
        pVideos->ReleaseDispatch();
          //*** leave ***
        return;
    }
}

void CMFCWallysVideoStoreDlg::OnTermvideoButton()
{
    // TODO: Add your control notification handler code here
    IVideosHandler* pVideos = NULL;
    //*** attempt to contact MFC Videos Handler and signal error if fail ***
    if (!pVideos->CreateDispatch("MFCMTSWallysVideos.VideosHandler.1"))
    {
          //*** Show Error to User ***
        MessageBox(
          _T("Wally's Currently Off-Line; Please Try Again Later!"),
            "MFCWallysVideoStore", MB_OK);
        //*** leave ***
        return;
    }
    IAccountsHandler* pAccounts = NULL;
    //*** attempt to contact MFC Accounts Handler and signal error if fail ***
    if (!pAccounts->CreateDispatch("MFCMTSWallysAccounts.AccountsHandler.1"))
    {
          //*** Show Error to User ***
        MessageBox(
          _T("Wally's Currently Off-Line; Please Try Again Later!"),
            "MFCWallysVideoStore", MB_OK);
        //*** leave ***
        return;
    }
    //*** try to update available copies and take user offline ***
    try
    {
         m_videoavailablecopies = pVideos->GetVideoAvailableCopies(
            m_videoname );
         m_videoavailablecopies++;
         pVideos->UpdateVideoEntryAvailableCopies( m_videoname,
              m_videoavailablecopies );
         //*** Release the IP ***
         pAccounts->UpdateAccountInUse( m_customername, FALSE );
         pVideos->ReleaseDispatch();
         pAccounts->ReleaseDispatch();
         //*** Show Success to User ***
         MessageBox(_T("Video terminated!"),"MFCWallysVideoStore", MB_OK);
    }
    catch( COleDispatchException* e )
```

```
    {
        //*** Show Error to User ***
       CString strError;
       strError = _T("Cannot Terminate Video Playback due to error: ");
       strError += e->m_strDescription;
       strError += _T(" Please Try Again Later!");
       MessageBox( strError ,"MFCWallysVideoStore", MB_OK);
       //*** release the pointer ***
       pVideos->ReleaseDispatch();
       pAccounts->ReleaseDispatch();
         //*** leave ***
       return;
    }
}

void CMFCWallysVideoStoreDlg::OnUpdatecustButton()
{
   // TODO: Add your control notification handler code here
   IAccountsHandler* pAccounts = NULL;
   //*** attempt to contact MFC Accounts Handler and signal error if fail ***
   if (!pAccounts->CreateDispatch("MFCMTSWallysAccounts.AccountsHandler.1"))
   {
        //*** Show Error to User ***
      MessageBox(
        _T("Wally's Currently Off-Line; Please Try Again Later!"),
           "MFCWallysVideoStore", MB_OK);
      //*** leave ***
      return;
   }
   //*** set customer info ***
   try
   {
        pAccounts->UpdateAccountCredit( m_customername, m_customercredit );
        pAccounts->UpdateAccountCharges( m_customername,  m_customerbill);
        pAccounts->UpdateAccountInUse( m_customername , m_customeronline);
        //*** Release the IP ***
        pAccounts->ReleaseDispatch();
        //*** Show Success to User ***
        MessageBox(_T("Customer Info Updated!"),"MFCWallysVideoStore", MB_OK);
   }
   catch( COleDispatchException* e )
   {
        //*** Show Error to User ***
      CString strError;
      strError = _T("Cannot Update Customer Info due to error: ");
      strError += e->m_strDescription;
      strError += _T(" Please Try Again Later!");
```

```
        MessageBox( strError ,"MFCWallysVideoStore", MB_OK);
        //*** release the pointer ***
        pAccounts->ReleaseDispatch();
          //*** leave ***
        return;
    }
}

void CMFCWallysVideoStoreDlg::OnUpdatevideoinfoButton()
{
    // TODO: Add your control notification handler code here
    IVideosHandler* pVideos = NULL;
    //*** attempt to contact MFC Videos Handler and signal error if fail ***
    if (!pVideos->CreateDispatch("MFCMTSWallysVideos.VideosHandler.1"))
    {
          //*** Show Error to User ***
        MessageBox(
           _T("Wally's Currently Off-Line; Please Try Again Later!"),
            "MFCWallysVideoStore", MB_OK);
        //*** leave ***
        return;
    }
    //*** Change video info ***
    try
    {
          pVideos->UpdateVideoEntryPrice( m_videoname, m_videorentalprice );
          pVideos->UpdateVideoEntryTotalCopies( m_videoname, m_videototalcopies );
          pVideos->UpdateVideoEntryAvailableCopies( m_videoname,
               m_videoavailablecopies );
          //*** Release the IP ***
          pVideos->ReleaseDispatch();
          //*** Show Success to User ***
          MessageBox(_T("Video Info Updated!"),"MFCWallysVideoStore", MB_OK);
    }
    catch( COleDispatchException* e )
    {
          //*** Show Error to User ***
        CString strError;
        strError = _T("Cannot Update Video Info due to error: ");
        strError += e->m_strDescription;
        strError += _T(" Please Try Again Later!");
        MessageBox( strError ,"MFCWallysVideoStore", MB_OK);
        //*** release the pointer ***
        pVideos->ReleaseDispatch();
          //*** leave ***
        return;
    }
```

```
1000. }
1001.
1002. void CMFCWallysVideoStoreDlg::OnUpdatevideosButton()
1003. {
1004.   // TODO: Add your control notification handler code here
1005.   IVideosHandler* pVideos = NULL;
1006.   //*** attempt to contact MFC Videos Handler and signal error if fail ***
1007.   if (!pVideos->CreateDispatch("MFCMTSWallysVideos.VideosHandler.1"))
1008.   {
1009.         //*** Show Error to User ***
1010.      MessageBox(
1011.           _T("Wally's Currently Off-Line; Please Try Again Later!"),
1012.              "MFCWallysVideoStore", MB_OK);
1013.      //*** leave ***
1014.      return;
1015.   }
1016.   //*** hold video name sent back ***
1017.   CString strVideoName;
1018.   BSTR bstrVideoName;
1019.   //*** get total videos in list ***
1020.   long lTotalVideos  = pVideos->GetTotalVideos();
1021.   //*** note that we have x + 1 records but 0th record is total videos ***
1022.   for (int i=1;i<=lTotalVideos;i++)
1023.   {
1024.        //*** get the name by number ***
1025.        pVideos->GetVideoNameByNumber( i, &bstrVideoName );
1026.        //*** convert string ***
1027.        strVideoName = bstrVideoName;
1028.        //*** put it in the list ***
1029.       SendDlgItemMessage(IDC_VIDEOLIST, LB_ADDSTRING,
1030.           0,(LPARAM)strVideoName.AllocSysString());
1031.   }
1032.   //*** Release the IPs ***
1033.   pVideos->ReleaseDispatch();
1034.
1035. }
```

***Listing 8-3** MFCWALLYSVIDEOSTOREDLG.CPP source code after modifications*

Here's the breakdown (since much of the code is repetitive, only the first use of a given technique is covered here):

- **Lines 8-11** This code puts in the files for using the MTS shared property components the application needs and for the three MTS components created in Chapter 7.
- **Lines 280-290** This code does the grunge work of connecting the application with the MTS-aware component that interacts with its database using COM techniques.

- **Lines 291-300** Once you've decided it is okay to create the account, the program makes the creation call. The key point to pick up on here is the absolute lack of MTS functionality at the client end! Although the MTS component checks the security role of the person making the request (i.e., it must be a manager rather than a clerk) and invokes a required transaction for the adding of the account, none of that is seen at the application end. It all takes place inside MTS when the component instance was created, and inside the MTS-aware component itself.
- **Lines 301-311** This code demonstrates error handling for the MFC application; notice that it handles the cleanup of the COM component.

# Creating an MTS Application with ASP

Since so much of MTS will undoubtedly be focused on working on and with the Internet and the World Wide Web, this book includes an example of using MTS with an Active Server Pages (ASP) script file. This file produces an HTML output which uses the ActiveX control (the example uses the ATL one, but you could switch to the MFC control without making any other changes) to accept user input of a video to watch and a customer name and password to use to order. The page contains a submit button that sends it to the ASP script for processing. Inside the ASP script, the code activates the ASP component and obtains display information from it (the list of videos available), as well as ordering a video and stopping video playback. You can create the ASP script in any environment you like; this example will use FrontPage Express.

## *Step-By-Step*

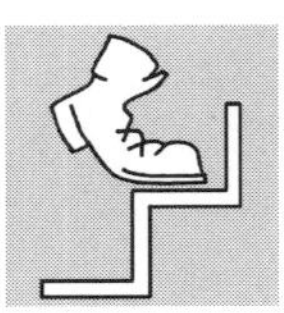

Start your favorite HTML authoring tool (I used Frontpage Express for this book). Create a new ASP file and save it as ASPWALLYSONLINEORDERING.ASP. Enter the source code in Listing 8-4 and save the file. (The ActiveX control entry can be used as is if you're using the CD projects, or you can put it in via a user interface if you've created it from scratch on your machine, since the GUID will be different.)

```
<html>
<HEAD>
<title>ASP Demo For MTS Applications</title>
</HEAD>
<BODY>
<p>
    <SCRIPT LANGUAGE="VBScript">
<!–
Sub videouserinterface1_OnTerminatePlayback()
Document.form1.actiontype.value = "stopvideo"
Document.form1.customername.value = Document.videouserinterface1.customername
Document.form1.customerpassword.value = Document.videouserinterface1.customerpassword
```

```
Document.form1.videoname.value = Document.videouserinterface1.videoname
Document.form1.connectiontype.value = Document.videouserinterface1.connectiontype
form1.submit
end sub
Sub videouserinterface1_OnUpdateVideoList()
Document.form1.actiontype.value = "updatevideos"
Document.form1.customername.value = Document.videouserinterface1.customername
Document.form1.customerpassword.value = Document.videouserinterface1.customerpassword
Document.form1.videoname.value = Document.videouserinterface1.videoname
Document.form1.connectiontype.value = Document.videouserinterface1.connectiontype
form1.submit
end sub
Sub videouserinterface1_OnOrderVideo()
Document.form1.actiontype.value = "ordervideo"
Document.form1.customername.value = Document.videouserinterface1.customername
Document.form1.customerpassword.value = Document.videouserinterface1.customerpassword
Document.form1.videoname.value = Document.videouserinterface1.videoname
Document.form1.connectiontype.value = Document.videouserinterface1.connectiontype
form1.submit
end sub
-->
    </SCRIPT>
    <OBJECT ID="videouserinterface1"
     CLASSID="CLSID:361BFD64-9A54-11D2-B7EA-00E02916C424">
    </OBJECT>
<%@ LANGUAGE = VBScript %>
<%
Dim fso, f , GigabitConnexAvailable
ControlString = Request.Form("actiontype")
CustomerNameString = Request.Form("customername")
CustomerPasswordString = Request.Form("customerpassword")
VideoNameString = Request.Form("videoname")
ConnectionType = Request.Form("connectiontype")
if ControlString = "ordervideo" then
  if connectiontype = 0 then
    Set fso = CreateObject("Scripting.FileSystemObject")
    Set f = fso.OpenTextFile("c:\gigaconnavail.txt", 1, True)
    f.Read GigabitConnexAvailable
   GigabitConnexAvailable = GigabitConnexAvailable - 1
    f.Close
    Set f = fso.OpenTextFile("c:\gigaconnavail.txt", 2, True)
    f.Write GigabitConnexAvailable
    f.Close
  end if
  Set objCrypto = Server.CreateObject("ATLASPWallysVideoManager.OnlineVideoManager")
  objCrypto.OrderVideo(CustomerNameString,CustomerPasswordString,VideoNameString)
  response.write("<SCRIPT LANGUAGE=""VBScript"">")
```

```
    response.write("Sub window_onLoad()")
    response.write("videouserinterface1.customername =" + objcrypto.customername )
    response.write("end sub")
    response.write("</SCRIPT>")
    set objCrypto = nothing
end if
if ControlString = "stopvideo" then
    if connectiontype = 0 then
      Set fso = CreateObject("Scripting.FileSystemObject")
      Set f = fso.OpenTextFile("c:\gigaconnavail.txt", 1, True)
      f.Read GigabitConnexAvailable
     GigabitConnexAvailable = GigabitConnexAvailable + 1
      f.Close
      Set f = fso.OpenTextFile("c:\gigaconnavail.txt", 2, True)
      f.Write GigabitConnexAvailable
      f.Close
    end if
    Set objCrypto = Server.CreateObject("ATLASPWallysVideoManager.OnlineVideoManager")
    objCrypto.TerminateVideo(CustomerNameString,VideoNameString)
    response.write("<SCRIPT LANGUAGE=""VBScript"">")
    response.write("Sub window_onLoad()")
    response.write("videouserinterface1.customername =" + objcrypto.customername )
    response.write("end sub")
    response.write("</SCRIPT>")
    set objCrypto = nothing
end if
if ( ControlString = "updatevideos" ) or ( ControlsString = "" ) then
    Set objCrypto = Server.CreateObject("ATLASPWallysVideoManager.OnlineVideoManager")
    dim counter1 as integer
    response.write("<SCRIPT LANGUAGE=""VBScript"">")
    response.write("Sub window_onLoad()")
    for counter1 = 1 to objCrypt.totalvideos
       objCrypto.getvideonamebynumber(counter1,nameholderstring)
       response.write("videouserinterface1.AddListItem(" + nameholderstring +")")
    next
    Set fso = CreateObject("Scripting.FileSystemObject")
    Set f = fso.OpenTextFile("c:\gigaconnavail.txt", 1, True)
    f.Read GigabitConnexAvailable
    f.Close
    if GigabitConnexAvailable > 0 then
       response.write("videouserinterface1.SetGigabitConnAvailability( TRUE )")
    else
     response.write("videouserinterface1.SetGigabitConnAvailability( FALSE )")
    end if
    response.write("end sub")
    response.write("</SCRIPT>")
    set objCrypto = nothing
```

```
107. end if
108. %>
109. </p>
110.     <FORM ACTION="-AspWallysOnlineOrdering.asp" METHOD="POST" NAME="form1">
111. <p>
112.         <INPUT TYPE=hidden NAME="customername">
113. </p>
114. <p>
115.         <INPUT TYPE=hidden NAME="customerpassword">
116. </p>
117. <p>
118.         <INPUT TYPE=hidden NAME="videoname">
119. </p>
120. <p>
121.         <INPUT TYPE=hidden NAME="connectiontype">
122. </p>
123. <p>
124.         <INPUT TYPE=hidden NAME="actiontype">
125. </p>
126.     </FORM>
127. <p> </p>
128. </BODY>
129. </html>
```

***Listing 8-4** ASPWALLYSONLINEORDERING.ASP source code after modifications*

Here's the breakdown of how the ASP and HTML code work to do the magic:

- **Lines 9-16** This HTML scripting code responds to the ActiveX event from the ActiveX control generated when the user clicks on the Terminate Video button. It sets up the hidden form fields and triggers the submission to the ASP page.
- **Lines 17-24** This HTML scripting code responds to the ActiveX event from the ActiveX control generated when the user clicks on the Update Video List button. It sets up the hidden form fields and triggers the submission to the ASP page.
- **Lines 25-32** This HTML scripting code responds to the ActiveX event from the ActiveX control generated when the user clicks on the Order Video button. It sets up the hidden form fields and triggers the submission to the ASP page.
- **Lines 35-37** This HTML code deploys the ActiveX control on the HTML page display. Notice that it does not set any of its properties, because the control starts in an uninitialized state and is then set up by ASP-generated code.
- **Lines 38-39** This ASP code sets up the ASP language and starts an ASP block.

- **Lines 40-45** This ASP code retrieves the hidden Form object data for use in calling the ASP component. Note that it cannot be obtained from the ActiveX control during this process because the control is created on the client and not the server where ASP code is executed!
- **Lines 46-65** This ASP code handles ordering a video. It creates the MTS-aware ASP component and calls its OrderVideo method. It then writes out a script block to be executed when the newly minted page loads that will put the current video list in the list box and also return the ASP component's status message in its CustomerName property. The somewhat cumbersome mechanism of writing a script block to hold the output from the component is required because the ASP component won't exist on the client machine, only on the server. Also notice that it keeps track of the connection type via the text file that must start out with the total gigabit connections available; whenever one is used it is reduced by 1 until it is zero. This will be used by the update code later.
- **Lines 66-85** This ASP code handles stopping a video. It creates the MTS-aware ASP component and calls its TerminateVideo method. It then writes out a script block to be executed when the newly minted page loads that will put the current video list in the list box and also return the ASP component's status message in its CustomerName property. The somewhat cumbersome mechanism of writing a script block to hold the output from the component is required because the ASP component won't exist on the client machine, only on the server. Also notice that it keeps track of the connection type via the text file that must start out with the total gigabit connections available; whenever one is stopped it is increased by 1. This will be used by the update code later.
- **Lines 86-108** This ASP code handles updating the videos display list box; it runs the first time the page is called because of its check for an empty actiontype field. It creates the MTS-aware ASP component and calls its GetVideoNameByNumber enumeration method. It then writes out a script block to be executed when the newly minted page loads that will put the current video list in the list box. The somewhat cumbersome mechanism of writing a script block to hold the output from the component is required because the ASP component won't exist on the client machine, only on the server. Notice that it sets the gigabit connection availability based on an external file which must be available on the server and contain a number greater than 0 for the availability.
- **Lines 109-129** This HTML scripting code creates hidden form fields that will hold the data from the ActiveX control on its trip back to the server. This is required because the ActiveX control is only created on the client, but the data is needed by the ASP code on the server.

You must now transport the ASP file to the server where it will live, and change the Action parameter in line 84 above to reflect the full URL of the server and the page so that the ASP code will run properly. You must also install and register the ASP component there, and make sure that the databases and MTS are installed and configured on the ASP-capable Web server as well.

## Where We Go From Here

You have now completed the full Wally's MTS application and components. Only two hurdles remain: getting the application to connect with MTS so you can test and deploy it, and moving the system, both applications and components, to your customers over the Internet. Chapters 9 and 10 answer these vital questions.

Chapter Nine

# Installing and Using MTS Components and Applications with MTS Explorer and SQL Server 7

Unlike many types of computer applications (even COM ones), an MTS application does not live on its own. Instead, MTS applications must have their components installed in the MTS run-time environment, so that MTS knows how to configure and support them. The utility that permits this configuration is called the MTS Explorer; a version of it exists on all operating systems that support MTS. With MTS Explorer, a developer or IT manager can install MTS-aware COM components; set their properties in regard to transactions, memory usage, and security; and even create self-installing executable files that automatically set up MTS components on a remote machine without further user or administrator intervention. This chapter takes you through the steps needed to install components in MTS Explorer, configure them into packages, and set the properties of the packages to support the expected behavior of the components. Finally, this chapter will guide you through running the three MTS applications created in Chapter 8. When you're done, you'll be ready to move out into the world of MTS and make your own components and applications.

## MTS Explorer Basics

Figure 9-1 shows the main display of the MTS Explorer (in Windows 98; in Windows NT 4 the display will have a tree control to the left similar to Windows Explorer). It has one window with one computer in it (the current one); if there were other computers available on the network they would be shown in the window as well.

*Figure 9-1*
*The MTS Explorer main display*

In both Windows 98 and Windows NT 4, you navigate in the main MTS Explorer window by double-clicking an icon. (In NT 4, you can also navigate via the left-hand tree control.) Starting with the My Computer icon (or its equivalent on your system), double-click on it to move one layer down in the MTS Explorer hierarchy (or expand its node in the tree control and click on the first exposed item). You'll see a display similar to Figure 9-2.

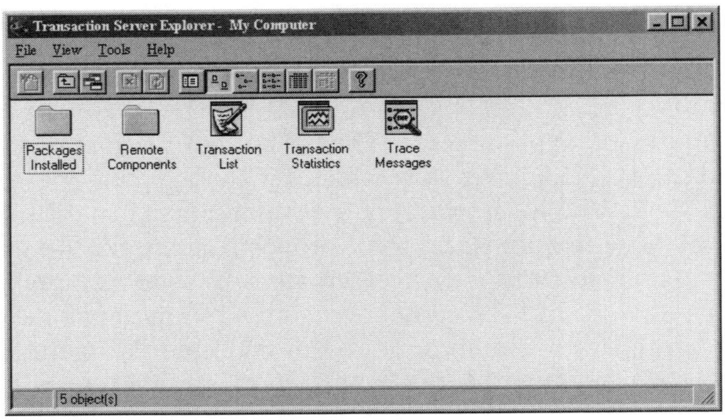


*Figure 9-2*
*The MTS Explorer Computer Elements display*

The second level of the display hierarchy shows you all the MTS elements present on a given computer. As you can see in the figure, this includes installed packages (which we'll get to a bit later), remote components (registered with the system but used via DCOM rather than COM), and three log files: a transaction list (all the transactions MTS has participated in since the log was last cleared), a set of transaction statistics (in graphical form to allow study of load levels for optimization purposes), and a log of debugging trace messages (to see exactly where a component in MTS has failed in a complex environment). The last three elements have their own separate viewers, which we'll cover later. For now, double-click on the Packages Installed icon or expand its node in the tree control and select the next item down. The display shown in Figure 9-3 appears.

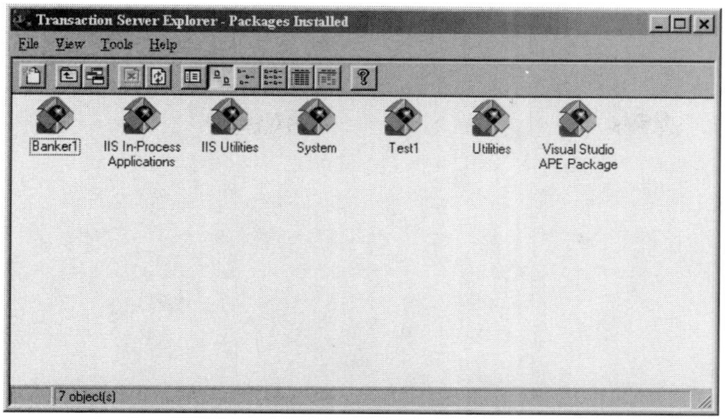


***Figure 9-3***
*The MTS Explorer Packages Installed display*

The third level of display shows the installed packages on the current computer; they appear as spheres with names under them. Packages are not the same as COM components, but rather are an MTS administrative fiction designed to allow developers and IT managers to group multiple COM elements into one convenient package for setting MTS properties like transaction requirements and security levels. We'll create our own packages for the ATL and MFC components we've created later on in this chapter. For now, select one of the displayed packages (Banker1 is good; it is installed with MTS as a demo, so most systems will have it) and double-click on it to open its level in the MTS Explorer. Figure 9-4 illustrates what you should see next.

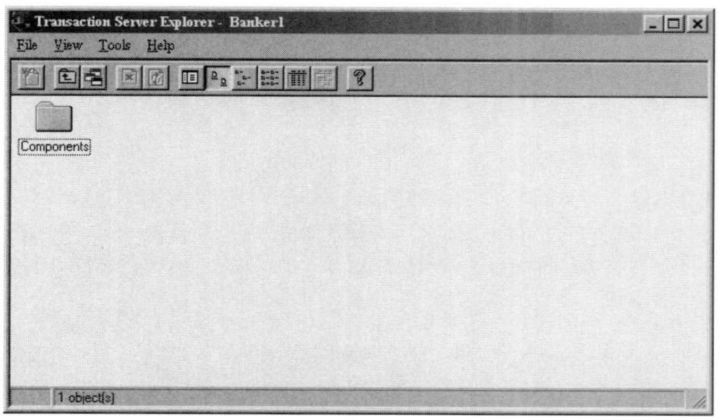


***Figure 9-4***
*The MTS Explorer Package Elements display*

This display is deceptively simple; it shows only a single file folder labeled Components. This serves as the gateway to all the MTS-aware components that are part of the current package. Double-click on it to move down and examine these COM components in detail.

Figure 9-5 shows an example of the components in a package (one of the utility ones). As you can see, each component has its own icon, with a caption that is its programmatic ID (ProgID in COM terms). This is a vital level of the MTS Explorer, because here is where you add, delete, and set properties for individual COM components in a given package. We'll utilize this display heavily later on; for now, double-click on one of the components, and you'll see the display illustrated in Figure 9-6.

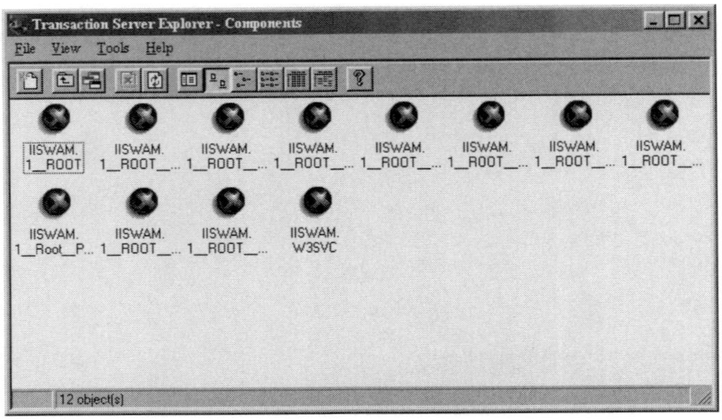


**Figure 9-5**
*The MTS Explorer Package Elements display*

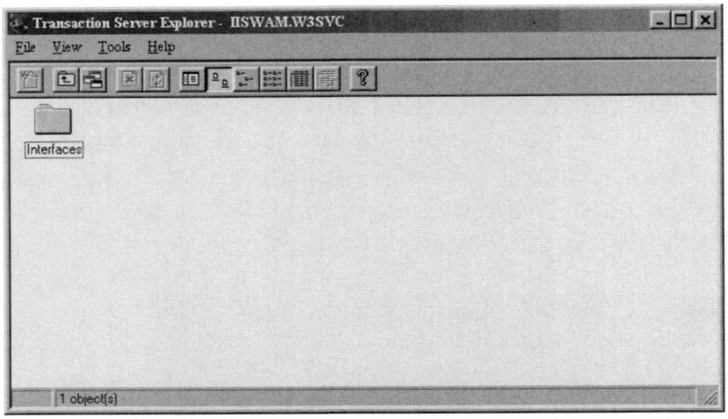


**Figure 9-6**
*The MTS Explorer Component Interfaces display*

At this level, the only available item are the interfaces supported by the component. It is mainly useful for changing component-specific properties. Double-click on the Interfaces folder and you'll move down to the display shown in Figure 9-7.

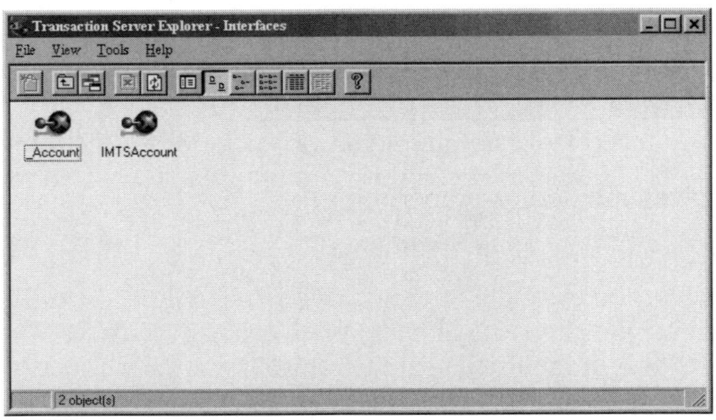


**Figure 9-7**
*The MTS Explorer Interfaces display*

Here you will see every interface supported by the MTS component. As you'll remember from our chapter on COM, interfaces are the way COM objects communicate with the outside world. All the clients of MTS components (including other MTS components!) must use these interfaces. If you experience a problem with failing to connect with an MTS component, this is a good place to check to see whether there is a spelling or other difference between the interface name you are using and the one the component provides to MTS. For now, double-click on one of the interfaces to move yet lower into the MTS hierarchy.

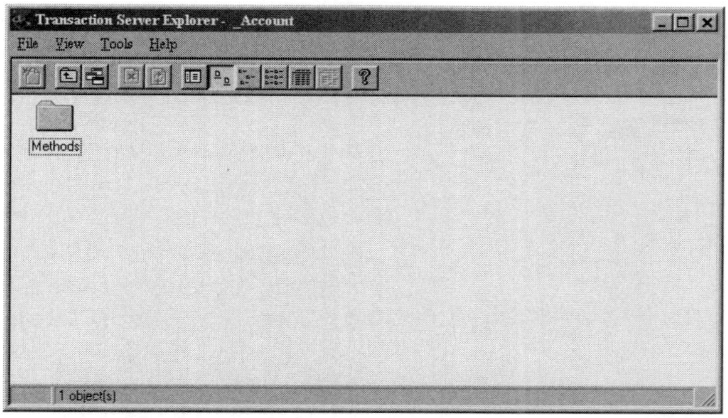


***Figure 9-8*** *The MTS Explorer Interface Methods/ Properties Access display*

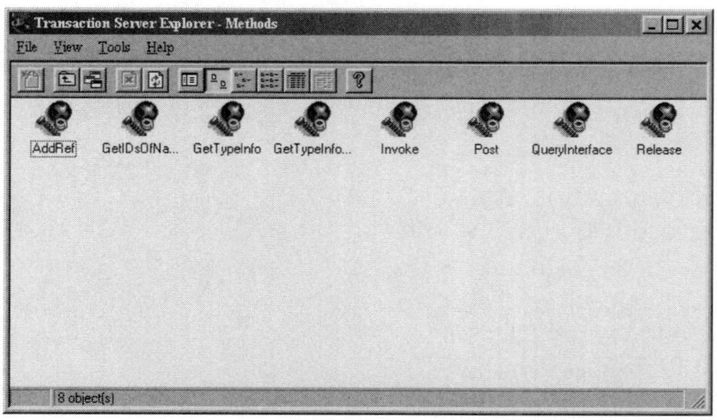


***Figure 9-9*** *The MTS Explorer Interface Actual Methods/ Properties Display*

Figure 9-8 will show either both Methods and Properties folders, or just one of them (i.e., only a Methods folder as is seen in the figure, or only a Properties folder). Double-click on one of these folders to move to the bottom level of the MTS hierarchy, as shown in Figure 9-9.

This is the end of the MTS hierarchy, and it illustrates all the properties or methods for a given MTS component interface (the figure shows methods). If you experience problems using a given MTS component, check this page to make sure that a given method or property is exported the way the application or other MTS component expects it (remember that COM can be case-sensitive!). To help you keep track of what given methods or properties do, you can select Properties as shown in Figure 9-10 from the File menu. Figure 9-11 shows the property page that appears from this menu selection; it allows administrators to enter a description of a given method or property in case it causes problems later.

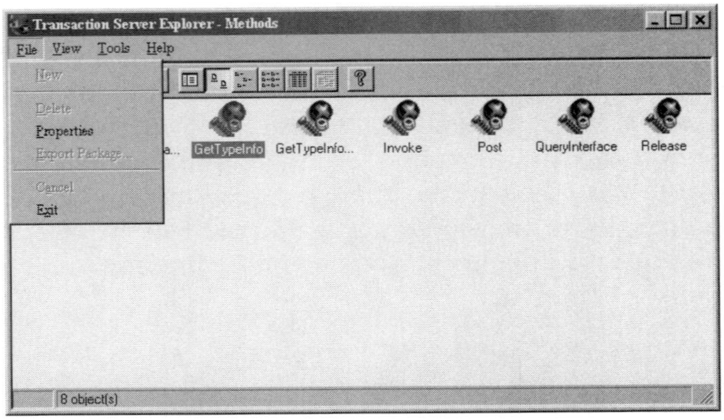


*Figure 9-10*
*Using the MTS Explorer File menu Properties option at the interface methods level*

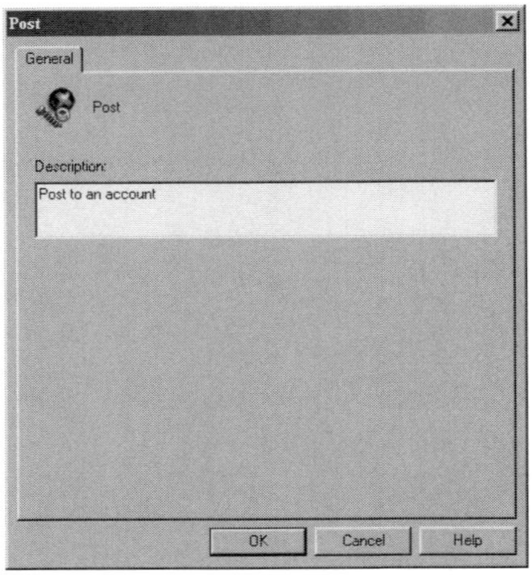


*Figure 9-11*
*Entering a method description in MTS Explorer*

Now move back up two levels (you can use the backup button on the MTS Explorer toolbar) to the main Interfaces display and again select Properties. You'll see the dialog shown in Figure 9-12 if you click on its left-hand (General) tab. This property page gives you a critical bit of information, namely the IID (Interface IDentifier) of the interface in Registry GUID format. If you are having trouble with a component, this value can be manually searched in the Registry to make sure things are as they should be there. You can also enter a description of the interface in the edit control.

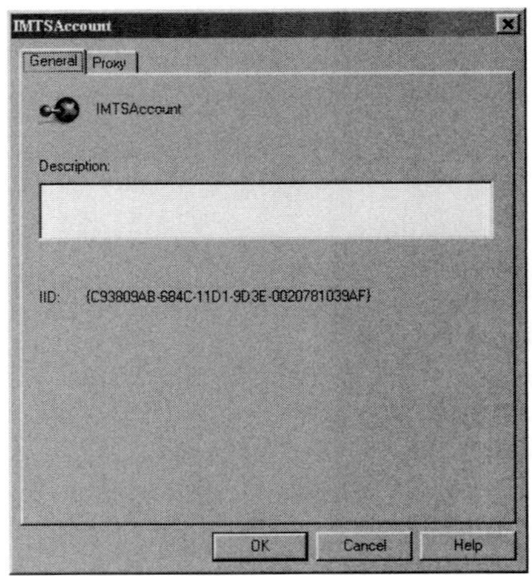


*Figure 9-12*
*Properties of a COM interface in MTS Explorer*

The right-hand (Proxy) tab of this property page gives administrators two more vital bits of COM information about the MTS component, as shown in Figure 9-13. The upper display gives the GUID and filename of the proxy/stub DLL used by the component (normally OLEAUT32.DLL); this is what is used to allow the component to work with the COM system to send data back and forth. If you experience data corruption in an MTS component, this is an essential place to check. The lower display gives the location and GUID of the Type Library associated with the

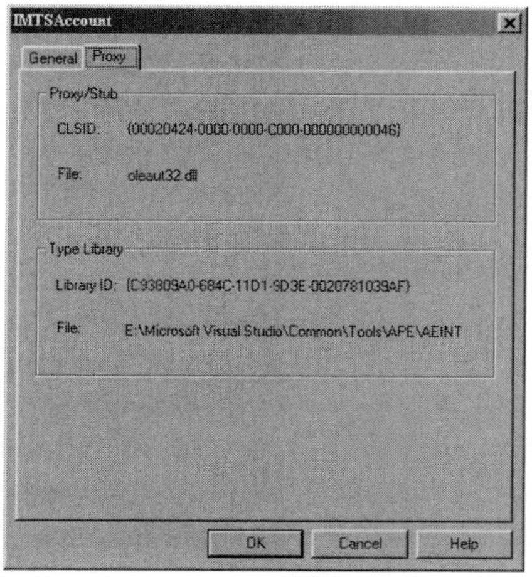


***Figure 9-13*** *Proxy/Stub and Type Library GUID and file values in MTS Explorer*

component; if a component has problems obtaining a component reference or using its methods, check for a problem with the TLB file given in this display.

Again move up two levels back to the Components level in the MTS hierarchy; select a component icon and then File|Properties. You'll see a display similar to Figure 9-14 if you click on the General tab of the property sheet. This display contains three key bits of data about the component: its filename and path, the CLSID of its COM server, and the package it is a part of (for the current instance; a component can participate in more than one MTS package at the same time). You can also enter a description of the component in the edit control. Now click on the Transaction tab to see a vital aspect of MTS Explorer configuration.

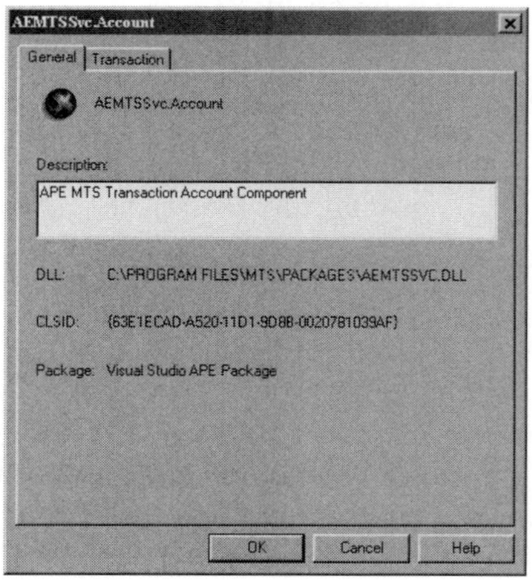


***Figure 9-14*** *Setting Component general properties in MTS Explorer*

MTS's main job is to maintain state across transactions from different databases. To do this, MTS Explorer needs information about what to do when a new instance (object in memory) is created for a given component. This tab of the component property sheet is where the developer or MTS administrator tells MTS what to do. There are, as shown in Figure 9-15, four possible states:

- **Requires a Transaction** This setting means that if an MTS transaction is not currently in progress when the new instance of the component is created, a new MTS transaction will be started for it. If an MTS transaction is currently under way for the component that creates the new component, the new component instance inherits that transaction instead.

- **Requires a New Transaction** This setting is identical to the previous one, except that even if an existing MTS transaction is under way, the new component instance gets a new transaction. (In practical terms, this means that success or failure of the new component's actions won't affect any other transaction, but it itself can have the benefits of a transactional environment.)
- **Supports Transactions** This setting indicates that if an MTS transaction is under way when a new instance of the component is created, it can participate in that transaction (via SetComplete, SetAbort, and other method calls to IObjectContext), but that if an MTS transaction is not in progress, it will still function correctly.
- **Does Not Support Transactions** This setting indicates that regardless of whether an MTS transaction is under way or not, the component will not participate in it and its changes to underlying databases will not report their status to MTS. However, if it is created as part of an ongoing transaction which fails, its changes will still be rolled back.

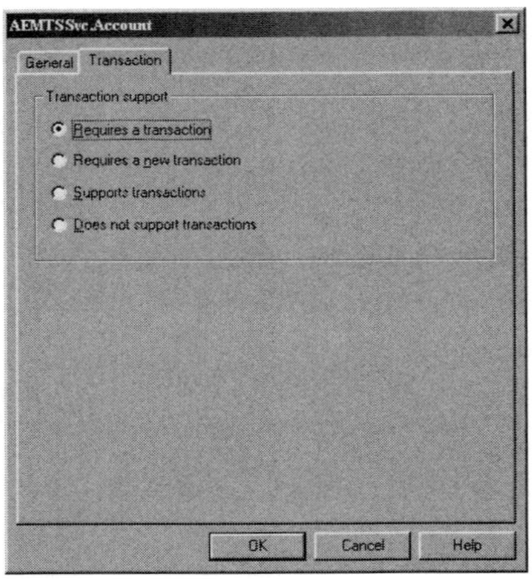


*Figure 9-15 Setting component transaction properties in MTS Explorer*

These essential settings are crucial to connecting your MTS components with the MTS system. A later section of this chapter will give you directions to set the MTS components you created in earlier chapters using this property page.

Again move up two levels, this time to the Package level of the MTS hierarchy. Again select a package and click on File|Properties. You'll see a display similar to that shown in Figure 9-16 if you click on the General tab of the property sheet dialog. This page gives you the GUID for the package (not really useful unless you are writing administration routines in C++, which we won't cover here), the name of the package in the MTS Explorer, and a place to enter your comments about what the package is supposed to do. Now click on the Advanced tab of the dialog box.

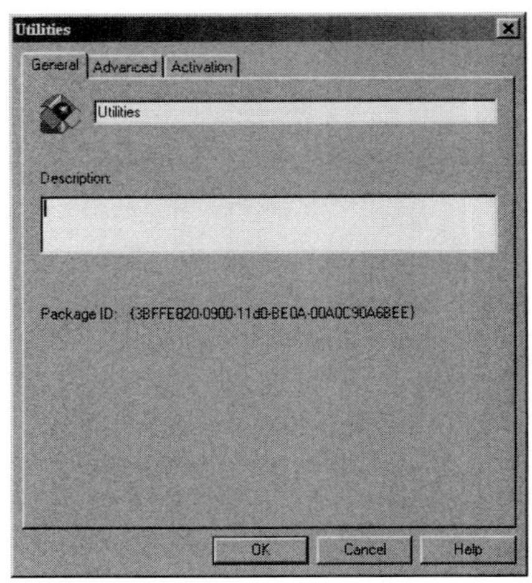


*Figure 9-16 Setting package general properties in MTS Explorer*

This page of the property sheet dialog is where several key settings for the package are controlled. The upper portion allows developers and administrators to determine whether to kill the server process containing the MTS elements as soon as it ends execution, or leave it around to be picked up by another MTS client after an interval in seconds that can be set in the edit control, or leave it running until MTS shuts down (the upper radio button). The lower portion of the display allows the administrator to disable both deletion of the package and making any changes to it; this is important in case some other users have privileges to access the MTS Explorer but not enough to access it at package level. Now click on the Activation tab of the dialog.

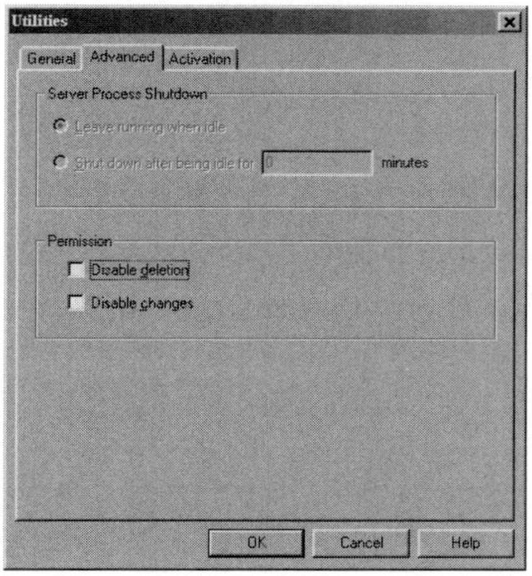


***Figure 9-17*** *Setting package advanced properties in MTS Explorer*

One of the key capabilities of MTS involves where components are created (for security purposes); this dialog allows developers and administrators to select creation either inside a client process (in which case security is disabled) or inside the server process for MTS (in which case security works normally).

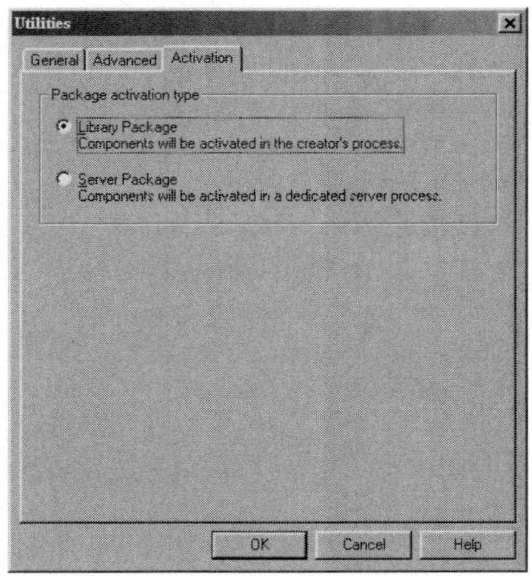


***Figure 9-18*** *Setting package activation properties in MTS Explorer*

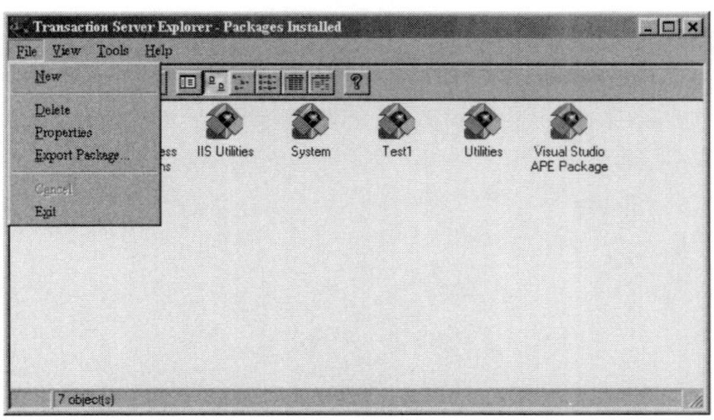


***Figure 9-19*** *Additional MTS Explorer menu options at the component level*

At the package level, there are two additional menu options available: Delete and Export Package, as shown in Figure 9-19. Selecting a package and then choosing the File|Delete menu option brings up the confirmation dialog shown in Figure 9-20. If you click on Yes, the package is deleted

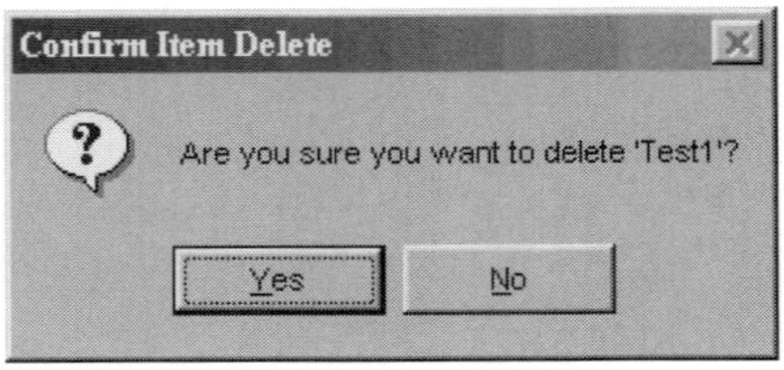


*Figure 9-20* The deletion confirmation dialog for an MTS package in MTS Explorer

from MTS but the underlying files are not, so you can continue to use them in other MTS packages or place them into another package (existing or newly created).

The other menu option is more sophisticated; it allows creation of a file that will contain information about all the components in the MTS package, and when this file is accessed from the MTS package wizard, it will arrange to re-create itself on the new computer. As shown in Figure 9-21, this menu selection brings up a configuration dialog which permits developers and administrators to select the directory to create the file, and whether or not to include the Role settings associated with it.

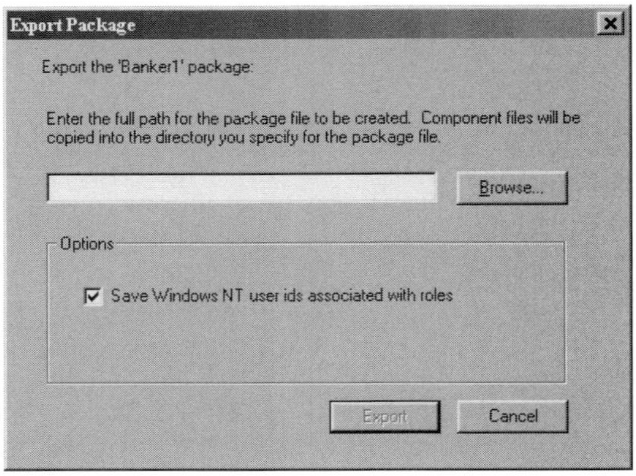


*Figure 9-21* Exporting a package in MTS Explorer

## Package Creation and Manipulation in MTS Explorer

As we noted in the previous section, the one essential skill to using MTS and MTS Explorer is the creation of packages, because to take advantage of MTS, an MTS-aware COM component must be installed in the MTS Explorer as part of a package. To do this, you first need to copy the MTS-aware COM components to the computer in question and place their information into its Registry. After that, you can start up the MTS Explorer and create a package for them.

To create a new MTS package, first start the MTS Explorer and navigate to the package level. Then select File|New. The Package Wizard dialog appears as shown in Figure 9-22.

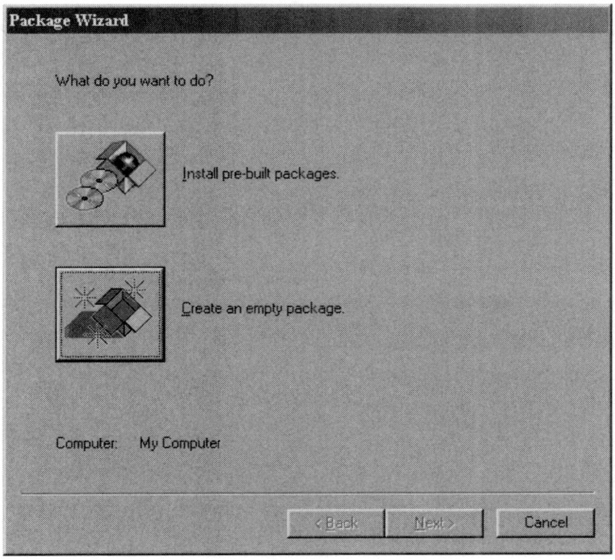


***Figure 9-22***
*The MTS Explorer Package Wizard dialog*

The figure shows the two basic options for creating a new MTS package: Either install a pre-built one (via the Export package option discussed in the last section) or create a new empty one. First, let's examine what happens when the first button is clicked; you will initially see a wizard page dialog similar to that in Figure 9-23.

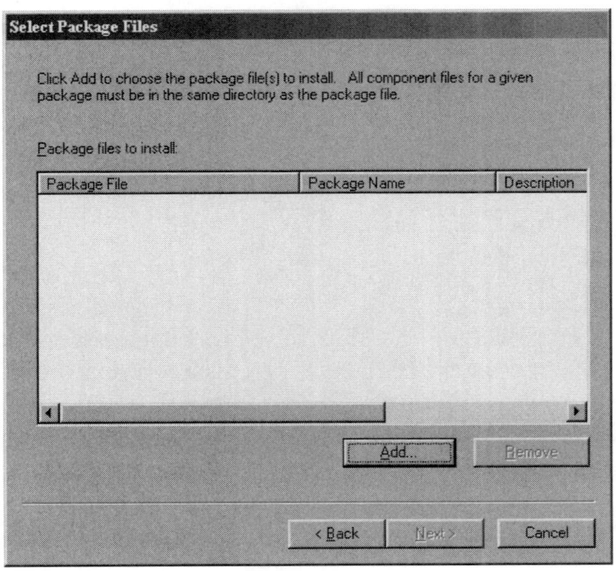


***Figure 9-23***
*The MTS Explorer Package Wizard package selection dialog*

This page of the wizard will usually come up blank as shown in the figure. It contains all the packages the wizard has currently scanned and is prepared to install on the current machine. To locate a package file and its associated

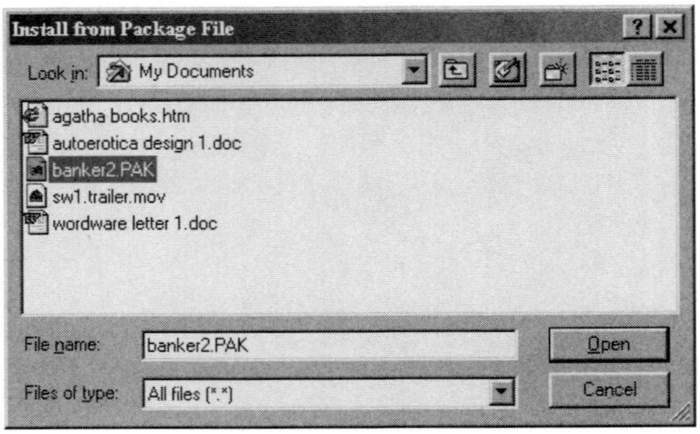


**Figure 9-24** *The MTS Explorer Package Wizard file selection dialog*

components (which must be in the same directory as it is in, as set up by the Export Package menu option), click on the Add button. A file selection dialog similar to that shown in Figure 9-24 will appear.

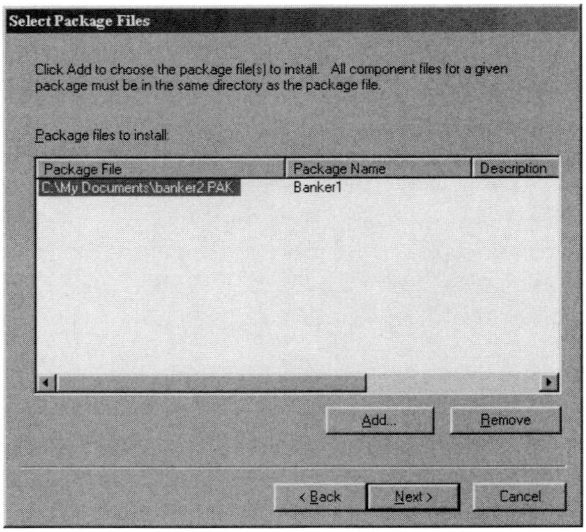


**Figure 9-25** *The MTS Explorer Package Wizard package selection dialog revisited*

This file selection dialog lets you hunt for the file created with the Export Package option. Note that in the figure, this file has the PAK extension. As of version 2.0, MTS does not enforce a file extension type for this file, so you can name it anything you like. Once you select a package file and click on the Open button, MTS will process the package and you'll return to the display shown in Figure 9-25.

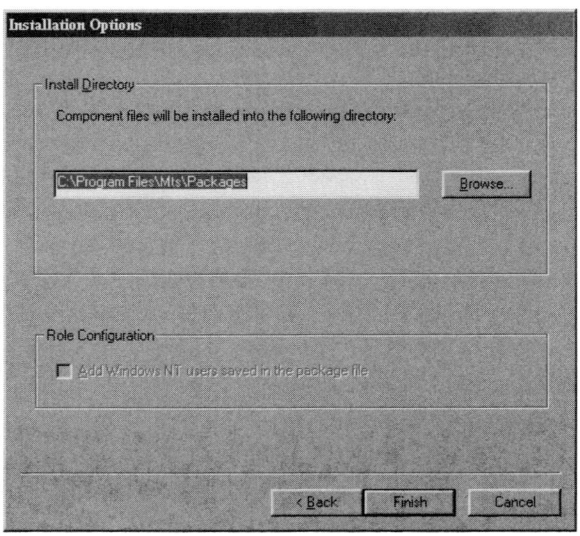


**Figure 9-26** *The MTS Explorer Package Wizard final page*

You can repeat this process for as many packages as you like. If you decide not to install a given package, click on it in the list and then press the Remove button. Once you've finished selecting all the packages to install, click on the Next button of the wizard to move to its final page, shown in Figure 9-26.

On the final wizard page for importing an MTS package, there is an edit control and Browse button to select the directory where the component files will be copied (the default is a directory off the main MTS one), and a check box to optionally automatically configure the security role information sent over with the package. When you click on Finish, the packages you've selected will have their files copied to the selected directory, have their MTS package information placed into the MTS Explorer, and optionally have their security roles configured.

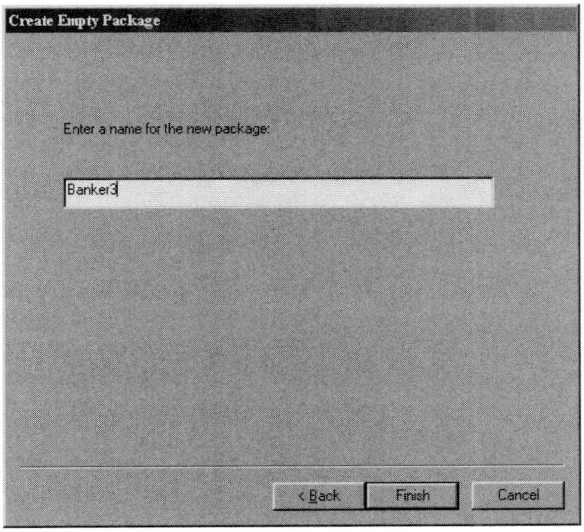


*Figure 9-27* The MTS Explorer Create Empty Package Wizard page

To create a new MTS package, select the lower button on the first wizard dialog page; if you do this, the wizard page shown in Figure 9-27 appears.

The only information you need to provide MTS to create a new empty MTS package is, as shown in the figure, its name. When you've entered it (it cannot conflict with existing names), click on Finish to create the new empty MTS package with that name. It will be assigned its "real" name (a GUID value) by MTS.

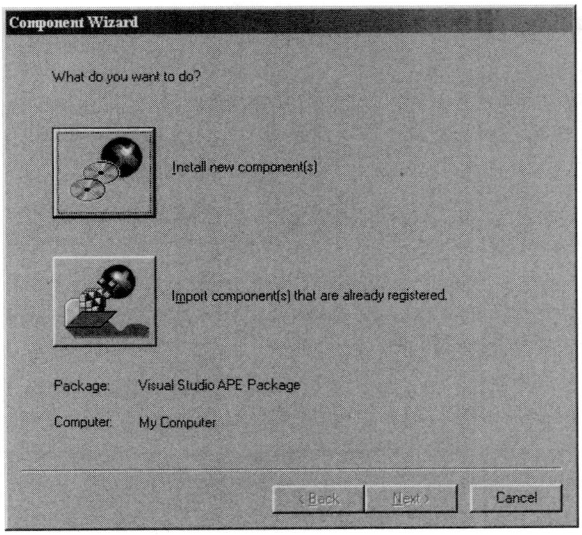


*Figure 9-28* The MTS Explorer Component Wizard page

Next, move into the newly created but empty MTS package. Again select the File|New menu option. A Component Wizard dialog will appear as shown in Figure 9-28.

This wizard also gives you two options: to install new COM components not in the Registry or to install COM components that are already registered. First, select the upper button; a display similar to that shown in Figure 9-29 will appear.

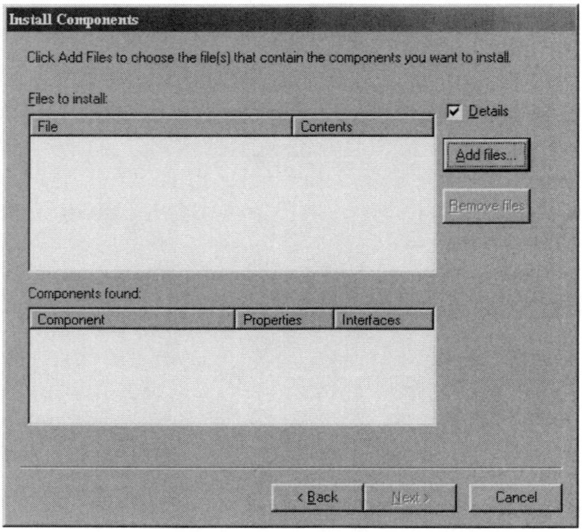


***Figure 9-29***
*The MTS Explorer Install Components page*

Initially this dialog will be empty as shown in the figure. To start the process of locating unregistered COM components to install in MTS, click on the Add Files button. A file search dialog similar to that in Figure 9-30 will be shown, allowing you to locate a DLL or OCX file for addition to the MTS system and COM system as well.

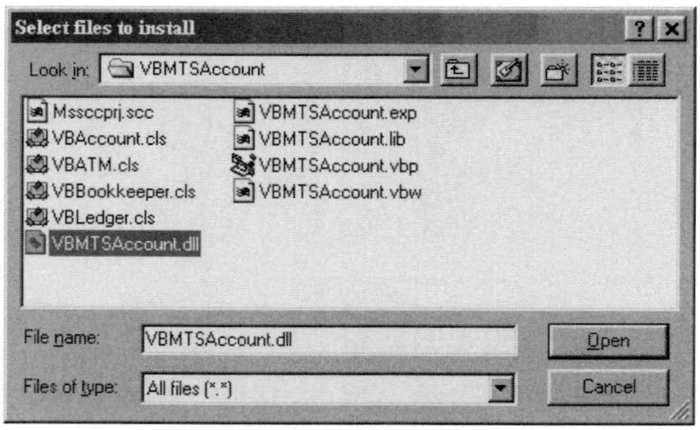


***Figure 9-30***
*The MTS Explorer file search dialog*

Use this dialog to locate the executable file for the COM server in question and click on Open. The MTS system will analyze the contents of the file and return to the display illustrated in Figure 9-31.

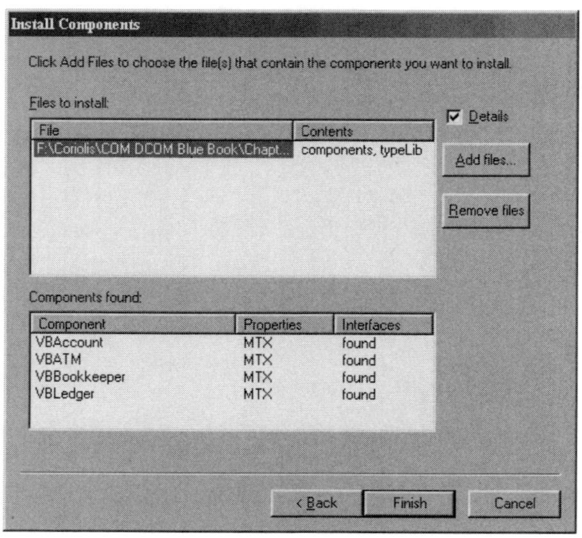


***Figure 9-31***
*The MTS Explorer Install Components page revisited*

This figure shows a sample importing of four MTS-aware components in a single COM server DLL. You can repeat this process to install as many components and their executables as you wish, but remember that all of them will be in the current package. When you are finished, click on the Finish button to perform both the COM and MTS installations. Figure 9-32 shows how the MTS Explorer display will show the newly registered and installed COM components as part of the current package.

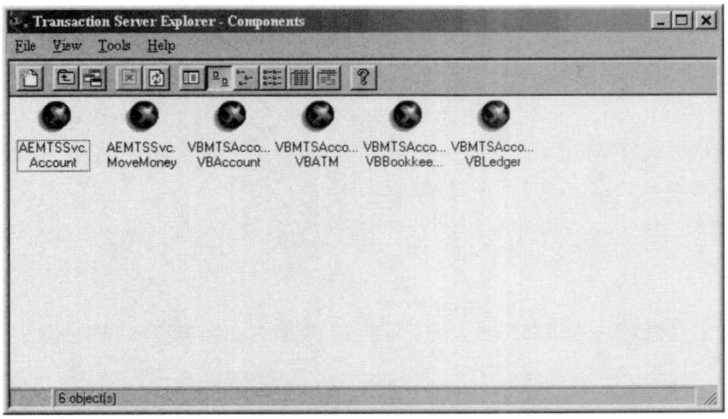


***Figure 9-32***
*The MTS Explorer showing newly installed and imported COM components*

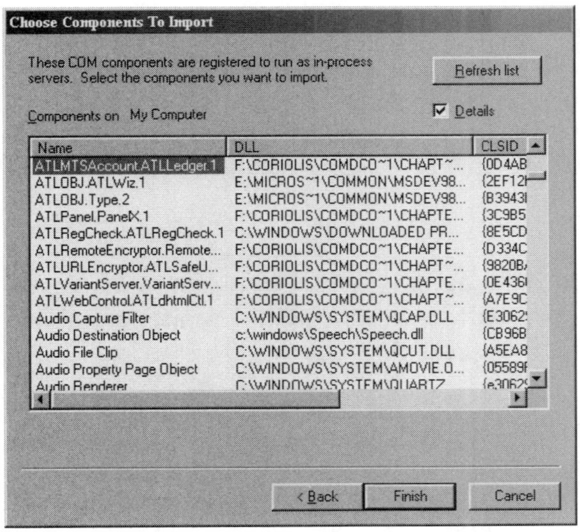


***Figure 9-33***
*The MTS Explorer component selection dialog*

The alternative method for installing COM components in MTS is to use existing ones that are already registered with COM in the Windows Registry. Figure 9-33 shows the wizard dialog that pressing the lower button in the Component Wizard dialog will display.

As shown in the figure, all the in-process (DLL) COM components registered on the current system are displayed. It is up to the developer/administrator to know which components are desired; this can perhaps be learned from their ProgID (shown to the left), their filename and path (shown in the middle), or in rare cases from their CLSID GUID value (shown to the right). Once a component has been located, select it and click on the Finish button of the wizard. As shown in Figure 9-34, the selected component will be installed in the current MTS package.

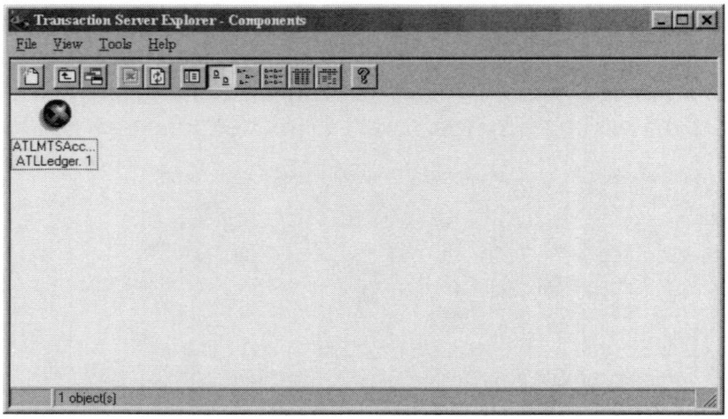


*Figure 9-34*
*An MTS component installed from an existing COM component in MTS Explorer*

# Creating the Packages for the Wallys Components

All the above is theory and illustration; let's get our hands dirty! The following section will give you step-by-step instruction in creating the packages for the ATL and MFC components of the online video store demonstration application created in Chapters 6 to 8. Then it will show you how to run the applications, both from the Windows environment and via a Web page, and verify that they are indeed connecting to MTS and working properly. Unlike some other step-by-step sections, this one won't show you figures as a guideline; instead, refer to the figures in the previous sections if you get lost.

## *Step-By-Step*

Copy the files for the ATL and MFC DLL and OCX executables to the machine where MTS will run (usually a server computer and preferably one with IIS installed if you want to test the ASP demonstration).

Start the MTS Explorer application.

Move down to the Packages level in the MTS Explorer hierarchy.

Using the wizard explained above, create a new empty MTS package named WallysVideoEmporium. Do the same for another empty MTS package named MFCWallysVideoEmporium.

Move into the WallysVideoEmporium MTS package. Using the wizard explained above, find the DLL and OCX files for the ATL components and import them into the package.

Repeat the previous step for the MFCWallysVideos MTS package with the MFC components executables.

Move back to the WallysVideoEmporium MTS package. Select the ATLMTSWallysVideos component and use its Properties dialog to set its Transaction attribute to Requires a Transaction. Do the same for the ATLMTSWallysAccounts component. Then select the ATLASPWallys-

VideoManager component, and set its Transaction attribute to Requires a New Transaction. Finally, select the ATLAxWallysVideosControl component and set its Transaction attribute to Supports Transactions.

Repeat the above steps for the MFC components of the same names.

Close MTS Explorer to save your changes.

## Creating the Sample Databases with SQL Server 7 Enterprise Manager

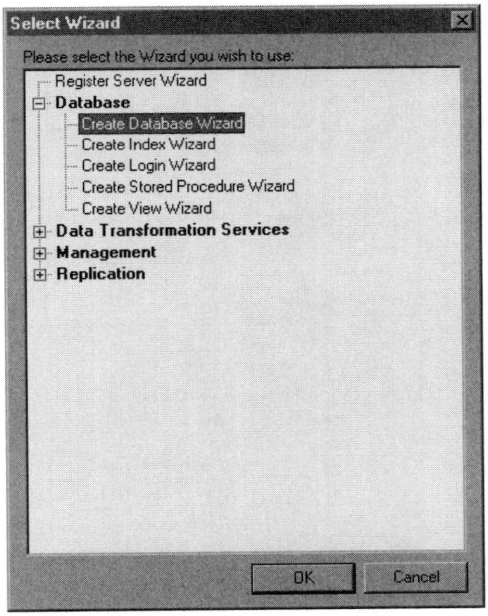


*Figure 9-35 The SQL Server 7 Enterprise Manager Wizard Selection dialog*

In order to use SQL Server 7 for the online video store demo application, you need to create two databases and populate them. To do this, start the SQL Server 7 Enterprise Manager from the Start menu. In the user interface, select the Databases entry, and then click on the Wizard icon or select Wizard from the Action menu. The Select Wizard dialog appears as shown in Figure 9-35.

The figure shows various wizards supported by SQL Server 7; expand the Database tree and select Create Database Wizard as shown in the figure. Click on OK to bring up the opening page of the Create Database Wizard. The welcome page of the Create Database Wizard appears; it lists the various things you can do with the wizard. Once you've read it, press Next to start the process. You'll then see a dialog very similar to that in Figure 9-36.

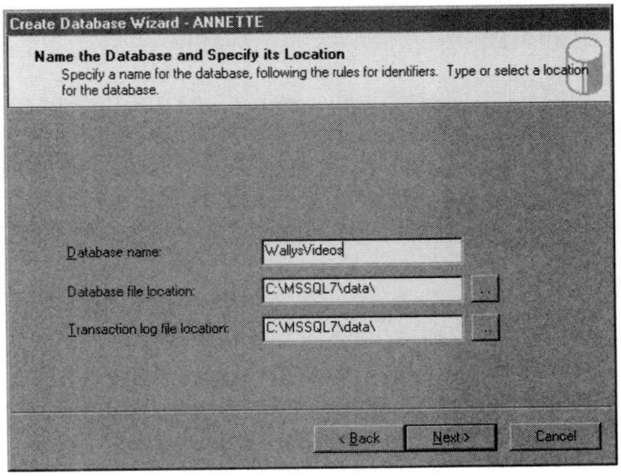


*Figure 9-36 The SQL Server 7 Enterprise Manager Create Database Wizard dialog names page*

In this page, you enter the name of the SQL Server 7 database to create and provide locations for its files (database and transaction log). Use the browse ellipsis (...) buttons beside the filename edit controls to navigate to a desired directory. Enter **WallysVideos** for the database name, and select an appropriate directory for its files. Then click on Next, and you'll see a dialog page very much like Figure 9-37.

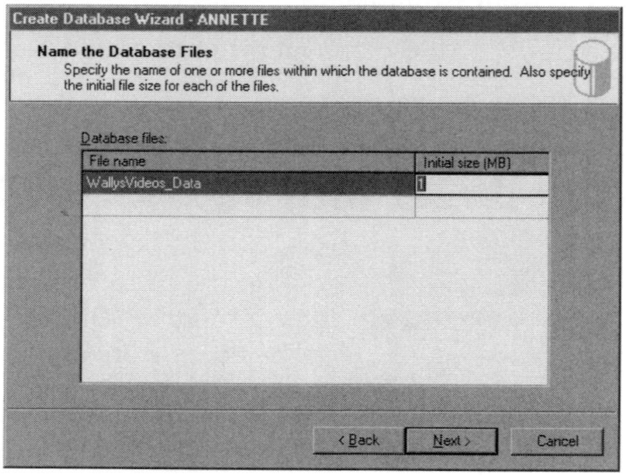


***Figure 9-37*** *The SQL Server 7 Enterprise Manager Create Database Wizard dialog database configuration page*

This page allows you to enter a name for the file (without an extension) that will hold the database's data. You can also select an initial size in megabytes. For now, leave the default selections unchanged and press Next. Move on to the dialog page shown in Figure 9-38.

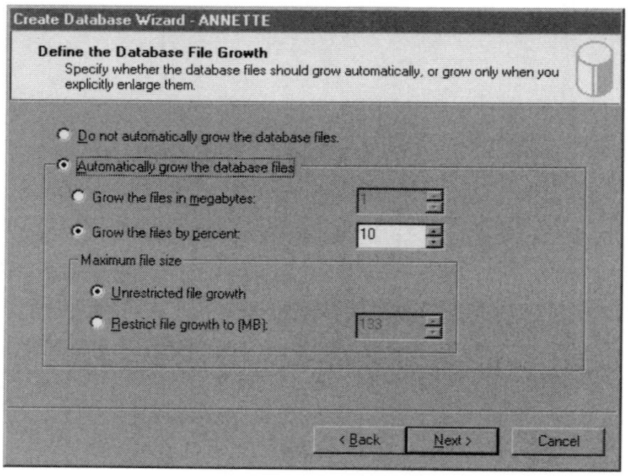


***Figure 9-38*** *The SQL Server 7 Enterprise Manager Create Database Wizard dialog database constraints page*

This page of the wizard allows you to control how the database file will grow over time. It allows you to prevent growth at all, or set it for percentage or megabyte-based growth. You can also set a maximum database file size if you wish. For this demo database, accept all the default settings and press Next.

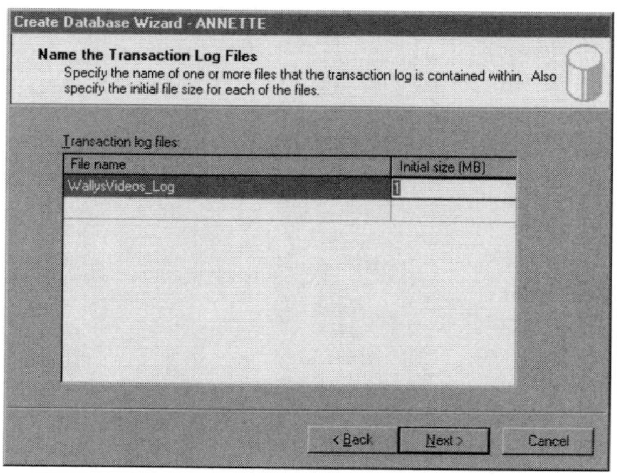


***Figure 9-39*** *The SQL Server 7 Enterprise Manager Create Database Wizard dialog transaction log configuration page*

The transcription log configuration page, shown in Figure 9-39, allows you to enter a name for the file (without an extension) that will hold the database's transaction logs. You can also select an initial size in megabytes. For now, leave the default selections unchanged and press Next. You'll move on to the dialog page shown in Figure 9-40.

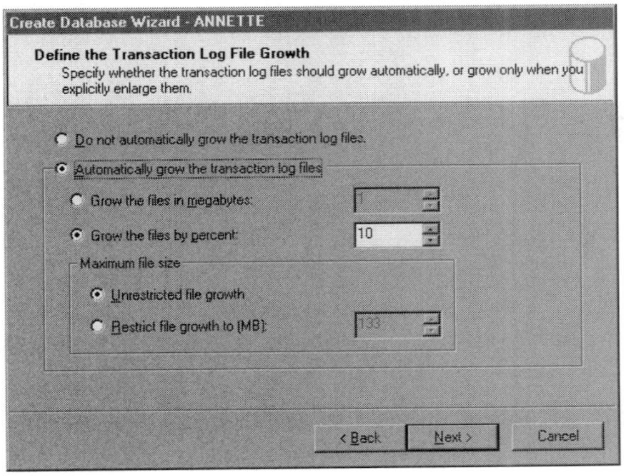


***Figure 9-40** The SQL Server 7 Enterprise Manager Create Database Wizard dialog transaction log constraints page*

This page of the wizard allows you to control how the transaction log file will grow over time. It allows you to prevent growth at all, or set it for percentage or megabyte-based growth. You can also set a maximum log file size if you wish. For this demo database, accept all the default settings and press Next. You'll move on to Figure 9-41, the completion page.

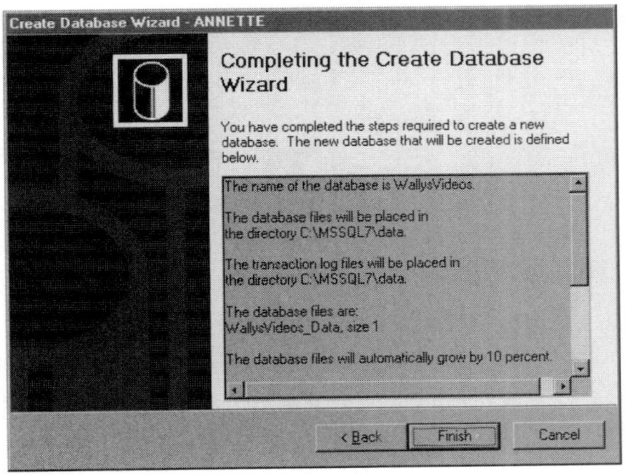


***Figure 9-41** The SQL Server 7 Enterprise Manager Create Database Wizard dialog completion page*

This dialog allows you to review your selections during the previous wizard pages. If you find you've made a mistake, you can go back and correct it. Once you press Finish, the database files and log files are actually completed. If no problems are encountered, you'll see a success dialog. If an error occurs, make sure you followed all the above directions correctly and retry.

At this point you have a created database with no structure except the minimum needed by SQL Server 7. To add structure, you need to define a table with your custom columns. To do this, open the WallysVideos database in the tree control, and click on the Tables entry. The pre-created tables are shown in the right-hand display. Right-click on the Tables entry, and select New Table as shown in Figure 9-42.

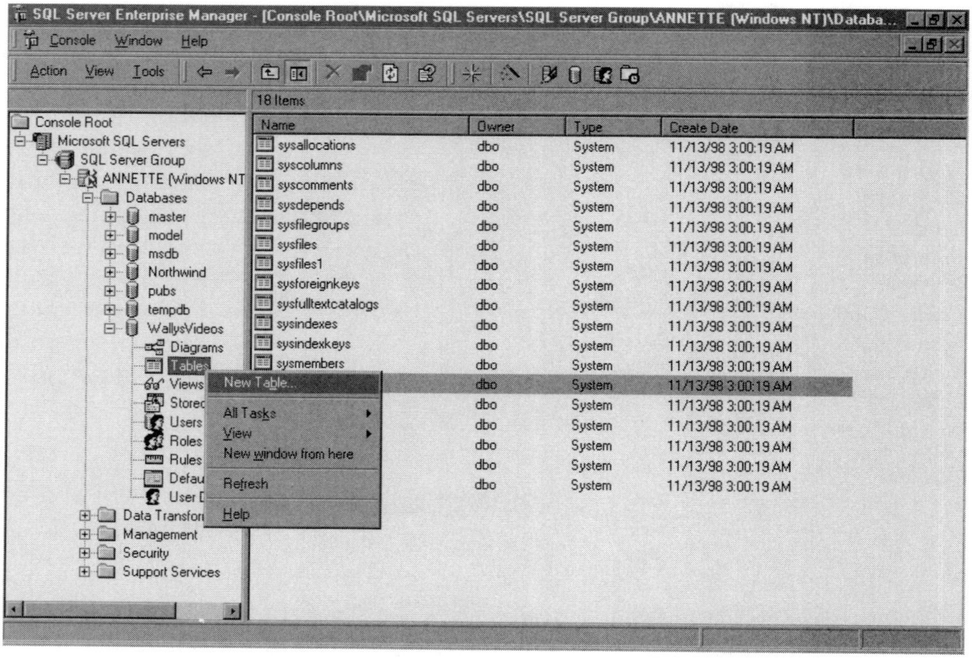

**Figure 9-42** *The SQL Server 7 Enterprise Manager New Table context menu option*

After a moment, the New Table Name Entry dialog appears. Enter **Videos** as the table name and click on OK.

After a brief delay, the display shown in Figure 9-43 appears, except without any of the column names or other information. Type in the names shown in the figure, and select the values shown from the appropriate drop-down lists. Click on the file icon to the upper left to save the data, then close the inner window (lower close button) to return to the main SQL Server Enterprise Manager display.

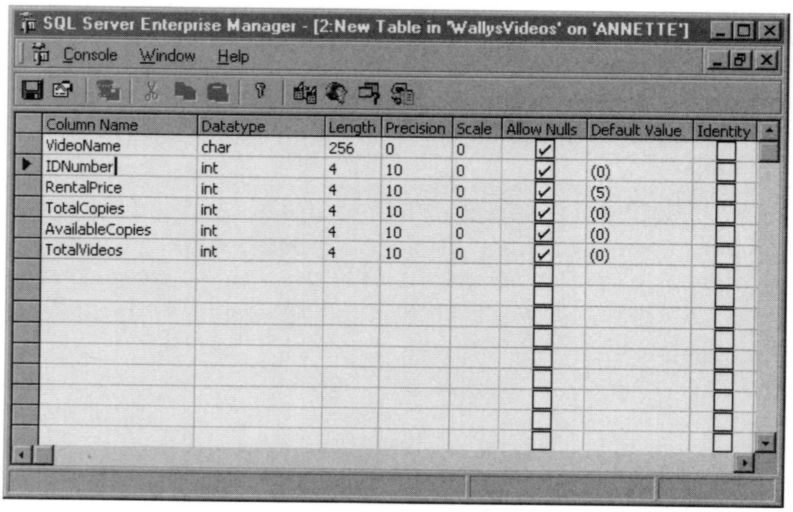

**Figure 9-43** *The SQL Server 7 Enterprise Manager Table Creation dialog*

Back at the Tables display, select the newly added Videos table, and right-click to bring up its context menu. Select OpenTable|Return All Rows. This will allow you to enter new information into the database.

After a moment, the display shown in Figure 9-44 will appear, except with only one row and no information. Enter the three rows (the editor automatically adds a new row as soon as any data is entered in the bottom empty one) shown in the figure. You do not need to save; the dialog automatically updates the database whenever any field is changed. Close the dialog when you are done; you have successfully entered the Videos database for the demo application.

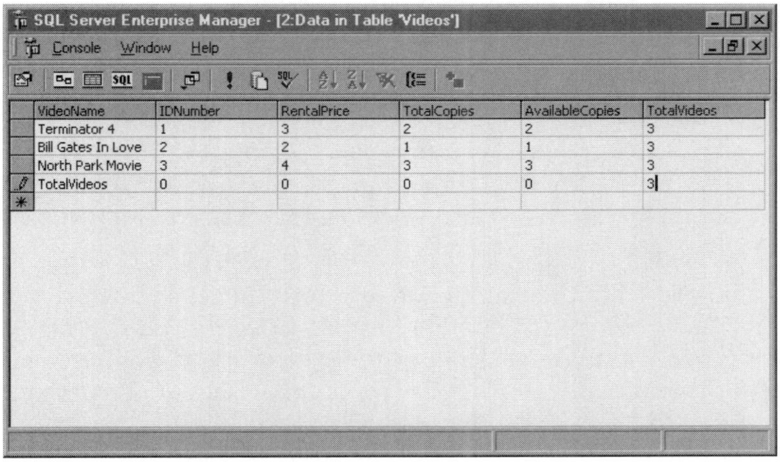


***Figure 9-44** The SQL Server 7 Enterprise Manager Table Editor*

Now again select the Databases entry, and then click on the Wizard icon or select Wizard from the Action menu. The dialog shows various wizards supported by SQL Server 7; expand the Database tree and select Create Database Wizard. Click on OK to bring up the opening page of the Create Database Wizard.

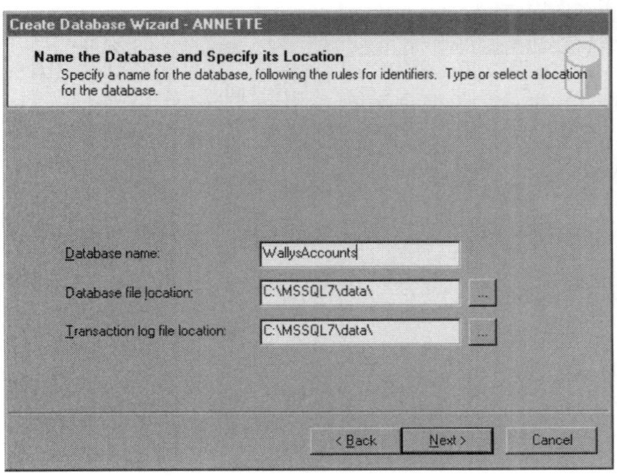


***Figure 9-45** The SQL Server 7 Enterprise Manager Create Database Wizard dialog names page*

The welcome page of the Create Database Wizard appears as before; it lists the various things you can do with the wizard. Once you've read it, press Next to start the process. You'll then see a dialog very similar to that in Figure 9-45.

In this page you enter the name of the SQL Server 7 database to create and provide locations for its files (database and transaction log). Use the browse ellipsis (...) buttons beside the filename edit controls to navigate to a desired directory. Enter **WallysAccounts** for the database name, and select an appropriate directory for its files. Then click on Next to bring up the database configuration page.

This page allows you to enter a name for the file (without an extension) that will hold the database's data. You can also select an initial size in megabytes. For now, leave the default selections unchanged and press Next.

You'll move on to the database constraints page, which allows you to control how the database file will grow over time. It allows you to prevent growth at all, or set it for percentage or megabyte-based growth. You can also set a maximum database file size if you wish. For this demo database, accept all the default settings and press Next.

The transaction log configuration page will appear. This page allows you to enter a name for the file (without an extension) that will hold the database's transaction logs. You can also select an initial size in megabytes. For now, leave the default selections unchanged and press Next.

You'll move on to the transaction log constraints page, which allows you to control how the transaction log file will grow over time. It allows you to prevent growth at all, or set it for percentage or megabyte-based growth. You can also set a maximum log file size if you wish. For this demo database, accept all the default settings and press Next.

The completion page will appear. This dialog allows you to review your selections during the previous wizard pages. If you find you've made a mistake, you can go back and correct it. Once you press Finish, the database files and log files are actually completed. If no problems are encountered, you'll see a success dialog. If an error occurs, make sure you followed the above directions correctly and retry.

At this point you have a created database with no structure except the minimum needed by SQL Server 7. To add structure, you need to define a table with your custom columns. To do this, open the WallysAccounts database in the tree control, and click on the Tables entry. The pre-created tables are shown in the right-hand display. Right-click on the Tables entry, and select New Table. Enter **Accounts** as the table name and click on OK.

After a brief delay, the display shown in Figure 9-46 appears, except without any of the column names or other information. Enter the names shown in the figure, and select the values shown from the appropriate drop-down lists. Click on the file icon to the upper left to save the data, then close the inner window (lower close button) to return to the main SQL Server Enterprise Manager display.

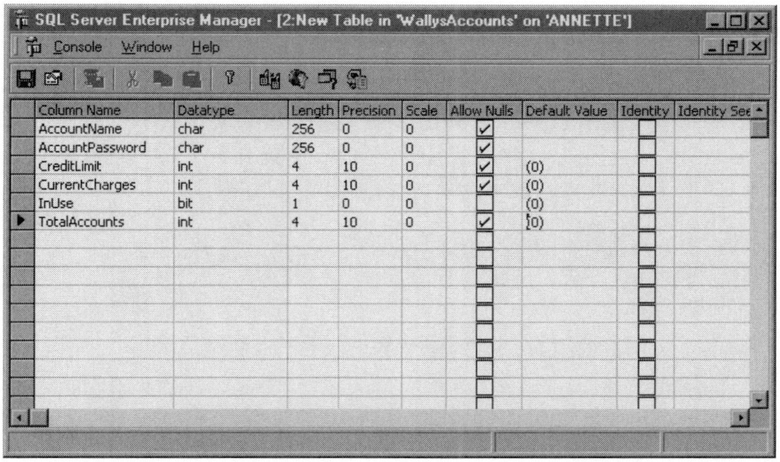


***Figure 9-46*** *The SQL Server 7 Enterprise Manager Table Creation dialog*

Back at the Tables display, select the newly added Accounts table, and right-click to bring up its context menu. Select OpenTable|Return All Rows. This will allow you to enter new information into the database.

After a moment, the display shown in Figure 9-47 will appear, except with only one row and no information. Enter the three rows (the editor automatically adds a new row as soon as any data is entered in the bottom empty one) shown in the figure. You do not need to save; the dialog automatically updates the database whenever any field is changed. Close the dialog when you are done; you have successfully entered the Accounts database for the demo application.

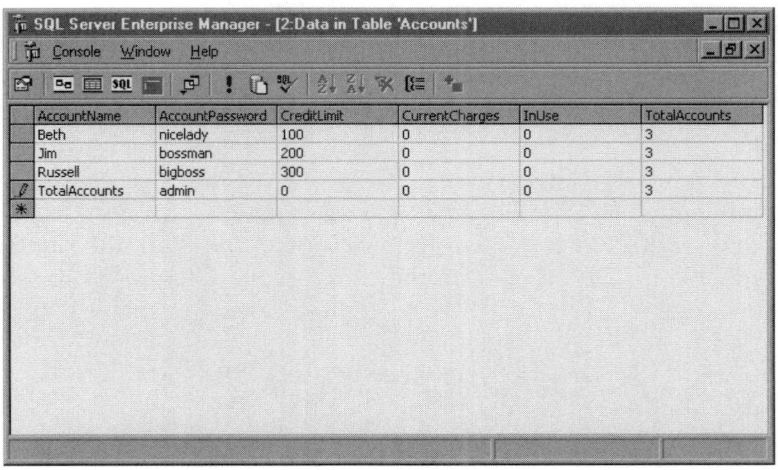


***Figure 9-47*** *The SQL Server 7 Enterprise Manager Table Editor*

# Creating the Sample Databases ODBC File DSN Entries

After you have created and populated the SQL Server 7 databases for the demo application, they still will not work correctly until they have been given a File DSN via the ODBC Configuration Wizard. The wizard is available via the ODBC Data Sources applet in Control Panel, as shown in Figure 9-48.

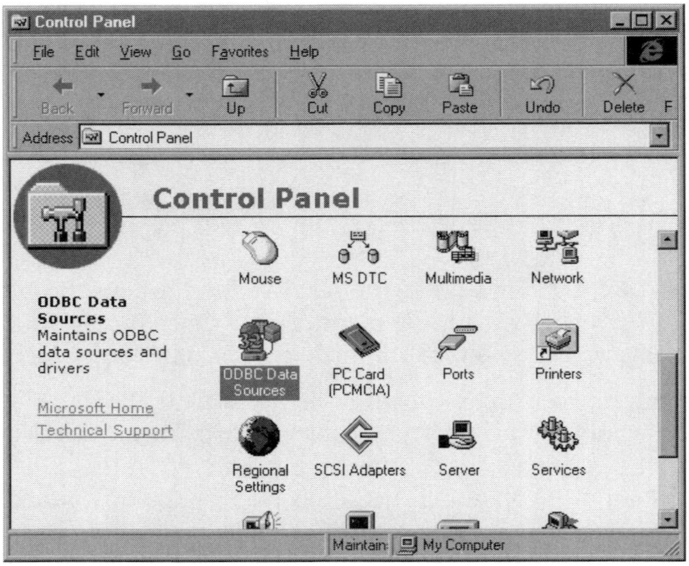


*Figure 9-48*
*The ODBC Data Sources applet in the Control Panel*

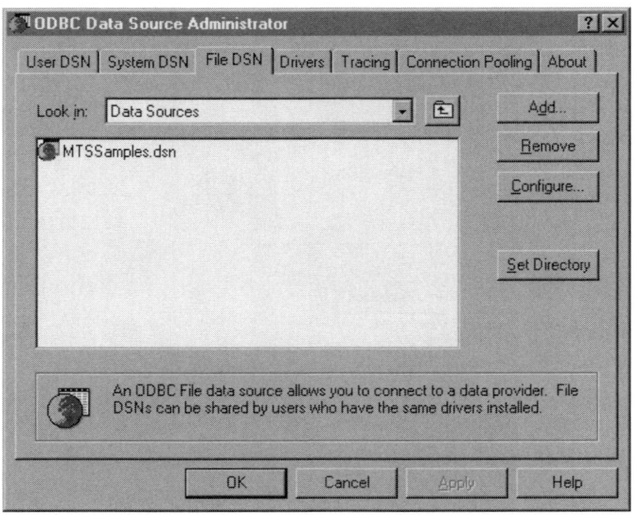


*Figure 9-49*
*The ODBC Data Source Administrator File DSN tab*

Once the ODBC Data Source Administrator dialog appears, click on the File DSN tab as shown in Figure 9-49. You may or may not see the MTSSamples entry; either way, click on the Add button to bring up the Create New Data Source Wizard.

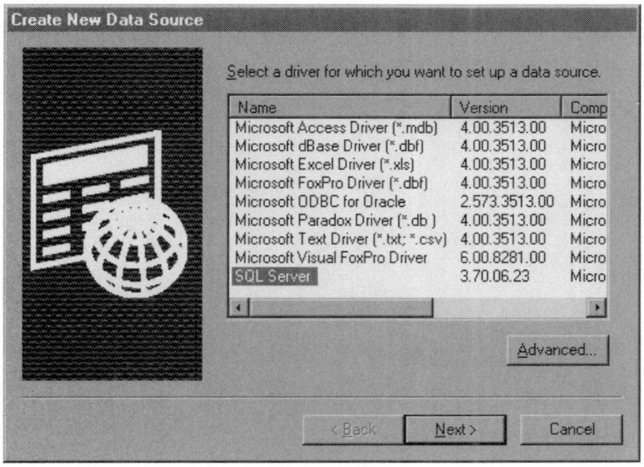


***Figure 9-50***
*The ODBC Data Source Create New Data Source Wizard driver selection page*

Figure 9-50 shows the driver selection page of the Create New Data Source Wizard from the ODBC Data Sources Control Panel applet. Scroll down if needed until you see the SQL Server entry and click on it to select it. Then click on Next to move to the next wizard page.

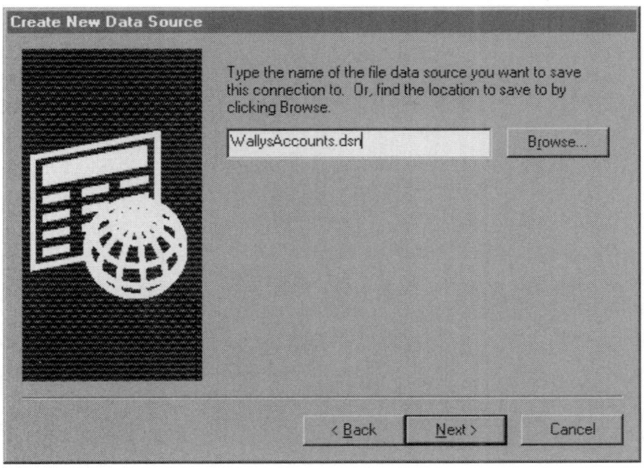


***Figure 9-51***
*The ODBC Data Source Create New Data Source Wizard DSN filename entry page*

The next page is the DSN filename entry page, illustrated in Figure 9-51. Enter **WallysAccounts.dsn** and then click on the Next button.

Next you'll see the completion page of the wizard. Click on Finish to start the DSN configuration process, administered via a SQL Server wizard.

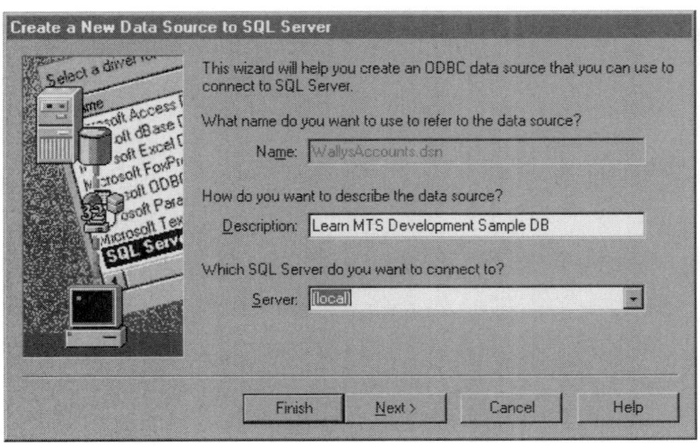


***Figure 9-52***
*The SQL Server DSN Creation Wizard first page*

Figure 9-52 shows the first page of the SQL Server DSN Creation Wizard. It allows you to enter a description of the DSN and to select from local or remote SQL Server installations. Enter **Learn MTS Development Sample DB** for the description, and select the appropriate copy of SQL Server from the drop-down list. Then click on the Next button.

The next page of the wizard controls security authentication for the DSN.

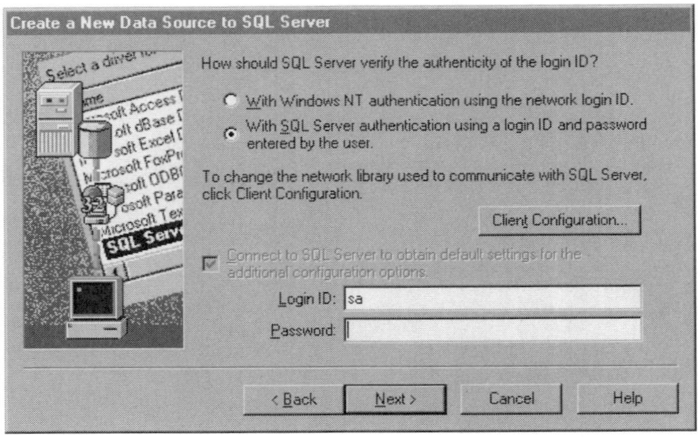


*Figure 9-53 The SQL Server DSN Creation Wizard authentication page*

Change the upper radio button to SQL Server rather than NT authentication, with a login of sa and no password. Figure 9-53 shows how the dialog should look when you are done. Click on the Next button to move on to the next page of the wizard.

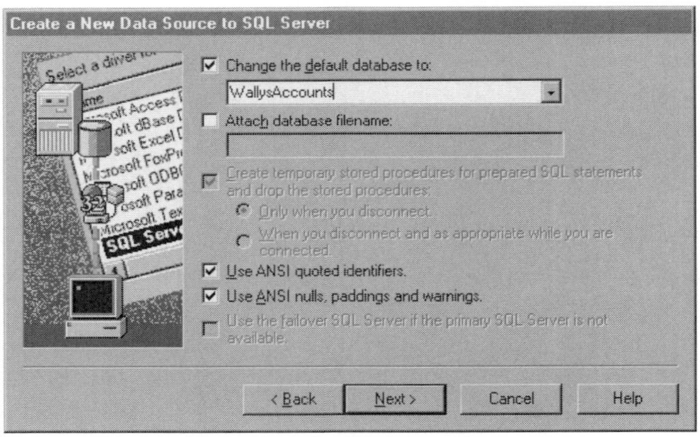


*Figure 9-54 The SQL Server DSN Creation Wizard database page*

Figure 9-54 shows the next page of the wizard, which requires you to select the database for the connection. Select the WallysAccounts database you created earlier, as shown in the figure. Leave the other selections at their defaults and click on the Next button.

The next page contains a number of advanced settings; for this demo database leave the defaults set and click on the Next button.

The last page of the wizard appears, listing all the choices you made in previous dialogs. If you need to change any of them, you must press Cancel and restart the process. To finish the process and create the DSN, click on OK. You can, however, test the DSN by clicking on the Test Data Source button.

If you have configured the DSN correctly, a success dialog will appear. Otherwise, an error dialog will appear, indicating one or more problems. In this case, click on Cancel and restart the process to fix the errors. Otherwise, click on OK to create the DSN.

Again click on the Add button of the ODBC Control Panel applet property page to bring up the Create New Data Source Wizard.

The driver selection page of the Create New Data Source Wizard from the ODBC Data Sources Control Panel applet appears. Scroll down if needed until you see the SQL Server entry and click on it to select it. Then click on Next to move to the next wizard page.

The next page is the DSN filename entry page, illustrated in Figure 9-55. Enter **WallysVideos.dsn** and then click on the Next button.

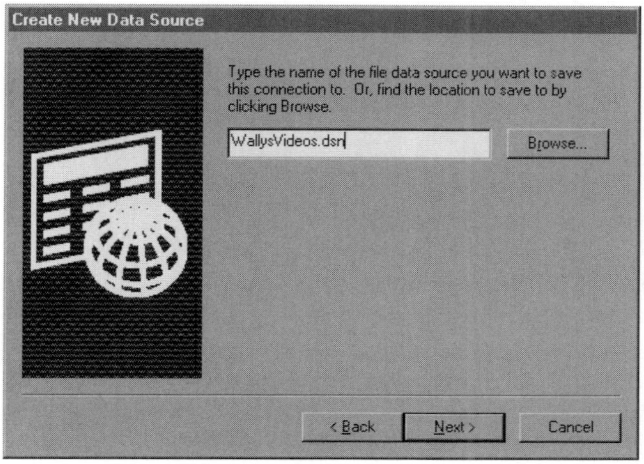


*Figure 9-55* *The ODBC Data Sources Create New Data Source Wizard DSN filename entry page*

Next you'll see the completion page of the wizard. Click on Finish to start the DSN configuration process, administered via a SQL Server wizard.

The first page of the SQL Server DSN Creation Wizard allows you to enter a description of the DSN and to select from local or remote SQL Server installations. Enter **Learn MTS Development Sample DB** for the description, and select the appropriate copy of SQL Server from the drop-down list. Then click on the Next button.

The next page of the wizard controls security authentication for the DSN. Change the upper radio button to SQL Server rather than NT authentication, with a login of sa and no password. Click on the Next button to move on to the next page of the wizard.

Figure 9-56 shows the next page of the wizard, which requires you to select the database for the connection. Select the WallysVideos database you created earlier, as shown in the figure. Leave the other selections at their defaults and click on the Next button.

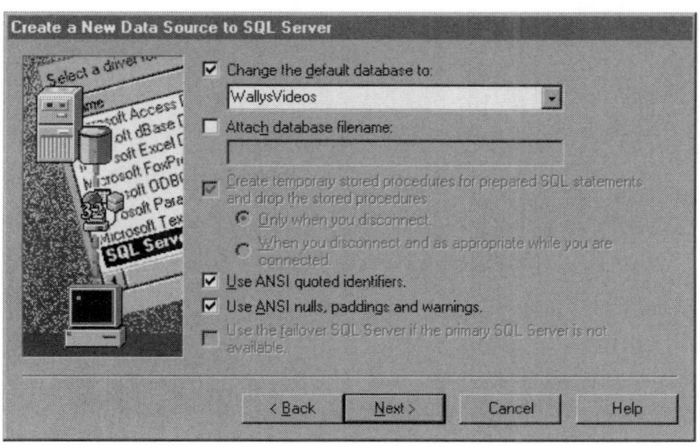


*Figure 9-56* *The SQL Server DSN Creation Wizard database page*

The next page contains a number of advanced settings; for this demo database, leave the defaults set and click on the Next button.

The last page of the wizard appears, listing all the choices you made in previous dialogs. If you need to change any of them, you must press Cancel and restart the process. To finish the process and create the DSN, click on OK. You can, however, test the DSN by clicking on the Test Data Source button.

If you have configured the DSN correctly, a success dialog will appear. Otherwise, an error dialog will appear, indicating one or more problems. In this case, click on Cancel and restart the process to fix the errors. Otherwise, click on OK to create the DSN. Once you've completed both the above processes, you should see the two new DSN entries shown in Figure 9-57. Click on OK to close the applet property sheet dialog.

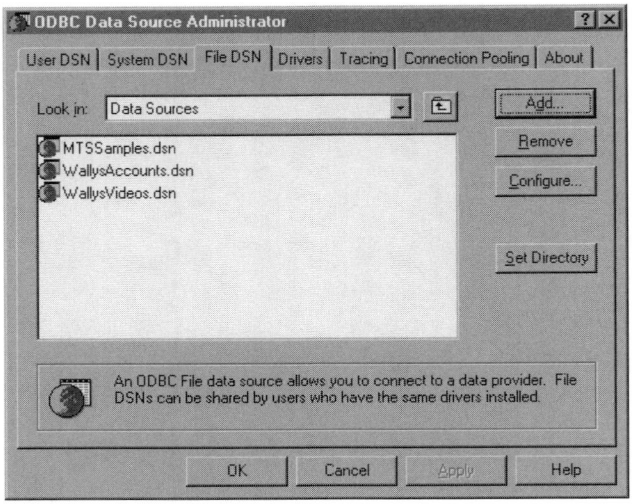


***Figure 9-57*** *The ODBC Data Source Administrator File DSN tab showing new DSN entries*

# Setting Security Roles in MTS Explorer

Once you have configured the MTS packages for the ATL and MFC applications you've created, you may wish to enable security for them to test this capability of the system. To do this, you need to start the MTS Explorer from the Start menu. Move down to the WallysVideoEmporium entry, open its components, and select the ATLMTSWallysAccount.AccountsHandler component. Open its Roles folder, then select New|Role from the Action button, as shown in Figure 9-58.

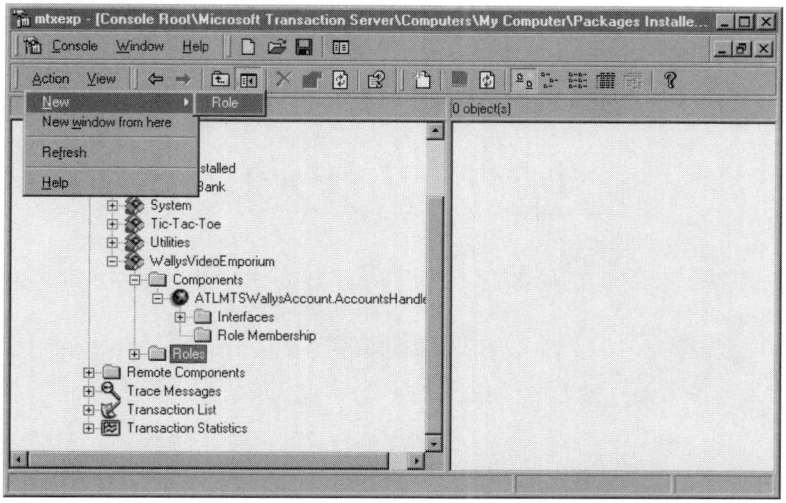


*Figure 9-58*
*The MTS Explorer Create New Role Action menu option*

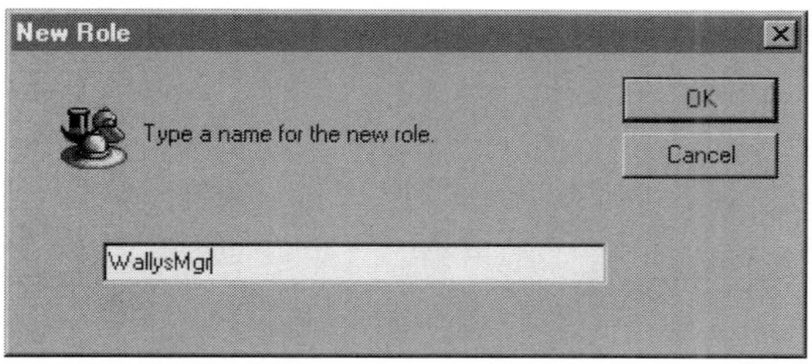


*Figure 9-59*
*The MTS Explorer New Role name entry dialog*

A dialog appears similar to that shown in Figure 9-59. Enter **WallysMgr** as the role name as shown in the figure, and click on OK.

As shown in Figure 9-60, the new role appears in the MTS Explorer under that folder; it indicates that MTS will support this role for that package.

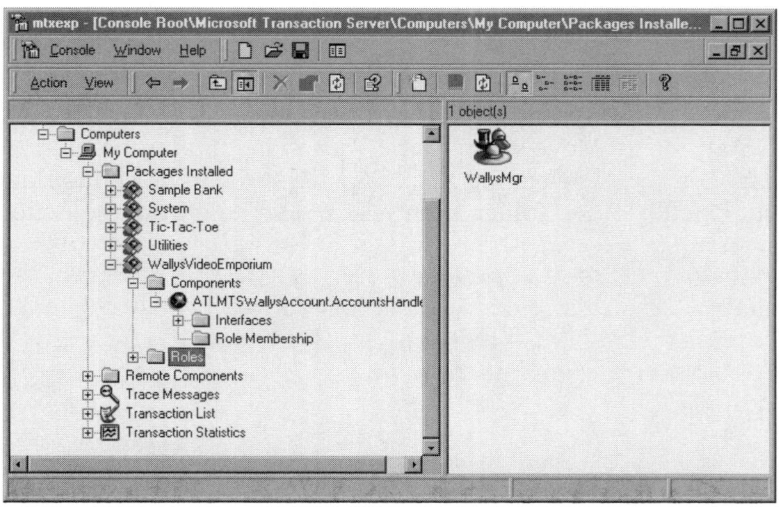


*Figure 9-60*
*The MTS Explorer showing the new role*

Expand the Users folder under the newly added role, and select New|User from the Action button, as shown in Figure 9-61.

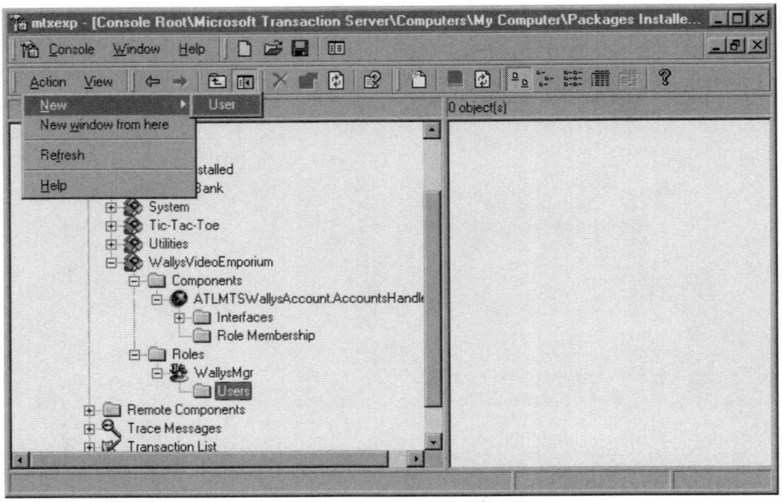


*Figure 9-61*
*The MTS Explorer Add New User to Role Action menu option*

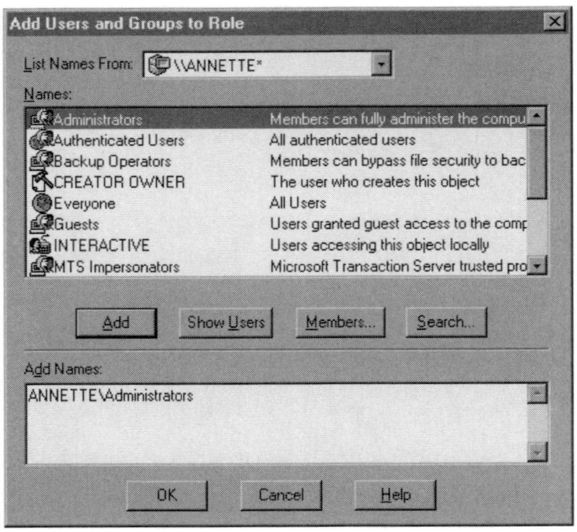


*Figure 9-62*
*The MTS Explorer Add Users to Role dialog*

A dialog appears similar to that shown in Figure 9-62. Select an appropriate user or group for the component and click on the Add button to make its members part of the selected role. When you are done, click on OK.

As shown in Figure 9-63, the new users for the role appear in the MTS Explorer under that folder; it indicates that MTS will accept anyone in the group (or the individual selected) as a valid member of the given role. Close MTS Explorer to complete the process.

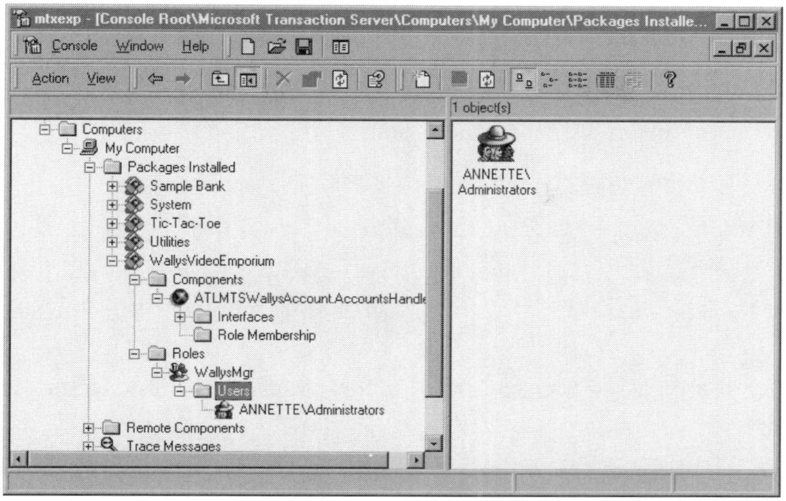


*Figure 9-63*
*The MTS Explorer showing the new user group in the role*

# Running the MTS Applications

Once you've installed the MTS packages for the fictional online video store, it is time to try out the applications that use them! The following sections show you how to use the ATL, MFC, and ASP applications to test out the components and their behavior in the MTS system.

## *Step By Step*

Start SQL Server for the machine where the ATL application will be run. MTS should already be started or configured to start when needed.

Run the ATLWallysVideos application. Enter one of the existing account names and passwords, or if you wish to test the role-based security, create a new account.

Now move to the order screen and select one of the existing videos with only one copy and order it. Since the users you entered should exist and have the money and the video is not being used, it should start "playing" for you.

Have another customer attempt to order the video the first one is currently "playing."

The customer should be marked as paying initially by the Accounts database. But when he hits the Videos database, he will learn that there isn't a copy available! This will cause the transaction to fail and an error dialog to be shown.

Back in the accounts display, notice that the second customer still has the starting available credit! MTS "rolled back" the invalid transaction! At the same time, note that the other user is down the appropriate amount since this transaction completed.

Terminate the playing video and shut down the application.

Now bring up the MFC application.

Repeat the ordering actions listed above.

Terminate the "playing" of the video and close the application.

Finally, if you have IIS available, set up the ASP page as noted in Chapter 8 and run the page in IE 4 or 5. You'll see an ordering display with the ActiveX control.

Enter the name and password of a customer and order a video with only one copy.

Now try to order the video for another customer. Again, you should get an error message.

Shut down the ASP page and return to either the ATL or MFC application. When you bring up the account, you'll see that it didn't lose the money because the ASP page's components were successfully transactioned by MTS.

Close the application. You have now utilized MTS in a full-featured e-commerce application environment!

## Where We Go From Here

You have learned about the last hurdle to standard MTS programming, namely the MTS Explorer, in this chapter; you already understand COM, ATL, MFC, ADO, and the MTS API. You might wonder what is left to learn about MTS development. The answer is: the Internet! Modern COM/MTS programmers usually have to deploy part or all of an MTS solution on the Internet/WWW as part of an e-commerce package. This requires mastery of a number of arcane skills, and the last chapter of this book will bring you up to speed on them.

Chapter Ten

# Putting MTS on the Internet

At this point, you're fully up to speed on all that Visual C++ 5.0 and/or 6 have to offer in terms of MTS. You can create and use MTS components and applications with the best of them, you understand the issues involved in creating MTS Automation Servers and ActiveX controls and clients in both ATL and MFC, and you're an ace with both the MTS Explorer and the underlying concepts behind MTS. So what's left? The Internet, that's what! More and more database developers are tasked by their clients to put DBMS (and thus MTS) functionality onto Web pages, either on a local intranet or the big, bad Internet/World Wide Web itself. Doing this requires an understanding of arcane issues totally unrelated to MTS or COM, and so the following sections will fill that essential gap. This chapter will add mastery of the LPK_Tool application for creating HTML License Keys, understanding of the ActiveX Control Pad and ActiveX SDK's Code Signing tools, and familiarity with the two major tools of Internet and World Wide Web functionality, FTP and Internet Explorer, to your MTS/COM skills inventory. Let's dig in! (Before we start, however, it is important to remember that in most places where you see "ActiveX" below, you can also substitute "COM," as in our MTS COM Automation components.)

## Using the LPK_Tool Application to Create HTML Run-time License LPK Files

Some components are sufficiently expensive that developers will want to control even their usage on WWW pages; the mechanism COM provides for this is called an LPK file. Visual C++ 5.0 and 6.0 include the LPK_TOOL.EXE application to assist with the creation of these files.

Figure 10-1 shows the location of the LPK_TOOL.EXE file on the Visual C++ 6.0 distribution CD. If you have floppy disks instead of a CD, see the Downloading the ActiveX SDK section below for an alternative location of the program.

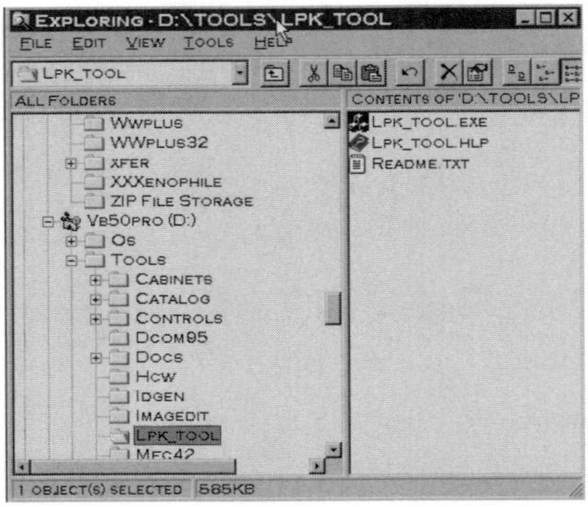


*Figure 10-1 The LPK_ TOOL.EXE file on the VC 6.0 distribution CD*

An LPK file is a text file that contains two very important pieces of information relative to Internet usage of COM components. The first element is a copyright notice that tells users not to download the file without permission; this hardly prevents it from happening but provides legal protection if a copyright infringement suit must be brought against unlicensed users of the software. The second is a MIME-encoded text string that contains the actual LPK license information.

Figure 10-2 shows the dialog which is the interface for LPK_TOOL.EXE. It consists of two list boxes and several command buttons. The left-hand list box shows all the COM elements currently registered on your computer; you can restrict it to only those controls which support licensing by checking the lower left-hand corner check box. To move a component to the right-hand list box, select it in the left-hand list box, and press the Add -> button. To remove a selected component from the right-hand list box, select it and press Remove ->.

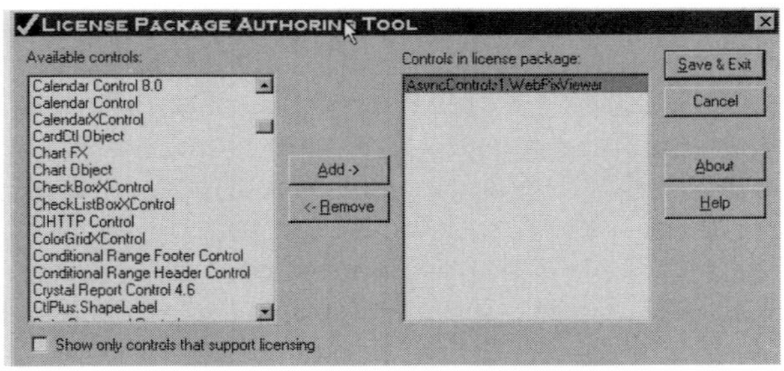


*Figure 10-2 The LPK_ TOOL.EXE file user interface*

The way that LPK files are used is vital in creating them! LPK files are required for each combination of licensed components on a given web page. In other words, if you have three instances of licensed controls on one page and two on another, you have to create a different LPK file for each page, containing the License Keys for each licensed control to be used on the page. Only one LPK file is allowed for a page (pages inside frames count as separate pages, however!), and every licensed control used on that page must have its License Key in the LPK file or the control will fail to create properly. Therefore, be sure to select all the components that will be used on a given HTML page when creating that page's LPK file.

Figure 10-3 shows the Save As dialog that appears when you press the Save & Exit button on the LPK_Tool main dialog box. Use it to navigate to the same location where you store the components to be uploaded to the web site for your OCX file and its HTML page(s); assign it a unique name based

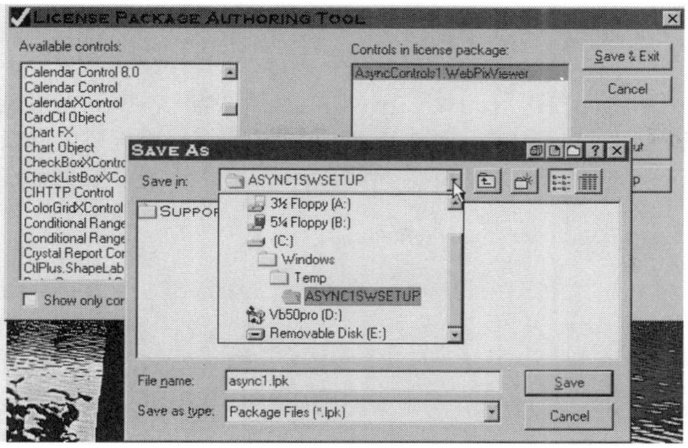


*Figure 10-3* *The LPK_TOOL Save As dialog for creating the LPK file*

on the page where the control will appear. Then press Save to actually create the LPK file.

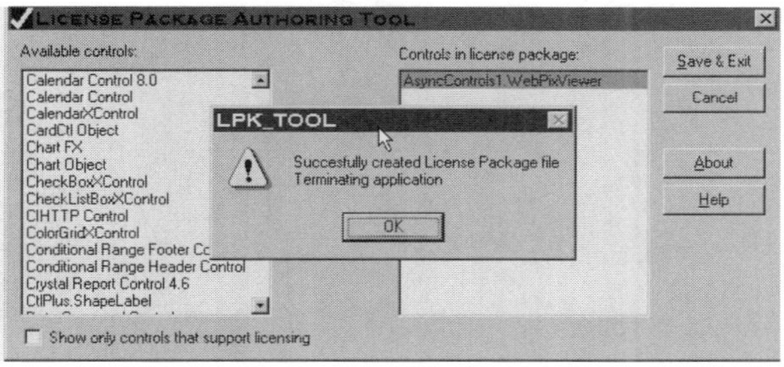


*Figure 10-4* *The LPK_TOOL success message final dialog*

Figure 10-4 shows the final dialog the LPK_Tool application will display after successfully creating the LPK file for the selected component group. Listing 10-1 shows the contents of a sample LPK file. The garbled characters at the end of the file contain the MIME-encoded License Key.

```
LPK License Package
////////////////////////////////////////////////////////////////////
//  WARNING:  The information in this file is protected by        //
//  copyright law and international treaty provisions.            //
//  Unauthorized reproduction or distribution of this file, or    //
//  any portion of it, may result in severe criminal and civil    //
//  penalties, and will be prosecuted to the maximum extent       //
//  possible under the law.  Further, you may not reverse         //
//  engineer, decompile, or disassemble the file.                 //
////////////////////////////////////////////////////////////////////
{3d25aba1-caec-11cf-b34a-00aa00a28331}
AUCU+GTTOBG32kRFU1QAAA=
AQAAAA=
1FByMCfSOBG32kRFU1QAABQAAABtAGsAagBpAGOAawBuAGkAbwBpAG4AbQB1AGoAbwBpAG4AZwBuAGcA=
```

***Listing 10-1*** *A sample LPK file*

## Downloading the ActiveX SDK

Figure 10-5 shows Internet Explorer at the download page for the ActiveX SDK from the Microsoft web site. If you wish to digitally sign your COM components, you will need to obtain a copy of the SDK from this site. The URL is:

**http://www.microsoft.com/intdev/sdk/**

Click on the Download link and follow the directions; a self-extracting compressed file containing the SDK will be downloaded by your browser and placed on your hard drive. Once you have downloaded the file (and its optional documentation), run the self-installing executable and it will place a copy of the SDK on your hard drive.

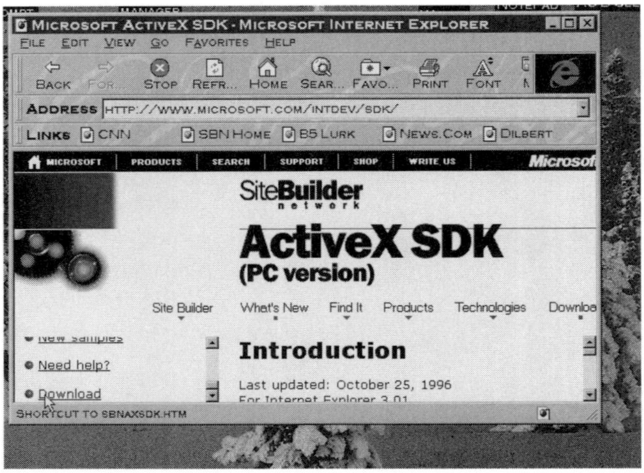


*Figure 10-5 Microsoft's download page for the ActiveX SDK*

Figure 10-6 shows the BIN subdirectory of the ActiveX SDK once it has been installed on a local computer. Notice it has two very important applications: LPK_TOOL.EXE (this is where to find it if you don't have the Visual C++ 5.0 or 6.0 CD) and SIGNCODE.EXE. The second file will be of vital importance in the next section about code signing. The rest of the SDK consists of various help files, documentation, and other tools to assist in creating Internet components for Microsoft Windows.

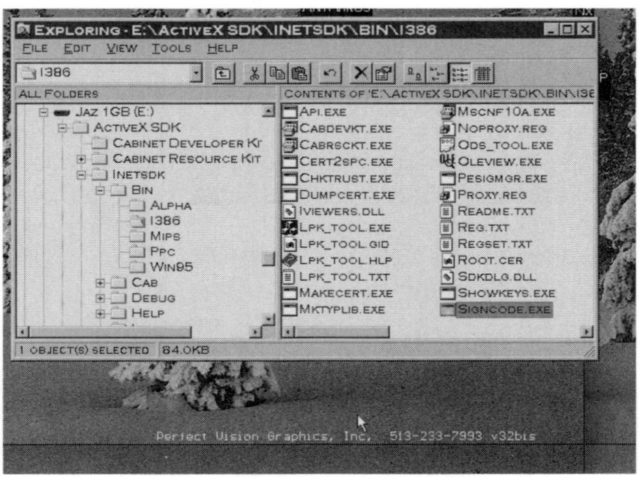


*Figure 10-6 The ActiveX SDK BIN subdirectory showing LPK_TOOL and SIGNCODE applications*

## Code Signing using Authenticode™—Obtaining an SPC

Authenticode™ is Microsoft's proprietary alternative to the Java sandbox security system. Java's *sandbox* is a term for the severe restrictions placed on Java applets; they cannot write to the local hard or floppy drives, cannot use most OS API calls, and otherwise can do very little beside show pictures and accept keyboard input. COM goes beyond this to allow much of the functionality of true application programs in its COM system, but at a price. The COM code element must be digitally "signed" for Internet Explorer or other Authenticode™-based systems to allow it to operate on the local machine. (You can alter the security settings to permit this, but it certainly is not recommended!) The process of adding a digital signature to a COM element is called *code signing*, and it requires two steps. The first you have already become acquainted with in the prior section, namely downloading the ActiveX SDK with the SIGNCODE.EXE application. The other step is to obtain an SPC (Software Protection Certificate) from a provider of such digital signatures. The one most commonly used is VeriSign. Figure 10-7 shows the VeriSign home page to acquire a digital signature. Its URL is: **http://digitalid.verisign.com/**. The following steps direct you through the process of obtaining your own personal SPC from VeriSign. (If you already have one or don't wish to obtain one, skip this section and the following one on actual code signing.)

*Figure 10-7 The VeriSign digital signature home page*

### Step-By-Step

Click on the Request a Digital ID image button. You should see a display similar to that shown in Figure 10-8 after the browser has navigated to the new page. These are the various kinds of SPCs available from VeriSign.

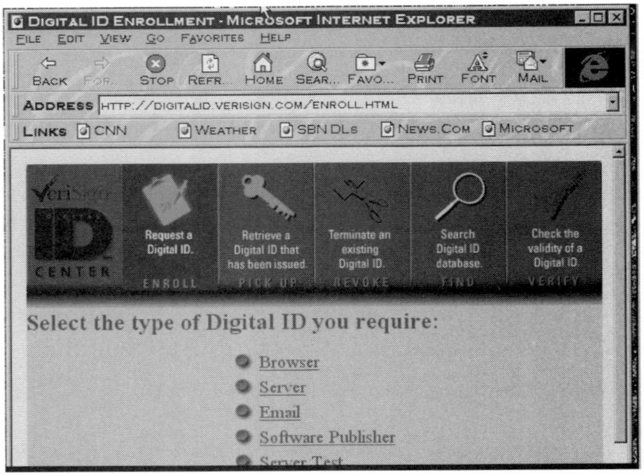


*Figure 10-8*
*The VeriSign SPC services page*

Click on the Software Publisher link. After the navigation is complete you should see a display similar to Figure 10-9.

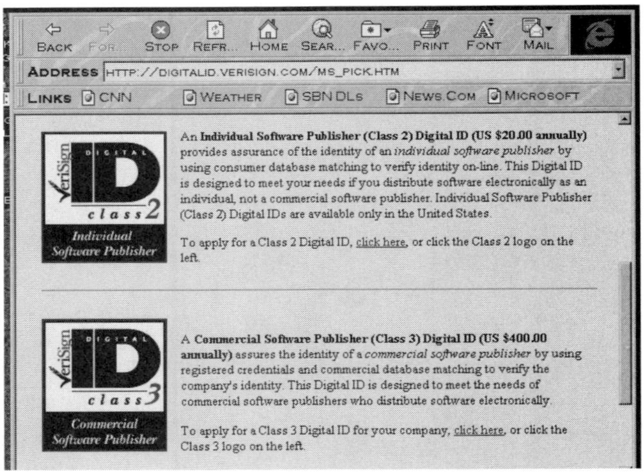


*Figure 10-9*
*The VeriSign Software Publisher SPC classes page*

There are two types of Software Publisher SPCs currently available, both of which are explained here. (Note that to use either service, a valid credit card with at least $20 credit is required. Also, Class 2 SPCs are only available at this time to United States residents.)

If you are an individual or a small business, click the Class 2 link or image. If you are a large business, click the Class 3 link or image.

The following steps are for the Class 2 SPC, but the Class 3 steps are very similar. You will see a display similar to Figure 10-10, which is the initial data entry screen for the SPC.

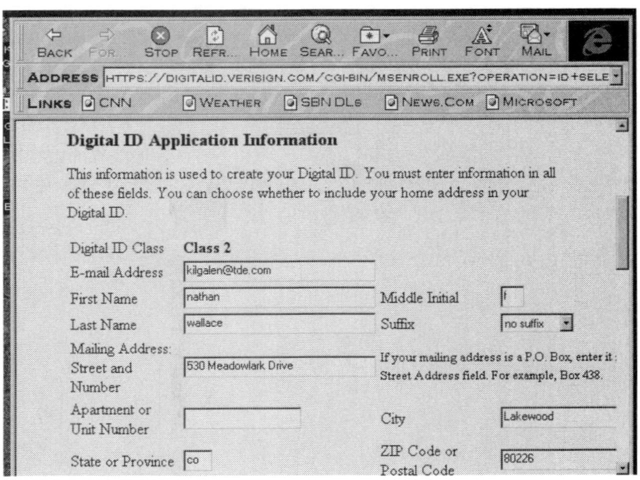


*Figure 10-10*
*Initial data entry screen for Class 2 VeriSign SPC*

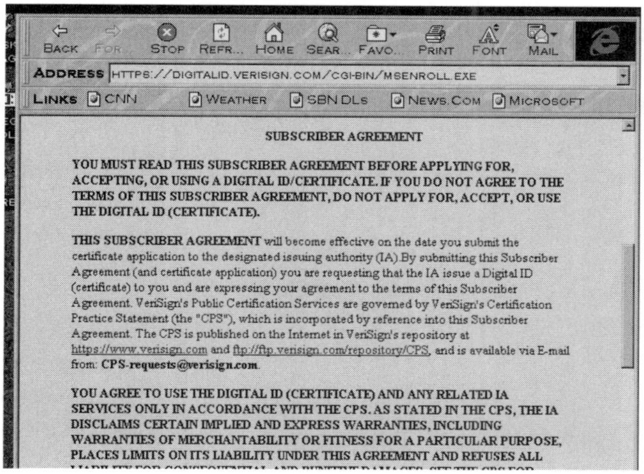


**Figure 10-11**
*SPC Subscriber Agreement page*

Fill out the data entry form very carefully. Obtaining the Class 2 SPC requires that your information be completely accurate and up to date! When you are finished, press the Submit image at the bottom of the page. You will then see a display similar to Figure 10-11, the Subscriber Agreement required to obtain the SPC.

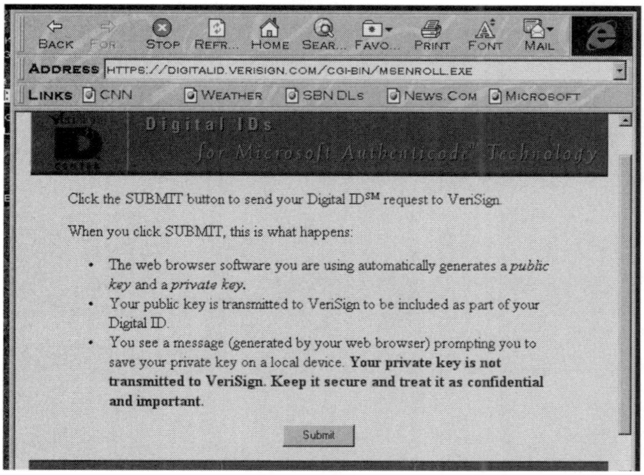


**Figure 10-12**
*SPC submission start screen*

The Subscriber Agreement is an absolute requirement to obtaining the SPC; it legally binds you to behave responsibly with whatever software is encoded using your SPC. After reading and agreeing with it, press the Accept image at the bottom of the page. You will then see a display similar to Figure 10-12, which is the display page to begin the actual process of obtaining your SPC.

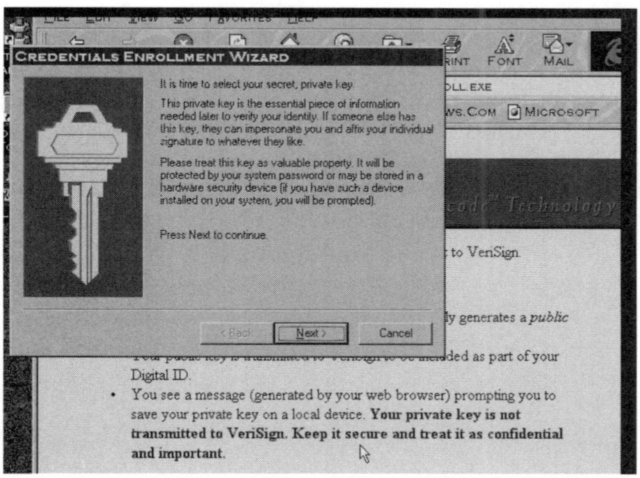


**Figure 10-13**
*Initial PVK Wizard display dialog*

Make sure there is a removable disk with about 500 K of space in whatever device you previously set up to hold your license files. Then press the Submit button. The browser will begin display of a series of wizard dialog boxes, the first of which is shown in

Figure 10-13. These wizards guide you through the automated process of acquiring your private portion of the SPC.

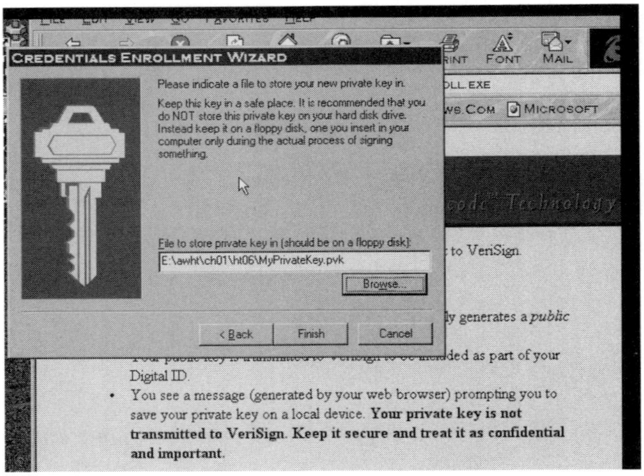


*Figure 10-14 Path entry dialog for the PVK Private Key File*

Press the Next button on the first wizard dialog box, and you will see a data entry dialog similar to that shown in Figure 10-14. It is used to enter the location of the removable media device you will use to store your Private Key File (PVK) for use in digitally signing files.

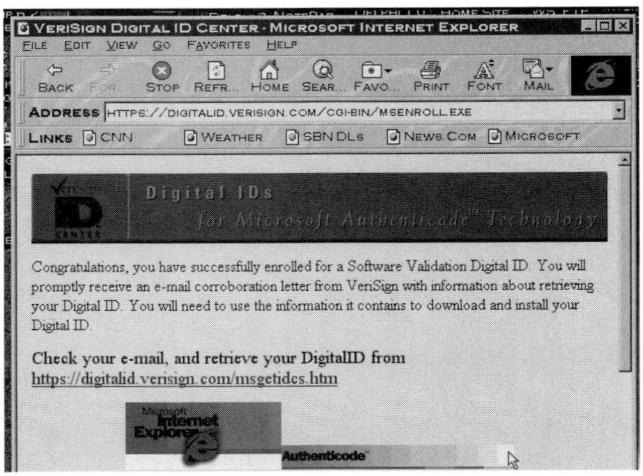


*Figure 10-15 URL display for retrieval of SPC file*

Use the Browse button to navigate to the drive and directory where you plan to store your PVK and SPC files. Then press Finish. The PVK file will be created and stored, and you will see a display similar to Figure 10-15, giving you the URL to return and obtain your SPC file.

At this point there will be a delay; if you are obtaining a Class 2 SPC it will be only a few moments, but if you are obtaining a Class 3 SPC it may be several days. Eventually you will receive an e-mail message similar to that shown in Figure 10-16, indicating you have been awarded the SPC you requested, or explaining why it was not awarded and giving you the steps to follow to correct the problem.

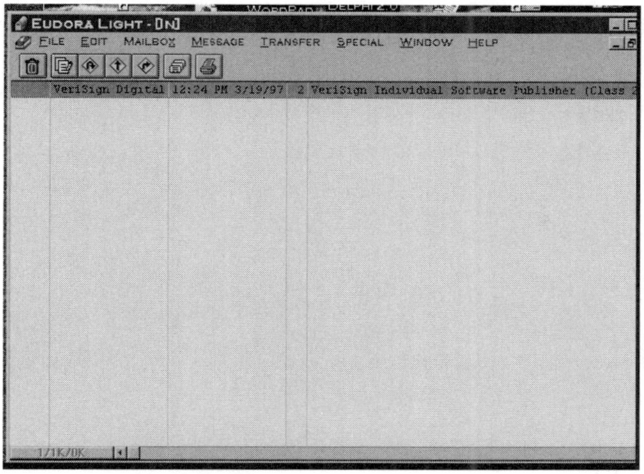


**Figure 10-16**
*E-mail client displaying VeriSign confirmation message*

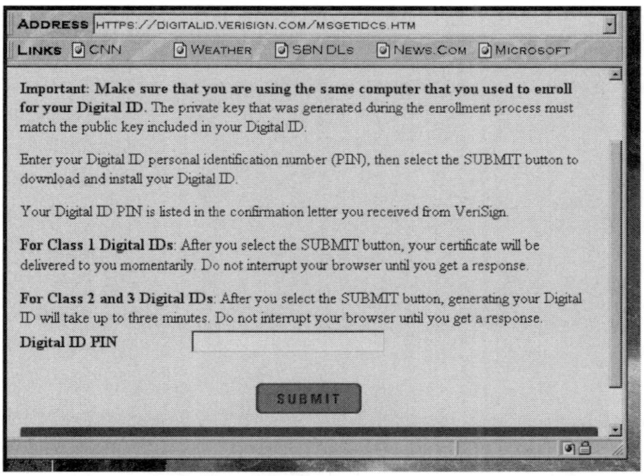


**Figure 10-17**
*VeriSign SPC PIN entry form*

At this point you should reactive your copy of Internet Explorer and navigate to the URL **http://digitalid.verisign.com/msgetiscs.htm**. You should see a display similar to that shown in Figure 10-17, which is a form to allow entry of your PIN to retrieve the SPC file.

The PIN is in the e-mail message shown in Figure 10-16. Enter it in the text box and press the Submit button. There will be a pause of up to several minutes while secured information is exchanged between VeriSign and your copy of Internet Explorer. Eventually you will see a display similar to Figure 10-18, unless a problem is encountered. In the latter case, you will be given a phone number to call and will be able to clear up the matter and resubmit your PIN. The display indicates the SPC file is ready to be placed on your removable media device.

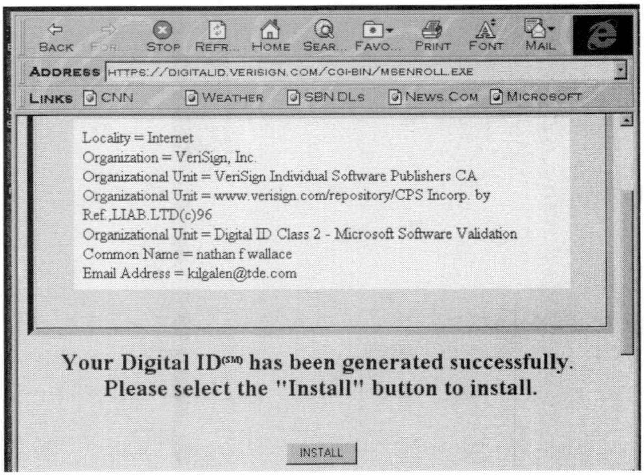


*Figure 10-18* SPC installation preparation screen

Pressing the Install button on the display will bring up the Credentials Enrollment Wizard dialog box shown in Figure 10-19. Make sure the removable disk with your PVK file is available to the system, and enter the same path for the SPC file. The IE application will, under control of the VeriSign page, write out your SPC file. You will then see a success dialog and should then remove the media with the software key, restoring it to the drive only when used to actually sign code.

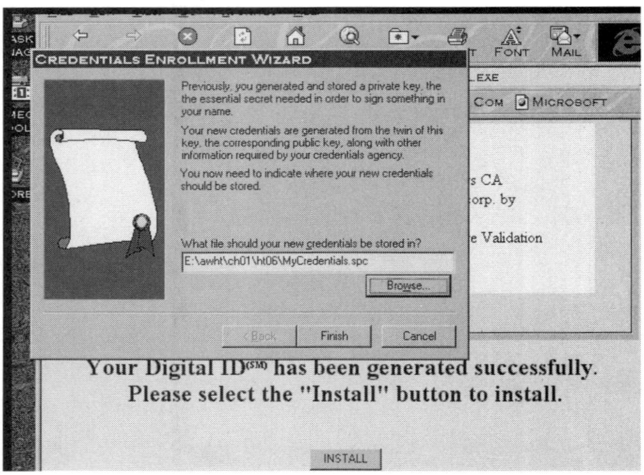


*Figure 10-19* SPC Credentials Enrollment Wizard dialog box

# Code Signing using Authenticode™—Digitally Signing Code

Now that you have obtained your SPC, here are the steps to actually sign code with it.

## *Step-By-Step*

First, bring up an MS-DOS window in the directory INETSDK\BIN of the ActiveX SDK. Enter **SIGNCODE** and press Return. Although you are running a DOS mode program, a set of wizard dialog boxes will appear to guide you through the code signing process, with the initial dialog shown in Figure 10-20.

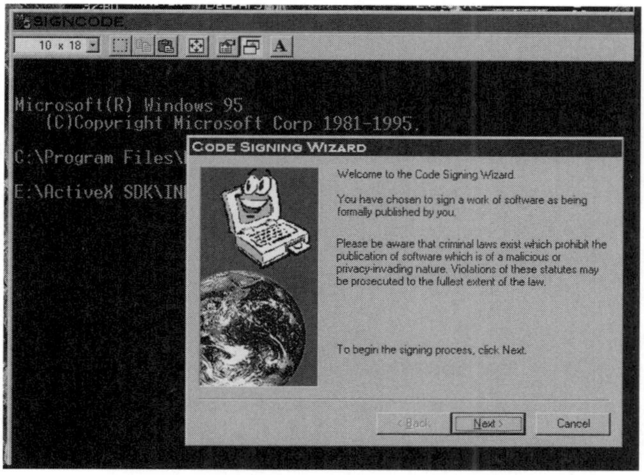


***Figure 10-20***
*Code Signing Wizard initial dialog*

(SIGNCODE.EXE can also be used from the DOS command line; see the ActiveX SDK documentation for details.)

Press Next on the initial dialog box. A new wizard dialog appears as shown in Figure 10-21. Fill in the top text entry control with the path and name of the CAB file you wish to sign. Give it a descriptive name in the middle text control. Finally, enter a URL for your web site or a README filename on the local drive.

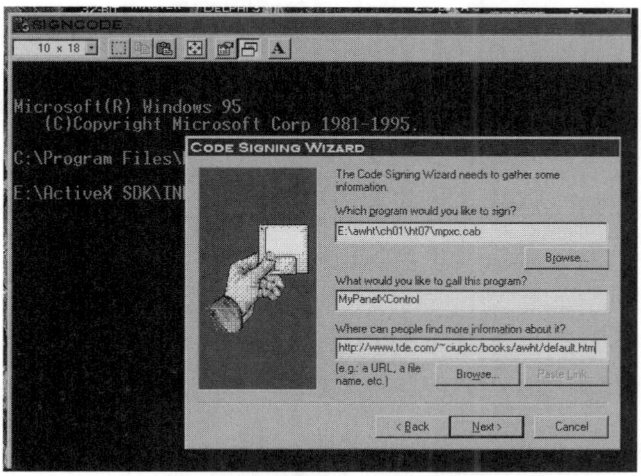


***Figure 10-21***
*Code Signing Wizard initial data acquisition dialog*

Make sure the removable media with your SPC and PVK files on it is available to the system. Press Next and the wizard dialog shown in Figure 10-22 will appear. It has two text controls which should already be filled in with the names and paths to the PVK and SPC files created in the section on obtaining an SPC above. If they are not, it is probably because you have not inserted the removable disk in the drive containing them; do so and use the Browse buttons to obtain the paths and filenames for your PVK and SPC files.

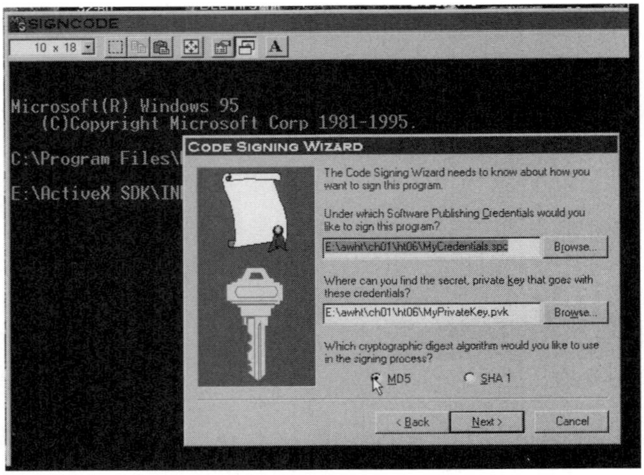


*Figure 10-22* *Code Signing Wizard PVK/SPC path entry dialog*

Pressing Next after completing the PVK and SPC file entry will bring up the dialog shown in Figure 10-23. It is a confirmation dialog which allows you to go back if needed and change parts of the code signing data.

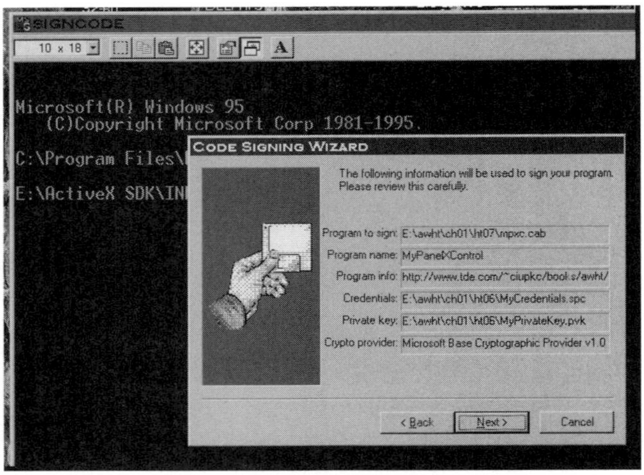


*Figure 10-23* *Code Signing Wizard data confirmation dialog*

Pressing Next moves you to the dialog shown in Figure 10-24. It is the final gateway prior to activating the code signing process; if for some reason you do not wish to continue the process, press Cancel; if you remember a needed data change, press Back.

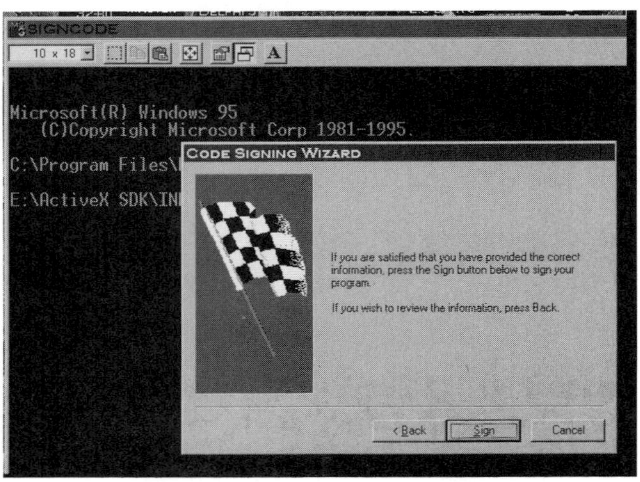


*Figure 10-24* *Code Signing Wizard final confirmation dialog*

Otherwise press Sign to actually sign your code.

Once the signing process is complete, you will see a success dialog similar to that shown in Figure 10-25. It indicates the file has been digitally signed and is ready for secure Internet, intranet, or World Wide Web usage. If for any reason you recompile or re-create the file, however, you must repeat the entire signing process! If the code signing process fails for any reason, an explanatory dialog box will appear; consult the ActiveX SDK documentation files for directions as to fixing the problem. (It is usually either an invalid SPC or PVK file or a problem with locating the file to be signed or the PVK or SPC files.)

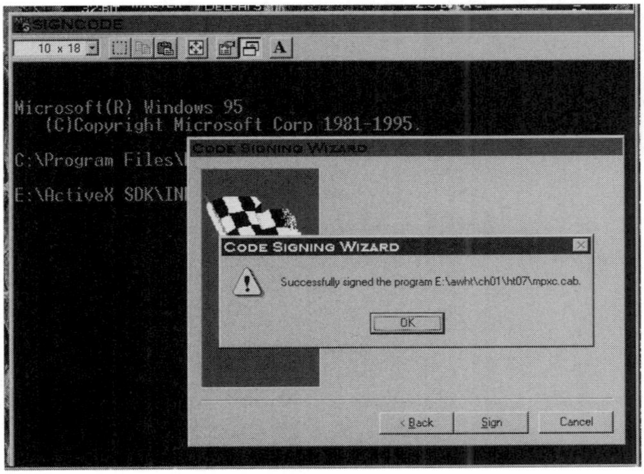


***Figure 10-25*** *Code Signing Wizard success dialog*

Once a file has been digitally signed, Microsoft provides a way to check the file prior to using it over the networks. This utility is called CHKTRUST, and it is another MS-DOS utility in the same directory as SIGNCODE. Activate another MS-DOS window, move to the \INETSDK\BIN\ directory, and enter **CHKTRUST -C** and the path to the signed CAB file. After a moment you should see a certificate display similar to that shown in Figure 10-26, except using your name and the distinctive name you gave the control in the wizard dialog illustrated in Figure 10-21. (If this dialog does not appear, then make sure you have the added -C and the correct filename and path on the command line for CHKTRUST.) You now have a signed, guaranteed safe CAB file with a COM component ready to be distributed over the World Wide Web!

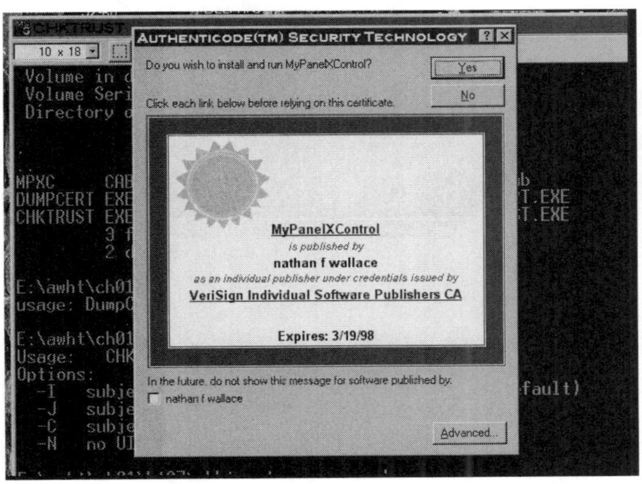


***Figure 10-26*** *Confirmation dialog showing code signing certificate*

## Obtaining and Using ActiveX Control Pad from Microsoft

Microsoft has kindly provided a very powerful utility for adding COM components to HTML pages, called ActiveX Control Pad. The URL to obtain it from Microsoft is **http://www.microsoft.com/workshop/author/cpad**. Figure 10-27 shows the download location at Microsoft's web site for obtaining it. Click on the Download link and follow directions to place the self-extracting install program on your hard drive. Then execute it, and it will install itself to your computer. Bring up the application, and you will see a display similar to Figure 10-28.

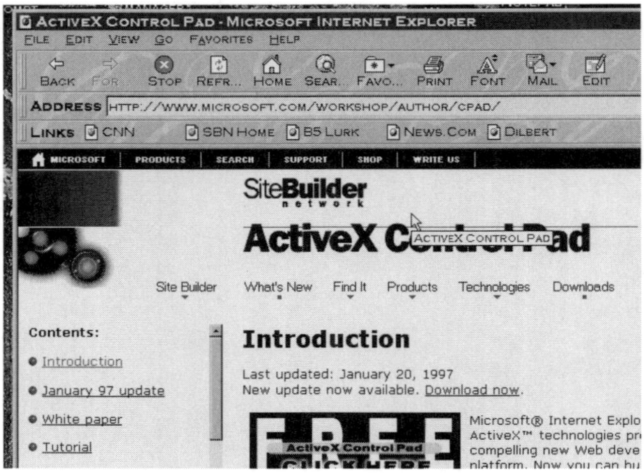


*Figure 10-27 Download page for ActiveX Control Pad from Microsoft*

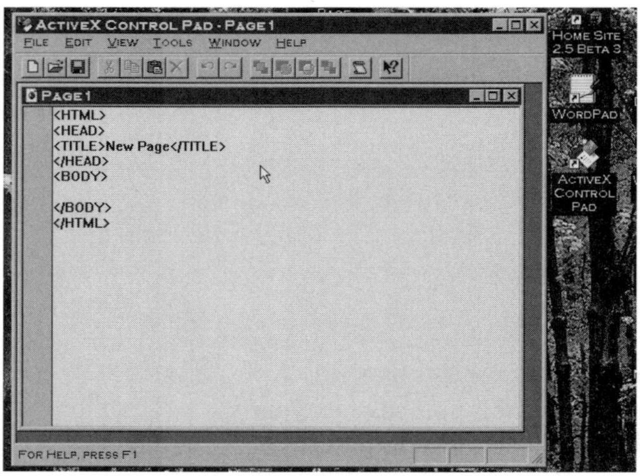


*Figure 10-28 ActiveX Control Pad's initial user interface*

There are four critical areas of functionality that the ActiveX Control Pad provides, over and above its Notepad-like text editor (which has no special HTML features, unfortunately): automatic insertion of <OBJECT> tags for COM components, including visual editing of the component desired; creation of the powerful new HTML Layout control layout files (called ALX but still HTML-based); visual editing and insertion of HTML layouts into HTML pages; and ActiveX scripting automation for both HTML pages and HTML layouts. Each of these areas is vital to effective use of COM components over the Internet, and has its own section below.

## Automatic COM <OBJECT> Tags/Visual Editing

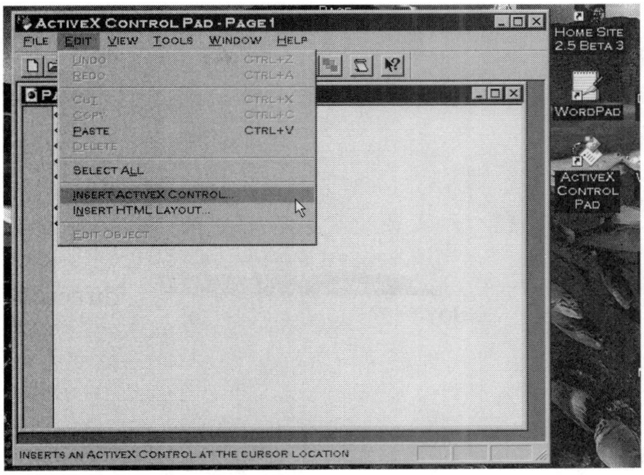


***Figure 10-29*** *The Edit | Insert ActiveX Control menu item*

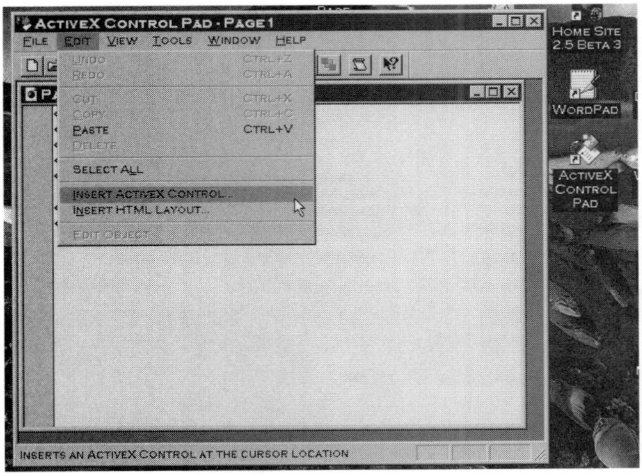


***Figure 10-30*** *A dialog box listing all available COM components*

Figure 10-29 shows the menu used to insert an ActiveX control into an HTML page. Selecting it causes the Control Pad to search the Registry for the computer and produce the dialog box shown in Figure 10-30, which lists all the available COM components on the host machine. Since this is a design activity, those controls that require license keys will not work unless the key is installed on the host computer.

Once you select the component to use (you can choose only one at a time since that's the way the <OBJECT> tag works), be prepared for a significant delay while the Control Pad convinces OLE to let it have the control; the less RAM and the more ActiveX controls you have on your system, the longer this will take (on my machine it's about five minutes!).

Figure 10-31 shows the various parts of the ActiveX Control Editor interface. The window marked "A" is the main visual editor pane. It allows you to size the control and observe its visual characteristics; however, it does not keep position information (unlike the HTML Layout control discussed below), so moving the control away from the top of the editor window has no net effect. The window marked "B" is the core of AXC editing in the Control Pad. It contains all the available properties for the control, and either accepts a value for them via typing into the upper text control (next to the Apply button) or supplies a drop-down list of values. Sometimes a custom editor button will appear to the right of the upper text control; pressing it will bring up a custom property editor for that particular property. The window marked "C" is not available for all controls, only those that support property pages. It's accessible from the right-click shortcut menu of the object inside the visual editing window, and is always the lowest "properties" entry there. It supplies user-written visual editing of property values for the control, as shown in the figure.

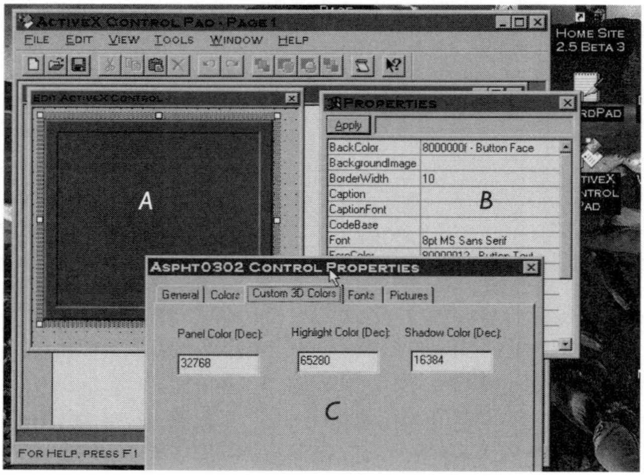


***Figure 10-31***
*ActiveX Control Pad's AXC editor interface*

Once you have made all the changes you like to the visual and informational state of the ActiveX control in the editors, click the close box of the main visual editor. This will close all the ActiveX control editor windows and cause the system to write out an <OBJECT> tag into the HTML file at the position of the cursor when the Edit menu option was invoked. This is shown in Figure 10-32, where I have accidentally placed the <OBJECT> tag in an invalid position, inside the HEAD block. (I moved it after discovering this...:)). Notice the <PARAM> tags written after the main <OBJECT> tag; these are where the custom values set in the ActiveX Editor are stored so the browser or another application can re-create them. Some defective controls don't correctly store their visual editing results this way, which will result in those settings being lost when the control is re-created in the target environment.

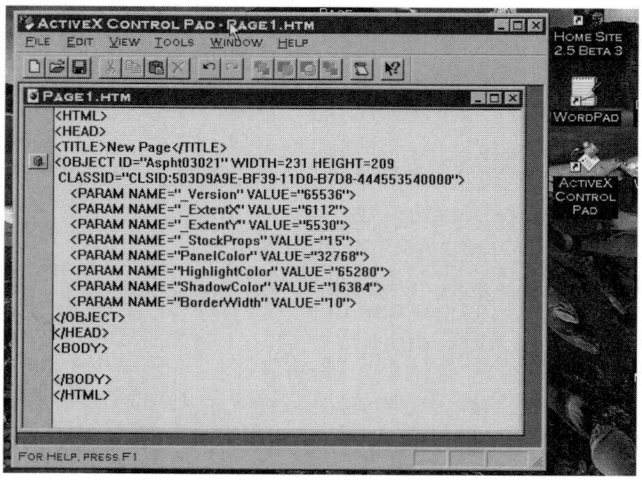


***Figure 10-32***
*An <OBJECT> tag inserted into the HTML by Control Pad*

## Creation of HTML Layout Controls

The big question is: What the heck is an HTML Layout control, and what has it got to do with Visual C++ 6.0 ActiveX control creation and usage? The answer lies in the usage part; HTML Layout controls are the hottest thing to come along since frames, maybe even HTML itself! Right now they are a supported extra requiring a download from Microsoft when a layout is first encountered. However, their functionality is already built into Internet Explorer 4.0 and is part of the Windows desktop in Windows 98. As to what they do, the answer is also simple: They provide three key elements previously missing from HTML: exact, pre-calculated two-dimensional placement of ActiveX controls on the HTML page, overlapping of controls along with transparency, and three-dimensional ordering of control display (also called *z-ordering*). With these capabilities, an HTML Layout allows a group of ActiveX controls on a web page to behave exactly like a Windows dialog: They always come up in the same positions with the same arrangement, no matter what HTML environment they are placed within. By clever use of z-ordering and transparency, sophisticated effects equal to those found in commercial games and multimedia presentations can be easily achieved.

At present, the only way to create HTML Layouts is with ActiveX Control Pad. They end up becoming data files for the HTML Layout control itself (which is itself an ActiveX control and must be directly inserted into the HTML to function), supplied with a nonstandard ALX file extension since although they are HTML-based, their tags are not supported by other browsers at the present time (such as Netscape's products). The ALX file(s) must be placed on the web site along with the HTM file that references them; Internet Explorer will automatically download both the HTM and ALX files to reconstruct the page as needed.

Using HTML Layouts requires configuring their principal visual component, called the Toolbox (like its counterpart in Visual C++ 6.0). To start the process, select the File|New HTML Layout menu option. After a relatively lengthy delay (about the same as for adding an ActiveX control, and heavily dependent on the individual state of your computer), the Layout Editor will appear, along with the Toolbox dialog. The Toolbox will initially have two tabs on its display. Click on the one marked Additional to move it into view; notice that it has room for additional controls. Right-click on the Toolbox dialog's Additional Page to bring up its shortcut menu, and select Additional Controls. You will see a display similar to Figure 10-33, as another dialog appears showing all the available controls on your computer. Unlike the ActiveX Editor, however, you can select multiple controls with this dialog box. When you select OK, all the controls you have checked will have a small image placed on the current palette of the Toolbox. You will then be able to visually click on them and drag their size on the Layout to position a new copy, just like in the Forms Editor Window of Visual C++! Select an interesting control or two and press OK, and observe as the system adds their icons to the palette.

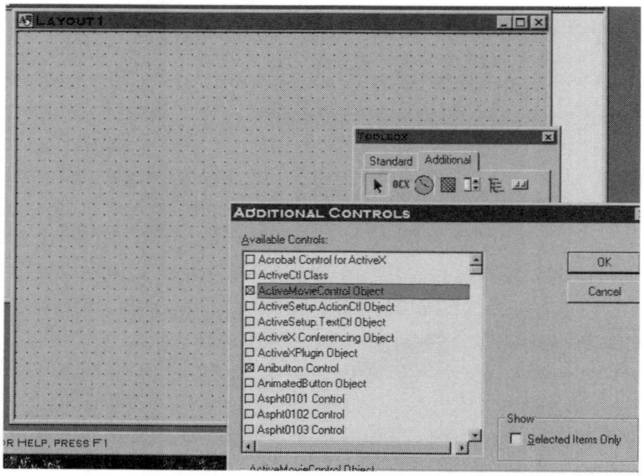


***Figure 10-33*** *Adding available controls to the HTML Layout Editor Toolbox*

There is also a way to add or modify the pages of the Toolbox dialog. Right-click on the tabs themselves, and a new shortcut menu will appear, as shown in Figure 10-34. This menu permits a number of important operations on the pages: adding and deleting a page, renaming a page, and changing its tooltip text. Also, pages can be saved into files for moving between copies of the Control Pad, either over the Internet or on different computers at the same location. Pages can also be moved from one position to another in the sequence of display. Once more pages are available than fit on the current size of the display, two small scroll buttons appear to the right of the tabs.

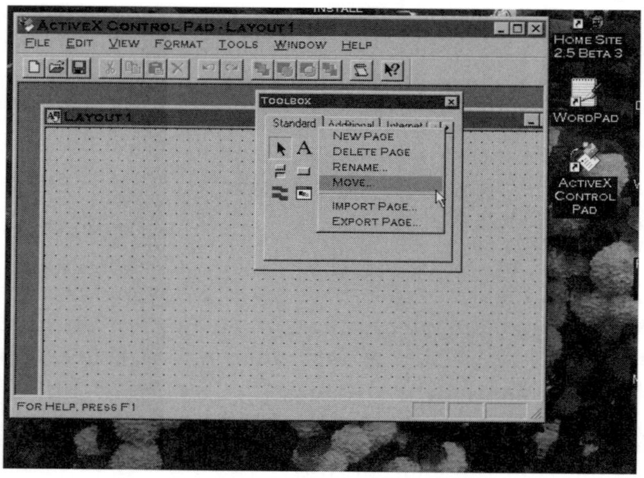


***Figure 10-34*** *Adding and modifying pages of the Toolbox dialog*

## Visual Editing of HTML Layout Controls

Figure 10-35 shows a sample HTML Layout being edited after construction. Notice the precise way in which the various controls are laid out; the control will maintain this appearance regardless of what HTML page it is displayed within! The controls shown in this page come from the Standard tab of the Toolbox, which includes Internet-ready versions of most of the controls provided with Visual C++ 5.0 or 6.0. Shown in the figure are a TextBox, a CommandButton, and an Image control. Also shown is a Custom control

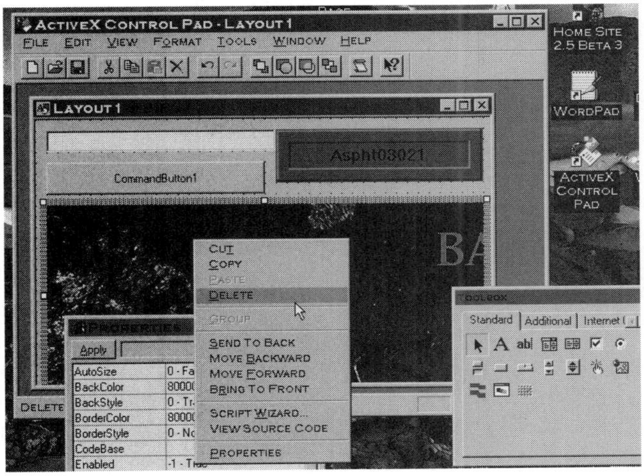


***Figure 10-35***
*An HTML Layout under construction*

created in another project; it was added using the functionality in the previous section and works just like the other controls.

To place a control on the Layout, simply click on it on the Toolbox, then click and drag on the Layout Editor pane to the desired size of the control. It will draw itself and add itself to the Layout as soon as you release the mouse. If you want to move it, simply click on it and drag its center; to change its size, click on it and drag an edge, just like in Visual C++. You can also cut, copy, and paste the controls just like in Visual C++; they always appear on the center of the Layout when pasted. Clicking outside the area of a control and dragging around multiple controls selects them as a group; there are special group menu options which are mainly used for OptionButton controls.

Controls can overlap, simply by placing them in such a way as to cause the effect. To determine which control is drawn "on top of" another control, use the four buttons showing overlapping controls on the toolbar, or use the Format menu options. You can make a given control go all the way in front of other controls, go all the way behind them, or incrementally move it forward or backwards. This is called "z-ordering," and is very powerful because, among other things, it can be controlled at run time with ActiveX scripting (discussed in the next section).

Controls have properties; these are accessible via the Properties dialog just like in Visual C++ and the other ActiveX Editor. There is a feature which is unique to the Layout, however: BackStyle. This property can be set to either opaque (the default) or transparent. If set to transparent, the background brush for the control is set to bsClear, meaning that when it draws itself, its background color won't show up, allowing things "behind it" (i.e., drawn previously in z-order) to be visible. Obviously, the control itself must not explicitly draw itself with an opaque brush style, or the effect won't take place; since many controls let Windows draw their background, however, the effect can be quite easily obtained and is very striking!

The other properties of the control are also accessible via the Properties dialog, and can trigger custom editors like the other ActiveX Editor did. Also, there is a shortcut menu for the controls in the Layout Editor that includes bringing up their property pages, showing the Script Wizard (explained below), and saving the HTML Layout and showing it in text form in Notepad or other default text editor. In addition, the shortcut menu supports the four z-order positioning choices.

Once a Layout is constructed as desired, it must be saved using the Save options of the toolbar or menus. Once saved, to show it in the HTML page, the menu option Edit|Insert HTML Layout must be chosen at the spot desired in the HTML code. A dialog will appear, prompting for the choice of Layout file; an <OBJECT> tag will then be written into the HTML to show the Layout at that point in the HTML stream. Unfortunately, there is no way at present to position two Layout controls effectively on either the same HTML page or a single Layout. In the case of multiple Layout controls on the same HTML page, they simply get treated like any other object and drawn in the sequence found in the HTML. The Layout control itself will not permit another copy of itself to be placed on it, to prevent stack explosions and other fun recursive catastrophes.

## ActiveX Script Wizard for HTML and ALX

But the real power of the ActiveX Control Pad, and in many ways of COM itself, is the feature called ActiveX scripting. It is a way for small program fragments, called *scripts*, written directly inside the HTML or ALX page itself, to directly manipulate the browser and other ActiveX controls, including HTML Layout controls and their embedded controls!

Books can and have been written on the subject of ActiveX scripting (including one by the author!), so the subject is much too large to be covered here in any real detail. But to give you enough information to get started, here is the scenario: Once you place an ActiveX control or other COM element on an HTML page, you cannot manipulate it using the editor tools used to create the page itself. Running in the browser, it can only be changed via the facility of scripting. By including small program elements written in VCScript language (a subset of Visual C++ itself) or in JScript (Microsoft's proprietary version of Netscape's JavaScript), you can achieve at run time in the browser what was previously only possible in the development environment! You can change properties, call methods, and respond to events, just as if the control was running in Visual C++ or the ActiveX Control Pad.

The key to including this incredible capability is the Script Wizard. It is shown in Figure 10-36, invoked from the HTML Layout Editor; it can also be called up from a regular HTML page in the main Editor. The Script Wizard consists of two large tree-view controls; the left-hand one is called the Events pane, and the right-hand one is the Actions pane. At the bottom is the Code pane, which is shown in List View mode in the figure. Using the Script Wizard is quite simple. You select the event to which you wish to add behavior in the Events pane (in the figure it is the Click event of the Command Button control on the Layout), and then select either the method you wish to invoke or the property you wish to change in the Actions pane. In the figure, the custom control's BackColor property is being changed. In List View mode, dialog boxes will appear to prompt you for values to add, and the calls to methods will simply be placed into the list of statements. This method is very useful for simple scripts and does not require a great deal of understanding of scripting, since the environment handles most of the work.

***Figure 10-36***
*The Script Wizard in the HTML Layout Editor*

However, if you need to get down and dirty, there is an alternative mode: Code View. In this mode, you must enter all the code yourself; clicking on methods and properties merely adds a line of code referencing that element without placing any other components, like equals signs, and without prompting you for new values.

The advantage of Code View mode is that you can enter most scripting statements by hand, such as variable declarations, changes to the parameters of procedures and functions, and new procedures and functions. The shortcut menu for the Actions pane also provides this capability, somewhat restrictedly. (It cannot declare local variables, for example.) Also, to call methods with parameters, you must use Code View mode, since those methods will not even be shown in List View mode. See Figure 10-37.

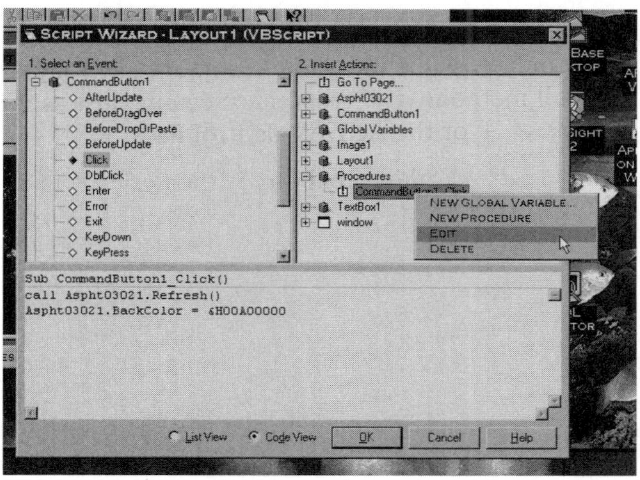


***Figure 10-37***
*The Script Wizard in Code View mode*

When you are finished adding your script, press OK and the appropriate <SCRIPT> tags will be written into the HTML or ALX file as appropriate.

The advantage of Code View mode is that you can enter most scripting statements by hand, such as variable declarations, changes to the parameters of procedures and functions, and new procedures and functions. The shortcut menu for the Actions pane also provides this capability, somewhat restrictedly. (It cannot declare local variables, for example.) Also, to call methods with parameters, you must use Code View mode, since those methods will not even be shown in List View mode.

Figure 10-38 shows the results of creating an HTML page with an ActiveX control, an HTML Layout control, and a script. Each of these code blocks has a small glyph in the left-hand gutter; clicking on it will bring up that element in the appropriate editor (ActiveX, HTML Layout, or Script Wizard). Saving the HTML file will allow all this useful functionality to come to life in Internet Explorer!

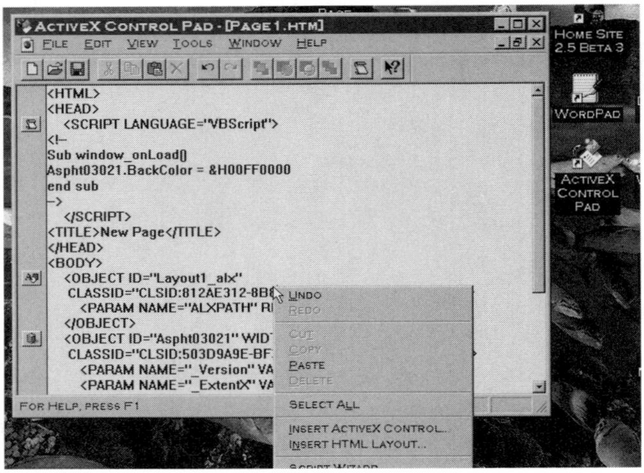


*Figure 10-38*
*A very functional HTML page*

## Obtaining and Using File Transfer Protocol (FTP) Software to Place COM Elements on the Internet

Now that you've gone to all the trouble of creating COM elements just for use on the Internet and World Wide Web, it seems appropriate to put them where they can be available on those networks! Unfortunately, neither Visual C++, nor ActiveX Control Pad, nor even Internet Explorer, will help you do this. Instead, you need a special type of Internet software called an "FTP client." While there is a text-mode version (shudder!) available from the DOS command line in Windows 95 and Windows NT, it seems more reasonable to find one that is Windows-based and nicely laid out. Fortunately, there is a shareware program called WS_FTP, written over ten years ago by John A. Junod, and now distributed commercially. Figure 10-39 shows the web site of the company that now markets WS_FTP, with the download location for a free evaluation copy. If you prefer freeware, you can also obtain older freeware versions of the program from many FTP sites using InfoSeek or Yahoo's search facilities. Also, many Internet service providers (ISPs) distribute the freeware version of WS_FTP to their customers, so check your computer for that filename, because it is very likely you already have it installed!

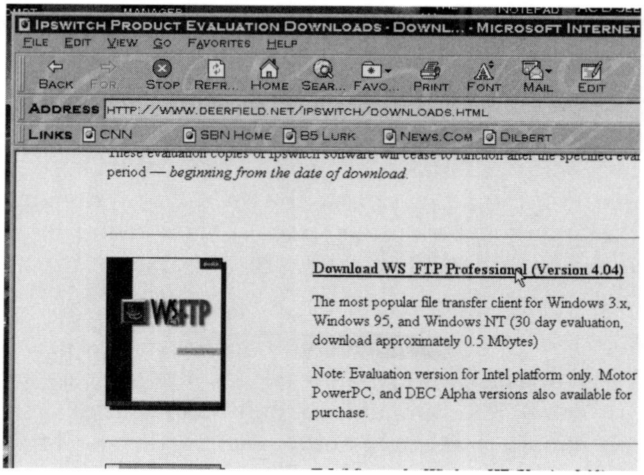


*Figure 10-39* Downloading WS_FTP FTP client

At this point, you may be wondering why all this bother! Well, the answer lies in the way the Internet and World Wide Web work. Browsers are designed to retrieve files from web and FTP server computers, not send them. The only way to move files around the Internet is FTP; it was one of the original protocols and is still the most widely used, since most download requests by browser software actually use the FTP protocol. In order to transfer your hand-written COM components and HTML/ALX files up to the web site you will be using, you need FTP!

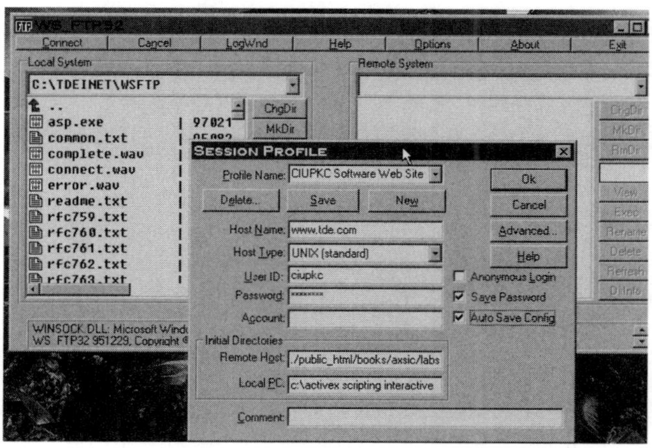


*Figure 10-40* The WS_FTP client startup screen

Figure 10-40 shows the WS_FTP client's startup screen. It is fairly typical of FTP software, so if you are using another graphical package, it should have the same functionality, just arranged a little differently.

Most of the problems encountered with FTP happen at login, so this section will attempt to anticipate most of them so you won't have to. First, notice the Profile Name box. It is a very good idea to enter a unique informational name for the web server you'll be using, and click the Auto Save Config check box so that your information only has to be entered once. If you choose not to save the configuration automatically, you can still save it manually from the File menu before you close the connection.

Next, note the Host Name box. This is where you enter the Internet address of the web server you will use. For this example, it is my web provider's address, **www.tde.com**; you would enter your own address, of course. You can also enter the "dotted decimal" version, like "158.158.12.140," but make sure you have it exactly right, or no end of problems will ensue! Do not enter path information to your own web pages here, or again you'll hopelessly confuse the poor thing and end up losing large amounts of cranial filaments.

Below Host Name is Host Type, a drop-down combo box. The UNIX option is standard, but you can also choose to autodetect the operating system of the web server or use one of the other choices. (If your provider is supporting Microsoft's Internet Information Server, the operating system may not appear in older versions and must be autodetected.) This is a vital choice; making the wrong one will end up either crashing the program or causing it to send bad data to your server.

The User ID field is your user name for the web server. If the server is for your personal web pages, it will be your ISP account user name; if it is for your business, it will be the company account's name. The Password field is the password, of course; make sure not to use it elsewhere on the display (like the comment field), as the records for the WS_FTP program are kept in ordinary text that anyone can examine if they get access to your computer.

The Account field is optional; it is used for larger servers that have account names in addition to a user name.

The Initial Directories area is used to store the information about startup directories the program will change to, both on the local machine and the remote machine. If either path is invalid, an error message will display but the connection will not be lost.

The Comment field can be used to store small text descriptions of the location to make it easier to distinguish between sites with similar names and profiles.

Aside from the Auto Save Config option mentioned earlier, there are two other possible settings for the login dialog. Anonymous Login is used for FTP sites that allow such connections; it won't be used for web server interactions. The Save Password option allows saving the password in an encrypted text block inside the normal text of the record; it is relatively safe and normally poses no security risk (not to mention making it a lot easier to use the system.)

Once you have filled out all the fields to your satisfaction, press OK and you will be connected to the server, if possible. There are several situations where connecting to the server may be impossible. One is that the server itself is down, making contact out of the question. Another common problem is traffic overload on larger and more popular servers, making getting a connection difficult and requiring multiple connection attempts over time. Finally, the network itself sometimes is either impossibly slow or down in some segments; in this case you will receive either an "unable to locate hostname" error from Winsock or hang after initial contact is made. In all these cases, the only solution is patience; either try again later, or keep trying until you get a good connection.

Figure 10-41 shows the WS_FTP client performing one of the most vital chores of maintaining a web site: adding new directories. The procedure is quite simple; navigate in the right-hand list box until you find the directory on your web server where you need the new directory created. Then press the MkDir button; the dialog box shown in the figure will appear. Enter a valid name (remember operating system peculiarities!) and press OK; the client will attempt to create the directory on the remote computer. If it succeeds, the display will flip to show the new directory in the list box; otherwise an error message dialog will appear. Once the directory is created, it can be navigated into, have subdirectories created under it, and so forth, just like any other directory on the remote machine. Other options available both on the remote and the local computer are explicitly changing the directory with ChgDir and removing a selected directory with RmDir. (Directories cannot be renamed; they have to be deleted and re-created.) Files can be viewed (downloaded into a viewer, best with text files only), executed either locally or remotely (where possible, often not on web servers), deleted, and renamed. In addition, the display can be refreshed and the actual text of the FTP directory output viewed with the DirInfo command.

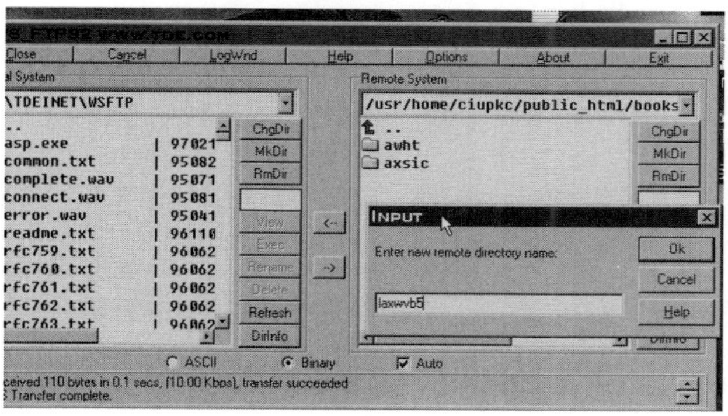


***Figure 10-41*** *The WS_FTP client adding a remote directory*

There are two other very important functions shown in the figure; the three type option buttons and the Log window. The type options are either ASCII or Binary, with an Auto check box as well. The default mode is Binary, which is an absolute requirement for all ZIP, CAB, EXE, DLL, OCX, and image files; they are all binary images and must be transmitted exactly as found. The other mode, ASCII, is used only for text files but has an advantage over binary: If the source computer is a Windows machine but the server is a UNIX computer, text files are handled differently between the two computers, which can result in inconsistencies in the display and manipulation of the text. Choosing ASCII mode will allow the system to determine which format is needed on each end, and add or remove control characters as needed. The Auto check box allows the program to attempt to determine for itself which mode is needed, by checking file extensions and other clues. The best way to use this feature is to keep it at Binary except when sending HTML and ALX files.

The Log window displays the actual text conversation going on between the local computer and the web server. It is only of real use to techno-weenies like the author, but if you start experiencing odd problems with files going up to your web server, this is the first place to look for error or warning messages or unusual events of any sort. Usually your web server administrator will ask for a copy of this data; you can use the LogWnd button at the top of the dialog box to bring the text up in Notepad and save it as a text file.

The other buttons at the top of the display control closing the current connection, making a new connection, and setting options for the program, most of which only apply for special, heavy-duty FTP use that we won't worry about. (They can be useful if you need them, though.)

Figure 10-42 shows the guts of FTP: a file upload. Here are the steps you take to perform this task: First, navigate to the directory on the local computer where the files to be stored are located; you can use the tree control or the explicit ChDir dialog box. Once there, use Ctrl and Shift to select the files you want to upload; then make sure you have the Binary/ASCII type setting correct (only use ASCII for HTML, TXT, and ALX files). Then press the –> button in the center of the two treeview controls. This will cause the upload to begin.

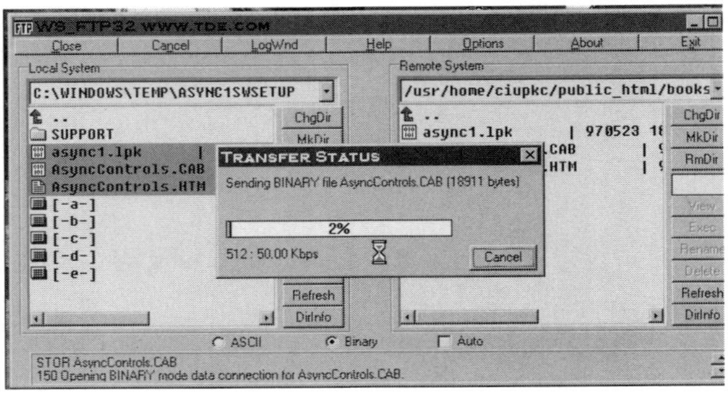


***Figure 10-42** The WS_FTP client uploading a file to the web server*

As each file is uploaded, a small dialog box will appear as shown in the figure; it will give the size of the file, the total bytes uploaded so far, and a visual gauge of the percentage of completion. The dialog is destroyed and re-created for each file, which makes things rather annoying with a lot of small files, because it unfortunately grabs both the mouse and keyboard focus each time it does this! Therefore, don't plan on doing anything else while you upload or download with WS_FTP.

Once the upload is complete, the new files will appear in the right-hand treeview control. Note that overwriting is normally silent; make sure you are where you want to be before sending files up! Also, be aware that UNIX is *case-sensitive* on filenames; MyFile and MYFILE are totally different files under UNIX, unlike DOS or Windows. (Windows NT is case sensitive, however!)

A final caveat regarding path names for web servers. Your account on the web server computer will have a somewhat different directory path than that used on the Internet or World Wide Web. The reason is something called *aliasing*. It is a trick UNIX and Windows NT administrators use to allow them to restructure their hard disks at will without breaking thousands of web pages every time they do so! Most paths that are appended to a web server

Internet address begin with the *tilde* character "~" (such as, "**http://www.tde.com/~ciupkc/index.html**".) The tilde character is the syntax for an alias; it causes the operating system to look up where "ciupkc" actually is and redirect the path there. This happens invisibly, and so your users think that your web files live in a "ciupkc" directory when they actually live in "**usr/home/ciupkc/public_html/**"!

The reason this is important is that FTP never heard of tildes!

Instead, you have to know where your account actually lives with FTP. Fortunately, most FTP servers for web servers look up the account of the user logging in (since they normally don't have access to other directories, for obvious reasons) and place the user in the directory that corresponds to their "tilde" address. Some don't, however, and in other cases you may need to access a different alias, such as with large corporate accounts. The key factor to remember in all of this is that the directory path you observe in the FTP client is, in most cases, not the one the user will see on the Internet! Consult your web server administrator for serious difficulties in this area; only they know for sure.

## Using Internet Explorer to Access COM Over the Internet and World Wide Web

At last, you are ready to look at the spiffy COM content you have laboriously authored, compressed, digitally signed, and painstakingly uploaded to your web server! Let's do it!

How?

Ah, I knew you were going to ask that! The answer is Internet Explorer.

Figure 10-43 shows Internet Explorer displaying a custom COM control created with Visual C++. Notice that all that is required is to type in the correct URL (uniform resource locator) for the web page; IE does the rest, downloading the COM components referenced in the HTML, creating the components in memory and obtaining any required support files from the web server or other location. All this is done automatically; all the user sees is the neato-keen COM functionality. And this is why COM will rule the Internet and WWW by the turn of the millennium! Rather than having to mess around with locating

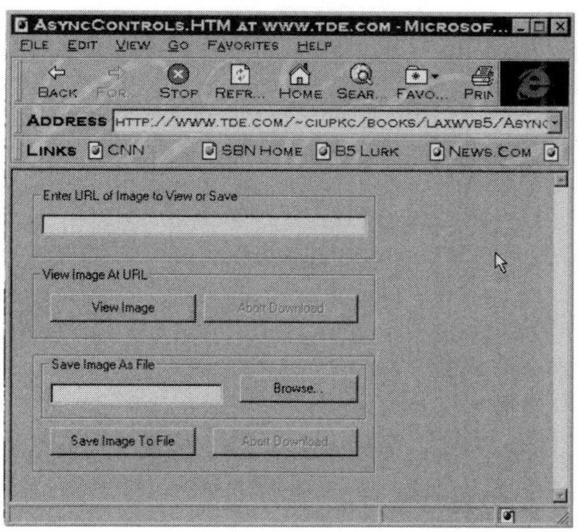


***Figure 10-43** Viewing a COM HTML page with Internet Explorer*

and downloading endless new plug-ins (many of which require payment and are often buggy!), the browser silently and quickly locates the needed COM elements, brings them onto the local hard drive, and runs them. Like HAL in the movie *2001*, Internet Explorer is almost too good a servant!

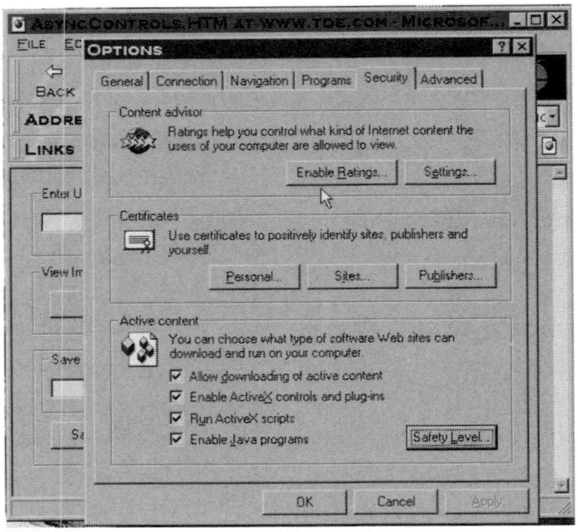

***Figure 10-44*** *IE's Active Content Options settings*

Fortunately, Microsoft has included several very important configuration options in Internet Explorer relating to Active Content. To access them, select View|Options from the main menu bar. Figure 10-44 shows the Security tab of the Options Property Pages dialog, which is where most of the Active Content features live.

There are four major sections to this page, and each deserves some scrutiny. The top section is used to control Content Ratings, which are ways to keep younger children from encountering web sites with inappropriate content. IE uses an industry standard rating system, which most commercial content providers and many individual pages support. The details on it are in the online help for IE.

The next section is an enhancement to the digital signature system you were shown how to use earlier in this chapter. Rather than having to download a certificate each time a signed control is encountered, this section allows setting a default acceptance for your own signature or that of other individuals (Personal), that of entire web sites (Sites), and those from Publishers (Publishers). The increasing level of acceptance does not compromise security, since all the accepted items must still have a valid digital signature; instead, it removes the time penalty to display repeated signature certificates from the same person or business when their content is regularly used.

The third section contains the most important settings in regard to Active Content. This group of four check box controls determines whether your copy of IE will permit downloading of COM elements not already on your local machine, whether it will allow COM elements to function once downloaded, whether it will permit embedded COM scripts to be run once downloaded, and whether Java applets and applications can be run once downloaded. Turning off all these options effectively kills COM for the browser, but there might be reasons for any one of them to be turned off briefly in a security threat environment.

The fourth element is contained behind the Safety Level button. Pressing it brings up the dialog box displayed in Figure 10-45.

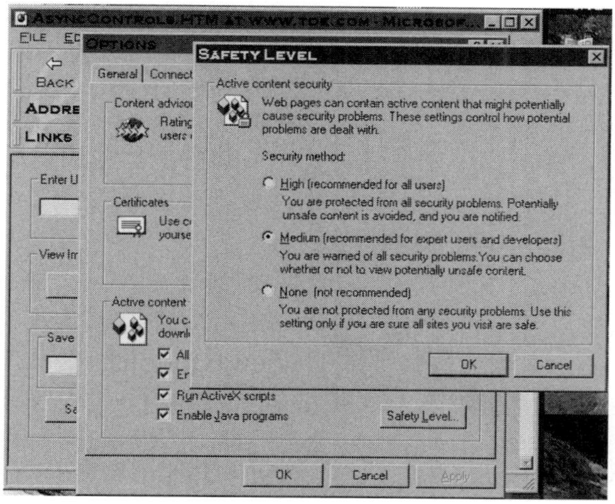


***Figure 10-45***
*IE's ActiveX safety settings*

The default setting is High, which refuses all ActiveX content that does not have a digital signature. The Medium setting is best used by developers such as ourselves, and only when we are developing our own work. This setting will allow non-signed ActiveX content to be downloaded and run, but will warn first and provide option levels for safety. The Low setting is only appropriate for completely isolated intranet environments or those behind extremely tight firewall security. It performs no signature checking and does not warn when any content is downloaded and executed.

You have probably heard quite a bit about the "security holes" in Internet Explorer. All of these holes require using the browser on Low or Medium security. None of them will happen on High security. So if in doubt, stay on High. (Also be sure you have the latest copy of IE; Microsoft is still giving it away for free as of this writing, so all it will cost you is a little download time and a few megabytes on your hard drive.)

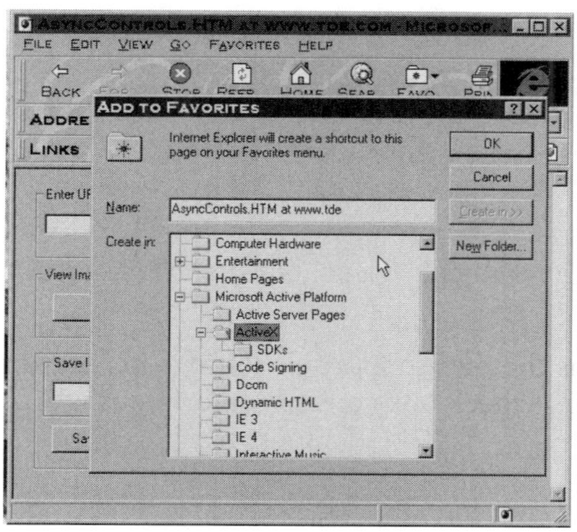


***Figure 10-46***
*IE's Favorites dialog*

Figure 10-46 shows the final figure for this chapter, the Favorites dialog of IE.

This dialog is activated whenever you cruise to a useful web site and select Add To Favorites from the menu. It allows you to create new Favorites folders, navigate among existing ones, and save the page in the one of your choice, with a modified title if desired. At first glance, this is pretty spiffy, right?

Well, it gets better! It turns out that the Favorites system of IE is nothing more than a set of directories under WINDOWS\FAVORITES\ on the hard drive! The actual favorites entries are stored as Internet shortcuts inside the directories, just like the shortcuts used for the Start menu or other program groups. What that means is that you can use your copy of Explorer to manipulate the Favorites system yourself. You can add directories, move them around, and even add and remove items with Explorer, without ever using the Favorites system of IE itself. And if you do choose the Organize Favorites menu item, don't be surprised at how similar the dialog used for this option is to Explorer; it's actually a junior copy of it.

Why bring up Favorites here? Well, in the process of testing the deployment of even the simplest of web sites, you'll be making a lot of trips to the same URL. Rather than typing it in over and over again, saving it once as a Favorite and then using the Favorite to go back to it can save huge amounts of typing.

## Mastering COM Over the Internet

Even though there isn't a thing about Visual C++ programming in this chapter, I think you'll agree it is complex! You've been on a whirlwind tour of the Internet aspects of the ActiveX SDK and code signing, ActiveX Control Pad, WS_FTP, and Internet Explorer. You've learned how to digitally sign your COM elements and create sophisticated HTML and ALX pages with ActiveX controls, HTML Layouts, and ActiveX scripting. You understand how to upload files onto your web server with WS_FTP, and how to download them with Internet Explorer, as well as how to determine what types of Active Content IE will permit under security considerations.

This brings us to the end of our journey into MTS; hopefully you have learned all that you need to know to start putting your data into the wild and wonderful world of transactions, COM, ADO, and the Internet. If you are interested in any of the companion technologies, please check out the other Wordware books on these topics (like ATL, MFC, or OLE DB). Happy coding!

# Index

# About the CD

The CD distributed with this book contains complete project source code for all the material in the book. To install the CD files:

1. Use the DOS XCOPY command as follows:

   Open a DOS window, then change to the drive containing the companion CD-ROM. Change to the **lmtsdcppweb** directory. (You must do this to avoid copying all the utilities to your hard drive.)

   Type **XCOPY /S*.*** followed by the drive and directory you want the files copied into, then press Enter. DOS will copy all the files (including the web files) to your hard drive. To avoid copying the web portion of the CD, change to the lmtsdcpp subdirectory before you type XCOPY.

2. Or, navigate using your favorite web browser to the Project link in the readme.htm file, and then to the individual chapters. Each chapter's page contains a set of links to its projects in a zip file. Click on the link to open a dialog that lets you select an appropriate location for the browser to copy the zip file to. The zip files have been creating using directory names; to unzip them and create the directory structure for the projects, simply use WinZip or PKUnzip with the same "use folder names" or "-d" options.

   Since each hands-on section assumes you start from scratch, you don't need any of these files to do the projects, but they're there if you want them. It's also a good idea to look at the readme.txt file on the CD for any last-minute typos, bug fixes, or updates to the book. Despite our best efforts, there are always a few loose ends!

**WARNING:** Opening the CD package makes this book nonreturnable.